CNE Training Guide: NetWare 4.1 Administration, Second Edition

Karanjit Siyan, Ph.D

New Riders

New Riders Publishing, Indianapolis, Indiana

CNE Training Guide: NetWare 4.1 Administration, Second Edition

By Karanjit Siyan, Ph.D

Published by:
New Riders Publishing
201 West 103rd Street
Indianapolis, IN 46290 USA

Printed in the United States of America 1 2 3 4 5 6 7 8 9 0

CIP data available upon request

Warning and Disclaimer

This book is designed to provide information about the NetWare network operating system. Every effort has been made to make this book as complete and as accurate as possible, but no warranty or fitness is implied.

The information is provided on an "as is" basis. The author(s) and New Riders Publishing shall have neither liability nor responsibility to any person or entity with respect to any loss or damages arising from the information contained in this book or from the use of the disks or programs that may accompany it.

Publisher	DON FOWLEY
Publishing Manager	EMMETT DULANEY
Marketing Manager	RAY ROBINSON
Managing Editor	TAD RINGO

ACQUISITIONS EDITOR
MARY FOOTE

DEVELOPMENT EDITOR
IAN SHEELER

PRODUCTION EDITOR
JOHN SLEEVA

COPY EDITORS
LAURA FREY
PATRICE HARTMANN
HOWARD PIERCE
ANGIE TRZEPACZ
LILLIAN YATES

TECHNICAL EDITOR
DAVE PARKES

ASSOCIATE MARKETING MANAGER
TAMARA APPLE

ACQUISITIONS COORDINATOR
TRACY TURGESON

PUBLISHER'S ASSISTANT
KAREN OPAL

COVER DESIGNER
JAY CORPUS

BOOK DESIGNER
SANDRA SCHROEDER

MANUFACTURING COORDINATOR
PAUL GILCHRIST

PRODUCTION MANAGER
KELLY DOBBS

PRODUCTION TEAM SUPERVISOR
LAURIE CASEY

GRAPHICS IMAGE SPECIALISTS
JASON HAND, CLINT LAHNEN,
LAURA ROBBINS, CRAIG SMALL,
TODD WENTE

PRODUCTION ANALYSTS
ANGELA BANNAN
JASON HAND
BOBBI SATTERFIELD

PRODUCTION TEAM
HEATHER BUTLER,
DAN CAPARO, KIM COFER,
JENNIFER EBERHARDT,
KEVIN FOLTZ, DAVID GARRATT,
ALEATA HOWARD,
ERICH J. RICHTER,
CHRISTINE TYNER

INDEXER
CHRISTOPHER CLEVELAND

About the Author

Karanjit S. Siyan is president of Kinetics Corporation. He has authored international seminars on Solaris & SunOS, TCP/IP networks, PC network integration, Novell networks, Windows NT, and expert systems using fuzzy logic. He teaches advanced technology seminars in the United States, Canada, Europe, and the Far East. Karanjit is actively involved in Internet research and holds a Ph.D in Computer Science. He has published articles in *Dr. Dobbs Journal, The C Users Journal*, and *Databased Advisor*.

Before working as an independent consultant, Karanjit worked as a senior member of technical staff at ROLM Corporation. As part of his consulting work, Karanjit has written a number of custom compiler and operating system development tools. Besides his interest in network security, his other interests include Unix-based, Novell-based, Windows NT-based, and OS/2 networks. Karanjit holds the ECNE certification for Novell-based networks and the Microsoft Certified Professional for Windows NT. His current book titles are *Internet Firewalls and Network Security, NetWare: The Professional Reference, Windows NT Server: The Professional Reference, NetWare TCP/IP and NFS, CNE Training Guide: NetWare 4 Administration*, and *CNE Training Guide: NetWare 4 Update*. He has also co-authored *LAN Connectivity, Banyan Vines: The Professional Reference, NetWare 4 for Professionals, Implementing Internet Security*, and *Downsizing to NetWare*. Karanjit is based in Montana where he lives with his wife, Dei. He can be reached through the Internet at `karanjit@siyan.com`.

Trademark Acknowledgments

All terms mentioned in this book that are known to be trademarks or service marks have been appropriately capitalized. New Riders Publishing cannot attest to the accuracy of this information. Use of a term in this book should not be regarded as affecting the validity of any trademark or service mark. NetWare is a registered trademark of Novell Inc.

Dedication

In dedication to the man who knew infinity:

Srinivasa Ramanujan (1887-1920)

for his dazzling mathematical genius that showed the potential of the human mind.

Acknowledgments

One of the more pleasurable tasks of being an author is to thank the people responsible for the success of a book. My heartfelt thanks to my wife, Dei, for her love and support. I wish to thank my father, Ahal Singh, and my mother Tejinder; my brothers, Harjit, Jagjit; my sisters, Kookie and Dolly. Thanks also to Margaret Cooper Scott, Cathryn and Bob Foley, Craig and Lydia Cooper, Robert and Janie Cooper, Heidi and Steve Bynum, and Barbara and Edward L. Scott (Scotty) for their love and support. Special thanks to Mother. Without her spiritual support, this book would not have been possible.

I would like to thank Learning Tree International for re-kindling my interest in teaching and writing. For readers interested in additional information on seminars taught by the author, call 800-421-8166 (U.S.), 800-267-1696 (Canada), or 0800282353 (U.K.). I wish to thank Bob Sanregret and Anders Amundson, who had no idea what they were starting when one fine day in July 1990, they innocently asked me the question, "Would you like to write a seminar on Novell networking?"

I wish to acknowledge the many people who have helped me along the way: Edward and Mary Kramer, Harpreet Sandhu, Bill Duby, Angela, Michael Anaast, Janice Culliford, my students Lisa, Debi, Sheri, Rondi; Daniel Gottsegen, David Stanfield, Jeffrey Wintroub, Dr. Wagner, Bill Joy, Professor Ramamoorthy, Professor G. S. Sanyal, Professor "M", Professor Kumar Subramaniam, Sunil Padiyar, Dwayne Walker, Rex Cardinale, mathematician D. R. Kaprekar, Mr. Gadre, Brad Koch, John Moriarty (Professor Moriarty!), Rick Adamson, Richard Beaumont, Rick Otto, Eric Garen, David Collins, Yo Amundson, Anders Amundson, Kristina Steeg, Mark Drew, Nancy Harrison, John Rutkai, David O'Neal, Doug Northcutt, Marti Lichtanski, Karen Snyder, Hy Yarchun, Hal Kane, Patrick Wolfe, Steve Blais, Susan Schneider, Beverly Voight, Marilyn Hilliard, Leslie Mezirow, Mike Murray, Stu Ackerman, and Bruce Wadman.

I especially wish to thank my friends, John Moriarty, Bob Sanregret, Rick Adamson, Marti Lichtanski, Terry Young, and Farshad Nowshadi, for their fine company and interesting dinner conversations on several continents. Terry Young and Farshad Nowshadi provided many stimulating discussions on the topic of NetWare 4.x. Special thanks go to Farshad for his *delightful* company, his helping hand with some of the questions, his teaching me some fine points on "sharing," and the importance of creating backups!

I wish to thank Novell for its technical innovation and leadership in defining and creating the popular PC-based network computing market, and for having the vision to create NetWare Directory Services. Credit must also be given to Novell for popularizing professional certification in the computing industry through their CNE/ECNE/CNA programs. Special thanks to Rose Kearsley of Novell for her tremendous help and support.

I wish to also thank Watcom, creators of the professional Watcom C++ 32-bit compiler that is used for developing NLMs for NetWare. Special thanks to Chris who was instrumental in providing the author with a copy of the Watcom compilers that the author used for exploring the NLM architecture.

Many thanks to the staff of Macmillan Computer Publishing. In particular, I wish to thank Emmett Dulaney, the Publishing Manager, for his zeal and attention to the creation of this edition. I also wish to thank Drew Heywood for his many suggestions, encouragement, and friendship. Thanks to John Sleeva and all the editors for their editorial skills.

Contents at a Glance

	Introduction	1
1	Introduction to NetWare 4.x	11
2	Introduction to NetWare Directory Services	99
3	NetWare 4.x File System	249
4	NetWare 4.x File System Security	343
5	NetWare Directory Services Security	403
6	Customizing the NetWare 4.x User Environment	533
7	Managing NetWare Servers	637
8	Configuring NetWare 4.x Printing	723
9	Network Fault Tolerance	799
10	NetWare 4.x Messaging Services	857
A	NetWare 3.x and NetWare 4.x Command Comparisons	883
B	Strategies for Preparing for and Taking the Exams	889
C	Answers to Chapter Test Questions	897
	Index	905

Table of Contents

Introduction   **1**

  How This Book Helps You   1
  Additional Help   3
    The Test Questions   *3*
    The Special Icons   *4*
  CNE Test Objectives   6
  Final Word   9

1 Introduction to NetWare 4.x   **11**

  Understanding Network Components   11
  Exploring LANs and WANs   13
  Using Network Operating Systems for
    Enterprise Networking   15
    NetWare Directory Services   *18*
    Logical Organization of the Network   *19*
    Single Login to the Network   *21*
  Making a Network Connection   22
    NetWare Workstation Connections   *30*
    The DOS Requester, IPXODI, and LSL   *34*
    NetWare DOS Requester Components   *38*
    The VLM Manager   *39*
    VLM Options   *40*
    Logging In to a NetWare 4.x Network   *42*
    VLM Functions   *44*
  Using NetWare Utilities   46
    NetWare Graphical User Interface Utilities   *46*
    DOS Menu-Based (Text) Utilities   *60*
    NetWare Command-Line Utilities   *65*
  Exploring Other NetWare 4.x Features   67
    Global Network Management   *68*
    Independence from Physical Location of Resources *68*

Learning About Improvements in the NetWare File System 70

   Block Suballocation 70

   NetWare File System Compression 72

   Data Migration 74

Understanding the Improved File System Security
  and Management 75

Learning About Support for Network Auditing 77

Exploring the Memory Management Architecture 79

Learning About Improvements in Client
  Networking Services 82

Exploring Integrated Storage Management
  Services (SMS) 84

Understanding Improvements
  in Network Print Services Architecture 85

Introducing Multiple Language Support
  (Internationalization) 86

Study Guide for the Chapter 88

Chapter Summary 88

Chapter Test Questions 89

2 Introduction to NetWare Directory Services **99**

Understanding NDS 100

Understanding NDS Logical Resources 101

Comparing NDS to the NetWare Bindery 105

Understanding the NetWare Directory Database 108

Classifying NDS Components 113

   Tree Structure of NDS 113

   Container Objects 115

   Leaf Objects 116

   Object Class and Schema 117

   Containers and Directories in File Systems 125

Naming Objects 126

Classifying Container Objects 129

   The [Root] Container Object 130

   The Country Container Object 133

   The Organization Object 134

   The Organizational Unit Object 134

   Attribute Types 136

Leaf Object Types   137
Object Properties   162
Exploring an NDS Tree Case Study   163
Using NDS Tools   166
   Setting Up the Network Administrator Tool
     (NWADMIN.EXE)   167
   Using the NetWare Administrator Tool   168
   Using the NETADMIN Utility   172
Understanding NDS Context   176
Specifying NDS Path Names   180
   Complete Name   180
   Partial Name   183
   Resolving a Partial Name   183
   Relative Distinquished Names Example Exercise   187
Naming Rules in NDS   191
   NDS Path   191
   Typeless Name   192
Setting the Name Context at the Workstation   193
Querying from the Command Line in NDS   195
   The CX Utility   195
   The NLIST Command   205
Using the NetWare Administrator Tool for NDS Queries   216
Understanding the Volume Object   219
Study Guide for the Chapter   219
Chapter Summary   220
Chapter Test Questions   220

3 NetWare 4.x File System   **249**

Using the NetWare File System   249
Exploring the Disk Subsystem   252
   Volumes   252
Understanding NetWare Directories and Files   257
Understanding Default NetWare Directory Structure   262
Understanding Directory Structure Organization   266
   Single-Volume Directory Structure   269
   Multiple-Volume Directory Structure   270
   Designing File System Directory Structure   271

Using Network File Storage Commands   271
    The NLIST Command   272
    The NDIR Command   273
    Directory Commands   282
    The NCOPY Command   282
    File Management with the NetWare Administrator   285
    The FILER program   286
    NetWare Directories and Files   289
Using Directory Mappings   291
    The MAP command   293
    Network Drives   304
    NDS Syntax with MAP Commands   309
    Directory Map Objects   311
    Creating a Directory Map Object   317
    Utilities Needed for Directory Management Tasks   318
    Salvaging and Purging files   320
    Managing Volume Space Usage   322
Chapter Study Guide   329
Chapter Summary   329
Chapter Test Questions   330

4 NetWare 4.x File System Security   **343**

Understanding Rights Access   343
    Assigning File System Rights   344
    Creating Group Objects Using NetWare Administrator   349
    Creating Group Objects Using NETADMIN   355
Understanding Directory Rights and File Rights   359
Understanding the Inherited Rights Filter   362
    Computing Effective Rights   363
Using the RIGHTS Command   367
    Viewing Rights to a Specific Directory   370
    Listing Trustees Using RIGHTS   370
    Granting and Revoking Rights Using the
      RIGHTS Command   371
    Observing Inherited Rights Using the
      RIGHTS Command   375
    Removing a User as a Trustee for a Directory   376
    Changing the Inherited Rights Filter   376

Using Attribute Security 377
Using the FLAG Utility 381
Using the FILER Utility 382
   Setting Directory Trustees and Attributes Using FILER 385
Study Guide for the Chapter 395
Chapter Summary 395
Chapter Test Questions 396

5 NetWare Directory Services Security **403**

Understanding Network Security 403
Using Login Security 404
   Account Restrictions 407
   Password Restrictions 409
   Time Restrictions 411
   Station Restrictions 413
   Intruder Limits 416
Understanding Login Authentication 417
   Accessing NDS Resources 419
Examining NDS Security Concepts 420
Understanding NDS Rights 423
Clarifying Terminology 425
Exploring Object Rights 426
   Supervisor Object Right 427
   Browse Object Right 427
   Create Object Right 428
   Delete Object Right 429
   Rename Object Right 430
Understanding the [Public] Trustee 431
Examining Default Object Rights 435
Understanding Inheritance of Object Rights 439
Examining the Inherited Rights Filter 442
Exploring Security Equivalence 444
Using Object Effective Rights 445
Calculating Object Effective Rights 451
   Case Study 1—Computing Effective Rights 452
   Case Study 2—Computing Effective Rights 455
   Case Study 3—Computing Effective Rights 457
   Case Study 4—Computing Effective Rights 460

Case Study 5—Computing Effective Rights   463
Case Study 6—Computing Effective Rights   466
Case Study 7—Computing Effective Rights   470
Case Study 8—Computing Effective Rights   473
Case Study 9—Computing Effective Rights   478
Case Study 10—Computing Effective Rights   481
Examining Property Rights   484
All Properties Right versus Selected Property Right   486
The Access Control List Property   487
NDS Rights and the File System   488
Calculating Property Effective Rights   491
Case Study 1—Computing Property Effective Rights   492
Case Study 2—Computing Property Effective Rights   494
Case Study 3—Computing Property Effective Rights   496
Guidelines for Implementing NDS Security   500
Comparing NetWare File System Security with
  NDS Security   502
Study Guide for the Chapter   507
Chapter Summary   508
Chapter Test Questions   508

6 Customizing the NetWare 4.x User Environment   **533**

Defining the User Network Environment   534
Preparing the PC as a Workstation   534
How DOS Is Loaded   535
DOS CONFIG.SYS Processing   540
AUTOEXEC.BAT Processing   543
STARTNET.BAT Processing   544
NET.CFG Processing   546
Login Validation and Account Restrictions   550
Processing of Network Requests   552
Login Scripts   555
Login Script Types   555
System Login Script   556
Profile Login Script   557
User Login Script   559
Default Login Script   560
The NO_DEFAULT Directive   562

Login Script Execution Order *563*

Upgrade Considerations for Login Scripts *566*

Rights to Execute Login Script Property Value *567*

NetWare Login Script Commands *568*

Complexity of Login Script Files *570*

Recommendations for Organizing Login Scripts *573*

Login Script Variables *592*

Novell Menus 595

Menu Temporary Files *598*

Example Menu Script *599*

Menu Parts *600*

Menu Commands *601*

Organizational Commands *602*

Menu Control Commands *609*

Menu Limitations 624

Customizing Menu Colors 625

Study Guide for the Chapter 626

Chapter Summary 626

Chapter Test Questions 627

7 Managing NetWare Servers   **637**

Understanding NLMs 637

Understanding the Core Operating System 643

Examining Server Memory Considerations 644

Using Server Commands 645

The ABORT REMIRROR Command *650*

The REMIRROR PARTITION Command *651*

The MIRROR STATUS Command *651*

The LIST DEVICES Command *653*

The SCAN FOR NEW DEVICES Command *653*

The MAGAZINE Command *654*

The MEDIA Command *656*

The RESTART SERVER Command *658*

The LANGUAGE Command *658*

Special Control Keys for Console Commands *666*

Using System Administration NLMs 667

Management NLMs *668*

Server Enhancement NLMs *676*

Using New NLMs in NetWare 4.x   693
   The DOMAIN NLM   *694*
   The DSREPAIR NLM   *698*
   The RTDM NLM   *700*
   The NWSNUT NLM   *702*
   The TIMESYNC NLM   *703*
   The DSMERGE NLM   *703*
   The CDROM NLM   *705*
   The KEYB NLM and International Language Support   *711*
   The SCHDELAY NLM   *712*
Learning Strategies for Protecting the NetWare Server   714
Study Guide for the Chapter   715
Chapter Summary   715
Chapter Test Questions   715

8 Configuring NetWare 4.x Printing   **723**

Understanding Network Printing Concepts   723
Understanding the Print Queue Object   727
The Printer Object   733
Understanding the Role of the Print Server and
  PSERVER.NLM   741
The Print Server Object   743
Loading of Printer Definitions   750
The NPRINTER Program   751
Interactions Among the Print Queue, Print Server, and
  Printer Objects   755
Configuring Network Print Services   758
The PCONSOLE Utility   759
The LOAD PSERVER Command   767
Examining Print Server Status Using PCONSOLE   769
Quick Setup Configuration   770
Sending a Print Job   772
   Printing Using NETUSER   *773*
   Printing Using CAPTURE   *774*
   Printing Using NPRINT   *778*
   Printing Using PCONSOLE   *779*

Network Printing Tools 781
    The PRINTCON Utility 782
    The PRINTDEF Utility 787
    Summary of Default Assignments and Printing Capabilities 788
Study Guide for the Chapter 790
Chapter Summary 791
Chapter Test Questions 791

9 Network Fault Tolerance **799**

Examining System Fault Tolerance 799
    SFT Level I 800
    SFT Level II 803
    SFT Level III 804
    UPS Monitoring 804
Overview of Backup Services 805
    Full Backup 806
    Incremental Backup 807
    Differential Backup 808
    Custom Backup 810
Examining Storage Management Service 810
    SMS Architecture 812
Using the SBACKUP Tool 815
Using SBACKUP 817
Using SBACKUP to Perform a Backup 822
Using SBACKUP to Perform a Restore 831
Restoring without Session Files 836
Using Restore Options for Restoring a File System 837
Using Custom Backup Options 840
Using SBACKUP and Compressed Files 843
Using SBACKUP Log and Error Files 844
Examining SBACKUP Rights and Security Issues ... 845
Backing Up DOS Workstations 846
Caveats when Using SBACKUP 846
Study Guide for the Chapter 848
Chapter Summary 848
Chapter Test Questions 849

10 NetWare 4.x Messaging Services   **857**

Components of Messaging Services   857
NetWare 4 MHS   859
   NetWare 4 MHS Installation Requirements   *860*
   Installing NetWare 4 MHS   *861*
   Post NetWare 4 MHS Installation Check   *863*
   Assigning MHS-Related Properties to NDS Objects   *868*
   Other MHS-Related NDS Objects   *872*
   Using FirstMail   *876*
Study Guide for the Chapter   878
Chapter Summary   878
Chapter Test Questions   879

A NetWare 3.x and NetWare 4.x Command Comparisons   **883**

B Strategies for Preparing for and Taking the Exams   **889**

How This Book Can Help You Prepare for Your Exams   890
Author's Technique on Memorization   891
Using the Test Questions in This Book   891
Registering for the Test   892
Taking the Test   893
   Form Test Versus Adaptive Test   *895*

C Answers to Chapter Test Questions   **897**

Chapter 1   897
Chapter 2   898
Chapter 3   899
Chapter 4   900
Chapter 5   900
Chapter 6   901
Chapter 7   902
Chapter 8   902
Chapter 9   903
Chapter 10   903

Index   **905**

Introduction

This book is designed for users and system administrators who plan to be working with NetWare 4.x-based networks. It will also help you in preparing for your CNE/CNA/CNI exams for the NetWare 4 Administration course.

How This Book Helps You

The information presented in this book will help you perform system administration tasks for small to medium size networks.

Chapter 1 introduces the network services that are available on a NetWare 4.x-based network. It defines the basic networking components that are used in a NetWare 4.x network, and how you can configure a DOS workstation to make a connection to the network and log in to the network. This chapter provides an overview of the different networking components that are used on a DOS workstation and the functions each component performs.

Chapter 2 introduces NetWare Directory Services (NDS) concepts and how NDS can be used to access and manage network resources. Understanding of NDS services is fundamental to managing NetWare 4.x because most network administration revolves around how the NDS is represented, accessed, and managed.

Chapter 3 discusses NetWare volumes and NetWare file system directory concepts. The default NetWare file system structure is presented with an explanation of how you can maximize its use. You will also learn about the NetWare file system organization and how to access NetWare directories using the different MAP command options.

Chapter 4 discusses the concepts of NetWare file system security that allow controlled access to data on the network. It covers file system concepts such as NetWare directory and file rights, directory and file trustees, inherited rights, and effective rights. You will learn how to implement file system security using the NetWare administration tools.

Chapter 5 explains how NetWare 4.x NDS security is implemented and how it can be used to limit access to only those parts of the NDS tree the user should have. This chapter discusses the different types of NDS security, such as object rights and property rights.

Chapter 6 discusses how to customize a user's network, including subjects such as setting up the workstation environment, understanding login scripts, implementing user account restrictions, writing custom login scripts, and simplifying access to NetWare applications using the Novell menus. You learn about the different types of login scripts: system, profile, user, and default. You learn about the different components of a NetWare 4.x menu system and learn how to set up and configure Novell menus.

Chapter 7 presents network management functions that can be performed from the server console. You will learn about the different management NLMs and console commands that can be used to manage the server.

Chapter 8 discusses NetWare 4.x printing issues. It presents the printing concepts used in NetWare 4.x and the basic components of network printing. You learn how to create and configure print objects. The properties of print objects such as print queue, printer, and print server objects are described in detail. The tools used for network print configuration are described in a hands-on fashion.

Chapter 9 describes the system fault-tolerance capabilities of NetWare 4.x. In addition to System Fault Tolerance, UPS (Uninterrupted Power Supply) and Storage Management Services backup services are discussed.

Chapter 10 describes NetWare 4.x messaging services.

Appendix A contains command comparisons between NetWare 4.x and NetWare 3.x utilities.

Appendix B contains hints and tips about preparing for exams. It also includes the procedures for registering for a test, not only in the U.S.A. and Canada, but also in other parts of the world.

Appendix C contains the answers to the chapter-ending questions.

Additional Help

As you go through this book, it would be best if you have at least one NetWare 4.x server and a workstation on a network that you can experiment with. Because you may not have access to such a system, when you are reading this book and preparing for your exams, many network administration tasks are presented in a guided-tour manner with plenty of screen shots, so that you can see how a task is performed. This is the next best thing to doing hands-on network administration tasks on the network.

The Test Questions

The book has extensive practice test questions that will be valuable not only for those preparing for CNE exams, but also those who want to acquire practical skills. A question can have more than one possible correct answer. If there is a single correct answer, it is indicated by a ○ (circle) placed next to each answer. If there are several correct answers, the choices have a □ (square) next to them. To get you used to this style, these circle and box icons are used with the test questions in this book. Some of the questions on the NetWare 4.x test require you to type in the answer instead of selecting from a number of alternatives. Also, the number of alternatives for a question can vary.

 The questions in this book are designed to test your understanding of the material in the book. The author and publisher, however, cannot guarantee that you will see exactly the same questions on the test. There has been a recent change in the type of questions that are asked on the CNE exams. The questions are conceptual; you are given case studies and asked to select the best answer. You may also be tested on procedures to perform network administration tasks. You may be asked, for example, to use a simulated version of the NetWare Administrator tool to create NDS objects with specified properties. Or you may be asked to assign file system and NDS rights using the NetWare Administrator tool. We therefore recommend that you study the material in this book on a NetWare 4.x network and become very familiar with the actual procedures for network administration tasks. It would be difficult to pass the exams by just studying the material in the book, and without having hands-on NetWare 4.x administration experience.

The Special Icons

Several icons are used throughout the book to help as a quick reference.

The Study Note Icon

 This icon is used to point out the specific areas of knowledge over which you are most likely to be tested. For instance, some tables in the book are referenced by a Study Note icon with the statement that you should be familiar with the contents of that table. It is generally a good idea to be familiar with all the information in the book, but when a piece of information is specifically referenced in a Study Note icon, it means that you should review the contents of the table before taking your exams because you are quite likely to be tested on it. A quick way to review the material in the book for preparing for the CNE exams is to browse through the book and go over the Study Notes.

The Practical Tip Icon

 This icon is used to point out information that you can apply directly in administering a NetWare 4.x network. These are items of information that you normally acquire after working with NetWare 4.x networks for some time.

The Author's Note Icon

These icons are comments or insights into the workings of NetWare that the author wishes to share with you. You are not likely to be tested over this information. The Author's Note is meant to provide additional insight which will give you confidence in understanding the inner workings of NetWare 4.x.

CNE Test Objectives

A major goal of this book is to teach you the practical side of NetWare 4.x administration. An equally important goal is to help you pass the CNE/CNA/CNI exams. The test objectives for the NetWare 4.x Administration exam are presented here for your reference.

Objectives, NetWare 4 Administration (Test 6521)

1. Activate, navigate, and find information in Novell online documentation.

2. Describe a network, including its basic functions and physical components.

3. Describe NetWare Directory Services (NDS) and explain its role on the network.

4. Describe the directory, including its functions and basic components.

5. Describe the function of the software necessary to connect a workstation to the network, including local operating systems, NetWare DOS Requester, communications protocols, and network board.

6. Define NetWare command-line utilities, describe how they are used, and activate help information for them.

7. Display volume, directory, and file information.

8. Map a network drive to a directory using a Volume object and a Directory Map object and navigate the directories of a volume.

9. Create, delete, rename, and move directories.

10. Describe the basic components of network printing and how they interrelate in processing a print job.

11. View the network printing information at the DOS command prompt and in MS Windows.

12. Set up a print job redirection with CAPTURE and print a document from a DOS application.

13. Describe the function of a User object and its property values.

14. Manage NDS objects by creating, deleting, renaming, and moving objects, and by entering and modifying property values.

15. Explain how to create a user home directory automatically while creating a User object; create user home directories.

16. Create User objects with the same property values using a User Template.

17. Describe and establish login security, including user account restrictions, time restrictions, station restrictions, and intruder detection.

18. Explain guidelines for planning and creating custom volumes and directories in the network file system.

19. List the system-created volumes and directories; describe their contents and function.

20. Identify the strengths and weaknesses of sample directory values.

21. Design and create a directory structure based on a given scenario.

22. Describe NetWare 4 file system security, including the concepts of directory and file rights, trustee assignments, inheritance, rights reassignment, Inherited Rights Filter (IRF), security equivalence, and effective rights.

23. Given a scenario, calculate a user's effective rights.

24. Perform basic security implementation tasks, such as assigning a trustee and granting rights, setting a directory IRF, creating a Group object and assigning members, and making a user security equivalent to another user.

25. Based on a scenario, create and implement a file system security plan that appropriately grants directory and file rights to a container, Group, and User objects, and sets directory IRFs.

26. Describe remote console management; list the steps necessary to set up a server for both SPX and asynchronous remote connections.

27. Use RCONSOLE.EXE to remotely access the server console, change between console screens, and activate the RCONSOLE Available Options menu.

28. Describe security strategies for a NetWare 4 server, such as setting a password on the monitor, setting a password for Remote Console, and placing the server in a secure location.

29. Recommend procedures that should execute during login.

30. Describe the process of creating menus.

31. Plan a simple menu using correct syntax.

32. Build, compile, execute, and debug menus.

33. Explain how access to the directory is controlled by object trustees, object rights, and property rights.

34. List and explain the automatic rights assignments that can occur in NDS.

35. Explain guidelines and considerations for managing NDS security.

36. Implement NDS security by making trustee assignments; modifying object, All Property, and Selected Property rights; setting Security Equivalence, and setting Inherited Rights Filter.

37. Describe the Directory tree, including container objects and sample Directory structures; discuss guidelines for organizing resources.

38. Demonstrate correct object-naming techniques.

39. Change the current context and navigate the Directory tree with CX.

40. Log in, map network drives, and redirect print jobs to resources in other contexts.

41. Grant rights to file system and network printing resources in other contexts.

42. Back up a NetWare server's file system.

43. Create NDS User, Group, Distribution List, and Organization Role objects as messaging service users and assign them user mailboxes.

Final Word

The author and publisher want you to use this book as both a study guide and a tool for continued learning. As your experience with NetWare 4.x increases, so will your need to understand the more complex features of NetWare 4.x (in general) and how they apply to your particular network. This book is designed to help you in this global approach to mastering network administration with NetWare 4.x.

Thank you for choosing *CNE Training Guide: NetWare 4.1 Administration, Second Edition*!

Introduction to NetWare 4.x

In this chapter you are introduced to network services that are available through a NetWare 4.x-based network. This chapter defines the basic networking components used in a NetWare 4.x network and teaches you ways to configure a DOS workstation for logging in to the network. You are also taught the different networking components that are used on a DOS workstation and the functions each component performs.

In addition, you are presented with an overview of the services and features available in NetWare 4.x.

Understanding Network Components

You can visualize a network as a system that connects computers in a manner that enables the computers to share information. The computers are classified based on the kinds of activities that are performed on them. Figure 1.1 displays a network with several types of computers. Some of these computers are dedicated for personal use by a network user. These are called workstations and can run a variety of different operating systems, such as DOS, OS/2, Macintosh OS, Unix, and Windows NT.

Figure 1.1

Network components.

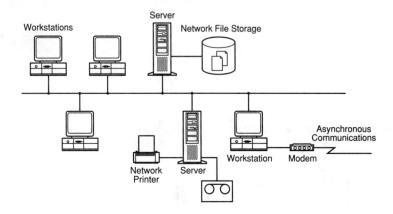

Other computers on the network provide specialized services that other computers can use. These computers are called servers and, depending on the services they provide, they are called file servers, database servers, and communication servers. A NetWare 4.x server is an example of a server that enables the sharing of resources, such as file services, to users on the network. Other types of servers provide database access or communications access and are, therefore, called database servers and communication servers. The network can also have larger computers such as minicomputers and mainframes that act as servers.

The operating system that runs on the servers is either a general-purpose operating system, such as Unix, OS/2, or Windows NT, or a specialized operating system, such as NetWare.

The workstation typically makes requests for services from servers and is therefore called a client of the network's server components. For communications to take place, the workstation needs to have physical network components, such as cabling and network cards, and network devices, such as repeaters (to amplify signals over long distances). Larger networks often have interconnecting devices such as bridges and routers to interconnect networks at OSI (Open Systems Interconnection model) layers two (data link) and three (network), respectively.

Exploring LANs and WANs

Figure 1.1 shows one possible type of a network. Because of the small distance span, such a network is called a *local area network* (LAN). Another type of network is the *wide area network* (WAN), which can span long distances. NetWare 3.x and early versions of NetWare were designed to run on LANs, where they provided workgroup computing solutions. You can use NetWare 3.x (and earlier versions) in WANs, but on large networks, current releases of NetWare 3.x begin to show weaknesses in the areas of network administration and communication. NetWare 4.x was designed to address these weaknesses and is utilized in both LANs and WANs.

NetWare 4.x can also be used for integrating LAN and WAN environments. Figure 1.2 and table 1.1 show the differences between LANs and WANs. A primary difference is that LANs are generally owned and operated by a department of an organization or a group of users, whereas WANs lease a commercial service or use expensive private technologies.

Local Area Networks   Wide Area Networks

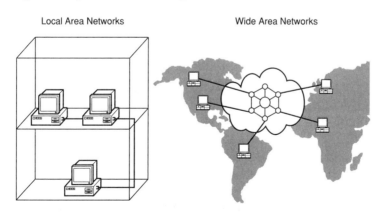

Figure 1.2
LANs and WANs.

13

Table 1.1
LANs and WANs

Parameter	Local Area Networks	Wide Area Networks
Ownership	Owned by departments and end users.	Not generally owned by an organization. Services are provided by commercial organizations.
Distance	Short: within a building or campus (less than 10 KM, typically).	Long: Across country, between countries.
Media Choices	Many: Twisted-pair, coaxial, fiber-optic, and so on.	Relatively few: Leased lines, telephone lines, fiber-optic.
Protocols	Many: IEEE 802 LAN protocols, TCP/IP, SPX/IPX, AppleTalk, ATM, and so on.	Relatively few: X.25, TCP/IP, ATM, and so on.
Data Transfer	Typically high-speed: 1 to 100 Mbps. Availability of ATM may blur the differences between LANs and WANs.	Typically low-speed: 2400 bps to 64 Kbps. Higher speed networks are becoming available. Availability of ATM may blur the differences between LANs and WANs.

As you can see from figure 1.2, LANs usually cover shorter distances. Most LANs today are based on a shared-media access technology that limits the distances across which LAN cabling can be run. This means that the network devices share a common network media, such as coaxial cabling or twisted-pair wiring, and have to use a method of communication that does not interfere with signals from other network devices using the same media. Examples of this are the CSMA/CD (Carrier Sense Multiple Access with Collision Detect) technology used in Ethernet

LANs and the Token Access technology used in token-ring networks. These shared-media access technologies are limited by distance and do not function efficiently over the longer distances required for WANs.

For LAN networks that have larger network bandwidths, switching technologies such as the type used in switched Ethernet, switched token ring, and Local ATM (LATM) networks can be used.

WANs must use underlying protocols that work well over longer distances. Examples of these are X.25, Frame Relay, SMDS, SONET, ATM, and so forth. Discussion of these technologies is beyond the scope of this book. You can refer to another book, *NetWare: The Professional Reference*, for more information on WAN technologies and Ethernet switch technologies.

The media choices that are available to LANs are wide-ranging and include such types as twisted-pair, coaxial cable (coax), fiber, wireless, and others. WANs are often limited to whatever media choices are already installed. A new media type is sometimes difficult and expensive to install over the long distances typical of WANs; likewise, the long distances might also affect right-of-way issues.

Using Network Operating Systems for Enterprise Networking

A network can consist of several LANs tied together with wide area links, as shown in figure 1.3. For a user to use printer or network volume storage resources, the user has to know the location of the resources. For earlier versions of NetWare, such as the one depicted in figure 1.3, the user needs to know the names of the file servers to which the printer and volume resources are attached. Before accessing a resource on a server, the user has to log in to that server.

Figure 1.3

An example of a NetWare-based network.

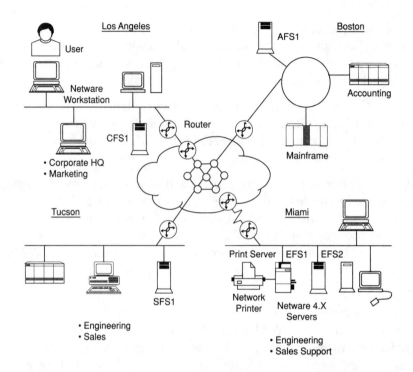

If the user needs to access a volume resource on another server, he or she has to attach to that server. Attaching and logging in to a server implies that the user needs accounts on each server that he or she intends to access. This approach works quite well in small networks that consist of less than 50 computers. On larger networks where there may be many servers, it is not easy for the user to remember the resources that are available on each of the servers. In such cases, it is much easier for the user to have a logical view of the network that hides the network's nonessential physical details. Figure 1.4 shows a logical view of the same network depicted in figure 1.3.

In the network's logical view, resources are organized into groups that are, in turn, organized into a hierarchy that reflects their usage, function, or geographical location. To utilize the resources on this network, the user logs in to this logical view of the network. Security mechanisms that are global in scope and apply to the entire network control access to network resources. In NetWare 3.x and 2.x, access to resources is controlled by security mechanisms that are local to each server (called the bindery). The bindery does not have network-wide significance;

the bindery-based services, therefore, are server-centric. To provide a single access to the network, the designers of NetWare 4.x created a global database called the *NetWare Directory Service*. The NetWare Directory Service is the mechanism used to supply a logical view of the network.

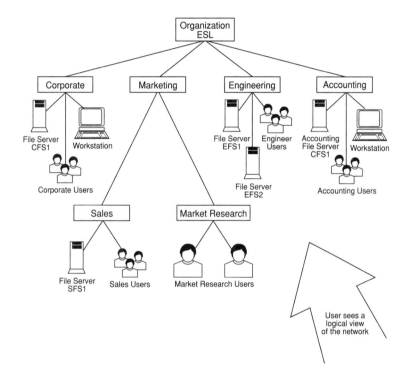

Figure 1.4

A logical view of a network.

The NetWare Directory Service's global database service is not confined to a single server; it represents network-wide resources. This distinction is the single most important difference between NetWare 4.x and NetWare 3.x/2.x. It is also the feature that affects many of the network administration tasks and network utilities. Many pre-NetWare 4.0 network administration tasks and utilities modified the network information in the bindery. The NetWare 3.x/2.x utilities cannot be used for NetWare 4.x because the information in a global database needs to be modified, and these older utilities have no concept of a global database, although they understand the bindery. Several older utilities have been consolidated into newer ones. These newer utilities have the capability to correctly modify the global database.

17

NetWare Directory Services

Before you can understand ways to administer and make a connection to a NetWare 4.x network, it is helpful to have a general understanding of the way NetWare Directory Services (NDS) works. NDS is the most distinctive feature of NetWare 4.x over earlier NetWare versions. It provides the network administrator and the user with a logical view of a network that hides the sometimes bewildering complexity of the actual physical network topology. An organization can arrange the logical view of its network in a way that meets the organization's needs and is easily recognizable to the network's users. Figure 1.5, for instance, presents a hierarchical view of the network that reflects the organization chart of a company and is recognizable by the company's network users. The physical details of the network (such as its type of cabling) and its interconnecting devices (such as routers and bridges) are not considered in figure 1.5. In other words, the network administrator and the user do not need to be aware of the physical nature of the network to use the network.

Figure 1.5

A logical network that reflects the hierarchy of an organization.

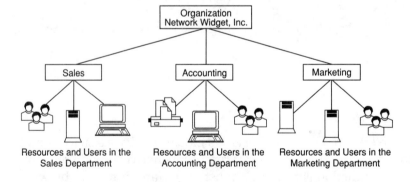

The logical view is possible because of NDS. NDS provides a distributed database that can act as a repository of information on all the shared resources on the network. The database is considered distributed because it does not physically reside on any single server on the network. The database is hierarchical because it provides a convenient grouping of resources by function, location, or organizational structure.

NDS is essentially a replacement for the bindery services that are part of the pre-NetWare 4.0 product line. The bindery in the earlier NetWare release is also a way of organizing resources, but the resources are specific to the server on which the bindery resides. The bindery cannot easily support information on other network nodes, and because it is organized as a flat database instead of a hierarchical database, it does not have any natural way of representing usage or organizational relationships between resources.

If you were to categorize some of the benefits of using NDS, they would be as follows:

◆ A logical organization of network resources

◆ A single login to the network

◆ A global network management view that you can centralize or distribute

◆ Independence from physical location of resources

◆ Resource sharing, such as file services and printer sharing

Novell's implementation of NetWare Directory Services for NetWare 4.x provides the following:

◆ Multiple levels of security

◆ Printer and file sharing

◆ Centralized or distributed network management

◆ Logical organization of network resources

Logical Organization of the Network

The logical organization of the network is a benefit that derives directly from the way you can group resources hierarchically in an organization's NetWare directory service representation (see fig. 1.5). This grouping is executed to reflect the way users want to use the network, making it easy for users and network administrators

19

to find the network resources without knowing the physical details of network connectivity. A user who needs to use a network resource has access to NDS objects in the database that contain information on the network resource. In NetWare 4.x, all network resources accessible by NetWare users are represented by NDS objects.

 NDS controls access to objects and resources on the network and eliminates redundant tasks such as adding a user account to multiple servers on the network.

An example of a network resource is a file server, which you can model as a File Server object. Inside this File Server object (see fig. 1.6) is information such as the name of the file server, its network address, location, and so forth. Information about the file server is described by the properties of the File Server object.

Figure 1.6

A file server represented as an object.

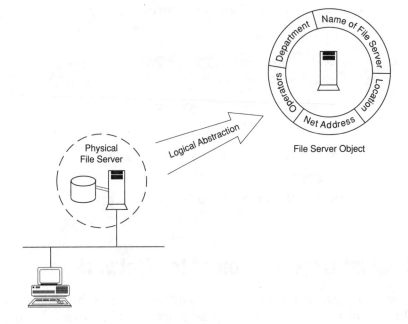

Single Login to the Network

A single login to a network (see fig. 1.7) enables a user to be authenticated just once in order to access all the resources on the network. After the user logs in, the network administrator can limit his or her access to resources on the network. For instance, all users, by default, are permitted to see the structure of an organization's directory, even though they cannot access all the objects in this directory unless explicitly given access by a network administrator. A single login to a network also simplifies the use of the network, because the user does not need to perform separate logins on multiple servers on the network.

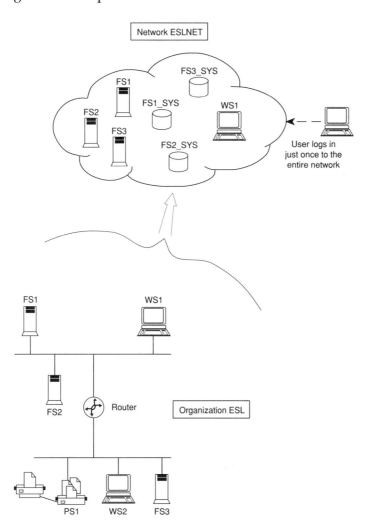

Figure 1.7

A single login to the network.

21

Before NetWare 4.0, the user was required to log in (or attach) explicitly by supplying a user name and password for every server to which he or she wanted access. The number of such concurrent connections was limited to eight. In addition, the network administrator had to create separate accounts on each server that the user needed to access. This easily became a burdensome task on large networks.

The single login to a network is possible because the user authentication takes place against a global network database (directory) that is not specific to a server. In figure 1.8 you can see that the first step to logging in to a network is the authentication of the user against information in the global directory. Once the user authentication is successful, the user is granted access to any resource on the network. The maximum number of concurrent connections to different NetWare servers is now 50; for pre-NetWare 4.0 versions, this limit is 8.

Figure 1.8

User authentication to the network.

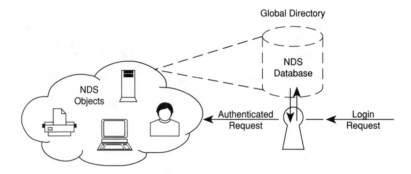

Making a Network Connection

The previous sections have described the purposes of an NDS tree and ways that you can use a single user login to log in to the entire network. This section discusses the components and procedures needed to make a network connection. Before a user can log in to the network, the user must make a connection to the network.

When a workstation makes a network connection in NetWare 4.x, it is not just connecting to a particular file server on the network, but is also connecting to a global database of resources accessible to users at any workstation. This global database contains the definition of the user accounts. The user can log in to the network using a valid user account in this global database that is implemented by NDS.

To make a network connection, you need additional hardware support in the form of a Network Interface Card (NIC) attached to the network. The NIC is responsible for the physical interface to the network. In addition to NIC hardware, networking software, consisting of the NetWare requester and communication protocols, is also needed to provide access to the NetWare 4.x network (see fig. 1.9). A communication protocol is a set of rules and regulations on ways to format and send messages between two computers. There are many choices of communication protocols in the industry today. NetWare servers and workstations typically use the IPX (Internet Packet Exchange) communication protocol. NetWare 4.x servers and workstations also can use other protocols such as TCP/IP for communication.

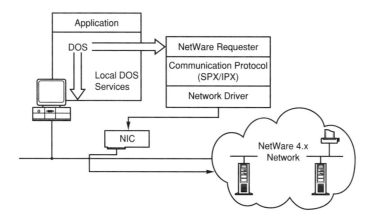

Figure 1.9

Workstation network components.

 Logging in to a NetWare 4.x network is accomplished by the following:

◆ Network client software

◆ NetWare Requester

◆ Communication protocols

◆ Network Interface Card (NIC) driver

Figure 1.10 shows workstation network components in relationship to the OSI model. The OSI model serves as a useful yardstick for comparing networking components. As you can see from this figure, the OSI model consists of seven layers. The lowest layer—the *physical layer*—deals with signal propagation. Data bits are suitably encoded using signaling techniques so that you can recover them at the end. The cable connections (MDI: "media dependent interface") and the signaling mechanism are part of the NIC of the workstation and correspond to OSI layer 1. OSI layer 1, therefore, is implemented by the NIC.

Figure 1.10

Network components
and the OSI model.

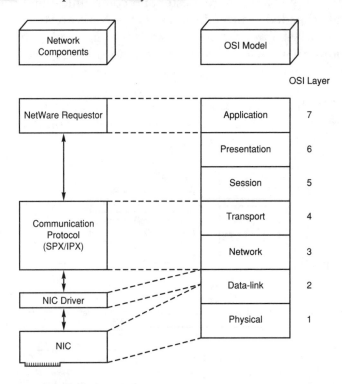

Layer 2 of the OSI model is called the *data link layer*; it deals with the grouping of bits to form a frame that is sent across the network. The data link layer manages the link between two network nodes. In the case of LANs, link management is implemented by media access control (MAC) techniques such as CSMA/CD for Ethernet and Token Access for token-ring networks. The data link layer function is handled by the NIC.

Layer 3 of the OSI model is called the *network layer* and deals with routing of packets on a network. In a simple LAN, there might be only one possible route between two network nodes. In more complex topologies, consisting of separate LAN segments connected via a router, multiple paths to a given destination may exist. The network layer figures out the best path to a destination.

Layer 4 of the OSI model is called the *transport layer* and deals with end-to-end data integrity. It is the job of this layer to ensure that data is sent reliably across the network. If packets are corrupted in transmission (because of noise and equipment malfunction) or arrive in the wrong order at the destination, the transport layer performs the necessary retransmission and proper ordering of packets to make the data stream reliable. In NetWare, the Sequence Packet Exchange (SPX) protocol is an example of a transport protocol that provides this reliability. Readers interested in more details on IPX/SPX can refer to *NetWare: The Professional Reference* from New Riders Publishing.

Layer 5 of the OSI model is called the *session layer* and deals primarily with session management. Layer 6 of the OSI model is called the *presentation layer* and deals with ways data are represented.

Layer 7 of the OSI model is called the *application layer* and deals with communication Application Programming Interfaces (APIs). The primary protocol NetWare uses at this layer is the NetWare Core Protocol (NCP). This protocol implements the NetWare core services for file, printer, and shared resource access. NetWare 4.x has extended the definitions of the NCP protocol to provide access to additional resource types and functions for NetWare 4.x.

The interface between layer 2 and layer 3 of the OSI model is provided by the network driver. The network driver understands the details of the NIC hardware and its parameter settings (interrupt request, I/O base address, and memory base address).

The network driver is written to Novell's Open Data Link Interface (ODI) specification. The ODI interface is discussed next.

The ODI specification enables a large number of network adapters to support different protocol stacks such as TCP/IP, OSI, SPX/IPX, and AppleTalk. Prior to ODI and similar mechanisms (NDIS and Packet Driver), a separate driver had to be written for each protocol stack; moreover, it was difficult to get these separate drivers to coexist on a workstation, making it hard to support more than one protocol stack.

The ODI specification

◆ enables network devices that use different protocols to coexist and share the same physical network.

◆ enables multiple protocols to share the same network adapter and cabling system.

◆ enables a network adapter driver to be written just once for different types of communication protocols.

The two key components of ODI layers are the Link Support Layer (LSL) and the Multiple Link Interface Driver (MLID). These components are shown in figure 1.11.

Figure 1.11

ODI components versus the OSI model.

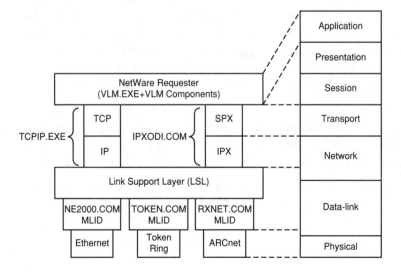

The Link Support Layer provides an ODI interface to the communication protocol. This interface enables multiple protocol stacks to coexist in harmony and even share the same network board driver. The ODI driver is also called the Multiple Link Interface Driver (MLID) because it can support multiple interfaces to communication protocols via the Link Support Layer.

The key components of ODI are as follows:

◆ Link Support Layer (LSL)

◆ Multiple Link Interface Driver (MLID)

In figure 1.11, the Ethernet, Token Ring, and ARCnet networking technologies correspond to layers 2 and 1 of the OSI model. NE2000.COM, TOKEN.COM, and RXNET.COM are the names of the MLID drivers. Other types of boards have different names. These drivers correspond to a portion of the data link layer and are written to interface with the Link Support Layer. The LSL does not map well onto the OSI model but represents the boundary between the data link layer and the network layer.

Because it provides the interface between MLID drivers and the upper-layer protocols, you can think of the Link Support Layer in terms of describing a portion of the data link layer and the lower portion of the network layer of the OSI model. The Link Support Layer is a key element in the ODI specification, providing a logical view of the network adapter and virtualizing it. The network layer software does not have to be rewritten to understand the low-level mechanics and operational details of a new network adapter. The network layer software sees a well-defined virtual interface to any network adapter.

The Link Support Layer

◆ acts as a switchboard to route packets to the correct protocol and correct ODI driver.

◆ implements the ODI specification.

The practical significance of the Link Support Layer is that the network layer protocol needs to be written only once to the ODI interface. When a new type of network adapter is built, the manufacturer writes an MLID driver for it that can hook into the LSL. The LSL provides the same logical interface to this board, and the protocol software does not need to be rewritten for the new network adapter.

The same MLID driver can support new types of protocol software as long as the protocols are written to the interface provided by LSL. The MLID driver is able to handle packets from different protocol stacks delivered to it by the LSL. After receiving the different protocol packets from the network, MLID forwards the packet to the LSL without interpreting the packet contents. The LSL is responsible for sending the packets to the correct protocol stack.

The MLID drivers are network adapter drivers that support the ODI specification. They can communicate with the Link Support Layer and are also called ODI drivers.

Configuration information for the ODI driver is kept in the NET.CFG file under the Link Driver section.

The ODI driver provides communications between the workstation software and the physical network components.

The configuration information for the MLID driver and protocol modules (IPXODI and TCP/IP) is kept in the NET.CFG file.

The LSL acts as a software switch, through which multiple protocol packet types travel and are delivered to the correct MLID or the correct protocol stack. In order to provide this routing, the LSL contains information about the MLIDs and the protocol stacks they support.

Then the MLID loads, and the LSL assigns a logical number to each network adapter. When a protocol stack loads and registers with the LSL, it is also assigned a logical protocol stack number. The LSL can support up to 16 protocol stacks.

The LSL module is specific to an operating system platform. This means that although LSL is available for DOS, OS/2, NetWare 3.x, NetWare external routers, and so forth, the actual LSL module cannot be interchanged between the operating systems. In DOS, for instance, LSL is loaded as a TSR (terminate-and-stay-resident) program and is implemented in the file LSL.COM; in OS/2 it is loaded as a device driver called LSL.SYS.

 The default Ethernet frame type for NetWare 4.x is ETHERNET_802.2 and is specified in the Link Driver section of the NET.CFG file.

Once the LSL module and the MLID drivers are loaded in memory, you can load the protocol modules. The native IPX/SPX protocol used with NetWare is implemented by the IPXODI.COM TSR program.

Figure 1.12 shows different protocol modules loaded at a workstation using the common LSL and an MLID.

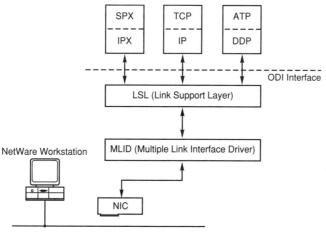

Figure 1.12

Multiple protocol stacks using MLID.

29

Benefits of using ODI include the following:

◆ Flexible configuration using the NET.CFG configuration file.

◆ Sharing of the same NIC by different protocols means fewer NICs and less hardware.

◆ The MLID needs to be written only once for an NIC, after which time you can use for communications any board that has the ODI interface.

◆ Multiple protocol support enables your workstation to communicate with different hosts using the protocols supported by the hosts.

NetWare Workstation Connections

Figure 1.13 shows the files that implement the different workstation components, and figure 1.14 shows ways that the network components and DOS interact. When a request is made for a network or DOS service, it is first seen by DOS. DOS then makes use of its redirection capabilities (introduced in DOS 3.1 and above) to send network requests to the VLM manager. Requests for local resources are handled by DOS itself.

Figure 1.13

NetWare 4.x DOS workstation connection components.

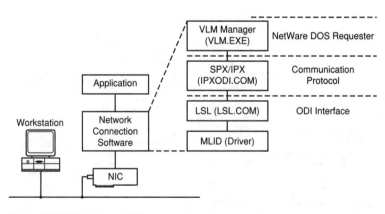

MLID = Multiple Link Interface Driver
VZM = Virtual Loadable Module

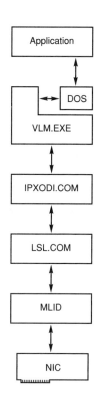

Figure 1.14

NetWare DOS
Requester and DOS.

To connect a DOS workstation to a NetWare 4.x network, you
need to perform the following steps:

1. Boot the workstation with DOS. Ensure that the
   LASTDRIVE=Z statement is present in the CONFIG.SYS file.
   Edit CONFIG.SYS with a text editor, if needed, to add this
   statement.

   The LASTDRIVE=Z statement is needed because DOS and
   the DOS Requester share a common drive table.

2. Load LSL.COM. Enter the following command at the DOS
   prompt:

   LSL

   LSL must be loaded prior to loading the MLID driver, because when the MLID driver loads, it connects with the NIC
   (initializes the NIC) and the LSL module. If the LSL module
   (LSL.COM) is not in memory, the MLID driver will not be
   able to link to the LSL layer.

31

3. Load the MLID driver. Enter the following command at the DOS prompt:

   NE2000 (Replace *NE2000* with your ODI driver)

   If there is more than one NIC at the workstation, you will need to load the MLID drivers for each of the NICs to be used for communications. Note that you can bind IPX to only one network board under DOS.

   Examples of MLID drivers include NE2000.COM for the NE2000 board, TOKEN.COM for IBM Token-Ring NICs, and SMC8000.COM for the SMC EtherCard PLUS family.

4. Load the communication protocol stack. Enter the following command at the DOS prompt:

   IPXODI

   For IPX/SPX, this is the IPXODI.COM driver. For TCP/IP, it is TCPIP.EXE.

5. Load the VLM.EXE program. Enter the following command at the DOS prompt:

   VLM

   VLM.EXE implements the Virtual Memory Manager program that manages the individual components called VLMs (Virtual Loadable Modules), which together implement the DOS Requester.

The VLMs replace the NetWare shell (NETX.COM or NETX.EXE) that was used in earlier versions of NetWare. The VLMs cannot coexist with the older shell's NETX.COM or NETX.EXE.

The CONFIG.SYS file must have the LASTDRIVE=Z statement for NetWare 4.x DOS workstations.

You might find it more convenient to place the commands listed in the preceding steps in a batch file to provide a network connection. This is done automatically when the DOS client software is installed using the DOS client INSTALL program. At the end of running the DOS client INSTALL program, a batch file called STARTNET.BAT is placed in the default directory \NWCLIENT on the workstation's hard disk. An entry is also placed in the startup AUTOEXEC.BAT file that calls the STARTNET.BAT file.

 The load sequence for loading network client software at a DOS workstation is as follows:

1. Load LSL.COM.

2. Load the MLID (ODI driver) for the NIC being used.

3. Load IPXODI.COM.

4. Load VLM.EXE.

An example of a STARTNET.BAT file for a XIRCOM PCMCIA Ethernet card is shown here:

```
@ECHO OFF
C:
CD \NWCLIENT
SET NWLANGUAGE=ENGLISH
LSL
CEODI
IPXODI
VLM
CD \
```

The STARTNET.BAT batch file is called using a call statement in the AUTOEXEC.BAT file:

```
@CALL C:\NWCLIENT\STARTNET.BAT
```

The CALL statement to the STARTNET.BAT file is placed in the beginning of the AUTOEXEC.BAT file. The CALL statement usually comes before the DOS PATH statement in the AUTOEXEC.BAT file that sets the local search drives. Some people modify the STARTNET.BAT file to change their directories to the first network drive and to issue the LOGIN command to log in to the network. This action can result in the PATH statement in the AUTOEXEC.BAT file executing after the user has logged in.

As a result of this procedure, the network search drives are replaced by the local search drives. To prevent this situation from occurring, move the call to the STARTNET.BAT to the end of the AUTOEXEC.BAT file, or at least after the PATH statement in the AUTOEXEC.BAT file.

The DOS client installation software can add the line

```
@CALL C:\NWCLIENT\STARTNET.BAT
```

in the AUTOEXEC.BAT file to automate connection to a network.

The DOS Requester, IPXODI, and LSL

When an application makes a request for services, DOS examines this request. If the request is for local network resources, the request is handled by DOS. If the request is for network resources, the request is sent to the DOS Requester. Beginning with DOS 3.1, DOS has had the capability of providing redirection services. The DOS Requester for NetWare (also called the NetWare DOS Requester) shares system tables, such as the drive table, with DOS (see fig. 1.15). DOS keeps track of which drive letter entries in the table are for DOS and which are for the DOS Requester. When an application makes a request for a file on a particular drive letter, after consulting the shared drive table, DOS is able to direct the request to the DOS Requester or local DOS system services.

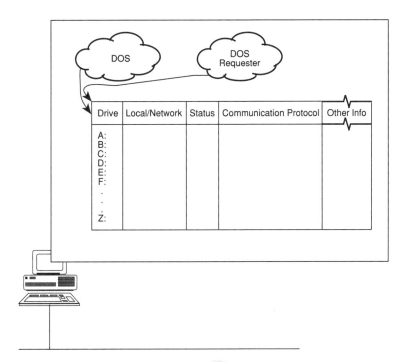

Figure 1.15

DOS Requester and DOS drive tables.

 The NetWare DOS Requester logically resides between workstation software and network services and enables communications between them.

The DOS Requester takes the application request and translates it into an equivalent NCP (NetWare Core Protocol) request. The NCP is used to carry requests for services to a NetWare file server. The NetWare file servers have an NCP server process that can handle multiple requests for network services and send the results of processing the NCP requests back to the sender. The NCP requests are then carried across the network by a transport communication protocol. The default communication protocol for a NetWare client is IPX (Internetwork Packet Exchange protocol).

In NetWare 4.x

◆ the request for a network service is first seen by DOS.

◆ DOS and the NetWare DOS Requester share a common drive table.

Application requests for network services are translated into NCP requests for services. The default communication protocol used for sending NCP requests is IPX.

The DOS Requester is implemented by Virtual Loadable Modules (VLMs). VLMs are a way of breaking up the monolithic NetWare shell (NETX.COM or NETX.EXE) found in earlier versions of NetWare into smaller components, each of which you can selectively load.

The communication protocol is implemented by TSR programs. The default IPX protocol is implemented by the IPXODI.COM program.

Though the name of the file makes no mention of the SPX (Sequenced Packet Exchange) protocol, the IPXODI.COM includes the SPX protocol. The SPX protocol is not normally used by NetWare 4.x. It is used in applications such as RCONSOLE (Remote Console) and for establishing connections between print servers and remote printers. These applications require a reliable virtual-circuit connection, which is implemented using the SPX protocol.

You can obtain help on the IPXODI options by typing the IPXODI /? command as shown here:

```
C:\NWCLIENT> IPXODI ?
NetWare IPX/SPX Protocol  v3.01 (941031)
(c) Copyright 1990-1994 Novell, Inc.  All Rights Reserved.
```

```
Available command line options:
/?      Display this help screen.
/D      Eliminate Diagnostic Responder - Reduces size by 3K.
/A      Eliminate Diagnostic Responder and SPX - Reduces size by 9K.

/C=[path\]filename.ext
        Specify a configuration file to use (Default is NET.CFG).

/U      Unload resident IPXODI from memory.
/F      Forcibly unload resident IPXODI from memory, regardless of
        programs loaded above it.  Using this option can cause a
        machine to crash if applications are still using IPX/SPX.
```

As you can see from the preceding help message, if the diagnostic responder used by some management programs to collect information on NIC statistics is not needed, using the /D option can reduce memory requirements by 3 KB. Using the /A option eliminates the diagnostic responder and SPX (not used for NetWare core services), which reduces memory requirements by 9 KB.

 If you are using RCONSOLE or a remote printer at the workstation, you should not use the /A option with IPXODI.

The Link Support Layer is implemented using LSL.COM for DOS. Like IPXODI.COM, the LSL.COM program is also a TSR. It must be loaded before loading the ODI driver. You can obtain the following LSL options by using the LSL ? command:

```
C:\NWCLIENT> LSL ?
NetWare IPX/SPX Protocol  v3.01 (941031)
(c) Copyright 1990-1994 Novell, Inc.  All Rights Reserved.

Available command line options:
/?      Display this help screen.
/D      Eliminate Diagnostic Responder - Reduces size by 3K.
/A      Eliminate Diagnostic Responder and SPX - Reduces size by 9K.

/C=[path\]filename.ext
        Specify a configuration file to use (Default is NET.CFG).
```

```
/U      Unload resident IPXODI from memory.
/F      Forcibly unload resident IPXODI from memory, regardless of
        programs loaded above it.  Using this option can cause a
        machine to crash if applications are still using IPX/SPX.
```

NetWare DOS Requester Components

The NetWare DOS Requester consists of a Manager program
called VLM.EXE, which upon loading loads the Virtual Loadable
Modules (VLMs). VLMs are readily identified by a VLM extension
and are program files that provide a specific function.

 NetWare DOS Requester consists of two major
components:

♦ Virtual Loadable Modules (VLMs)

♦ VLM Manager

VLMs provide the same flexibility at the workstation that
NetWare Loadable Modules (NLMs) provide at the server. NLMs
are software modules that you can load on the server and dynamically link to perform a desired function. Similarly, VLMs are
software modules that are loaded at the workstation to provide a
desired function. Figure 1.16 shows a comparison of VLMs and
NLMs. Novell has specified ways to write NLMs, and many third-
party vendors provide management capabilities and applications
that you can connect directly to internal NetWare resources, with
the NLM acting as an extension of the operating system. As the
use of VLMs becomes more popular, third-party products that
extend the workstation's network capability will increase. As new
VLMs become available, they can connect to the VLM-bus in
figure 1.16 and provide a clean way of extending the capability of
the network client software.

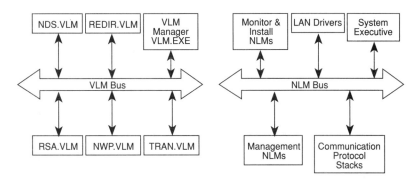

Figure 1.16

The VLM-bus versus the NLM-bus.

 When VLM.EXE loads, it loads and activates the NetWare DOS requester.

The VLM Manager

The VLM Manager, implemented by VLM.EXE, is a TSR and can manage VLM program files written to the VLM specification.

The data flow and communications between VLMs are managed by the VLM manager. The VLM manager is also responsible for handling application requests and forwarding them to the appropriate VLM that can process the request. It also manages memory services on behalf of the VLMs, such as a VLM's need for memory allocation and deallocation.

 The VLM Manager is responsible for the following:

◆ Managing data flow and communications between VLMs

◆ Forwarding application requests to the appropriate VLM for processing

◆ Controlling VLM access to memory at the workstation

39

After the VLM Manager loads, the VLM program files (those with a VLM extension) are loaded in a default order if the USE DEFAULT=ON option is specified in the NET.CFG file's NetWare DOS Requester section. The NET.CFG is a configuration file that is used by the workstation communication software.

If USE DEFAULT=ON is not specified, the VLMs are loaded in an order that must be specified in the NET.CFG file.

The VLM Manager will look for VLMs in the current directory. If you want to load VLMs from another directory, you can use the /C=directory option to specify an alternate directory. You can also specify an alternate NET.CFG. The only way to get the VLMs themselves from outside the current directory is to specify the full path on the VLM= line in NET.CFG.

Some benefits of using VLMs include the following:

◆ Only needed components are loaded. This reduces workstation memory overhead.

◆ Because the requester consists of a smaller number of components, each of these components has a better chance of being loaded in upper memory (memory between 640 KB and 1 MB) than if it was one large module.

◆ Using VLMs opens up the workstation architecture for development by third parties who can write additional VLM components.

VLM Options

The VLM Manager has a number of options, including using expanded, extended, or conventional memory; using alternate configuration files; and unloading the VLM TSR program without rebooting the workstation. You can see these options by typing this command:

```
VLM /?
```

The following output shows the help messages for the different VLM options:

```
C:\NWCLIENT> VLM /?
VLM.EXE      - NetWare virtual loadable module manager  v1.20
(941108)
(c) Copyright 1994 Novell, Inc.  All Rights Reserved.
Patent pending.

Available command line options:
/?      Display this help screen.
/U      Unload the VLM.EXE file from memory
/C=[path\]filename.ext
        Specify a configuration file to use (Default is NET.CFG).
/Mx     The memory type the VLM.EXE file uses where x is one of the
        following:
        C = Conventional memory.
        X = Extended memory (XMS).
        E = Expanded memory (EMS).
/D      Display the VLM.EXE file diagnostics.
/PS=<server name>
        Preferred server name to attach to during load.
/PT=<tree name>
        Preferred tree name to attach to during load.
/Vx     The detail level of message display where x is one of the
        following:
        0 = Display copyright and critical errors only.
        1 = Also display warning messages.
        2 = Also display VLM module names.
        3 = Also display configuration file parameters.
        4 = Also display diagnostics messages.
```

The more important of these options are summarized in table 1.2.

Table 1.2
Important VLM Commands and Options

VLM Command	Description
VLM /C=[*path*]*filename*	Loads DOS Requester using the configuration file's filename instead of the default NET.CFG.
VLM /MC	Loads DOS Requester in conventional memory.

41

Table 1.2, Continued
Important VLM Commands and Options

VLM Command	Description
VLM /ME	Loads DOS Requester in expanded (EMS) memory.
VLM /MX	Loads DOS Requester in extended (XMS) memory.
VLM	Loads DOS Requester. VLMs loaded are those in the current directory or those specified in the NET.CFG file.

The VLM.EXE program automatically selects the best possible memory use: extended memory first (if extended memory drivers are loaded), expanded memory second (if expanded memory drivers are loaded), and conventional memory only in the absence of enhanced memory options.

 Study the options in table 1.2 .

Logging In to a NetWare 4.x Network

Figure 1.17 shows the steps necessary to log in to the network. After the VLM Manager loads, it searches for the nearest active server. A connection between the workstation and the server is established, and the first network drive is mapped according to the FIRST NETWORK DRIVE statement in the NetWare DOS Requester section of the NET.CFG file. This is usually set to drive F: (see fig 1.17). The first network drive is mapped to the SYS:LOGIN directory of a server volume. The phrase "mapping a drive" means that the DOS workstation can access the remote file system SYS:LOGIN by using the same DOS commands that are used to access a local drive, such as drive C:. A sample NET.CFG file, used for connecting to a NetWare 4.x network, is shown next.

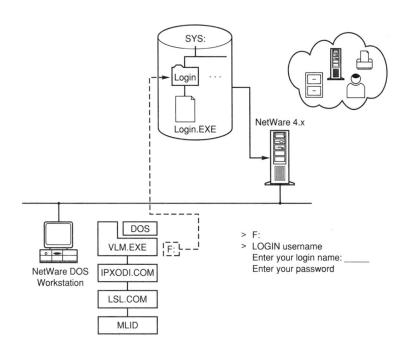

Figure 1.17

Logging in to the network.

```
Link Driver CEODI
 FRAME  Ethernet_802.2
 INT  5
 PORT 380
 MEM  d0000
 IOWORDSIZE 16

NetWare DOS Requester
 FIRST NETWORK DRIVE = F
```

NET.CFG has a number of section headings. In this example of the NET.CFG file, the section headings are Link Driver CEODI and Net-Ware DOS Requester. The section headings always begin in the first column of the file. Under the section heading are configuration statements that pertain to that section. These statements are in-dented by at least one character or a tab. The statements in the Link Driver section deal with the driver configuration, and the state-ments under the NetWare DOS Requester are for the VLM.EXE.

After VLM loads, it maps as a network drive the drive specified in the FIRST NETWORK DRIVE statement in NET.CFG.

At this point, changing your current drive to the F: drive makes the programs in that drive (SYS:LOGIN directory) accessible. One of the programs in the F: drive is LOGIN.EXE. When the program LOGIN.EXE is run, it prompts for the user name and password. If these are entered correctly, the user is logged in to the user account on the network. Thus, the steps to complete the login process are as follows:

```
F:
LOGIN
Enter your user name: username
Enter your password: secretpassword
```

 Executing LOGIN.EXE from the mapped network drive activates the login procedure.

Login is the mechanism or procedure that requires you to identify yourself in order to gain access to the network resources that network security permits you to access.

VLM Functions

There are currently 13 VLMs that are loaded if the USE DEFAULT=ON option is specified in the NetWare DOS Requester section of the NET.CFG file. For a NetWare 4.x client enabled for directory services, the order in which the VLMs are loaded reflects the order in which they are used. If you do not want to load a VLM, you can delete it or rename it. PNW.VLM, for example, is used to support Personal NetWare. If you are not using Personal NetWare, you can delete or rename the PNW.VLM file.

The default load order is listed here:

1. CONN.VLM

2. IPXNCP.VLM

3. TRAN.VLM

4. SECURITY.VLM

5. NDS.VLM

6. BIND.VLM

7. PNW.VLM

8. NWP.VLM

9. FIO.VLM

10. GENERAL.VLM

11. REDIR.VLM

12. PRINT.VLM

13. NETX.VLM

Table 1.3 provides a description of the VLM functions. The list is not exhaustive; it lists only the important VLMs that are within the scope of this book.

Table 1.3
VLM Table Summary of the Major VLMs

VLM Name	Brief Description
BIND.VLM	Bindery emulation—child of NWP.VLM
CONN.VLM	Connection table manager
FIO.VLM	File input/output for network requests
GENERAL.VLM	Provides miscellaneous functions for other VLMs such as NETX.VLM and REDIR.VLM
IPXNCP.VLM	Transport Protocol Processing using IPX—child of TRAN.VLM
NDS.VLM	NetWare Directory Services—child of NWP.VLM

continues

Table 1.3, Continued
VLM Table Summary of the Major VLMs

VLM Name	Brief Description
NETX.VLM	Shell compatibility
NWP.VLM	NetWare Protocol Multiplexor
PNW.VLM	Personal NetWare VLM
PRINT.VLM	Print redirector
REDIR.VLM	Redirector
RSA.VLM	Background authentication service
TRAN.VLM	Transport protocol multiplexor

Using NetWare Utilities

Now that you have learned to log in to the network, what kind of network tasks can you perform? This section gives you a guided tour of some basic NetWare utilities.

NetWare 4.x provides for the following basic utilities:

◆ NetWare graphical user interface programs

◆ DOS menu-based (text) utilities

◆ Command-line utilities

NetWare Graphical User Interface Utilities

NetWare graphical user interface utilities are available for MS Windows and OS/2. These utilities are bundled with NetWare 4.x and are installed when the server is installed. If you are familiar with MS Windows-based applications, you will feel at home using these utilities. The NetWare graphical user interface utilities include programs such as the following:

◆ NWUSER (NetWare User Utility)

◆ NWADMIN (NetWare Administrator)

◆ DynaText (GUI online help)

Figure 1.18 shows the top level screen for the NWUSER utility.

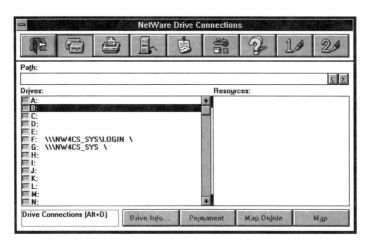

Figure 1.18
The NWUSER screen.

Guided Tour to Using NWUSER

You are now presented with a guided tour for using the NWUSER utility.

Throughout this guided tour and others dealing with GUI utilities, the following terms will be used. If you have never used MS Windows, these terms may be helpful to you.

Left-click on X	Position the mouse pointer on X and click the left button of the mouse once.
Click on X	Same as left-click on X.
Double-click on X	Position the mouse pointer on X and click the left button twice in rapid succession.
Right-click on X	Position the mouse pointer on X and click the right button of the mouse once.

To open the NWUSER utility, follow these steps:

1. Log in as an Admin user to the network. If the server is in the same context as the User object definition, you can simply specify your user name—otherwise you will have to specify your complete name. Refer to Chapter 2, "Introduction to NetWare Directory Services," for a discussion on contexts and complete names. This guided tour assumes that you have MS Windows installed and configured for the NetWare User Utility.

2. Start MS Windows by typing

   WIN

   You should see a screen similar to that in figure 1.19.

Figure 1.19

The MS Windows startup screen.

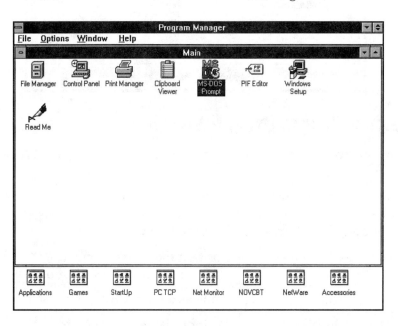

3. Find the group icon labeled NetWare and double-click on it. You should see program items in the NetWare group similar to those shown in figure 1.20.

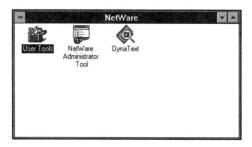

Figure 1.20

The NetWare group
program items.

4. Double-click on the User Tools icon. You should see drive mappings for the NetWare Drive Connections similar to those in figure 1.21.

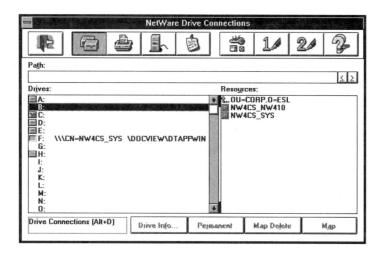

Figure 1.21

NetWare Drive
Connections.

For sending messages, perform the following steps:

1. Click on the Messages icon, which looks like a note button:

2. If you don't see any users in the Resources panel, find the file server on the Connections panel and click on it.

3. Click on a user's name to send a message.

49

4. Type a message in the message area in the top half of the screen by clicking in that message area once and typing the message.

5. Click on the Send button in the bottom right corner of the screen.

6. If you want to clear a message that you receive from another user, select the OK button.

To send a message to a group of users, follow these steps:

1. Highlight a user by pressing the Ctrl key and clicking on the user name.

2. Enter a message in the message box and click on the Send button.

To create a network drive mapping, you can assign a network drive to a directory on a server volume:

1. Click on the network drive icon:

You should see your screen change (see fig. 1.22).

Figure 1.22

The NetWare Drive Connections screen.

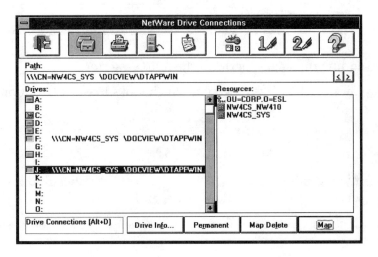

2. Highlight drive K: and double-click on the Volume object displayed on the Resources panel. You should see a list of directories in the Volume object on your screen (see fig. 1.23).

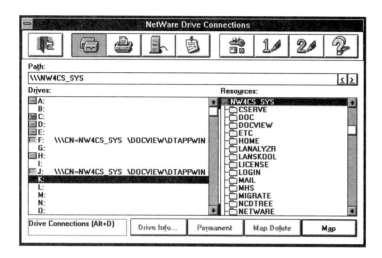

Figure 1.23
The NetWare Drive Connections screen.

3. Click on the PUBLIC directory and then click on the Map button in the bottom right corner of the screen. You should see a new drive mapping created (see fig. 1.24).

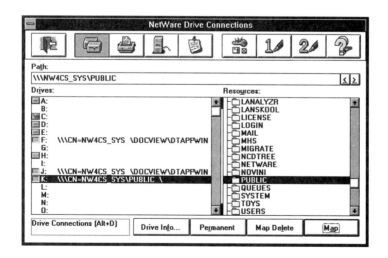

Figure 1.24
New drive mapping created.

51

Practice deleting the drive mapping you just created by performing the following steps:

1. Highlight the newly created drive mapping.

2. Click on the Map Delete button on the bottom of the screen.

 You can create a drive mapping by dragging a directory from the right panel and dropping it on top of a network drive in the left panel of the screen. To remove a drive mapping, you can highlight the drive mapping and drag it away from the left panel.

1. Repeat the preceding actions and create a drive mapping of S: to the SYSTEM directory.

2. Make the map drive permanent by using the Permanent button. The permanent drive mapping, when created, exists in all applications and DOS sessions started from within MS Windows.

Using the Login and Logout options, you can log out and log back in from within the NetWare User Utility:

1. Highlight the NetWare Connections icon:

2. Click on your network tree icon from the Connections panel on the left, and select the Logout button.

3. You are now logged out. Verify by selecting the Drive Connections button. You should see no drive mappings.

4. Log in again by selecting the Login button from the NetWare Connections screen. You should see a Login to NetWare dialog box.

5. Enter your user login name and password to log back in.

Examine the NetWare settings:

1. Click on the NetWare Settings button:

You should see the NetWare Settings dialog box (fig. 1.25).

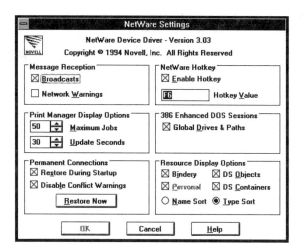

Figure 1.25
The NetWare Settings dialog box.

2. Notice that the NetWare Hotkey is enabled and set to a default value of F6. Additionally, note that you can enable and disable the restoration of permanent drive connections during Windows startup.

3. Select OK.

4. Exit the NetWare User Utility by using the following button:

5. Press the F6 key and notice that you are in the NetWare User Utility application. If pressing F6 does not work, verify that you have enabled the hot key correctly.

6. Exit Windows, go back to the DOS prompt, and log out of the network.

Online NetWare Manuals via DynaText

NetWare DynaText is a graphical utility that works with Windows 3.1 (or higher) to make online manuals accessible through a graphical user interface (GUI). Figure 1.26 shows a sample DynaText screen.

Figure 1.26

A Sample DynaText screen.

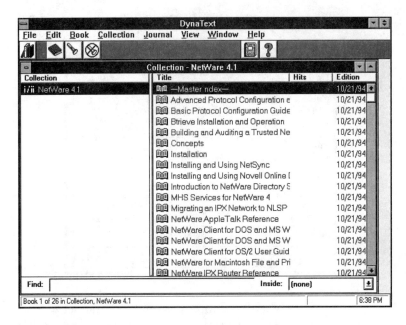

All the NetWare manuals are available in DynaText format. A list of these manuals and a brief description of their contents follows:

◆ **Master Index**

This index links to all places in the manuals. Click on a link marker to go to a place in the manual in which a term or topic can be found.

◆ **NetWare AppleTalk Reference**

This reference provides the information you need to understand the AppleTalk protocol stack for NetWare servers. It describes configuration parameters for the AppleTalk protocol stack.

◆ **Btrieve Installation and Reference Manual**

Btrieve is a popular and efficient record manager bundled as an NLM in NetWare servers. This manual contains information on installing, configuring, executing, and monitoring the Btrieve record management system for NetWare servers.

◆ **Concepts**

This is a glossary of NetWare-related terms with a tutorial description of what each term means. Topics are listed alphabetically in categories ranging from AAA to ZZZ.

◆ **NetWare Client for DOS and MS Windows User Guide**

This manual helps you set up and install your client software. It introduces you to the client tools for managing your client on a NetWare network. The manual covers concepts and procedures for installing and using NetWare client software on NetWare 2.x, 3.x, and 4.x networks.

◆ **NetWare Client for DOS and MS Windows Technical Reference**

This manual describes the parameters needed to configure NetWare workstation software on NetWare 2.x, 3.x, and 4.x networks.

◆ **Installation**

This contains information on how to install a new NetWare 4.x server.

◆ **NetWare IPX Router Reference**

This manual provides the information you need to understand the IPX protocol for the router. It describes the IPX configuration parameters.

◆ **NetWare for Macintosh File and Print Services**

This manual explains how to install, configure, and maintain the NetWare for Macintosh software.

◆ **Using MacNDS Client for NetWare 4**

This manual describes the NetWare for Macintosh MacNDS client software. The MacNDS client software enables access to NetWare 4 NDS services from Macintosh workstations.

55

◆ **MHS Services for NetWare 4**

This manual explains the NetWare MHS (Message Handling Service) services, and explains how to install and manage it. The guide also describes how to use the FirstMail client software.

◆ **Installing and Using NetSync**

This manual explains how to install and use the NetSync utility. NetSync is a management utility that enables you to manage NetWare 3.x servers from the NetWare Directory Services.

◆ **Introduction to NetWare Directory Services**

This manual introduces you to the basics of NDS and helps you plan the NDS tree.

◆ **New Features**

This manual introduces you to features that are unique to NetWare 4.x.

◆ **NetWare Client for OS/2 User Guide**

This manual describes the installation and configuration of NetWare Client software for OS/2 workstations. This client software can be used for both NetWare 3.x and NetWare 4.x. The manual contains information on accessing network services form Virtual DOS machines and setting up Named Pipes and NetBIOS protocol support.

◆ **Print Services**

This helps you with NetWare 4.x printing concepts and how you can set up, load, and use network printing utilities. It contains some troubleshooting tips and guidelines for network print services.

◆ **Supervising the Network**

This helps you to set up and administer the network after you complete the NetWare 4.x installation. It covers issues such as managing NDS, NetWare files and directories, creating login scripts, NetWare server maintenance, network auditing, and backing up and restoring data.

◆ **Utilities Reference**

This contains information on how to use NetWare utilities, such as Text workstation utilities, server utilities, and GUI-based utilities. It also contains information on NDS bindery objects and their properties.

◆ **Upgrade and Migration**

This manual describes upgrading to NetWare 4.x from other NetWare servers, such as NetWare 2.x or 3.x and IBM LAN Server.

◆ **TCP/IP Reference**

TCP/IP is a de facto protocol for connecting heterogeneous systems together. This manual discusses how TCP/IP can be configured and managed on the NetWare 4.x server. It explains the concepts in relationship to NetWare's implementation of TCP/IP.

◆ **Building and Auditing a Trusted Network Environment with NetWare 4**

This describes an overview of the security requirements for large networks and how NetWare 4 auditing can be used to meet these requirements.

◆ **System Messages**

This is a list of all possible system and warning messages that you may encounter in configuring NetWare 4.x. It lists the messages according to the modules that generate them, and there are over 150 modules. It explains the possible cause of the error message and the action you can perform to fix it.

Starting DynaText

The online documentation can be viewed using DynaText. The following is an outline of the procedure for using DynaText:

1. Log in to the network.

   Make sure that the DOS environment language variable NWLANGUAGE is set correctly. For example, for the

57

English language, use the following in the AUTOEXEC.BAT or STARTNET.BAT file:

```
SET NWLANGUAGE=ENGLISH
```

The NWLANGUAGE environment variable should normally be set when you perform the client installation.

2. Start MS Windows.

3. Start the NetWare group by double-clicking on it.

4. Double-click on the DynaText icon. You should see the DynaText screen (see fig. 1.27).

Figure 1.27

The opening
DynaText screen.

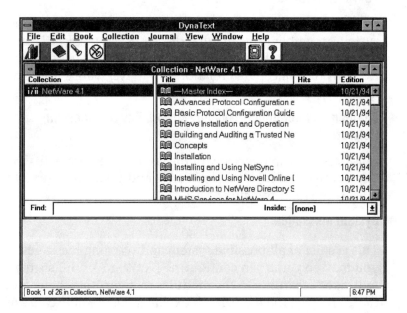

5. Ensure that the Collection NetWare 4.x Manuals is high-lighted on the left of the screen, if you have multiple manuals installed.

6. Open the Concepts manual by double-clicking on it. You should see the start of the manual (see fig. 1.28).

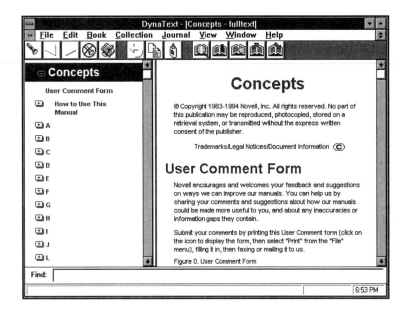

Figure 1.28

The Concepts
manual screen.

7. On the bottom of the screen is a Find box. Click within this box and type this string:

   `NET.CFG`

   If you find only one or no occurrences of the string, make sure you start the search from the beginning of the manual.

8. Repeat the search for this string:

   `IPXODI`

9. Exit the Concepts manual (double-click on the icon in the top left corner).

10. Search for the string LOGIN in all the manuals. You should see a report on the number of books that were matched. If you press OK, you will see the number of matches in each book.

11. See if you can answer the following questions:

    a. In what number of books was the string LOGIN found?

    b. Which manual had the maximum string matches, and what number of matches were there in this manual?

12. Explore the Help option in the menu bar. Use it to find out ways the search options could be used.

13. Explore any other topics of interest to you.

DOS Menu-Based (Text) Utilities

The DOS text-based utilities are utilities that use the extended character set, such as line drawing characters. Figure 1.29 shows an example of the NETUSER menu-based tool. These tools are based on a modified C-Worthy utility library.

Figure 1.29

The NETUSER main screen.

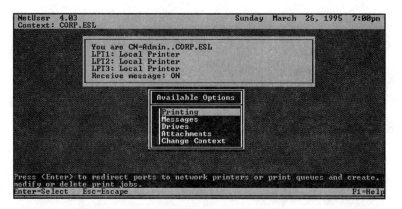

The following are examples of other menu-based text utilities:

- ◆ NETUSER
- ◆ NETADMIN
- ◆ FILER

The text utilities make use of the special control keys shown in table 1.4.

60

Table 1.4
Text Utility Control Keys

Key	Action
Up/Down arrow keys	Move between menu choices
Enter	Selects menu option
Esc	Goes back to previous menu
F1	Obtains help
F3	Modifies an option
F5	Marks an option
F10	Saves changes and continues
Alt+F10	Exits menu
Ins	Adds item to list
Del	Deletes item from list

You will now be presented with a guided tour of using the text-based utility, NETUSER. NETUSER provides many of the capabilities of the NetWare User Utility from a menu-driven text utility.

Throughout this guided tour and other guided tours dealing with text-based utilities, the following terms will be used:

Select option X from Y	Use the up/down arrow keys to highlight X from menu with title Y and press the Enter key.
Mark option X	Highlight option X and press the function key F5.

Sending Messages

To send a message to another user, follow these steps:

1. Log in to the network.

2. Start the NETUSER utility by typing the following:

   NETUSER

   Highlight the Messages option.

3. Press Enter with the Messages option highlighted from Available Options. You should see a screen similar to figure 1.30.

Figure 1.30

Messages option in NETUSER.

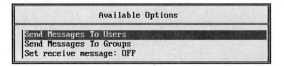

4. Select the Send Messages To Users option from Available Options. You should see a screen similar to figure 1.31.

Figure 1.31

The Send Messages option in NETUSER.

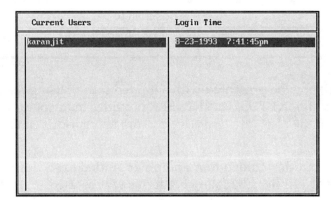

5. Highlight a user's name to send a message, and press Enter.

6. Type a message in the message area on the bottom half of the screen.

7. Press Enter to send the message.

8. If you want to clear a message that you receive from another user, press Ctrl+Enter.

To send a message to a group of users, follow these steps:

1. Mark several users by highlighting their user names and pressing the F5 key.

2. Press Enter.

3. Enter a message in the message box and press Enter again.

4. Verify that your messages have been sent.

5. Press Esc once to return. You should see the screen in figure 1.32.

Figure 1.32

Checking receive message status.

What is the current status of "Receive message"? (Look for the gray box on the top half of the screen.)

1. Select the option "Set receive message: ..." a few times and observe the changes on your screen.

2. Set the Receive message option to OFF. You should see the screen in figure 1.33.

Figure 1.33

Setting Message options to not receive messages.

3. Select Drives and then Drive Mapping. You should see the screen in figure 1.34.

Figure 1.34

The Current Drive
Mappings screen.

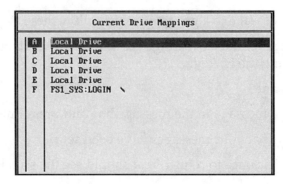

Figure 1.34

The Current Drive
Mappings screen.

4. Press Ins. Note that the net drive letter that appears is the next unassigned network drive.

5. Press Enter. You should see the Select Directory screen (see fig. 1.35).

Figure 1.35

Select Directory
in NETUSER.

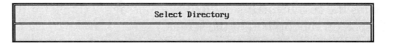

6. You can enter a directory name or press Ins to browse through a list of directories and select a directory.

7. Map to the network directory SYS:PUBLIC and press Enter.

8. You will be asked if you want to map root this drive. Select No for now (later you can practice using the map root option and observe any differences). You should see a new drive mapping (see fig. 1.36).

   You will learn about the map root drive option later in this book.

Select the option Attachments from the main NETUSER screen:

1. Use the F1 key and the Ins key to discover the meaning of this option.

2. Toggle the function key F4 from the Attachments screen and observe the screen changes.

3. Exit the NETUSER utility by pressing Esc a few times and answering Yes to exit, or by using Alt+F10 and answering Yes to exit.

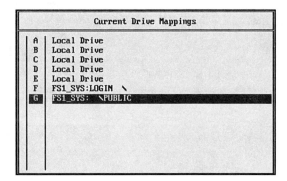

Figure 1.36
Newly created drive.

NetWare Command-Line Utilities

NetWare command-line utilities are executed at the shell command prompt. These utilities are located in the SYS:PUBLIC and SYS:SYSTEM directories. Their general syntax is as shown here:

```
COMMAND_NAME [Parameters]    [/Options]
```

Examples of some of these utilities are as follows.

To list information on users currently logged in, use

```
NLIST USER /A
```

To send message to users who must be logged in, use

```
SEND "message" to user
```

To obtain help on commands NLIST and SEND, use

```
NLIST /?
SEND /?
```

Figures 1.37 and 1.38 show help on the SEND command.

Figure 1.37

SEND /? Help—
Screen 1.

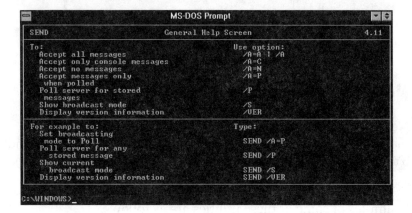

Figure 1.38

SEND /? Help—
Screen 2.

Table 1.5 shows the important options for the SEND commands.

Table 1.5
Important SEND Commands and Options

SEND Command	Description
SEND /A=N	Accept no messages (including console messages).
SEND /A=C	Accept only console messages.
SEND /A or SEND /A=A	Accept all messages.
SEND "message" to loginname	Send message to login name.
SEND "message" to groupname	Send message to group name.

Obtaining Help on Command-Line Utilities

The command-line utilities have a /? switch that gives additional help information on ways to use these utilities. This switch is very convenient, because help is available from the command line without invoking any other online documentation. Typing illegal command-line parameters also results in help screens being displayed. You can see the NDIR help screen by using the following command:

```
>NDIR /?
```

Help is also available in the menu utilities via function key F1. This help is context-sensitive. The menu utilities such as FILER and PCONSOLE use the familiar C-Worthy Menu interface. Unlike previous versions of NetWare, using the F1 key twice (F1,F1) does not display extended help information.

NetWare 4.x online help is available through the DynaText application that runs under Windows. DynaText is a valuable tool for quickly looking up information on a topic.

Exploring Other NetWare 4.x Features

You have seen ways that a workstation makes a network connection in a NetWare 4.x network. After you are logged in, NetWare 4.x provides you with a number of useful features. This section provides you with an overall understanding of these features and capabilities.

NetWare 4.x features include the following:

◆ NetWare Directory Services (NDS)

◆ Improvements in NetWare file system support

◆ Improved file system security and management

◆ Support for network auditing

◆ Simplified and more efficient memory management architecture

67

- Improvements in client networking services
- Integrated Storage Management Services (SMS)
- Improvements in network print services architecture
- Multiple language support (internationalization)
- Simplified installation and upgrade procedures
- Online NetWare manuals via DynaText

Global Network Management

In pre-NetWare 4.0, the network management tasks had to be performed separately on each NetWare server, because network management usually resulted in a modification of the bindery, and the bindery was specific to each server. To perform network management tasks, the bindery (a local database of network resources on a specific server) had to be modified on each server.

Because the NDS is a global database, global network management is possible where the network administrator can administer the network resources from any place on the network (see fig. 1.39). Also, as you will learn later, the network administrator can delegate responsibility to other users who serve as network administrators. In pre-NetWare 4.0, the responsibility was delegated to a fixed number of user account managers, workgroup managers, and other operators; in NetWare 4.x, many levels of network administrators with varying degrees of responsibilities can exist.

Independence from Physical Location of Resources

In pre-NetWare 4.0-based networks, the resources were described in a server bindery and were dependent on that server. A classic example of this was NetWare printer definitions that were tied to a specific server. If the printer had to be relocated to another server, the bindery representation of the printer had to be moved to another server (see fig. 1.40). In a large network that is in a state of flux, this shuffle can become a major task.

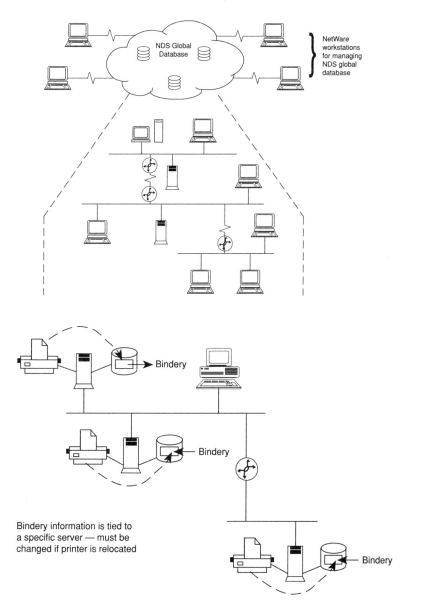

Figure 1.39

Global network management.

Figure 1.40

Bindery representations of printer definitions.

In NetWare 4.x, the resource definitions are not tied to any specific server or a physical location on the network. This means that a user can access a resource without worrying about the physical location of the resource and ways to reach it. Changes to network resources are made to the NDS objects that are part of a global database. The user can access the NDS object from any station on the network, provided he or she has been granted security permission for the resource.

Learning About Improvements in the NetWare File System

One of the strengths of NetWare has always been a fast and efficient file system. This has always been central to NetWare's popularity and ability to act as a file server. In NetWare 4.x, the file system has been improved. Some of these improvements are the result of new features called block suballocation, compression, and migration.

Block Suballocation

NetWare 4.x enables the disk block size selected at installation time to be 4, 8, 16, 32, or 64 KB (where 1 KB is 1024 bytes). This capability also existed in NetWare 3.x. However, in NetWare 3.x, if a 200-byte file was created on a volume that had a disk block size of 4 KB, a 4 KB block of storage would be allocated and the remaining 3,896 (4,096 – 200) bytes would not be available for use. This represents a wasted space of 95 percent, and if the disk block size was 64 KB, the wasted space would be even greater. Figure 1.41 shows how block suballocation in NetWare 4.x works.

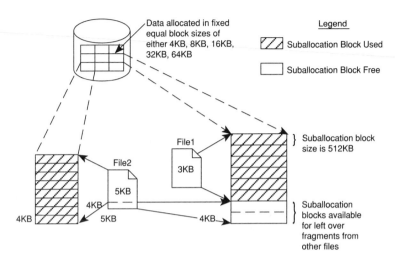

Figure 1.41

Block suballocation.

In NetWare 4.x, the unused disk block space is used in 512-byte suballocation units. This means that in the example of creating a 200-byte file, a 512-byte suballocation within the 4 KB disk block would be used. The remaining seven 512-byte suballocation blocks would be available for sharing by the leftover fragments of other files. If all these suballocation blocks were used, in the NetWare 4.x example there would be wasted space of only 312 (512 – 200) bytes out of a total of 4,096 bytes—only 8 percent wasted space. Also, if the file sizes and leftover fragments were multiples of 512 bytes, there would be no wasted space.

 Understand how block suballocation works in terms of how many suballocation units are used for a file of a given size.

You can define *block suballocation* as a mechanism in NetWare 4.x that enables small files and files that are not multiples of the disk block size to share space in a disk block that would otherwise go to waste. The improved utilization in disk space is accompanied by the extra overhead in the operating system to maintain the status of disk blocks that have been suballocated, but because caching is used, the impact of this overhead is minimal.

71

Disk suballocation is enabled by default during a NetWare volume's installation. You can explicitly disable it during installation.

 Always allocate a disk block size of 64 KB for maximum gain in server disk performance, because the software and disk subsystems perform at an optimum at this block size.

NetWare File System Compression

Studies have shown that the processor utilization of many NetWare servers in real life networks does not often exceed 50 percent. In heavily loaded servers, it is not uncommon to see processor utilization higher than 90 percent, but such situations are relatively rare for servers that are predominantly being used for file and print services. The designers of NetWare 4.x decided to use this unutilized processor bandwidth for useful background tasks such as file system compression. Today there are many disk compression utilities available for DOS. However, these utilities decompress disk blocks as they are read and recompress when they are written. This process causes the disk to appear slow because of the compression operation that accompanies each read or write operation.

In NetWare 4.x, file compression is performed in the background. You can set certain parameters at the file server to control the frequency at which compression can be performed in the background. When a file is retrieved, it is decompressed. The file blocks that are immediately decompressed are available for use, even as the rest of the file is being decompressed by special decompression threads (see fig. 1.42). Usually, the file remains in the decompressed state for a certain period of time that is controllable at the server. You also can control the status of the compressed file—whether it should be left in the compressed state or decompressed state after it has been accessed. The compression of files is always performed in the background.

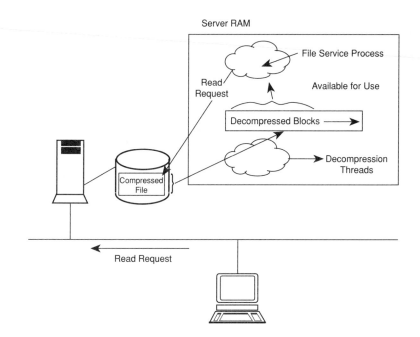

Figure 1.42
Read of a
compressed file.

By using the file compression feature, you can increase effective disk space without adding new server drives. The amount of savings in disk space depends on the nature of repeated characters or binary patterns in the file and is very high for text files. It is not uncommon to see savings of 63 percent or more because of file compression. This means that 500 MB of files can take up as little as 185 MB (at 63 percent compression) of disk space. With disk space being at a perennial premium on file servers, this is a great advantage.

A file is not compressed unless NetWare sees a certain gain in disk space. The network administrator can exercise explicit control by flagging files and directories for immediate compression or never to be compressed. The network administrator can exercise control of compression using SET commands from the server console.

You can enable or disable the compression option during installation of a volume on the NetWare server. The default is that compression is enabled, which means that NetWare will try to compress a file if it has not been used for some time, as long as a minimum savings in disk space is possible.

Data Migration

Data migration enables infrequently used files to be moved to a near-line or off-line storage medium. Examples of near-line storage are optical disk libraries (also known as jukeboxes), and examples of off-line storage are tape backup devices. When data migration occurs, NetWare 4.x still sees the data on the NetWare volumes, because the directory entries for the migrated files are still on the NetWare volume. If a file is accessed and it has been migrated, the file is brought back (de-migrated) to the NetWare volume (see fig. 1.43). The net effect of data migration is that valuable disk space is freed up. When combined with compression, data migration is a very effective way of saving disk space.

Figure 1.43

Data migration.

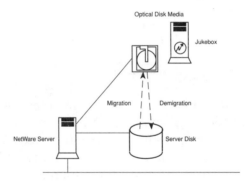

Some of the earlier Control Data Corporation's supercomputers used data migration, but NetWare 4.x is the first one to popularize its use among PC-based network operating systems (NOS).

You can enable and disable data migration when you install the NetWare volume. You can also mark files for migration by using NetWare utilities such as FILER and the FLAG command.

The High Capacity Storage System (HCSS) enables data migration to be implemented. HCSS is a storage and retrieval system that can extend the capacity of a NetWare server by integrating optical libraries into the NetWare file system. HCSS can work in conjunction with data migration, so that you can move migrated files from the faster but lower-capacity NetWare volumes to the slower but higher-capacity media that comprise the HCSS.

As far as the user is concerned, the operation of data migration and HCSS is transparent. Files that have been migrated to HCSS are accessed with the same commands as files that reside on the NetWare volume. If a migrated file is accessed, it is automatically de-migrated.

 With the help of NDIR, FILER, NWADMIN, or the SERVMAN.NLM, you can ascertain whether a file has been migrated by seeing if its M (migrate) attribute is set.

Migration is performed on an individual file basis depending on the last time the file was accessed, called the least recently used criteria, and the current volume usage. Least recently used criteria for files refers to files that are the least active, or that have not been accessed for the longest time. If the current volume usage exceeds a capacity threshold, data migration occurs. Capacity threshold is defined as the percentage of the server's disk that is used before data migration begins.

Understanding the Improved File System Security and Management

Access to the NetWare 4.x-based network is performed when the user logs in to a network's NetWare directory. Each organization has its own network directory tree that reflects the usage and security needs of network users. As part of implementing network security, access to parts of the network directory tree are controlled by explicit trustee assignments. Figure 1.44 shows the different steps that must occur before a user is granted access to a file on a volume. These include login authentication, NDS security, and NetWare file system security.

Figure 1.44

NetWare 4.x security.

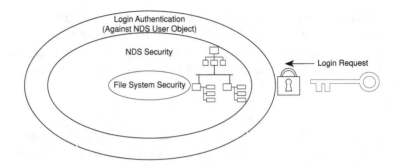

When a user logs in to the network, the user specifies the name of the NDS object that represents the user account. The user's login name and password are used to build a personalized key that is used to authenticate a user's right to access the network. The actual algorithm that is used to build the personalized key is RSA, which stands for Rivest, Shamir, and Adelman, the original creators of the famous public encryption key algorithm. Novell licensed this technology from RSA, Inc., for use with NetWare 4.x.

When the user is authenticated on the network, the user must have rights to directory objects that represent resources on the network. This is seen in figure 1.44, where a user has to pass through the NDS Security. For example, in order to access files on a volume, the user must have certain rights to the volume object in the directory tree.

After the user is authenticated by the NDS, the user's access to a file is controlled by the File and Directory Trustee rights. These rights are the same as those for the NetWare 3.x servers.

Network management is done by the network administrator. An initial user account called ADMIN is created when a directory tree is first established. This is equivalent to the SUPERVISOR user in pre-NetWare 4.0, except that the ADMIN user has network-wide responsibility. The ADMIN user account can be deleted or renamed; in that sense it does not have any special significance. This contrasts with the SUPERVISOR account in NetWare 3.x and 2.x servers, which could not be renamed or deleted. Because the ADMIN account can be deleted, care should be taken to ensure that other users have the equivalent of supervisory rights to the directory tree before the ADMIN account is deleted.

For secure environments, rename the ADMIN account so that an unauthorized user cannot use the supervisor's username to try to break system security.

The ADMIN user can create other user objects anywhere in the directory tree. This is usually done in such a manner that the users can access resources in the directory tree easily for ease in implementing security on the network.

The network administrator can delegate different levels of network responsibility to users, such as the authority to create other user objects but not delete them, or the responsibility of managing part of a directory tree but not accessing the information represented by the objects. This makes it possible to have multiple levels of network administrators in a manner that is more flexible than the NetWare 3.x approach of workgroup managers and user account managers.

You can more finely control security in NetWare 4.x by creating assistant supervisors who can administer network resources but who do not have access to data that needs to be protected from view, such as payroll data or other financial data of an organization. You can implement this control by setting the NDS object rights. Object rights control access to NDS objects in the NDS tree. To control access to information inside the NDS objects, you need another type of object right called the Object Property right.

Learning About Support for Network Auditing

In NetWare 4.x, you can designate a user as an auditor. The auditor acts independently of the network administrator to audit critical activities on the network. The auditors can also audit past and present transactions on the network for any security breaches (see fig. 1.45). It is important to understand why network auditors need to be independent of the network administrator. The network administrator of the directory tree, unless specifically restricted, has unrestricted access to data and resources on the network. As a result, an organization has to place great trust in the network administrator. If this trust is betrayed, the network administrator can cause a great deal of damage to an organization's data and privacy of data.

Figure 1.45

Auditing in NetWare 4.x.

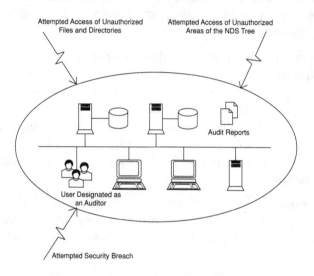

Auditing enables auditor users to monitor actions on the network, including that of the network administrator. For this reason, an auditor should not have Supervisor rights or Supervisor-equivalent rights. An auditor's main function is to track events on the network, but they are unable to modify data on the network, other than the Audit Data and Audit History files.

Auditing should not be confused with accounting features of earlier NetWare versions. Accounting enables the tracking of resource usage on the networks, such as disk blocks read and written to, storage charges, and service requests. This accounting capability is still available in NetWare 4.x.

Auditing enables the monitoring of critical events on the network such as logins and logouts, file operations, directory services object operations (creations, deletions, reads, and writes), directory object events, user events, and trustee modifications. To audit files, auditing is enabled at the volume level. For directory objects, auditing must be enabled at the container object level. Container objects are used in the NDS tree for organizational purposes and are discussed in the next chapter. When enabled, log files are created to track audited operations.

The primary utility for implementing auditing is AUDITCON, a menu-based text utility.

Exploring the Memory Management Architecture

NetWare 3.x was a great improvement over NetWare 2.2 in the way memory was managed on the server. However, there were a few problems with memory management under NetWare 3.x, as seen in figure 1.46. In NetWare 3.x, memory was managed in five pools, each serving a different purpose. The pools were for purposes such as permanent memory, movable cache, nonmoveable cache, and semi-permanent memory.

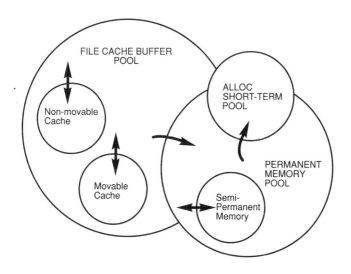

Figure 1.46

NetWare 3.x memory management.

As the names suggest, each memory pool served a special purpose. To meet temporary high demands, memory pools were permitted to borrow memory from the file cache buffer memory; but once borrowed, this memory was not returned. Under certain conditions, it was possible for this memory leakage to occur to the point that the file cache buffer memory was severely depleted, and this resulted in a severe degradation in server performance. To reset the memory pools, the server had to be restarted.

In a manner similar to the way NetWare 3.11 was an improvement over NetWare 2.x, NetWare 4.x memory management is a considerable improvement over NetWare 3.11. For one thing, there are no separate memory pools (see fig. 1.47). There is only one main pool and that is the file cache memory. All memory used by processes running on the server is borrowed against this pool and completely returned to it when the process terminates, at which time the returned memory becomes available to other processes. As a result, memory management is simpler because there is only one pool instead of five. Also, because memory management is simpler, it takes fewer processor cycles to accomplish, and memory allocation is therefore faster.

Figure 1.47

NetWare 4.x memory management.

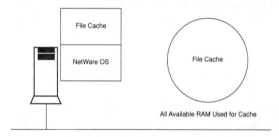

Some of the features of NetWare 4.x memory management include the following:

- ◆ Improved server performance, because memory management is an important resource for server processes.

- ◆ Integration with the paged memory architecture of the Intel processors.

- ◆ Ring protection to control damage caused by misbehaved NLMs.

◆ Easier to write applications for the NLM developer, because memory management is simpler.

A controversial aspect of NetWare 3.x memory usage is that all programs—the kernel and applications—run in ring 0 of the Intel 80386 architecture. The Intel 80386 architecture defines 4 rings: rings 0 to 3 (see fig. 1.48). The purpose is to have the operating system kernel run at ring 0, and other programs at one of the outer rings. Programs running at ring 3 can access the RAM used by other programs running in ring 3 but cannot directly access RAM for programs running at rings 2, 1, or 0. If the operating system kernel is running in ring 0, a program at ring 3 would have to make an inter-ring gate call to make service requests from the operating system kernel. If the program crashes, it cannot affect the operating system kernel. This architecture makes the system more reliable at the cost of reduced speed because of the inter-ring call overhead. An example of an operating system that uses the ring architecture is OS/2.

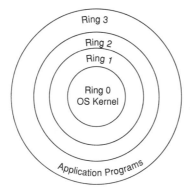

Figure 1.48

Intel 80386 processor ring architecture.

NetWare 3.x does not use the ring architecture. The NetWare 3.x operating system, NLMs, and all server processes run in ring 0. What NetWare 3.x loses in reliability, it gains in simplicity and speed.

In NetWare 4.x, all NLMs by default run in ring 0. However, the network administrator can configure the server to run NLMs that are loaded in an outer ring so that offending programs cannot cause the operating system kernel that runs in ring 0 to crash. As new NLMs are added to the server, you can load them in an outer ring for a trial period. They will run a little slower there because they have to make an inter-ring call. If the NLMs prove to be reliable, you can add them to ring 0, where they can run faster.

When purchasing NLMs from third parties, check to see if they are designed to run in an outer ring of the Intel processor (80386 and higher). Not all NLMs can run in an outer ring.

Learning About Improvements in Client Networking Services

The NetWare 4.x networking software for workstation operating system clients includes better support for DOS, MS Windows, and OS/2 (see fig. 1.49). DOS and MS Windows now use a DOS Requester, ODI support, and Packet Burst Protocol support.

Figure 1.49

Multiple client support in NetWare 4.x.

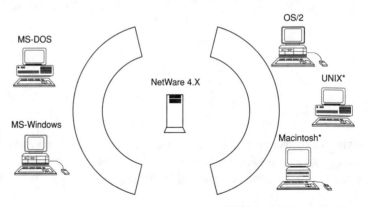

*UNIX, Macintosh support not in initial release of Netware 4.0

The DOS Requester enables the redirector capability of later releases of DOS via the interrupt mechanism INT 2F (hex) to be used. The earlier NetWare shell used the DOS INT 21 (hex) mechanism and a software multiplexor mechanism to direct the request to appropriate system services. Because of the additional overhead of the software multiplexor mechanism, it was slightly less efficient. In NetWare 4.x, the DOS Requester actually consists of a number of smaller components that need to be loaded only if the service is needed. These smaller components are called Virtual Loadable Modules (VLMs) and are loaded and managed by the VLM Manager (VLM.EXE). VLMs give you the flexibility of selectively loading only the services that are needed. VLMs are designed to understand NetWare Directory Services, and there is even a VLM component (NETX.VLM) that can be used to communicate with bindery-based servers.

The ODI support is the Open Data Link interface that provides an interface for protocol stacks to talk to network boards that represent layer 2 (the data link layer) of the OSI model. The ODI interface was also available in earlier NetWare client software.

The Packet Burst Protocol enables transmission of multiple packet requests and packet replies. It is similar to the window flow-control mechanism used in other protocol suites and is an improvement over the single-packet request/response behavior of the earlier NCP packet transmissions. The Packet Burst Protocol was added to later releases of NetWare 3.x and is also available for NetWare 4.x.

The Packet Burst Protocol is particularly useful for multiple NCP packet requests and packet replies, where a number of requests or replies can be acknowledged by a single acknowledgment packet. This eliminates some of the overhead of the round-trip delay when a sender has to wait for the last packet that was sent to be acknowledged before transmitting the next packet. It also results in fewer packets being sent, and this results in reduction of network traffic and reduced time for processing packets.

Another enhancement in NetWare 4.x is support for Large Internet Packet (LIP). Earlier NetWare routers were limited in the size of the Internet packet that could be supported. With LIP, this limit has been removed, and the larger packet sizes that are common in token ring networks (4 KB to 16 KB) and Ethernet networks (1.5 KB) are possible.

Exploring Integrated Storage Management Services (SMS)

Storage Management Services (SMS) in NetWare 4.x provide data on the network to be backed or restored in a common data format and in a manner that is hardware- and software-independent. A Target Service Agent (TSA) program is run on each device that needs to be backed up, and it is the target for the backup program. These targets include workstations and NetWare 3.x and 4.x servers (see fig. 1.50).

Figure 1.50

SMS and TSAs.

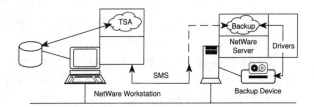

The SBACKUP program is an example of a program that uses SMS for backup and restore operations. SBACKUP is an NLM that runs on a NetWare server. The NBACKUP functionality of earlier NetWare releases is now consolidated in SBACKUP.

SMS consists of a number of other modules, such as the Storage Management Data Requester (SMDR), that are used to pass commands between SBACKUP and the TSAs. TSAs are device drivers that use the Storage Device Interface (SDI) to communicate between the SBACKUP program and the storage devices (see fig. 1.51).

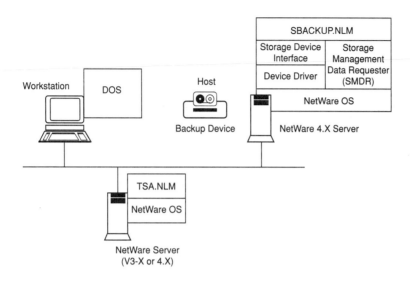

Figure 1.51
SMS architecture.

 Besides SBACKUP you may want to consider a number of third-party backup schemes that use SMS. These provide a simpler and streamlined user interface and many advanced backup options.

Understanding Improvements in Network Print Services Architecture

In NetWare 3.x, print services were defined as part of the print server definition, and the only way to do a network print job was to submit the print job to a print queue. In NetWare 4.x, you can still send the network print jobs to the network print queue, but you can also send print jobs to the printer object in the NDS tree.

Other improvements in NetWare 4.x printing include the following:

◆ Simpler installation in comparison to NetWare 3.x

◆ Support for a larger number of printers (up to 256) on a single print server

85

◆ The ability to set up remote printers on NetWare servers

Printing issues are covered in greater detail in later chapters.

Introducing Multiple Language Support (Internationalization)

Because the character of NetWare has become international in scope, NetWare 4.x has introduced support for international languages to NLMs and network utilities. This means that you can set messages and options associated with utilities in the language of the user. The default language is English, but you can add support for other languages during installation.

It is even possible to have different language NLMs running on the server at the same time, or have one user using the system utility NETADMIN in French and another user using the same utility in Italian. It is important to understand that the language support does not mean that NetWare is capable of translating messages between users using different languages. For example, if the SEND utility is used by a French language user to send a message in French to another user who is set up to use Italian, NetWare is not smart enough to translate the message from French to Italian.

Even though the language may be the same, there may be differences in the manner in which dates, times, and numbers are formatted. A classic example of this is English, which is spoken in both the U.S.A. and the U.K. The default format for representing dates in the U.S.A. is mm/dd/yy (for example, 10/16/93). In the U.K., the default date format would be dd/mm/yy (for example, 16/10/93). The formatting is not just dependent on the language but can change across different locales for the same language.

Example of the date, time, and number formats for U.S.A, U.K., France, and Germany are shown in table 1.6.

Table 1.6
Format Differences for Countries

Country	Number Format	Time Format	Date Format
U.S.A.	355,113.22	11:55:00 PM	10/16/93
U.K.	355,113.22	23:55:00	16/10/93
Germany	355.113,22	23:55:00	16.10.93
France	355 113,22	23:55:00	16.10.93

The ability to support differences in language and format representations is called internationalization. Internationalization in NetWare is supported through unicode representation, which is a standard for representing data in 16 bits instead of the familiar 8-bit ASCII.

NetWare 4.x distribution comes in CD-ROM. Distribution on high-density floppy disks is available at an additional cost by sending in the request form that accompanies the NetWare 4.x distribution.

Installing NetWare 4.x on CD-ROM saves time during installation, because the copying of the files from the distribution media is much faster. This leads to a simpler and faster implementation.

You can attach the CD-ROM drive to the server that is being installed, or to a remote workstation. Figure 1.52 shows the different possibilities for CD-ROM configuration. The CD-ROM drive is shown as an external unit to the workstation or server. Internal CD-ROMs are also possible.

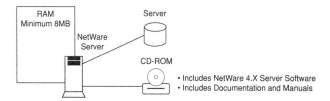

Figure 1.52

NetWare 4 installation using CD-ROM distribution.

Study Guide for the Chapter

If you are preparing for the NetWare 4.x Administration exams, review the chapter with the following goals:

1. Understand and identify all the new capabilities in NetWare 4.x. Use the Study Notes as a quick review.

2. Pay particular attention to memory protection, NDS services, enhanced client services, and block suballocation.

3. After studying this chapter, attempt the sample test questions for this chapter. If you miss the answers to a question, review the appropriate topic until you understand the reason for the correct answer.

Chapter Summary

In this chapter, you have examined the basic networking components that are used in a NetWare 4.x network. You have learned to configure a DOS workstation to make a connection to the network and log in to the network. You have learned about the different networking components that are used on a DOS workstation and the functions each component performs.

NetWare 4.x represents an exciting change in the way large enterprise-wide area networks are supported. The principal change has been the introduction of NDS. NDS enables you to superimpose a logical structure or view on a physical network, which makes the network easier to use and administer.

Because NDS is central to accessing resources on the network, security is integrated into NDS. When a user logs in, that user is authenticated at the NDS level.

Other improvements to NetWare 4.x have been made in the area of storage management services, enhanced client support, enhanced and integrated utilities, and better online documentation.

Chapter Test Questions

Test questions can have a single correct answer or multiple correct answers. When a single answer is desired, this is indicated by a ○ notation that precedes the possible answers. Some questions require you to select more than one answer; these are indicated by the □ preceding each answer. Taking practice quizzes will not only test your knowledge but will also give you confidence when you take your exam.

1. A NetWare 4.x server _____.

   ○ A. runs workstation software and server software

   ○ B. runs the same software as a NetWare workstation

   ○ C. runs networking software that allows it to share its resources and services with other users on the network

   ○ D. runs networking software that allows it to use resources and services on other network servers and workstations

2. The NetWare server provides which of the following services to users of NetWare workstations?

   ○ A. Distributed

   ○ B. Shared

   ○ C. Centralized

   ○ D. Global

3. Typically, the workstation that makes requests is called a _____.

   ○ A. redirector

   ○ B. shell

   ○ C. client

   ○ D. service requester

4. Novell's implementation of NDS for NetWare 4.x provides
   _____.

   ☐ A. file system security only

   ☐ B. multiple levels of security

   ☐ C. general database services

   ☐ D. logical organization of network resources

   ☐ E. global data access services

5. NetWare Directory Services _____.

   ☐ A. eliminates the need to create user objects

   ☐ B. eliminates the need to create user and group objects

   ☐ C. eliminates redundant tasks such as adding a user
           account to multiple servers on the network

   ☐ D. provides access to network resources

   ☐ E. provides a general database service

6. An NDS benefit is _____.

   ○ A. access to a general database

   ○ B. logical organization of network resources

   ○ C. no need to create user objects

   ○ D. group login to the network

7. Logging in to a NetWare 4.x network is accomplished by
   _____.

   ○ A. NetWare DOS Requester

   ○ B. DOS

   ○ C. NetWare shell

   ○ D. OS/2

8. A necessary component for logging in to a NetWare 4.x network is _____.

   ○ A. NETX.COM

   ○ B. NetWare shell

   ○ C. A Network Interface Card (NIC) Driver

   ○ D. VLM.COM

9. An ODI benefit is that it allows _____.

   ○ A. network devices that use same protocols to share the same physical network

   ○ B. network devices that use different protocols to coexist and share the same physical network

   ○ C. network devices that use different protocols to interoperate

   ○ D. workstations using different protocols to communicate with a NetWare server using IPX protocol

10. Logging in to a NetWare 4.x network is accomplished by using _____.

   ☐ A. a Network Interface Card (NIC) Driver

   ☐ B. VLM.COM

   ☐ C. DOS

   ☐ D. communication protocols

   ☐ E. NetWare DOS Requester

   ☐ F. OS/2

   ☐ G. NetWare shell

11. ODI allows multiple protocols to _____.

   ☐ A. share the same network adapter and cabling system

   ☐ B. coexist as long as they are running at different workstations

   ☐ C. coexist at a workstation

   ☐ D. use the same NetWare server

91

12. ODI allows _____.

   ☐ A. a network adapter driver to be written just once for different types of communication protocols

   ☐ B. multiple protocols to share the same network adapter and cabling system

   ☐ C. multiple protocols to coexist as long as they are running at different workstations

   ☐ D. multiple protocols to coexist at a workstation

13. The key components of ODI are _____.

   ☐ A. Link Support Layer (LSL)

   ☐ B. NE2000.COM

   ☐ C. Multiple Link Interface Driver (MLID)

   ☐ D. IPX.COM

14. The Link Support Layer _____.

   ☐ A. must be loaded after the ODI driver

   ☐ B. acts as a switchboard to route packets to the correct protocol and correct ODI driver

   ☐ C. must be loaded before the ODI driver

   ☐ D. provides communications between the workstation software and network services

   ☐ E. provides a network redirector function

15. Which module implements the ODI specification?

   ○ A. IPXODI.COM

   ○ B. VLM.EXE

   ○ C. IPX.COM

   ○ D. LSL.COM

   ○ E. NETX.EXE

   ○ F. NE2000.COM

16. The MLID is _____.

☐ A. used to refer to network adapter drivers that support the ODI specification

☐ B. a set of special network adapters that support the ODI specification

☐ C. used to communicate between the network adapter and the Link Support Layer

☐ D. a protocol that stands for Multiple Layer Internetworking Device

☐ E. a protocol module that implements the SPX/IPX protocols

17. Configuration information for the ODI driver is kept in the _____ file.

○ A. CONFIG.SYS

○ B. AUTOEXEC.BAT

○ C. NET.CFG

○ D. NET.DAT

○ E. STARTNET.BAT

18. The Link Support Layer is implemented by which of the following for a DOS workstations?

○ A. LSL.SYS

○ B. LSL.COM

○ C. LINK.COM

○ D. LINKS.COM

○ E. LINKS.SYS

19. The default frame type for NetWare 4.x is _____.

○ A. ETHERNET_SNAP

○ B. ETHERNET_II

○ C. ETHERNET_802.3

○ D. ETHERNET_802.2

93

20. The CONFIG.SYS file for NetWare 4.x DOS workstations must have _____.

    ○ A.   DEVICE=HIMEM.SYS

    ○ B.   DEVICE=SMARTDRV.SYS

    ○ C.   LASTDRIVE=Z

    ○ D.   LASTDRIVE=E

21. The load sequence for loading network client software at a DOS workstation is _____.

    ○ A.   MLID driver, LSL.COM, IPXODI.COM, VLM.EXE

    ○ B.   LSL.COM, IPXODI.COM, MLID driver, VLM.EXE

    ○ C.   LSL.COM, MLID driver, IPXODI.COM, VLM.EXE

    ○ D.   MLID driver, IPXODI.COM, LSL.COM, VLM.EXE

22. The DOS client installation software can add the _____ in the AUTOEXEC.BAT file to automate connecting to a network.

    ○ A.   CALL C:\NWCLIENT\STARTNET.BAT

    ○ B.   STARTNET.BAT

    ○ C.   NETSTART.BAT

    ○ D.   CALL C:\NWCLIENT\NETSTART.BAT

23. The NetWare DOS Requester _____.

    ○ A.   must have the LASTDRIVE=E statement set in the NET.CFG file

    ○ B.   can coexist with the older NetWare shell

    ○ C.   logically resides between workstation software and network adapter and enables communications between them

    ○ D.   logically resides between workstation software and network services and enables communications between them

24. In NetWare 4.x, the request for a network service is first seen by _____.

   ○ A. the NetWare shell
   ○ B. DOS
   ○ C. DOS and then by the NetWare shell
   ○ D. the DOS Requester

25. Application requests for network services are translated into _____.

   ○ A. IPX request for services
   ○ B. NCP request for services
   ○ C. SPX request for services
   ○ D. IP request for services

26. The NetWare DOS Requester is implemented by _____.

   ○ A. DLLs
   ○ B. NLMs
   ○ C. VLMs
   ○ D. the NetWare shell

27. When VLM.EXE loads, it loads _____.

   ○ A. and activates the NetWare DOS Requester
   ○ B. the IPXODI.COM, if it is not already loaded
   ○ C. the LSL.COM
   ○ D. the VLMs and the ODI interface modules

28. VLM Manager is a _____ and is implemented by _____.

   ○ A. device driver, VLM.EXE
   ○ B. TSR, VLM.EXE
   ○ C. device driver, VLMs
   ○ D. TSR, VLMs

95

29. The VLM Manager is responsible for _____.

    ☐ A. managing VLMs and NLMs

    ☐ B. loading the NetWare shell and associated protocol modules

    ☐ C. managing device drivers loaded from the CONFIG.SYS file

    ☐ D. controlling VLMs and access to memory at the workstation

    ☐ E. managing data flow and communications between VLMs

30. Benefits of using VLMs are _____.

    ☐ A. only needed components are loaded, which reduces workstation memory overhead

    ☐ B. coexistence of NetWare shell and the NetWare DOS Requester

    ☐ C. because the requester consists of smaller number of components, each of these components has a better chance of being loaded in upper memory than if it was one large module

    ☐ D. it opens up the workstation architecture for development by third parties who can write additional VLM components

    ☐ E. the ability to load all dependent protocol modules on demand priority

31. The command to load the DOS Requester using the configuration file ALTER.CFG in the directory C:\CONFIG, instead of the default NET.CFG, is _____.

    ○ A. VLM ALTER.CFG

    ○ B. VLM /C=C:\CONFIG\ALTER.CFG

    ○ C. VLM /D=C:\CONFIG\ALTER.CFG

    ○ D. VLM

32. The command to load DOS Requester in expanded memory is _____.

   ○ A. VLM /ME

   ○ B. VLM /M=EXP

   ○ C. VLM /MC

   ○ D. VLM /M=E

   ○ E. VLM /M=X

   ○ F. VLM /M=C

33. When VLM loads _____.

   ○ A. it maps the next drive specified after the LASTDRIVE statement in CONFIG.SYS as a network drive

   ○ B. it maps the drive specified in the NETWORK DRIVE statement in NET.CFG as a network drive

   ○ C. it maps the drive specified in the FIRST NETWORK DRIVE statement in NET.CFG as a network drive

   ○ D. it maps the drive specified in the FIRST NETWORK DRIVE statement in the NetWare DOS Requester section of the NET.CFG as a network drive

34. Which of the following statements can be found in the NET.CFG file for a NetWare 4.x workstation for mapping the first network drive to F?

   ☐ A. Frame ETHERNET_802.2

   ☐ B. LASTDRIVE=Z

   ☐ C. NetWare DOS Requester

   ☐ D. FIRST NETWORK DRIVE=Z

   ☐ E. FIRST NETWORK DRIVE=F

2

CHAPTER

Introduction to NetWare Directory Services

NetWare Directory Services (NDS) is perhaps the single most important feature of NetWare 4.x. It enables a network consisting of many servers to be treated as a single network that you can easily administer. By using NDS, you can treat all network resources as logical resources. You can group the logical resources together to represent their logical relationships, and you can administer them from any workstation on the network. Network administration is reduced to managing the resources in the NDS database. This chapter will teach you basic NDS concepts and ways you can use NDS to access and manage network resources. An understanding of NDS services is fundamental to managing NetWare 4.x, because access to network resources revolves around the ways that NDS is represented, accessed, and managed.

Understanding NDS

NetWare Directory Services (NDS) is a distributed global database of services and resources that are available on the network. The term *global* implies the existence of a single database that is shared by all servers on the network, and is available to users from any point on the network. Most resources important to network management on the network have an entry in this global database.

Conceptually, this database exists when Directory Services is installed, and it is not tied to any physical resource such as a server. In practice, because NDS is implemented as a database, it must be stored on storage devices on the network (such as physical volumes that are associated with physical servers). Because the size of the NDS database can become very large, the NDS database is not stored at any central site (except for very small networks). Reliability concerns also figure in this storage decision. Portions of the NDS database are distributed on volume storage devices at strategic locations on the network. These subdivided elements of the NDS are called *partitions*.

NDS is

♦ a distributed global database of network resources and services.

♦ not confined to a central site or location.

♦ stored on strategically located storage volumes on the network.

NDS provides the following benefits:

♦ Mapping between a physical resource and its logical name in the NDS database

♦ Logical organization of network resources independent of the location of physical resources

- ◆ A single global database that you can access from any point on the network, providing for management of network resources

- ◆ A uniform method of managing all resources through the NDS database

- ◆ Dynamic mapping between an NDS object and the physical resource it represents

Understanding NDS Logical Resources

NDS logical resources are represented by objects. Because these logical resources are associated with NDS, they are often called *NDS objects*. You can look at NDS objects conceptually as records in a global database (see fig. 2.1). The network resources that you can represent as NDS objects include network printers, network volumes, NetWare file servers, AppleTalk Filing Protocol servers, user accounts, and so on.

Each NDS object holds information about the logical resource it represents. Information about an object is stored as properties of the object. Because you can view an NDS object as a record, the properties are similar to the fields of a record (see fig. 2.2). For example, the properties of a User object include the user's login name, last name, groups the user belongs to, user's telephone number, and so forth. Figure 2.3 provides examples of NDS Resource objects and their properties. The figure shows some of the properties of a User object and a NetWare Server object. The properties are listed in the property column, and represent the categories or types of information you can store in the object.

Figure 2.1

Viewing NDS as a global database.

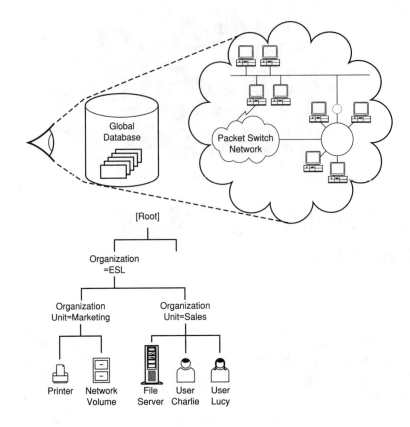

Figure 2.2

Properties of objects.

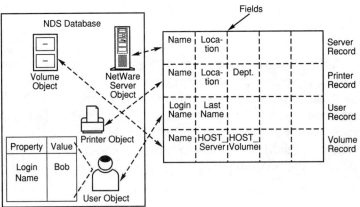

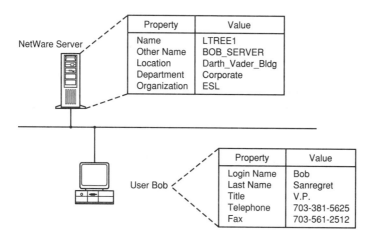

Figure 2.3

Example NDS objects and property values.

The actual information stored in a property is listed in the Value column and is called a *property value*. Some properties are crucial and must have a value associated with them. These are mandatory, or required, properties. An example of a mandatory property for all NDS objects is the *name* property, called the *common name*. If the name property is not defined, an object cannot be referenced. The *last name* property for User objects is mandatory.

Some of the NetWare Server object's properties are also shown in figure 2.4. You can view these properties using the NetWare Administrator GUI tool. This figure shows that you can specify the Department, Organization property for the Server object. The properties Net Address, Status, and Version cannot be changed by the administrator, and represent the current status of the physical file server.

Author's Note
In NetWare 3.x there was an optional Full Name property for user accounts. But in NetWare 4.x the last name property is mandatory. This might seem strange at first because the last name property does not seem to serve any crucial technical function in the NDS database. The answer to this mystery lies with X.500, on which the NDS is based. Although certain properties are

continues

explicitly defined as being mandatory in X.500, others are optional. Many of the properties defined in NDS User objects are taken directly from the X.500 definition. In X.500, the last name property for User objects is called the *surName property*, and this is mandatory. NDS defines the last name property as mandatory to be compliant with X.500.

Figure 2.4

NetWare server properties.

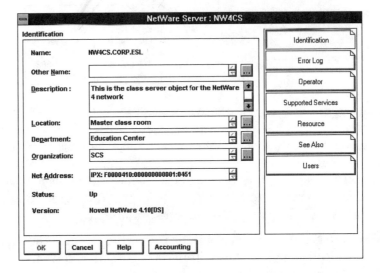

Certain properties in NDS are defined for informational purposes and are optional properties. Examples of these are a user's telephone number, fax number, user's title, and electronic mail address. Many objects have an optional See Also property.

Property values can be single-valued or multivalued. If a property is single-valued, you can define no more than one value for that property. An example of this is the network address property of a NetWare File Server object. Multivalued properties can have more than one value defined. An example of this is the telephone number property for User objects. You can define multiple telephone numbers for a User object.

Author's Note

Property values can be numeric, a string, or in some special format, such as a network address on an IPX network (4-byte network address, 6-byte node address, 2-byte socket number). In X.500 terms, the properties of an object are called its *attributes*. The actual format of the value of a property is defined by the attribute syntax for that property/attribute.

Practical TIP

For your company or organization, define which of the optional properties should have values defined for them. It is generally a good idea to define optional properties for information purposes so that you can query the NDS database for information on these property values. Certain organizations, however, might not want to give out telephone numbers or other information about users. In this case, certain properties might not be defined, or NDS security might be used to enable only certain users to view information on the NDS objects.

Comparing NDS to the NetWare Bindery

NDS treats all resources on the network as objects belonging to a global database. This global database (directory) represents the network and has a structure that corresponds to a logical view of the network. The directory is not kept in a centralized location, but portions of it (*partitions*) are distributed across servers on the network; it can, therefore, be described as a *distributed database*. This is different from the approach used in pre-NetWare 4.0-based networks, in which the resources on a server were centrally located in a flat database called the *bindery*. Because the bindery served as a centralized database, it was a potential single point of failure. Also, the bindery could only define resources available on the server on which it was resident, it lacked the global nature of NDS.

 NDS provides a global directory that represents a logical view of the network.

The directory database in NDS is organized in a hierarchical fashion. This hierarchical structure maps well onto the organizational structure of most companies; moreover, you can use the structure to represent logical relationships between network resources, such as the grouping of resources under a node that represents a specific department. It is interesting to contrast the differences between the NDS and the NetWare 3.x bindery, because the differences provide insight into the improved manner in which network resources are managed in NetWare 4.0. Table 2.1 summarizes the differences between the NDS and the NetWare bindery.

Table 2.1
NDS Versus the NetWare Bindery

Attribute/Feature	NDS	Bindery
Structure	Hierarchical	Flat
Users	Network-wide	Server-centered
Login	Network-wide	Server-centered
Passwords	Single password	Password per server
Groups	Network-wide	Server-centered
Location	Distributed	Server-centered

In earlier versions of NetWare, the bindery was used to keep information on network resources in a flat database. This flat database did not represent the logical relationship between network resources. The bindery was server-centered, and was used to store information on resources available at a NetWare server, rather than the entire network. As a result of this limitation, tasks such as user account creation had to be performed on each server separately. User and group accounts had to be stored in the bindery of the server on which they were defined. The concept of a network-wide user account did not exist. There was an attempt to provide this capability using NNS (NetWare Name Service), but this was not very successful, and was never popular because of a number of problems dealing with its implementation.

 Because the bindery is implemented as a flat database, it is not used to represent logical relationships between network resources.

The NDS structure is hierarchical. This enables NDS to represent relationships between network resources in a manner that is more comprehensible for the user and the network administrator. The logical representation of resources in the NDS is called an NDS object. The NDS can also be used to store information about objects so that you can query this information in much the same way as you can a telephone directory. For instance, you can use the User object information to keep data such as phone numbers, fax numbers, electronic mail and other addresses, locations, and so forth. User and group accounts in the NDS are network-wide in scope, and this eliminates the network administrator's need to create user and group accounts on each server to which the user needs access.

Many tasks such as user/group account creation, which in earlier releases of NetWare had to be done separately on each server, are eliminated because the user/group account needs to be created just once in the directory. After you create the user account, you can assign it rights to any network resource that is represented in the NDS, such as NetWare volumes and network printers. Another benefit of the NDS is that the user needs to remember just one password to the network. Once validated, the user's trustee assignments provide the user with necessary access privileges to network resources.

NDS eliminates the need for creating separate user and group accounts on each NetWare server. NDS enables the creation of User and Group objects that have a network-wide scope.

It is important to understand that NDS provides control of directory resources such as servers and volumes, but not control over the contents of volumes, such as files and directories. The trustee right mechanisms used in NetWare 3.x are still used to provide access to files and directories.

 NDS provides control over directory information on network resources, not control over files or directories on a network volume.

Understanding the NetWare Directory Database

NDS is a global, distributed database that records information about network resources hierarchically. The distributed nature of NDS enables it to store information concerning many types of objects, such as users, printers, servers, and volumes that are of interest to the network's user community (see fig. 2.5). The distributed information is actually stored on NetWare servers throughout the network in a manner that is transparent to the user. A directory synchronization mechanism is used, so that directory changes in any part of the NDS database are propagated throughout the network. In other words, NDS synchronizes itself to present a consistent view of itself to the rest of the network. Directory synchronization takes place automatically without user intervention. The network administrator can set certain parameters to minimize the effect of directory synchronization on network traffic.

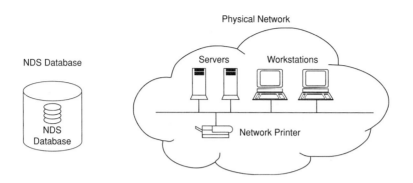

Figure 2.5

The NDS database.

For security reasons, NDS is kept as a hidden data area on a storage volume. NDS presents a hierarchical view of itself to the rest of the world. Access to any portion of NDS is controlled by a new set of object trustee assignments made on NDS objects.

The hierarchy in NDS is often described in terms of a directory tree, such as the one shown in figure 2.6.

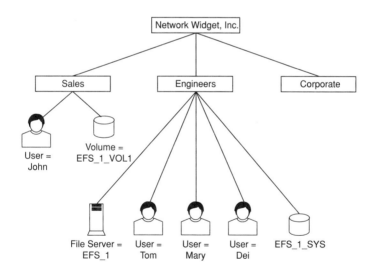

Figure 2.6

Hierarchical NDS tree for Network Widgets, Inc.

The hierarchical relationship enables network resources to be organized in a manner that reflects the ways the network is used, instead of the physical topology and connectivity of the network. You can make the directory organization more closely match the

109

user's view of the network. For example, in figure 2.6, engineers Tom, Mary, and Dei of the organization Network Widgets, Inc. have user accounts defined under the departmental unit (called organization unit, in NDS terminology) Engineers. Figure 2.7 shows that the users are in different physical locations. In figure 2.7, engineers Tom and Mary are shown to be in Dallas and user Dei is in Los Angeles. Because they all belong to a group of engineers, however, they will have similar needs to access network resources. Under these circumstances it makes sense to group them in an organization unit called Engineers, regardless of their physical location.

Figure 2.7

Physical network for Network Widgets, Inc.

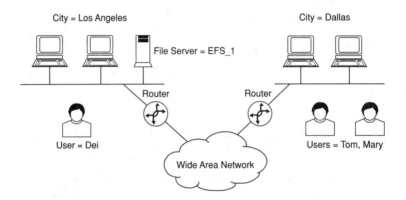

The file server for the engineers of Network Widgets, Inc. is currently defined in Los Angeles. Should there be a need in the future to physically move the server to Dallas, you can move the file server without changing the NDS view of the network. The file server EFS_1 is still under the organization unit of Engineers in the NDS tree. In figure 2.6, you can see that volume EFS_1_SYS, which is physically attached to the server EFS_1, is in the organization unit Engineers because it is primarily used by the engineers of the company. Another volume, called EFS_1_VOL1 also is physically attached to server EFS_1, but its NDS representation is kept in the organization unit Sales because it is primarily used by members of the sales team. Volume EFS_1_VOL1 might be kept in the Sales organization unit because the group Sales does not yet have its own file server. This discussion shows that you can place network resources in the NDS tree according to their use and the user's view of the network, rather than by physical location of the resource.

NDS is based on the CCITT X.500 standard. CCITT stands for Consultative Committee for International Telephone and Telegraphy, and is an international body that develops standards in the area of data communications. Its members comprise the standard-making bodies of various countries. CCITT publishes and updates standards periodically at four-year intervals.

NDS is not in complete compliance with X.500 because NDS is largely based on the 1988 X.500 recommendations. The X.500 standard has further evolved into the 1992 X.500 specification, but this was not available to NDS designers, who began work on NDS before 1992.

Author's Note

For strategic reasons you can expect Novell's implementation of NDS to comply with the international consensus on X.500 when this becomes universal. The protocol mechanism for keeping the NDS database updated when changes are made to it (directory synchronization) is another area of expected change. This has not been completely specified in the X.500 standards. As a result of this oversight, Novell, like many other X.500 vendors (DEC, Retix, etc.), has had to design its own directory services synchronization protocol to deal with directory synchronization. Many X.500 vendors, including Novell, are seeking common ways to implement X.500-compliant synchronization methods and services. Novell provides an API to exchange data between other name services, making it possible to build name service gateways to other name services.

NDS complies closely with X.500 recommendations. Details of the kinds of objects that make up the directory are specific to NetWare-based

continues

networks. You can add other general classes of objects that are not Novell-specific to the NDS directory by making use of the NDS programming APIs. This capability makes it possible to integrate it with other vendors' X.500 directory implementations. The schema (type of objects in a database) of NDS is extensible, which means the NDS database is extensible.

The NDS database is called the *Directory Information Base* (DIB) in the X.500 specification. Novell's documentation uses the terms NDS database or NDS tree, and these are the terms that will be used throughout this book.

NetWare Directory Services is

◆ a distributed, hierarchical database.

◆ a global database.

◆ referred to as the directory database or directory tree.

◆ represented as hidden files on servers.

◆ stored on NetWare 4.x servers.

◆ compliant with X.500 naming rules.

◆ used to store information on network resources.

◆ a mechanism for providing distributed information service on many types of data.

NDS provides

◆ a logical view of the network that reflects the way the network is used.

◆ an information database that replaces the earlier NetWare bindery.

◆ access to the same information regardless of the client location.

Classifying NDS Components

NDS employs a hierarchical structure, and uses a specific terminology to describe its components. Although some of the terms have been derived from CCITT's X.500 recommendations, others are specific to Novell. Before you can obtain a working understanding of NDS, you must understand the vocabulary and terms used to describe NDS.

Tree Structure of NDS

The NDS database is organized as a hierarchical tree. Computer scientists use the term *tree* to describe a method of representing data beginning from a single point, called the *root*. The root of this tree has *branches*, which can, in turn, branch off to other branches or *leaves*. Figure 2.8 illustrates this tree concept, along with a picture of the NDS tree.

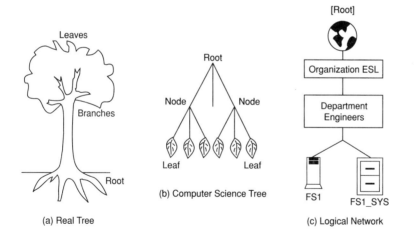

Figure 2.8

NDS tree components.

The tree has a single root, an important detail because the NDS database also has a single root. If you have several NDS databases constructed separately from each other, they will have separate roots. At the moment, no way exists to dynamically exchange NDS information between NDS trees with their own separate roots. Tools exist for combining several separate NDS trees (each with its own root) into a single, larger NDS tree. An example of such a tool is DSMERGE, which enables two NDS trees to be merged.

The root of the tree describes the first level of the tree, and is also used to describe the entire tree. The [Root] object cannot be created using any of the NetWare administration tools. It is created during the installation of a NetWare 4.x server, at which time you have the opportunity to install the Server object in an existing NDS tree or define a separate NDS tree with its own [Root]. Once defined, the [Root] object cannot be renamed, moved, or deleted.

You can have only one [Root] per NDS tree. The [Root] object cannot be renamed, moved, or deleted.

The [Root] object can contain only Country, Organization, and Alias objects.

A branch from the root of a tree leads to another object on the tree, and describes a complete subtree. An object on a tree that contains other objects is called a *container* object (all nodes of a tree represent a logical concept of an organization or a resource, and are called *objects*). A branch of a tree can, therefore, be seen as a container object plus all the objects underneath it.

The NDS tree is used to represent the hierarchical structure of the NDS database.

A branch of an NDS tree is a container object and all the objects underneath it.

An NDS tree has a single root that is named [Root].

Container Objects

An NDS container is an object that contains other objects, such as resource and service objects, and other containers. Containers provide a practical way of organizing objects by departments, geographic locations, work groups, projects, common usage of network resources, or any other criteria that make it easier to use the network.

Container objects provide a convenient way to organize other objects into groups (see fig. 2.9)—a key advantage of NDS. Besides facilitating a logical organization of the NDS tree, you can use container objects as groups that you can assign certain security rights, which then affect the security rights of all objects in that container.

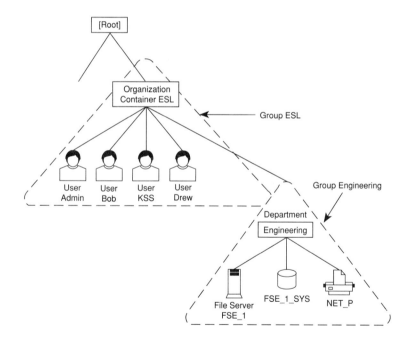

Figure 2.9

Container objects as groups.

Besides the [Root] object, the NDS defines the following container objects:

- ◆ Country
- ◆ Organization
- ◆ Organizational Unit

A container's type is referred to as its *object class*. Each container type previously listed has a separate object class definition. An object class definition defines the rules that govern the object's existence in the NDS tree. That the Country container can exist directly underneath the [Root] object is an example of such a rule. It cannot be contained in the Organization or Organizational Unit containers. This rule is described in the Containment Classes structure rules for NDS objects.

Container objects are used for

- ◆ organizing the NDS database.
- ◆ grouping objects in a logical way that reflects network use.
- ◆ assigning a common set of security rights to objects within the container.

Leaf Objects

An object in the tree that does not (and cannot) contain any other nodes is called a *leaf* object. A leaf object is similar to a leaf of a real tree—it has no other branches and leaves coming from it. A leaf object acts as a terminal point in the tree and represents a network resource or service (see fig. 2.10). A leaf object can exist only inside a container object.

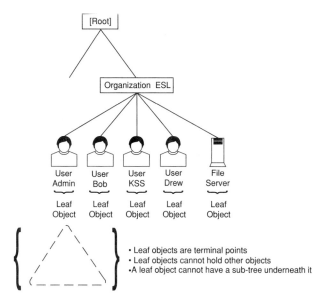

Figure 2.10
Leaf objects.

 A leaf object

◆ cannot contain other objects.

◆ acts as a terminal point in the tree.

◆ represents a network resource or service.

◆ can exist only in a container object.

Object Class and Schema

A NetWare 4.x-based network can have many different types of network resources and services, and each is described by a special type of leaf object. Earlier, you learned about file server and print server objects. These are examples of leaf objects. The object definition (also called object type) for an object in the NDS database is called its *object class*. In database technology terms, the collection of the different object definitions possible in the database, their scope and rules of existence, and their operation within the database, is called the *schema*.

117

Because the NDS tree is a globally distributed database, database terms are sometimes used to describe the NDS tree, and you should be familiar with them. The NDS schema is, therefore, a collection of object class definitions for objects such as file servers, computers, printers, print servers, and so forth (see fig 2.11). When an object of a type that can exist in the NDS schema is created, the object class is said to be *instantiated*. The object class implies the potential for an object of that class to exist in the database; it does not imply the existence of an object of that type. The object class must be instantiated (created) before an object belonging to that category can exist.

Figure 2.11

The NDS schema.

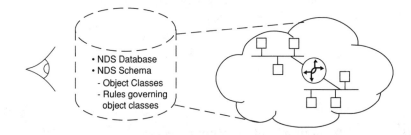

Each different type of network resource that can exist in an NDS database is called an *object class*.

The collection of the different object definitions possible in the database, their scope and rules of existence, and their operation within the database, is called the *schema*.

In the example shown in figure 2.8, the objects ESL and Engineers are examples of container objects. They are container objects because they can, in turn, contain other objects. The objects FS1 and FS1_SYS are examples of leaf objects. These leaf objects are the terminal points in the tree, and cannot contain other objects.

A container that has objects defined in it is a *parent* container to the objects that it contains. Although some object classes can contain other objects, other objects cannot. For instance, leaf object classes cannot contain any other object classes. Container object classes can contain other object classes, but there are rules that govern the kind of container class objects that can exist in other container class objects. These structural rules are called *Containment Class rules* and define where one type of object class can occur in relation to another object class. An object can exist in or be subordinate to only the objects listed among the object's containment classes. Table 2.2 shows the containment class rules for container objects.

Table 2.2
Containment Class Rules for Container Objects

Container Object	Containment Classes (Can Exist In)	Can Contain
[Root]	Cannot exist under any object. Parent to all objects.	Country Alias (Alias can be to another Country object only)
Country	[Root]	Organization Organizational Unit Alias (Alias can be to an Organization or Organizational Unit object only)
Organization	[Root] Country	Organizational Unit leaf objects
Organizational Unit	Organization Organizational Unit	Organizational Unit leaf objects

 Understand the containment rules in table 2.2.

NDS objects have a definition hierarchy similar to that used in object-oriented programming languages. The structural rules for objects define the concept of an Immediate Superclass. An object is "derived" from its immediate superior class.

At the topmost level is an object called Top. Top is the superclass of all objects. All NDS objects are directly or indirectly derived from Top. Top is the only class that has no superclass.

When an object has a superclass, the object's definition is said to be derived from this superclass. This means that the object's attributes (properties) are those defined by the superclass object plus any additional properties peculiar to that object. Another way to say this: An object inherits some of its properties from its parent object.

An example of derivation is shown in figure 2.12, in which the Alias object class is derived from the Top superclass. The only new attribute/property defined in the Alias object class is the alias Object Name; all other properties of the Alias object class are inherited from the Top superclass.

Figure 2.12

Deriving an Alias object from the Top Class object.

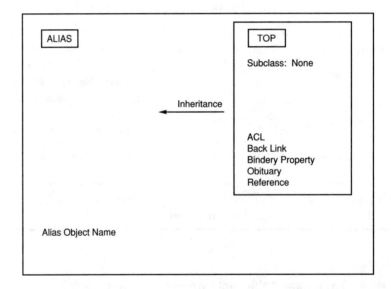

You can express the definition of the Alias object by using the formalism of ASN.1 (Abstract Syntax Notation Revision 1) as shown in the following:

```
alias OBJECT-CLASS
SUBCLASS OF Top
MUST CONTAIN {aliasObjectName}
```

ASN.1 is a standard that deals with rules of encoding and describing structural properties of application-level data. ASN.1 is part of the ISO (International Organization of Standards) recommendations for the presentation layer (layer 6) of the OSI (Open Systems Interconnection) Reference model, and is the language used by protocol designers to describe upper-layer application protocols.

Another interesting definition is that of the User class. The User class is actually derived from the Organizational Person superclass. This means that the User class has all the information types defined in the Organizational Person superclass, as well as any additional attributes defined for the User class. The Organizational Person class is derived from the Person class, which is, in turn, derived from the Top superclass. This inheritance is shown in figure 2.13. In formal terms, the derivation of the User class is defined as follows:

```
Person OBJECT-CLASS
    SUBCLASS OF Top
    MUST CONTAIN { commonName,  surName }
    MAY CONTAIN  { description, telephoneNumber,
        fullName, seeAlso }

Organizational Person OBJECT-CLASS
    SUBCLASS OF Person
    MAY CONTAIN {  EMail Address,
                   Facsimile Telephone Number,
                   Locality Name, // Not implemented in NDS
                   Organizational Unit Name,
                   Physical Delivery Office Name,
                   Postal Address,
                   Postal Code,
                   Postal Office Box,
                   State or Province name,
                   Street Address,
                   Title }
        CONTAINMENT {Organization,
                   Organizational Unit }
        NAMED BY   {Common Name,
                   Organizational Unit Name }

User OBJECT-CLASS
    SUBCLASS OF Organizational Person
```

```
MAY CONTAIN {Account Balance,
                Allow Unlimited Credit,
                Group Membership,
                Higher Privileges, // Not implemented
                Home Directory,
                Language,
                Last Login Time,
                Locked By Intruder,
                Login Allowed Time Map,
                Login Disabled,
                Login Expiration Time,
                Login Grace Limit,
                Login Grace Remaining,
                Login Intruder Address,
                Login Intruder Attempts,
                Login Intruder Reset Time,
                Login Maximum Simultaneous,
                Login Script,
                Login Time,
                Message Server,
                Minimum Account Balance,
                Network Address,
                Network Address Restriction,
                Password Allow Change,
                Password Expiration Interval,
                Password Minimum Length,
                Password Required,
                Password Unique Required,
                Passwords Used,
                Print Job Configuration,
                Printer Control,
                Private Key,
                Profile,
                Public Key,
                Security Equals,
                Server Holds }
```

The X.500 standard defines two subclasses (derived classes) from the Person class. These are the Residential Person and Organizational Person subclasses. The Residential Person object class is not defined in NDS. This is used in X.500 to define directory services similar to those found in phone books.

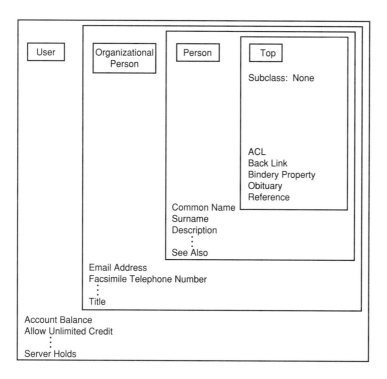

Figure 2.13
User object class
derivation.

Objects belonging to object classes, such as Person and Organizational Person, do not exist as objects in an NDS database. They are used for object derivation and construction only and are therefore called *noneffective* classes. Classes such as User, Group, and so on, can have their objects exist in an NDS tree. Such classes are called *effective* classes.

You can only use an effective class to create NDS objects. An object class used to create NDS objects is called the created object's base class. It follows, therefore, that you can use only an effective class as a base class for an object. Sometimes, in object-oriented programming languages, the term *parent class* is used as a synonym for *base class*. In NDS terminology, the term *parent class* is used for container objects that contain other objects, and is not used to describe the object derivation hierarchy.

The NDS base schema defines the following noneffective classes:

◆ Device

◆ Organizational Person

- Partition
- Person
- Resource
- Server
- Top

The NDS base schema defines the following effective object classes:

- AFP Server
- Alias
- Bindery object
- Bindery Queue
- Computer
- Country
- Directory Map
- Group
- Locality
- NCP Server
- Organization
- Organization Role
- Organizational Unit
- Printer
- Print Server
- Profile
- Queue
- Unknown
- User
- Volume

The Higher Privileges attribute in the user class definition is not currently implemented. This attribute is meant to activate certain privileges on a temporary basis and then deactivate them. Users of Unix systems will readily recognize that the su (supervisor command) on a Unix system enables an already logged-in user to assume root (supervisor) privileges after proper password authentication. You can expect the Higher Privileges attribute, if it becomes implemented, to provide a similar capability.

The Message Server attribute for the User object class is set to the Server object that stores and forwards broadcast-type messages.

Containers and Directories in File Systems

Containers are similar to directories in a file system. A directory in a file system can contain other subdirectories and files. Similarly, a container in NDS contains other subcontainers and leaf objects (network resources and services; see fig 2.14). You can use a directory in a file system for organizing files. Containers in NDS are used to organize network resources. One difference between an NDS tree and a file system directory tree is that there are limitations in the NDS tree as to where container and leaf objects can occur.

No limit to the NDS tree depth exists. For practical reasons, you might want to limit the depth of the NDS tree.

 No limit to the NDS tree depth exists. The NDS tree has restrictions on where you can place certain object classes. File system directory trees do not have this restriction.

Each container typically represents an organization, department within an organization, workgroup center, responsibility center, geographical location, and shared information network usage. The container and its relationship with other objects in the tree must be planned carefully.

Figure 2.14

Containers versus
directories for
file systems.

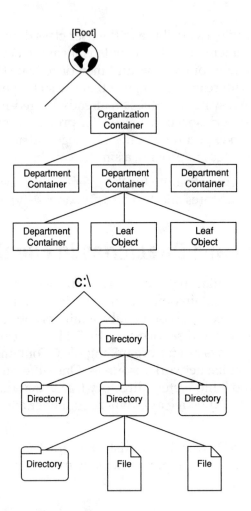

Naming Objects

All objects of the NDS tree must have a name, called the *object
name*. The root of the tree has the fixed object name of [Root].
Object names are case-insensitive. This means that two objects
with the name NW4CS_SYS and nw4Cs_sYs have the same object
name. Therefore, [root] and [Root] refer to the same object—the
root of the directory tree.

Objects that are directly in the same container cannot have the same name. Therefore, in figure 2.15, the container ENGINEERS cannot have two Volume objects with the names NW4CS_SYS and nw4Cs_sYs. It is not even possible for two objects that have a different object class to have the same name. Container ENGINEERS, therefore, cannot have a file Server object named ZAPHOD and a User object named ZAPHOD. These two objects can, however, exist in different containers, as shown in figure 2.16.

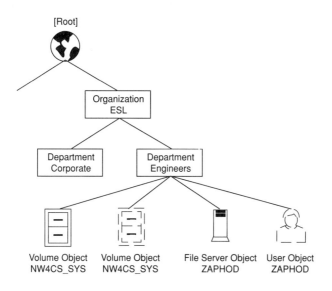

Figure 2.15
Object names in a container.

Even though object names are case-insensitive, the case of the name at the time of the object's creation is preserved for display purposes. This means that if you create an object named mY_worKstation, it will appear in the case used for the object name at the time the object was created. You can rename both leaf and container objects.

To make object names consistent and more readily understandable, it is important for an organization to have guidelines about object-naming conventions.

Figure 2.16

The same object names in different containers.

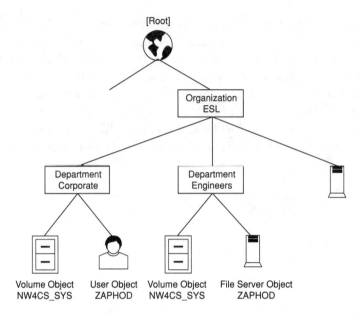

Object names

◆ must be unique in the same container level regardless of the object type they represent.

◆ are case-insensitive, but appear in the case that was used to create them.

◆ can be renamed only if they are leaf objects.

You can use up to 64 characters, consisting of alphanumeric characters, dashes, underscores, parentheses, and even spaces, in an object name. If spaces are used, you will have to enclose the object name in quotation marks (") to be recognized in command-line utilities and login scripts. For simplicity, you might want to avoid this. It is even possible to construct a name with a single blank. Figure 2.17 shows an interesting example of an NDS tree that has two objects with blank names. The first container object under ESL and the User object underneath it have blank object names. Even though blank names are permitted, it is a good idea to avoid them.

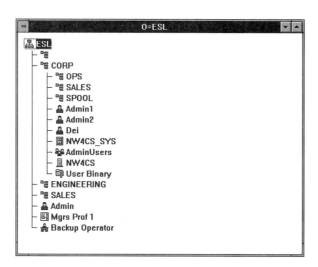

Figure 2.17
Blank name objects.

Brackets, periods, and percent signs are not permitted in object names. A few special characters such as plus (+), period (.), and the equals sign (=) must be preceded by a backslash (\). In general, it is a good idea to avoid using special characters in object names, as the names then become confusing and difficult to use and remember.

NDS even enables you to use characters that are designated illegal in the documentation for creating names of objects. They are not, however, guaranteed to work consistently in the NDS-based commands and utilities. For this reason, it is best to avoid them.

Classifying Container Objects

NDS supports four types of container objects, as follows:

◆ The [Root] object

◆ The Country object

129

♦ The Organization object

♦ The Organizational Unit object

Figure 2.18 shows the icons used to represent these different container objects. These icons appear when you use the Windows-based network administration tools. The US container, in this figure, represents the Country object. The containers AT&T, DEC, ESL, ESL_KSS, LG, LTREE, MITEL, RSA, SCS, WELFLEET, and WIDGET all represent Organization container objects. The containers ACCOUNTING, CORP, R&D, and SALES represent Organizational Unit container objects.

Figure 2.18

Symbolic representations of container objects.

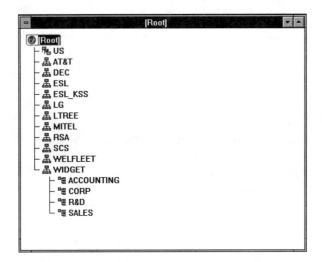

The [Root] Container Object

The most frequently used container objects are the Organization object and the Organizational Unit object. You can have only one [Root] object per NDS tree. The [Root] object cannot be renamed or deleted. It can have rights to other objects, or other objects can have rights to it.

It is possible to install NetWare 4.x on separate LANs, each with its own [Root] object. This can easily happen if the network is built in different segments, and final connectivity of the separate network segments is done at a later time. Under these circumstances, several [Root] objects can exist, each describing a different tree. Now, if you connect the network segments together, the networks represented by the different [Root] objects are not able to communicate (see fig. 2.19) through normal NDS mechanisms for current releases of NDS. Future releases may support NDS mechanisms for communicating between NDS trees.

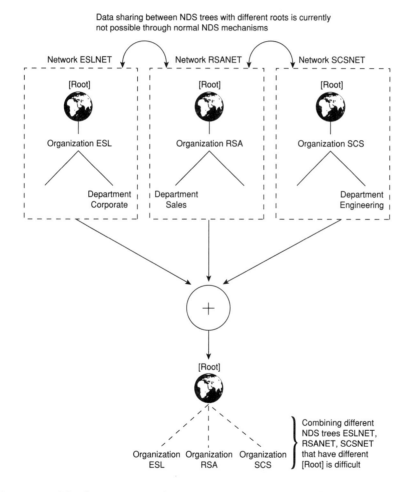

Figure 2.19

Multiple [Root] objects and sharing of data.

It is possible, however, to have two servers FS1 and FS2, each defined in its own unique tree TREE1 and TREE2. You could log in to FS1 under TREE1 as a valid NDS user. If you map a drive to a volume on FS2, using the NetWare 3.x syntax, NetWare automatically switches to bindery emulation mode and attempts to connect you. You then have access to the FS2 object, even though the FS2 object is in a separate NDS tree. Follow these steps:

1. Log in to TREE1 as a valid NDS user.

2. Enter **MAP N:= FS2/SYS:**.

   This is the NetWare 3.x syntax, which causes NetWare to switch to bindery-emulation mode.

 When installing a NetWare 4.x server that is not the first server installed on the network, you should physically connect this NetWare 4.x server to the rest of the network, so that the server can be installed as part of the NDS tree. You can also use the DSMERGE tool to merge two NDS trees.

 For extremely secure environments it might be desirable to have separate [Root] objects. This ensures that users in a directory tree under one [Root] cannot access or communicate with users under another [Root].

The [Root] object can contain only Country, Organization, and Alias objects. Of these, Country and Organization are container objects, and Alias is a leaf object.

 The only container objects that you can place directly under [Root] are Country and Organization objects.

The only objects that you can place under [Root] are Country, Organization, and Alias objects.

The Country Container Object

The Country object is part of the X.500 recommendations. Figure 2.20 shows an NDS tree with the two-letter designations for several countries. From this figure you can see that the Country object must be placed directly below the [Root] object. The Country object is optional. If used, it must occur directly under the [Root] object.

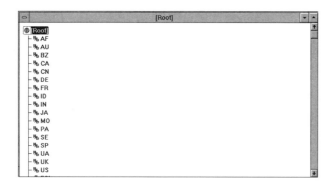

Figure 2.20

Country objects in an NDS tree.

The Country object can contain only Organization and Alias objects.

 An Alias object is the only leaf object that both the [Root] and Country containers have in common. Also, the only leaf object [Root] can contain is the Alias object.

 The only container object that the Country container can have is Organization.

Country object names can consist of only two characters.

The Organization Object

The Organization object represents the name of the organization. Figure 2.21 shows an NDS tree that has Organization objects. Notice the special icon used to represent the Organization object. At least one Organization object must be used in an NDS tree. It can occur directly under the [Root] object or a Country object. In figure 2.21, the organization objects CISCO, HP, IBL, IBM, MS, and NOVELL are placed directly underneath the Country object US. Also, organizations such as AT&T, DEC, ESL, ESL_KSS, LG, LTREE, MITEL, RSA, SCS, WELLFLEET, and WIDGET are placed directly underneath the [Root] object. These are the only places in which the NDS schema allows an Organization object to be placed.

Figure 2.21
Organization objects.

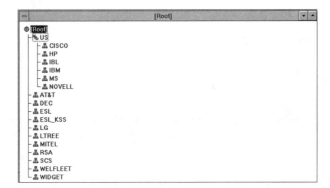

The Organization object can contain any leaf object and Organization Unit object, but it cannot contain another Organization object.

 You can place the Organization object underneath either the [Root] or the Country object only.

The Organizational Unit Object

Because organizations are usually subdivided into specialized functions, such as by department, network usage, common jobs, location, work groups, responsibility centers, and so forth, you can use the Organizational Unit object to represent the organization's subdivision. The Organizational Unit must occur under an Organization object or another Organizational Unit object. An Organizational Unit cannot occur directly under the [Root] object or Country object.

Figure 2.22 shows examples of an Organizational Unit object and the different locations in the NDS tree in which it can occur. The organizations HP, MS, and NOVELL that are in the Country container object have Organizational Units such as CORP, ENGINEERING, MARKETING, and DISTRIBUTION directly underneath them. The organization ESL_KSS that is directly underneath the [Root] has organizational units CORP, ENG, and SALES underneath it. Notice that CORP is used as an organizational unit name in more than one organization. The object-naming rules require an object name to be unique only within the same level of the container, and this enables the same object names to be used in different containers.

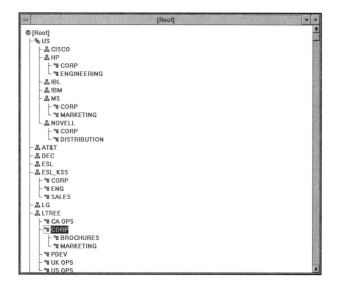

Figure 2.22

Organizational Unit objects.

In figure 2.22, organization LTREE has an Organizational Unit named CORP underneath it. CORP, in turn, has two other Organizational Units, BROCHURES and MARKETING, directly underneath it. Many organizations typically have subdivisions within a department.

The Organizational Unit object can contain any leaf object and Organizational Unit object.

The Organizational Unit object

◆ can occur in an Organization or Organizational Unit object.

◆ can contain any leaf object.

Attribute Types

As part of the X.500 system of naming objects, each object type is represented by an attribute designator. Country objects, for example, have the attribute type C. This means that the Country object US is represented as:

C=US

The other container objects, Organization and Organizational Unit, have the attribute types of O and OU, respectively. The organization IBM, therefore, is represented by:

O=IBM

and an organizational unit SALES is represented by:

OU=SALES

A leaf object that represents a resource or a service has the attribute type designator CN (for *common name*). A file server named NW4CS, therefore, is represented as:

CN=NW4CS

The different attribute types are summarized in table 2.3. All attribute types except the one for [Root] are part of the X.500 recommendations.

Table 2.3
Attribute Type Designators

Object	Container/Leaf	Attribute Type
[Root]	Container	No special attribute type. Designated by [Root] itself.
Country	Container	C
Organization	Container	O
Organizational Unit	Container	OU
Leaf Object	Leaf	CN

Leaf Object Types

Leaf objects are the actual representations of network resources. Other objects, such as [Root], Country, Organization, and Organizational Unit, are logical in nature and are used for organizational purposes.

The NDS schema, by default, permits the following leaf objects:

◆ AFP Server

◆ Alias

◆ Computer

◆ Directory Map

◆ Group

◆ NetWare Server

◆ Organizational Role

◆ Print Server

- Printer

- Print Queue

- Profile

- User

- Volume

- Bindery

- Bindery Queue

- Distribution List

- Message Routing Group

- External Entity

- Messaging Server

- Unknown

Each leaf object is discussed next.

AFP Server Objects

The AFP Server leaf object's current use is for informational purposes only. It represents an AppleTalk Filing Protocol (AFP) server that is on your network. This can be a Macintosh computer running the AFP protocols, or even a VAX server emulating AFP protocols. You can use the AFP server to store information such as network addresses, users, and operators. One of NDS's benefits is that you can query it for information in a manner similar to databases. If you have an AFP Server object for each AppleTalk server on your network (see fig. 2.23), therefore, you can make general queries, such as, "Show me all AppleTalk servers in container O=IBL."

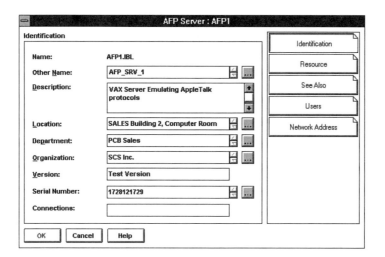

Figure 2.23
The AFP Server object.

Alias Objects

The NDS system is hierarchical in nature, and the object-naming syntax (as you will learn later in this chapter) consists of listing the NDS objects, beginning from the leaf, all the way up to the top of the tree. If you try to reference an object that is not in your container, the naming syntax becomes complicated, especially for end users who do not have the training to understand NDS naming conventions (see fig 2.24).

NDS permits the definition of an object called the Alias object. An Alias object can point to a leaf or a container object. This capability is similar to the concept of symbolic links used in operating systems such as Unix, except that Unix symbolic links apply to file systems, whereas Alias objects are links to leaf objects in the NDS tree.

You can enter the value for the Aliased object directly or by selecting the Browse icon next to this field, which shows the Select Object dialog box (see fig. 2.25). In this figure, because the Alias object is being created under [Root], the only possible objects that you can alias are the Organization and Country objects. An attempt to alias another object produces an error message.

Figure 2.24

Accessing another
object by means
of alias.

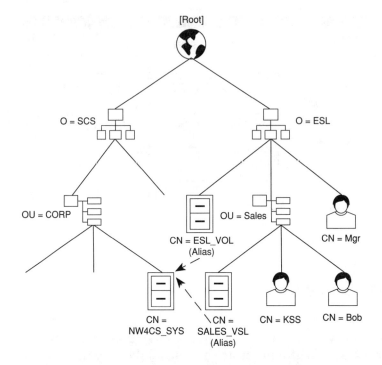

Figure 2.25

Alias object creation.

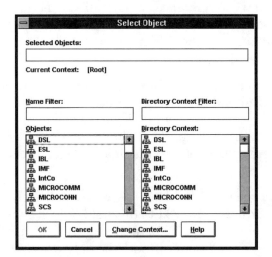

Computer Objects

A Computer object is used to represent a non-server computer such as a workstation, minicomputer, or mainframe. You can even use it to represent a *router*, which is a specialized computer with multiple network boards and routing logic implemented in firmware or software. A Computer object can contain information such as network addresses, computer serial numbers, computer operators, and so forth (see fig. 2.26).

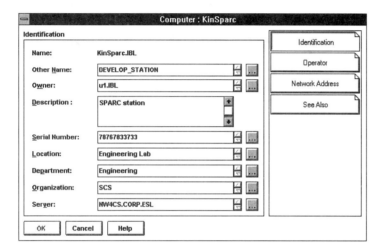

Figure 2.26

A Computer object.

Directory Map Objects

A Directory Map object contains a reference or pointer to a directory on a Volume object anywhere in the NDS tree. Currently, MAP objects are used only with the MAP command, which enables a workstation drive letter to refer to a network directory on a server. Using Directory Map objects can simplify the MAP command, which enables you to point to Volume objects in other containers.

A login script, a sequence of instructions that is executed when a user logs in, illustrates an important use of the MAP command. Login scripts are primarily used to set up a user's network environment. Consider a situation in which a login script containing

141

the MAP command maps the drive letter G: to a directory in Volume object FS1_VOL in container O=ESL. If, at a later point, the Volume object is moved to another container, or if the directory path is changed, the mapping becomes invalid and all references to the former location of the Volume object and directory subsequently change. If, however, the Directory Map object is used to perform the mapping in the login script, only the Directory Map reference to the new volume/directory location changes, and the login scripts do not change. Figure 2.27 shows a Directory Map object in an NDS tree with some of its properties.

Figure 2.27

A Directory
Map object.

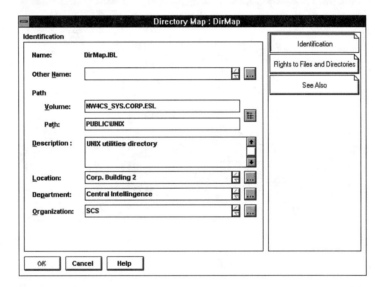

Group Objects

A Group object is used to refer to a collection of users in the NDS tree, and can only refer to a collection of User objects. The Group object is used to conveniently assign a number of users the same security rights. Figure 2.28 illustrates the concept of groups. In figure 2.29, the users belong to the same container. This is the most common use of groups. The Group object permits users from other containers to belong to the same group.

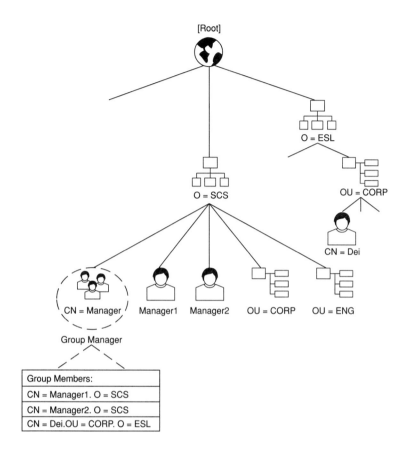

Figure 2.28

The concept of groups.

The Group object is similar to the concept of groups in NetWare 3.x, except that Group is an NDS object instead of a Bindery object. There are, moreover, no default groups such as group EVERYONE that, by default, contain all users created on the NetWare 3.x server. To achieve the effect of a group such as EVERYONE, you can use container objects. By using the container name, you can treat all objects created in a container as a group. A Group object has a group membership property, which is a list of User objects defined anywhere in the NDS tree.

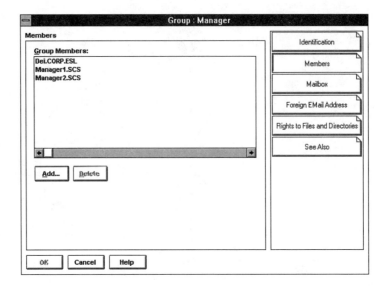

Figure 2.29

The Group object membership property.

Members of a Group object can only be User objects. On the other hand, you can use container objects as groups, but any leaf object or other container object can comprise a member of a container object. You can use container groups to provide a hierarchical relationship between groups that is not possible with Group objects and the groups used in NetWare 3.x. For instance, in NetWare 3.x, a group cannot contain other groups. This means the subset relationship between groups does not exist. By using containers that have a natural hierarchical relationship between them, subset relationships between groups is possible.

NetWare Server Objects

The NetWare Server object represents the physical NetWare server on a network. This is the object that provides NCP (NetWare Core Protocol) services. Some of the services provided by this object are represented as special objects in the NDS tree that reference the NetWare server. An example is the Volume object, which can be part of the physical NetWare server but is represented as a separate Volume object.

The NetWare Server object is created during installation. One of the parameters that you specify as part of the installation process

144

is the container in which the NetWare server should be placed. The NetWare Server object contains information such as the physical location of the Server object, its network address, the service it provides, and so forth.

The NetWare Server object is referenced by other objects in the NDS tree. An example is the Volume object, which references the NetWare server that acts as its host server. Without the NetWare Server object, you could not reference the Volume object and, hence, the files on the volume.

Figure 2.30 shows a NetWare Server object in an NDS tree, and some of its properties. Notice that the status of the server is shown as being Up, and its IPX address is IPX:F0004101:000000000001:0451. The F0004101 refers to the eight-hexadecimal-digit internal network number of the NetWare server; 000000000001 refers to the 12-hexadecimal-digit node number; and 0451 refers to the four-hexadecimal-digit socket number for receiving NCP requests. The 000000000001 is a 12-hexadecimal-digit node number and is different from the hardware address of the board, sometimes also called the node address or the MAC (Media Access Control) address. The version number of the server is reported as Novell NetWare v4.10[DS]. The DS stands for Directory Services. For NetWare 4, this node number is always 1 when associated with a NetWare server.

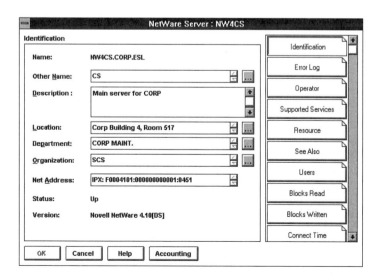

Figure 2.30

The NetWare
Server object.

Organizational Role Objects

The Organizational Role object refers to a position or role with which a set of responsibilities and tasks are associated within a department or organization. An example of such a role is the backup operator, who needs access to certain volumes to perform the backup operation. Another example is the print server operator. You can assign a User object to be an occupant of the Organizational Role object. In this case, the User object inherits all the rights that have been assigned to the Organizational Role object (see fig. 2.31). If the responsibility for performing the task is passed on to another user, you can change the user occupant of the Organizational Role object to reflect this.

Figure 2.31

The relationship between the User object and the Organizational Role object.

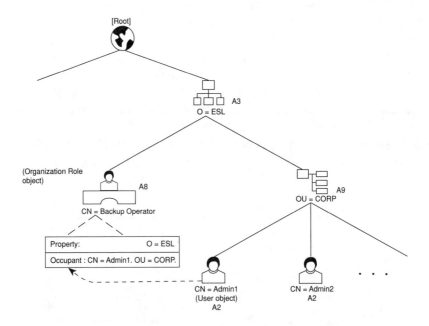

The Organizational Role object is useful in situations where the task performed by the organizational role does not change, but the person fulfilling that role does change. For example, the person assigned to perform backup tasks can change depending on the workload of individuals in an organization. Instead of changing the rights of the user for performing a certain task, you can assign these rights to the Organizational Role object. The occupant of the Organizational Role object can be changed, and this gives the assigned occupant sufficient rights to perform the organizational role's task. Figure 2.32 shows the Organizational Role object and the individual occupying that role. You can assign only User objects to the property occupant. Figure 2.32 indicates that the occupant of the organizational role is the User object CN=Admin1.OU=CORP.O=ESL.

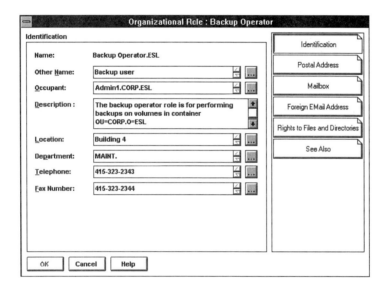

Figure 2.32

The Organizational Role object.

Print Server Objects

A Print Server object describes the services provided by the NetWare Print Server. The Print Server object is created by the utilities PCONSOLE and NWADMIN (NetWare Administrator Tool), and contains a reference to all the Printer objects it services.

Figure 2.33 shows the Print Server object and some of its properties in the NDS tree. Notice that the print server has a property called the Advertising Name, the name used by the print server to advertise its services using SAP (Service Advertising Protocol). The status of the Print Server in the example indicates that it is down.

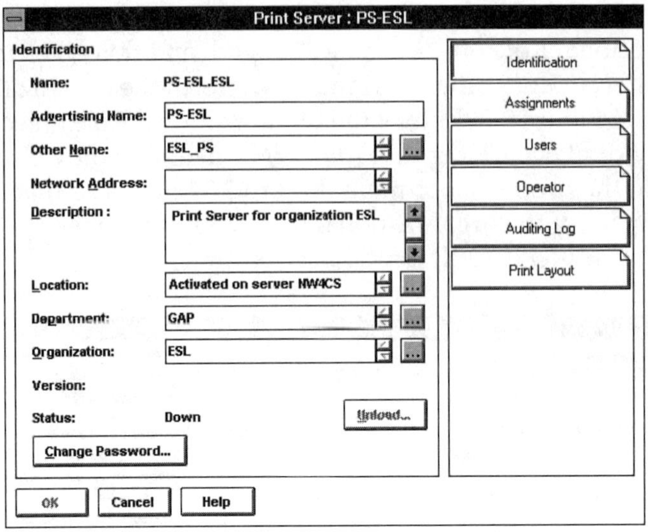

Figure 2.33

The Print Server
object.

Print Queue Objects

The Print Queue object is used to describe the network print queues, and contains a reference to the Volume object on which the actual print jobs are stored. The Printer object is assigned to a Print Queue object. Print jobs sent to the Printer object go to the associated print queue. As in NetWare 3.x, print jobs can also be sent to the print queue.

Figure 2.34 shows the Printer Queue object in the NDS tree. Notice that the Volume property indicates the Volume object that is used to support the print queue. Print queues are stored in the QUEUES directory on the specified volume.

Printer Objects

The Printer object is used to describe the physical network printer device. The Print Queue object references the Volume object on which the actual print jobs are stored. Printer objects are assigned to print queues. Print jobs sent to the Printer object go to the associated print queue. As in NetWare 3.x, print jobs can also be sent specifically to the print queue.

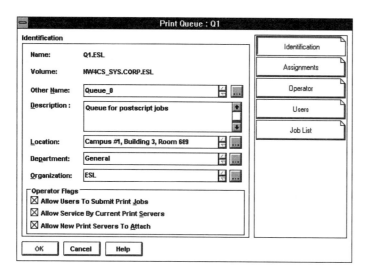

Figure 2.34

The Print Queue object.

There are additional restrictions for sending jobs to Printer objects. For instance:

◆ You must be a user of all the objects assigned to the Print queues.

◆ You must have Browse NDS rights to the Printer object and all assigned Print Queue objects.

◆ You need to designate a default queue for the Printer object.

Figure 2.35 shows a Printer object in the NDS tree, and the properties of the Print object that contains references to other printer-related objects. In figure 2.35, the Print Queues property list has just one Queue object assigned to it at a priority of 1 (highest). This means that print jobs sent to the Printer object will be sent to the queue represented by the object CN=Q1.O=ESL. The Print Server this printer services is CN=PS-ESL.O=ESL.

Figure 2.35

The Printer object
and the Assignment
properties.

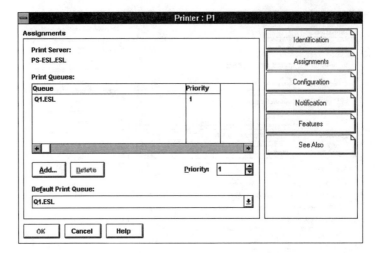

Figure 2.35

The Printer object
and the Assignment
properties.

Profile Objects

The Profile object represents common actions that are performed during login processing—specifically, a login script that is shared by a number of users. Different containers can hold the User objects that share the login script.

The Profile object is listed as a property of a User object, and is executed when an individual uses the User object to log in to the network. Other types of login scripts, such as the system login script and user login scripts, exist. These scripts, however, are properties of the container object and the User object, and do not exist as separate NDS objects. The Profile object is the only login script type that can exist as an independent NDS object.

Figure 2.36 shows a Profile object in an NDS tree, and the login script contained in the Profile object.

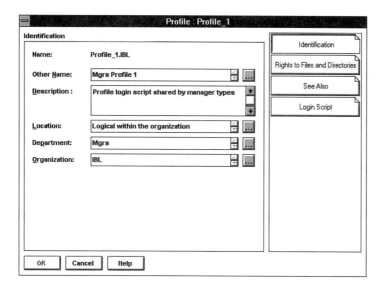

Figure 2.36
The Profile object.

User Objects

A User object represents the user account of the individual logging in to the network. This is the most important object as far as the user is concerned. Changes made to this object affect the user directly. A User object must exist for every user that needs to log in to the network. The User object is defined in the NDS tree, which makes it different from NetWare 3.x, in which User objects were defined on a server. Using this single User object, an individual can access all the servers and other network resources to which the user has been assigned rights.

Some of the attributes (called *properties* in NDS terms) of the User object include: a home directory on a Volume object to which the user has rights, login restrictions, intruder lock out mechanism enabling/disabling, and so forth.

Figure 2.37 shows a User object defined in the NDS tree and some of its properties.

Figure 2.37

The User object.

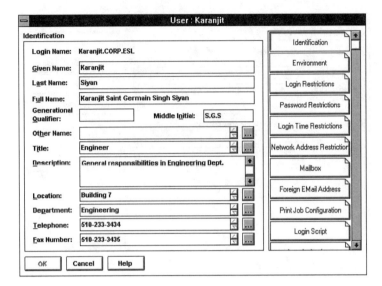

A User object with the special name USER_TEMPLATE functions as a template for creating default property values for User objects within that container. Only one USER_TEMPLATE object can exist within a container (such as Organization, or Organizational Unit) that enables the creation of such objects.

Volume Objects

The Volume object represents the physical volume that is attached to the server. It also represents data storage and the file system on the network, and is used to store print jobs associated with a network queue.

Although the Volume object appears to be independent of the NetWare server, the Volume object has a logical connection to the NetWare Server object to which it is attached. For this reason, Volume objects have a property called the *host server*, which associates the volume with its host NetWare server (see fig 2.38).

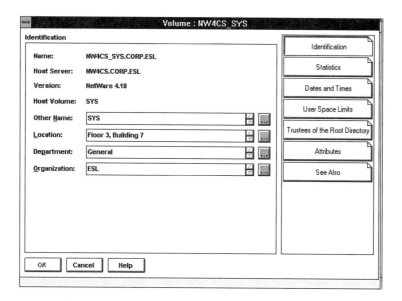

Figure 2.38
The Volume object.

The Volume object is created when the NetWare 4.x server is first installed in a container. The volume is given a default NDS name that consists of the name of the NetWare 4.x server, followed by an underscore, and the name of the physical volume such as SYS, VOL1, and so forth. The physical name of a volume is the name given when the volume is first initialized as part of the installation process using INSTALL NLM.

> NDS *Volume object name = Object Name of*
> *Server _ Physical Volume Name*

If, therefore, the NetWare Server object name is NW4CS, the first physical volume on it that has the name SYS has an NDS name of NW4CS_SYS. If the server has a second volume named VOL1, its NDS name is NW4CS_VOL1.

Bindery Objects

The Bindery object is created when you place a NetWare 3.x service in the NDS tree as part of the upgrade or migration utility. The internals of this object cannot be managed by NDS. The

153

Bindery object is used to provide bindery emulation services, which enable a NetWare 4.x server to be accessed by NetWare 3.x client software that expects to see a bindery-based server.

To access NetWare 4.x servers by NetWare 3.x client software, the SET BINDERY CONTEXT parameter needs to be set at the NetWare server. This parameter is set by default during installation of the NetWare server to the context in which the server is installed. You can additionally define up to 16 containers for the bindery context or up to 255 characters for the bindery context, depending on which limit is reached first. Bindery objects are created only when there is no equivalent object type within the set of standard NDS object types. Certain utilities such as SBACKUP.NLM and AUDITCON.EXE use bindery emulation, and do not work correctly if BINDERY CONTEXT is not set.

Bindery Queue Objects

The Bindery Queue object represents a NetWare 3.x print queue placed in the NDS tree as part of the upgrade or migration process. It is used to provide compatibility with bindery-based utilities and applications.

Distribution List

The Distribution List object was defined starting with NetWare 4.1. A Distribution List object represents a collection of objects that have mailboxes. You can assign objects such as the Organizational Unit, Group, or User objects to a distribution list. This enables you to send the same message to many different recipients by sending it to the Distribution List object.

Distribution lists can be nested. In other words, a distribution list can have other distribution lists as members. However, members of distribution lists do not have security equivalence to the Distribution List object.

Figure 2.39 shows some of the properties of a distribution list. The MailBox page button describes the Mailbox Location property, which is the name of the messaging server that contains the mailboxes. The Mailbox Location is a property of Organization, Organizational Role, Organizational Unit, Distribution List, Group, and User objects in NetWare Directory Services.

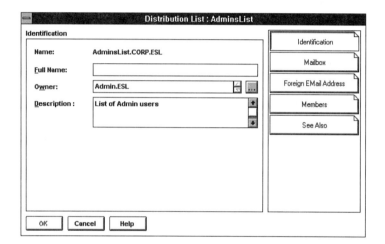

Figure 2.39

The Distribution List object.

Message Routing Group

The Message Routing Group object was defined starting with NetWare 4.1. A Message Routing Group object represents a cluster of messaging servers in the NDS tree. Because the messaging servers do frequent synchronizations among themselves, you should try to avoid connecting message servers in a message routing group through expensive or low-speed remote links. All messaging servers connected to the same message routing group send messages directly among themselves.

Figure 2.40 shows some of the message routing group properties. The Name field is the name you assign to the Message Routing

155

Group object. The Postmaster General is the User object who owns and administers the Messager Routing Group. The Postmaster General can modify the Message Routing Group object and its attributes (it has Supervisor object right to the Message Routing Group).

Figure 2.40

The Creation dialog box for a Message Routing Group object.

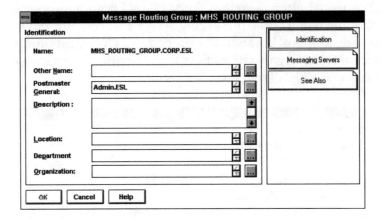

Note that a user who has the following rights is called a *Postmaster:*

◆ Supervisor access to the MHS (Message Handling System) Messaging Server object.

◆ Supervisor access to the Mailbox Location, Mailbox ID, and EMail Address properties of users of the MHS Messaging Server.

◆ Read access to the Message Routing Group that the MHS Messaging Server is in.

You will learn more about object and property rights later in this book.

External Entity

The External Entity object was defined starting with NetWare 4.1. An External Entity object represents a non-native NDS object or service that is imported into NDS or registered with NDS. An example of this might be a non-MHS e-mail address. By importing the non-MHS e-mail address into NDS, you can build an integrated address book for sending mail.

External entities are particularly useful if your messaging environment contains non-MHS Messaging Servers, such as SMTP (Simple Mail Transfer Protocol) hosts, SNADS (Systems Network Architecture Distribution Services) nodes, or X.400 MTAs (Message Transfer Agents). You can then add e-mail addresses of users and distribution lists for these non-MHS servers to the NDS. These non-NDS objects are added as external entities. Having done this, the non-MHS addresses are not accessible by the native NDS messaging applications. This enables MHS users to select non-MHS users and lists from a directory list.

An External Entity object has an External Name property that specifies the NDS name of the External Entity, and a Foreign E-mail Address property that specifies the user's mailbox, which is in a foreign messaging system. Figure 2.41 shows that the foreign e-mail address is an SMTP mailbox, with the address SMTP:karanjit@siyan.com. The e-mail address karanjit@siyan.com is in the format of the SMTP (Internet e-mail) address. Messages sent to this user can be delivered to an SMTP gateway.

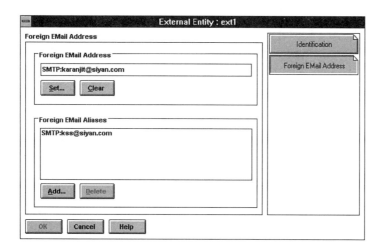

Figure 2.41

The External Entity object.

It is important to note that an NDS object can have a mailbox property or a foreign E-mail address property, but not both. These E-mail property values can be assigned when you create an object or at a later time.

Messaging Server

The Messaging Server object is a leaf object that represents a message server program, typically running on a NetWare server. The purpose of the messaging server is to route messages delivered to it. If a message recipient has a mailbox that is local to the Messaging Server, the message is delivered locally; otherwise, the message is transferred to other message servers. Message servers act as store-and-forward message transfer agents.

For those familiar with the OSI definition of a Message Transfer Agent (MTA), the Messaging Server is an MTA.

The NetWare 4.x servers ship with the MHS.NLM, which implements the MHS Messaging Server. Figure 2.42 shows some of the properties of a Messaging Server.

Unknown Objects

The Unknown object represents an NDS object, the object class of which cannot be determined because its NDS information has been corrupted.

An Unknown object appears if you bring the server down and then up again while specifying a different server name or delete the Server object. New volume names appear, and the old volume names become unknown objects. Also, if you remove the object that an alias Volume object points to, the Alias object appears as an Unknown object.

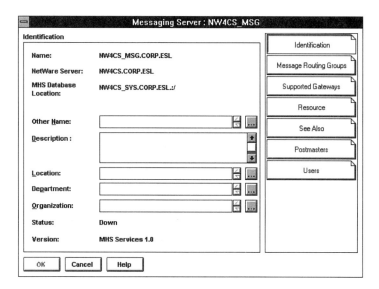

Figure 2.42
Messaging Server
properties.

Unfortunately, if you have an existing server in a DS tree and you decide to rename the server, only the server name is changed automatically. The Volume objects will still have the old server name and volume name. You have to change the Volume object name manually. The old volume names do not become Unknown objects.

 Too many Unknown objects in an NDS tree can signal NDS directory corruption. Running the DSREPAIR utility can fix this problem.

Table 2.4 summarizes the previous discussion and briefly describes each type of leaf object.

Table 2.4
Leaf Object Descriptions

Leaf Object Class	Meaning
AFP Server	An AppleTalk File Protocol Server. Used for informational purpose.

continues

Table 2.4, Continued
Leaf Object Descriptions

Leaf Object Class	Meaning
Alias	A link to another object. This is a substitute name for an object that points to another object in the NDS tree.
Computer	An object that represents a computer: workstation, minicomputer, mainframe, and so on. It is used for informational purposes.
Directory Map	An object that makes it possible to perform a simple drive mapping to another container. Makes it easier to maintain login scripts.
Group	An object whose members can be other objects. Similar to the concept of groups in NetWare 3.x, except that Group is an NDS object, instead of a Bindery object.
NetWare Server	Represents a NetWare server on a network. This is the object that provides NCP (NetWare Core Protocol) services. Some of the services provided by this object are represented as special objects in the NDS tree that references the NetWare server.
Organizational Role	Represents a position that has a certain set of defined tasks and responsibilities, and can be performed by any user assigned that role.
Print Server	Represents the Print Server service.
Print Queue	Represents the network print queue that holds the print jobs before they are printed.
Printer	Represents a network printer that can accept print jobs sent to it.
Profile	Represents an object that can be used for sharing of common actions that are performed during the login processing, regardless of whether they are in the same container.

Leaf Object Class	Meaning
User	The object that represents the user account. Used to contain information on the users who use the network.
Volume	The object that represents data storage on the network. Used to represent the file system on the network used for storing files and print jobs associated with a network queue.
Bindery object	The object created when placing a NetWare 3.x service in the NDS tree as part of the upgrade process. Internals of this object cannot be managed by NDS. It is used to provide bindery emulation services.
Bindery Queue	Created as part of the upgrade process. It represents a NetWare 3.x print queue.
Distribution List	Represents a list of mail boxes or other distribution lists. This simplifies sending the same E-mail to a group of users. Distribution lists can contain other distribution lists.
Message Routing Group	Represents a group of messaging servers that can transfer messages directly amongst themselves.
External Entity	Represents a non-native NDS object/service that is imported into NDS or registered in NDS. For example, MHS services can use External Entity objects to represent users from non-NDS directories such as SMTP, SNADS, X.400, etc. This enables MHS to provide an integrated address book for sending mail.
Messaging Server	A Message Transfer Agent for e-mail applications.
Unknown	Represents an NDS object whose object class cannot be determined because its NDS information has been corrupted. Running DSREPAIR can fix this problem.

Object Properties

Objects have attributes called *properties* that represent the types of information that you can store in the object. In this sense, an NDS object is similar to a record in a database, and the properties of the object are similar to the different field types that you can have in a record.

Figure 2.43 shows the File Server object. The File Server object, in this figure, shows such properties as Name, Network Address, and Location. The actual value assigned for each property is called the *property value*. A property value is an instance of the property type. Some object properties are mandatory and critical for proper use of the object. Other properties are descriptive and used for informational and documentation purposes, which enables the use of the NDS as a database of management information.

Figure 2.43

NDS object and properties.

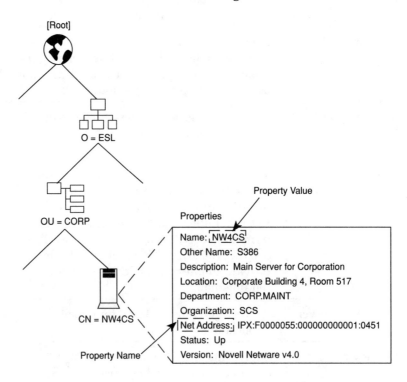

The critical values are filled out by the network administrator at the time of the object's creation. The network supervisor, who has Write access to properties, can fill out at a later time the values that are used for information and documentation. An example of User object properties, which are for informational purposes, is the list of telephone and fax numbers for the user, and the user's postal address and job title. A User object's name property is mandatory.

The type of information that is stored in an NDS object is called a *property*.

The value of an information item that is stored in an NDS object is called a *property value*.

Some object properties are mandatory; others are optional and are used for descriptive purposes.

Fill out as many property values for an object as you have information for because the NDS tree can be used as a database of information that you can query by using tools such as NLIST.

You can have single-value or multivalue properties. A property such as the login name of the user is single-valued, whereas the telephone number for a user is multivalued and represented as a list of values.

Exploring an NDS Tree Case Study

Consider the organization MICROCON, which makes advanced semiconductor devices. Its manufacturing plants and research labs are in San Jose, but its marketing and sales department is in New

York. The San Jose facility has a VAX computer, a NetWare 4.x file server used for manufacturing and testing, and another NetWare 4.x server for R&D. The R&D engineers are Rick and James; the manufacturing engineers are Tom and Bill. Ed is the network administrator of the entire network.

The New York facility has two file servers, NY_FS1 and NY_FS2, that are shared by all the users at that facility. Kirk is the overall network administrator. The SALES department is a department within the MARKETING group. Currently, the salespeople are Janice, Jane, and John. Ron works in the Marketing department, which at the moment is understaffed.

A diagram of MICROCON's physical network is shown in figure 2.44. Figure 2.45 shows the NDS tree structure for this organization. Because users Ed and Kirk have network administrator responsibilities, their User objects are defined directly under the containers OU=ENGINEERING and OU=MARKETING. Shared resources used by all users of the San Jose and New York networks also are assigned directly within these containers. Examples of these shared resources are the printer FS1_PRT and the file servers NY_FS1 and NY_FS2. File servers FS1 and FS2 are placed in the containers OU=MANUFACTURING and OU=R&D. The SALES division is defined as a subcontainer of OU=MARKETING. The salespeople's User objects are defined in the OU=SALES container.

Using the previous example, draw a physical network and an NDS tree for the organization Electronic Systems Lab (ESL) based in London, with facilities in Toronto, New York, and Paris. ESL's research labs are located in Paris and Toronto, with marketing in New York and administration and sales in London. A support staff of network administrators in London manages the entire network. Network services and hardware support at other sites are performed by local contractors. Each location has its own servers and printers.

Although other locations have a single file server and two network printers attached to the file server, London and New York both have two file servers each and three network printers. As the company grows, it is expected that additional servers will be added. All locations have their own print servers. The locations are tied together with communications links that run at 1.544 Mbps. The local networks used at each site are based on Ethernet.

Make reasonable assumptions for data that is not provided in this case study. For instance, you might have to invent names for users at each location, and decide which of the users are going to be network administrators.

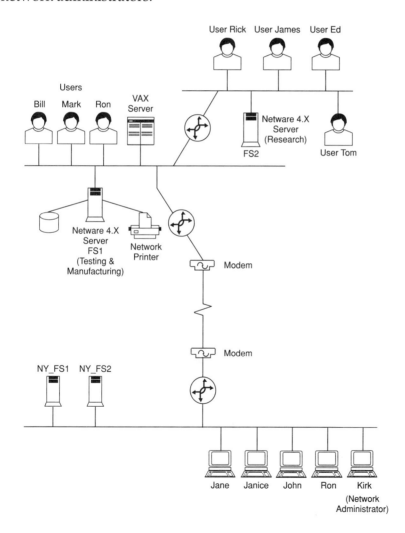

Figure 2.44

The MICROCON physical network.

Figure 2.45

The MICROCON NDS tree.

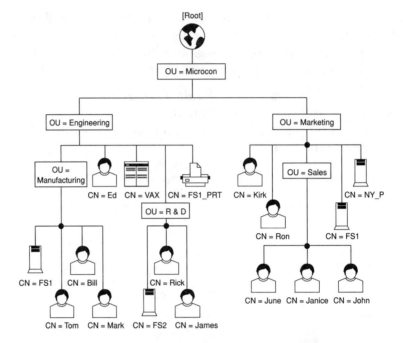

When you design the NDS tree for ESL, consider the following:

◆ Decide the depth of the tree. What number of container levels do you need?

◆ List all container objects that you need. Justify why you need each container.

◆ Give appropriate names for container objects. Should they correspond to departments or geographical locations?

◆ Do you need one Organizational Unit, or more than one?

Using NDS Tools

The two primary tools for creating, deleting, and moving NDS objects are:

◆ Network Administrator Tool (NWADMIN.EXE)

◆ NETADMIN

Another tool for user batch creation is UIMPORT. UIMPORT is similar to the NetWare 3.x MAKEUSER tool. Because UIMPORT is outside the scope of this book, it is not discussed here.

The Network Administrator Tool is a Windows and OS/2 GUI (Graphical User Interface) tool that you can use to manage NDS objects, whereas the NETADMIN tool is a text utility for creating NDS objects using C-Worthy menus.

Setting Up the Network Administrator Tool (NWADMIN.EXE)

To set up the NWADMIN.EXE tool, you must have installed the NetWare 4.x server and the DOS/Windows client software. The following steps show ways to set up the NWADMIN tool for MS Windows.

If one does not already exist, you must set up the NetWare program group in Program Manager. To set up the NetWare program group, follow these steps:

1. Make sure that you are logged in to the NetWare 4.x network.

2. Select the File menu from Program Manager.

3. Select the New option from the File menu.

4. Select Program Group from the New Program Object dialog box and select the OK button.

5. In the Program Group Properties box, type **NetWare** in the Description field. In the Program Group File field, type **C:\WINDOWS\NWUTILS.GRP** (or whichever is the Windows directory). Select OK.

If one does not already exist, perform the following steps to create a program item for NetWare Administrator Tool:

1. Highlight the NetWare program group.

2. Select the File Menu from the Program Manager.

3. Select the <u>N</u>ew option from the <u>F</u>ile menu.

4. Select the Program <u>I</u>tem from the New Program Object dialog box and select the OK box.

5. In the Program Item Properties box, type **NetWare Adminis-trator Tool** in the Description field. In the Command Line field, type **Z:\PUBLIC\NWADMIN**. In the Working Directory field, type **Z:\PUBLIC**. Select OK.

   You can specify a network drive other than Z:. Z: is used because you are likely to have at least one search drive, and this will be mapped to search drive Z:. You will have to make sure that this search drive is not "root mapped."

   Select Yes when the message "The specified path points to a file might not be available during later Windows sessions. Do you want to continue?" appears. This message appears because the path is a network drive, and unless you are logged in to the network, the network drive will not be available.

The program item for NWADMIN should appear in the NetWare program group.

Using the NetWare Administrator Tool

This section gives you a guided tour of the creation of the NDS tree structure shown in figure 2.46, using the NetWare Administrator Tool and assuming that you are familiar with MS Windows.

You should be very familiar with performing the operations of creating and deleting containers using the NWADMIN tool. A simulated NWADMIN tool is used in the test engine for the CNE exams.

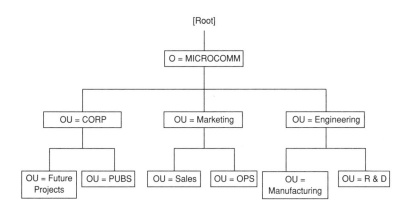

Figure 2.46

A sample NDS tree.

1. Log in to the network as an Administrator account.

   When the NDS services are first installed (at the time the first NetWare 4.x server is installed), a default network administrator user object Admin is created that has supervisor privileges to the entire NDS tree. You can use the Admin user object to login to the network.

2. Activate the NetWare Group and launch the NetWare Administrator Tool program item (double-click on the NetWare Administrator icon).

   You should see a screen similar to that shown in figure 2.47, which shows the NDS tree beginning from the current container.

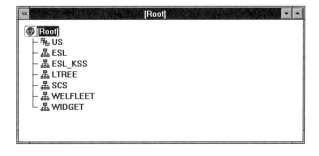

Figure 2.47

The NetWare Administrator menu.

3. To see the NDS tree beginning from the [Root], Select the **V**iew menu. Select the Set C**o**ntext option.

Set the current context to [Root]; which you can do by entering [Root] in the context field or by using the Browse button to browse through the NDS tree and select the context that you want to set as the current context.

4. Highlight the [Root] object. You can do this by clicking on it once.

5. Right-click on the [Root] object to see a list of operations that you can perform under the [Root]. Select Create.

You should see a list of objects that you can create under the [Root] object, as seen in figure 2.48.

Figure 2.48

New objects under [Root] container.

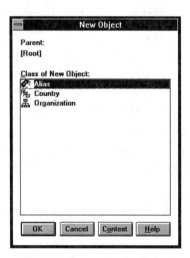

6. Select the Organization object and click OK. You should see a dialog box for creating the Organization object (see fig. 2.49).

Enter the name of the Organization shown in figure 2.46, and select the Create button. You should see the name of the newly created organization MICROCOMM appear in the NDS tree.

7. Highlight MICROCOMM and right-click. Select Create. You should see a list of objects that you can create under the Organization object (see fig. 2.50).

Compare figure 2.50 with figure 2.48. Notice that the list of objects that you can create under an Organization object is much larger.

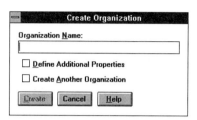

Figure 2.49

The Create Organization dialog box.

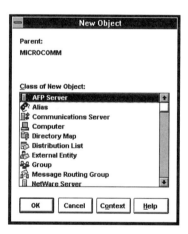

Figure 2.50

New objects under the Organization container.

8. Select the Organizational Unit object and click on OK. You should see a dialog box for creating the Organizational Unit object (see fig. 2.51).

   Enter the name of the Organizational Unit CORP, shown in figure 2.46, and select the **C**reate button. You should see the name of the newly created Organizational Unit CORP appear in the NDS tree if you double-click on MICROCOMM.

9. Repeat steps 7 and 8 to create Organizational Unit container objects for MARKETING and ENGINEERING as shown in figure 2.46. You can check the box labeled Create **A**nother Organizational Unit to speed up creation of objects of the same class.

Figure 2.51

The dialog box for creating the Organizational Unit container.

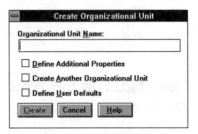

10. Repeat previous steps to create the rest of the organization as shown in figure 2.46.

11. Delete the NDS tree you have just created. You cannot delete a container object that has objects defined in it. You must, therefore, begin with the bottommost objects and delete them first.

    To delete an object, right click on the object and select the Delete operation. Alternatively, highlight the object and select the **O**bject menu, and select the Delete operation from the menu.

To delete a group of objects, perform the following steps:

1. Open the container by double-clicking on it.

2. Highlight the first object to be deleted. Click on the last object to be deleted while holding the Shift key. You should see the objects between the first and the last object highlighted.

3. Press the Delete key.

You can also use the Ctrl key to highlight non-contiguous objects upon which you want to perform operations.

Using the NETADMIN Utility

This section gives you a guided tour of the creation of the NDS tree structure using the NETADMIN tool. NETADMIN is a text-based utility that provides a similar functionality to the NetWare Administrator tool. As a system administrator, it is very useful to be able to perform NDS operations using NETADMIN, because you might run into situations where MS Windows is not installed at a NetWare workstation. NETADMIN can work directly on top of DOS, and does not require MS Windows.

The guided tour's goal for this session is to accomplish the same objectives as in the previous section, so that you can compare the differences between the NetWare Administrator and the NETADMIN tools.

1. Log in to the network as an Administrator account.

   When the NDS services are first installed (at the time the first NetWare 4.x server is installed), a default network administrator user object, Admin, is created that has supervisor privileges to the entire NDS tree. You can use the Admin user object to log in to the network.

2. The NETADMIN utility is located in the SYS:PUBLIC directory, and you must have a search path to that directory for the NETADMIN command to work correctly.

   To invoke the program NETADMIN, enter:

   `NETADMIN`

   You should see the NETADMIN screen shown in figure 2.52.

Figure 2.52

NetAdmin options.

The current context is seen on top of the screen under the label Context. If this is not set to [Root], perform the following steps to set it to [Root]:

   a. Select "Change context."

   b. Type [Root] when asked to "Enter context:".

   c. Press Enter to go back to the NETADMIN main menu with the changed context.

3. Select "Manage objects." You should see a list of objects and their classes under the [Root] container (see fig. 2.53).

Figure 2.53

Object classes under [Root] using NetAdmin.

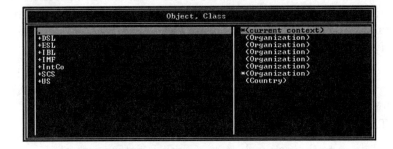

4. Press the Insert key. You should see a list of objects that you can create under [Root] (see fig. 2.54).

Figure 2.54

Object classes under [Root] using NetAdmin.

5. Select "Organization" to create an Organization object. You should see a box for creating the Organization object (see fig. 2.55).

Figure 2.56

NetAdmin box for creating an Organization container.

Enter the name of the organization shown in figure 2.46. You can elect to create a User Template for the Organization object at this point or defer this action until later.

6. Press F10 to save changes and perform the create operation.

When prompted to create another Organization object, answer No. You should see the name of the newly created organization appear in the Object, Class list.

174

7. Highlight the newly created organization and press Enter. Notice that your context has changed to the organization.

8. Press Insert to create an object. You should see a list of objects that you can create under the Organization object (see fig. 2.56).

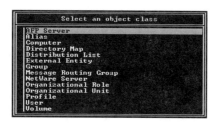

Figure 2.56

Object classes under Organization container using NetAdmin.

9. Select the "Organizational Unit" choice to create an Organization object. You should see a box for creating the Organizational Unit object (see fig. 2.57).

Figure 2.57

The NetAdmin box for creating an Organizational Unit container.

Enter the name of the Organizational Unit shown in figure 2.46. You can elect to create a User Template for the organization object at this point or defer this action till later.

10. Press F10 to save changes and perform the create operation.

11. When asked to create another Organizational Unit object, answer Yes and repeat the previous steps to create all the other Organizational Unit objects.

12. Review figure 2.46 and repeat the previous steps to create the rest of the organization, as shown in figure 2.46.

13. Delete the NDS tree you have just created. You cannot delete a container object that has objects defined in it. You must, therefore, begin with the lowest objects and delete them first.

To delete an object, highlight it from the Object, Class list and press the Delete key. You will be asked to confirm your delete operation. You can also delete several objects by marking them with the F5 key and then pressing the Delete key.

Understanding NDS Context

NDS context is a term used to describe the position of an object in the NDS tree in terms of the container that contains the object. For example, in figure 2.58 the context of object Admin is container ESL, and the context of the File Server object FSP_1 is in container CORP.

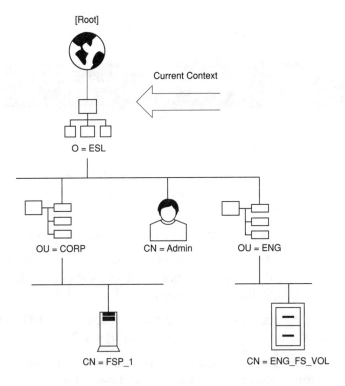

• Partial name of FSP_1 is CN = FSP_1. OU = CORP
• Partial name of ENG_FS_VOL is CN = ENG_FS_VOL. OU = ENG
• Partial name of Admin is CN = Admin

The context of an object is important because some NDS utilities require you to know the position (or location) of the object in the NDS tree. In general, you must know the object's position (context) so that you can find it. (There are commands, such as the NLIST command, that help you find the object's position in the NDS tree, if you know its name. These will be discussed later in this chapter). The context of an object affects the ways the object is referenced.

The context can also be seen as a *pointer* that locates the object's position in the NDS tree. The context is described by listing, from left to right, the NDS names of the container objects, separated by periods (.). The order of listing of container objects is to begin with the immediate container and work your way up to the root. Therefore, the context of object Admin in figure 2.58 is Admin.ESL or CN=Admin.O=ESL because only one container exists. The [Root] container object is not listed because it is always implied that the topmost container is [Root]. In the second method of representing the NDS context, an object-type designator such as O (Organization) is used. Both forms are valid, with the second form using attribute-type designators.

The position of an object in an NDS tree is called its *context*. It locates where you can find an object in the NDS tree. The *context* of an object refers to its container. The context can never be set to a leaf object (because leaf objects cannot contain other objects).

Another example is the context of object FSP_1 in figure 2.58:

FSP_I.CORP.ESL

or

CN=FSP_I.OU=CORP.O=ESL

The [Root] container object is not listed, because it is always implied that the topmost container is [Root]. In the second form of NDS context representation, the object-type designators CN (Leaf Object), OU (Organization Unit), and O (Organization) are used.

A special type of context called the *current context* indicates the current position of the *attached workstation* in the NDS tree. An attached workstation is one that is connected (logically speaking) to the NDS tree by means of the network.

When the network client software loads, it makes a connection to the NDS tree. If DOS is used as the workstation software, it can maintain only one current context at a time for each DOS session. You can set the workstation's current context only to container objects and *not* leaf objects, because a context is defined as the position of the immediate *container* that contains the object in the NDS tree.

The current context is the default reference point used by the workstation to find other objects in the NDS tree. It is used in the same manner as the concept of the *current directory* in a file system. Just as the current directory cannot be set to a file name, the current context cannot be set to a leaf object.

The *current context* is an attached workstation's current position in the NDS tree.

You can use the current context as a reference point to find other objects in the tree.

Leaf objects that are in the current context of a workstation are referred to by their object names. For instance, if a workstation's current context is CORP.ESL, the user of that workstation can reference objects FS1 and PS1 by their common names:

> FS1

or

> CN=FS1
> PS1

or

> CN=PS1

It is not essential to use the full NDS name of the object in this case. This is a great convenience to the user of the workstation. Resources that are not in the current context cannot be referred to by their leaf names only; you must specify the NDS path name of the object. Objects FS2 and PS2, in figure 2.59, must be referenced by their NDS path names.

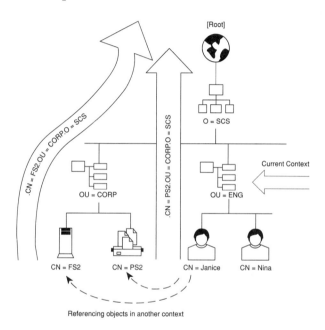

Figure 2.59

Referencing objects in another context.

Referencing objects in another context

 Study Note

You can refer to NDS objects that are in the current context of a workstation by their leaf object names.

NDS objects that are not in the current context of a workstation must be referred to by their NDS path name.

Group frequently accessed resources in the user's context to simplify access to these objects.

179

Specifying NDS Path Names

In the previous section, you observed that objects not in the current context of a workstation must be defined by their NDS path names. There are three ways of specifying NDS path names:

◆ By its complete name (also called Distinguished Name)

◆ By a typeless name

◆ By a partial name (also called Relative Distinguished Name)

 In the Novell documentation, the terms complete name and partial name are used. In the latest versions of the tests, the X.500 terms of Distinguished Name and Relative Distinguished Name are used.

Complete Name

A *complete name* is the name of an NDS object that includes the leaf name and the names of the containers that contain the leaf object, beginning from the leaf object and going up the tree to the [Root] object. The object names are specified with their attribute name abbreviation (attribute type). The complete name must always begin with a period (.). Periods between object names that make up the NDS name are used as separators for the object names. The complete name is also called the Distinguished Name (DN).

This is an important point to note: The leading period has a different meaning than other periods used in the NDS object name; it signifies that the name is a complete name, and that you can reference the object by *enumerating* its path—listing the object name and its containers—all the way to the root object.

The general syntax of the complete name of an object is:

```
.CN=leaf_object.[OU=org_unit_name.{OU=org_unit_name}].O=org_unit.[C=country]
```

In the previous syntax, the [] brackets and the {} braces are *meta characters* that have a special meaning. The [] indicates that the contents between the [] are optional. The {} indicates that you can have zero or more occurrences. The leading period is required for complete names. Without the leading period, the complete name becomes a partial name.

To summarize some of the rules of a complete name: the syntax for a complete name always begins with a period, followed by the NDS path of the object all the way up to the root. Because you can have only one [Root] per NDS tree, the [Root] object is not listed as part of the NDS tree. If an attribute type is used to qualify the object name in the NDS path, it will have the following form:

```
attribute_type_abbreviation=object_name
```

The *attribute_type_abbreviation* will be CN for leaf object, OU for Organizational Units, O for Organization, and C for Country. After the name of the object, the list of containers beginning with the most immediate container, and continuing all the way to the [Root] container are enumerated. Because you can have only one [Root], the root object is not listed. The square brackets around the Organizational Unit list indicate that the OUs are optional. Examples of types of complete names follow:

```
.CN=leaf_object.O=org_unit.C=country
```

or

```
.CN=leaf_object.O=org_unit
```

or

```
.leaf_object.org_unit
```

The last example is a typeless complete name, which does not have the attribute types. The C=*country* has been left out of the syntax example of the complete name, because the Country object is optional.

The most general case of the complete name lists the Organizational Units, a single Organization, and a Country name as shown in the following:

```
.CN=leaf_object.OU=org_unit_name.OU=org_unit_name.O=org_unit.C=country
```

181

In the previous syntax example, only two Organizational Unit objects are shown, but there could be any number of these objects.

In figure 2.60, the complete names of objects FS1, PS1, PRINT_1, PRINT_2, and PS2 follow:

.CN=FS1.OU=REGION_A.O=HAL

.CN=PS1.OU=REGION_A.O=HAL

.CN=PRINT_1.OU–OPS.OU=SALES.O–HAL

.CN=PRINT_2.OU=SALES.O=HAL

.CN=PS2.O=HAL

Figure 2.60

The NDS tree for complete name examples.

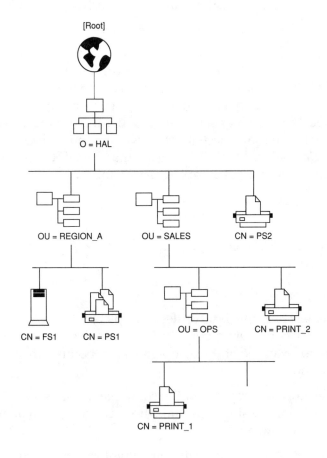

Partial Name

A partial name for an NDS object is its NDS path relative to the current context. This is in contrast to the complete name that lists the NDS path objects relative to the root of the tree. A partial name is similar to specifying the name of a file relative to the current directory, and a complete name is similar to specifying the name of a file, using its complete path name that lists all the directories beginning from the root. The partial name is also called the *Relative Distinguished Name* (RDN).

Author's Note

In X.500, the object's full path name, with reference to its position in the NDS tree, is called its *Distinguished Name* (DN); and the name relative to a context is called the Relative Distinguished Name (RDN). The NDS term for this is *complete name*. The Distinguished Name of an object is formed by adding the RDN of the object to the DN of the object's parent. You should be familiar with the X.500 terms for taking the test.

The X.500-equivalent term for the NDS database is the *Directory Information Base* (DIB), and the NDS tree is referred to as the *Directory Information Tree* (DIT) in X.500 terminology.

Resolving a Partial Name

The NDS must resolve the partial name to a complete name. This is done by appending the current context to the partial name and adding a period at the beginning to indicate a complete name, as in the example that follows:

Complete Name = .Partial Name.Current Context

Another example will help clarify the preceding rule:

If the current context is OU=CORP.O=ESL, the partial name for object HP_PR1 that is in the same context is CN=HP_PR1. NDS forms the complete name by appending the current context OU=CORP.O=ESL to the partial name CN=HP_PR1, and adding a period at the beginning.

Current context	OU=CORP.O=ESL
Partial name	CN=HP_PR1
Complete name	.CN=HP_PR1.OU=CORP.O=ESL

The main purpose of a partial name is to simplify the names for NDS objects that are in the current context or in the vicinity of the current context.

The examples so far have been of objects in the current context. In figure 2.61, the object FSP_1 is not in the same context as the current context that is set to O=ESL. In this case, the partial name of FSP_1 is the object name plus the list of all the containers leading up to the current context O=ESL. In other words, the partial name for FSP_1 is:

CN=FSP_1.OU=CORP

Similarly, if the current context is O=ESL, the partial name of ENG_FS_VOL is:

CN=ENG_FS_VOL.OU=ENGI

If the current context is O=ESL, the partial name of Admin is:

CN=Admin

What if the current context is *not* set to a container that is part of the complete name leading up to the root? In this case, appending a period (.) at the end of the NDS name refers to the previous container. In figure 2.61, the current context is OU=ENG.O=SCS. If the object DEI_FS in OU=CORP is to be referenced, you can use the partial name

CN=DEI_FS.OU=CORP.

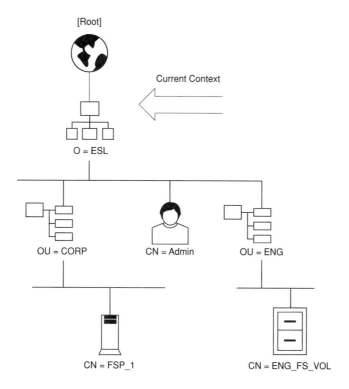

Figure 2.61

The partial name for objects not in current context, but in the same tree branch.

[Root]

Current Context

O = ESL

OU = CORP   CN = Admin   OU = ENG

CN = FSP_1   CN = ENG_FS_VOL

- Partial name of FSP_1 is CN = FSP_1. OU = CORP
- Partial name of ENG_FS_VOL is CN = ENG_FS_VOL. OU = ENG
- Partial name of Admin is CN = Admin

The trailing period (.) refers to the parent container of the current context, which in this case is O=SCS. The partial name of the object DEI_FS with respect to the container O=SCS is CN=DEI_FS.OU=CORP, but because the current context is in a different tree branch (current context is OU=ENG.O=SCS and not O=SCS), a trailing period must be added.

If the current context in figure 2.62 were OU=OPERATIONS.OU=ENG.O=SCS, you could refer to the same object, CN=DEI_FS, by the partial name

CN=DEI_FS.OU=CORP..

Figure 2.62

The partial name for objects when the current context is in a different branch of the NDS tree.

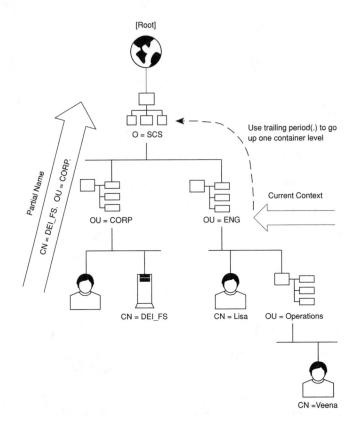

Two trailing periods signify two parent containers above the current context. Because the current context is OU=OPERATIONS.OU=ENG.O=SCS, the two trailing periods refer to the container O=SCS.

The trailing period can occur *only* in partial names.

A summary of the trailing period rules follows:

1. A single trailing period rule at the end of the NDS partial name removes a *single* object name from the current context.

2. The resulting name, formed by removing a leftmost object from the current context, is appended to the partial name.

3. A leading period is added to form a complete name.

Relative Distinquished Names Example Exercise

The Relative Distinguished Names for objects HP_PR1, FS1, VOL1, FS2, and BOB in figure 2.63 are listed in table 2.5 for different current context settings.

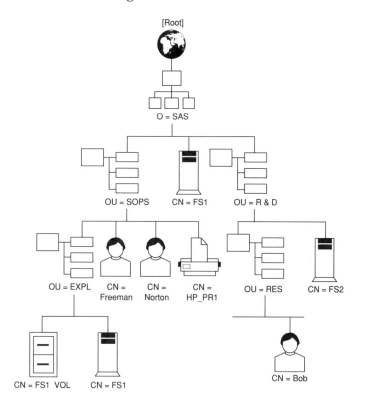

Figure 2.63

The NDS tree for Relative Distinguished Name examples.

Table 2.5
Partial Name Examples

NDS Object	Current Context	Relative Distinguished Name
HP_PR1	[Root]	CN=HP_PR1.OU=SOPS.O=SAS
HP_PR1	O=SAS	CN=HP_PR1.OU=SOPS

continues **187**

Table 2.5, Continued
Partial Name Examples

NDS Object	Current Context	Relative Distinguished Name
HP_PR1	OU=SOPS.O=SAS	CN=HP_PR1
HP_PR1	OU=R&D.O=SAS	CN=HP_PR1.OU=SOPS.
HP_PR1	OU=RES.OU=R&D.O=SAS	CN=HP_PR1.OU=SOPS..
HP_PR1	OU=EXPL.OU=SOPS.O=SAS	CN=HP_PR1.
FS1	[Root]	CN=FS1.O=SAS
FS1	O=SAS	CN=FS1
FS1	OU=SOPS.O=SAS	CN=FS1.
FS1	OU=EXPL.OU=SOPS.O=SAS	CN=FS1..
FS1	OU=R&D.O=SAS	CN=FS1.
FS1	OU=RES.OU=R&D.O=SAS	CN=FS1..
FS1_VOL1	[Root]	CN=FS1_VOL1.OU=EXPL.OU= SOPS.O=SAS
FS1_VOL1	O=SAS	CN=FS1_VOL1.OU=EXPL.OU=SOPS
FS1_VOL1	OU=SOPS.O=SAS	CN=FS1_VOL1.OU=EXPL
FS1_VOL1	OU=EXPL.OU=SOPS.O=SAS	CN=FS1_VOL1
FS1_VOL1	OU=R&D.O=SAS	CN=FS1_VOL1.OU=EXPL.OU=SOPS.
FS1_VOL1	OU=RES.OU=R&D.O=SAS	CN=FS1_VOL1.OU=EXPL.OU=SOPS..
FS2	[Root]	CN=FS2.OU=R&D.O=SAS

NDS Object	Current Context	Relative Distinguished Name
FS2	O=SAS	CN=FS2.OU=R&D
FS2	OU=SOPS.O=SAS	CN=FS2.OU=R&D.
FS2	OU=EXPL.OU=SOPS.O=SAS	CN=FS2.OU=R&D..
FS2	OU=R&D.O=SAS	CN=FS2
FS2	OU=RES.OU=R&D.O=SAS	CN=FS2.
BOB	[Root]	CN=BOB.OU=RES.OU=R&D.O=SAS
BOB	O=SAS	CN=BOB.OU=RES.OU=R&D
BOB	OU=SOPS.O=SAS	CN=BOB.OU=RES.OU=R&D.
BOB	OU=EXPL.OU=SOPS.O=SAS	CN=BOB.OU=RES.OU=R&D..
BOB	OU=R&D.O=SAS	CN=BOB.OU=RES
BOB	OU=RES.OU=R&D.O=SAS	CN=BOB

Study Note

Study the examples in table 2.5 so that you thoroughly understand the formation of Relative Distinguished Names.

Author's Note

The X.500 standard defines ways that Distinguished Names are exchanged between OSI systems. Typically this is done using ASN.1 (Abstract Syntax Notation 1), which unambiguously transmits the Distinguished Names

continues

189

across the network. When dealing with implementations of NDS, you must have a textual representation of these distinguished names. The X.500 standard does not define the ways the textual strings for Distinguished Names are to be represented. Contrary to popular belief, Novell's syntax for complete names for the NDS is not the only way to represent Distinguished Names. This does not mean that Novell is not compliant with X.500, because the standard does not define the textual representation of the DN.

An interesting X.500 implementation that was developed at University College, London is available as part of the ISODE (ISO Development Environment) release called QUIPU. You can obtain ISODE by contacting:

University of Pennsylvania
Department of Computer and Information Science
Moore School
Attn: ISODE Distribution
200 South 33rd Street
Philadelphia, PA 19104-6319
USA
Phone: 215-898-8560

QUIPU (pronounced kwi-poo) is named after the manner in which information was stored by the Inca of Peru. Writing was not used by the Inca. Instead, they used a system of knotted colored strings to encode information. The strings were attached to a larger rope to form a device known as the Quipu. The Quipu could only be read by trained people and contained information about property locations and rights throughout the Inca empire.

An NDS object with the name .CN=KSS.OU=
R&D.OU=ENG.O=SCS.C=US will be named in the
following manner in QUIPU:

@C=US@O=SCS@OU=ENG@OU=R&D@CN=KSS

Notice that in QUIPU, objects are written left to
right, beginning from the root of the DIT and
moving down the tree to the object. This is in
contrast to NDS where objects, though written from
left to right, are listed beginning from the object
and moving up the tree.

To move up one level from the current context, the
NDS syntax is:

CN=KSS.OU=SCS.

To move up one level in QUIPU, the syntax is:

@OU=SCS.CN=KSS

You can decide for yourself which system is superior for the textual names of DNs.

Naming Rules in NDS

This section summarizes the naming rules discussed in many of
the examples in this chapter. There are three important concepts
that deal with the NDS path, typeless naming, and period rules.

NDS Path

The NDS path name consists of a list of object names that are
written left to right, beginning with the referenced object, and
leading up to the [Root] object or the current context. If the object
name is preceded by a period (.), the object names refer to the
complete name and must lead up to the [Root]. If the NDS path
name does not have a leading period, it refers to a partial name.

Typeless Name

The complete name of the object, in addition to beginning with a period, uses the attribute type names CN, OU, O, and C to designate the type of the object as being a Common Name, Organizational Unit, Organization, and Country object respectively.

Typeless names are NDS names that do not have the attribute type designators of CN, OU, O, or C. The following are examples of typeless names:

Mary.CORP.IBM

.Lisa.CORP.ESL

OPS.ICS.US

.Linda.SALES.LONDON.UK

When NDS encounters a typeless name, it resolves it to a complete name and supplies the appropriate attribute types.

The use of typeless names involves less typing on the part of the network administrator and can simplify the use of NDS names.

Author's Note

Prior to NetWare 4.1, Novell did not recommend the use of the Country object because the NetWare 4 libraries and clients assumed that the top-level container was an Organization container. In the NetWare 4.02 release, it was possible to use Country objects in typeless names, if the current context included a Country object and it had the same number of objects as the name being resolved. All of these complex rules of resolving typeless names have been removed in NetWare 4.1 (and higher).

With current releases of NetWare 4, NDS resolves the typeless name correctly whether it includes a Country object or not.

If your organization wants to interoperate with the AT&T NetWare Connect Services (ANCS), and other X.500 Directories that use the North American Directory Forum (NADF), you should design your directory with the Country object at the top. You should also follow the NADF naming standards for X.500 environments.

Setting the Name Context at the Workstation

NetWare 4.x client software provides the ability to set the current context as a user logs in to the workstation. This is provided by the Name Context configuration setting in the NET.CFG file. The NET.CFG file is processed at the time the NetWare client software drivers and the network requester software are launched.

The format of the name context is:

```
NAME CONTEXT = "NDS Path of Context"
```

The NET.CFG statements are case-insensitive; thus you enter them in upper- or lowercase.

Suppose you desire to set the current context at the time of login for user Bob to:

> OU=CORP.O=SCS

You can do this by including the statement

```
Name Context = "OU=CORP.O=SCS"
```

in the NET.CFG file.

 You cannot enter a leading period (.) in the name context parameter. For example, the following is illegal:

```
NAME CONTEXT = ".OU=CORP.O=SCS"
```

The following sample of an NET.CFG file has the name context set to OU=CORP.O=ESL. The Name Context specification must occur in the NetWare DOS Requester section.

```
LINK DRIVER SMC8000
      FRAME ETHERNET_802.2
      INT    3
      PORT 280
      MEM  D0000
NetWare DOS Requester
      FIRST NETWORK DRIVE = F
      NAME CONTEXT = "OU=CORP.O=SCS"
```

You can explicitly change the name context by using the CX (Change Context) command, before logging in to the network. Placing the name context statement in the NET.CFG is a convenience to the user, as it simplifies access to the network resources the user most frequently uses. For this reason, it is best to place the name context to the container that holds the resources a user is most likely to use. If the name context of a user is set to the container that holds the User object, login to the network is possible by using the command:

```
LOGIN UserLoginName
```

For user BOB this would be as simple as:

```
LOGIN BOB
```

If the name context is set to a different context than the location of the user object, the user has to use the NDS path to the User object.

```
LOGIN  NDSPathToUserObject
```

For user BOB, whose User object is defined in OU=CORP.O=SCS, this would be:

```
LOGIN   .CN=BOB.OU=CORP.O=SCS
```

or

```
LOGIN   .BOB.CORP.SCS
```

The second form demonstrates the use of the typeless complete name, whereas the first form shows the User object referenced by its complete name with attribute-type designators.

Querying from the Command Line in NDS

Besides NETADMIN, two primary command-line utilities for browsing the NDS tree are:

- ◆ CX(Change Context)
- ◆ NLIST (Network List)

Used together, the CX and NLIST utilities provide a flexible and powerful mechanism for browsing and searching NDS object names and properties.

The CX Utility

The CX utility is used to change the current context. When used by itself, without any parameters and options, you can employ it to find out the current context. Thus the command CX from the DOS prompt, as shown in the following example, indicates that the current context is set to O=ESL.

```
F> CX
ESL
F> CD
F:\SYSTEM
```

The command in bold is the command a user types in, and the other text is the system's response. In the preceding commands F> is the system (DOS) prompt and the O=ESL and the F:\SYSTEM are the results that appear after the respective execution of the CX and CD commands.

The CX command is very similar to the CD command, which enables the user to display or change the current directory for a file system. It is important to keep in mind that the CX operates on the NDS context and not the file system directory.

Changing the NDS directory context does not change the current file system directory. Therefore, in the previous example, the CX

195

command reveals that the current context is O=ESL and the CD command reveals that the current directory is F:\SYSTEM. Changing the current context will have no effect on the current directory setting, and changing the current directory will have no effect on the current context setting.

The commands that follow refer to the NDS tree in figure 2.64.

Figure 2.64

An NDS tree example for CX commands.

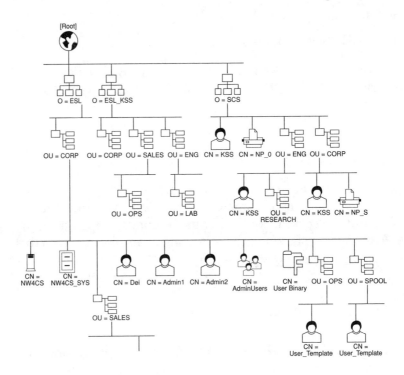

To change the current context to OU=CORP.O=ESL, you can issue the following command:

```
F> CX   .OU=CORP.O=ESL
CORP.ESL
```

Notice that the CX command always returns the current context; this is a quick check to see if the CX command works correctly.

In the preceding command the complete name .OU=CORP.O=ESL was used. You can also use typeless names, because no Country object exists in the NDS tree. For instance, the command that follows has the same effect as the preceding command.

```
F> CX  .CORP.ESL
CORP.ESL
```

To go back one container level above, you can issue the command:

```
F> CX  .
ESL
```

The period (.) following the CX command means that you want to change your context to the parent container. You can combine periods to go up several container levels. The example that follows illustrates this:

```
F> CX
CORP.ESL
F> CX ..
[Root]
```

In the preceding example, the current container is OU=CORP.O=ESL. Using the command CX.., go two container levels up, which in this case is the [Root] container.

What would happen if you tried to go three container levels above if your current context is OU=CORP.O=ESL?

```
F> CX
CORP.ESL
F> CX ...
CX-4.20-260: An internal system error occurred during CX's attempt
to canonicalize the context: (...)
```

If an attempt is made to change the context to a location that does not exist in the NDS tree, an error message appears.

To change the context to the [Root] you can use the /R option:

```
F> CX /R
[Root]
```

To view all container objects (tree structure) below your current context or specified context you can use the /T option:

```
F> CX
[Root]
F> CX /T
```

Figure 2.65 shows the output of the CX /T command issued from the [Root].

Figure 2.65

The CX /T command from the [Root].

```
[Root]
  +ESL
  |   +CORP
  |   |   +OPS
  |   |   +SALES
  |   +SALES
  |   +ENG
  +DSL
  |   +
  +SCS
  |   +CORP
  |   +ENG
  |        +RESEARCH
  +US
  +IBL
  |   +CORP
  |   +ENG
  |   +MKTG
  |   +SALES
  +IMF
  +IntCo
  |   +US
  |   |   +Accounting
  |   |   |   +AP
  |   |   |   +AR
  |   |   + AR
  |   |   + AP
  |   + UK
  |   + CA
  |   + IN
  + MICROCOMM
  +ESL_KSS
       +CORP
       +SALES
       |   +OPS
       +ENG
            +LAB
```

You can combine the /R with other options such as /T. If /R is combined with /T, the CX /T command is issued from the root of the tree, but the context is not changed. You can, thus, type the commands:

```
F> CX .CORP.ESL
CORP.ESL
F> CX /T /R
```

```
F> CX
CORP.ESL
```

The command CX /T /R produces the same output as in figure 2.60, but the context before and after executing the command remains the same (OU=CORP.O=ESL).

The /A (or /ALL) option enables you to view all objects at or below the current context. It is meant to be used in conjunction with options like the /T option.

```
F> CX
CORP.ESL
F> CX /T /A
```

The command CX /T /A produces an output that is shown in figure 2.66.

You can combine the CX /T /A command with the /R option. For instance:

```
F> CX
CORP.ESL
F> CX /T /A /R
F> CX
CORP.ESL
```

The CX /T /A /R will show all objects beginning from the [Root], but the context will remain the same (OU=CORP.O=ESL) before and after executing the commands.

To view only container objects at a specified level, you can use the /CONT option:

```
F> CX
CORP.ESL
F> CX /CONT
```

You can combine the /CONT command with /A to see all objects within the container only:

```
F> CX
CORP.ESL
F> CX /CONT /A
```

Figure 2.67 shows the output of using the CX /CONT /A command in the current context OU=CORP.O=ESL.

Figure 2.66

The CX /T /A command from the OU=CORP.O=ESL context.

```
*** Directory Services Mapping ***
CORP.ESL
    +NW4CS
    +NW4CS_SYS
    +NW4CS_VOL1
    +Dei
    +Backup Operator
    +Admin1
    +Q_0
    +PS_0
    +P_0
    +PF
    +Anonymous
    +NW4KS
    +BackupOp
    +Jan
    +WMgr
    +HACKER
    +UNIXUSER
    +Linksys Ps1
    +QLINK1
    +PLINK1
    +NW4CS_VOLS
    +S386+543
    +Everyone
    +Guest
    +Karanjit
    +QUEUE_0
    +QUEUE_1
    +QUEUE_2
    +QUEUE_3
    +Students
    +Nobody
    +Nogroup
    +Nfsgroup
    +User2
    +Kss
    +Test
    +User1
    +Corporate
    +Engineers
    +Marketing
    +Newuser
    +Q_NETSYNC
    +PS_NETSYNC
    +P_NETSYNC
    +Serial Printer
    + {S386_QUEUE_0}
    + {S386_QUEUE_1}
    + {S386_QUEUE_2}
    + {S386_QUEUE_3}
    + unixprinter
    + AdminUsers
    + User Binary
    +OPS
    |     + USER_TEMPLATE
    + SALES
        +USER_TEMPLATE
```

```
*** Directory Services Mapping ***
CORP.ESL
    +NW4CS
    +NW4CS_SYS
    +NW4CS_VOL1
    +Dei
    +Backup Operator
    +Admin1
    +Q_0
    +PS_0
    +P_0
    +PF
    +Anonymous
    +NW4KS
    +BackupOp
    +Jan
    +WMgr
    +HACKER
    +UNIXUSER
    +Linksys Ps1
    +QLINK1
    +PLINK1
    +NW4CS_VOLS
    +S386+543
    +Everyone
    +Guest
    +Karanjit
    +QUEUE_0
    +QUEUE_1
    +QUEUE_2
    +QUEUE_3
    +Students
    +Nobody
    +Nogroup
    +Nfsgroup
    +User2
    +Kss
    +Test
    +User1
    +Corporate
    +Engineers
    +Marketing
    +Newuser
    +Q_NETSYNC
    +PS_NETSYNC
    +P_NETSYNC
    +Serial Printer
    + {S386_QUEUE_0}
    + {S386_QUEUE_1}
    + {S386_QUEUE_2}
    + {S386_QUEUE_3}
    + unixprinter
    + AdminUsers
    + User Binary
    +OPS
    + SALES
```

Figure 2.67

The CX /CONT /A command from the OU=CORP.O=ESL context.

What is the difference between the CX /CONT /A and the CX /T /A command? Compare figure 2.67 with figure 2.66. The CX /CONT /A displays all objects in the current context only, whereas the CX /T /A displays all objects in the current context and in the containers below the current context.

If the CX /CONT /A is combined with the /R option, what output appears?

```
F> CX
CORP.ESL
F> CX /CONT /A /R
F> CX
CORP.ESL
```

Figure 2.68 shows the output of using the CX /CONT /A /R command in the current context OU=CORP.O=ESL. Notice that the current context before and after executing this command does not change, even though the /R option displays the tree starting from the [Root] object.

Figure 2.68

The CX /CONT /A /R command from the OU=CORP.O=ESL context.

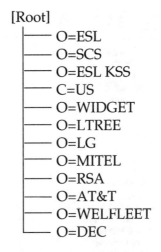

```
[Root]
       ┌───── O=ESL
       ├───── O=SCS
       ├───── O=ESL KSS
       ├───── C=US
       ├───── O=WIDGET
       ├───── O=LTREE
       ├───── O=LG
       ├───── O=MITEL
       ├───── O=RSA
       ├───── O=AT&T
       ├───── O=WELFLEET
       └───── O=DEC
```

You can use the CX command with typeless and partial names. If the current context in figure 2.64 is O=ESL, for instance, the partial typeless name to change the context to OU=CORP.O=ESL is:

```
F> CX
ESL
F> CX  CORP
CORP.ESL
```

If the current context is O=ESL, the partial typeless name to change the context to OU=SALES.OU=CORP.O=ESL is:

```
F> CX
ESL
F> CX  SALES.CORP
SALES.CORP.ESL
```

If the current context is [Root], the partial typeless name to change context to O=SCS is:

```
F> CX
[Root]
F> CX SCS
SCS
```

If the current context is O=SCS, the partial typeless name to change context to O=ESL is:

```
F> CX
SCS
F> CX ESL.
ESL
```

The preceding example uses the trailing period rule to go one container above the current context.

If the current context is OU=CORP.O=SCS, the partial typeless name to change context to OU=SALES.OU=CORP.O=ESL is:

```
F> CX
CORP.SCS
F> CX SALES.CORP.ESL..
ESL
```

The previous example uses the trailing period rule to go two containers above the current context.

To view additional help on using the CX command, type the following command

```
CX /?
```

The screens in figure 2.69 show the two help screens that appear after you type the CX /? command. Table 2.6 also summarizes many common CX options.

Figure 2.69

The CX /? Help screens.

CX	Options Help	v4.00

Syntax: CX [new context] [R] [/T | CONT] [/ALL]] [/C] [/?]

To:	Use:
view all container objects below the current or specified context.	/T
view container objects at the current or specified level.	/CONT
modify /T or /CONT to view ALL objects at or below the context	/ALL
change context or view objects relative to root	/R

For example, to:	Type:
view directory tree below the current context	CX /T
view containers within a specific context	CX .O=Novell /CONT

CX	General Usage Help	v4.00

Purpose: View and set current context.
Syntax: CX [new context] [/Root] [/[Tree | CONT] [/All]] [/C] [/?]

New context:
   A context can be entered either relative to your current context or
   as a distinguished name relative to the directory root.
   Use trailing periods (.) to change to a context relative to a higher
   level of your current context.
   To change to a context relative to the root of the directory put a period
   at the beginning of the new context or use the /Root flag.

To view your current context type CX
Current context is OU=Engineering.O=Novell

For example, to change context:	Type:
O=Novell	CX
OU=Testing.OU=Engineering.O=Novell	CX OU=Testing
OU=Marketing.O=Novell	CX OU=Marketing.

Table 2.6
Common CX Options

Command	Description
CX .	Change context to one container above current context.
CX	Display current context.

Command	Description
CX /R	Change context to root of NDS tree.
CX /T	View all container objects below current or specified context.
CX /T /A	View all objects in current context and below. The /A is an abbreviation for /All.
CX /CONT	View container objects at current or specified context only.
CX /CONT /A	View all objects at current context or specified context only.
CX *new_context*	Changes context to specified context.
CX /?	Obtain CX help screens.

 Use figure 2.69 and table 2.6 as a summary of the CX options before you take your exams.

The NLIST Command

By using the NLIST command, you can view information on different object classes. The information appears in a convenient tabular form. NLIST is the fundamental command-line utility for extracting information on NDS objects. You can use NLIST to set up general-purpose queries that will search NDS objects based on a number of search criteria, such as on:

◆ Property values

◆ Existence of properties

◆ Specific branch of the NDS tree

205

If you want to search for all the active users that are connected to the network, use the /A option, such as the command:

```
F> NLIST USER /A
Object Class: User
Current context: ESL
Conn            = The server connection number
*               = The asterisk means this is your connection
User Name = The login name of the user
Address         = The network address
Node            = The network node
Login time      = The time when the user logged in
User Name                                       Address       Node
*Admin                                          [E8022]     [C024282D]
One user object was found in this context.
One user object was found.
```

The output of all NLIST commands produces a legend that describes the columns for the tabular information that is displayed.

An asterisk next to a connection means that the connection is your connection to the server. The output of this command is equivalent to the USERLIST /A command in NetWare 3.x.

To see all user objects defined in the current context and subcontainers, use the /S option:

```
F> CX
OU=CORP.O=ESL
F> NLIST USER /S
Object Class: User
Current context: CORP.ESL
User name= The name of the user
Dis           = Login disabled
Log exp    = The login expiration date, 0 if no expiration date
Pwd        = Yes if passwords are required
Pwd exp  = The password expiration date, 0 if no expiration date
Uni          = Yes if unique passwords are required
Min          = The minimum password length, 0 if no minimum
User Name                               Dis  Log Exp Pwd  Pwd Exp Uni Min
------------------------------------------------------------------------
Dei                                     No   0-00-00 No   0-00-00 No   0
Admin1                                  Yes  0-00-00 Yes  0-00-00 No   8
Admin2                                  No   9-01-99 No   0-00-00 No   5
```

```
A total of 3 USER objects was found in this context.
Object Class: User
Current context: SPOOL.CORP.ESL
User Name                     Dis  Log Exp Pwd  Pwd Exp Uni Min
- - - - - - - - - - - - - - - - - - - - - - - - - - - - - - - - - - -
USER_TEMPLATE                 No   0-00-00 No   0-00-00 No   0
One USER object was found in this context.
Object Class: User
Current context: SALES.CORP.ESL
User Name                     Dis  Log Exp Pwd  Pwd Exp Uni Min
- - - - - - - - - - - - - - - - - - - - - - - - - - - - - - - - - - -
USER_TEMPLATE                 No   0-00-00 No   0-00-00 No   0
One USER object was found in this context.
Object Class: User
Current context: OPS.CORP.ESL
User Name                     Dis  Log Exp Pwd  Pwd Exp Uni Min
- - - - - - - - - - - - - - - - - - - - - - - - - - - - - - - - - - -
USER_TEMPLATE                 No   0-00-00 No   0-00-00 No   0
One USER object was found in this context.
A total of 6 USER objects was found.
```

As you can see from the last two NLIST commands, the output always begins with the Object Class that is specified in the NLIST command. The Current Context is listed next, followed by the information returned by NLIST for the current context.

The NLIST USER /S command was issued from the context OU=CORP.O=ESL. It lists all the users found in the context OU=CORP.O=ESL and all users defined in subcontainers below this context. There is a total of three User objects defined in the context OU=CORP.O=ESL. User Dei is not disabled and has no login expiration dates. User Dei also does not have unique password or minimum password length restrictions. User Admin1, on the other hand, is disabled and has required password, unique password, and eight-character minimum password length restrictions. User Admin2 is not disabled, but the login account expires on 9-1-99, and although no password uniqueness is enforced for this user, the minimum password length is five characters. The subcontainers OU=SPOOL.OU=CORP.O=ESL, OU=SALES.OU=CORP.O=ESL and OU=OPS.OU=CORP.O=ESL are searched next.

Each reveals a User object with the name USER_TEMPLATE, which—like user Dei in the container above—has no restrictions. You will learn later that you can use the user USER_TEMPLATE in a container as a model for other users created within that container.

To see property details for a specific user, such as user DEI, use the following command:

```
F> NLIST USER=DEI  /D
Object Class: User
Current context: CORP.ESL
User: Dei
      Name: Dei
      Object Trustees (ACL):
            Subject: Dei
            Property:  [All Properties Rights]
            Property Rights: [ R   ]
      Object Trustees (ACL):
            Subject: Dei
            Property: Login Script
            Property Rights: [ RW  ]
      Object Trustees (ACL):
            Subject: [Public]
            Property: Default Server
            Property Rights: [ R   ]
      Object Trustees (ACL):
            Subject: [Root]
            Property: Group Membership
            Property Rights: [ R   ]
      Object Trustees (ACL):
            Subject: Dei
            Property: Print Job Configuration
            Property Rights: [ RW  ]
      Object Trustees (ACL):
            Subject: [Root]
            Property: Network Address
            Property Rights: [ R   ]
       Full Name: Dei Siyan
      Given Name: Dei
      Group Membership: Manager.SCS..
```

```
     Home Directory:
            Volume Name: NW4CS_SYS
            Path: USERS\Dei
            Name Space Type: DOS
     Middle Initial: G
     Language:
            English
     Default Server: NW4CS
     Object Class: User
     Object Class: Organizational Person
     Object Class: Person
     Object Class: Top
     Revision: 5
     Security Equal To: Manager.SCS..
     Last Name: Siyan
     Title: Finance Controller
- - - - - - - - - - - - - - - - - - - - - - - - - - - - - - - - - - - - - - - - - - - -
```

```
One User object was found in this context.
One User object was found.
```

The output of the NLIST USER=Dei /D command gives detailed information on the properties for that object. Some of the properties that are listed for the user are [All Properties Rights], Login Script, Default Server, Group Membership, Printer Job Configuration, Network Address, Home Directory, Language, Full Name, Given Name, Middle Initial, Group Membership, Language, Title, and Last Name.

Author's Note

Notice that in the NLIST USER=Dei /D command, the following lines appear at the end:

```
Object Class: User
Object Class: Organizational Person
Object Class: Person
Object Class: Top
```

The preceding lines indicate the derivation hierarchy for User object Dei. The base class for User object Dei is User class. This is derived from the Organizational Person superclass, which is derived from the superclass Person, which is, in turn, derived from superclass Top.

continues

The derivation principles used in NDS were discussed earlier in this chapter.

To search for user KSS in the current container and all subcontainers:

```
F> CX
SCS
F> NLIST USER=KSS /S
Object Class: User
Current context: SCS
User name= The name of the user
Dis          = Login disabled
Log exp      = The login expiration date, 0 if no expiration date
Pwd          = Yes if passwords are required
Pwd exp  = The password expiration date, 0 if no expiration date
Uni          = Yes if unique passwords are required
Min          = The minimum password length, 0 if no minimum
User Name                               Dis  Log Exp Pwd  Pwd Exp
Uni Min
KSS                                     No   0-00-00 No   0-00-00
No   0
One USER object was found in this context.
Object Class: User
Current context: CORP.SCS
User Name                               Dis  Log Exp Pwd  Pwd Exp
Uni Min
-----------------------------------------------------------------
KSS                                     No   0-00-00 No   0-00-00
No   0
One USER object was found in this context.
Object Class: User
Current context: ENG.SCS
User Name                               Dis  Log Exp Pwd  Pwd Exp
Uni Min
KSS                                     No   0-00-00 No   0-00-00
No   0
One USER object was found in this context.
```

The NLIST USER=KSS /S command finds all occurrences of User object KSS in current context and all subcontainers.

To see all printer objects within current context and all subcontainers:

```
F>CX
SCS
F> NLIST PRINTER /S
Current context: SCS
Partial Name                                        Object Class
----------------------------------------------------------------
NP_0                                                Printer
One PRINTER object was found in this context.
Current context: CORP.SCS
Partial Name                                        Object Class
NP_0                                                Printer
One PRINTER object was found in this context.
A total of 2 PRINTER objects was found.
```

To search for a specific property value for an object class such as the User object class, in the current context and all subcontainers:

```
F> CX
SCS
F> NLIST USER SHOW "Telephone Number"  /S
Object Class: User
Current context: scs
User: Manager1
     Telephone: 310-434-3344
User: Manager2
     Telephone: 310-444-4435
User: KSS
     Telephone: 415-333-4655
A total of 3 User objects was found in this context.

Object Class: User
Current context: ENG.scs
User: AMY
     Telephone: 310-444-4354
One User object was found in this context.

Object Class: User
Current context: CORP.scs
User: Linda
     Telephone: 510-233-3432
One User object was found in this context.

A total of 5 User objects was found.
```

211

If the /S option were left out in the preceding command (NLIST USER SHOW "Telephone Number"), only the phone numbers for users in the current context of OU=CORP.O=SCS would be displayed.

To see a specific value for a specific object, use

```
F> CX
CORP.ESL
F> NLIST SERVER=NW4CS SHOW "Network Address"
Object Class: Server
Current context: CORP.ESL
Server: NW4CS
IPX/SPX Network Address
Network: F0000055
Node: 1
Socket: 451
One SERVER object was found in this context.
One SERVER object was found.
F> CX .O=SCS
SCS
F> NLIST PRINTER="NP_0" SHOW "Location" /S
Current context: SCS
Printer: NP_0
Location: Building 6, Room 404
-----------------------------------------------------------------

One PRINTER object was found in this context.
Current context: CORP.SCS
Printer: NP_0
Location: Engineering Lab Bldg, Printer Room 5
-----------------------------------------------------------------

One PRINTER object was found in this context.
A total of 2 PRINTER objects was found.
```

In the NLIST SERVER command, the network address of server NW4CS is queried. The network address that is reported is the internal software address of the server, which consists of the internal network number, the socket number, and the node number, which is always set to 1. The internal network number is selected during installation, and the socket number identifies the file service process that handles incoming requests. The NLIST PRINTER command shows the location of the Printer object NP_0.

The /S option helps find this Printer object in the current context of O=SCS and all subcontainers. Without the /S option, only the Printer object located at Building 6, Room 404 would be found, and the Printer object at location Engineering Lab Bldg, Printer Room 5 would not show up.

To search for all objects with a specific property value, use the WHERE option with the NLIST command:

```
F> CX
SCS
F> NLIST USER WHERE "Title" EQ ENGINEER
Object Class: User
Current context: SCS
User name= The name of the user
Dis          = Login disabled
Log exp   = The login expiration date, 0 if no expiration date
Pwd          = Yes if passwords are required
Pwd exp   = The password expiration date, 0 if no expiration date
Uni          = Yes if unique passwords are required
Min          = The minimum password length, 0 if no minimum
User Name                         Dis  Log Exp Pwd  Pwd Exp Uni Min
------------------------------------------------------------------

KSS                               No   0-00-00 No    0-00-00
No  0
One USER object was found in this context.
One USER object was found.
F> NLIST USER=KSS SHOW TITLE
Object Class: User
Current context: SCS
User: KSS
Title: Engineer
One USER object was found in this context.
One USER object was found.
```

In the preceding commands, the quotation marks (") are placed around property names and values that have spaces around them; otherwise, they are optional. Also the EQ operator for comparison can be replaced by the equal symbol (=). This means that each of the following commands are equivalent and produce the same results.

```
NLIST USER WHERE "Title" EQ ENGINEER

NLIST USER WHERE "Title" = ENGINEER

NLIST USER WHERE "Title" = "ENGINEER"
```

213

```
NLIST USER WHERE Title = "ENGINEER"

NLIST USER WHERE Title = ENGINEER
```

The common NLIST options are summarized in table 2.7.

Table 2.7
Common NDS Options

Command	Description
NLIST USER /A	Displays active users logged in to the network.
NLIST VOLUME /S	Displays all volumes in the current context and sub containers.
NLIST USER=Dei /D	Shows detail property values for a user.
NLIST USER=KSS /S	Searches for a specific object in current context and all subcontainers.
NLIST SERVER=FS1 SHOW "Network Address"	Shows a specific property for a specific Server object.
NLIST PRINTER WHERE "LOCATION"=LAB	Searches for objects that have a specific property value.
NLIST /?	Displays top level help screen for NLIST.

The help screens obtained from using the NLIST /? command are displayed in figures 2.70 to figures 2.74. Figure 2.70 is the top level help, and the other figures are the specific help screens described in the top level help. These help screens are shown here for your reference.

Use figures 2.70 to 2.74, and table 2.7 as a summary for studying the NLIST command before taking the certification test.

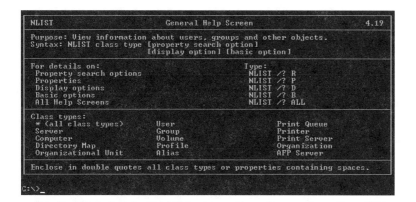

Figure 2.70

NLIST /?: Top-level help screen for NLIST.

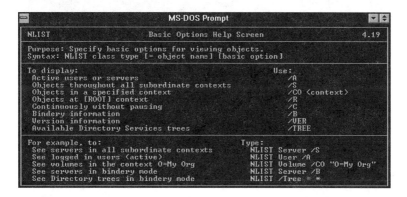

Figure 2.71

NLIST /? B : Basic Options help screen for NLIST.

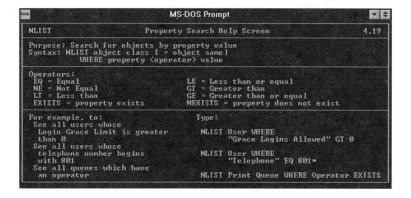

Figure 2.72

NLIST /? R : Property Search Options help screen for NLIST.

Figure 2.73

NLIST /? P :
Properties help screen
for NLIST.

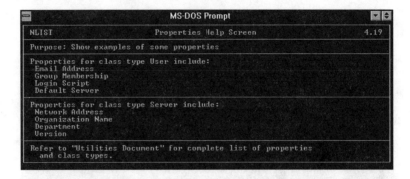

Figure 2.74

NLIST /? D : Display
Options help screen
for NLIST.

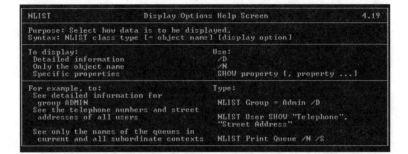

Using the NetWare Administrator Tool for NDS Queries

NDS queries can also be generated using a graphical user interface tool such as the NetWare Administrator Tool.

Launch the Search option by performing the following steps:

1. Launch the NetWare Administrator Tool.

2. Highlight the container object from which the search is to be carried out. If you want to search the entire NDS tree, highlight the [Root] object.

3. Select the **O**bject menu.

4. Select the Searc**h** option from the Object menu.

After the preceding steps, you should see a screen similar to that shown in figure 2.75. Start From is the beginning point of the search, and you can set it to any container object in the NDS tree. You can use the Browse icon, next to this value, to browse for an appropriate container, as shown in figure 2.76. You also can search the entire subtree by checking the box labeled Search Entire Subtree.

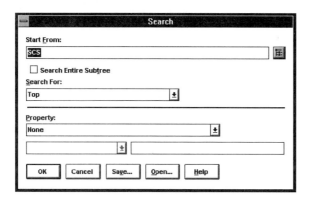

Figure 2.75

The Search dialog box in the NetWare Administrator tool.

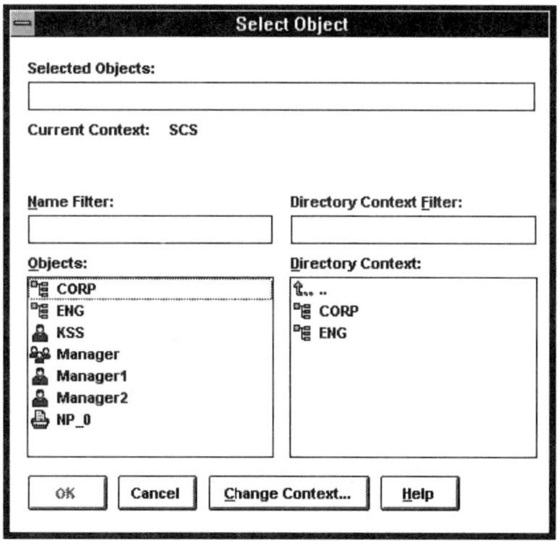

Figure 2.76

The Select Object dialog box used for setting the value of Start From in the Search option.

Several other object classes are listed in the Search For files. In addition to the standard object classes, you can use additional classifications to aid in finding the objects. These additional classifications are listed in table 2.8.

The Properties list box enables you to select from the different properties that you want to search for. The comparison operators include Equal, Not Equal To, Not Present, and Present. A field exists in which you can enter the actual property value that you want to search for.

Table 2.8
Additional Object Classifications for the Search Option

Object Classification	Description
Device	Includes all computer and printer objects.
Locality	This classification is not currently used by NDS; it can be used by third-party products and tools.
Organizational Person	Lists all users.
Partition	Used by the Partition Manager tool to indicate containers that are on the top of a separate partition.
Person	Includes all users.
Resource	Includes Printer Queue and Volume objects.
Server	Includes NetWare Server, Print Server, and AFP server.
Top	Includes every object in the container that is being searched.

Figure 2.77 shows the results of searching all Organizational Unit objects in the container O=SCS, and its subcontainers. This figure shows that there are three Organizational Unit objects that were found:

```
OU=CORP.O=SCS
OU=ENG.O=SCS
OU=RESEARCH.OU=ENG.O=SCS
```

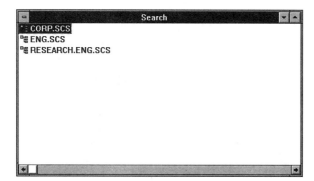

Figure 2.77

Search results for all Organizational Units in O=SCS.

Understanding the Volume Object

One object exists that is both an NDS object and a File System object. This is the *Volume object*. It has characteristics of both a File System object and an NDS object. As an NDS object, the Volume object is managed by NDS, but its components consist of directories and files.

Study Guide for the Chapter

If you are preparing for the NetWare 4.x System Administration exams, review the chapter with the following goals:

1. Understand and identify the NDS components and their properties. Use the study notes as a quick review.

2. Pay particular attention to examples of Current Context, Distinguished Names, Typeless Names, and Relative Distinguised Names. Also review the differences between container and leaf objects, and the use of the CX and NLIST utilities. Be very familiar and comfortable using NWADMIN.

3. After studying this chapter, attempt the sample test questions for this chapter. If you miss the answers to a question, review the appropriate topic.

Chapter Summary

In this chapter, you have learned the basics of NetWare Directory Services. The NDS represents an exciting way of managing the network as a logical entity. Because NDS is a key service in NetWare 4.x, many details of its operations were provided in this chapter. One concept that was covered was NDS as a global database for network management. This global database is accessible from any point on the network. The nature of the NDS objects was examined, and each different type of leaf and container object was described in detail. The NDS naming rules were described with respect to several examples. Among the key concepts that were covered were current context, complete names, typeless names, partial names, and period rules.

The NDS utilities CX and NLIST, and their most important options, were discussed, and numerous examples of the ways they could be used were provided.

Chapter Test Questions

Test questions can have a single correct answer or multiple correct answers. Single-answer questions are indicated by a ○ notation that precedes the possible answers. Some questions require you to select more than one answer; these are indicated by the ☐ preceding each answer. Not all the questions are multiple choice. Occasionally, you might get a question that asks you to type in an answer. The answer in this case is usually a one-word answer. The answer is not case-sensitive; so you can type in the answer in lower- or uppercase.

You will notice a large number of questions on NetWare 4.x container/leaf identification and NDS names. This is probably the most frequent type of question you will be asked on material covered in this chapter.

Some of the questions that are based on material from this chapter will have a picture of an NDS tree and an associated question.

Because the NDS tree and the question do not often fit on a single screen (the MS Windows screen used in the CNE testing), they are often split into two screens. The first screen has the NDS tree diagram and the second screen has the question. You can use a menu button to see each screen. Unless you have a very good memory, you should get into the habit of quickly drawing the essential details of the NDS tree (scrap paper will be provided for you while you are taking the test), so you can save time in answering these questions.

1. NDS can be subdivided into elements called _____.

   A. volumes

   B. partitions

   C. directories

   D. replicas

   E. segments

2. In a NetWare 4.x network, network resource information is stored in _____.

   A. a bindery

   B. text files

   C. Btrieve files

   D. NDS

3. The [Root] object can contain only the _____ objects.

   A. Country

   B. Organizational Unit

   C. User

   D. Organization

   E. Profile

4. The container OU=CORP.O=IBL can have _____.

  ☐ A. two file server objects named CORP_FS and corp_FS

  ☐ B. a printer object named ZEPHYR and a file server named ZEPHYR

  ☐ C. a User object named SHIVA and a file server named ZEOS

  ☐ D. a print server object named [PRINT]

  ☐ E. a file server named CORP FS

5. Which of the following objects can the [Root] container have?

  ○ A. user

  ○ B. printer

  ○ C. bindery

  ○ D. alias

  ○ E. NetWare Server

  ○ F. none of the above

6. Which of the following are true for the [Root] object?

  ☐ A. There can be only one [Root] per NDS tree.

  ☐ B. The [Root] object cannot be renamed.

  ☐ C. The [Root] object can be deleted.

  ☐ D. The [Root] object cannot be deleted.

7. The Country object can contain the following container object:

  ○ A. [Root]

  ○ B. Country

  ○ C. Organization

   ◯ D. Server

   ◯ E. Alias

   ◯ F. Organizational Unit

   ◯ G. none of the above

8. Which of the following are container objects that cannot be underneath the Organization object?

   ☐ A. Country

   ☐ B. Organization

   ☐ C. Server

   ☐ D. Alias

   ☐ E. Organizational Unit

9. Which container object can be placed under the Organizational Unit object?

   ◯ A. Country

   ◯ B. Organization

   ◯ C. Server

   ◯ D. Alias

   ◯ E. Organizational Unit

   ◯ F. [Root]

10. Which of the following leaf objects can be used to simplify creation of login scripts?

   ◯ A. Map

   ◯ B. Link

   ◯ C. Directory Map

○ D. Alias

○ E. Map Directory

11. Which of the following objects represents a login script?

○ A. Group

○ B. Organizational Role

○ C. Organizational Unit

○ D. Profile

○ E. Directory Map

12. Which of the following objects indicates a corruption in the NDS?

○ A. Queue

○ B. Unknown

○ C. Strange

○ D. Invalid

○ E. Profile

13. Which of the following is a tool for creating a batch of User objects?

○ A. SYSCON

○ B. NETADMIN

○ C. UIMPORT

○ D. NetWare Administrator (NWADMIN)

○ E. FILER

14. Given the NDS tree for organization shown below, what is the Distinguished Name for object ALLY_FS?

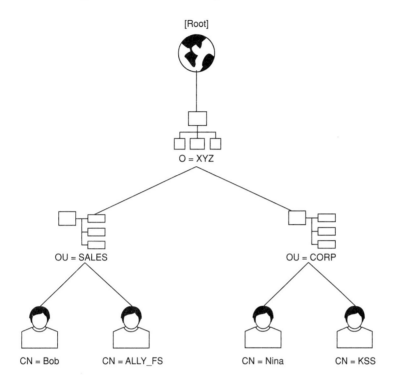

- ○ A. .CN=ALLY_FS
- ○ B. .CN=ALLY_FS.OU=SALES
- ○ C. .CN=ALLY_FS.OU=SALES.O=XYZ
- ○ D. CN=ALLY_FS.OU=SALES.O=XYZ

15. Given the NDS tree for organization shown below, what is the Distinguised Name for user Nina?

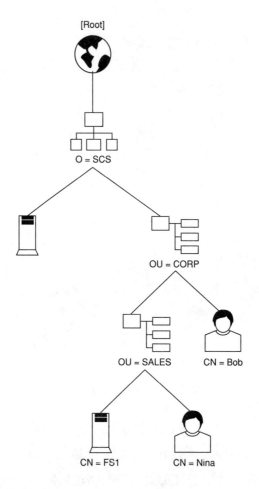

- ○ A. .CN=Nina
- ○ B. .CN=Nina.OU=SALES.OU=CORP.O=SCS
- ○ C. CN=Nina.OU=SALES.OU=CORP.O=SCS
- ○ D. .CN=Nina.OU=CORP.O=SCS
- ○ E. .CN=Nina.OU=SCS

16. Given the NDS tree for organization shown below, what is the Distinguished Name for object FSP?

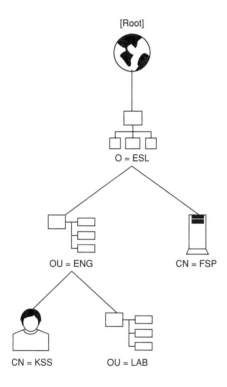

- A. .CN=FSP
- B. .CN=FSP.OU=ENG.O=ESL
- C. .CN=FSP.OU=ESL
- D. .CN=FSP.O=ESL
- E. CN=Nina.OU=ENG.O=ESL

17. Given the NDS tree for organization shown below, what is the Distinguished Name for object FS4?

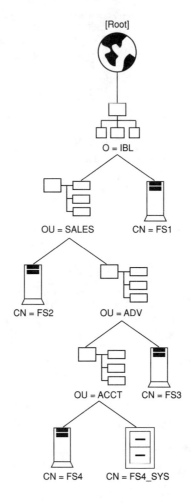

○ A. .CN=FS4

○ B. .CN=FS4.O=IBL

○ C. CN=FS4.OU=ACCT.OU=ADV.OU=SALES.O=IBL

○ D. .CN=FS4.OU=ACCT.OU=ADV.OU=SALES.O=IBL

○ E. .CN=FS4.OU=ADV.OU=SALES.O=IBL

18. Given the NDS tree for organization shown below, what is the Distinguished Name for object FS1?

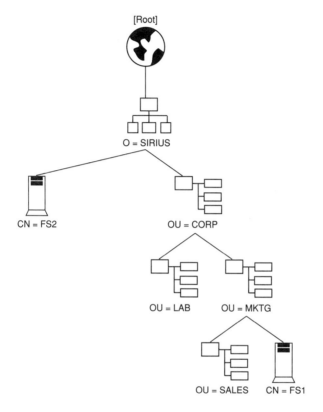

○　A.　.CN=FS1

○　B.　.CN=FS1.O=SIRIUS

○　C.　.CN=FS1.OU=CORP.O=SIRIUS

○　D.　.CN=FS1.OU=LAB.OU=CORP.O=SIRIUS

○　E.　.CN=FS1.OU=MKTG.OU=CORP.O=SIRIUS

19. Given the NDS tree shown below, what is the Relative Distinguished Name of object PR1 if the current context is set to [Root]?

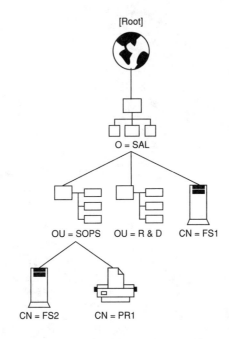

○ A. .CN=PR1.OU=SOPS.O=SAL

○ B. CN=PR1.OU=SOPS.O=SAL

○ C. CN=PR1

○ D. CN=PR1.OU=SOPS

○ E. CN=PR1.OU=R&D.O=SOPS

20. Given the NDS tree shown below, what is the Relative Distinguished Name of object Jim if the current context is set to O=SAL?

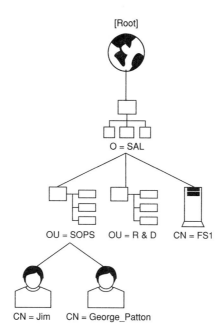

○ A. .CN=Jim.OU=SOPS.O=SA

○ B. CN=Jim.OU=SOPS.O=SAL

○ C. CN=Jim

○ D. CN=Jim.OU=SOPS

○ E. CN=Jim.OU=R&D.O=SOPS

21. Given the NDS tree shown below, what is the Relative Distinguished Name of object George_Patton if the current context is set to OU=SOPS.O=SAS?

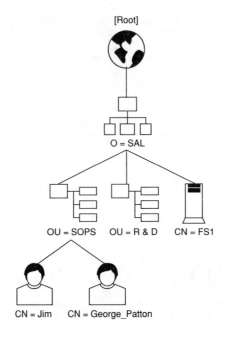

- ○ A. .CN=George_Patton.OU=SOPS.O=SAL
- ○ B. CN=George_Patton.OU=SOPS.O=SAL
- ○ C. CN=George_Patton
- ○ D. CN=George_Patton.OU=SOPS
- ○ E. CN=George_Patton.OU=R&D.O=SOPS

22. Given the NDS tree shown below, what is the Relative Distinguished Name of object Freeman if the current context is set to OU=R&D.O=SAS?

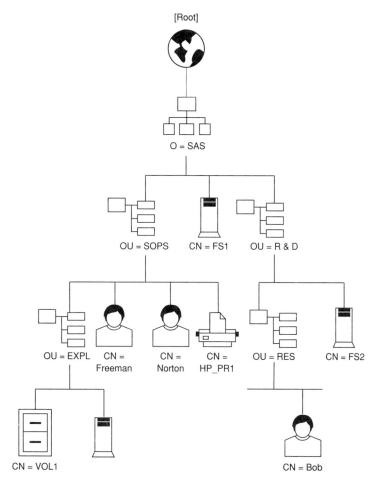

[Root]

O = SAS

OU = SOPS   CN = FS1   OU = R & D

OU = EXPL   CN = Freeman   CN = Norton   CN = HP_PR1   OU = RES   CN = FS2

CN = VOL1   CN = Bob

○ A. .CN=Freeman.OU=R&D.O=SAS

○ B. CN=Freeman.OU=R&D.

○ C. CN=Freeman.OU=SOPS.

○ D. CN=Freeman.OU=SOPS..

○ E. CN=Freeman.OU=SOPS.O=SAS..

23. Given the NDS tree shown below, what is the Relative Distinguished Name of object Norton if the current context is set to OU=LAB.OU=R&D.O=SAL?

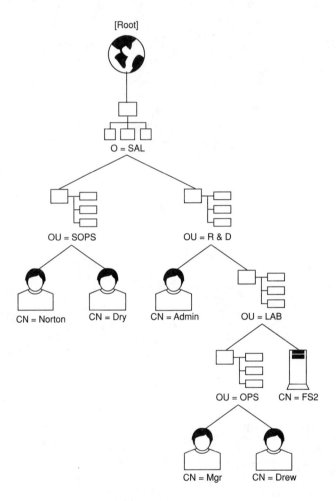

- ○ A. .CN=Norton.OU=R&D.O=SAL

- ○ B. CN=Norton.OU=R&D.

- ○ C. CN=Norton.OU=SOPS.

- ○ D. CN=Norton.OU=SOPS..

- ○ E. CN=Norton.OU=SOPS...

24. Given the NDS tree shown below, what is the Relative Distinguished Name of object Norton if the current context is set to OU=OPS.OU=LAB.OU=R&D.O=SAL?

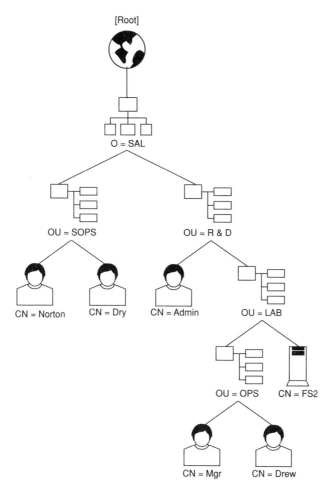

- A. .CN=Norton.OU=R&D.O=SAL
- B. CN=Norton.OU=R&D.
- C. CN=Norton.OU=SOPS.
- D. CN=Norton.OU=SOPS..
- E. CN=Norton.OU=SOPS...

235

25. Given the NDS tree shown below, what is the Relative Distinguished Name of object FS1 if the current context is set to [Root]?

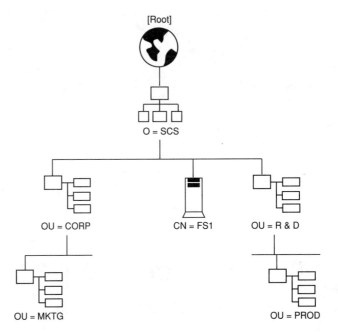

- ○ A. CN=FS1
- ○ B. CN=FS1.O=SCS
- ○ C. CN=FS1.
- ○ D. CN=FS1..
- ○ E. CN=FS1...

26. Given the NDS tree shown below, what is the Relative Distinguished Name of object FS1 if the current context is set to O=SCS?

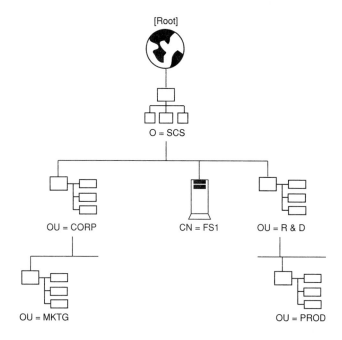

- ○ A. CN=FS1
- ○ B. CN=FS1.O=SCS
- ○ C. CN=FS1.
- ○ D. CN=FS1..
- ○ E. CN=FS1...

27. Given the NDS tree shown below, what is the Relative Distinguished Name of object FS1 if the current context is set to OU=CORP.O=SCS?

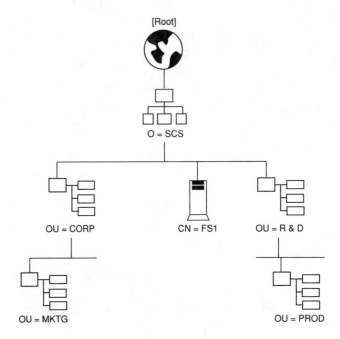

- ○ A. CN=FS1
- ○ B. CN=FS1.O=SCS
- ○ C. CN=FS1.
- ○ D. CN=FS1..
- ○ E. CN=FS1...

28. Given the NDS tree shown below, what is the Relative Distin-guished Name of object FS1 if the current context is set to OU=R&D.O=SCS?

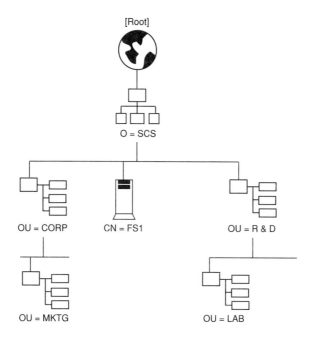

- ○ A. CN=FS1
- ○ B. CN=FS1.O=SCS
- ○ C. CN=FS1.
- ○ D. CN=FS1..
- ○ E. CN=FS1...

29. Given the NDS tree shown below, what is the Relative Distinguished Name of object FS1 if the current context is set to OU=PROD.OU=R&D.O=SCS?

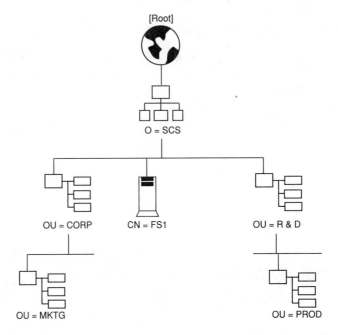

- ○ A. CN=FS1
- ○ B. CN=FS1.O=SCS
- ○ C. CN=FS1.
- ○ D. CN=FS1..
- ○ E. CN=FS1...

30. Given the NDS tree shown below, what is the Relative Distinguished Name of object FS1 if the current context is set to OU=OPS.OU=LAB.OU=R&D.O=SCS?

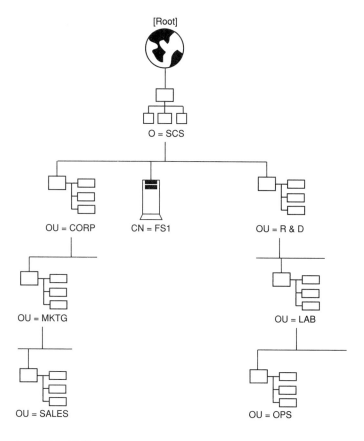

- ○ A. CN=FS1
- ○ B. CN=FS1.O=SCS
- ○ C. CN=FS1.
- ○ D. CN=FS1..
- ○ E. CN=FS1...

31. Which of the following names is a partial typeless name?

    ☐ A. .CN=Veena

    ☐ B. Veena

    ☐ C. .Veena.CORP.SCS

    ☐ D. .CN=Veena.OU=CORP.O=SCS

    ☐ E. .FS1.SALES.ESL

    ☐ F. FS1.SALES.ESL

32. The container IN is a Country object, and the container LA is an Organization object. Which of the following are valid names?

    ☐ A. .CN=NQ_0.OU=MKTG.O=LA

    ☐ B. .CN=NP_0.OU=CORP.O=IN

    ☐ C. .CN=NP_1.OU=SALES.O=SCS.C=IN

    ☐ D. .NP_1.SALES.SCS.O=IN

    ☐ E. .KSS.CORP.IBL.OU=IN

33. To set the default context to OU=CORP.O=SCS, use the following statement in the NET.CFG file:

    ○ A. NAME CONTEXT OU=CORP.O=SCS

    ○ B. "NAME CONTEXT" = OU=CORP.O=SCS

    ○ C. NAME CONTEXT = "OU=CORP.O=SCS"

    ○ D. NAME CONTEXT "OU=CORP.O=SCS"

    ○ E. NAME CONTEXT = ".OU=CORP.O=SCS"

34. To change context to one container above the current context, use the command _____.

   ○ A. CX

   ○ B. CX /R

   ○ C. CX .

   ○ D. CX /T

   ○ E. CX /T /A

   ○ F. CX /CONT

35. To view current context, use the command _____.

   ○ A. CX

   ○ B. CX /R

   ○ C. CX .

   ○ D. CX /T

   ○ E. CX /T /A

   ○ F. CX /CONT

36. To view container objects at current context only, you can use the command _____.

   ○ A. CX

   ○ B. CX /R

   ○ C. CX .

   ○ D. CX /T

   ○ E. CX /T /A

   ○ F. CX /CONT

37. The command NLIST SERVER=FS1 SHOW "Network Address" performs the following task:

   ○ A. Displays active users logged in to the network.

   ○ B. Displays all volumes in the current context and subcontainers.

   ○ C. Shows detailed property values for a user.

   ○ D. Searches for a specific object in current context and all subcontainers.

   ○ E. Shows a specific property for a specific server object.

   ○ F. Searches for objects that have a specific property value.

   ○ G. Displays top level help screen for NLIST.

38. The command NLIST PRINTER WHERE "LOCATION"=LAB performs the following task:

   ○ A. Displays active users logged in to the network.

   ○ B. Displays all volumes in the current context and subcontainers.

   ○ C. Shows detailed property values for a user.

   ○ D. Searches for a specific object in current context and all subcontainers.

   ○ E. Shows a specific property for a specific User object.

   ○ F. Searches for objects that have a specific property value.

   ○ G. Displays top level help screen for NLIST.

39. Name the GUI utility that allows you to access the NDS database.

40. Name the text utility that allows you to access the NDS database.

41. Which command-line utility allows you to search the NDS database?

42. What is an object's position in the NDS tree called?

43. The current context can be changed by _____.

☐ A. CD

☐ B. CO

☐ C. CX

☐ D. NETADMIN

☐ E. SYSCON

☐ F. NWADMIN

44. The USER_TEMPLATE object can be created _____.

☐ A. at the same time as objects Organization and Organizational Unit are created

☐ B. at the same time as objects Organization and Country are created

☐ C. at the same time as objects Organizational Unit and Country are created

☐ D. as a separate step using NETADMIN

☐ E. as a separate step using NWADMIN

45. Which of the following are Distinguished Name?

    ☐ A. BRAD.CORP.SCS

    ☐ B. .CN=JIM.O=JFK

    ☐ C. CN=ADMIN.O=JAL

    ☐ D. .CN=KSS.OU=OPS.OU=LAB.O=ESL

46. Which of these are typeless names?

    ☐ A. CN=Amy.O=ESL

    ☐ B. Linda.CORP.O=SCS

    ☐ C. James

    ☐ D. James.SALES.IBM

47. The primary command-line utilities for accessing NDS resources are _____.

    ☐ A. CX

    ☐ B. NETADMIN

    ☐ C. NLIST

    ☐ D. NETUSER

    ☐ E. FILER

48. To change your current context to OU=OPS.OU=LABS.O=SED, given that your current context is OU=SALES.OU=CORP.O=SED, the command can be _____.

    ☐ A. CX OU=OPS.OU=LABS.O=SED

    ☐ B. CX .OU=OPS.OU=LABS.O=SED

    ☐ C. CX OU=OPS.OU=LABS..

    ☐ D. CX .CN=OPS.OU=LABS.O=SED

    ☐ E. CX .OPS.LABS.SED

    ☐ F. CX .OPS.LABS.SED.

49. To view the tree structure and all objects below the current context, the command is _____ .

   ○   A.   CX /T
   ○   B.   CX /A
   ○   C.   CX /T /A
   ○   D.   CX /ALL

50. To change the context of the workstation at time of login, you can _____ .

   ○   A.   use the CX /LOGIN command
   ○   B.   use the LOGIN /CX command
   ○   C.   set NAME CONTEXT in NET.CFG
   ○   D.   set NAME CONTEXT in VLM.CFG

51. The command to see all active users in the current context is _____ .

   ○   A.   NLIST /A
   ○   B.   NLIST /A USER
   ○   C.   NLIST /USER /A
   ○   D.   NLIST USER /A

52. To view property details on user Veena in current container and all subcontainers, use _____ .

   ○   A.   NLIST USER=Veena /D
   ○   B.   NLIST USER=Veena /D /A
   ○   C.   NLIST USER=Veena /D /S
   ○   D.   NLIST USER:Veena /D /SUB

NetWare 4.x File System

This chapter discusses NetWare volume and directory concepts, examines the default NetWare file system structure, and shows you how to manage the NetWare file system using tools that come with the NetWare 4.x operating system. You also learn about the NetWare file system organization and how to access NetWare directories using the different options of the MAP command.

Using the NetWare File System

One of the major features of a NetWare server is a NetWare file system that can be accessed by NetWare clients. Because this NetWare file system is shared by many users, the following points are important:

- ◆ The NetWare file system on the server should be well-organized and easy to maintain.

◆ Users must share the file system on the server without violating system security or the privacy of other users.

◆ Access to the file system should be intuitive and consistent with the workstation operating system used by the client.

◆ The speed of accessing the server's file system should be comparable to the speed of accessing a workstation's local hard disk.

The NetWare system and utilities are organized into standard directories. Users can be assigned a home directory in which they can keep personal files. If a directory contains system programs meant for network administration, these programs can be restricted for use by network administrators only. Files on the server can be accessed by the workstation's operating system commands. This makes access to the network files simple and intuitive.

Home directories are described in more detail in the section "Understanding Directory Structure Organization" later in this chapter.

Because most LANs operate at speeds in the order of megabits per second, access to the server's file system is very fast. Reading and writing a network file to the server is comparable to the speed of reading and writing to a local disk.

Other benefits of NetWare file storage include the following:

◆ Users can share data.

◆ Access to file resources is improved.

◆ Security of data is improved.

◆ Privacy of data can be protected.

◆ Management and backup of data is centralized.

The NetWare file system is an extension of the workstation's file system (see fig. 3.1). A Macintosh station views the NetWare file system with the FINDER interface, and a DOS workstation views the file system as a number of remote drives designated by letters such as F:, G:, H:, and so on. The default *name space* support is DOS. Name space refers to the capability of the NetWare server to provide alternate views of the NetWare file system. The NetWare file system's chameleon-like capabilities are important because a workstation operating system can view the NetWare file system using its own file system conventions.

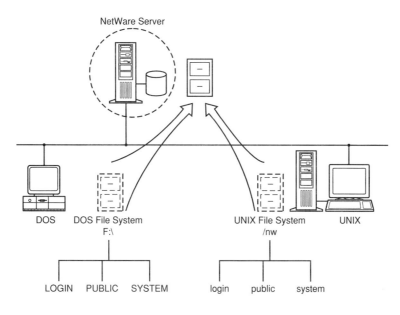

Figure 3.1

Multiple name space support for NetWare clients.

NetWare offers name-space support for the Unix, Macintosh, and OS/2 operating systems, meaning the clients of those operating systems can access the NetWare file system. Unix workstation support comes with NetWare for NFS products. Macintosh workstation support comes with NetWare for Macintosh products. OS/2 client support is bundled with the NetWare 4.x distribution as NetWare OS/2 Client Requester software.

The default name-space support for the NetWare file system is DOS.

NetWare 4.x includes client support for DOS, OS/2, Macintosh, and Unix workstations.

251

The OS/2 name space provides support for long file names under Windows NT and Windows 95.

Exploring the Disk Subsystem

The NetWare 4.x operating system presents a logical view of the server's disk. The server's disk is organized into three key areas:

◆ Volumes

◆ Directories

◆ Files

Internally, NetWare manages the disk as a sequence of disk blocks of fixed size. This block size is selectable for NetWare 4.x upon installation (for each volume that is installed) with values of 4 KB, 8 KB, 16 KB, 32 KB, and 64 KB. Treating the disk as a sequence of blocks lets the NetWare file system be independent of the physical disk structure, such as the sectors, cylinders, and disk platters (surface area).

Unused drive letters (usually F: through Z:) are assigned to directories on the server for DOS and OS/2 workstations. After NetWare makes this logical association, the server directories can be treated as extensions to the local disk subsystem. The server's remote file system can be accessed with workstation operating system commands by using a network drive letter.

Volumes

A server's disk is organized into volumes (see fig. 3.2). *Volumes* are logical divisions of the space on a server's disk. A volume is the highest-level division of NetWare's file system and roughly corresponds to the partitions of a DOS disk. Although DOS disk partitions are designated by single-drive letters such as C: and D:, the NetWare physical volume names consist of 2 to 15 characters, such as SYS and VOL1. You can only have one NetWare partition per physical drive.

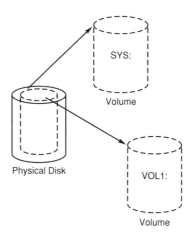

Figure 3.2

NetWare volumes on
a server.

A NetWare volume can consist of the entire physical disk, a portion of the disk, or several disks.

A NetWare 4.x server can support 64 volumes. A volume's maximum size is 32 TB (terabytes), which is greater than the capacity of current disks on the market. NetWare 4.x enables a logical volume to span several server disks. This is called *volume spanning*. A volume can consist of as many as 32 volume segments. Each volume segment is a NetWare partition.

The details of a volume's name, size, and segments are recorded in a Volume Definition Table.

A volume's capability of spanning several disks is advantageous for applications with extremely large files that won't fit onto a single disk. This feature also enables several I/O operations to be done simultaneously, because the volume can have a number of separate disks and disk controllers that provide simultaneous access to it. Requests to access a volume don't have to be queued up. As long as the requests refer to an area of the volume that's on a separate disk, those requests can be processed by the separate disk controllers and drives.

Volume spanning does have its negative features, however. If any of the disks comprising a volume fails, the entire volume fails. When volumes span multiple hard drives, Novell recommends that SFT Level II disk mirroring or duplexing be used to prevent data loss as a result of drive failure; however, this can be a very expensive solution when large disks are involved.

253

The first volume in a NetWare server is always named SYS:. This volume holds the NetWare NOS and its program and data files. Other volumes can have names of 2 to 15 characters.

The physical name of the first volume that the NetWare server will mount is SYS.

Keep volume names simple. The first volume after SYS: for example, can be labeled VOL1:, the next one VOL2:, and so on. You can alternatively give more descriptive names for volumes.

NetWare volumes are referred to by a *volume name*, which can be of two types:

◆ Physical volume name

◆ Volume object name

The syntax of these volume names is discussed in the following sections.

Physical Volume Names

Physical volume names should maintain compatibility with the NetWare 3.x naming convention. Volumes attached to server FS1 with the physical names of SYS and VOL1, for example, can be referred to by the following NetWare 3.x syntax:

FS1/SYS: to reference the SYS volume

FS1/VOL1: to reference the VOL1 volume

The physical volume name must follow several naming rules, including:

◆ It must be between 2 and 15 characters.

◆ It must end in a colon (:) when a reference to the volume is made.

◆ It can contain only legal characters, as follows:

A to Z

0 to 9

$ ~ - _ # ! % ^ &) (} {

◆ The following are illegal characters in volume names:

space ( ), backslash (\), period (.), comma (,)

◆ A backslash (\) or forward slash (/) must separate the NetWare server name from the volume name, as follows:

```
FS1/SYS:
FS1\VOL1:
```

◆ Different servers can have the same physical volume name, because a physical volume name can be qualified by the server name, as shown in the following example:

FileServerName\PhysicalVolumeName

```
FS1\VOLA:
FS2\VOLA:
```

Remember the volume name rules listed in this section for your exams.

The physical volume name is created during server installation (see fig. 3.3).

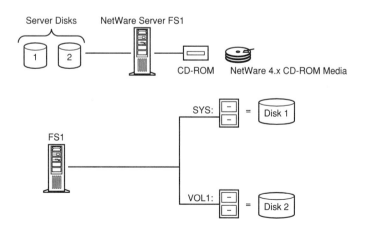

Figure 3.3

NetWare volumes created at installation.

255

Volume Object Names

A Volume object name is created with the physical volume name during server installation (see fig 3.4). Every physical volume name has an NDS object name counterpart. The Volume object name for a physical volume is its NDS object name. The Volume object is placed in the same context as the File Server object, and its name is derived from the file server using the following rule: *The default Volume object name is a concatenation of the File Server object name, the underscore character (_), and the physical object name.*

Figure 3.4

Volume object naming.

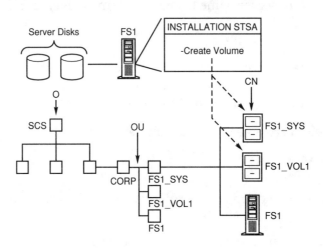

A volume with the physical name PhysicalVolumeName and attached to the server called ServerName has the following Volume object name:

`ServerName_PhysicalVolumeName`

Table 3.1 provides examples of the application of this rule.

Table 3.1
Examples of Building Volume Object Names

Server Name	Physical Volume Name	Volume Object Name
FS1	SYS:	FS1_SYS
LTREE1	VOL1:	LTREE1_VOL1
FS_CORP	CORP_VOL:	FS_CORP_CORP_VOL
KSS_FS	APP$ENG!VOL	KSS_FS_APP$ENG!VOL

The Volume objects contain properties such as the *host server name* and the *physical volume name* that refer to the Server object and its physical name. Though the Volume object names are created in the context in which the File Server object is placed, they can be moved to a different context. You should keep the Volume objects in their default context (same as server context) because they're most likely to be used by User objects defined in this context. Keeping Volume objects in their default context also helps avoid confusion with the location of Volume objects.

Because Volume object names refer to the Volume object in the NDS tree, you can use the NDS syntax to refer to its name. To refer to the Volume object name FS1_SYS in the context OU=CORP.O=SCS, you can use any of the following:

```
.CN=FS1_SYS.OU=CORP.O=SCS
.FS1_SYS.CORP.SCS
FS1_SYS          (if current context is OU=CORP.O=SCS)
```

Understanding NetWare Directories and Files

A volume can be divided into directories and files, and directories can be further divided into subdirectories. Directories and subdirectories help users organize files.

NetWare supports a hierarchical file structure. Figure 3.5 illustrates the hierarchy of dividing a volume into directories and files. For DOS workstations, the file and directories follow the 8.3 naming rule—that is, eight-character file names with three-character extensions. Because DOS is the default name space for the NetWare file system, DOS rules for naming directories should be used for DOS workstations. The following is a summary of the DOS name space restriction rules:

◆ A file name is limited to eight characters.

◆ The extension is optional and can contain at most three characters.

◆ Legal characters are as follows:

A to Z

0 to 9

$ ~ - _ # ! % ^ &) (} {

◆ The following characters are illegal:

space, backslash, period (except to indicate an extension), comma

◆ Subdirectories in the same directory that are at the same level must have unique names.

Figure 3.5

NetWare directory structure versus DOS directory structure.

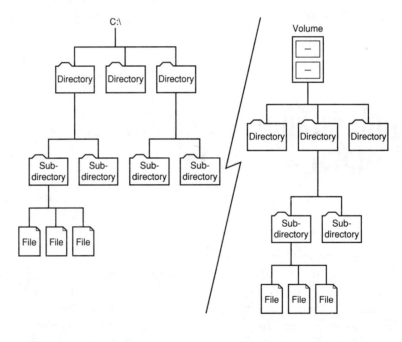

DOS Directory Structure   NetWare Directory Structure

 Study Note Remember the DOS name rules for NetWare files listed in this section.

You can refer to a file on this server using the NetWare 3.x file naming syntax. In this case, bindery emulation is used to resolve the file name. In the NetWare 3.x syntax, the full path name of the file consists of the following:

```
[serverName/]volName:dir1{/dir2}/fileName
```

The directory separator delimiter character can be a forward slash (/) or backslash (\). Examples of NetWare path names are as follows:

- ◆ KSS/SYS:PUBLIC/SCRIPTS/STUDENTS.SCR

- ◆ SYS:APPS\README.DOC

- ◆ VOL1:BRIGHT/DOC\MANUAL.DOC

In the first example, the path name includes the name of the server KSS. The volume name is SYS. The first directory is PUBLIC, and the subdirectory is SCRIPTS. The file name is STUDENTS.SCR.

In the second example, the optional server name is not listed. This implies that the server name of the default server will be used. Under the volume name SYS: is the directory APPS that contains the file README.DOC.

In the third example, the optional server name again is not listed. The volume name is VOL1:; the directory name is BRIGHT. BRIGHT has a subdirectory named DOC that contains the file MANUAL.DOC. Both the forward slash (/) and backslash (\) are used as directory separators. Although either one is all right, you should use one consistently.

Because a NetWare volume is a leaf object in the NDS tree, the directories and file path names can use the NDS syntax to refer to the volume name. Figure 3.6 shows the path name for subdirectories ENG and CORP that are in the COMMON subdirectory in the Volume object FSDEV_SYS. The Volume object is in the context OU=CORP.O=LGROUP. If the current context is O=LGROUP, the following partial NDS names can be used to refer to the Volume object:

```
FSDEV_SYS.CORP.LGROUP
```

```
CN=FSDEV_SYS.OU=CORP.O=LGROUP
```

259

Figure 3.6

NDS syntax for file names.

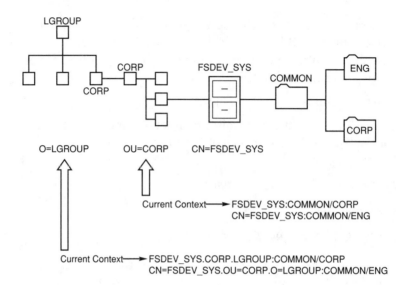

To refer to the subdirectory CORP or ENG, the Volume object name must contain the file directory path as a prefix (COMMON/ CORP or COMMON/ENG). The Volume object name and the directory path are separated by the colon (:) delimiter. Therefore, the CORP and ENG directories can be referred to by the following syntax, if the current context is O=LGROUP:

```
FSDEV_SYS.CORP.LGROUP:COMMON/CORP
CN=FSDEV_SYS.OU=CORP.O=LGROUP:COMMON/ENG
```

If the current context is OU=CORP.O=LGROUP, the following partial NDS names can be used to refer to the Volume object:

```
FSDEV_SYS
```

```
CN=FSDEV_SYS
```

To refer to the subdirectory CORP or ENG, the Volume object name must contain the file directory path as a prefix (COMMON/ CORP or COMMON/ENG). Therefore, the CORP and ENG directories can be referred to by the following syntax, if the current context is OU=CORP.O=LGROUP:

```
FSDEV_SYS:COMMON\CORP
CN=FSDEV_SYS:COMMON/ENG
```

Again, you can use the backslash (\) or forward slash (/) to separate file directory names.

Instead of using partial names for the Volume object (as in the previous examples), you also can use complete names, as shown in the following example (notice that complete names must have a leading period):

```
.FSDEV_SYS.CORP.LGROUP:COMMON/CORP
.CN=FSDEV_SYS.OU=CORP.O=LGROUP:COMMON/ENG
```

The first example uses typeless complete names for the Volume object, and the second example uses complete names with attribute type designators (CN, OU, O).

The normal method of naming files is to start from the top of the directory tree and enumerate the directories separated by the delimiter backslash (\) or forward slash (/), all the way down to the file or directory. The NDS naming convention, however, is the opposite of this. Here, you start with the *bottom* of the tree and list the object names separated by the delimiter period (.) all the way up to the [Root] object. The [Root] object isn't listed because a NDS tree can have only one root.

When you name file directories using the NDS syntax, you're combining the NDS and file-naming conventions. Figure 3.7 shows that these two conventions can be thought of as going up a hill to list the NDS path name. The colon character, listed at the peak of the hill, marks the switch to the file-naming convention. The file-naming convention lists the file directories beginning with the root directory and goes down the hill to the file or directory.

In summary, when combining NDS syntax for volume names with NetWare file system directory syntax, remember the following:

◆ Path names in NDS syntax are listed from bottom to top.

◆ Path names in a NetWare file system are listed from top to bottom.

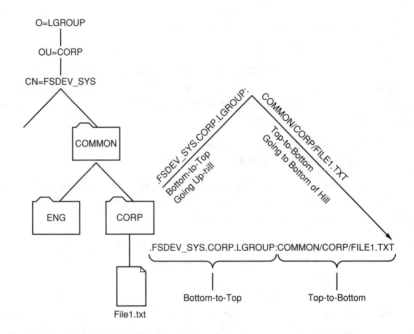

Figure 3.7

Combining NDS syntax and file-naming syntax.

Understanding Default NetWare Directory Structure

During server installation, a default directory structure is created in the first installed volume. This directory structure is listed in figure 3.8. Table 3.2 shows the purpose of each of the major default directories.

The NLS subdirectories under the LOGIN, PUBLIC, and SYSTEM directories contain the unicode files for international language support. The NLS directory contains further subdirectories that identify the installed language support. If the default language ENGLISH is installed, subdirectories will be named LOGIN\NLS\ENGLISH, PUBLIC\NLS\ENGLISH, and SYSTEM\NLS\ENGLISH.

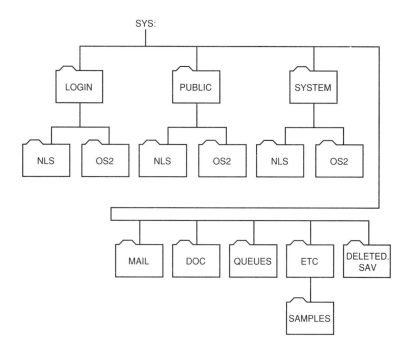

Figure 3.8

Default directory structure on first volume of each server.

The DOC directory is created if you've installed the online DynaText files and documentation. The QUEUES directory is created if the volume is used for implementing storage for print queues.

Table 3.2
Default Directories

Installed Directory	Description
SYS:LOGIN	Contains LOGIN.EXE, CX.EXE, and other programs for logging in to the network.
SYS:PUBLIC	Contains NetWare commands and utilities available to users.
SYS:SYSTEM	Contains files used by the system administrator and the NetWare operating system. NLMs (NetWare Loadable Modules) also are kept here.

continues

Table 3.2, Continued
Default Directories

Installed Directory	Description
SYS:MAIL	Mail directory. Usually empty in NetWare 4.x but may have subdirectories if upgrading from NetWare 3.x.
SYS:DOCVIEW	Contains DynaText Viewer program files and documentation.
SYS:DOC	Contains the actual data files for DynaText.
SYS:QUEUES	Contains directories for NetWare print queues.
SYS:ETC	Contains files for configuring TCP/IP. SYS:ETC/SAMPLES contains sample files that can be customized.
SYS:DELETED.SAV	Contains file from directories that can be salvaged (deleted but not purged).
NLS subdirectories	The NLS subdirectories are created in SYS:LOGIN, SYS:PUBLIC, and SYS:SYSTEM. They contain the message and Help files for national languages support for the utilities found in these directories.

Remember the default installed directories and their purpose as listed in table 3.2.

The LOGIN directory contains the NetWare utilities LOGIN.EXE, NLIST.EXE, CX.EXE, and several others. The LOGIN directory also holds the operating system boot images created by the DOSGEN program for diskless workstations. Some LAN managers keep other copies of programs that they want to be widely available to users without restrictions, such as a program for detecting viruses.

The default access rights to the SYS:LOGIN directory prevent modification of programs in this directory. Care must be exercised to see that these default access rights are not changed. Otherwise, the LOGIN directory can become a place through which a virus attack can spread.

The PUBLIC directory contains the NetWare utilities used by most users; for this reason it is added to the search path. A copy of LOGIN.EXE, NLIST.EXE, and CX.EXE also are kept here in case they become corrupted in the LOGIN directory. Again, care must be taken to limit access to SYS:PUBLIC for running NetWare utilities and not modifying them accidentally or maliciously.

The SYSTEM directory contains the NetWare operating system files and system programs. Access to SYS:SYSTEM should be limited to system administrators and special management utilities that might need to access SYS:SYSTEM.

The SYSTEM directory contains the NetWare Loadable Modules for the operating system, startup files (.NCF), and server drivers. This is because SYS:SYSTEM is the default search path for NLMs loaded from the server console.

Earlier versions of NetWare distributed an e-mail program called MAIL. The e-mail messages were stored in the user ID subdirectory in SYS:MAIL, along with the user's login script. Distribution of the e-mail program was discontinued, but the name of the directory (MAIL) was kept the same. In earlier NetWare versions, the MAIL directory contained the login scripts for the users defined on the NetWare server. In NetWare 4.x, login scripts are kept in the NDS database as a property of a User, Profile, Organization, or Organizational Unit object. If you're upgrading a NetWare 3.x server to a NetWare 4.x server, the older login files that are kept in the MAIL directories will be kept in the SYS:MAIL directory, even though these login scripts will not be used when logging in as an NDS user. If you are running bindery emulation in the SYS:MAIL directory, these login files will be used. Also, the correct SYS:MAIL directory can be created by entering LOGIN <username> /b.

Understanding Directory Structure Organization

Novell recommends that a directory structure be used to help organize the network files and directories. Figure 3.9 shows one possible structure, with separate directories for different DOS versions, users' home directories, applications, and configuration information.

Figure 3.9

Recommended directory structure.

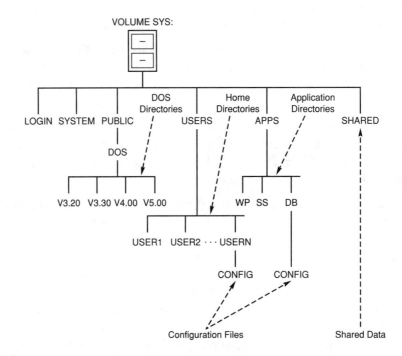

 Please study the Novell recommendation on the different types of directory structures carefully. You may be presented with a scenario of a number of applications and users on a server and asked about the best selection among several NetWare file system directory configurations. These directory configurations will be presented graphically.

The DOS directories hold different versions of DOS programs and utilities installed on NetWare workstations. This capability is useful for keeping a shared copy of the DOS versions used by workstations.

Because many versions of DOS can be used on the network, Novell recommends the directory structure shown in figure 3.9 for storing DOS programs. To support this directory structure, NetWare defines a number of login script variables. These script variables can be used to specify directories in the login script, and are mapped into values shown in figure 3.9. Thus, the login script variable %MACHINE can map into values IBM_PC or COMPAQ, and the script variable %OS_VERSION can map into version numbers such as V3.20, V3.31, V5.00, and V6.20. Depending on the DOS version and machine type, the appropriate network directory can be specified by using the generic script variables. The value of script variables such as %MACHINE can be explicitly controlled by the *LONG MACHINE TYPE* parameter in the NET.CFG workstation configuration file. The procedures for creating login scripts are described in Chapter 6.

All workstations should use the same DOS version to minimize maintenance problems, but this is not always possible. If users of the network belong to different departments that have different budgets, the departments might be using different DOS versions. Also, some older network applications might only work with a particular DOS version. The DOS directory should have a copy of COMMAND.COM for each DOS version supported on the network; having these copies in the DOS directory ensures proper exit from applications when the transient copy of the overwritten COMMAND.COM needs to be written back.

 Note If the directory structure shown in figure 3.9 is used, you must be careful to avoid license infringements. Each user on a DOS workstation must have a license.

A *home directory* is a directory on the server disk reserved for a user to keep personal files. The user usually has unrestricted access to the home directory because the home directory is an extension of the local disk space at the user's workstation.

Home directories can be organized under a directory named USERS or HOME. The users' home directories can be created as subdirectories under the parent USERS or HOME directory. Users get full access to their home directories when the home directory is created using utilities such as NETADMIN, NWADMIN, and UIMPORT. Users are free to organize their home directories any way they want. The home directory should be the same as the user's login name to assist in its identification, and to enable the use of common script files that can refer to a user's home directory by using the login script variable %LOGIN_NAME.

In secure environments, you might want to remove the Supervisor and Access Control rights for users to their home directories. These rights enable the users to grant access for their home directories to other users on the network.

Application directories are used for network applications on the network. You can install applications in their own subdirectories under a common directory called APPS. These directories are shared by all users, so only application programs and data files that need to be shared should be kept here. Temporary files created during the execution of an application should not be kept here, unless the application can recognize the temporary files created by different users and subsequently remove those files on application exit.

Always try to keep the TMP and TEMP variables pointed at a local drive when creating and accessing NetWare files, because this avoids network traffic.

Configuration directories can be created for individual user customization or for all users. This supports applications that maintain separate configuration files for each user. An example of such an application is a WordPerfect program that stores a configuration file for users based on their three-letter initials. If users need to modify the configuration files, you should keep the configuration files in the CONFIG directory under the user's home directory. If configuration files need to be maintained by the application, they should be placed in the application's directory.

The Shared data directory acts as a clearinghouse for distributing information. You can use NetWare file system security to ensure that only designated users have access to this directory. Many network administrators prefer not to have the shared data directory, because it requires periodic maintenance to ensure that old files are removed.

Single-Volume Directory Structure

Figure 3.10 shows an example of a one-volume directory structure. This assumes that only one volume is on the server and you are dealing with a very small number of users who need access to the server. In this figure, the users' home directories are created directly under the root of volume SYS, instead of under the USERS or HOME directory. You can, if you want, create the home directories under a common USERS or HOME directory. Figure 3.10 also shows separate CORP and ACCT directories to maintain applications for different departments (Corporate and Accounting) in separate directories.

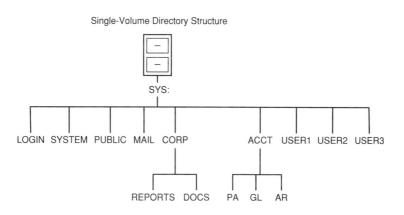

Single-Volume Directory Structure

Figure 3.10

Single-volume directory structure.

Multiple-Volume Directory Structure

Figure 3.11 shows an example of a multiple-volume directory structure. This assumes that the server contains multiple volumes, and that volumes are dedicated for a specific use, such as the following:

◆ Applications

◆ Department

◆ Workgroup

Figure 3.11

Multiple-volume directory structure.

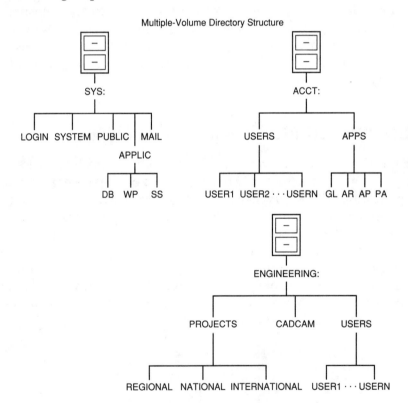

Multiple-Volume Directory Structure

In figure 3.11, the SYS: volume holds the standard NetWare file systems in the LOGIN, PUBLIC, and SYSTEM directories. Certain applications common to all departments are stored in the SYS:APPLIC directory. Volume ACCT is dedicated for accounting department users and the applications they use, and volume ENGINEERING is dedicated for engineering applications and engineering users' home directories.

Designing File System Directory Structure

A number of factors should be considered before a file system directory structure is established, including the following:

◆ The types of applications network users need

◆ Whether applications and data should be in the same or different directories

◆ Whether applications are shared by all users or shared by small user groups

◆ What information needs to be shared by users

◆ Implementing and maintaining file system security

You can expect to apply these criteria in some of the questions on the CNE exams.

Using Network File Storage Commands

The system administrator can manage the network file storage using the following commands and utilities:

◆ NLIST

◆ NDIR

◆ NCOPY

◆ RENDIR

◆ FILER

◆ NetWare Administrator

◆ NETADMIN

These commands are discussed in the following sections.

The NLIST Command

A brief overview of the many options of the NLIST command can be obtained by using the NLIST /? command. Many of the options were discussed in Chapter 2, "Introduction to NetWare Directory Services."

The NLIST VOLUME command displays information on volume subjects, such as the following:

◆ Object class

◆ Current context

◆ Volume name

◆ Host server

◆ Physical volume

◆ Number of Volume objects

Figure 3.12 shows the output of the NLIST VOLUME /S command. In this example, the current context is O=ESL. Several Volume objects were found in the subtree O=ESL. When you use the NLIST VOLUME command without any options, you must be in the proper context to see the Volume objects. To see all Volume objects in subcontainers, you can use the /S option. The /CO option, which uses the context specified for the NLIST command, is very useful. For example, to view all Volume objects in Organization O=SCS, type the following:

```
NLIST VOLUME   /S   /CO "O=SCS"
```

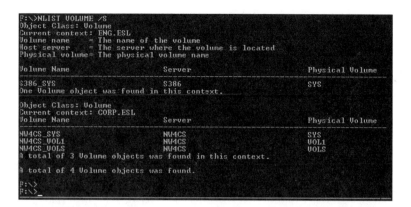

Figure 3.12

The NLIST VOLUME /S command.

Some other useful NLIST VOLUME commands are listed in table 3.3. The examples are not exhaustive, but are listed so that you can understand how the NLIST VOLUME command can be used.

Table 3.3
NLIST VOLUME Command Examples

Task	Command
List information on volumes in current context	NLIST VOLUME
List information on volumes and subcontainers in current context	NLIST VOLUME /S
List only names of volumes in current context	NLIST VOLUME /N
List detailed information on volumes in current context	NLIST VOLUME /D

The NDIR Command

The NDIR command is the network version of the DOS DIR command. It performs the following functions:

◆ Displays information on volume statistics.

◆ Displays directory/file contents, including ownership information and effective rights.

273

◆ Searches for specific files/directories.

◆ Searches directories/files sorted by different criteria.

The NDIR command syntax is shown in figures 3.13 through 3.19. These figures can be obtained using the NDIR /? command. Use these figures as a quick review of the NDIR options when preparing for your CNE exams.

Figure 3.13

NDIR General Usage Help.

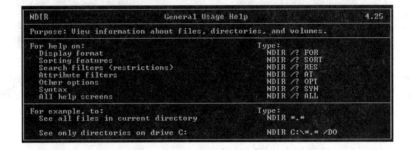

Figure 3.14

NDIR Format Specification Help.

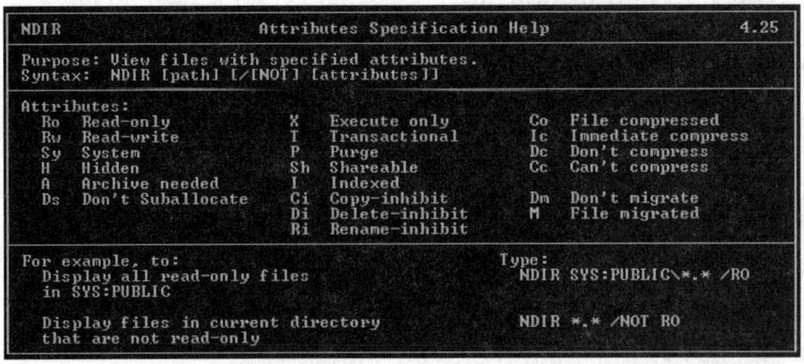

Figure 3.15

NDIR Attributes Specification Help.

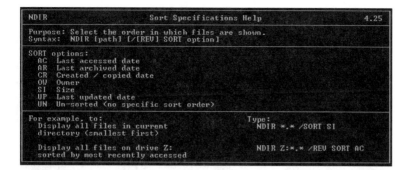

Figure 3.16

NDIR Sort
Specifications Help.

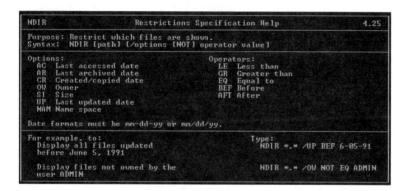

Figure 3.17

NDIR Restrictions
Specification Help.

Figure 3.18

NDIR Options Help.

Figure 3.19

NDIR Syntax Help.

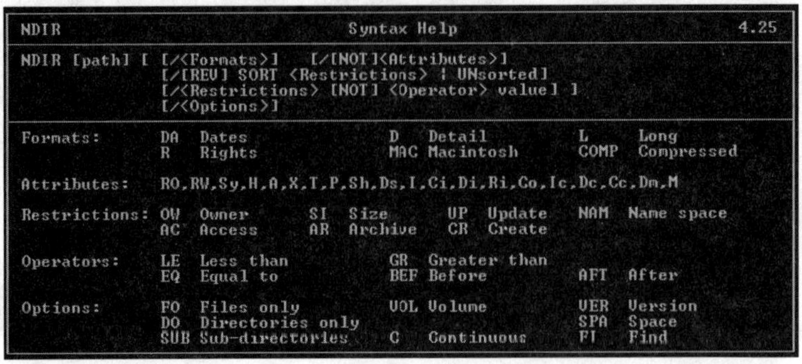

```
NDIR                          Syntax Help                        4.25

NDIR [path] [ [/<Formats>]    [/[NOT]<Attributes>]
              [/[REV] SORT <Restrictions> | UNsorted]
              [/<Restrictions> [NOT] <Operator> value] ]
              [/<Options>]

Formats:      DA  Dates            D   Detail       L    Long
              R   Rights           MAC Macintosh    COMP Compressed

Attributes:   RO,RW,Sy,H,A,X,T,P,Sh,Ds,I,Ci,Di,Ri,Co,Ic,Dc,Cc,Dm,M

Restrictions: OW  Owner        SI  Size       UP  Update   NAM  Name space
              AC  Access       AR  Archive    CR  Create

Operators:    LE  Less than             GR  Greater than
              EQ  Equal to              BEF Before       AFT  After

Options:      FO  Files only            VOL Volume       VER  Version
              DO  Directories only                       SPA  Space
              SUB Sub-directories   C   Continuous       FI   Find
```

Here's an example of the use of the NDIR command:

```
F:\>NDIR SYS:PUBLIC
Files         = Files contained in this path
Size          = Number of bytes in the file
Last Update   = Date file was last updated
Owner         = ID of user who created or copied the file
FS1/SYS:PUBLIC\*.*
Files         Size      Last Update       Owner
ALLOW.BAT     26        9-24-92  11:48a   FS1
APLASER2.PDF  2,986     1-17-92   3:23p   FS1
APPIMAGE.PDF  327       10-25-89 11:49a   FS1
APPLASER.PDF  1,281     8-14-90   3:57p   FS1
:
:
    16,335,472  bytes (24,903,680  bytes in 380 blocks allocated)
           167  Files
             4  Directories
```

Figure 3.20 shows the output of the NDIR /VOLUME command. This command shows statistics on the current volume. The statistics are for volume NW4CS/SYS:. It displays the total volume space, deleted space not yet purgeable, space remaining on volume, and space remaining on volume for the user who issued the command. The NDIR /VOLUME command also displays volume compression information if compression is enabled for the volume.

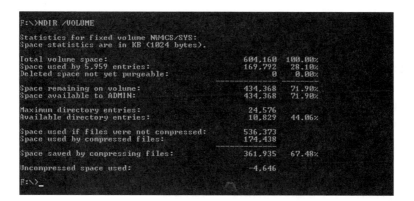

Figure 3.20

NDIR /VOLUME
command output.

The NDIR /DO command displays only information on directories. Figure 3.21 shows an example of this command's output. The NDIR /DO command was issued from the root of volume NW4CS/SYS:. It shows that nine directories were found and shows the Inherited Rights Filter (IRF) for each directory, the effective rights for the directory for the user issuing the command, and the directory-creation time stamp. Notice that certain default directories such as SYS:LOGIN, SYS:PUBLIC, SYS:SYSTEM, SYS:DELETED.SAV were created during installation. This is a quick way of determining when a particular installation was done. The owner of the directory also is displayed.

```
F:\>NDIR /DO
Directories       = Directories contained in this path
Filter            = Inherited Rights Filter
Rights            = Effective Rights
Created           = Date directory was created
Owner             = ID of user who created or copied the file

NW4CS/SYS:*.*
Directories       Filter        Rights        Created        Owner
----------------  -----------   -----------   --------------  --------------------
DEI               [SRWCEMFA]    [SRWCEMFA]    6-27-93  8:29p  Admin
DELETED.SAV       [--------]    [SRWCEMFA]    6-27-93  1:30p  [Supervisor]
DOC               [SRWCEMFA]    [SRWCEMFA]    6-27-93  2:17p  NW4CS.CORP
ETC               [SRWCEMFA]    [SRWCEMFA]    6-27-93  1:37p  [Supervisor]
LOGIN             [SRWCEMFA]    [SRWCEMFA]    6-27-93  1:30p  [Supervisor]
MAIL              [--------]    [SRWCEMFA]    6-27-93  1:30p  [Supervisor]
NOVINI            [SRWCEMFA]    [SRWCEMFA]    6-27-93  2:35p  NW4CS.CORP
PUBLIC            [SRWCEMFA]    [SRWCEMFA]    6-27-93  1:30p  [Supervisor]
SYSTEM            [--------]    [SRWCEMFA]    6-27-93  1:30p  [Supervisor]
            9  Directories

F:\>
```

Figure 3.21

The NDIR /DO
command.

277

The NDIR /FO command displays only information on files. Figure 3.22 shows an example of this command's output. It shows that the root of the SYS: volume has three files: BACKOUT.TTS, TTS$LOG.ERR, and VOL$LOG.ERR. These are important files for the network administrator to know. The first two deal with the Transaction Tracking System (TTS) that enables incomplete transactions to be backed out. The VOL$LOG.ERR shows errors that have been recorded for that volume.

Figure 3.22

The NDIR /FO command.

```
F:\>NDIR /FO
Files            = Files contained in this path
Size             = Number of bytes in the file
Last Update      = Date file was last updated
Owner            = ID of user who created or copied the file

NW4CS/SYS:*.*
Files                      Size Last Update    Owner
-------------------- ------------- ---------------- --------------------------
BACKOUT.TTS               16,384  7-31-93  3:09p [Supervisor]
TTS$LOG.ERR                1,999  7-31-93  3:09p [Supervisor]
VOL$LOG.ERR                1,441  7-31-93  3:09p [Supervisor]


        19,824  bytes (49,152  bytes in 3 blocks allocated)
            3  Files


F:\>
```

To list directory information only within the current directory and all subdirectories within the current directory, you can use the /SUB option, as follows:

```
NDIR   /DO   /SUB
```

To list only files in the current directory and all subdirectories within the current directory, use the following command:

```
NDIR   /FO   /SUB
```

To list all directories within the current directory and all subdirectories in the SYS: volume that have the letters WAN as part of the directory name, you can use the /SUB option, as follows:

```
NDIR   SYS:*WAN*   /DO   /SUB
```

To display a list of files only sorted by the last modified (updated) time stamp, use the following command:

```
NDIR  /FO /SORT UP
```

To display a list of files sorted by the most recently accessed time stamp, type the following command:

```
NDIR  /FO /SORT AC
```

To sort a directory list of files by size, with the largest file first (reverse sort), type the following command:

```
NDIR  /FO /REV SORT SI
```

For details of other sort options, refer to figure 3.16.

To list files that have not been modified before a certain date (Oct 16, 1993), type the following command:

```
NDIR /FO /UP BEF 10-16-93
```

To list files that have been modified after a certain date (Nov 20, 1993), type the following command:

```
NDIR /FO /UP AFT 11-20-93
```

To list files in SYS:PUBLIC that have long file names (such as those supported by NFS and OS/2 name spaces), type the following:

```
NDIR  SYS:PUBLIC   /L
```

or

```
NDIR SYS:PUBLIC /LONG
```

To list all files in SYS:DATA directory that have a Read Only attribute, type the following command:

```
NDIR SYS:DATA\*.*   /RO
```

To list all files in SYS:DATA directory that *do not* have a Read Only attribute, type the following command:

```
NDIR SYS:DATA\*.*   /NOT RO
```

To display all files owned by user KSS, type this command:

```
NDIR SYS:*.* /SUB   /OW EQ KSS
```

To display all files not owned by Admin, type the following command:

```
NDIR SYS:*.* /SUB   /OW NOT EQ Admin
```

To display additional information on compressed files, type this command:

```
NDIR   /COMP
```

The /COMP option displays compressed and uncompressed sizes of each compressed file as well as the percentage of space saved as a result of compression.

Examples of useful NDIR options are summarized in table 3.4.

Table 3.4
NDIR Examples

Option	Meaning
/SUB or /S	Display information on subdirectories also.
/C	Continuous display. Do not pause for user input if more than one screen of display information.
/SORT	Sort in ascending order. Sort criteria is file name (default).
/REV SORT	Sort in descending order. Sort criteria is file name (default).
/VER	Displays version number stored in NetWare utility program files.
/COMP	Displays compression information on files.
/FO	Displays files only.
/DO	Displays directories only.
/OW	Owner information. Example: /OW EQ ADMIN.
/LONG or /L	Shows long file name space support for non-DOS name spaces such as NFS, OS/2, and Unix.

Be familiar with the use of the NDIR options listed in table 3.3.

NDIR wild card searches work differently than in DOS. The asterisk (*) is used to match zero or more characters. In DOS, the asterisk matches any file-name pattern. The following commands show the differences between the DOS DIR and NetWare NDIR wild cards. The examples show the wild card pattern *W*.* on the directory list of the F:\USERS\KARANJIT directory for the DOS DIR and NetWare NDIR commands. The DOS version used in the examples is DOS 5. The directory has three files. Notice that the DIR *W*.* matched all files in the directory, whereas the NDIR *W*.* found only the single file that correctly matches this file pattern:

```
> DIR *W*.*

 Volume in drive F is SYS
 Directory of F:\USERS\KARANJIT

AWK           EXE     36027 07-04-92   3:21p
COPYQM        COM     28451 12-10-92   5:30p
TEST          TXT         2 06-10-93   4:34p

      3 file(s)      64480 bytes
                 103972864 bytes free


>NDIR   *W*.*

NDIR is searching the directory.  Please wait...
Files               = Files contained in this path
Size                = Number of bytes in the file
Last Update         = Date file was last updated
Owner               = ID of user who created or copied the file


NW4CS/SYS:USERS\KARANJIT\*W*.*
Files               Size            Last Update      Owner
_____            _____          _____      _____

AWK.EXE             36,027          7-04-92  3:21    Admin

        36,027  bytes (49,152  bytes in 3 blocks allocated)
            1   File
```

Directory Commands

Many of the DOS commands that work with the DOS file system also can be used with the NetWare file system. Examples of such commands are the DOS MD (Make Directory) and RD (Remove Directory) commands.

NetWare supports a RENDIR command that's used for renaming directories. It has the following syntax:

```
RENDIR  directory_path [TO]  new_directory_path
```

The following are examples of this command:

```
RENDIR  SYS:APPS/SHARED SYS:APPS/COMMON
RENDIR F:\USERS\KIMS  TO  F:\USERS\KIMJ
```

The RENDIR command also can be used on local drives to rename directories on local hard disks:

```
RENDIR  C:\UTILS TO BIN
```

The previous command renames C:\UTILS to C:\BIN.

 The RENDIR command can be used to rename NetWare directories and local directories.

The NCOPY Command

The NCOPY command copies files or directories from a server directory to a server directory without using the workstation as an intermediate point (see fig. 3.23). This command preserves NetWare file extended attributes that are different from those available in DOS.

Figure 3.23 also shows the differences between the DOS COPY command and the NCOPY command. The DOS COPY command copies data to the workstation and then back from the workstation to the server. This involves a considerable amount of network traffic. With the NCOPY command, the file's destination and source are at the same server, and no network traffic is involved.

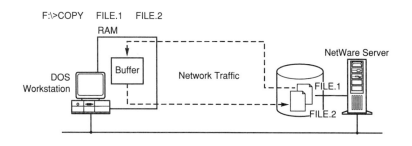

Figure 3.23

DOS COPY command versus NCOPY command.

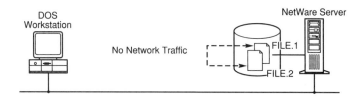

The general syntax for the NCOPY command is as follows:

```
NCOPY   source_path  [TO]  destination_path
```

To copy file SYS:DATA\X.TXT to VOL1:COMMON\DATA, type the following command:

```
NCOPY  SYS:DATA\X.TXT  VOL1:COMMON\DATA
```

When the previous copy command is executed, no traffic is generated because the volumes are on the same server. If the source and destination volumes are attached to different servers, network traffic is generated—as seen in the following example that shows a copy of a file between servers FS1 and FS2:

```
NCOPY  FS1/SYS:DATA\X.TXT  FS2/SYS:DATA\X.TXT
```

To copy all files in the current directory to another location—including subdirectories and empty subdirectories—use the following command:

```
NCOPY  FS1/SYS:CONFIG  /S  /E
```

The /C option ensures that only DOS information is copied. NetWare extended-attribute information is copied without the /C option. To copy file MYFILE.DOC to another location and not preserve NetWare extended attribute information, type this command:

283

```
NCOPY MYFILE.DOC SYS:APPS/WP  /C
```

If you want to be notified that non-DOS file information (NetWare extended attributes) will be lost when the NCOPY command is used, add the /I option to the command. This option is also valuable if you're copying name-space information to a volume that does not support it. The /I option warns you if the name space information will not be copied.

The /R option for the NCOPY command copies the file in the compressed state. If a compressed file is copied, it's copied to the destination in an uncompressed state. To force the copying of a file in the compressed state, you can use the /R (Retain Compression) option.

If you are copying a file to a different volume, that volume should have compression enabled. Compression is enabled for a volume during volume installation time. You can use the /RU (Retain Uncompressed) option to force the copying of a file in the compressed state—even if the destination volume doesn't support NetWare's compression. An example of this use could be copying a file temporarily to a local DOS drive. Data in the copied file cannot be accessed unless it is copied back to a NetWare volume that has compression enabled. Thus, to copy the file SYS:APPS/DATA/GL.DAT to the C: drive in a compressed state, type the following:

```
NCOPY SYS:APPS/DATA/GL.DAT  C:\   /RU
```

The /M option copies files that have an archive bit set and then clears the archive bit. This enables the copying of files that have not been backed up.

If you want to copy files that need to be backed up to another location and be notified if extended file information will not be copied, type the following:

```
NCOPY *.* H:\BCPY  /M  /I
```

The NCOPY command has an /F option that works with *sparse files*. Sparse files have one or more empty blocks. Examples of applications that use sparse files are graphical, imaging, and database applications. The /F option forces the NCOPY command to write the empty disk blocks when copying sparse files. An example of the /F option follows:

```
NCOPY FSDB/VOLDB:APPS/DATA/*.*  FSBK/SYS:BU    /F
```

Figure 3.24 shows the help obtained using the NCOPY /? command. This figure shows the details of other NCOPY options.

Study the NCOPY examples in this section and the NCOPY options listed in figure 3.24.

Figure 3.24

NCOPY General Help (NCOPY /?).

File Management with the NetWare Administrator

The NetWare Administrator (NWADMIN) can be used for managing files and directories as well as salvaging and purging files. It's a GUI utility that runs under MS Windows. The NWADMIN program is normally associated with management of NDS objects, but can be used for managing files and directories in a volume because the Volume object is an NDS object. Double-clicking on an NDS object reveals the subdirectories stored in that volume. The information is displayed in a graphical tree (see fig. 3.25).

Figure 3.25

Using the NWADMIN program for file and subdirectory management.

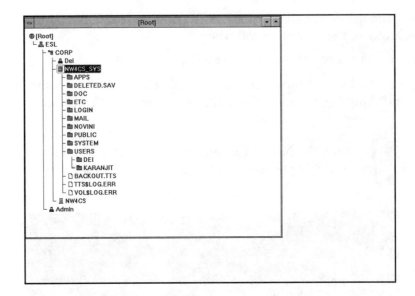

Figure 3.25 displays the subdirectories for Volume object NW4CS_SYS in the context OU=CORP.O=ESL. The directories are listed in alphabetical order. The home directories for user DEI and KARANJIT are also displayed under the USERS directory. The file names BACKOUT.TTS, TTS$LOG.ERR, and VOL$LOG.ERR at the root of the Volume object NW4CS_SYS also are displayed. To examine the contents of any directory, you can highlight and select that directory (double-click if you're using a mouse).

 The NetWare Administrator (NWADMIN) can be used for file management.

The FILER program

The FILER program is a text-based menu utility that enables you to perform the following tasks:

◆ View volume, directory, and file information

◆ Delete, move, and copy multiple files

- ◆ Delete entire directory structures

- ◆ Set up search filters

- ◆ Salvage and purge files

Figure 3.26 shows the FILER main menu and the options that are available.

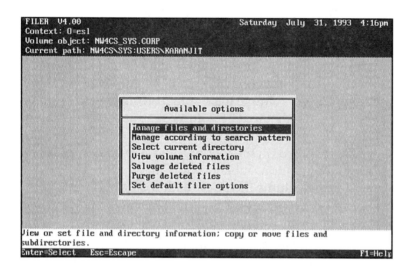

Figure 3.26

The FILER main menu.

The *Manage files and directories* option displays a list of subdirectories and files in the current directory. Selecting a directory displays its contents. Selecting a file enables you to copy, view, or move a file. Additionally, you can view and set file information such as file attributes, owner, Inherited Rights Filter (IRF), file trustees, creation date, last accessed date, last archived date, and last modified date. You also can display a list of rights for a file.

To perform operations on a directory, you must highlight the directory and press F10. For directories, you can copy a subdirectory's files, copy a subdirectory's structure, move a subdirectory's structure, make it your current directory, view trustees of the directory, or view/set directory information.

The *Manage according to search pattern* option enables you to select files and directories that only match a certain pattern. The default search pattern is *.* for all directories and files. You can select to exclude or include patterns for files and directories. You also can search based on file or directory attributes.

The *Select current directory* option enables you to select the current directory path.

The *View volume information* option enables you to observe volume statistics, volume features, and volume creation and modification date and time stamps. Volume statistics include total volume space in KB, active space used, deleted space not yet purgeable, space remaining on volume, maximum directory entries, and directory entries available. The volume features include volume type (removable, non-removable, and so on), volume block size, name spaces installed on the volume, and installation features (compression, migration, suballocation, and auditing). The dates and times for the volume include creation date and time, volume owner, last modified date and time, and last archived date and time. The last user to archive the volume also is shown.

The *Salvage deleted files* option enables you to view/recover deleted files, salvage from deleted directories, and set salvage options.

The *Purge deleted files* option enables you to select the file name patterns to purge by. In NetWare, files that have been deleted can be set to be recoverable, unless they're purged. When files are purged, they cannot be recovered. The default is * (all files).

The *Set default filer options* option enables you to control filer settings that affect its behavior. You can, for example, configure a filer to confirm deletions, confirm file copies, confirm file overwrites, preserve file attributes, notify you if name-space information is lost, copy sparse files, copy compressed files, and force files to be copied in compressed form.

Certain applications can store files in sparse format. This means that because most of the file blocks contain repeated patterns (all zeros, for example), the file can be maintained by the application in a special sparse format. If the copy files sparse format is set, NetWare does not expand the file to its non-sparse format while making a file copy.

 Make sure you know the capabilities of FILER listed in this section.

NetWare Directories and Files

This section shows you how to use the commands and utilities discussed in the previous sections. Follow these steps:

1. Log in as an Administrator user to the network. The login command is LOGIN *admin_user_name*.

2. Change your context to [Root], as follows:

   `CX /R`

3. Use the NLIST VOLUME command to find information on the volume, as follows:

   `NLIST VOLUME`

   Notice that no volumes have been found. This is because using the NLIST VOLUME command without any options lists only objects of object class VOLUME in the current context. The current context is set to [Root], which cannot contain leaf objects such as Volume objects.

4. To search for Volume objects in all subcontainers, type the following command:

   `NLIST VOLUME /S`

5. Make a list of all contexts under which a Volume object can be found.

The number of Volume objects reported by the NLIST command might be more than the actual number of physical Volume objects. This would be the case if some of the Volume objects are alias objects that point to other Volume objects. The NLIST command does not distinguish between alias object names and the real object names.

6. Change your context to the container that has the Volume object. To observe information on the Volume object, type the following command:

   ```
   NLIST VOLUME
   ```

   The NLIST VOLUME command also reports information on the current context that the volume has found, the host server name on which the volume is located, and the physical name of the volume.

7. To see only the object name, use the /N option, as follows:

   ```
   NLIST VOLUME /N
   ```

8. To see detailed information on the Volume object, use the following command:

   ```
   NLIST VOLUME /D
   ```

9. If there is a Volume object in a different container, you can use the /CO option to see information on it without first changing your context. If, for example, you want to see information on the Volume object in the container OU=ENG.O=SCS, use the following command:

   ```
   NLIST VOLUME /CO   .OU=ENG.O=SCS
   ```

The previous command lists information on Volume objects in another context without changing your current context. You might want to use the command CX to verify that your context has not changed.

The following steps show you how to explore the volume with the NDIR command.

1. To list only the subdirectories under SYS:SYSTEM, type the following:

   ```
   NDIR SYS:SYSTEM /S /DO
   ```

2. To list only the files under SYS:SYSTEM, type the following:

   ```
   NDIR SYS:SYSTEM /S /FO
   ```

3. To find the smallest file in the SYS:SYSTEM directory, type the following:

   ```
   NDIR SYS:SYSTEM /FO /SORT SI
   ```

   The first file displayed is the smallest file.

4. To find the largest file in the SYS:SYSTEM directory, type the following:

   ```
   NDIR SYS:SYSTEM /FO /REV SORT SI
   ```

   The first file displayed is the largest file.

   You also could use the NDIR SYS:SYSTEM /SORT SI command, in which case the last file listed is the largest file.

5. To list all executable files in SYS: and its subdirectories that have been updated after 6-1-93 (June 1, 1993), type the following:

   ```
   NDIR SYS:*.EXE /FO /SUB /UP AFT 6-1-93
   ```

6. To list all executable files in SYS:PUBLIC and its subdirectories that were accessed prior to 1993, type the following:

   ```
   NDIR SYS:PUBLIC\*.EXE /FO /SUB /AC BEF 1-1-93
   ```

Using Directory Mappings

To make use of the NetWare file system, the workstation assigns one of the available network drives to a directory on the server. This process is called *mapping a network drive*. Figure 3.27 shows the available drive letters. Drive letters from A: to E: are usually reserved for local drives, and drives F: to Z: can be used for network drives. The figure also shows search drive mappings, which will be discussed later in the chapter.

291

Figure 3.27

Local, network, and search drives.

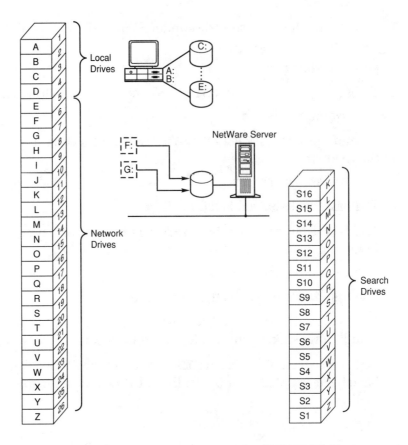

NetWare 4.x requires that you have the LASTDRIVE=Z statement in the CONFIG.SYS file of the NetWare DOS workstation, because the drive table data structure is shared by both DOS and the NetWare requester. The FIRST NETWORK DRIVE statement can be used in the NetWare DOS Requester section of the NET.CFG file to assign which drive letter will be used as the first network drive. If the FIRST NETWORK DRIVE statement isn't used, the first drive letter that isn't used for a local drive or device becomes the first network drive.

The NetWare shell that was used with older versions of NetWare used the LASTDRIVE statement in the NET.CFG to define the last local drive available to the workstation. The next drive letter after the LASTDRIVE letter became the first network drive. Because the default value of LASTDRIVE was E:1 E:, the first network drive became F:. To preserve compatibility with the older convention of starting the first network drive as F:, many NetWare 4.x installations set FIRST NETWORK DRIVE=F in the NetWare DOS Requester section of the NET.CFG file.

 In NetWare 4.x DOS workstations, the LASTDRIVE=Z statement must be in the CONFIG.SYS file.

The MAP command

The MAP command assigns a drive letter to a NetWare server directory. The general syntax of the MAP command is shown in figures 3.28 and 3.29. In figure 3.28, you can see that the MAP command has a number of parameter options that precede the drive letter. These options will be discussed next. The = *path* syntax specifies a directory path and is used when performing a drive mapping. When the DEL (or REM) option is used with the MAP command, the directory path is not specified.

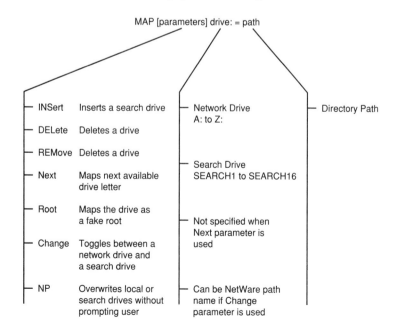

Figure 3.28
The MAP command.

293

Figure 3.29

MAP General Help
(MAP /?).

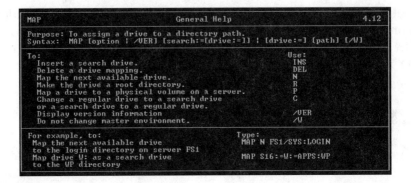

 You should be familiar with the MAP command options listed in figures 3.28 and 3.29.

Here are a few examples of use of the MAP commands:

```
MAP F: = SYS:PUBLIC
MAP G: = SYS:USERS
MAP H: = SYS:
```

The drive letters and their associated network directories are shown in figure 3.30.

Figure 3.30

Examples of the MAP command.

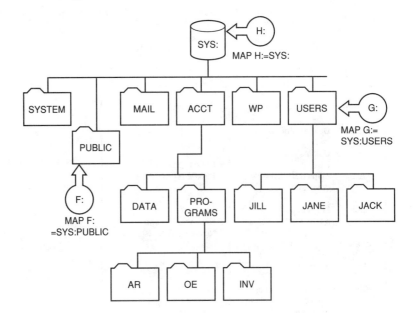

Search Drives and the MAP INS Option

In DOS, you can use the PATH command to specify the order in which directories are searched (if a program file isn't found in the current directory). The directories specified in the PATH command are stored in a DOS environment variable of the same name (PATH).

You can't include NetWare directories as part of the PATH command using the NetWare syntax for a directory. Consider a situation in which a DOS station has the following setting for the PATH environment variable before logging on to a NetWare server:

```
PATH=C:\WP51;C:\BIN;C:\BC\BIN;C:\WC386\BIN
```

To add a NetWare directory SYS:PUBLIC\UTIL to the beginning of the search path, you might be tempted to use the following DOS PATH command:

```
PATH=SYS:PUBLIC\UTIL;C:\WP51;C:\BIN;C:\BC\BIN;C:\WC386\BIN
```

This command, however, won't work because most commands are executed at the workstation. For a DOS workstation, this means that the command will be executed under DOS. When DOS tries to process the SYS:PUBLIC\UTIL directory in the PATH environment variable, it gets confused by the SYS:. It expects to see a one-letter drive; instead, it finds a three-letter name, SYS. NetWare provides an easy way out of specifying network directories as part of the search path by making use of search drives.

Search drives are shown in figure 3.27. Sixteen are available, and they are labeled SEARCH1 through SEARCH16. The common abbreviation is to replace the word SEARCH with the letter S. Thus, the first search drive can be abbreviated as S1 and the sixteenth search drive is abbreviated as S16.

Search-drive assignments are made using the MAP command, and they specify the order in which directories—including network directories—are to be searched. This is similar to the way the PATH command operates under DOS, except that the search drives also enable you to work with network directories.

Thus, in the preceding example, if you want to include the network directory SYS:PUBLIC\UTIL as part of the search path, you use these MAP commands:

```
MAP S1:=SYS:PUBLIC\UTIL
```

or

```
MAP INS S1:=SYS:PUBLIC\UTIL
```

The first MAP command maps search drive 1 (SEARCH1) to the network directory SYS:PUBLIC\UTIL, causing this directory to be searched first. The second MAP command (with the INS option) is similar to the first, but has a subtle difference. The INS option inserts SYS:PUBLIC\UTIL as the first search drive. *Inserting* means that if the first search drive was assigned previously, it is pushed down the list to become the second search drive, and the later MAP INS S1:=SYS:PUBLIC\UTIL command causes SYS:PUBLIC\UTIL to become the first search drive. This push-down effect is shown in figure 3.31.

Figure 3.31

The push-down effect of using the MAP INS command.

Search Drive	Single Drive Letter Assignment	Search Directory		Search Drive	Single Drive Letter Assignment	Search Directory
S1	Z:	SYS:PUBLIC	→	S1	Z:	SYS:PUBLIC/UTIL
S2	Y:	SYS:SYSTEM		S2	Y:	SYS:PUBLIC
				S3	X:	SYS:SYSTEM

MAP INS S1: = SYS : PUBLIC/UTIL

In the preceding figure, the search drives are shown before and after the MAP INS command is issued. Notice that the search drive assignments are pushed down one level after the MAP INS command is issued.

After the MAP S1:=SYS:PUBLIC\UTIL command is issued to map search drive 1, it also changes the DOS PATH environment variable. It does this by assigning an unused drive letter, starting with Z:, to the network directory and inserting Z: in the DOS PATH environment variable. Thus, the DOS PATH environment variable before the MAP S1=SYS:PUBLIC/UTIL command looks like this:

```
PATH=C:\WP51;C:\BIN;C:\BC\BIN;C:\WC386\BIN
```

Then, after the MAP command is issued, drive letter Z: is mapped to SYS:PUBLIC\UTIL and inserted in the DOS PATH environment variable, which looks like this:

```
PATH=Z:.;C:\WP51;C:\BIN;C:\BC\BIN;C:\WC386\BIN
```

DOS now understands the single letter Z: as another network directory letter and is no longer confused by a directory name such as SYS:PUBLIC\UTIL. DOS searches drive Z: as it would any local drive. The period (.) is a symbol for the current directory and, when used in "Z:." in the PATH environment variable, indicates that the current directory Z: mapped to (SYS:PUBLIC\UTIL) will be searched.

Drive letters for search drives are assigned beginning with Z: and moving up to K:. As an example, search drive 1 is assigned letter Z and search drive 16 is assigned letter K. The reason for the reverse order is that drive letters for applications are usually assigned beginning with drive F: and moving down. This minimizes conflicts in drive letter assignments between applications and search drives.

Note Application drive letters can be safely assigned up to drive J:. If you use drives beyond J: (such as K:), a conflict occurs when you use up the maximum of 16 search drives. That's because search drive 16 also wants to use letter K.

continues

297

This scenario isn't uncommon in complex NetWare user environments. The network manager is sometimes left wishing that the English alphabet had more than 26 letters or that DOS used a different scheme.

Search drive mappings only affect the user's session. That is, if the MAP command is used to map to a network directory, this mapping is only for the user issuing the MAP command. Other users on the network aren't affected. The shell is responsible for keeping the drive mappings for a session. When a user logs out of a server by using the LOGOUT command, the drive mappings are removed from the drive-map table kept by the shell.

The only way to make the drive mappings permanent every time the user logs in is to automate the execution of the MAP commands when the user logs in to the network. One way of doing this is through login scripts.

MAP commands build a network search path by placing them in a login script file. A login script defines a user's network environment. Login scripts are the network equivalent of the DOS AUTOEXEC.BAT file. Login scripts are discussed in detail in Chapter 6, "Customizing the NetWare 4.x User Environment."

The most frequently used search drives should be listed first to minimize unnecessary searches. This is particularly true for network search drives, because searching them generates network traffic. Consider an example in which a user needs applications and programs stored in the local drives more often than access to programs on network drives. If the network drives are listed before local drives in the search path, unnecessary traffic is generated while searching for programs in network drives although the program actually resides in the local drives. In this case, the user should have local search drives listed before network search drives.

You cannot map to a network directory unless you have access rights to that directory. Attempting to map to a network directory for which you do not have access rights results in an error message.

The MAP INS S16 Option

If you attempt to map a search drive that is not yet defined, the next logical search drive is assigned as a search drive. Consider the following example, in which a NetWare session has three search drive mappings:

```
MAP INS S1:=SYS:PUBLIC
MAP INS S2:=SYS:PUBLIC\BIN
MAP INS S3:=SYS:APPS\BIN
```

If an attempt is made to perform the following mapping, the next search drive mapping that is assigned is S4: and *not* S16:

```
MAP INS S16:=SYS:APPS\DB
```

This is because search drive S16: doesn't exist, and the next available search drive is S4:. Search drive S16: is typically used for this purpose because it's the last search drive. Any other search drive that isn't used exhibits the same behavior when used in the MAP command. For example, consider if the only search drives that exist are described by the following MAP commands:

```
MAP INS S1:=SYS:PUBLIC
MAP INS S2:=SYS:PUBLIC\BIN
MAP INS S3:=SYS:APPS\BIN
```

Then, using search drive S16: that does not exist, in the following MAP command:

```
MAP INS S16:=SYS:APPS\WP
```

maps search drive S4: to SYS:APPS\WP.

Because the last possible search drive in NetWare is search drive 16 (S16:), the MAP INS S16 command is most commonly used to assign the next search drive letter.

The MAP NEXT Option

The MAP NEXT, or MAP N, command assigns the next available drive as a network drive. Consider the following example, in which only network drive F: has been assigned:

```
MAP  F: = SYS:USERS\JOHN
```

Then, these MAP NEXT commands:

```
MAP NEXT SYS:USERS\JOHN\DATA
MAP N SYS:DATA
MAP NEXT FS1/VOL1:DATA
```

assign network drive G: to SYS:USERS\JOHN\DATA, network drive H: to SYS:DATA, and network drive I: to FS1/VOL1:DATA, respectively. The second form of the MAP command shows that N is an abbreviation for option NEXT.

After the MAP NEXT command executes, it reports the network drive that has been assigned. The MAP NEXT command is a convenient way to provide network drive mappings using a simpler syntax when it does not matter which network drive is assigned, as long as it is not a network drive that is already in use.

The MAP ROOT Option

Consider the following MAP command with the ROOT option:

```
MAP ROOT G: = KSS/VOL1:DEVELOP/BIN
```

In this command, drive G: is mapped to VOL1:DEVELOP/BIN on server KSS. In addition, specifying the ROOT option roots G: to the network directory KSS/VOL1:DEVELOP/BIN. When a drive is *rooted* to a network directory, the network directory behaves as the root of the file system. Because the root directory is the top-level directory, one cannot go up the directory by using DOS commands such as the following:

```
CD ..
CD \
```

The security of the network directory is protected by providing a fake root. A fake root also helps in the installation of single-user applications on the NetWare server. Some single-user applications install in the root directory. If these applications are installed on the server, the root directory on the server volume can become cluttered. A fake root lets the single-user application be installed in a subdirectory on the server.

Remember that the only way you can legally install a single-user application on the server is to have a license for as many copies of the single-user application as there are users.

You can abbreviate the ROOT option with the letter R. Thus, the following MAP statements are equivalent:

```
MAP ROOT G: = KSS/VOL1:DEVELOP/BIN
MAP R G: = KSS/VOL1:DEVELOP/BIN
```

The MAP ROOT command is also useful to overcome the 63 character limitation of the current working directory for DOS workstations that use VLMs.

The MAP NP Option

The MAP NP option enables a local or search drive mapping to be overridden without prompting the user. Its general syntax is as follows:

```
MAP NP  [Option] Drive: = DirectoryPath
```

Thus, to override the local drive mapping D:, use this command:

```
MAP NP G: = SYS:USERS/KSS/BIN
```

To override a search drive mapping for search drive S3 that may already exist, use the following command:

```
MAP NP S3: = SYS:USERS/DORSH/BIN
```

301

In NetWare, the CD command alters the drive mapping, so use it with care. Consider what would happen if you used the following command from the local C: drive prompt:

```
C:\> CD SYS:COMMON\DATA
```

This would map your C drive to SYS:COMMON\DATA. You would then lose access to your C: drive. You can regain access to the local drive C: with the following command:

```
MAP DEL C:
```

You would have a similar problem for a network driver as shown next. Consider the situation when Z: is mapped as a second drive to SYS:PUBLIC. Execute this command:

```
Z: CD\
```

You'll notice that you have lost your search drive mapping to SYS:PUBLIC. To recover, execute the command:

```
CD \PUBLIC
```

The MAP CHANGE Option

The MAP CHANGE option converts a search drive to a network drive.

Consider a network administrator who just installed an application in network drive J: that's mapped to NW4CS_SYS:APPS\WP. The network administrator now wants to test the application by placing it in the search drive. The administrator issues this command:

```
MAP CHANGE J:
```

The command also could be given in the abbreviated form, as follows:

```
MAP C J:
```

302

If the next available search drive is S10:, you should see the following displayed as a result of executing any of the previous MAP CHANGE commands:

```
S10: = J:.  [NW4CS_SYS: \]
```

If you want to remove the search drive and make it a regular drive, you can use the MAP CHANGE to toggle back to the network drive, as follows:

```
MAP C S10:
```

Throughout these operations, drive J: still is mapped to SYS:APPS\WP. Even when J: is mapped as a search drive, the association between J: and SYS:APPS\WP is maintained.

Using the MAP Command without Options

One of the most common forms of the MAP command is to use it by itself to display current drive mappings.

If the MAP command is issued without options, you see an output similar to the following:

```
F:\USERS\KSS> MAP
Drives A, B, C, D, E map to local disk
Drive F:= NW4CS_SYS:USERS\KSS
Drive G:= NW4CS_SYS:COMMON\DATA
_     Search Drives    _
S1:  = Z:.[NW4CS_SYS: \PUBLIC]
S2:  = Y:.[NW4CS_SYS: \]
S3:  = C:\BIN
S4:  = C:\WINDOWS
```

This MAP output shows that drives A, B, C, D, and E are assigned to local disks. Drive F is the next available network drive and is mapped to NW4CS_SYS:USERS\KSS, the user's home directory. Drive G is mapped to NW4CS_SYS:COMMON\DATA.

The search-drive mappings are listed separately. Search drives S1 and S2 are mapped to NW4CS_SYS:PUBLIC and NW4CS_SYS:\. Search drives S3 and S4 are mapped to C:\BIN and

303

C:\WINDOWS, respectively. The last two search drives are in the following DOS PATH environment variable before logging in to the network:

```
PATH=C:\BIN;C:\WINDOWS
```

The network search drive mapping assignments caused these search drives to be pushed down as search drives S3 and S4.

Network Drives

The best way to learn about network drive assignments is to experiment with them. This section gives you steps to follow to test drive mappings.

1. Log in as Admin or using a valid user account

2. Type the following command:

   MAP

   The MAP command by itself can be used for examining the current drive mappings. The output for this command appears something like that shown following (the details depend on the way your login script has been set up):

   ```
   Drives A, B, C, D, E map to local disk
   Drive F: = NW4CS_SYS:USERS\KSS
   Drive G: = NW4CS_SYS:COMMON\DATA
   _    Search Drives   _
   S1:  = Z:. [NW4CS_SYS: \PUBLIC]
   S2:  = Y:. [NW4CS_SYS: \]
   S3:  = C:\BIN
   S4:  = C:\WINDOWS
   ```

3. Issue a MAP command to map drive I: to SYS:PUBLIC, as follows:

   ```
   MAP I:=SYS:PUBLIC
   ```

   Verify that your mapping has been successful by issuing the MAP command.

4. Try to map to a directory that does not exist, as follows:

   ```
   MAP J:=SYS:DEVELOP
   ```

You should see a message saying that "Directory [SYS:DEVELOP] cannot be located."

5. Map to a directory for which you don't have access. To perform this step, you must create a directory called SYS:DEVELOP/BIN—using a Supervisor account—and then log in as a user who does not have Supervisor rights:

```
MAP J:=SYS:DEVELOP/BIN
```

If you don't have access permissions to this directory, you receive an error message indicating that the directory is not locatable.

If you understand NetWare file system rights (covered in the next chapter), you might want to perform the extra step of logging in as an Admin user. Assign Read and File Scan rights of SYS:DEVELOP to the user you're working with, and then try to map drive H: to the directory SYS:DEVELOP when logged in as a non-supervisor user:

```
MAP J:=SYS:DEVELOP/BIN
```

This time you should be able to perform the mapping successfully.

6. To delete the drive J: mapping, issue the following command:

```
MAP DEL J:
```

7. To map drive J: to the same directory I: is mapped to, issue the following command:

```
MAP J:=I:
```

Issue the MAP command to verify this mapping.

8. You don't have to use the NetWare network directory syntax of specifying the volume name to map to a network directory. Try mapping as follows:

```
MAP H:=F:\PUBLIC
```

The preceding command maps H: to the same volume to which F: is mapped, starting from the root and going down to the PUBLIC directory.

9. Experiment with search drives in the next few sections.

   Note the current search drives by typing the MAP command, as follows:

   ```
   MAP
   ```

   The MAP command displays current drive mappings and search-drive mappings. It might appear similar to the following:

   ```
   Drives A, B, C, D, E map to local disk
   Drive F: = NW4CS_SYS:USERS\KSS
   Drive G: = NW4CS_SYS:COMMON\DATA
   Drive H: = NW4CS_SYS:   \PUBLIC
   Drive I: = NW4CS_SYS:   \PUBLIC
   Drive J: = NW4CS_SYS:   \PUBLIC

   _    Search Drives    _
   S1:  = Z:. [NW4CS_SYS: \PUBLIC]
   S2:  = Y:. [NW4CS_SYS: \]
   S3:  = C:\BIN
   S4:  = C:\WINDOWS
   ```

   Notice that the MAP command displays the search drive mappings. In the previous search drive, 1 is mapped to NW4CS_SYS:\PUBLIC.

   Now, issue the DOS PATH command to display the current DOS search path, as follows:

   ```
   PATH
   ```

   You should see a response that appears similar to the following:

   ```
   PATH=Z:.;Y:.;C:\BIN;C:\WINDOWS
   ```

   Notice that the PATH command is consistent with the current search drive mappings.

10. Issue a command to insert SYS:DEVELOP/BIN as the first search drive, as follows:

    ```
    MAP INS S1:=SYS:DEVELOP/BIN
    ```

    Examine the changed drive mappings by typing the MAP command. Compare the search drive mappings with those in step 9.

Also, examine the DOS PATH environment variable by typing the PATH command, as follows:

```
PATH
```

The results of the PATH command appear similar to the following:

```
PATH=X:.;Z:.;Y:.;C:\BIN;C:\WINDOWS
```

Compare the DOS PATH environment variable with that in step 9. Notice that the DOS PATH environment variable has been modified to reflect the changed search driver mappings.

11. Delete the first search drive mapping, as follows:

```
MAP DEL S1:
```

Examine the new search drive mappings and the DOS PATH environment variable using the commands outlined in step 10. These should have the same values as in step 9.

12. Try deleting a drive that does not exist, as follows:

```
MAP DEL S16:
```

If the search drive S16 doesn't exist, trying to delete it produces an error message.

13. You can add a search drive at the very end. You probably have less than 16 search drive mappings for your current login session. If so, type this command:

```
MAP INS S16:=SYS:DEVELOP
```

Now, examine the search drive mappings by using the following NetWare command:

```
MAP
```

Notice that search drive 16 wasn't created. Instead, a search drive was created with a number one greater than the previous search drive. Using the MAP INS S16 command is a convenient trick to add search drives to the end of the current search drive list without having to know the number of the last search drive.

14. Use the MAP command on a local directory:

```
MAP INS S16:=C:\
```

Examine the new search drive mappings and the DOS PATH environment variable using the MAP and PATH commands. Notice that the directory C:\ is now in the search drive list and the DOS PATH environment variable.

If you do not have a hard drive, you can use floppy drive A:. If you have a diskless workstation, you cannot perform this part of the experiment.

15. Map the drive H: to SYS:PUBLIC by using the following command:

```
MAP H:=SYS:PUBLIC
```

Make H: the current drive and use the DOS change directory command to go up one level to the root SYS:, as follows:

```
H:
CD ..
```

Now issue the MAP command to find out the current search drive mappings.

Notice that the drive mapping of drive H: was changed by the CD command.

16. Repeat step 15 with a fake root MAP command.

Root map the drive H: to SYS:PUBLIC by using the following command:

```
MAP R H:=SYS:PUBLIC
```

Make sure H: is the current drive and issue the DOS CD command to go up one level to the root SYS:, as shown here:

```
H:
CD ..
```

Now, issue the MAP command to find out the current search drive mappings. Notice that, unlike the situation in step 15, the change directory command was not able to go above the fake root.

17. If you inadvertently wipe out the DOS PATH environment variable, the search drives are not effective.

    Try the following command to delete the DOS PATH:

    ```
    F:
    CD \
    SET PATH=
    ```

    Now type the MAP command. Unless your current directory is SYS:PUBLIC where the MAP command is kept, you see the following message:

    ```
    Bad command or file name
    ```

    Change to the SYS:PUBLIC directory where the MAP.EXE (command program file) is kept by typing the following command:

    ```
    CD \PUBLIC
    ```

    Now, type the MAP command. You should see that the search drive mappings have also been wiped out.

One trick is that MAP <drive> := will pick up the current working directory and make that a mapped drive.

NDS Syntax with MAP Commands

Because the Volume object is an NDS object, the NDS syntax can be used to refer to the Volume object, regardless of the current context of the user. Figure 3.32 shows an NDS tree for Organization ESL, where the current context is OU=OPS.OU=SALES.O=ESL. The Volume objects CORP_SYS and ENG_VOL are in the contexts OU=CORP.O=ESL and OU=ENGINEERING.O=ESL, respectively.

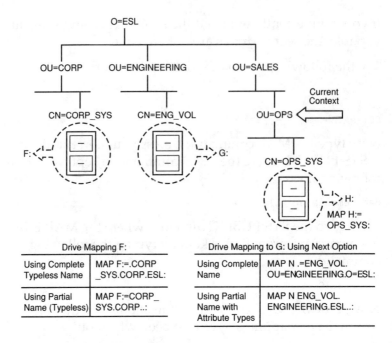

Figure 3.32

Assigning network drives to Volume objects in an NDS tree.

Drive Mapping F:	
Using Complete Typeless Name	MAP F:=.CORP _SYS.CORP.ESL:
Using Partial Name (Typeless)	MAP F:=CORP_ SYS.CORP..:

Drive Mapping to G: Using Next Option	
Using Complete Name	MAP N .=ENG_VOL. OU=ENGINEERING.O=ESL:
Using Partial Name with Attribute Types	MAP N ENG_VOL. ENGINEERING.ESL..:

To create a drive mapping F: to the root of Volume object CORP_SYS, you can use either of the following commands:

```
MAP F: = .CORP_SYS.CORP.ESL:
```

or

```
MAP F: = CORP_SYS.CORP..:
```

The first version of the MAP command uses a typeless complete name to refer to the Volume object. The second version uses a partial name (relative to the current context OU=OPS.OU=SALES.O=ESL) to refer to the Volume object.

You may be asked questions on which MAP command is legal, given a scenario of a volume with a file system directory structure in an NDS tree.

To map the next available drive (G:) to ENG_SYS using the NEXT option, you can use either of the following commands:

```
MAP N .CN=ENG_VOL.OU=ENGINEERING.O=ESL:
```

or

```
MAP N  ENG_VOL.ENGINEERING.ESL..:
```

The first command uses a complete name with attribute type designators (CN, OU, O) to refer to the Volume object. The second command uses a partial name (relative to the current context OU=OPS.OU=SALES.O=ESL) to refer to the Volume object.

Finally, to map H drive to the OPS_SYS volume, you can use any of the following MAP commands:

```
MAP H: = .OPS_SYS.SALES.ESL:
```

or

```
MAP H: = OPS_SYS:
```

or

```
MAP H: = CN=OPS_SYS:
```

The first command uses a typeless complete name to refer to the Volume object. The second command uses a partial name (relative to the current context OU=OPS.OU=SALES.O=ESL) to refer to the Volume object. Because the Volume object is in the current context, notice you can refer to the Volume object by its common name. The third example of the MAP command is also a partial name, but uses attribute type CN to name the Volume object.

The simplest syntax for referring to a Volume object in a MAP statement is if the Volume object is in the current context. If users need frequent access to a Volume object in another context, consider defining an alias to that Volume object in the current context. The users can refer to the volume using a simplified NDS name.

Directory Map Objects

If a Volume object is moved to another location in the NDS tree or renamed (see fig. 3.33), all batch files and login scripts that refer to the old volume position have to be changed. In figure 3.33, the Volume object ENG_VOL is moved from the context OU=ENGINEERING.O=ESL to OU=CORP.O=ESL. Prior to moving the object, the drive K: was mapped to the PUBLIC directory of the ENG_VOL using the NDS path name for the Volume object, as follows:

```
MAP K: = .ENG_VOL.ENGINEERING.ESL: PUBLIC
```

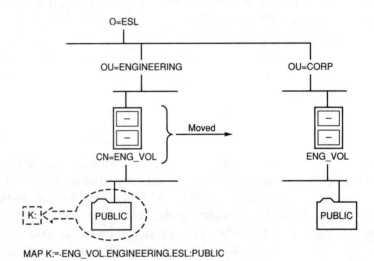

MAP K:=.ENG_VOL.ENGINEERING.ESL:PUBLIC

After the relocation of the Volume object name, the previous drive mapping K: is no longer valid. To map drive K: to the PUBLIC directory using the NDS path name, the new drive mapping should be:

```
MAP K: = .ENG_VOL.CORP.ESL: PUBLIC
```

To avoid the kind of problems mentioned previously, you need to be able to create a drive mapping that's independent of the position of the Volume object. This can be done using a Directory Map object.

The *Directory Map object* provides location-independent mapping. This object contains a volume/directory path (see fig. 3.34). Figure

3.35 shows a Directory Map object in the context OU=ENGINEERING.O=ESL. The Directory Map object refers to the PUBLIC directory in the ENG_VOL. To map a drive to the PUBLIC directory using the Directory Map object, issue the following command:

```
MAP K: = ENG_PUBLIC
```

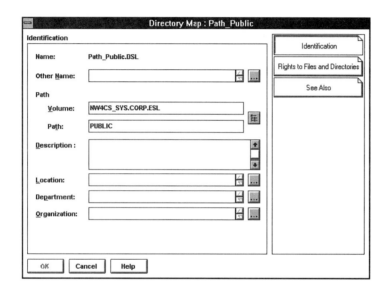

Figure 3.34

Directory Map object properties.

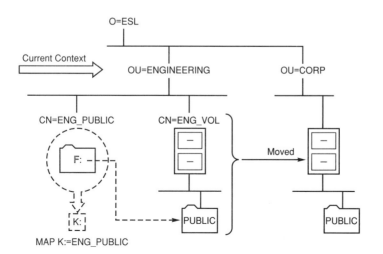

Figure 3.35

Location-independent mapping using Directory Map object.

313

If the ENG_VOL Volume object is moved to the context OU=CORP.O=ESL, the volume/directory path property of the Directory Map object ENG_PUBLIC must be changed, but the mapping to PUBLIC directory does not change.

 The Directory Map object can be used to provide location-independent mapping.

Figures 3.36 and 3.37 show further examples of the use of Directory Map objects.

Figure 3.36

Network drive mappings to directories on different volumes.

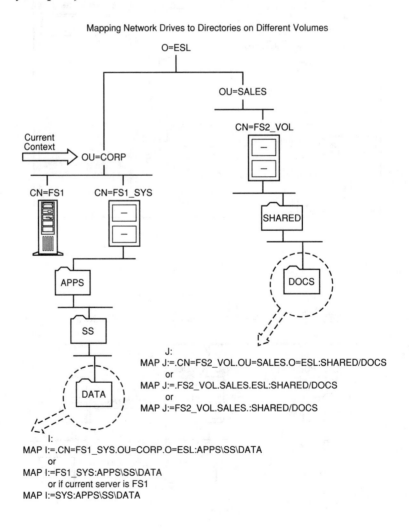

Mapping Network Drives to Directories on Different Volumes

O=ESL

OU=SALES

CN=FS2_VOL

Current Context

OU=CORP

CN=FS1   CN=FS1_SYS

SHARED

APPS

DOCS

SS

J:
MAP J:=.CN=FS2_VOL.OU=SALES.O=ESL:SHARED/DOCS
or
MAP J:=.FS2_VOL.SALES.ESL:SHARED/DOCS
or
MAP J:=FS2_VOL.SALES.:SHARED/DOCS

DATA

I:
MAP I:=.CN=FS1_SYS.OU=CORP.O=ESL:APPS\SS\DATA
or
MAP I:=FS1_SYS:APPS\SS\DATA
or if current server is FS1
MAP I:=SYS:APPS\SS\DATA

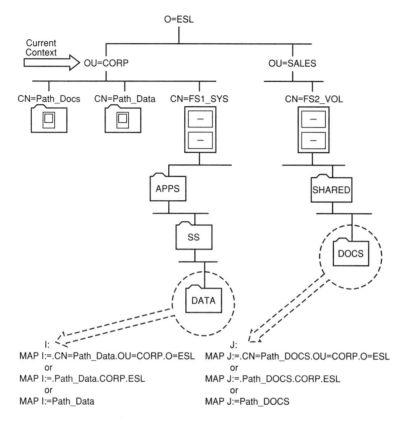

Figure 3.37

Network drive mappings using Directory Map objects.

Figure 3.36 shows Directory Mappings to different Volume objects. Assume that the current context in the NDS tree is OU=CORP.O=ESL. A drive mapping of I: to the APPS\SS\DATA directory for the Volume object FS1_SYS can be written in any of the following forms:

```
MAP I: = .CN=FS1_SYS.OU=CORP.O=ESL:APPS\SS\DATA
```

or

```
MAP I: = ESL_SYS:APPS\SS\DATA
```

or

```
MAP I: = SYS:APPS\SS\DATA
```

The first version of the MAP command uses a complete name for the Volume object with attribute type designators (CN, OU, O).

315

The second version refers to the partial name of the Volume object, and because the Volume object is in the current context, the common name of the Volume object can be used. The third version uses the physical name of the Volume object and can be used if the user initially connects to the file server FS1.

In the tree branch under the container OU=SALES, a drive mapping of J: to the SHARED\DOCS directory for the Volume object FS2_VOL can be written in any of the following forms:

```
MAP J: = .CN=FS2_VOL.OU=SALES.O=ESL:SHARED/DOCS
```

or

```
MAP J: = .FS2_VOL.SALES.ESL:SHARED/DOCS
```

or

```
MAP J: = FS2_VOL.SALES.:SHARED/DOCS
```

The first form of the MAP command uses a complete name for the Volume object with attribute type designators (CN, OU, O). The second form refers to the typeless complete name of the Volume object. The third form uses the partial name of the Volume object (relative to the current context OU=CORP.O=ESL).

The mappings shown in figure 3.36 can be simplified using Directory Map objects, as shown in figure 3.37. In figure 3.37, two Directory Map objects, CN=Path_Docs and CN=Path_Data, are created. The Directory Map object CN=Path_Docs contains a mapping to the SHARED\DOC directory for Volume object CN=FS2_VOL.OU=SALES.O=ESL, and the Directory Map object Path_Data contains a mapping to the APPS\SS\DATA directory for Volume object CN=FS1_SYS.OU=CORP.O=ESL. The drive mappings of I: and J: in the example in figure 3.36 can now be expressed in terms of the Directory Map objects, as follows:

```
MAP I: = .CN=Path_Data.OU=CORP.O=ESL
```

or

```
MAP I: = .Path_Data.CORP.ESL
```

or

```
MAP I: = Path_Data
```

The first form of the MAP command uses the complete name with attribute types (CN, OU, O) for the Directory Map object. The second form uses a typeless complete name, and the third form uses a partial name for the Directory Map object. Because the Directory Map object is in the current context, the common name of the Directory Map object can be used for the partial name.

The drive mappings for J:, using directory name object, are as follows:

```
MAP J: = .CN=Path_Docs.OU=CORP.O=ESL
```

or

```
MAP J: = .Path_Docs.CORP.ESL
```

or

```
MAP J: = Path_Docs
```

The first form of the MAP command uses complete name with attribute types (CN, OU, O) for the Directory Map object. The first form of the MAP command uses the typeless complete name of the Directory Map object. The third form uses a partial name for the Directory Map object. Because the Directory Map object is in the current context, the common name of the Directory Map object can be used for the partial name.

Creating a Directory Map Object

To create a Directory Map object using the NetWare Administrator, perform the following steps:

1. Start NetWare Administrator while logged in as an Admin user.

2. Highlight the container where you want to create the Directory Map object.

3. Right-click the mouse button and select **Create**.

4. Select the entry for Directory Map, and select OK.

5. You should see a panel for creating a Directory Map object (see fig. 3.38).

317

6. Enter the Directory Map object name in the field Directory Map <u>N</u>ame.

7. Enter the volume name and path in the <u>V</u>olume and <u>P</u>ath fields.

You can select the Browse icon, next to the volume and path, to graphically locate the Volume object and the directory you want the Directory Map object to point to.

 You may be asked to use a simulated version of NWADMIN to create a Directory Map object.

Figure 3.38

The Create Directory Map object panel.

Utilities Needed for Directory Management Tasks

NetWare provides a number of utilities needed for directory management tasks. Some of the same tasks can be performed by a number of utilities. Tables 3.5 and 3.6 summarize the directory and file management tasks and NetWare utilities that can be performed by them.

Table 3.5
Directory Management Tasks

Tasks	NetWare Utilities
Move a directory structure	NetWare Administrator, FILER
Remove a directory and subdirectories	NetWare Administrator, FILER
Remove multiple subdirectories simultaneously	NetWare Administrator, FILER
Delete only contents of a directory	NetWare Administrator, FILER
Create a directory	NetWare Administrator, FILER
Modify directory information such as creation date, last access date, owner, and attributes	NetWare Administrator, FILER
View directory information such as creation date, last access date, owner, and attributes	NetWare Administrator, FILER, NDIR
Rename a directory	NetWare Administrator, FILER, RENDIR
Copy a directory structure while maintaining NetWare attributes	NetWare Administrator, FILER, NCOPY

If you are using NWADMIN or FILER to move directories or files from one volume to another, the rights will not be transferred.

Table 3.6
File-Management Tasks

Tasks	NetWare Utilities
Modify file information such as creation date, last access date, owner, and attributes	NetWare Administrator, FILER
View file information such as creation date, last access date, owner, and attributes	NetWare Administrator, FILER, NDIR
Copy files while maintaining NetWare attributes	NetWare Administrator, FILER
Copy files	NetWare Administrator, FILER, NCOPY
Salvage/Purge deleted files	NetWare Administrator, FILER
Set a file or directory to purge upon deletion	NetWare Administrator, FILER

Salvaging and Purging Files

Files that have been deleted can be salvaged at any time. NetWare keeps a record of the salvageable files in the SYS:DELETED.SAV directory.

The following steps show how salvage/purge operations can be performed using the NetWare Administrator:

1. Double-click on Volume object from within NetWare Administrator.

2. Highlight the directory on which salvage operations are to be done.

3. Select the Tools menu of the NetWare Administrator.

4. Select Salvage.

5. Select the List button. You should see a list of files that can be salvaged (see fig. 3.39).

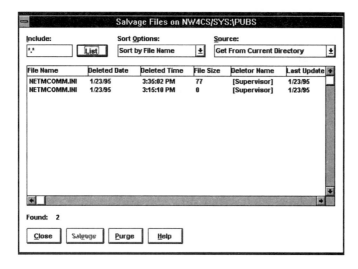

Figure 3.39

Salvage options in NetWare Administrator.

6. If you want to salvage a file, highlight the file and select the Salvage button.

7. If you want to purge a file, highlight the file and select the Purge button.

8. Press the Close button when done.

Files that are deleted are saved until the user deliberately purges them, or until the NetWare server runs out of unused disk blocks on the volume. If the NetWare server runs out of unused disk blocks before the files are explicitly purged, NetWare deletes the files on first-in, first-out basis.

If you have confidential files, you should purge them after deleting them. You can do this using the NetWare Administrator FILER utility. When you purge deleted files, only the files that you own are removed from the system—unless you have Supervisor file system rights.

321

Salvage and Purge operations can be performed using the NetWare Administrator or the FILER utilities. The salvageable files are kept in the SYS:DELETED.SAV directory.

For security and space-saving reasons, you might want to purge certain files as soon as they're deleted. You can have NetWare perform this operation for you automatically if you flag the file or directory with the purge attribute. If a directory is flagged with a purge attribute, any file deleted from that directory is immediately purged. You can set the Purge NetWare attribute on files or directories using the NetWare Administrator, FILER, or the FLAG command.

 You can set the Purge NetWare attribute on files or directories using the NetWare Administrator, FILER, or the FLAG command.

Managing Volume Space Usage

NetWare 4 has several features for managing space on volumes. Management of volume space consists of the following tasks:

- ◆ Display volume space information
- ◆ Locate a file by its access date, owner and size
- ◆ Restrict volume space usage
- ◆ Change file and directory ownership
- ◆ Set file compression attributes
- ◆ Set file migration attributes

Display Volume Information

You can display volume space information using the following:

◆ NDIR /VOLUME

◆ NetWare Administrator

Figure 3.20 (discussed earlier in the chapter) shows the output of the NDIR /VOLUME command. This command displays total volume space, space used by directory entries, space remaining on volume, space available to user running the NDIR /VOLUME command, maximum directory entries, available directory entries, and amount of space saved because of compression.

The same information can also be viewed in a more graphical form using the NetWare Administrator. The following is an outline of using the NetWare Administrator to view volume information:

1. Right-click on the Volume object from the NetWare Administrator.

2. Select Details.

3. Select Statistics page button. You should see a screen similar to the following (see fig. 3.40).

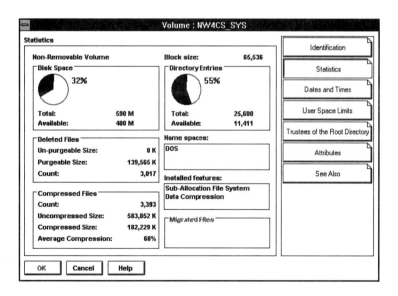

Figure 3.40

The Volume statistics screen.

Locate a File by Its Access Date, Owner, and Size

When you're running out of disk space, it's helpful to have a report of the files on a volume by their access date, owner, and size. You can use the NDIR command with different options to generate this report. The NDIR command was discussed earlier in this chapter, so only the commands for performing specific tasks are listed here.

To list files not used after some time, use the following command:

```
NDIR *.* /ACCESS BEF date /S
```

Replace *date* with a date, such as 10-1-94.

To list files owned by a specific user, use the following command:

```
NDIR *.* /OWNER=name  /S
```

Replace *name* with the user name.

To list files by largest file size first, use the following command:

```
NDIR *.* /REV SORT SIZE /S
```

To list files larger than a specific size, use the following command:

```
NDIR *.* /SIZE GR bytesize
```

Replace *bytesize* with the number representing the size of the file in bytes.

Restrict Volume Space Usage

NetWare provides you with the ability to manage volume disk space by user or by directory. User space restrictions must be set independently—one each volume. You can use the NetWare Administrator or NETADMIN to restrict disk space for users. Volume objects have a User Space Limits property. This is a multi-valued property to which you can add a user's name and the amount of space he is permitted for that volume.

Figures 3.41 and 3.42 show the User Space Limits property for a Volume object using the NetWare Administrator or NETADMIN. The screens show that users Guest, HACKER, and Jan have restricted space on the volume, and all other users do not have space restrictions.

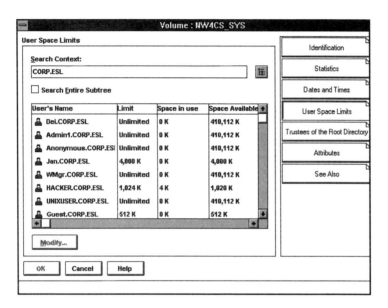

Figure 3.41

Viewing User Space Limits setting using NetWare Administrator.

Figure 3.42

Viewing User Space Limits setting using NETADMIN.

 You can limit the amount of space for a user on a per volume basis using:

◆ NetWare Administrator

◆ NETADMIN

You can use the NetWare Administrator or FILER to restrict disk space for a specific directory. This means that the space used by files in the specified directory cannot exceed a certain value. Directories have a Restrict Size property that can be accessed from the Facts page button using the NetWare Administrator.

325

Figure 3.43 shows the Restrict Size property for a directory using the NetWare Administrator. This figure shows that the directory ETC is restricted to a space of 6400 KB with 6272 KB of space available to it. Figure 3.44 shows the same information using the FILER utility.

Figure 3.43

Restrict Size property for a directory using NetWare Administrator.

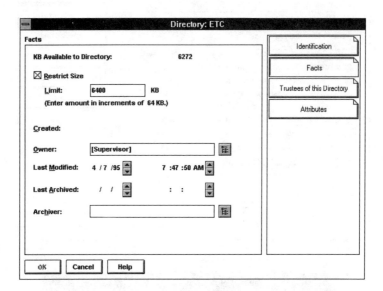

 You can limit the amount of space in a directory using:

◆ NetWare Administrator

◆ FILER

Change File and Directory Ownership

The amount of space a user has is calculated based on the owner-ship property of files and directories. The user who creates a file or directory becomes the owner. If a user is responsible for copy-ing a large number of files or directories to a volume, that user automatically becomes the owner of the files that are copied. If you do not want the disk space charge to accrue to the user, you must change the ownership of these files. You can change the ownership of a file using NetWare Administrator.

Figure 3.44 shows that there's a Browse icon next to the Ownership property. You can use this to change the ownership of a directory or file.

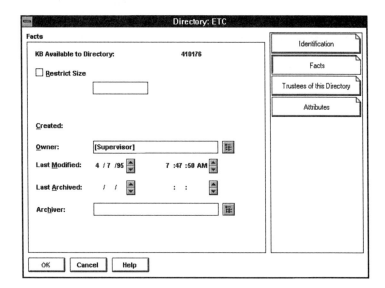

Figure 3.44

Ownership property of a directory/file.

Set File Compression Attributes

You can conserve disk space by enabling file compression. File compression is enabled when the volume is created during the server installation. Once enabled for a volume, file compression cannot be permanently disabled unless you re-create the volume.

Whether a file is to be compressed is determined by a number of factors. Files and directories have a number of special attributes that determine the file's compression. For example, if the file is marked with the Immediate Compress (Ic) attribute, the file is compressed immediately. After the compression, the Immediate Compress attribute is reset. You can also set the Don't Compress (Dc) attribute to inform NetWare not to compress a file. The Immediate Compress and Don't Compress attributes apply to files and directories. Another attribute, called the Compress (Co) attribute applies to files only. The Compress attribute indicates whether a file has been compressed, and is a status attribute only.

If the flags do not prohibit compression, the file is compressed—if it hasn't been accessed for a specified time or controlled by a SET parameter that is set on the NetWare server console (SET DAYS UNTOUCHED BEFORE COMPRESSION). The disposition of a file after it's decompressed upon access is determined by a server console SET parameter (SET CONVERT COMPRESSED TO UNCOMPRESSED OPTION). The compression start and stop times are also controllable through SET parameters (SET COMPRESSION DAILY CHECK STARTING HOUR, SET COMPRESSION DAILY CHECK STOP HOUR).

You can also determine if there should be a minimum percentage gain in compression for the compression to take place (SET MINIMUM COMPRESSION PERCENTAGE GAIN). The default for minimum compression percentage gain is 2 percent. You can also control the percentage of disk space on a volume that is required to be free in order for file decompression to permanently change the compressed file to the uncompressed state (SET DECOMPRESS PERCENT DISK SPACE FREE TO ALLOW). This can be used to prevent newly decompressed files from entirely filling up the volume. The time interval between displaying warning alerts—when the file system is not permanently changing compressed files to decompressed files due to insufficient disk free space—is also controllable (SET DECOMPRESS FREE SPACE WARNING INTERVAL).

The file compression attributes for files and directories can be changed using the NetWare Administrator and FILER.

Set File Migration Attributes

Data migration can be used to transfer inactive files to a near-line storage, with the files still appearing as part of the volume storage. Popular implementation of the near-line storage are optical juke boxes. Data migration can be used in conjunction with previously mentioned techniques to manage space on volumes.

Data Migration is a function of the High Capacity Storage System (HCSS). If HCSS is installed, data migration statistics can be displayed using NetWare Administrator, FILER, and NDIR.

The Don't Migrate (Dm) attribute can be set for files and directories. This attribute can be used to prevent files and directories from being migrated. Another attribute, Migrate (M), applies to files only and is a status attribute that indicates whether a specific file has been migrated.

Chapter Study Guide

If you're preparing for the NetWare 4.x Administration exams, review the chapter with the following goals in mind:

1. Understand the NetWare file-system Organization.

2. Pay particular attention to default directory name structures and their meanings, and the different types of MAP commands.

3. After studying this chapter, attempt the sample test questions that follow. If you miss an answer, review the appropriate topic until you understand the reason for the correct answer.

Chapter Summary

This chapter discussed NetWare volumes and directories concepts. You learned about the default NetWare file system structure and how to manage the NetWare file system using tools that come with the NetWare 4.x operating system. You also learned about the NetWare file-system Organization and how to access NetWare directories using the different options of the MAP command.

Chapter Test Questions

The following questions can have one correct answer or multiple correct answers. Where a single answer is correct, they are indicated by a ○ notation that precedes the possible answers. If more than one answer is correct, they are preceded by a □. Some questions are presented in different ways, so that you can recognize them even when the wording is different. Practice quizzes not only test your knowledge, they give you confidence when you take your exam.

1. Benefits of NetWare file storage include _____.

   □ A. sharing of data

   □ B. printer sharing

   □ C. access to file storage resources on the network

   □ D. directory replication

2. The default name space support for the NetWare file system is _____.

   ○ A. Unix

   ○ B. NFS

   ○ C. DOS

   ○ D. OS/2

   ○ E. Macintosh

3. NetWare 4.x includes client support for _____.

   □ A. DOS

   □ B. DOS/MS Windows

   □ C. VMS

   □ D. OS/2

   □ E. IBM's MVS

4. NetWare 4.x volumes _____.

☐ A. are a logical division of the space available on a server's disk or another storage volume such as a CD-ROM

☐ B. are stored on DOS partition space

☐ C. represent the highest level division of the NetWare file system

☐ D. are limited to a size of 64 GB

5. Which of the following statements about NetWare 4.x volumes are true?

☐ A. NetWare volumes are limited to a size of 32 TB

☐ B. NetWare volumes are stored on DOS partition space

☐ C. NetWare volumes represent the highest level division of the NetWare file system

☐ D. NetWare volumes can support DOS, OS/2, and Macintosh name spaces only

6. A NetWare volume can have a maximum size of _____.

○ A. 32 GB

○ B. 64 GB

○ C. 256 GB

○ D. 32 TB

○ E. 64 TB

7. A NetWare volume can have a maximum of _____ volume segments.

○ A. 16

○ B. 32

○ C. 48

○ D. 64

○ E. 128

331

8. What is the three-letter physical name of the first volume of a NetWare server.

9. Which of these are *not* legal physical volume names?

   ☐ A. X:

   ☐ B. CD:

   ☐ C. NETWARE_40:

   ☐ D. LONG_VOLUME_CD:

   ☐ E. MY VOLUME:

10. Given the following NDS tree that shows a file directory PUBLIC/BIN in the Volume object FSC_SYS in context OU=CORP.O=SCS, which of these are valid file directory names, assuming that the current context is OU=SALES.O=SCS.

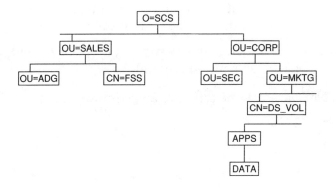

   ☐ A. CN=CORP.O=ESL:PUBLIC\BIN

   ☐ B. FSC_SYS.CORP.:PUBLIC/BIN

   ☐ C. FSC_SYS.CORP..:PUBLIC\BIN

   ☐ D. .FSC_SYS.CORP.SCS:PUBLIC/BIN

   ☐ E. FSC_SYS:PUBLIC/BIN

   ☐ F. .CN=FSC_SYS.OU=CORP.O=SCS:PUBLIC/BIN

11. Given the following NDS tree that shows a directory APPS/ DATA in the Volume object DS_VOL in context OU–MKTG.OU=CORP.O=SCS, which of these are valid file directory names, assuming that the current context is OU=ADG.OU=SALES.O=SCS?

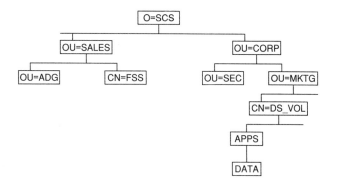

☐ A. CN=DS_VOL.OU=MKTG.OU=CORP:APPS\DATA

☐ B. DS_VOL.MKTG.CORP:APPS/DATA

☐ C. DS_VOL.MKTG.CORP.:APPS\DATA

☐ D. DS_VOL.MKTG.CORP..:APPS\DATA

☐ E. .DS_VOL.MKTG.CORP.SCS:APPS/DATA

☐ F. .CN=DS_VOL.OU=MKTG.OU=CORP.O=SCS:APPS \DATA

12. Given the following NDS tree that shows a directory COMMON\CONFIG in the Volume object NW4CS_VA in context OU=LAB.OU=ENG.O=MICROCONN, which of these are valid file directory names—assuming that the current context is OU=LAB.OU=ENG.O=MICROCONN?

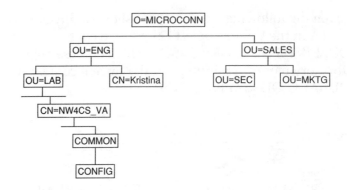

- [ ] A. CN=NW4CS_VA.OU=LAB.OU= ENG.O=MICROCONN: COMMON\CONFIG

- [ ] B. .NW4CS_VA.LAB.ENG.MICROCONN :COMMON\CONFIG

- [ ] C. NW4CS_VA.LAB.ENG.MICROCONN. :COMMON\CONFIG

- [ ] D. NW4CS_VA.LAB.ENG.MICROCONN.. :COMMON\CONFIG

- [ ] E. NW4CS_VA:COMMON\CONFIG

13. Given the following NDS tree that shows a file directory PUBLIC/BIN in the Volume object FSC_SYS in context OU=CORP.O=SCS, which of these are valid file directory names, assuming that the current context is OU=CORP.O=SCS?

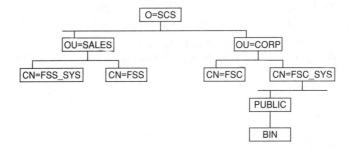

☐ A. CN=CORP.O=ESL:PUBLIC\BIN

☐ B. FSC_SYS.CORP.:PUBLIC/BIN

☐ C. FSC_SYS.CORP..:PUBLIC\BIN

☐ D. .FSC_SYS.CORP.SCS:PUBLIC/BIN

☐ E. FSC_SYS:PUBLIC/BIN

☐ F. .CN=FSC_SYS.OU=CORP.O=SCS:PUBLIC/BIN

14. Given the following NDS tree that shows a directory APPS/DATA in the Volume object DS_VOL in context OU=MKTG.OU=CORP.O=SCS, which of these are valid file directory names, assuming that the current context is OU=SEC.OU=CORP.O=SCS?

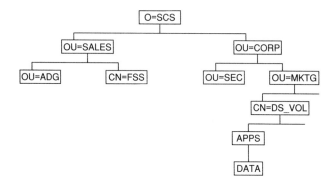

☐ A. CN=DS_VOL.OU=MKTG.OU=CORP:APPS\DATA

☐ B. DS_VOL.MKTG.CORP:APPS/DATA

☐ C. DS_VOL.MKTG.CORP.:APPS\DATA

☐ D. DS_VOL.MKTG.:APPS\DATA

☐ E. DS_VOL.MKTG.CORP..:APPS\DATA

☐ F. VOL.MKTG.CORP.SCS:APPS/DATA

☐ G. .CN=DS_VOL.OU=MKTG.OU=CORP.O=SCS:APPS\DATA

15. Given the following NDS tree that shows a directory COMMON\CONFIG in the Volume object NW4CS_VA in context OU=LAB.OU=ENG.O=MICROCONN, which of these are valid file directory names, assuming that the current context is OU=SEC.OU=SALES.O=MICROCONN?

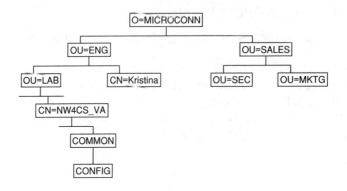

- ☐ A. .CN=NW4CS_VA.OU=LAB.OU= ENG.O=MICROCONN: COMMON\CONFIG

- ☐ B. CN=NW4CS_VA.OU=LAB.OU= ENG.O=MICROCONN: COMMON\CONFIG

- ☐ C. .NW4CS_VA.LAB.ENG.MICROCONN: COMMON\CONFIG

- ☐ D. NW4CS_VA.LAB.ENG.MICROCONN..: COMMON\CONFIG

- ☐ E. NW4CS_VA.LAB.ENG..:COMMON\CONFIG

- ☐ F. NW4CS_VA:COMMON\CONFIG

16. Which of the following are directories that are installed in the first volume of a NetWare 4.x server during server installation?

- ☐ A. PUBLIC

- ☐ B. USERS

- ☐ C. LOGIN

☐ D. APPS

☐ E. SYSTEM

☐ F. ETC

17. To list information on volumes in current context only, you can use _____.

○ A. NLIST VOLUME /S

○ B. NLIST VOLUME

○ C. NLIST /VOLUME

○ D. NLIST VOLUME /N

○ E. NLIST VOLUME /L

18. To list all Volume objects in the tree branch O=UE, you can use _____.

○ A. NLIST VOLUME O=UE /S

○ B. NLIST VOLUME /S /O=UE

○ C. NLIST VOLUME /S /D /O=UE

○ D. NLIST VOLUME /S /CO="O=UE"

○ E. NLIST VOLUME /S /CO "O=UE"

○ F. NLIST VOLUME /L

19. To show statistics on the current volume, you can use the _____ command.

○ A. NDIR /VOLUME

○ B. NDIR VOLUME

○ C. NDIR /STATISTICS

○ D. NDIR /D

20. To sort a directory listing of files by size, with the largest file first, use _____.

  ○ A. NDIR /FO /SORT LA

  ○ B. NDIR /FO /SORT SI

  ○ C. NDIR /FO /REV SORT SI

  ○ D. NDIR /REV SORT SI

21. To list all files in SYS:DATA directory that have a Read-Only attribute, use _____.

  ○ A. NDIR SYS:DATA*.* /Read-Only

  ○ B. NDIR SYS:DATA*.* =RO

  ○ C. NDIR SYS:DATA*.* /RO

  ○ D. NDIR SYS:DATA*.* /ATTR=RO

22. To display all files owned by user KSS on volume SYS:, use _____.

  ○ A. NDIR SYS:*.* /SUB /TRUSTEE EQ KSS

  ○ B. NDIR SYS:*.* /SUB = KSS

  ○ C. NDIR SYS:*.* /SUB /OW EQ KSS

  ○ D. NDIR SYS:*.* /SUB /O EQ KSS

23. To display all files not owned by Admin on volume SYS:, use _____.

  ○ A. NDIR SYS:*.* /SUB /OW NOT EQ Admin

  ○ B. NDIR SYS:*.* /SUB /NOT OW EQ Admin

  ○ C. NDIR SYS:*.* /SUB /TRUSTEE NOT EQ Admin

  ○ D. NDIR SYS:*.* /SUB != Admin

24. Which of the following utilities can be used to access and manage NetWare files?

  ☐ A. NETADMIN

  ☐ B. NWADMIN

☐ C. FILER

☐ D. UIMPORT

☐ E. DSPACE

25. The Directory Map object can be used to _____.

○ A. store directories mapped in the login script file

○ B. list files in the Directory Map object

○ C. provide location independent mapping to directories

○ D. provide location dependent mapping of directories

26. If the current context is O=IAF, which of these are valid names for referring to Volume object name for VOL1 on file server EMERALD in container OU=LAB under O=IAF?

☐ A. VOL1_EMERALD.LAB

☐ B. EMERALD_VOL1.LAB

☐ C. EMERALD_VOL1.LAB.IAF

☐ D. .EMERALD_VOL1.LAB.IAF

☐ E. .CN=EMERALD_VOL1.OU=LAB.O=IAF

☐ F. .VOL=EMERALD_VOL1.OU=LAB.O=IAF

27. Which directory contains files that can be salvaged?

○ A. SYS:SYSTEM/DELETED.DAT

○ B. SYS:DELETED.DAT

○ C. SYS:SYSTEM/DELETED.SAV

○ D. SYS:DELETED.SAV

28. Which command can be used to show information on Volume object?

○ A. NLIST /VOL

○ B. NLIST /VOLUME

   ○ C. NLIST VOL

   ○ D. NLIST VOLUME

29. Which of the following utilities can be used for accessing and managing files and directories?

   ☐ A. NWADMIN

   ☐ B. NETADMIN

   ☐ C. FILER

   ☐ D. NETUSER

   ☐ E. PCONSOLE

30. Given that you need to assign the first search drive to SYS:PUBLIC\UTILS and preserve any existing search drive mappings, you would use the following command:

   ○ A. MAP S1=SYS:PUBLIC\UTILS

   ○ B. MAP INS S1=SYS:PUBLIC\UTILS

   ○ C. MAP S1:=SYS:PUBLIC\UTILS

   ○ D. MAP INS S1:=SYS:PUBLIC\UTILS

31. Given that you need to assign the next network drive to PUBLIC\UTILS in Volume object FS2_SYS in the container OU=SALES.O=SCS, you would use the following command:

   ○ A. MAP N SALES.SCS:FS2_SYS/PUBLIC/UTILS

   ○ B. MAP NEXT SALES.SCS.FS2_SYS:PUBLIC/UTILS

   ○ C. MAP N .FS2_SYS.SALES.SCS/PUBLIC/UTILS

   ○ D. MAP N .FS2_SYS.SALES.SCS:PUBLIC/UTILS

32. The directory _____ contains programs and utilities for network supervisors.

   ○ A. SYS:SYSTEM

   ○ B. SYS:LOGIN

○ C. SYS:MAIL

○ D. SYS:PUBLIC

33. A shared data directory can be used for _____.

○ A. storing a user's login script files only

○ B. storing network applications

○ C. storing private files belonging to user

○ D. storing common files belonging to all users

34. A network drive usually refers to _____.

○ A. a directory on the local hard disk or floppy

○ B. a directory on the search path

○ C. a directory on a NetWare Volume object

○ D. a file on a NetWare server

35. Given that you need to assign the first search drive to SYS:PUBLIC\UTILS and preserve any existing search drive mappings, you would use the _____ command.

○ A. MAP S1=SYS:PUBLIC\UTILS

○ B. MAP INS S1=SYS:PUBLIC\UTILS

○ C. MAP S1:=SYS:PUBLIC\UTILS

○ D. MAP INS S1:=SYS:PUBLIC\UTILS

36. You wish to delete the drive mapping N: that is assigned to the directory path FS3/SYS:SHARED\COMMON. The command to perform this is _____.

○ A. MAP DEL N:=FS3/SYS:SHARED\COMMON

○ B. MAP DEL N:=

○ C. MAP DEL N:

○ D. MAP DEL N:\

37. To map the next available drive to SYS:LOGIN\LANFAN, you can use the _____ command.

   ○ A. MAP INS N:=SYS:LOGIN\LANFAN

   ○ B. MAP INS N:

   ○ C. MAP N:=SYS:LOGIN\LANFAN

   ○ D. MAP N SYS:LOGIN\LANFAN

38. The ROOT option of the MAP command is useful when you want to _____.

   ○ A. test the MAP command by faking its operation without performing the actual mapping

   ○ B. assign a fake drive to a network directory

   ○ C. install an application in a network subdirectory when the application expects to be installed in the root directory

   ○ D. install an application in the root directory of a network volume

39. The network drive G: is mapped to SYS:APPS/BIN. To make this a search drive, which of the following commands can be used?

   ○ A. MAP C INS S16:=G:

   ○ B. MAP CHANGE G:

   ○ C. MAP CHANGE SEARCH G:

   ○ D. MAP C SYS:APPS/BIN

4

CHAPTER

NetWare 4.x File System Security

This chapter teaches the concepts of NetWare file system security. This security system controls user access to data on the network. You can learn about file system concepts such as NetWare directory and file rights, directory and file trustees, inherited rights, and effective rights. You also can learn how to implement file system security using the NetWare administration tools.

Understanding Rights Access

After a user successfully logs in to the server, NetWare file system security controls access to directories and files on the server. Figure 4.1 shows the different layers of security through which a user needs to go before being granted rights to the NetWare file system. From this figure, you can see that NetWare security consists of the following three levels:

- ◆ Login authentication
- ◆ NetWare Directory Services security
- ◆ NetWare file system security

The focus of this chapter is on NetWare file system security.

Figure 4.1

NetWare layered security.

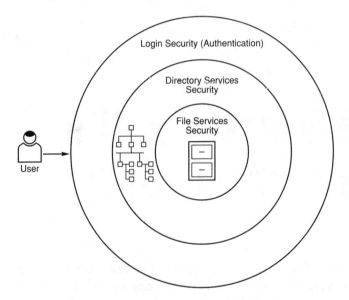

Assigning File System Rights

NetWare file system security is implemented by a NetWare administrator user who has the rights to implement file system security. The administrator grants access to the NetWare file system to users and other objects.

Figure 4.2 shows a user in the act of exercising rights to a directory. The user wants to read and write to files in a directory, but the NetWare NOS must determine whether the user has sufficient privileges to exercise these rights.

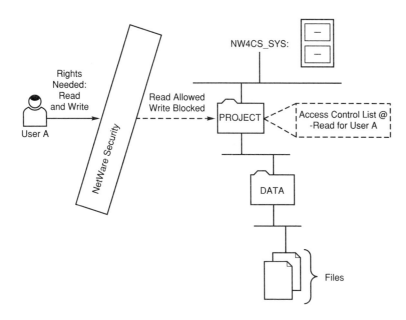

Figure 4.2

Exercising rights to a NetWare file system.

A user can be given trustee assignment explicitly. This means that the trustee assignment is assigned on an individual user basis. Figure 4.3 shows that a user is assigned explicit rights to a directory. Setting individual rights for a large number of users can be a very tedious process and difficult to maintain. Many users have similar needs to access directories and files on the server. Consider an example in which all engineers in the engineering department may need access to the same directories. To change an access right for all users becomes a time-consuming and repetitious task. To help with the management and administration of users with similar needs, NetWare uses the concept of groups.

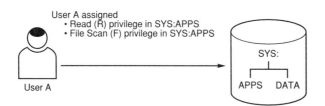

Figure 4.3

Assigning rights on a user basis.

A *group* is a collection of network users who have the same access privileges to directories and files on the server. All managers, for example, can be considered members of a group called MGRS. In Figure 4.4, group MGRS is implemented as a Group object in context O=SCS. The group MGRS can be given a trustee assignment in a manner similar to that for individual users; the difference being that all members of the group automatically inherit the trustee assignments for that group. If a user needs rights that group MGRS has, he or she can be made a member of the group MGRS. If a user no longer needs these rights, he or she can be removed as a member of group MGRS.

Figure 4.4

Assigning rights on a group basis.

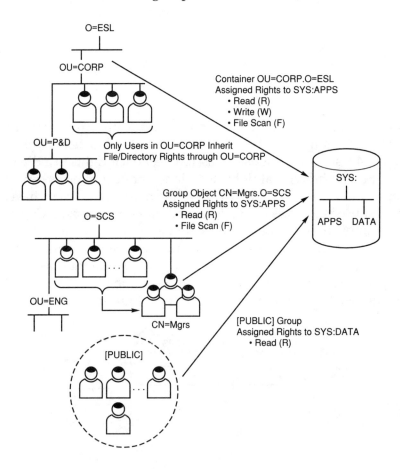

User objects can be members of more than one group. The total rights for a user is the sum of all the rights inherited by virtue of membership to all groups. If a user has Read and Write TA (trustee assignment) to directory SYS:COMMON/DATA because of membership in Group object ACCOUNTING, and Read, Create, and Erase TA to the same directory because of membership in group ENGINEERS, then the user has a TA of Read, Write, Create, Erase to SYS:COMMON/DATA. The user has, in other words, the sum of all rights by virtue of membership to groups ACCOUNTING and ENGINEERS.

If rights are to be assigned to a group of users, the preferred way is through containers or Group objects.

Container objects also can be used for assigning file and directory rights to users in that container (refer to figure 4.4). Containers in the NDS tree have "group" semantics because the members of a container object are the objects defined in that container. When a container is made a trustee of a file or directory, User objects in that container inherit the trustee rights.

Rights also can be assigned via a special group [Public]. [Public] is an implicit group. All users connected to the network are automatically members of group [Public]. If rights are granted through [Public], any user can gain access to directories and files for which [Public] is a trustee. The normal NetWare security mechanisms are bypassed. Unless there is a special reason for bypassing NetWare security, you should avoid granting file/directory rights through [Public]. In Chapter 5, "NetWare Directory Services Security," you are taught that the reason [Public] was created as an implicit group is to give certain default NDS rights to all connected users for an NDS tree.

NDS defines an Organizational Unit object. Users can be assigned members of the Organizational Unit object, and this Organizational Unit object can be made a trustee, in which case all members of the Organizational Unit object inherit the trustee rights. The Organizational Unit object provides a similar functionality as the NetWare Group object for assigning rights. The major difference between the Organizational Unit and the Group object is that the Organizational Unit object is formally defined in the X.500 standard from which NDS was derived. NetWare Group objects is a direct translation of the NetWare 3.x (and 2.x) group concept, and is specific to NetWare-based networks. You may want to use Organizational Role objects if you are interfacing with other X.500 systems.

Another way of assigning rights is through *security equivalence*, a property of the User object. That lists the users and groups through which a user gains rights.

NetWare 4.x has no default group objects such as group EVERY-ONE that existed for NetWare 3.x. If you are upgrading a NetWare 3.x server to a NetWare 4.x server, however, the Group object Everyone, which exists on the NetWare server, is created as an NDS Group object in the same context where the server that has been upgraded resides. An example of the Group object Everyone can be seen in figure 4.5. The server NW4CS in this figure was upgraded from a NetWare 3.x server.

Figure 4.5

Group Everyone in a NetWare 3.x upgraded server.

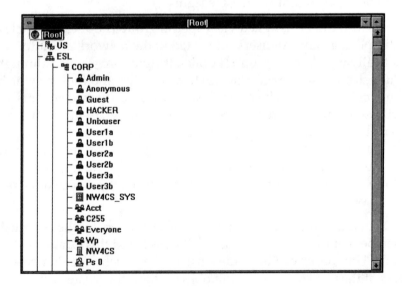

NetWare file system rights can be assigned to individual objects, container objects, and Group objects. Assigning rights on an individual basis can be done when you are dealing with special circumstances for that object. An example of this is assigning a user specific rights to a home directory. By default, when User objects and home directories are created, the User object is given all rights to the home directory. These rights are specific to the user and are granted on an individual basis.

Group objects and their membership can be defined using the NetWare Administrator or the NETADMIN utility. A Group object can have members only of object class user. A Group object cannot be a member of another Group object.

Because Group objects are a preferred way for assigning rights to a large group of users, Group object creation using the NetWare Administrator and NETADMIN are discussed next. The actual details of the meanings of the individual file system and trustee rights are discussed in the section "Understanding Directory Rights and File Rights."

Group objects used for assigning rights can be created using NETADMIN and NWADMIN.

Creating Group Objects Using NetWare Administrator

To create a Group object using the NetWare Administrator, perform the following steps:

1. Start NetWare Administrator while logged in as an Admin user.

2. Highlight the container where you want to create the Group object.

3. Right-click the mouse button and select Create.

4. Select the entry for "Group," and select OK. A panel for creating a Group object appears.

5. Enter the Group object name in the Group **N**ame field.

6. Check the box **D**efine Additional Properties, because you want to define members to this group.

7. Select the **C**reate button.

   The property dialog box for the newly created Group object appears (see fig. 4.6).

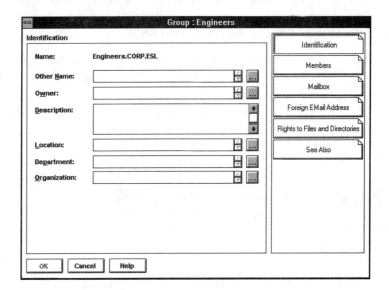

The property names in figure 4.6 describe the identification of the Group object. Except for the group name, all of these properties are optional. For documentation purposes, it is a good idea to fill out these group properties.

8. To assign members, select the page button "Members." The membership list for the group appears (see fig. 4.7). Because this is a newly created Group object, it has no members defined.

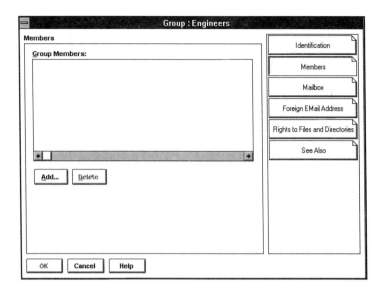

Figure 4.7

Group object
properties—Members.

9. Assign members by selecting the **A**dd button.

   The Select Object dialog box appears (see fig. 4.8). The right
   panel in this dialog box shows the NDS directory context,
   and the left panel shows the User objects in that context. Only
   User objects appear, because only users can be members of a
   Group object. If you want to select User objects in a different
   context as members of the Group object, you can use the up
   arrow in the directory context to move to the parent container or double-click on a container object to change directory context to that container. The current directory context is
   displayed in the dialog box.

10. Figure 4.8 shows several User objects in the context O=UNE.
    You can mark several User objects at once by clicking on each
    object while holding down the CTRL key. If the User objects
    that you want to select are in a group, you can mark the first
    User object by clicking on it; then move to the last object and
    click on it while holding down the Shift key.

Figure 4.8

The Select Object dialog box for adding users as members.

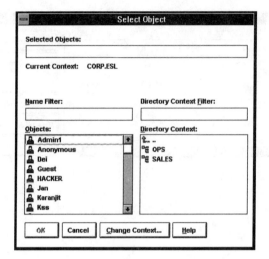

11. After selecting the User objects, select the OK button.

    You should see the selected User objects added as members to the group (see fig. 4.9).

Figure 4.9

Group object—added members.

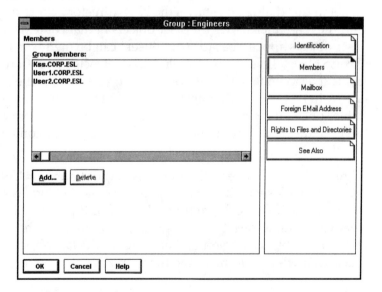

12. To add more User objects, select the **A**dd button. To delete members from this group, select the **D**elete button.

13. Now, group membership has been defined.

    To save your changes, select OK at the bottom of the Group object properties box.

    To assign rights to files and directories for this group, select the page button Rights to Files and Directories and go to the next step.

14. Figure 4.10 shows that there are currently no rights assigned to this Group object.

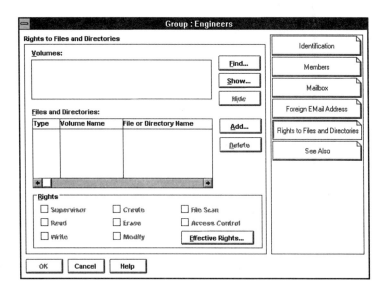

Figure 4.10

Assigning rights to Group objects.

To add rights to Group object, select **A**dd.

The Select Object dialog box appears.

The right panel in this dialog box shows the NDS directory context. The left panel shows the files and directories for selected Volume object. If no Volume objects are in this directory context, you can use the up arrow in the directory context to move to the parent container or double-click on a container object to change directory context to that container. The current directory context is displayed in the current context field.

15. After you select the Volume object, double-click on it to reveal the directories and files in the Volume object in the Directory Context panel. You then can select the file or directory to which the Group object should be assigned rights. Figure 4.11 shows that the ETC directory in Volume object NW4CS_SYS in the directory context OU=CORP.O=ESL was selected.

Figure 4.11

Select directory for assigning rights to Group objects.

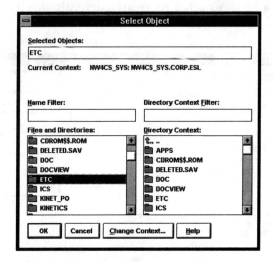

16. Select OK to accept the file or directory.

An entry for the selected directory to which rights can be assigned appears (see fig. 4.12). The list of possible rights is shown in the bottom of the dialog box. You can select the rights and press OK to save changes. The rights you selected are now the rights to the users belonging to the group "Engineers."

The explanation of the meaning of the individual rights is covered later in this chapter.

To see rights assigned for a Group object, select the Show button in figure 4.12 and the Volume object for which rights have been assigned.

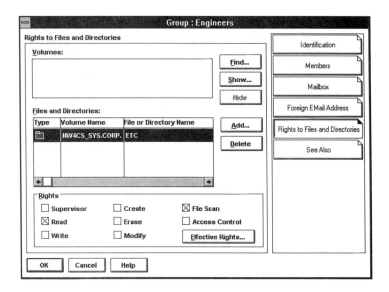

Figure 4.12

Directory to which rights are assigned for Group object.

Creating Group Objects Using NETADMIN

To create a Group object using NETADMIN, perform the following steps:

1. Start NETADMIN while logged in as an Admin user.

2. Select Change Context and the context in which you want to create the Group object. You can use the Ins key to browse through the NDS tree and select the context. After you select the context, press F10 to accept this as your context.

 The context changes made within NETADMIN (and any other Novell text-based utility) are for the duration of execution of this utility. When you quit the utility, the current context reverts to the context that existed before running these utilities.

3. Select Manage Objects.

A list of objects in the current context appears (see fig. 4.13).

Figure 4.13

Objects in selected context within NETADMIN.

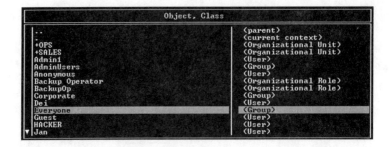

4. Press Ins to create the Group object.

   A list of object classes that can be created in the current context appears (see fig. 4.14).

Figure 4.14

Object classes that can be created in container.

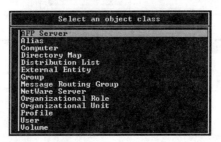

5. Select the Group object class.

6. Enter the new group name in the Create Group Object window.

   NETADMIN informs you that the Group object has been created, and also asks you if you want to create another Group object. You can create as many Group objects as you want. When you select "No" to stop creating Group objects, the newly created Group object is shown (see fig. 4.15). The newly created Group object in figure 4.15 is Consultants.

7. Highlight the newly created object, and press F10.

   A list of actions that you can perform on the newly created group appears (see fig. 4.16).

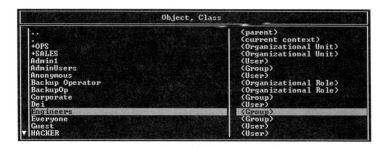

Figure 4.15

Newly created Group object in NETADMIN.

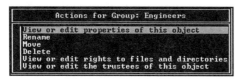

Figure 4.16

Actions on newly created Group object.

8. Select View or edit properties of this object.

   A list of properties grouped by Identification, Group members, and See also appears (see fig. 4.17).

Figure 4.17

View or Edit property option for Group object.

9. Select Group members.

   A list of members of this group appears. The list initially is empty for a newly created group.

10. Press Ins to add members to this group.

    A window asking you to enter a group member opens. Press Ins to browse directory contexts and select User objects as group members. To select a group of users in a directory context, use the F5 key to mark the User objects and press Enter.

    Figure 4.18 shows a number of users added to the newly created group.

Figure 4.18

Members added to
Group object.

11. Press F10 to accept the added group members. You are then prompted to Save Changes.

12. Press Esc to go back to the list of actions that you can perform on the newly created Group object.

    Now, group membership has been defined. To assign rights to files and directories for this group, select View or edit rights to files and directories.

13. A form for editing rights to files and/or directories appears (see fig. 4.19).

Figure 4.19

NETADMIN form for editing rights to files and/or directories.

For Volume object name, press Enter or Ins to enter the volume where the file or directory resides. Press Ins to browse and select the Volume object name, or type the NDS name of the Volume object and press Enter.

For Beginning path, press Enter or Ins to enter the file or directory path. Press Ins to browse and select the path, or type in the path name.

For Directories/Files, press Enter to select if you want to view directories, files, or both when you are making a trustee assignment.

For Trustee search depth, press Enter and select either Current Directory or All subdirectories for viewing files and directories in current directory only or in all subdirectories.

Figure 4.20 shows an example of a completed form.

Figure 4.20

Completed
NETADMIN form with
rights to files and/or
directories.

14. Press F10 to display the trustee list.

15. Press Ins to add a trustee list.

16. Select the directory or file to which a trustee should be added.

   The default rights for the directory or file appear (see fig 4.21).

Figure 4.21

Default rights for a
directory.

17. To change a default trustee right, highlight it and press Enter.

   A list of trustee rights that have been granted appears. To
   remove a right, highlight it and press Del. To add a right,
   press Ins to display the list of trustee rights that have not
   been granted. Select the rights you want to add and press
   Enter.

18 Use the F5 key to mark several rights. Use F10 to save your
   changes.

19. Use Esc or the shortcut key Alt+F10 to exit NETADMIN.

Understanding Directory Rights and File Rights

Table 4.1 shows the NetWare 4.x directory rights. NetWare 4.x
directory and file rights are the same as those in NetWare 3.x,
except that the NetWare 3.x Supervisory rights are called Supervisor rights in NetWare 4.x, and the NetWare 3.x term IRM (Inherited Rights Mask) is called IRF (Inherited Rights Filter) in
NetWare 4.x.

Table 4.1
NetWare Directory Trustee Rights

Name	Description
S*	*Supervisor* rights to all directory/ subdirectories/files
R	*Read* rights to open files in a directory, read contents, and execute
W	*Write* rights to open and write (modify) contents of files
C	*Create* rights to create files and subdirectories in a directory
E	*Erase* rights to delete a directory, its files, and its subdirectories
M	*Modify* rights to change directory and file attributes and rename
F	*File Scan* rights to view names of subdirectories and files
A	*Access Control* rights to other users, modify trustee rights, IRM

*NOTE: NetWare 2.2 does not have Supervisor rights; NetWare 3.x calls its relative equivalent *Supervisory* rights.

The Read and Write rights in table 4.1 permit the reading and writing of files in a directory. Both of these rights are needed to perform updates on files in a directory. Reading and writing also imply that the user has a right to open files in a directory, because the user cannot do a read or write without opening the files.

The Create and Erase rights are necessary for creating files and subdirectories and for removing them. The Modify rights can be used for the changing of file attributes. Without Modify rights, you cannot use NetWare commands such as FLAG to change file attributes.

The File Scan right allows a user to view names of files and subdirectories. If you do not want a user to see file names in a directory, you can remove the File Scan right. The user can execute DIR or NDIR (NetWare DIR command) but does not see the names of files in the directory. If you know the name of a file, however, you still can access it.

The Access Control rights allow other users to modify trustee rights and the IRF (Inherited Rights Filter). IRF is discussed a little later. This means that a user who has Access Control rights to a directory can use a NetWare utility like FILER to assign rights to other users for this directory. Access Control rights must be assigned with care to trusted users.

Table 4.2 shows file level rights for NetWare 4.x. In NetWare 4.x and 3.x, trustee assignment can be made at the file level. This is unlike NetWare 2.x where a trustee assignment can be made only at the directory level. NetWare 4.x and 3.x permit a finer level of control over files in a directory. The author's experience has been that in most situations, such a fine level of control is not needed, but that it is helpful to have it in situations that need this level of control. The trustee rights for files are similar to that for directories, except that the scope of these rights is limited to an individual file. The same symbols as the ones used for directory trustee rights are used. The Create right for a file means the right to salvage a file after it has been deleted. This is a little different from the Create right for a directory, which implies creating files and subdirectories in a directory.

Table 4.2

NetWare 4.x File Trustee Rights

Name	Description
S	*Supervisor* rights to all rights to the file
R	*Read* rights to open a file, read contents, and execute a program
W	*Write* rights to open and write (modify) contents of a file

continues

Table 4.2, Continued
NetWare 4.x File Trustee Rights

Name	Description
C	*Create* rights to salvage a file after the file has been deleted
E	*Erase* rights to delete a file
M	*Modify* rights to change a file's attributes and rename a file
F	*File Scan* rights to view the name of a file and its full path name
A	*Access Control* rights to modify file's trustee assignments and IRM

Trustee assignments can be controlled by four utilities: RIGHTS, FILER, NETADMIN, and NWADMIN. The NetWare 3.x GRANT, REVOKE, REMOVE, and ALLOW utilities are combined into the RIGHTS command-line utility. Another less familiar way of assigning a trustee assignment can be done using a batch utility for creating users called UIMPORT.

Understanding the Inherited Rights Filter

A directory or file has a maximum potential right that can control the effective rights a user can have for a directory (or file). Figure 4.23 illustrates this concept, where the individual components of the NetWare directory/file rights are Read, Write, Create, Erase, Modify, File Scan, and Access Control. In figure 4.22, a filter is shown to block out certain rights. In NetWare, the Inherited Rights Filter (IRF) acts like this filter. It can block out any right, except Supervisor rights.

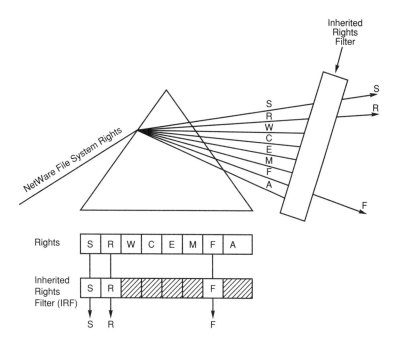

Figure 4.22

Inherited Rights Filter.

Whenever a new directory (or file) is created, the maximum potential rights it can have are all rights. That is, the Inherited Rights Filter is [SRWCEMFA] (the individual letters in the square brackets are the first letters of the individual rights). The IRF can be used to exercise control over the effective rights to a directory (or file).

The Inherited Rights Filter for files and directories can be modified by RIGHTS, FILER, NWADMIN, and NetAdmin.

Computing Effective Rights

A user may have rights assigned to a directory, but the IRF controls the actual or effective rights a user can exercise in a directory. Effective rights can be obtained from trustee assignment and Inherited Rights Filter by applying some rules of combination. These rules of combination are illustrated in figures 4.23 and 4.24 for directories and files.

Figure 4.23

Effective rights for directories.

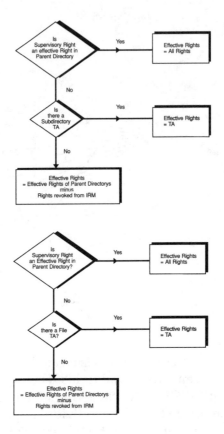

Figure 4.24

Effective rights for files.

At first glance, the rules of combination look a little complex, but after you study a few examples, you can begin to appreciate the logic in them. The examples that follow are for determining effective rights for directories. The user can construct similar examples for determining effective rights for a file based on the rules in figure 4.24.

Example 1: If no explicit trustee assignment has been granted to a subdirectory, the effective rights for the subdirectory are determined by the logical AND of the Inherited Rights Filter of a subdirectory and the parent directory's effective rights (see fig. 4.25).

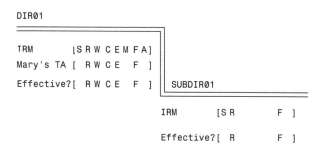

Figure 4.25

Assigning effective rights for a subdirectory.

The effective rights of subdirectory SUBDIR01 are the logical AND operation shown below:

```
Effective rights of parent DIR01  [    R W C E  F  ]
IRF for SUBDIR01                   [ S  R        F  ]
-------------------------------------------------------------
Effective rights for SUBDIR01      [    R        F  ]
```

Example 2: If an explicit trustee assignment has been granted to a subdirectory, the effective rights for the subdirectory are the same as the explicit trustee assignment, regardless of Inherited Rights Filter of the subdirectory (see fig. 4.26). In other words, an explicit TA overrides any IRF setting.

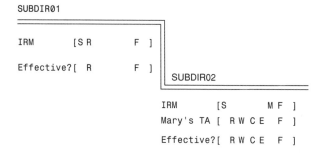

Figure 4.26

Explicit trustee assignment and effective rights for a subdirectory.

Effective rights to subdirectory SUBDIR02 follow:

```
IRF for SUBDIR02             [ S  R        M F  ]
TA for SUBDIR02             [    R W C E    F  ]
-------------------------------------------------------------
Effective rights for SUBDIR02   [    R W C E    F  ]
```

Example 3: If Supervisory rights are granted to the parent directory, the user has all rights for the subdirectories and files, regardless of a subdirectory's trustee assignment and Inherited Rights Filter (see fig. 4.27). Care must be exercised in assigning Supervisory rights.

Figure 4.27

Assigning Supervisory rights.

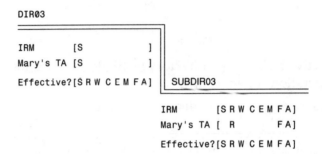

```
DIR03

IRM        [S              ]
Mary's TA  [S              ]
Effective?[S R W C E M F A]    SUBDIR03

                               IRM        [S R W C E M F A]
                               Mary's TA  [ R           F A]
                               Effective?[S R W C E M F A]
```

Author's Note

The rules of computing effective rights have been designed so that effective rights flow down subdirectories, and if no explicit TA is made, the effective rights are modified by the IRF. Whenever an explicit TA is made, a new set of effective rights flow down subdirectories. This is in contrast to pre-NetWare 2.2 versions where trustee assignments flow down subdirectories instead of effective rights. In these situations, unexpected rights can be inherited by users if new subdirectories are created. The Inherited Rights Filter concept and the rules of combination were introduced in NetWare 2.2 and NetWare 3.x to overcome these problems, except that the Inherited Rights Filter is called Inherited Rights Mask in NetWare 2.2 and 3.x.

The effective rights can be examined by the NetWare utility FILER or the command-line utility RIGHTS. You also can examine effective rights using NetWare Administrator (NWADMIN) and NETADMIN.

366

Using the RIGHTS Command

Examples of using the RIGHTS command follow:

```
RIGHTS
```

The output may resemble the following:

```
NW4CS\SYS:\PUBLIC
Your rights for this directory are: [SRWCEMFA]
Supervisor rights to directory.        (S)
Read from a file in a directory.       (R)
Write to a file in a directory.        (W)
Create subdirectories and files.       (C)
Erase directory and files.             (E)
Modify directory and files.            (M)
Scan for files and directories.        (F)
Change access control.                 (A)
```

The user has all rights to the SYS:PUBLIC directory. Because the command was issued while the user was logged in as user Admin, the results are as expected because the user Admin has all rights.

The general syntax for using RIGHTS is shown in figures 4.28 to 4.33.

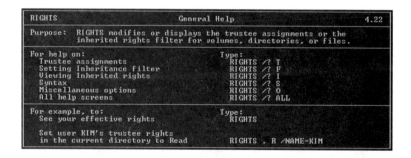

Figure 4.28

RIGHTS /? General Help Summary.

Figure 4.29

RIGHTS /? T
Summary.

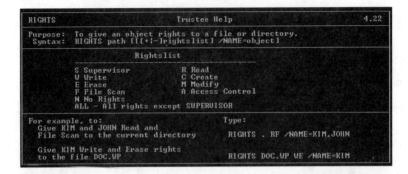

Figure 4.30

RIGHTS /? F
Summary.

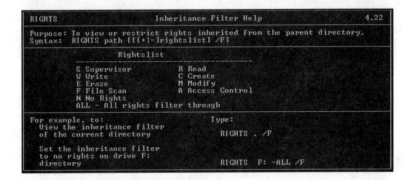

Figure 4.31

RIGHTS /? I
Summary.

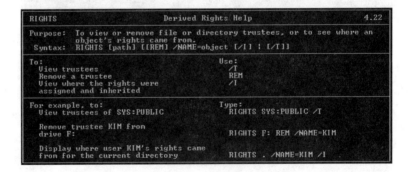

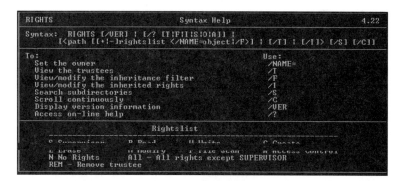

Figure 4.32

RIGHTS /? S
Summary.

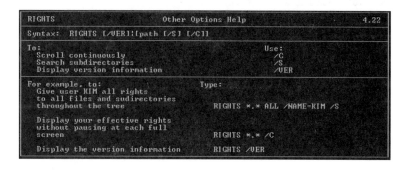

Figure 4.33

RIGHTS /? O
Summary.

The RIGHTS command enables you to:

◆ View and set the rights of a directory or file

◆ View trustee assignments to a specified directory

◆ See inherited rights

◆ View and set the Inherited Rights Filter

The examples that follow illustrate these actions.

Study RIGHTS usage in the examples that follow.

Viewing Rights to a Specific Directory

To view the rights for user KSS in SYS:USERS/KSS directory, use the following command:

```
F:\>RIGHTS SYS:USERS/KSS
NW4CS\SYS:USERS\KSS
```

The output is as follows:

```
Your rights for this directory are:   [ RWCE F ]
Read from a file in a directory.      (R)
Write to a file in a directory.       (W)
Create subdirectories and files.      (C)
Erase directory and files.            (E)
Scan for files and directories.       (F)
```

This command was issued by user KSS while logged in under his account.

Listing Trustees Using RIGHTS

You can use the /T option to see a list of trustees for a directory.

To view the trustee assignments for a specified directory, such as SYS:USERS/KSS, use the following command:

```
F:\> RIGHTS SYS:PUBLIC  /T
NW4CS\SYS:\PUBLIC
User trustees:
    CN=KSS.OU=CORP.O=SCS          [ R    F ]
- - - - - - - - - -
Group trustees:
    CN=Everyone.OU=CORP.O=ESL     [ R    F ]
- - - - - - - - - -
Other trustees:
    OU=CORP.O=ESL                 [ R    F ]
```

Note that group Everyone is not a predefined group under NetWare. It appears in the preceding example because the server was upgraded from NetWare 3.x to NetWare 4.x.

The output of the previous RIGHTS command shows that a User object, a Group object, and a container object have rights to NW4CS\SYS:\PUBLIC.

The User object CN=KSS.OU=CORP.O=SCS, the Group object CN=Everyone.OU=CORP.O=ESL, and the container object OU=CORP.O=ESL all have Read and File Scan rights to NW4CS\SYS:\PUBLIC.

Because the container object has Read and File Scan rights to NW4CS\SYS:\PUBLIC, all User objects in the container have Read and File scan rights to NW4CS\SYS:\PUBLIC.

The /T option lists all trustees that have been given an explicit trustee assignment to SYS:PUBLIC. While NWADMIN and NETADMIN also can display this information, using the previous RIGHTS command is simpler (and usually faster).

Granting and Revoking Rights Using the RIGHTS Command

You can use the /NAME= option to specify the NDS object that must be assigned rights to a file or directory.

The general syntax of RIGHTS using the /NAME= option is the following:

```
RIGHTS  directory_file_name  [+¦-]rights  /NAME=objectname
```

To set the rights for user KSS in SYS:USERS/KSS directory so that the user has all rights except Supervisor rights, the command is the following:

```
F:\> RIGHTS SYS:USERS/KSS   CRWEMFA /NAME=.KSS.CORP.SCS
NW4CS\SYS:USERS
Directories                                                 Rights
------------------------------------------------------- ----------
KSS                                                     [ RWCEMFA]
```

Rights for one directory were changed for .KSS.CORP.SCS.

To remove the Erase and Create rights for user KSS in SYS:USERS/KSS directory, use the following command:

```
F:\> RIGHTS SYS:USERS/KSS   -C-E   /NAME=.KSS.CORP.SCS
NW4CS\SYS:USERS
Directories                                                        Rights
----------------------------------------------------------------  ----------
KSS                                                               [ RW   MFA]
```

Rights for one directory were changed for .KSS.CORP.SCS.

 According to Novell documentation the command

```
RIGHTS SYS:USERS/KSS   -CE   /NAME=.KSS.CORP.SCS
```

should be the same as the command

```
RIGHTS SYS:USERS/KSS   -C-E   /NAME=.KSS.CORP.SCS
```

But, in version 4.01 of the RIGHTS command, the first RIGHT command only removes the Create right and not the Erase right.

Using the + option to add a right works correctly. The following two commands, therefore, have the same effect.

```
RIGHTS SYS:USERS/KSS   +CE   /NAME=.KSS.CORP.SCS
```

```
RIGHTS SYS:USERS/KSS   +C+E   /NAME=.KSS.CORP.SCS
```

To add the Create right back for the user KSS in SYS:USERS/KSS directory, use the following command:

```
F:\> RIGHTS SYS:USERS/KSS   +C   /NAME=.KSS.CORP.SCS
NW4CS\SYS:USERS
Directories                                                        Rights
----------------------------------------------------------------  ----------
KSS                                                               [ RWCEMFA]
```

Rights for one directory were changed for .KSS.CORP.SCS.

Two User objects KSS are in contexts CORP.ESL and CORP.OSCS. To assign both users all rights—except Supervisor right—to the current directory, use the following command:

```
RIGHTS . ALL /NAME=.CN=KSS.OU=CORP.O=ESL,.CN=KSS.OU=CORP.SCS
NW4CS\SYS:USERS
Directories                                                  Rights
---------------------------------------------------------    ----------
KSS                                                          [ RWCEMFA]
```

Rights for the directory were changed, first for .CN=KSS.OU=CORP.O=SCS.

```
NW4CS\SYS:USERS
Directories                                                  Rights
---------------------------------------------------------    ----------
KSS                                                          [ RWCEMFA]
```

Rights for the directory were then changed for .CN=KSS.OU=CORP.O=ESL.

Notice that the period (.) can be used for the current directory name. Also, note that ALL means all rights except the Supervisor right. The /NAME= option enables you to list a number of NDS names.

To remove all rights (except Supervisor, if given) for the two User objects KSS in contexts CORP.ESL and CORP.OSCS, use the following command:

```
RIGHTS . -ALL /NAME=.CN=KSS.OU=CORP.O=ESL,.CN=KSS.OU=CORP.OSCS
NW4CS\SYS:USERS
Directories                                                  Rights
---------------------------------------------------------    ----------
KSS                                                          [        ]
```

Rights for the directory were then changed for .CN=KSS.OU=CORP.O=SCS.

```
NW4CS\SYS:USERS
Directories                                                      Rights
------------------------------------------------------------- -----------
KSS                                                            [         ]
```

Rights for one directory were changed for
.CN=KSS.OU=CORP.O=ESL.

Notice that all rights have been removed for the two User objects.

```
RIGHTS . -ALL /NAME=.CN=KSS.OU=CORP.O=ESL,.CN=KSS.OU=CORP.SCS
NW4CS\SYS:USERS
Directories                                                      Rights
------------------------------------------------------------- -----------
KSS                                                            [         ]
```

Rights for one directory were changed for
.CN=KSS.OU=CORP.O=SCS.

```
NW4CS\SYS:USERS
Directories                                                      Rights
------------------------------------------------------------- -----------
KSS                                                            [         ]
```

Rights for one directory were changed for
.CN=KSS.OU=CORP.O=ESL.

Notice that all rights have been removed for the two User objects.

Table 4.3 shows the rights letter codes that can be used with the
RIGHTS command.

Table 4.3
Rights Letter Codes in the RIGHTS Command

Rights Letter Codes	Description
ALL	Grants all rights except supervisor
N	Revokes all rights
S	Supervisor right
C	Create right

Rights Letter Codes	Description
R	Read right
W	Write right
E	Erase right
M	Modify right
F	File Scan right
A	Access Control right
+	Adds the right to existing rights
-	Removes a right from existing rights

Observing Inherited Rights Using the RIGHTS Command

The /I option enables you to see how the inherited rights contribute to effective rights.

To see your inherited rights for SYS:PUBLIC for the user KSS defined in container OU=CORP.O=SCS, use the following command:

```
F:\>RIGHTS SYS:PUBLIC  /NAME=.KSS.CORP.SCS  /I
Name= .KSS.CORP.SCS
Path                                      Rights
---------------------------------------------------- ------
NW4CS\SYS:
Inherited Rights Filter:                  [                    ]
Inherits from above:                      [                    ]
         _____
Effective Rights =                        [                    ]
---------------------------------------------------- ------
```

375

```
NW4CS\SYS:\PUBLIC
Inherited Rights Filter:               [SRWCEMFA          ]
Inherits from above:                   [                  ]
KSS.CORP.SCS                           [ R     F          ]
                   ----------------
Effective Rights =                     [ R     F          ]
-------------------------------------------------------- ------
```

The /I option enables you to see inherited rights. It shows you the sequence of steps for computing rights.

Removing a User as a Trustee for a Directory

When you precede the /NAME= with the keyword REM, the names listed in the /NAME parameter are removed as trustees to the file or directory. This method is different from removing trustee rights. Removing trustee rights can remove rights, including all rights, but the user is still listed as a trustee.

To remove user .KSS.CORP.ESL as a trustee of SYS:USERS/KSS, use the following command:

```
RIGHTS SYS:USERS/KSS  REM /NAME=.KSS.CORP.ESL
NW4CS\SYS:USERS\KSS
User .KSS.CORP.ESL is no longer a trustee of the specified
directory.
Trustee .KSS.CORP.ESL was removed from the directory.
```

Changing the Inherited Rights Filter

You can use the /F option to examine or change the Inherited Rights Filter. To see the current IRF for SYS:USERS/KSS, use the following command:

```
RIGHTS SYS:USERS/KSS  /F
NW4CS\SYS:USERS
```

```
Directories                                                    Rights
------------------------------------------------------------   ----------
KSS                                                            [SRWCEMFA]
```

You can precede a right with a + or - to add or remove that right from the IRF. You can remove all rights from the IRF, except the Supervisor right.

To remove the Write right from the IRF for SYS:USERS/KSS, use the following command:

```
RIGHTS SYS:USERS/KSS   -W    /F
NW4CS\SYS:USERS
Directories                                                    Rights
------------------------------------------------------------   ----------
KSS                                                            [SR CEMFA]
```

To set the IRF for SYS:USERS/KSS to [SR F], use the following command:

```
RIGHTS SYS:USERS/KSS   SRF    /F
NW4CS\SYS:USERS
Directories                                                    Rights
------------------------------------------------------------   ----------
KSS                                                            [SR    F ]
```

Using Attribute Security

Individual files or directories can be assigned attributes that can override a user's effective rights. In figure 4.34, USER1 has Read, Write, Create, and Erase effective rights to SYS:APPS/DATA. But the file FILE.1 is flagged with a Delete Inhibit attribute, and this prevents the file from being deleted, even though the user has Erase effective rights to the directory.

Figure 4.34

Use of Attribute
security.

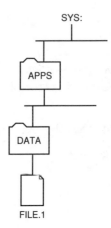

Figure 4.34

Use of Attribute
security.

Directory attributes and file attributes common to both
NetWare 3.x and 4.x are illustrated in tables 4.4 and 4.5. File
and Directory attributes are set by the FLAG command. Type
FLAG /? to see help on setting file and directory attributes.

Table 4.4
Directory Attributes for NetWare 3.x, 4.x

Directory	Meaning Attribute
D	The *Delete Inhibit* attribute prevents a directory from being erased.
H	The *Hidden* attribute hides a directory from a DOS DIR command.
P	The *Purge* attribute purges all files in a directory when deleted.
R	The *Rename Inhibit* attribute prevents a directory from being renamed.
Sy	The *System* attribute similar to H; used for system directories.

Table 4.5
File Attributes for NetWare 3.x, 4.x

File	Meaning Attribute
A	The *Archive Needed* attribute is automatically assigned to files modified after backups.
CI	The *Copy Inhibit* attribute restricts copy rights for Macintosh users.
DI	The *Delete Inhibit* attribute prevents files from being erased.
X	The *Execute Only* attribute prevents files from being copied, and is permanent.
H	The *Hidden* attribute hides a file from a DOS DIR scan.
I	The *Indexed* attribute speeds access to large files; automatically assigned for files with over 64 FAT entries.
P	The *Purge* attribute purges a file when deleted.
Ro	The *Read only* attribute cannot write to, erase, or rename files.
Rw	The *Read Write* attribute is the default setting for a file.
R	The *Rename Inhibit* attribute prevents a file from being renamed.
S	The *Sharable* attribute enables a file to be used by more than one user.
Sy	The *System* attribute is similar to H; used for system files.
T	The *Transactional* attribute protects against incomplete operations on files.

Additional NetWare 4.x directory and file attributes are listed in table 4.6.

Table 4.6
Additional NetWare 4.x Attributes

Attribute	File/Directory	Abbreviation	Description
Migrate	File	M	Indicates that the file has migrated to near-line storage.
Don't Migrate	File/Directory	Dm	Prevents a file or the files in a directory from migrating.
Compress	File	Co	Indicates whether a file has been compressed.
Don't Compress	File/Directory	Dc	Prevents a file or the files in a directory from being compressed.
Immediate Compress	File/Directory	Ic	Marks a specified file or files in a directory marked for compression as soon as the OD can perform compression.
Can't Compress	File	Cc	Indicates that a file cannot be compressed because of limited space-saving benefit.

The attributes Migrate (M), Compress (Co), and Can't Compress (Cc) are status attributes and indicate the status of individual files only. The attributes Don't Migrate (Dm), Don't Compress (Dc), and Immediate Compress (Ic) apply to both files and directories and specify actions that are to be performed or prevented from occurring.

The Data Migration feature is installed using INSTALL.NLM and requires a near-line-storage media that acts as a secondary storage area to the primary hard disk storage area.

The compression feature is enabled or disabled on a volume-by-volume basis during installation. It can be further controlled by a variety of SET parameters.

Using the FLAG Utility

The NetWare 4.x FLAG utility consolidates the functions of the NetWare 3.x FLAG, FLAGDIR, and SMODE commands. You can use a single FLAG utility to change both the file and directory attributes and the search mode for executable files. The FLAG utility also enables you to change the owner of a directory or a file.

The functions of the FLAG utility also can be performed by the FILER menu utility.

Figure 4.35 shows a summary of the FLAG command usage.

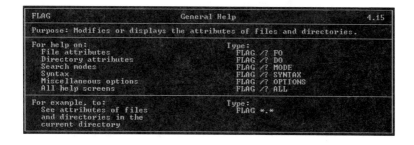

Figure 4.35

FLAG /? Help Summary.

Using the FILER Utility

The FILER utility combines the functions of the NetWare 3.x FILER, SALVAGE, DSPACE, and VOLINFO utilities.

FILER can be used to perform many file-, directory-, and volume-related tasks.

You can use FILER to perform the following tasks:

- ◆ Viewing file contents and directories

- ◆ Viewing/setting directory and file rights

- ◆ Viewing/setting directory and file attributes

- ◆ Copying, moving, and deleting files

- ◆ Deleting entire subdirectory structure (including non-empty subdirectories)

- ◆ Limiting disk space on a volume and directory

- ◆ Purging and salvaging files and directories

Figure 4.36 shows the main menu for FILER when the command FILER is run at a workstation.

Figure 4.36

The FILER main menu.

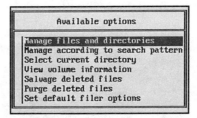

The Manage files and directories option in the main menu shows you a list of directories and files in the current directory (see fig. 4.37).

The Manage according to search pattern option in the main menu gives you the ability to set search patterns for the files and directories to view (see fig. 4.38).

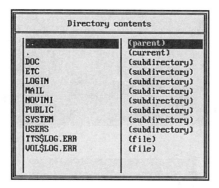

Figure 4.37

FILER Directory contents.

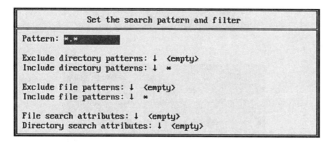

Figure 4.38

Managing according to search patterns.

The Select current directory option in the main menu gives you the ability to set the current directory (see fig. 4.39). The current path is displayed on the top of the screen.

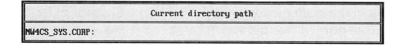

Figure 4.39

Setting the current directory.

The View volume information option in the main menu gives you the ability to view statistics, features, and date and time information for a volume (see fig. 4.40). The volume information is shown in figures 4.41, 4.42, and 4.43.

Figure 4.40

Viewing volume information.

Figure 4.41

FILER volume statistics.

Figure 4.42

FILER volume features.

Figure 4.43

FILER volume dates and times.

The Salvage deleted files option in the main menu gives you the ability to view/recover deleted files, salvage from deleted directories, and set salvage options (see fig. 4.44). The Purge deleted files option in the main menu enables you to set a file pattern for all files to be purged (see fig. 4.45).

Figure 4.44

FILER salvage deleted files options.

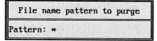

Figure 4.45

FILER purge deleted files options.

The Set default filer options option in the main menu gives you the ability to confirm deletions, copy operations, and overwrites (see fig. 4.46). It also enables you to specify what file attributes should be preserved, and if you should be notified if you are going to lose file attribute information when copying from one name space to another.

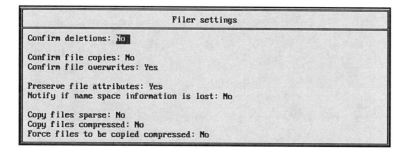

Figure 4.46

Filer settings.

You also can specify whether the files should be copied in their sparse format. NetWare 4.x enables the implementation of sparse files, which are common in database applications when a file may currently contain only a few of the total records that the file can contain. Because the valuable data is a small portion of the overall file size, a sparse representation of a file that occupies much less space can be designed. You also can specify whether or not to copy files in a compressed format.

Setting Directory Trustees and Attributes Using FILER

To set directory rights and attributes using FILER, use the following procedure as a guideline:

1. Log in as Admin and run FILER.

2. Select the Manage files and directories option from the Available Options menu.

3. Highlight a directory for which you want to set the directory trustees and attributes, and press F10.

4. To view trustee assignments to the directory, select Rights list from the Subdirectory Options menu.

   A list of trustee assignments to the directory appears (see fig. 4.47).

Figure 4.47

Using FILER to view trustee assignments to a directory.

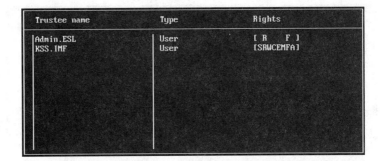

5. Press Esc to return to the Subdirectory Options screen.

6. To set directory trustee assignments or attributes, select View/Set directory information from the Subdirectory Options menu, after highlighting a directory and pressing F10. Information on the directory appears (see fig. 4.48).

Figure 4.48

Using FILER to view directory information.

7. To assign a trustee to the directory, select the Trustees field, then press Enter.

   A list of trustees to the directory appears.

   To remove a trustee, highlight the trustee and press Del.

   To add a trustee, press Ins. A list of objects in the current context that can be assigned as trustees to the directory appears. Select the trustee(s) and press Ins. To select more than one trustee, mark them using F5.

   Figure 4.49 shows that two new trustees have been added using this step. These trustees are the Group object CN=Mgrs.OU=CORP.O=ESL and the User object CN=UNIXUSER.OU=CORP.O=ESL.

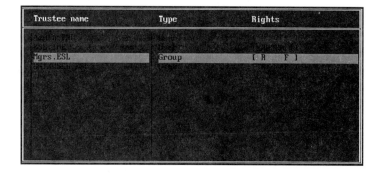

Figure 4.49

Using FILER to add trustees.

8. Press Esc to return to the directory information screen.

9. To set attributes for the directory, select the Directory attributes field and press Enter.

   A list of attributes that have been set for the directory appears.

   To remove an attribute, highlight the attribute and press Del.

   To add an attribute, press Ins. A list of other attributes that can be assigned to the directory appears (see fig. 4.50). You can use the F5 key to mark several directory attributes to set.

Figure 4.50

The list of other attributes that can be assigned to a directory.

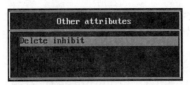

10. Press Enter to see a list of directory attributes to be assigned (see fig. 4.51). Figure 4.51 shows that the Purge attribute and Delete Inhibit attribute have been set.

Figure 4.51

The list of attributes set for a directory.

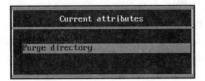

11. Press Esc to return to the directory information screen.

12. To change IRF for a directory, select the Inherited Rights Filter field from the directory information screen and press Enter.

    To remove a right, highlight the attribute and press Del.

    To add a right, press Ins (see fig. 4.52) and select the right. After selecting the right, press Enter to see the new IRF, and Esc to go back to the directory information screen.

Figure 4.52

Modifying IRF using FILER.

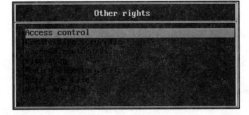

Setting File Trustees and Attributes Using FILER

To set file rights and attributes using FILER, use the following procedure as a guideline:

1. Log in as Admin and run FILER.

2. Select the Manage files and directories option in the Available Options menu.

3. Highlight the file for which you want to set file trustees and attributes, then press F10.

4. To view trustee assignments to the directory, select Rights list from the File options menu.

   A list of trustee assignments to the file appears (see fig. 4.53).

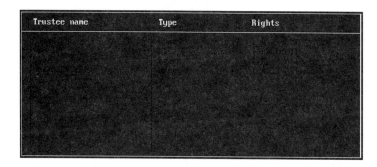

Figure 4.53

Using FILER to view trustee assignments to a file.

5. To set file trustee assignments or attributes, select View/Set file information from the File options menu, after highlighting a file and pressing F10.

   Information on the file appears (see fig. 4.54).

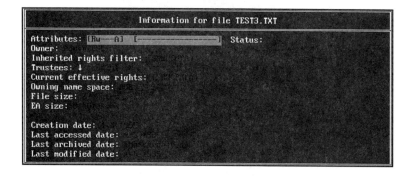

Figure 4.54

Using FILER to view file information.

6. To assign a trustee to the file, select the Trustees field, then press Enter.

   A list of trustees for the file appears.

   To remove a trustee, highlight the trustee and press Del.

   To add a trustee, press Ins. A list of objects in the current context that can be assigned as trustees to the file appears. Select the trustee(s) and press Ins. To select more than one trustee, mark them by using the F5 key.

7. Press Esc to return to the file information screen.

8. To set attributes for the file, select the Attributes list from the file information screen.

   A list of attributes that have been set for the directory appears.

   To remove an attribute, highlight the attribute and press Del.

   To add an attribute, press Ins. A list of other attributes that can be assigned to the file appears (see fig. 4.55). You can use the F5 key to mark several file attributes to set.

Figure 4.55

The list of other attributes that can be assigned to a file.

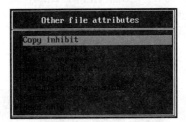

Other file attributes

Copy inhibit

9. Press Enter to see a list of file attributes to be assigned.

10. Press Esc to return to the file information screen.

11. To change IRF for a file, select Inherited rights filter from the file information screen and press Enter.

    To remove a right, highlight the attribute and press Del.

    To add a right, press Ins and select the rights. After selecting the rights, press Enter to see the new IRF, and Esc to go back to the file information screen.

Assigning Trustee Rights Using NetWare Administrator

Use the following steps as a guideline to assign rights to a file
directory using the NetWare Administrator:

1. Start NetWare Administrator while logged in as Admin.

2. Highlight the Volume object on which the directory/files
   resides. You might need to browse the tree until you find the
   Volume object you want.

3. Double-click on the Volume object to see an expanded view
   of directories/files in the volume.

4. Right-click on the selected directory/file.

5. Select Details. The property dialog box for the directory/file
   opens. Figure 4.56 shows the property screen for a directory
   attribute.

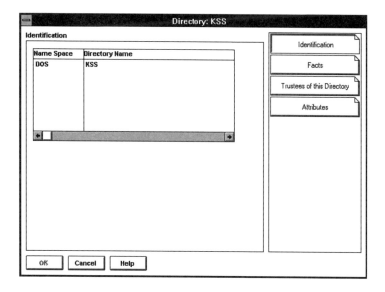

Figure 4.56

The properties
of a directory.

The remaining steps use the directory as an example. The
procedure for assigning rights to a file are similar to the
procedure previously described.

6. Select the Trustees of this Directory page button. A list of trustees appears in the Trustees panel (see fig. 4.57).

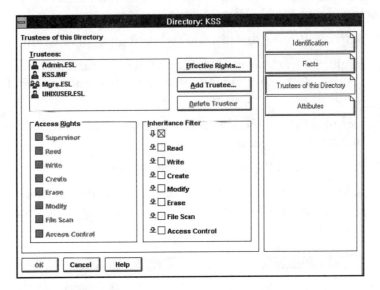

7. To see trustee assignments for a listed trustee, highlight the trustee (see fig. 4.58).

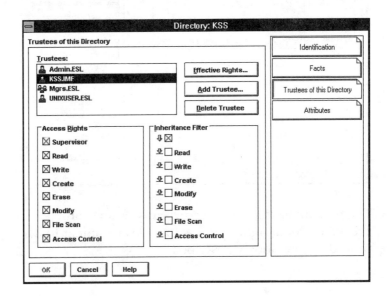

In figure 4.58, the trustee assignment for user KSS.IMF is
[CRWEMFA] as seen in the bottom half of the figure.

8. To see effective rights for a trustee, select the button **E**ffective
Rights.

You see the effective rights for the selected trustee (see fig.
4.59). The browse button on the Effective Rights screen can be
used to determine effective rights for other trustees.

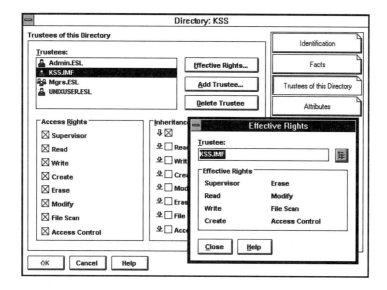

Figure 4.59

The Effective
Rights screen.

9. To add a trustee, select the **A**dd Trustee button.

Use the Select Object dialog box to select a trustee.

Figure 4.60 shows that a new trustee, the Group object
Engineers.CORP.ESL, has been assigned. This trustee has the
rights [R F] to the NW4CS_SYS:USERS directory.

393

Figure 4.60

New trustee added.

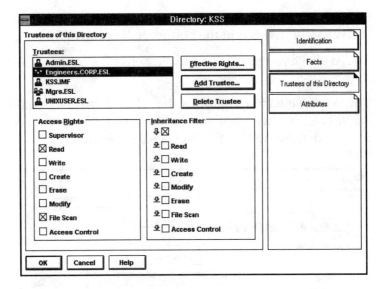

Figure 4.60

New trustee added.

10. To delete a trustee, select the **D**elete Trustee button.

11. To add directory attributes, select the Attributes page button. The Directory Attributes for the directory appear (see fig. 4.61).

Figure 4.61

The Directory Attributes screen.

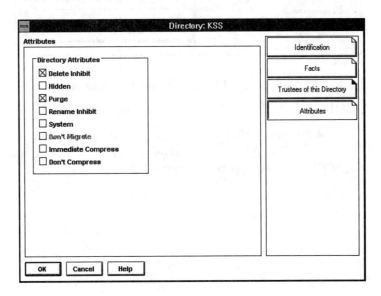

To set an attribute, check the box for that attribute. If an attribute is grayed out, it means that feature has not been enabled for the Volume object.

 Practice using the NetWare Administrator to assign and view file system rights to users, groups, and containers. You may be asked to perform these tasks using a simulated NetWare Administrator tool.

Study Guide for the Chapter

If you are preparing for the NetWare 4.x Administration exams, review the chapter with the following goals:

1. Understand the NetWare file system security rights concepts.

2. Pay particular attention to the tools used to implement NetWare file system security, and the procedure for assigning rights.

After studying this chapter, attempt the sample test questions for this chapter. If you miss the answers to a question, review the appropriate topic.

Chapter Summary

In this chapter, you learned about the concepts behind NetWare file system security and how to use NetWare file system security to control access to data on the network. You also learned about file system concepts such as NetWare directory and file rights, directory and file trustees, inherited rights, and effective rights. You were given a guided tour of some of the critical steps that need to be performed to implement file system security using the NetWare administration tools.

Chapter Test Questions

Test questions can have a single correct answer or multiple correct answers. A ○ notation preceding possible answers indicates that a single answer is desired. Some questions require you to select more than one answer; these questions are indicated by the □ preceding each answer. Certain questions are repeated in different ways so that you can recognize them even when the wording is different. Taking practice quizzes not only tests your knowledge, it also gives you confidence when you take your exam.

1. The default IRF for a newly created directory is _____.

   ○ A. SRWCEMFA

   ○ B. SRWF

   ○ C. SRCEMFA

   ○ D. RWCEMFA

2. Using RIGHTS one can remove all rights from the IRF except _____.

   ○ A. Access Control

   ○ B. Modify

   ○ C. Supervisor

   ○ D. File Scan

3. If a trustee assignment is given to a directory, _____.

   ○ A. the effective rights for the directory depends on the Inherited Rights Mask

   ○ B. the effective rights for the directory depends on the Inherited Rights Filter

   ○ C. the effective rights for the directory depends on the Maximum Rights Mask

   ○ D. the effective rights for the directory is the same as the trustee assignment

4. For a directory that has not been given an explicit trustee assignment, _____.

○ A. the effective rights for the directory depends on the Inherited Rights Filter and the parent directory's trustee assignment

○ B. the effective rights for the directory depends on the Inherited Rights Filter and the parent directory's effective rights

○ C. the effective rights for the directory depends on the Maximum Rights Filter of the parent's directory

○ D. the effective rights for the directory is the same as the Inherited Rights Filter

5. For a subdirectory that has no explicit trustee assignment, the effective rights are determined by _____.

○ A. rights derived from group EVERYONE

○ B. rights derived from parent's trustee assignment

○ C. the effective rights of the parent directory, less what is disallowed by the IRF of the subdirectory

○ D. the trustee assignment of the parent directory, less what is disallowed by the IRF of the subdirectory

6. User John is a member of group WPUSERS. The group WPUSERS has a TA of [R WCE] for SYS:WP. John tries to create a new directory SYS:WPUSERS\JOHN. Which of the following is true?

○ A. The IRF for JOHN for directory SYS:WPUSERS\JOHN is [SRWCEMFA].

○ B. The IRF for JOHN for directory SYS:WPUSERS\JOHN is [S].

○ C. The IRF for JOHN for directory SYS:WPUSERS\JOHN is [R WCE].

○ D. No IRF is set, because JOHN does not have rights to create a directory.

7. The group Acct has a TA of [R F] in SYS:PUBLIC. The Administrator creates a subdirectory SYS:PUBLIC\SCRIPTS and SYS:PUBLIC\UTILS. What rights does the user Bob have in these directories?

   ○ A. No rights

   ○ B. [SRWCEMFA] because the IRF for the subdirectories is [SRWCEMFA]

   ○ C. [R F]

   ○ D. Insufficient information

8. Bill has the following trustee and IRF settings:

   For Directory DIR01:

   IRF is [S   ]
   TA is [RWCE   F]

   For Directory DIR01\SUBDIR01:

   IRF is [SR   ]

   What are Bill's effective rights for DIR01\SUBDIR01?

   ○ A. [R]

   ○ B. [SR]

   ○ C. [RWCE F]

   ○ D. No Rights

9. Nina has the following trustee and IRF settings:

   For Directory DIR01:

   IRF is [S W E   ]
   TA is [RWCE   F]

   For Directory DIR01\DIR02:

   IRF is [SRW   F]

   For Directory DIR01\DIR02\DIR03:

   IRF is [RW CEM A]

   TA is [R   ]

What are Nina's effective rights for DIR01\DIR02\DIR03?

- ○ A. [RW CEM A]
- ○ B. [R]
- ○ C. [RW]
- ○ D. [W]

10. Lisa has the following trustee and IRF settings:

For Directory DIR01:

IRF is [S W E   ]
TA is [RWCE F]

For Directory DIR01\DIR02:

IRF is [SRW   F]

For Directory DIR01\DIR02\DIR03:

IRF is [RW CEM A]

The file attribute for DIR01\DIR02\DIR03\FILE.1 is set to [S Ro]

What operations can Lisa perform on FILE.1?

- ○ A. Read and Write to file
- ○ B. Read only
- ○ C. Read only and share file with other users
- ○ D. No operations

11. The RIGHTS SYS:DATA -R /NAME=JAN command _____.

- ○ A. removes a trustee right from a user or a group for a file or directory
- ○ B. removes file access for a trustee
- ○ C. removes a user or group from a trustee list for a file or directory
- ○ D. removes all permissions to a file or directory

12. Setting the Read Only attribute file also sets the following attributes on the file:

   ○ A. DI Sy

   ○ B. RI DI

   ○ C. H RI

   ○ D. S DI

13. NDS Group objects used for assigning rights can be created using _____.

   ○ A. NETADMIN

   ○ B. FILER

   ○ C. SYSCON

   ○ D. MAKEUSER

14. Giving a user Supervisor file system rights to the root of a server volume _____.

   ○ A. is not possible because only the Supervisor user and equivalent are allowed this permission

   ○ B. gives a user all file system rights to the volume

   ○ C. gives a user all rights to a volume only if that user is a supervisor equivalent

   ○ D. gives a user all rights to all volumes on the file server

15. Assigning a user a trustee assignment of Write to a directory _____.

   ○ A. assigns the user write rights to files in a directory, but open rights must be granted separately to allow writes

   ○ B. assigns the user the right to open and write to files in the directory

   ○ C. assigns the user write rights but denies him or her open rights

   ○ D. assigns the user write rights but denies him or her read rights

16. Assigning the user Access Control rights to a directory
_____.

   A. gives the user the right to change directory and file attributes and rename the directory

   B. gives the user the right to assign rights to other users and to modify trustee assignments and inherited rights filter

   C. gives the user the right to modify contents of a directory

   D. gives the user the right to control access to all files and directories by modifying his attributes

17. User Mary has an IRF of [S] in the directory SYS:COMMON and an IRF of [S A] in SYS:COMMON\DATA.

   Trustee assignments of [R W] have been given to Mary for SYS:COMMON\DATA and [W] for the SYS:COMMON directory.

   What are Mary's effective rights in SYS:COMMON?

   A. W

   B. R W

   C. S A

   D. R

18. To see a list of trustee assignments for directory SYS:DATA, you can use the command _____.

   A. RIGHTS SYS:DATA /F

   B. RIGHTS SYS:DATA /T

   C. RIGHTS SYS:DATA /S

   D. RIGHTS SYS:DATA /I

19. To see the IRF for directory SYS:DATA, you can use the command _____.

    ○ A. RIGHTS SYS:DATA /F

    ○ B. RIGHTS SYS:DATA /T

    ○ C. RIGHTS SYS:DATA /S

    ○ D. RIGHTS SYS:DATA /I

20. To see the inherited rights for directory SYS:DATA, you can use the command _____.

    ○ A. RIGHTS SYS:DATA /F

    ○ B. RIGHTS SYS:DATA /T

    ○ C. RIGHTS SYS:DATA /S

    ○ D. RIGHTS SYS:DATA /I

5

CHAPTER

NetWare Directory Services Security

NetWare Directory Services (NDS) provides a logical view of the network resources and provides access to these resources in a uniform manner. The user needs to log in to the network just once. Once logged in, access to network resources is controlled by NDS security.

In this chapter, you learn how NetWare 4.x NDS security is implemented, and how it can be used to provide access to only those parts of the NDS tree to which the user should have access.

Understanding Network Security

NetWare 4.x security includes the traditional NetWare 3.x security dealing with login security and file system security. NetWare 4.x adds an additional component called the NDS security. The three elements of NetWare 4.x security are as follows:

- ◆ Login security

- ◆ NDS security

- ◆ File system security

Figures 5.1 and 5.2 show the NetWare 3.x and NetWare 4.x security. Chapter 4, "NetWare 4.x File System Security," deals with file system security. At each of the levels (or elements) of security, a number of tools and options exist. To implement security effectively on a network, you need to understand how to implement the different options at each level and which tools NetWare 4.x provides to implement network security.

The three components of NetWare 4.x security are

- ◆ Login security

- ◆ NDS security

- ◆ File system security

Using Login Security

The login security in figures 5.1 and 5.2 has a number of components. Login security controls who can gain initial entry into the network. The login authentication of a user must be done against the User object stored in the global NDS database. A user logging in as an object CN=KARANJIT in container O=ESL must, for example, type in the following command after initial attachment to the network:

```
LOGIN .CN=KARANJIT.O=ESL
```

or

```
LOGIN .KARANJIT.ESL
```

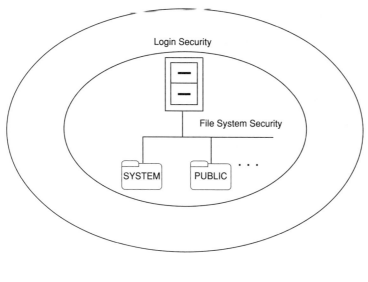

Figure 5.1

NetWare 3.x network security.

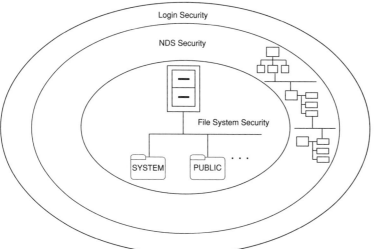

Figure 5.2

NetWare 4.x network security.

The first login command specifies the complete name of the User object. The second form uses the typeless complete name. This assures that the user can log in from any context in the NDS tree. The context, you recall from the discussion in Chapter 2, "Introduction to NetWare Directory Services," is the location (pointer) in the NDS tree. Partial names also can be used by the user to log in to the network. If the current context is [Root], for example, the following commands can be used:

```
LOGIN CN=KARANJIT.O=ESL
```

or

```
LOGIN KARANJIT.ESL
```

If the current context is O=ESL, the container that holds the User object, the following command can be used:

```
LOGIN CN=KARANJIT
```

or

```
LOGIN KARANJIT
```

Before a user can successfully log in, the user has to pass through several login restriction checks (see fig. 5.3). These login restrictions are as follows:

◆ Account restrictions

◆ Password restrictions

◆ Station restrictions

◆ Time restrictions

◆ Intruder limits

The login restrictions in figure 5.3 are initiated on NDS objects through the NetWare Administrator or the NETADMIN tools.

Figure 5.3

The Login
Restrictions.

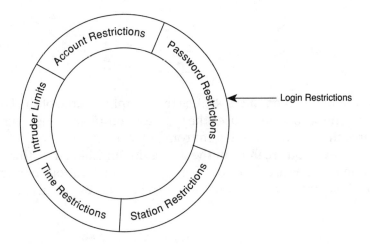

Account Restrictions

Account restrictions can be controlled by changing the account restriction properties for a User object. Account restrictions include the ability to restrict a User object in the following ways:

- ◆ Disabling the user account
- ◆ Setting an expiration date on the user account
- ◆ Limiting concurrent connections

Figure 5.4 shows the account restriction properties for a User object. In this figure, the account is enabled, as indicated by the absence of the check in the Account Disabled check box. The account is set to expire 8/22/99 at 2:00:00 AM. Also, the concurrent connections are limited to three. This limitation means that the user CN=KARANJIT.O=ESL can log in to no more than three stations at the same time.

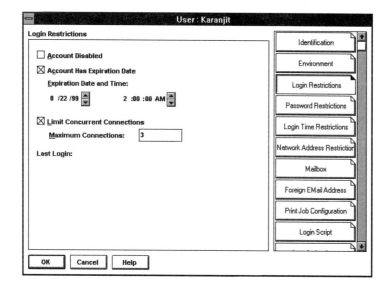

Figure 5.4

The Login Restrictions dialog box.

To get to figure 5.4, you need to perform the following actions:

1. Log in to the network with Administrator privileges to at least a portion of the NDS tree that has User objects defined.

2. Start the NetWare Administrator Tool. You should see a screen similar to figure 5.5.

   Set the context of the NDS tree so you can see the entire NDS tree. You can set the context by performing the following steps:

   ◆ Select View menu.

   ◆ Select Set Context from the View menu.

Figure 5.5

NetWare
Administrator
showing NDS tree.

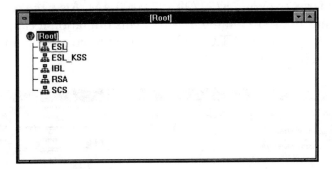

3. Examine a container that has User objects defined.

   Highlight a User object and examine its properties by double-clicking on the User object or by right-clicking on the User object and selecting the Details option.

   Figure 5.6 shows the properties of the User object.

4. Select the Login Restrictions page button, and you see the dialog box for setting Account Restrictions (refer to fig. 5.4).

Note that account restrictions can be used to:

◆ Disable the user account

◆ Set an expiration date on the user account

◆ Limit concurrent connections

408

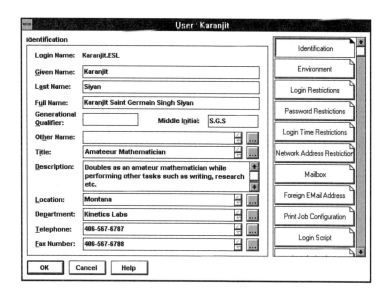

Figure 5.6

Properties of User
object
CN=KARANJIT.O=ESL.

Password Restrictions

Password restrictions are properties of a User object. Password restrictions include the ability to restrict a user's password in the following ways:

◆ Enables users to change (or not change) their passwords.

◆ Requires a password, or disables this requirement.

◆ Enforces a minimum password length, or has no control on the minimum password length.

◆ Forces (or does not force) users to change passwords periodically. The periodicity of change can be set from 1 to 365 days and can be set to start at any date and time.

◆ Forces (or does not force) users to set unique passwords.

◆ Limits grace logins to a specific number from 1 to 200.

Figure 5.7 shows the password restriction properties for a User object. In this figure, the user is enabled to change his or her password. A password is required, and its minimum length is five. The user is forced to change passwords periodically at

intervals of 40 days. The current password expires on 4/3/95 at
2:00:00 AM. The password that a user enters must be unique from
previous passwords the user used. The user is allowed a limit of
six grace logins after the password expires. If the user does not
change the password in the specified number of logins, the account is disabled. It can be re-enabled by an administrator.

Figure 5.7

The Password
Restrictions dialog
box.

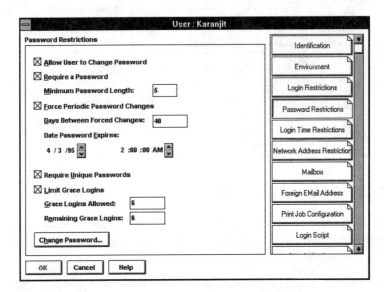

To get to figure 5.7, you need to perform the following actions:

1. Log in to the network with administrator privileges to at least
   a portion of the NDS tree that has User objects defined.

2. Start the NetWare Administrator Tool.

3. Examine a container that has User objects defined.

4. Highlight a User object and examine its properties by double-
   clicking on the User object, or by right-clicking on User object
   and selecting Details option.

5. Select the Password Restrictions page button, and you see the
   dialog box for setting password restrictions (see fig. 5.7).

Password restrictions can

♦ enable users to change their password.

♦ require a password.

♦ enforce a minimum password length.

♦ force users to change passwords periodically at intervals from 1 to 365 days.

♦ force users to set unique passwords.

♦ limit grace logins to a specific number from 1 to 200.

Time Restrictions

Time restrictions are properties of a User object. Time restrictions can be used to restrict a user's login ability in the following ways:

♦ The user can log in during specific days of the week only.

♦ The user can be restricted to log in at specific times only.

♦ The granularity of time interval that can be set for logging in is 30 minutes.

Figure 5.8 shows the login time restriction properties for a User object. In this figure, the user is enabled to log in on weekdays only. Access on Saturday and Sunday is denied during those times shaded in gray. On weekdays, the user is not able to log in from 10 pm to 12 am or from 12 am to 4 am. This limitation means that the user can log in only from Monday through Friday between 4 am and 10 pm.

If users are logged in and reach a restricted time, the system gives a five-minute warning, saying that they need to log out. If users are still logged in after five minutes, the system will forcibly log them out. Any unsaved information will be lost.

Figure 5.8

The Time Restrictions
dialog box.

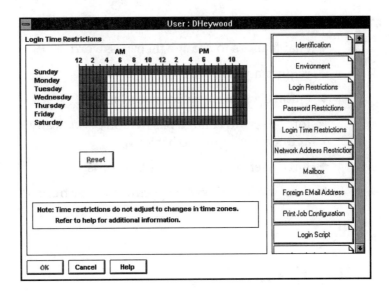

While NDS uses a universal network time based on Greenwich
Mean Time (GMT), and adjusts for time zone differences, login
restrictions do not account for time zone differences. For example,
if you live in a geographical region that uses US Mountain Time,
and you set the time restrictions during Mountain Daylight
Savings Time (MDT) to permit weekday access from 8 am to 8 pm,
then time restrictions will be off by one hour when your region
goes back to US Mountain Standard Time (MST). This means that
users who arrive at 8 am, when the time is set to Mountain Standard Time, will not be able to log in until 9 am. This is because the
NetWare server time on the server they initially attach to is ad-
justed back one hour but the login time restrictions are not ad-
justed. To compensate for time differences within a time zone, you
can set login time restrictions with a buffer of one hour before and
after normal login time restrictions.

To get to figure 5.8, you need to perform the following actions:

1. Log in to the network with Administrator privileges to at
   least a portion of the NDS tree that has User objects defined.

2. Start the NetWare Administrator Tool.

3. Examine a container that has User objects defined.

4. Highlight a User object and examine its properties by double-clicking on User object, or by right-clicking on User object and selecting Details option.

5. Select the Login Time Restrictions page button, and you see the dialog box for setting Time Restrictions (see fig. 5.9).

NetWare 4.x time restrictions can be used to:

◆ restrict a user to log in during specific days of the week

◆ restrict a user to log in at specific times of the day

◆ set the time interval a user can log in at intervals of 30 minutes

Station Restrictions

Station restrictions (also called network address restrictions) include the capability to restrict a user's ability to log in to specific workstations. In NetWare 4.x, the station restrictions are more powerful and general than NetWare 3.x. Station restrictions in NetWare 3.x can be done only on the hardware address (MAC address) of the workstation's network board. In NetWare 4.x, station restrictions include the ability to restrict based on a protocol address. For this reason, the station restrictions also are called network address restrictions in NetWare 4.x. Network address restrictions are properties of a User object and enable you to restrict logins based on network addresses such as the following:

◆ IPX/SPX

◆ SDLC

◆ AppleTalk

◆ OSI

413

♦ TCP/IP

♦ Ethernet/Token Ring

The Network Address formats for some of the previous address types are shown in figures 5.9 through 5.11.

The IPX/SPX address format (see fig. 5.9) consists of a 4-byte network number and a 6-byte hardware address. The hardware address is the MAC (Media Access Control) address of the network board.

Figure 5.9

IPX/SPX address restriction.

The TCP/IP address format (see fig. 5.10) is the IP address and consists of a 4-byte logical address that is expressed in a dotted-decimal notation. Each of the 4 bytes that make up the IP address is expressed in its equivalent decimal number (range 0 to 255) and separated by a dot (.).

Figure 5.10

TCP/IP address restriction.

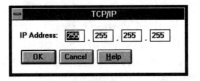

The Ethernet/Token Ring address format shows the SAP (Service Access Point) address and a 6-byte MAC address. The SAP is a 2-byte field that is part of the Logical Link Control (LLC, also called IEEE 802.2) that could be used with frame types such as ETHERNET_802.2, ETHERNET_SNAP, TOKEN-RING, and TOKEN-RING_SNAP. The 6-byte MAC address is broken down into a 3-byte BLOCKID and a 5-byte Physical Unit ID (PUID). The terms BLOCKID and PUID are used with IBM's SNA or SAA networks. For LAN usage, these fields are considered to be one long field that can be used to code the station's MAC address.

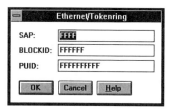

Figure 5.11

Ethernet/Token Ring address restriction.

To see the network address restriction screens shown in figures 5.9 to 5.11, you need to perform the following steps:

1. Log in to the network with administrator privileges to at least a portion of the NDS tree that has User objects defined.

2. Start the NetWare Administrator Tool.

3. Examine a container that has User objects defined.

4. Highlight a User object and examine its properties by double-clicking on the User object, or by right-clicking on User object and selecting Details option.

5. Select Network Address Restrictions page button, and you see the dialog box for setting address restrictions.

 Network address restrictions are properties of a User object. They enable you to restrict logins based on the following address types:

♦ IPX/SPX

♦ SDLC

♦ AppleTalk

♦ OSI

♦ TCP/IP

♦ Ethernet/Token-Ring

Intruder Limits

Intruder limits are set in a container object by selecting the Intruder Detection page button in the container's properties using the NetWare Administrator. Intruder limits apply to all User objects within the container (see fig. 5.12). They limit the user's access to the network if an incorrect password is typed in too many times.

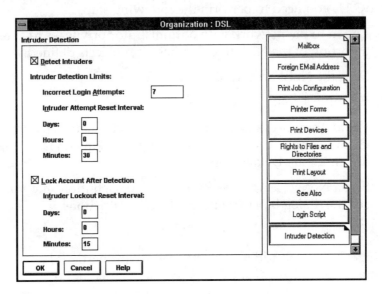

You can also set intruder limits by using NETADMIN. This procedure is outlined next:

1. Highlight the container for which intruder detection is to be set using NETADMIN.

2. Press F10.

3. Select the View or edit properties of this object option.

4. Select Intruder Detection. You will see the same type of information displayed as in figure 5.12.

The user account is locked if it exceeds the intruder detection limits. The network administrator can use the Intruder Lockout Detection screen for the User object to see the number of incorrect login attempts and the station address that was used by the intruder.

To enable login for a locked user, deselect the Account Locked check box. Enabling a user's account, once it has been locked, requires Supervisor rights.

To get to figure 5.12, you need to perform the following steps:

1. Log in to the network with Administrator privileges to at least a portion of the NDS tree that has User objects defined.

2. Start the NetWare Administrator Tool.

3. Examine a container that has intruder limits defined.

4. Right-click on container object and select the Details option.

5. Select the Intruder Detection page button, and you see the dialog box for accessing the Intruder Detection screen.

Intruder Detection is set in a container object and applies to all User objects within the container.

Intruder limits are used to lock a user's access to the network if an incorrect password is typed in too many times.

The container objects on which intruder detection can be set are:

♦ Organization

♦ Organizational Unit

Understanding Login Authentication

When a user first logs in to the network, the network authenticates the user against the information stored in the user's object, such as the user's login name and password. Once authenticated, further requests are validated to ensure that the requests originate from the user's workstation and that they have not been illegally altered in transit across the network. NetWare 4.x's authentication mechanism takes place in the background, with no more direct user involvement after the user types in the object and password correctly. In other words, further authentication takes place in the background and is transparent to the user. The authentication of a user is done on each session basis. If the user logs out of the network, background authentication ceases until the user attempts to log in to the network again.

NetWare 4.x authentication is done on a session-by-session basis and takes place continuously in the background (see fig. 5.13). Background authentication is done during a specific user session, but ceases when a user logs out and exits from the session.

Authentication is used to ensure that only a valid user could have sent the message, and that the message came from the workstation where the initial authentication data was created. It validates that only the sender could have built the message, and that the message has not been illegally modified during transit across the network. It also guarantees that the message is for the current session only, thus eliminating the threat from play-back attacks, where an attempt is made to capture a valid session and play it back on the network.

Authentication ensures that:

◆ only a valid user could have sent the message

◆ only the purported user could have built and sent the message

◆ the message has come from a workstation where the initial authentication data was created

◆ the message has not been tampered with during transit across the network

◆ the message applies to the current session

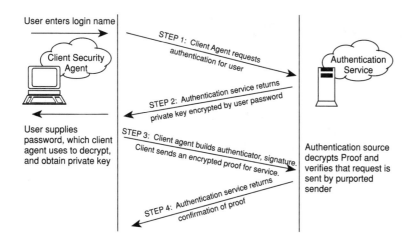

Figure 5.13

NetWare 4.x login authentication.

User enters login name

Client Security Agent

STEP 1: Client Agent requests authentication for user

Authentication Service

STEP 2: Authentication service returns private key encrypted by user password

User supplies password, which client agent uses to decrypt, and obtain private key

STEP 3: Client agent builds authenticator, signature. Client sends an encrypted proof for service.

Authentication source decrypts Proof and verifies that request is sent by purported sender

STEP 4: Authentication service returns confirmation of proof

NetWare 4.x provides a scheme for continual background authentication after the initial authentication is complete. This provision makes it difficult to assume the identity of a legitimate user connection.

Accessing NDS Resources

When a client accesses a network resource represented by an NDS object, the NDS locates that resource in the NDS tree and verifies that you are a valid user and have proper permissions to access that resource. The sequence of steps that are performed are listed, next:

1. Client requests NDS resource.

2. NetWare server responds.

3. NDS locates object in the directory.

4. Resource location is identified.

5. NDS checks client has a valid name and appropriate permissions.

6. Client is connected to the resource.

419

Examining NDS Security Concepts

After the user is validated for network services, the NDS security is used to determine the network resources (NDS objects) to which the user is allowed access. The kinds of operations a user is permitted to perform on an NDS object and files and directories in volumes on the network require certain rights. The operations permissible on NDS objects are called *NDS object rights* and the operations permissible on a NetWare file system are the *file system rights*.

Several examples can be given of how NDS object rights are useful. Suppose a user wants to view the structure of a tree. Should the user be enabled to view the directory structure? Viewing the structure (also called browsing) of a tree would be very valuable for a user if the user needs to find out what network resources are available on the network. One of the object rights is called Browse, which enables the user to view the directory structure. Other useful rights are Create, Delete, or Rename. You do not want an ordinary user to have these rights. An administrator user should have a special right called the Supervisor right that grants the administrator all privileges to a directory object.

Figure 5.14 shows that if object rights could not be inherited, explicit rights would have to be assigned at each directory and container level. This would involve greater security administration than is needed in most cases. Using inheritance can simplify the assignment of rights, as seen in figures 5.15 and 5.16.

When a right is assigned to a container object, should all objects in that container get those rights? Objects in a container that receive rights from a parent (superior object) container are said to inherit rights. Inheritance is a very important property and is used in object rights to simplify the assignment of rights. Consider the situation of an Organizational Unit container that has 1,000 objects underneath it (see fig. 5.14).

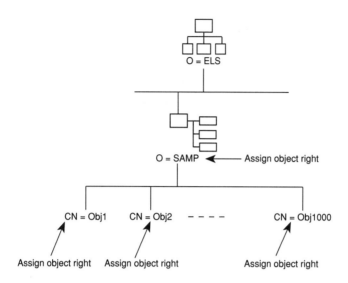

Figure 5.14

If object rights could not be inherited.

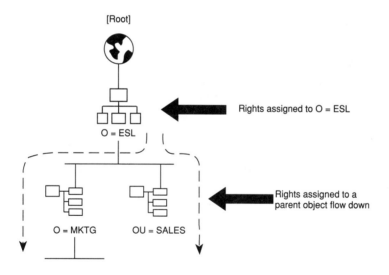

Figure 5.15

Inheritance in object rights for NetWare 4.x.

421

Figure 5.16

Blocking inheritance of object rights in NetWare 4.x.

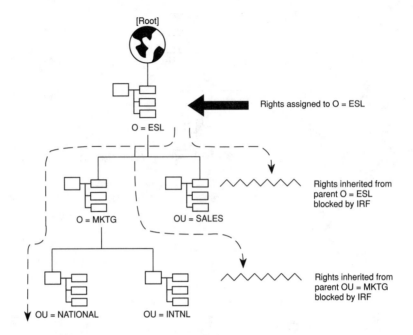

For the most part, a user/group needs the same rights to all the objects in that container. If objects could not inherit rights from their parent container, each one of the 1,000 objects would have to be granted a right individually! Most administrators would not appreciate performing such a task. If, on the other hand, objects could inherit rights, the desired object right could be granted just once for the Organizational Unit container (see fig. 5.15). What if some objects in the container needed a different set of rights (see fig 5.16)? In this case, a mechanism to block the flow of rights below a certain container is needed. This mechanism is called the *Inherited Rights Filter* (IRF) and is discussed in greater detail in a later section of this chapter.

Another important question is the following: Do you want any network administrator to have complete control over the NDS tree for the entire organization? Such control would give this user access to all network resources. Many large organizations are reluctant to grant such access. NDS object rights provide the ability to restrict access to portions of the NDS tree, even to administrator users. Care should be used to prevent a situation where no one has administrative rights to a portion of the NDS tree.

Understanding NDS Rights

NDS provides for two types of rights. The rights to perform operations on the NDS tree structure, and the rights to perform operations on properties of an object (see fig. 5.17). These two types of rights are quite different.

NDS rights that deal with the structure of objects in the NDS tree are called *object rights*. These are used to view and manage objects in the NDS tree.

NDS rights that deal with the ability to access the values stored in the properties of an object are called *property rights*. Property rights deal with what a user can do with the values of a property.

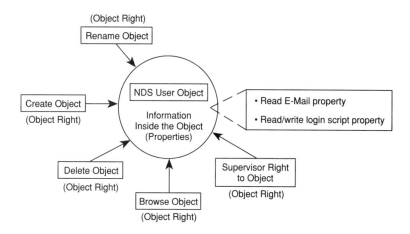

Figure 5.17

Object versus property rights.

When working with the NDS structure, for instance, you might need to browse the tree, or rename an object. When you are examining the properties of an object, the Browse right is not meaningful. You typically want to be able to read the value of a property or to write to it. You might want a user to have Read access to his or her e-mail address property, for example, but you might not want the user to change his or her e-mail address. You might, on the other hand, enable users to modify their login scripts. In this case, they need to have Write access to the login script property for their User object.

423

An NDS object that is granted an explicit right is called the *trustee* of the object (see fig. 5.18). The trustee can be any object in the NDS tree. It is easy to understand that User objects and Group objects can be trustees, because they all deal with users. But it might seem strange, at first, to think of a container object as a trustee to another object.

Figure 5.18

Trustee of an object and rights to an object.

Chapter 2, "Introduction to NetWare Directory Services," discusses that container objects are a convenient way of grouping NDS objects into a logical structure that reflects the organization of an enterprise. Container objects can be considered as groups where the members of the container are the NDS objects in the container. Making a container a trustee to another object gives all objects in that container rights to the designated object. These rights, furthermore, flow down to other containers and objects, unless explicitly blocked at a tree level.

In summary, the two types of NDS rights are the following:

◆ Object rights

◆ Property rights

The next few sections discuss object rights first. A discussion of property rights follows.

An NDS object that is granted a specific (explicit) right is called the trustee of the object.

Two types of NDS rights are object rights and property rights.

The specific (explicit) right that is granted to an NDS object is called a trustee assignment. The two types of trustee assignments are:

424

◆ Object trustee assignment

◆ Property trustee assignment

Clarifying Terminology

When a right is assigned to an object A for another object B, the object A is called a trustee of object B. The process of granting this right is called a *trustee assignment*. Often, the object that has been granted the right and the right that has been granted are called a trustee assignment. A trustee can be any other object. In NetWare 3.x, a trustee could be a user account or a group account. In NetWare 4.x, other leaf objects and container objects can also be made trustees.

When a User object is a trustee, the user who is logged in as the User object can perform the operations allowed by the trustee assignment. When a container is made a trustee of an object, all objects in that container can perform the operations allowed by the trustee assignment. Similarly, when a Group object is made a trustee for an object, all User objects listed in the Group object's Group Membership property can perform the operations allowed by the trustee assignment.

Author's Note

A procedural difference is found in adding rights in NetWare 4.x compared with adding rights in NetWare 3.x. In NetWare 3.x, when SYSCON was used to assign trustee assignments, you selected the user who was to be given the trustee assignment first. After having selected the user, you then assigned rights to that user. When veteran NetWare 3.x users attempt to do this using the NetWare Administrator tool in NetWare 4.x, they tend to select the user first and then try to give trustee assignments to that user, just as they are accustomed to doing in NetWare 3.x.

continues

In NetWare 4.x, however, you must first go to the object of which the user is being made a trustee, and then make trustee assignments to that object. Keeping this clear in your mind avoids potential confusion in assigning rights.

Exploring Object Rights

Object rights are assigned to an object in the NDS tree and control the operations that can be performed on the object as a whole. They do not control access to information within the object, except for one important exception. This is a situation when a Supervisor object right has been granted to an NDS object. Granting the Supervisor object right gives full control over the information inside the object, but Supervisor right, like any other right, can be blocked by an Inherited Rights Filter (IRF).

Control of information kept inside the object (property) is accomplished by property rights.

Table 5.1 shows the different object rights that are possible.

Table 5.1
Object Rights

Object Right	Abbreviation	Meaning
Supervisor	S	Grants all rights. Assigning this right automatically gives Supervisor rights to the object's All Properties (discussed later in this chapter).
Browse	B	Grants the right to see an object in the NDS tree. When a request is made to search for an object, its name is returned.

Object Right	Abbreviation	Meaning
Create	C	Applies to container objects only. Gives the right to create a new object within the container. Cannot be given to leaf objects because they cannot contain subordinate objects.
Delete	D	Grants the right to delete an NDS object. Only leaf objects and empty container objects can be deleted.
Rename	R	Grants the right to rename an object. Applies to leaf and container objects.

Supervisor Object Right

The Supervisor right grants all possible rights to the User object. An object with Supervisor rights has full access to the information inside the object. This right is an exception. Normally, the object rights do not affect access to the contents of the object.

A special right called the All Properties right is used to describe all the properties. When a Supervisor object right is assigned, a Supervisor property right also is assigned, which means that all access to the information inside the object is given if an object has the Supervisor object right. Needless to say, this right must be given with care. If you find it necessary, you can block the Supervisor right to branches of an NDS tree by removing this right from the Inherited Rights Filter for the top-level container for a tree branch.

Browse Object Right

The Browse object right is, perhaps, the most common right given. For readers familiar with NetWare file system security, the Browse object right is similar to the File Scan right for file systems.

427

A Browse right for an object gives the trustee the ability to see the object's name in the NDS tree. Without this right (if a Supervisor right is not given), the object is hidden from the user's view.

If a Browse right is not granted to a trustee for a container, the trustee is denied access to all containers and objects within that tree branch. The default is to give everyone the Browse right to the [Root] object. Because all objects in a directory tree are under the [Root] object, the Browse right is inherited (it also can be said that it flows down) by all objects in the NDS tree.

If, for security reasons, you want to deny access to users in a specific part of the NDS tree, you can do so by blocking the Browse right (using the IRF) for the container that represents the tree branch.

Create Object Right

The Create object right gives the trustee the ability to create subordinate objects underneath the container. Because leaf objects cannot have subordinate objects beneath them, the Create right is not assignable to leaf objects. Figure 5.19 shows an attempt to assign an object right to a leaf object, such as the User1.CORP.ESL. Notice that the object right Create is not shown as an option for this user.

Figure 5.19

Create right not possible for leaf objects.

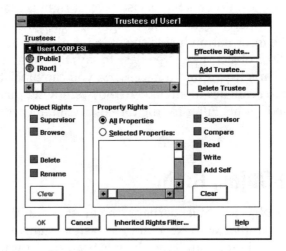

You also must have Browse rights, in addition to Create rights to a container, before you can create an object underneath the container. The Browse right is usually inherited because [Public] is assigned the Browse right to the [Root] object. You do not need the Browse right to change to a context using the CX command.

Delete Object Right

This right grants the trustee the right to delete an object. A container object can be deleted only if it has no other objects underneath it. You must delete the leaf and subcontainer objects before you can delete a container. This rule is primarily in effect to prevent inadvertent damage to the NDS tree. This is similar to files and directories; you cannot delete the directory unless it is empty (all files are removed).

If a file server is active, its object cannot be deleted. Again, this limitation is for reasons of security, so that access to the file server is not lost while users are connected to it.

You can delete a file server's Volume object, even while user's are logged in to it! This action can have disastrous consequences, because users cannot access the volume using NDS. Do not try this on a production system! To safeguard this from happening, remove the Delete right in the Inherited Rights Filter.

If someone manages to delete the Volume object, try the following fix:

1. Create a Volume object using NetWare Administrator or NETADMIN.

continues

429

2. If an error message is generated:

   a. reboot the server.

   b. connect to the server using VLM /PS=*servername*. Replace *servername* with name of server that has the physical Volume whose Volume object representation was deleted.

3. Log in as Admin and start NetWare Administrator.

   a. Create a Volume object.

4. Specify the Host Server property to be the NDS name of server, and Host Volume to be SYS.

Alternatively, you can try the following:

1. LOAD INSTALL.NLM at the server.

2. Select Maintenance/Selective Install option.

3. Select Directory Options.

4. Select Install/Reinstall mounted volumes into the directory. You are asked to log in to the NDS as Admin. INSTALL then prompts you to add deleted volumes back into the NDS structure. The volume is placed in the current server context.

Rename Object Right

The Rename object right enables the trustee to change the Name property for the object. Both leaf and container object names can be changed. In pre-NetWare 4.02 releases, only the leaf object names could be changed.

Decide on the names of the container objects with careful consideration. You might want to take into account how easily recognizable the container name is to users of the network, its length (should not be too long), and its appearance, as seen in the NDS tree (lowercase, uppercase, or combination of both).

Understanding the [Public] Trustee

Earlier, it was mentioned that everyone is given the Browse right. Readers familiar with NetWare 3.x might recall that everyone received the Read and File Scan (RF) rights to SYS:PUBLIC through the group called EVERYONE. No default group is called EVERYONE (or a similar name) in NetWare 4.x. So the problem is, how do you assign the Browse right to all users in the tree?

The problem is further compounded by the fact that the Browse right would be nice to have for users who are not logged in to the network, but merely attached.

The difference is that users who are logged in to the network have been authenticated by NDS. Users who are attached have a connection to the SYS:LOGIN directory of a NetWare file server so that they can have access to the LOGIN.EXE, CX.EXE, NLIST.EXE and other programs. With this connection, they can log in to the network, or search the NDS tree for the name of a resource. The network security, in most cases, is not threatened if a user can see the names of network resources. In extremely secure environments, the Browse right can be revoked from any part of the NDS tree. Another benefit of the Browse right that is available to attached users and workstations is that it permits the NDS to interface with third-party tools or other X.500 implementations that might need to search Novell's NDS (DIB—Directory Information Base, in X.500 terms), for names of resources and its tree structure.

In order to solve this problem, the designers of NDS created an implicit group called [Public]. An implicit group is different from an explicit group (such as Group objects). Membership to an implicit group is implied by other means. In the case of the group [Public], all workstations that are attached (connected to but not logged in, as yet) to a NetWare 4.x network, automatically are members of the group [Public], making it possible to assign rights to workstations that are not authenticated by NetWare 4.x.

[Public] is an implied group and includes all users who have a network connection, even though they might not be authenticated by the network.

You must take care when assigning rights to [Public]. Otherwise, non-authenticated connections to the network can have excessive rights to the network.

Other operating systems, such as Windows NT, also have the concept of an implicit group, where membership to certain groups is implied to users accessing a Windows NT station across a network.

When the server is first installed, the group [Public] is made a trustee of [Root] and given the Browse object right to the [Root] object. Figure 5.20 illustrates this trustee assignment, and figure 5.21 shows the NetWare Administrator screen that depicts the assignment of these rights. The Browse object right is inherited by all containers and their sub-containers, down to the individual leaf objects because [Public] has the Browse object right. This right enables a user to browse the directory tree.

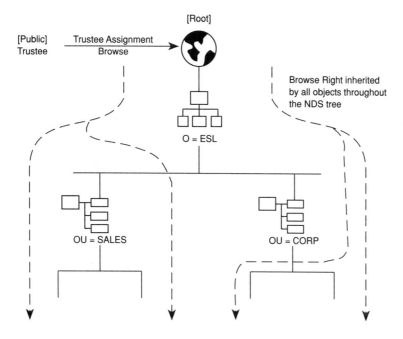

Figure 5.20

The Browse right to trustee [Public] on [Root] object.

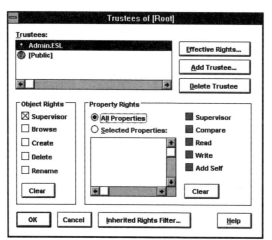

Figure 5.21

The NetWare Administrator showing default trustee assignments to [Root] object.

Situations might occur when you want users to browse only portions of the NDS tree, rather than allow the entire NDS tree to be browsed. In those cases, the default trustee assignment of Browse for [Public] to [Root] object can be removed, and this right

433

can be assigned to the root container (top of tree branch) for which the user needs to see directory resources. See figures 5.22 and 5.23, which illustrate this concept. These figures show that the Browse right can be granted to all connected users to a specific tree branch. In figures 5.22 and 5.23, the root of this tree branch is at the organization object level O=ESL; it also could be at a lower level in the tree, such as at an Organizational Unit level.

Figure 5.22

The Browse right to trustee [Public] for container O=ESL.

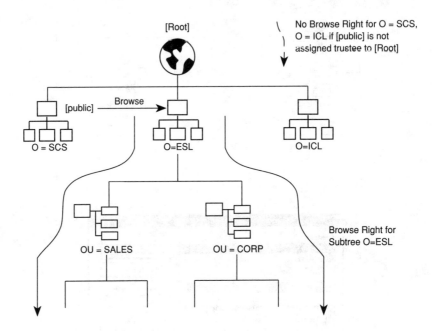

Figure 5.23

The NetWare Administrator showing Browse right to [Public] for container O=ESL.

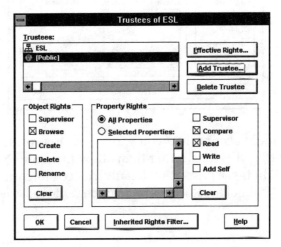

[Public] is similar to the NetWare 3.x group EV-ERYONE with the difference that:

- [Public] does not have an explicit membership; that is, users cannot be added or deleted.

- Membership to [Public] is based on being connected to the network.

Examining Default Object Rights

NetWare 4.x sets certain default system rights to simplify the number of administration tasks that would otherwise have to be performed. One of these default rights is the Browse right that the [Public] trustee gives to the [Root] object. Other default rights are discussed in the following paragraphs.

The container object that contains the SYS: Volume object receives the Read and File Scan (RF) rights to the SYS:PUBLIC directory of the Volume object. These rights are indicated in figure 5.24, which shows that the CORP.ESL container that is the parent container of the server Volume object is given the access rights of Read and File Scan. This allows all objects, such as User and Group objects, defined in that container to inherit these rights.

In essence, this is equivalent to assigning Read and File Scan rights to group EVERYONE in NetWare 3.x. If you have upgraded your server from NetWare 3.x to NetWare 4.x, and if the group EVERYONE had Read and File Scan rights to SYS:PUBLIC, you will also see the Group object EVERYONE in the container where the upgraded NetWare 4.x server and volume objects are installed. You should also see the Group object EVERYONE as a trustee to SYS:PUBLIC with Read and File Scan rights.

Figure 5.24

The rights to
SYS:PUBLIC.

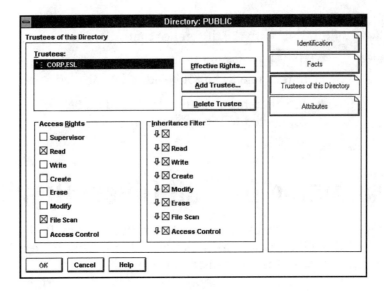

The initial user Admin is by default given the Supervisor object right to [Root]. This means that the Admin user inherits Supervisor object rights to all objects and their contents in the NDS tree. For this reason the password to the initial Admin user must be guarded with care. The Admin user by default is placed in the Organization object container and is named Admin. For security reasons, it might be advisable to rename this User object first and then move it to another context.

The User object, by default, has the following object trustees assigned to it:

1. The [Root] object is made a trustee to the User object and is given the Browse object right (see fig. 5.25), which means that any NDS object can browse the User object.

2. If the creator of the User object is not the Admin user, who has Supervisor rights, the creator is made a trustee with Supervisor rights to the newly created object.

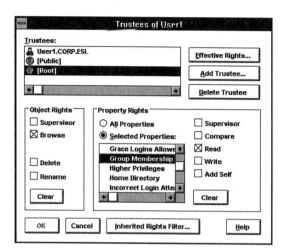

Figure 5.25

The Default [Root] trustee assignment for User object.

Another default right is that the creator (Admin) of the server object is given the Supervisor object right to the server object. Assigning Supervisor rights to server objects also gives Supervisor rights to All Properties. Supervisor All Properties right also implies Write property right to the ACL property of the server object. Anyone who has the Write property right to the ACL property of the server object is given Supervisor right to the root of the server's volumes. It is implied that assigning the Supervisor right to a server object gives all file system rights to volumes attached to that server.

The default rights assigned during NDS installation, file server object installation, and User object creation are summarized in tables 5.2, 5.3, and 5.4.

Table 5.2
Default NDS Rights During NDS Installation

Trustee	NDS Right	Comments
Admin	[S] object right to [Root]	Allows Admin user to administer the entire NDS tree.

continues

Table 5.2, Continued
Default NDS Rights During NDS Installation

Trustee	NDS Right	Comments
[Public]	[B] object right to [Root]	Allows users to view the NDS tree using CX and NLIST in the SYS:LOGIN directory without first being authenticated by the NDS tree.

Table 5.3
Default NDS Rights During Server Installation

Trustee	NDS Right	Comments
Server object creator	[S] object right to server object	Allows creator (usually administrator of container) to administer the server object.
[Public]	[R] (Read) property right to Messaging Server property	Allows network messaging clients to identify the messaging server assigned to the server.
Server	[S] object right to server object	Allows privileged processes running on server to modify parameters in the server object.

Table 5.4
Default NDS Rights for User Object

Trustee	NDS Right	Comments
[Public]	[R] (Read) property right to Default Server property of User object	Allows network clients to identify the default server for the user.

Trustee	NDS Right	Comments
[Root]	[R] (Read) property right to Network Address and Group membership property of User object	Allows authenticated network clients of the NDS tree to identify the login network address and the group memberships of the user.
User	[R] (Read) property right to All Properties of User object	Allows user to read the values of any property stored in the User object.
	[RW] (Read, Write) property rights to the Login Script property for the User object	Allows users to change their login scripts.
	[RW] (Read, Write) property rights to the Print Job Configuration property for the User object	Allows users to change their print job configurations.

Understanding Inheritance of Object Rights

When an object trustee assignment is made, the right granted to the trustee is *inherited* by all objects subordinate to it. In the case of container objects, all leaf objects in the container and all Organizational Units inherit this right. This inheritance of rights is sometimes called the *flowing down* of rights.

If an object is given an explicit trustee assignment at a lower level in the tree, any object rights that were inherited from above are overwritten.

439

Figure 5.26 shows an example of an NDS tree, where User object KSS is made a trustee of the Organization container O=ESL. The trustee assignment that has been given is the [B C D] rights. This is the right to Browse, Create, and Delete objects. The container O=ESL has two Organizational Units: OU=CORP and OU=ENG. The rights assigned to user KSS for O=ESL flow to these Organizational Units. The Organizational Unit objects inherit the [B C D] right. The [B C D] right for trustee KSS, in turn, flows down to the Organizational Units below OU=CORP and OU=ENG. It is important to realize that the [B C D] right is only for a specific trustee; in this case, the trustee is the User object.

Figure 5.26

Example of inheritance of object rights.

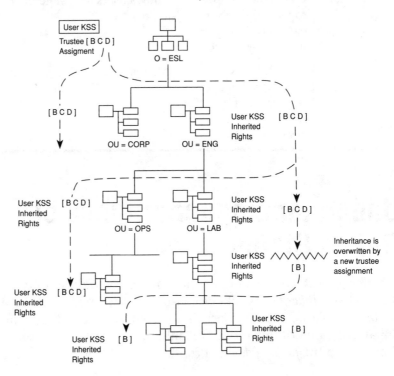

The rights assigned to Organizational Unit container OU=ENG flow to its two organizational units, OU=OPS and OU=LAB. The rights inherited by OU=LAB container flow further down the tree, but the OU=R&D Organizational Unit has an explicit trustee assignment of [B] for User object KSS. This explicit trustee assignment overrides the trustee assignment user KSS inherits for OU=R&D from the parent container OU=LAB. The trustee assignment for User object KSS becomes the new right of [B]. This new right flows down to subordinate containers below OU=R&D. In figure 5.26, these subordinate containers are OU=LASER and OU=NNET. User object KSS inherits the rights of [B] to these containers.

It also is interesting to see that in OU=OPS, underneath the OU=ENG container, no explicit trustee assignment was given to user KSS. In this case, the trustee assignment [B C D] flows down and is inherited by the OU=MAINT container that is subordinate to OU=OPS.

Besides an explicit trustee assignment that overrides any inherited rights, inheritance also can be controlled by the use of the Inheritance Rights Filter. This topic is discussed next.

The NDS rights that are inherited are different from the NetWare file system rights. Object rights granted to a Volume object are not inherited by the file directories in that Volume object.

You must be careful about assigning rights to top-level containers. Assigning rights to the [Root] container gives User objects that right to the entire tree, unless this right is explicitly removed using IRF.

Examining the Inherited Rights Filter

The Inherited Rights Filter (IRF) is a part of a property of the object, called the ACL property (also called the Object Trustees property). It can be used to control which rights are allowed to be inherited from above.

Every NDS object has an IRF. The default value of the IRF is all object rights [S B C D R], meaning that an NDS object has the potential to inherit all rights. The IRF often is confused with the actual object right. The sole purpose of the IRF is to block a right from flowing down. The IRF cannot be used to block an explicit trustee assignment.

 The explicit trustee assignment overrides any Inherited Rights received from above and causes the IRF to be ignored.

The IRF functions in a manner similar to the Inherited Rights Filter for NetWare 4.x file system (same as NetWare 3.x, Inherited Rights Mask, except for the name change). The important difference is that the Supervisor right can be removed for IRF for NDS. In the NetWare file system, the Supervisor right cannot be removed from the IRF for a file or directory.

When the Supervisor right is removed from the IRF for an NDS object, the Supervisor right is essentially blocked from that tree branch. Before removing a Supervisor right from the IRF of an NDS object, you must make another object a trustee with explicit Supervisor rights for that object.

Figure 5.27 shows an attempt to remove the Supervisor right for an NDS object. The trustee, CORP.ESL, is highlighted in the Trustees box, which means that the operations that are performed are in relationship to this trustee object. An attempt was made to remove the Supervisor right from the IRF. Figure 5.27 shows the error message that you see when an unsuccessful attempt was made to clear this box.

Figure 5.27

An attempt to remove Supervisor right from an IRF for a container object.

The reader who is interested in experimenting with this should try the following:

1. Log in as an Admin user and start the NetWare Administrator.

2. Right-click on a container and select Trustees of this Object.

3. Highlight the container in the Trustee List box and select the Inherited Rights Filter button.

4. You should see the Inherited Rights Filter screen.

5. Click on any of the object rights in the Filter panel. The rights should be exposed for your view.

6. Try to remove the Supervisor object right by clicking on the box against it. You should see the error message in figure 5.27.

If an explicit Supervisor trustee assignment to an object exists, the Supervisor object right can be removed from the IRF. In this case, though, the Supervisor right is blocked. At least one object can manage the object and its subordinate objects.

Though the Supervisor right can enable a trustee to perform all operations on an object, it is a good practice to assign the other rights in case the Supervisor right is removed accidentally. From the preceding discussion, you can determine that NetWare 4 checks to see if at least one trustee that has a Supervisor right exists before allowing the Supervisor right to be removed; but you still might want to assign other rights as a precautionary measure.

443

Exploring Security Equivalence

A User object can be granted all the security rights of another NDS object. This situation is called *security equivalence* and is a property of the User object. Figure 5.28 shows that user Dei is made security equivalent to the users Jan.CORP.ESL and Lisa.ESL, organization role BackupOp.CORP.ESL, group Mgrs.ESL and the Organizational Unit SALES.ESL. This example indicates that Dei inherits, by the definition of security equivalence, whatever rights the previously mentioned objects have. These rights are in addition to the rights that user Dei already has.

Figure 5.28

The security equivalence property of a User object.

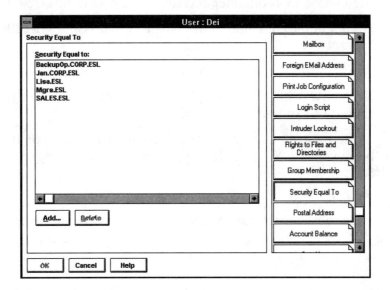

 Security equivalence is a property of the User object. You may be asked questions on security equivalences, such as when you should make use of security equivalences. These points are discussed in this section.

Because security equivalence is a property of the User object, the user must not have the right to make changes to this property. If a user has the Write property right to the security equivalence property and the Write property right to the ACL property of an Admin User object, the user could assign an Admin User object as one of the values for the security equivalence property. This action would give the user all the rights the Admin user has. The default for a newly created user is that users can read their security equivalence property. You should not normally have to change this value.

One situation in which security equivalence might be particularly useful is when a user in an organization needs access to files and directories of another user. This user could be made security equivalent to the user whose files and directories need to be accessed. To perform this task, you need to have the Write property right for the User object (property rights are discussed later in this chapter).

Using Object Effective Rights

An object's effective rights are the rights that a user actually has to the object. The effective rights are not the same as the rights inherited from a parent container, because these could be blocked by the IRF. Also, a user can have a right blocked, but might inherit that right because a group to which the user belongs has an explicit or inherited trustee assignment for the object. By the same token, an effective right is not the same as an explicit trustee assignment. A user can inherit other rights because a group to which the user belongs has an explicit or inherited trustee assignment for the object.

The effective rights need to be calculated for each situation. Because of the hierarchical structure of the NDS tree, a right can be inherited from a number of sources. This possibility makes the determination of the origin of NDS rights an interesting and challenging task.

Consider the example in figure 5.29. To compute the effective rights of user KSS to the Printer object HP_PRINTER, you must consider effective rights that come from any of the following sources:

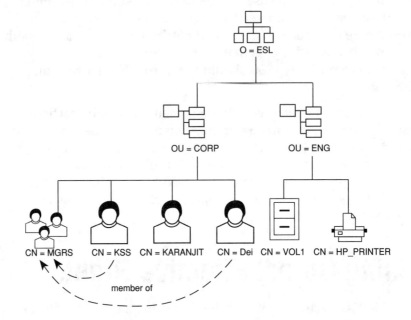

1. Explicit trustee assignment: This assignment includes the trustee assignment on HP_PRINTER that lists user KSS as a trustee (see fig. 5.30).

2. Inherited from trustee's parent container: Trustee assignment on HP_PRINTER that lists OU=CORP as a trustee. This assignment also includes a trustee assignment on HP_PRINTER that lists other parent containers, such as O=ESL and [Root], as trustees. This is because the user KSS is in the tree branch with these objects as roots of the tree branch (see fig. 5.31).

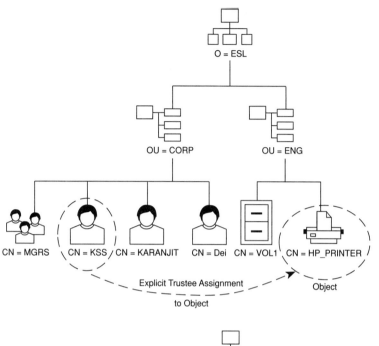

Figure 5.30

Effective object rights: explicit trustee assignment.

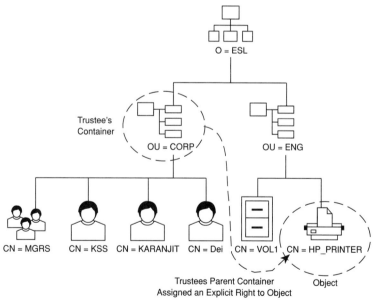

Figure 5.31

Effective object rights: inherited from trustee's parent container.

3. Inherited from direct assignment to object's container: Trustee assignment on the container OU=ENG that lists user KSS as a trustee (see fig. 5.32). The rights assigned must pass through the object HP_PRINTERs IRF.

Figure 5.32

Effective object rights: inherited from direct assignment to object's container.

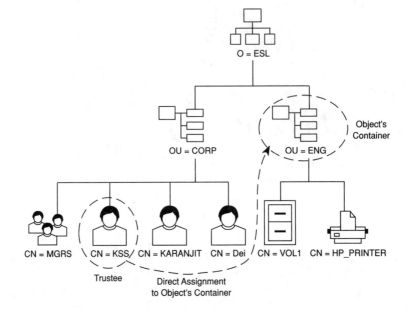

4. Inherited from assignment of trustee's container to object's container: Trustee assignment on the container OU=ENG that lists User object KSS's parent containers such as OU=CORP, O=ESL and [Root] as a trustee (see fig. 5.33). The rights assigned must pass through the object HP_PRINTER's IRF.

5. Trustee assignment to a Group object: Any trustee assignment made to the Group object MGRS of which the user KSS is a member (see fig. 5.34).

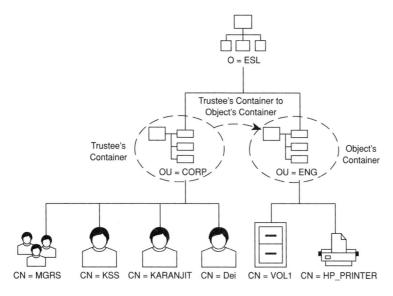

Figure 5.33

Effective object rights: inherited from assignment of trustee's container to object's container.

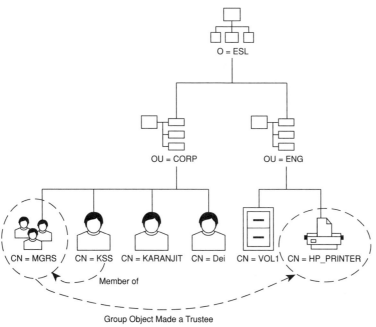

Figure 5.34

Effective object rights: trustee assignment to a Group object.

449

6. Trustee assignment to a security equivalent object: If user KSS is made a security equivalent to object KARANJIT, any right that the user KARANJIT has to HP_PRINTER automatically is inherited by user KSS (see fig. 5.35).

Figure 5.35

Effective object rights: trustee assignment to a security equivalent object.

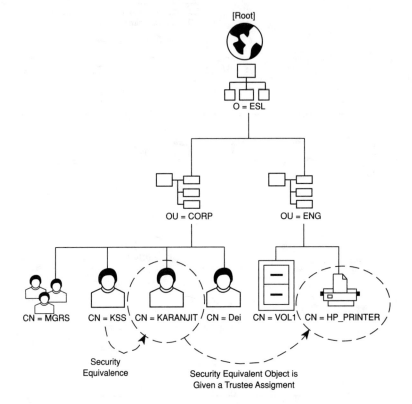

Study the different ways, listed in this chapter, that an object could derive its effective rights.

As you can determine from the previous discussion, you must consider the following in order to compute effective rights:

◆ The rights explicitly granted to a User object.

◆ The rights inherited from above, minus the rights revoked by the IRF. If an explicit trustee assignment exists, it overrides any inherited rights for that particular trustee.

- The rights granted to container objects between the object and the [Root], which applies to container objects that are between the object and the [Root] and the trustee and the [Root].

- The rights granted through security equivalence.

The next section presents case studies to give you practice in computing effective rights.

Calculating Object Effective Rights

Understanding how effective rights are computed for an object in the NDS tree is extremely important for NetWare 4.x administration. For this reason, many case studies are presented to help you understand how effective rights work in NetWare 4.x.

Figure 5.36 shows a worksheet that can be used for computing effective rights. This figure also shows a partial directory tree with the containers O=ESL, OU=CORP, and OU=ACCTG. The worksheet for computing effective rights shows the entries for each of these containers. For each container, entries are shown for the following:

- Inherited Rights Filter (IRF)

- Inherited rights

- Trustee assignment

- Effective rights

While practicing how to compute effective rights, you should discover that the worksheet is an invaluable aid because it systematically shows the rights at each level. With more experience and practice in computing effective rights, you might be able to dispense with the use of a worksheet and compute effective rights more directly.

Figure 5.36

Worksheet for computing effective rights.

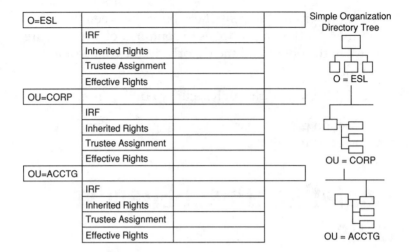

O=ESL				Simple Organization Directory Tree
IRF				
Inherited Rights				
Trustee Assignment				O = ESL
Effective Rights				
OU=CORP				
IRF				
Inherited Rights				
Trustee Assignment				
Effective Rights				OU = CORP
OU=ACCTG				
IRF				
Inherited Rights				
Trustee Assignment				
Effective Rights				OU = ACCTG

Ten case studies are presented, with a discussion of solutions for each case study. The case studies range from the simple to the complex. Ten case studies might seem to be a lot, but the more practice you have, the more confident you should feel, not just for passing the exams, but also for real-life tasks of designing security on a NetWare 4.x network.

Case Study 1—Computing Effective Rights

Figure 5.37 shows a directory tree for organization IBL. Drew becomes a trustee of Organization O=IBL and receives Browse, Create, and Rename rights. The IRFs for the containers follow:

```
IRF for O=IBL      [S B C D R]
IRF for OU=CORP    [  B C D  ]
IRF for OU=MKTG    [S     D R]
```

Calculate Drew's effective rights in containers O=IBL, OU=CORP, and OU=MKTG. Assume that Drew does not inherit rights from any other source than the ones listed in the case study.

Figure 5.38 shows the completed worksheet containing the answers. The explanations for entries in the worksheet are presented.

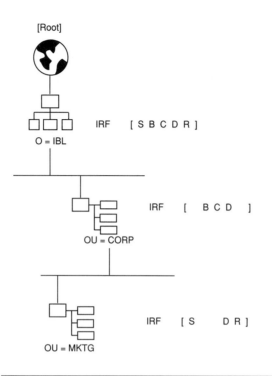

Figure 5.37

A directory tree for organization IBL.

O = IBL			
	IRF	S B C D R	
	Inherited Rights	None	
	Trustee Assignment	B C R	Drew
	Effective Rights	B C R	
O = CORP			
	IRF	B C D	
	Inherited Rights	B C	
	Trustee Assignment	None	
	Effective Rights	B C	Drew
O = MKTG			
	IRF	S D R	
	Inherited Rights	No Rights	
	Trustee Assignment	None	
	Effective Rights	No Rights	Drew

Figure 5.38

The completed worksheet.

453

Entries for O=IBL

The IRF, according to the case study, is [S B C D R]. No rights are inherited from above, and therefore, the entry for Inherited Rights is None. An explicit trustee assignment of [B C R] has been given to the user. The explicit trustee assignment overrides any other inherited rights, so the effective rights for the user in container O=IBL are the same as the explicit trustee assignment. That is, Drew's effective rights for O=IBL are [B C R].

Entries for OU=CORP

The IRF, according to the case study, is [B C D]. The rights inherited from above are the effective rights of the parent container masked with the IRF for this container:

```
IRF                            [    B C D    ]
Effective rights of parent  [    B C      R]
_____
Inherited Rights               [    B C      ]
```

The masking operation is a logical AND operation, which means that an entry needs to be in the IRF rights and Effective rights of the parent container for it to be in the final result.

The Inherited Rights for OU=CORP are [B C]. Because no trustee assignment is made in OU=CORP, the effective rights are the same as the Inherited Rights. That is, Drew's effective rights for OU=CORP are [B C].

Entries for OU=MKTG

The IRF, according to the case study, is [S D R]. The rights inherited from above are the effective rights of the parent container masked with the IRF for this container:

```
IRF                            [S        D R ]
Effective rights of parent  [    B C      ]
_____
Inherited Rights               [             ]
```

The Inherited Rights for OU=MKTG are [   ], or No Rights.

Because no trustee assignment is made in OU=MKTG, the effective rights are the same as the Inherited Rights. That is, Drew's effective rights for OU=MKTG are No Rights.

Case Study 2—Computing Effective Rights

Figure 5.39 shows a directory tree for organization IAF. Hari becomes a trustee of Organization O=IAF and receives Browse, Create, Delete, and Rename rights. The IRFs for the containers follow:

```
IRF for O=IAF      [S B C D R]
IRF for OU=CORP    [S B C D  ]
IRF for OU=MKTG    [S B     R]
```

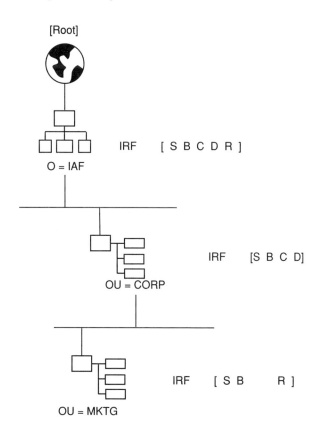

[Root]

O = IAF   IRF   [S B C D R]

OU = CORP   IRF   [S B C D]

OU = MKTG   IRF   [S B   R]

Figure 5.39

Object effective rights: NDS tree for case study 2.

Calculate Hari's effective rights in containers O=IAF, OU=CORP, and OU=MKTG. Assume that Hari does not inherit rights from any other source.

Figure 5.40 shows the completed worksheet containing the answers. The explanations for entries in the worksheet are presented next.

Figure 5.40

Object effective rights: worksheet for case study 2.

O = IBL			
	IRF	S B C D R	
	Inherited Rights	None	
	Trustee Assignment	B C D R	Hari
	Effective Rights	B C D R	

O = CORP			
	IRF	S B C D	
	Inherited Rights	B C D	
	Trustee Assignment	None	
	Effective Rights	B C D	Hari

O = MKTG			
	IRF	S B R	
	Inherited Rights	B C D	
	Trustee Assignment	None	
	Effective Rights	B	Hari

Entries for O=IAF

The IRF, according to the case study, is [S B C D R]. No rights are inherited from above, and therefore, the entry for Inherited Rights is None. An explicit trustee assignment of [B C D R] has been given to the user. The explicit trustee assignment overrides any other inherited rights, so the effective rights for the user in container O=IAF are the same as the explicit trustee assignment. That is, Hari's effective rights for O=IBL are [B C D R].

Entries for OU=CORP

The IRF, according to the case study, is [S B C D]. The rights inherited from above are the effective rights of the parent container masked with the IRF for this container:

```
IRF                       [S  B C D   ]
Effective rights of parent [   B C D  R]
_____
Inherited Rights          [   B C D   ]
```

The masking operation is a logical AND operation, which means that an entry needs to be in both the rights for it to be in the final result.

The Inherited Rights for OU=CORP are [B C D]. Because no trustee assignment is made in OU=CORP, the effective rights are the same as the Inherited Rights. That is, Hari's effective rights for OU=CORP are [B C D].

Entries for OU=MKTG

The IRF, according to the case study, is [B C D R]. The rights inherited from above are the effective rights of the parent container masked with the IRF for this container:

```
IRF                       [  S B       R ]
Effective rights of parent [    B C D    ]
_____
Inherited Rights          [    B        ]
```

The Inherited Rights for OU=MKTG are [B   ]. Because no trustee assignment is made in OU=MKTG, the effective rights are the same as the Inherited Rights. That is, effective rights for OU=MKTG are [B   ].

Case Study 3—Computing Effective Rights

Figure 5.41 shows a directory tree for organization SCS. Dei becomes a trustee of Organization O=SCS and receives Browse, Create, Delete, and Rename rights. Dei also is given a trustee assignment of [B C D R] to OU=LAB. The IRFs for the containers follow:

```
IRF for O=SCS    [S  B       ]
IRF for OU=ENG   [S  B       ]
IRF for OU=LAB   [S  B  C   R]
```

Figure 5.41

Object effective rights: NDS tree for case study 3.

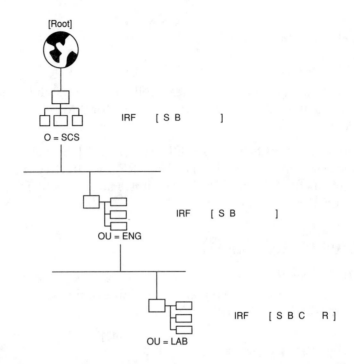

Calculate Dei's effective rights in containers O=SCS, OU=ENG, and OU=LAB. Assume that Dei does not inherit rights from any other source.

Figure 5.42 shows the completed worksheet containing the answers. The explanations for entries in the worksheet are presented next.

Entries for O=SCS

The IRF, according to the case study, is [S B]. No rights are inherited from above, and therefore, the entry for Inherited Rights is None. An explicit trustee assignment of [B C D R] has been given to the user. The explicit trustee assignment overrides any other inherited rights, so the effective rights for the user in container O=SCS are the same as the explicit trustee assignment. That is, effective rights for O=SCS are [B C D R].

```
O = SCS
          IRF                 S B
          Inherited Rights    None
          Trustee Assignment     B C D R        Dei
          Effective Rights       B C D R
 OU = ENG
          IRF                 S B
          Inherited Rights      B
          Trustee Assignment  None
          Effective Rights      B
  OU = LAB
          IRF                 S B C    R
          Inherited Rights      B
          Trustee Assignment     B C D R        Dei
          Effective Rights       B C D R
```

Figure 5.42

Object effective rights: worksheet for case study 3.

Entries for OU=ENG

The IRF, according to the case study, is [S B]. The rights inherited from above are the effective rights of the parent container masked with the IRF for this container:

```
IRF                        [S   B       ]
Effective rights of parent [    B C D  R]
_____
Inherited Rights           [    B       ]
```

The masking operation is a logical AND operation, which means that an entry needs to be in both the rights in order for it to be in the final result.

The Inherited Rights for OU=ENG are [B]. Because no trustee assignment is made in OU=ENG, the effective rights are the same as the Inherited Rights. That is, Dei's effective rights for OU=ENG are [B].

Entries for OU=LAB

The IRF, according to the case study, is [S B C R]. The rights inherited from above are the effective rights of the parent container masked with the IRF for this container:

```
IRF                            [ S B C        R   ]
Effective rights of parent     [     B             ]
───────────────────────
Inherited Rights               [     B             ]
```

The Inherited Rights for OU=LAB are [B]. Because an explicit trustee assignment of [B C D R] is made in OU=LAB, the effective rights are the same as the explicit trustee assignment. That is, Dei's effective rights for OU=LAB are [B C D R].

Case Study 4—Computing Effective Rights

Figure 5.43 shows a directory tree for organization SCS. Karanjit becomes a trustee of Organization O=SCS and receives Supervisor rights. Karanjit also is given a trustee assignment of Browse, Create, Delete, and Rename to OU=ENG. The IRFs for the containers follow:

```
IRF for O=SCS      [S B  C D R ]
IRF for OU=ENG     [S B  C     ]
IRF for OU=LAB     [  B      R ]
```

Figure 5.43

Object effective rights: NDS tree for case study 4.

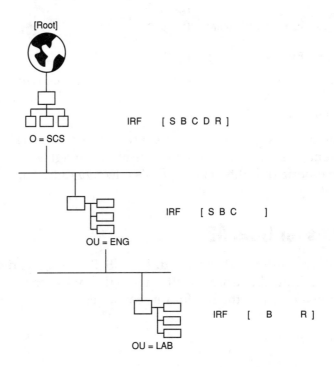

[Root]

O = SCS   IRF   [S B C D R]

OU = ENG   IRF   [S B C   ]

OU = LAB   IRF   [B   R]

Calculate Karanjit's effective rights in containers O=SCS, OU=ENG, and OU=LAB. Assume that Karanjit does not inherit rights from any other source.

Figure 5.44 shows the completed worksheet containing the answers. The explanations for entries in the worksheet are presented next.

O=SCS			
	IRF	S B C D R	
	Inherited Rights	None	
	Trustee Assignment	S	Karanjit
	Effective Rights	S (B C D R)	
OU=ENG			
	IRF	S B C	
	Inherited Rights	S (B C D R)	
	Trustee Assignment	B C D R	Karanjit
	Effective Rights	B C D R	
OU=LAB			
	IRF	B R	
	Inherited Rights	B R	
	Trustee Assignment	None	
	Effective Rights	B R	Karanjit

Figure 5.44

Object effective rights: worksheet for case study 4.

Entries for O=SCS

The IRF, according to the case study, is [S B C D R]. No rights are inherited from above, and therefore, the entry for Inherited Rights is None. An explicit trustee assignment of [S] has been given to the user. The explicit trustee assignment overrides any other inherited rights, so the effective rights for the user in container O=SCS are the same as the explicit trustee assignment. That is, Karanjit's effective rights for O=SCS are [S (B C D R)]. The rights in parentheses of (B C D R) are implied rights. If the trustee has Supervisor rights, the trustee automatically has the other rights.

461

Entries for OU=ENG

The IRF, according to the case study, is [S B C]. The rights inherited from above are the effective rights of the parent container masked with the IRF for this container:

```
IRF                         [S  B       ]
Effective rights of parent  [S (B C D R)]
_____
Inherited Rights            [S (B C D R)]
```

The masking operation is a logical AND operation, which means that an entry needs to be in both the rights for it to be in the final result.

The Inherited Rights for OU=ENG are [S (B C D R)]. Because a trustee assignment of [B C D R] is made in OU=ENG, the effective rights are the same as the explicit trustee assignment, and override any inherited rights. That is, Karanjit's effective rights for OU=ENG are [B C D R]. An interesting fact about this case study is that the inherited rights to OU=ENG were all object rights. But by explicitly assigning lesser rights, the greater rights inherited from above are overridden.

Entries for OU=LAB

The IRF, according to the case study, is [B R]. The rights inherited from above are the effective rights of the parent container masked with the IRF for this container:

```
IRF                         [   B     R  ]
Effective rights of parent  [   B  C D R  ]
_____
Inherited Rights            [   B     R  ]
```

The Inherited Rights for OU=LAB are [B R]. Because no explicit trustee assignment is made in OU=LAB, the effective rights are the same as the Inherited Rights. That is, Karanjit's effective rights for OU=LAB are [B R].

Case Study 5—Computing Effective Rights

Figure 5.45 shows a directory tree for organization KJBR. John becomes a trustee of Organizational Unit OU=LAB and receives the Supervisor right. Group object OWNERS received a trustee assignment of Browse and Create for Organization O=KJBR. John is a member of this group.

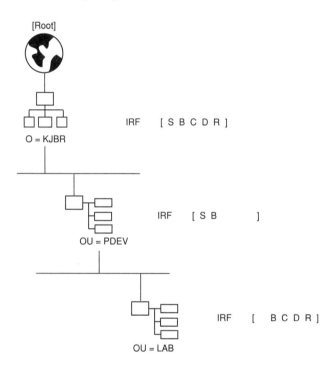

Figure 5.45

Object effective rights: NDS tree for case study 5.

The IRFs for the containers are shown here:

```
IRF for O=KJBR , [S B C D R ]
IRF for OU=PDEV [S B      ]
IRF for OU=LAB  [  B C D R ]
```

Calculate John's effective rights in containers O=KJBR, OU=PDEV, and OU=LAB. Assume that John does not inherit rights from any other source.

Figure 5.46 shows the completed worksheet containing the answers. The explanations for entries in the worksheet are presented next.

463

Figure 5.46

Object effective rights: worksheet for case study 5.

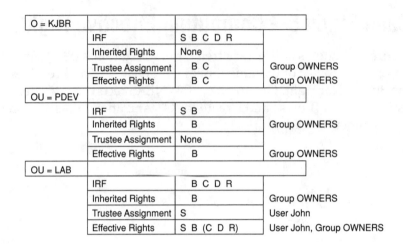

O = KJBR			
IRF	S B C D R		
Inherited Rights	None		
Trustee Assignment	B C		Group OWNERS
Effective Rights	B C		Group OWNERS

OU = PDEV			
IRF	S B		
Inherited Rights	B		Group OWNERS
Trustee Assignment	None		
Effective Rights	B		Group OWNERS

OU = LAB			
IRF	B C D R		
Inherited Rights	B		Group OWNERS
Trustee Assignment	S		User John
Effective Rights	S B (C D R)		User John, Group OWNERS

Entries for O=KJBR

The IRF, according to the case study, is [S B C D R]. No rights are inherited from above, and therefore, the entry for Inherited Rights is None. An explicit trustee assignment of [B C] has been given to the group OWNERS, of which John is a member. The explicit trustee assignment overrides any other inherited rights, so that the effective rights for the user in container O=KJBR are the same as the explicit trustee assignment. That is, John's effective rights for O=KJBR are [B C]. The worksheet also shows that the effective rights computed are for Group object OWNERS, of which John is a member. When calculating effective rights, remember that you can avoid confusion by keeping track of the sources of the rights because it is possible to have rights from several sources.

Entries for OU=PDEV

The IRF, according to the case study, is [S B]. The rights inherited from above are the effective rights of the parent container masked with the IRF for this container:

```
IRF                        [S   B          ]
Effective rights of parent [    B C        ]
_____
Inherited Rights           [    B          ]
```

The masking operation is a logical AND operation, which means that an entry needs to be in both the rights for it to be in the final result.

The Inherited Rights for OU=PDEV are [B], and the source is the Group object OWNERS. Because no trustee assignment is made in OU=PDEV, the effective rights are the same as the inherited rights. That is, John's effective rights for OU=PDEV are [B], and the source of this right is group OWNERS.

Entries for OU=LAB

The IRF, according to the case study, is [B C D R]. The rights inherited from above are the effective rights of the parent container masked with the IRF for this container:

```
IRF                        [   B C D R   ]
Effective rights of parent [   B C       ]
_____
Inherited Rights           [   B         ]
```

The Inherited Rights for OU=LAB are [B   ], and the source is group OWNERS.

An explicit trustee assignment of [S] has been given to user John. The explicit trustee assignment overrides any other inherited rights for user John only. The last point is important to understand. Inherited rights of [B] exist, but this is through group OWNERS. So the explicit right of [S] for user John does not override the inherited rights for group OWNERS, which is the reason that it is so important to keep track of the source of the rights. The effective rights in this case are the sum of the inherited rights from group OWNERS and the explicit trustee assignment for user John.

```
Inherited Rights for group OWNERS   [   B         ]
Trustee Assignment for user John    [ S           ]
_____
Effective Rights                    [ S B (C D R ) ]
```

The effective rights are through membership to group OWNERS and through assignment to User object John, and they are [S B (C D R)]. The (C D R) rights are implied because of the presence of the Supervisor [S] right.

If the trustee assignment of Supervisor right was revoked from user John for OU=LAB, user John still would have the Browse right from membership to Group object OWNERS. And, if the user John was removed as a member of group OWNERS, John still would have the explicit Supervisor right granted to him for OU=LAB and the implied rights of (B C D R).

Case Study 6—Computing Effective Rights

Figure 5.47 shows a directory tree for organization KJBR. Bob becomes a trustee of Organizational Unit OU=LAB and receives the Supervisor right. Bob is a member of two Group objects: group OWNERS and group MGRS. The Group object OWNERS has been given a trustee assignment of Browse and Rename rights for Organization O=KJBR. The Group object MGRS has been given a trustee assignment of Browse, Create, and Delete right for Organization Unit OU=PDEV.

Figure 5.47

Object effective rights: NDS tree for case study 6.

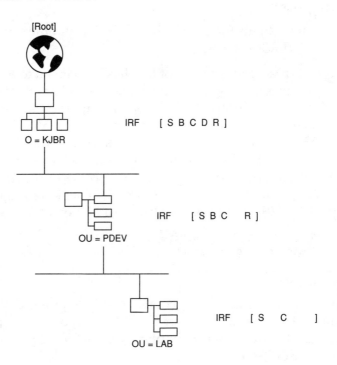

The IRFs for the containers are shown here:

```
IRF for O=KJBR     [S B C D R ]
IRF for OU=PDEV    [S B C   R ]
IRF for OU=LAB     [S   C     ]
```

Calculate Bob's effective rights in containers O=KJBR, OU=PDEV, and OU=LAB. Assume that Bob does not inherit rights from any other source than the ones listed in the case study.

Figure 5.48 shows the completed worksheet containing the answers. The explanations for entries in the worksheet are presented next.

Figure 5.48

Object effective rights: worksheet for case study 6.

O = KJBR		
IRF	S B C D R	
Inherited Rights	None	
Trustee Assignment	B R	Group OWNERS
Effective Rights	B R	

OU = PDEV		
IRF	S B C R	
Inherited Rights	B R	Group OWNERS
Trustee Assignment	B C D	Group MGRS
Effective Rights	B C D R	Group MGRS, OWNERS

OU = LAB		
IRF	S C	
Inherited Rights	C	Group MGRS
Trustee Assignment	S	User Bob
Effective Rights	S (B) C (D R)	User Bob, Group MGRS

Entries for O=KJBR

The IRF, according to the case study, is [S B C D R]. No rights are inherited from above, and therefore, the entry for Inherited Rights is None. An explicit trustee assignment of [B R] has been given to the group OWNERS, of which Bob is a member. The explicit trustee assignment overrides any other inherited rights for group OWNERS, so the effective rights for Bob in container O=KJBR are the same as the explicit trustee assignment. That is, Bob's effective rights for O=KJBR are [B R]. The worksheet also shows that the effective rights that were computed are for Group object OWNERS, of which Bob is a member. When calculating effective rights in cases where rights could be from several sources, you should keep track of the sources of the rights to avoid confusion.

Entries for OU=PDEV

The IRF, according to the case study, is [S B C R]. The rights inherited from above are the effective rights of the parent container masked with the IRF for this container:

```
IRF                           [S  B C  R            ]
Effective rights of parent    [   B    R            ]
_____
Inherited Rights              [   B    R            ]
```

The masking operation is a logical AND operation, which means that an entry needs to be in both the rights for it to be in the final result.

The Inherited Rights for OU=PDEV are [B R], and the source is the Group object OWNERS. An explicit trustee assignment of [B C D] is made to OU=PDEV through group MGRS.

The explicit trustee assignment overrides any other inherited rights for group MGRS only. The explicit right of [B C D] for group MGRS does not override the inherited rights for group OWNERS, which is the reason that it is so important to keep track of the source of the rights. The effective rights in this case are the sum of theinherited rights from group OWNERS and the explicit trustee assignment for group MGRS, and Bob is a member of both.

```
Inherited Rights for group OWNERS   [    B    R           ]
Trustee Assignment for group  MGRS  [    B C D             ]
_____
Effective Rights for Bob            [    B C D R           ]
```

The effective rights are through membership to group OWNERS and MGRS.

If the user Bob was removed as a member of group OWNERS, Bob still would have the explicit [B C D] rights granted to him by membership to MGRS. And, if Bob was removed as a member of group MGRS, Bob still would have the inherited [B R] rights granted to him by membership to OWNERS.

Entries for OU=LAB

The IRF, according to the case study, is [S B C]. The rights inherited from above are the effective rights of the parent container masked with the IRF for this container:

```
IRF                        [ S  B  C       ]
Effective rights of parent [    B  C  D  R ]
_____
Inherited Rights           [    B  C       ]
```

The Inherited Rights for OU=LAB are [S B C], and the source is group MGRS.

An explicit trustee assignment of [S] has been given to user Bob. The explicit trustee assignment overrides any other inherited rights for user Bob only. The last point is important to understand. Inherited rights of [B C] exist through group MGRS. The explicit right of [S] for user Bob, therefore, does not override the inherited rights for group MGRS, which is the reason that it is so important to keep track of the source of the rights. The effective rights in this case are the sum of the inherited rights from group MGRS and the explicit trustee assignment for user Bob.

```
Inherited Rights for group  MGRS   [     C        ]
Trustee Assignment for user Bob    [ S            ]
_____
Effective Rights                   [ S B C (D R ) ]
```

The effective rights are through membership to group MGRS and through assignment to User object Bob, and they are [S B C (D R)]. The [(D R)] rights are implied because of the presence of the Supervisor [S] right.

If the trustee assignment of Supervisor right was revoked from user Bob for OU=LAB, user Bob still would have the Create and Browse rights from membership to Group object MGRS. And, if the user Bob was removed as a member of group MGRS, Bob still would have the explicit Supervisor right granted to him for OU=LAB, and the implied rights of (B C D R).

Case Study 7—Computing Effective Rights

Figure 5.49 shows a directory tree for organization MicroCon. JConnor becomes a trustee of Organizational Unit OU=RESEARCH and receives the Supervisor, Create, Delete, and Rename rights. JConnor also becomes a trustee of OU=LAB and receives the Create right. [Public] receives the Browse right to organization O=MicroCon.

Figure 5.49

Object effective rights: NDS tree for case study 7.

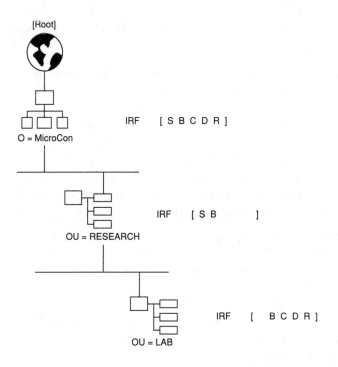

The IRFs for the containers follow:

```
IRF for O=MicroCon      [S B C D R ]
IRF for OU=RESEARCH     [S B       ]
IRF for OU=LAB          [   B C D R ]
```

Calculate JConnor's effective rights in containers O=MicroCon, OU=RESEARCH, and OU=LAB. Assume that JConnor does not inherit rights from any other source than the ones listed in the case study.

Figure 5.50 shows the completed worksheet containing the answers. The explanations for entries in the worksheet are presented next.

O = MicroCon			
IRF	S B C D R		
Inherited Rights	None		
Trustee Assignment	B	[Public]	
Effective Rights	B		

OU = RESEARCH			
IRF	S B		
Inherited Rights	B	[Public]	
Trustee Assignment	S C D R	User JConnor	
Effective Rights	S B C D R	User JConnor, [Public]	

OU = LAB			
IRF	B C D R		
Inherited Rights	B C D R	User JConnor, [Public]	
Trustee Assignment	C	User JConnor	
Effective Rights	B C	User JConnor, [Public]	

Figure 5.50

Object effective rights: worksheet for case study 7.

Entries for O=MicroCon

The IRF, according to the case study, is [S B C D R]. No rights are inherited from above, and therefore, the entry for Inherited Rights is None. An explicit trustee assignment of [B] has been given through [Public], of which JConnor automatically is a member. The explicit trustee assignment overrides any other inherited rights for [Public] (of which there are none), so the effective rights for JConnor in container O=MicroCon are the same as the explicit trustee assignment. That is, JConnor's effective rights for O=MicroCon are [B]. The worksheet also shows that the Effective rights that were computed are for [Public], of which JConnor is a member. When calculating effective rights where there could be rights from several sources, you should keep track of the sources to avoid confusion.

Entries for OU=RESEARCH

The IRF, according to the case study, is [S B]. The rights inherited from above are the effective rights of the parent container masked with the IRF for this container:

```
IRF                          [S  B        ]
Effective rights of parent   [   B        ]
_____
Inherited Rights             [   B        ]
```

The masking operation is a logical AND operation, which means that an entry needs to be in both the rights for it to be in the final result.

The Inherited Rights for OU=RESEARCH are [B], and the source is [Public]. An explicit trustee assignment of [S C D R] is made to OU=RESEARCH for user JConnor.

The explicit trustee assignment overrides any other inherited rights for user JConnor only. The explicit rights of [S C D R] for user JConnor does not override the inherited rights of [B], whose source is [Public], which is the reason that it is so important to keep track of the source of the rights. The effective rights in this case are the sum of the inherited rights from [Public] and the explicit trustee assignment for user JConnor.

```
Inherited Rights for [public]            [    B       ]
Trustee Assignment for user JConnor      [  S     C D R ]
_____
Effective Rights for JConnor             [  S B C D R ]
```

The effective rights are through [Public] and trustee assignment to JConnor.

Entries for OU=LAB

The IRF, according to the case study, is [B C D R]. The rights inherited from above are the effective rights of the parent container masked with the IRF for this container:

```
IRF                          [   B  C   D  R  ]
Effective rights of parent   [S  B  C   D  R  ]
_____
Inherited Rights             [   B  C   D  R  ]
```

The Inherited Rights for OU=LAB are [B C D R   ], and the sources are [Public] and user JConnor. JConnor's contribution to this right is [C D R], and [Public]'s contribution is [B]. An explicit trustee assignment of [S] has been given to user JConnor. The explicit trustee assignment overrides any other inherited rights for user JConnor only. JConnor has inherited rights of [C D R], so the explicit right of [C] for user JConnor overrides the inherited rights of [C D R]. The effective rights in this case are the sum of the inherited rights from [Public] and the explicit trustee assignment for user JConnor.

```
Inherited Rights for [Public]          [   B                  ]
Trustee Assignment for user JConnor    [ S   C D R            ]
_____
Effective Rights for JConnor           [   B C D R            ]
```

The effective rights are through membership to [Public] and through assignment of the [C] right to User object JConnor.

If the Trustee Assignment of the Create right was revoked from user JConnor for OU=LAB, user JConnor still would have the Browse right from [public]. And, if the [Public] with Browse right was removed as a trustee for O=MicroCon, user JConnor still would have the explicit Create right granted to him for OU=LAB.

Case Study 8—Computing Effective Rights

Figure 5.51 shows a directory tree for organization MicroCon. BWayne becomes a trustee of each of the container objects O=MicroCon, OU=RESEARCH, OU=LAB. For O=MicroCon, BWayne receives Supervisor right; for OU=RESEARCH, BWayne receives Browse, Create, and Delete rights; and for OU=LAB, BWayne receives the Create and Delete rights. [Public] is given the Browse and Rename rights to organization O=MicroCon.

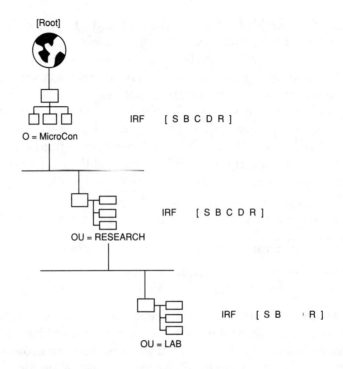

The IRFs for the containers follow:

```
IRF for O=MicroCon      [S B C D R ]
IRF for OU=RESEARCH     [S B C D R ]
IRF for OU=LAB          [S B     R ]
```

Calculate BWayne's effective rights in containers O=MicroCon, OU=RESEARCH, and OU=LAB. Assume that BWayne does not inherit rights from any other source than the ones listed in the case study.

Figure 5.52 shows the completed worksheet containing the answers. The explanations for entries in the worksheet are presented next.

O = MicroCon			
	IRF	S B C D R	
	Inherited Rights	None	
	Trustee Assignment	B R S	[Public] BWayne
	Effective Rights	S B (C D) R	[Public], BWayne
OU = RESEARCH			
	IRF	S B C D R	
	Inherited Rights	S B (C D) R	[Public], BWayne
	Trustee Assignment	B C D	BWayne
	Effective Rights	B C D R	[Public], BWayne
OU = LAB			
	IRF	S B R	
	Inherited Rights	B R	[Public], BWayne
	Trustee Assignment	C D	BWayne
	Effective Rights	B C D R	[Public, BWayne]

Figure 5.52

Object effective rights: worksheet for case study 8.

Entries for O=MicroCon

The IRF, according to the case study, is [S B C D R]. No rights are inherited from above, and therefore, the entry for Inherited Rights is None. An explicit trustee assignment of [B R] has been given through [Public], of which BWayne is automatically a member. The explicit trustee assignment overrides any other inherited rights for [Public] (of which there are none). BWayne also receives an explicit trustee assignment of Supervisor for O=MicroCon. So, the effective rights for the user BWayne in container O=MicroCon are the sum of the rights through [Public] and through an explicit assignment.

```
Inherited Rights for [public]        [   B        R  ]
Trustee Assignment for user BWayne   [S              ]
_____
Effective Rights for BWayne          [S  B  (C D) R  ]
```

The Effective rights are through membership to [Public] and through assignment to User object BWayne of the [S] right. The [(C D)] rights are implied because of the Supervisor [S] right.

Entries for OU=RESEARCH

The IRF, according to the case study, is [S B C D R]. The rights inherited from above are the effective rights of the parent container masked with the IRF for this container:

```
IRF                        [S  B  C D  R ]
Effective rights of parent [S  B (C D) R ]
_____
Inherited Rights           [S  B (C D) R ]
```

The masking operation is a logical AND operation, which means that an entry needs to be in both the rights for it to be in the final result.

The Inherited Rights for OU=RESEARCH are [S B (C D) R], and the sources are [Public] and BWayne. BWayne's contribution to the effective rights is [S], and [Public]'s contribution is [B R].

An explicit trustee assignment of [B C D] is made to OU=RESEARCH for user BWayne. The explicit trustee assignment overrides any other inherited rights for user BWayne only. The explicit right of [B C D] for user BWayne overrides the Supervisor (S) right in the inherited rights. With the Supervisor right gone, only the [B R] right in the Inherited rights mask for [Public] remains. The explicit assignment of [B C D] for BWayne cannot override inherited rights from another source, such as [Public], which is the reason that it is so important to keep track of the source of the rights. The effective rights in this case are the sum of the inherited rights from [Public] and the explicit trustee assignment for user BWayne.

```
Inherited Rights for [Public]        [    B      R   ]
Trustee Assignment for user BWayne   [    B C  D     ]
_____
Effective Rights for BWayne          [    B C  D  R  ]
```

The effective rights are through [Public] and trustee assignment to BWayne. Please also note that the Browse right is contributed by both [Public] and BWayne. If the Browse right is removed from either [Public] or BWayne, but not both, user BWayne still would have the Browse right.

Entries for OU=LAB

The IRF, according to the case study, is [S B R]. The rights inherited from above are the effective rights of the parent container masked with the IRF for this container:

```
IRF                        [S  B        R  ]
Effective rights of parent [   B  C  D  R  ]
                           _____
Inherited Rights           [   B        R  ]
```

The Inherited Rights for OU=LAB are [B   R], and the sources is [Public] and user BWayne. BWayne's contribution to this right are [B], and [Public]'s contribution is [B R]. An explicit trustee assignment of [C D] has been given to user BWayne. The explicit trustee assignment overrides any other inherited rights for user BWayne only. BWayne has inherited rights of [B]. So, the explicit right of [C D R] for user BWayne overrides the inherited rights of [B] for BWayne. The effective rights in this case are the sum of the inherited rights from [Public] and the explicit trustee assignment for user BWayne.

```
Inherited Rights for [Public]       [   B        R  ]
Trustee Assignment for user BWayne  [      C  D      ]
                                    _____
Effective Rights for BWayne         [   B  C  D  R  ]
```

The effective rights are through membership to [Public] and through assignment to User object BWayne of the [C D] right.

If the trustee assignment of the Create and Delete rights were revoked from user BWayne for OU=LAB, user BWayne still would have the Browse and Rename rights from [Public]. And, if the [Public] with Browse and Rename rights was removed as a trustee for O=MicroCon, user BWayne still would have the explicit Create and Delete right granted to the user for OU=LAB.

Case Study 9—Computing Effective Rights

Figure 5.53 shows a directory tree for organization SCS.

Figure 5.53

Object effective rights: NDS tree for case study 9.

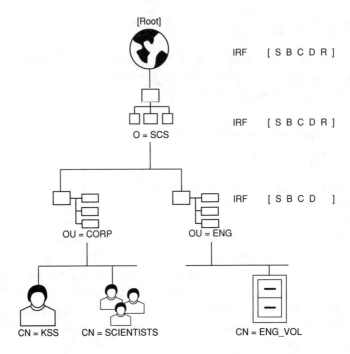

[Public] is given the Browse right to the [Root] object. User KSS is given the Create right to O=SCS. The Organizational Unit OU=CORP is given the Create and Delete right to OU=ENG. The Group SCIENTISTS is given the [C D R] rights to O=SCS. User KSS is a member of group SCIENTISTS.

The IRFs for the containers follow:

```
IRF for [Root]    [S B C D R ]
IRF for O=SCS     [S B C D R ]
IRF for OU=ENG    [S B C D   ]
```

Calculate KSS's effective rights in containers [Root], O=SCS, and OU=ENG. Assume that KSS does not inherit rights from any other source than the ones listed in the case study.

Figure 5.54 shows the completed worksheet containing the answers. The explanations for entries in the worksheet are presented next.

[Root]			
	IRF	S B C D R	
	Inherited Rights	None	
	Trustee Assignment	B	[Public]
	Effective Rights	B	
O = SCS			
	IRF	S B C D R	
	Inherited Rights	B	[Public]
	Trustee Assignment	C D R	User KSS / Group SCIENTISTS
	Effective Rights	B C D R	[Public], User KSS, Group SCIENTISTS
OU = ENG			
	IRF	S B C D	
	Inherited Rights	B C D	[Public], User KSS, Group SCIENTISTS
	Trustee Assignment	C D R	Org Unit CORP
	Effective Rights	B C D R	[Public], User KSS, Group SCIENTISTS, Org Unit CORP

Figure 5.54

Object effective rights: worksheet for case study 9.

Entries for [Root]

The IRF, according to the case study, is [S B C D R]. No rights are inherited from above, and therefore, the entry for Inherited Rights is None. An explicit trustee assignment of [B] has been given through [Public], of which KSS is automatically a member. The explicit trustee assignment overrides any other inherited rights for [Public] (of which there are none). So, the effective rights for the user KSS in container [Root] are the same as the explicit rights through [Public].

Entries for O=SCS

The IRF, according to the case study, is [S B C D R]. The rights inherited from above are the effective rights of the parent container masked with the IRF for this container:

```
IRF                         [S  B  C  D  R     ]
Effective rights of parent  [   B              ]
_____
Inherited Rights            [   B              ]
```

479

The masking operation is a logical AND operation, which means that an entry needs to be in both the rights for it to be in the final result.

The Inherited Rights for O=SCS are [B], and the source is [Public].

An explicit trustee assignment of [C] is made to O=SCS for user KSS. The explicit trustee assignment overrides any other inherited rights for user KSS only. Group SCIENTISTS has an explicit trustee assignment of [C D R], which overrides any inherited rights for group SCIENTISTS, if any occurred. The effective rights are the sum of the inherited rights for [Public], and explicit trustee assignments for user KSS and group SCIENTISTS.

```
Inherited Rights for [Public]              [     B          ]
Trustee Assignment for user KSS            [        C       ]
Trustee Assignment for group SCIENTISTS    [        C D R   ]
_____
Effective Rights for KSS                   [     B C D R    ]
```

Entries for OU=ENG

The IRF, according to the case study, is [S B C D]. The rights inherited from above are the effective rights of the parent container masked with the IRF for this container:

```
IRF                        [S  B  C  D     ]
Effective rights of parent [   B  C  D  R  ]
_____
Inherited Rights           [   B  C  D     ]
```

The Inherited Rights for OU=ENG are [B C D], and the sources of these rights are [Public], user KSS, and group SCIENTISTS. KSS's contribution to this right is [C], [Public]'s contribution is [B], and group SCIENTISTS' contribution is [D]. An explicit trustee assignment of [C D R] has been given to container OU=CORP, of which user KSS and group SCIENTISTS are member objects. The explicit trustee assignment overrides any other inherited rights for user container OU=CORP only.

```
Inherited Rights for KSS, [public], group SCIENTIST   [ B C D   ]
Trustee Assignment for container OU=CORP              [   C D R ]
_____
Effective Rights for KSS                             [ B C D R ]
```

Case Study 10—Computing Effective Rights

Figure 5.55 shows a directory tree for organization SCS.

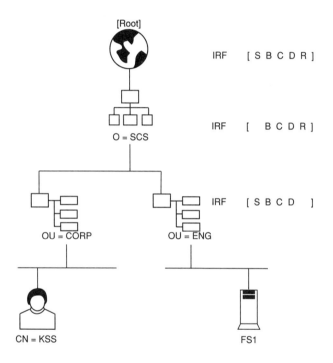

IRF   [S B C D R]

IRF   [B C D R]

IRF   [S B C D   ]

Figure 5.55

Object effective rights: NDS tree for case study 10.

[Public] receives the Browse right to the [Root] object. The Organizational Unit container OU=CORP receives the Rename right to OU=ENG and the Supervisor right to O=SCS. User KSS receives a trustee assignment of Browse, Create, Delete, and Rename to O=SCS.

The IRFs for the containers follow:

```
IRF for [Root]     [S B C D R ]
IRF for O=SCS      [  B C D R ]
IRF for OU=ENG     [S B C D   ]
```

Calculate KSS's effective rights in containers [Root], O=SCS, and OU=ENG. Assume that KSS does not inherit rights from any source other than the ones listed in the case study.

Figure 5.56 shows the completed worksheet containing the answers. The explanations for entries in the worksheet are presented next.

Figure 5.56

Object effective rights: worksheet for case study 10.

[Root]			
	IRF	S B C D R	
	Inherited Rights	None	
	Trustee Assignment	B	
	Effective Rights	B	
O = SCS			
	IRF	B C D R	
	Inherited Rights	B	
	Trustee Assignment	B C D R / S	User KSS OU = CORP
	Effective Rights	S B C D R	
OU = ENG			
	IRF	S B C D	
	Inherited Rights	S B C D	KSS, OU = CORP
	Trustee Assignment	R	OU = CORP
	Effective Rights	B C D R	

Entries for [Root]

The IRF, according to the case study, is [S B C D R]. No rights are inherited from above, and therefore, the entry for Inherited Rights is None. An explicit trustee assignment of [B] has been given through [Public], of which KSS is automatically a member. The explicit trustee assignment overrides any other inherited rights for [Public] (of which there are none). So, the effective rights for the user KSS in container [Root] are the same as the explicit rights through [Public].

Entries for O=SCS

The IRF, according to the case study, is [B C D R]. The rights inherited from above are the effective rights of the parent container masked with the IRF for this container:

```
IRF                       [ B  C  D  R  ]
Effective rights of parent  [ B           ]
_____
Inherited Rights          [ B           ]
```

The masking operation is a logical AND operation, which means that an entry needs to be in both the rights for it to be in the final result.

The Inherited Rights for O=SCS are [B], and the source is [Public].

An explicit trustee assignment of [B C D R] is made to O=SCS for user KSS. The explicit trustee assignment overrides any other inherited rights for user KSS only. Group OU=CORP has an explicit trustee assignment of [S], which would override any inherited rights for OU=CORP, if there were any. The effective rights are the sum of the inherited rights for [Public], and explicit trustee assignments for user KSS and OU=CORP.

```
Inherited Rights for [Public]      [    B        ]
Trustee Assignment for user KSS    [    B C D  R  ]
Trustee Assignment for OU=CORP     [ S           ]
_____
Effective Rights for KSS           [ S  B C D  R  ]
```

Entries for OU=ENG

The IRF, according to the case study, is [S B C D]. The rights inherited from above are the effective rights of the parent container masked with the IRF for this container:

```
IRF                       [S  B  C  D     ]
Effective rights of parent  [S  B  C  D  R  ]
_____
Inherited Rights          [S  B  C  D     ]
```

The Inherited Rights for OU=ENG are [S B C D], and the sources of these rights are [Public], user KSS, and OU=CORP.

KSS's contribution to this right is [B C D R], [Public]'s contribution is [B], and OU=CORP's contribution is [S]. An explicit trustee assignment of [R] has been given to container OU=CORP, of which user KSS is a member object. This explicit trustee assignment overrides any other inherited rights for user container OU=CORP only. OU=CORP has an inherited rights value of [S], and this is overridden by the new trustee assignment of [R]. All that remains of the inherited rights are just the [B C D R].

```
Inherited Rights for KSS, [public]        [  B   C D   ]
Trustee Assignment for container OU=CORP  [          R ]
_____
Effective Rights for KSS                  [  B   C D R ]
```

Examining Property Rights

Property rights are used to control access to information inside an NDS object. All objects have properties, because all objects are used to store information. An object can have many properties, and different objects can be expected to have different properties. A Volume object, for example, has a host server property with a value that is the name of the NetWare server with which the volume is associated.

This property does not exist for a User object, however. Similarly, a user has a group membership property that does not exist for a Volume object. The group membership is an example of a property that is multi-valued. Another example is the telephone number property. A user can have several phone numbers, so the telephone property for the user has the characteristic of accommodating multiple values. The location property of an object is single-valued, because an object can have only one location.

Table 5.5 lists the property rights that are defined for an NDS object.

Table 5.5
Property Rights Summary

Property Right	Abbreviation	Meaning
Supervisor	S	Grants all rights to All properties.
Compare	C	Grants the right to compare the value to a property. Does not enable you to see the value.
Read	R	Grants the right to read the value of a property. Read includes the Compare right, even if the Compare is not explicitly given.
Write	W	Grants the right to add, remove, change any values to the property.
Add or Delete	A	Applies to list property values Self such as group membership. Grants the trustee the right to add/remove itself from the property value. The trustee cannot add/delete other values of the property. Useful for mailing lists, group lists.

The Supervisor property right grants all rights to a property. This property can be blocked by the Inherited Rights Filter, if you so desire.

The Compare property right grants the right to compare the value of a property. A trustee with the Compare property right enables a trustee to compare the property value to any value. The result of this comparison is a logical True, if there is a match; and a logical

False, if there is no match. This property right is useful for NDS tools that need to check for the existence of a specific value. The Compare right does not give you the right to read a property value. This right is granted by a special property value.

The Read property right grants the right to read a value for a property. This property right is useful for NDS tools that need to display selected property values of an NDS object. If a trustee can read the value, it follows that the trustee should be able to compare the property value against another value. For this reason, a Read property right includes the Compare property right.

The Write property right allows the property value to be changed. Some property values are multi-valued. In this case, the Write property enables the trustee to remove or add values to the property.

The Add or Delete Self property right allows the addition of a new property value or the removal of an existing property value. This right applies to multi-valued properties such as group memberships, mailing lists, or the Access Control List (ACL). The Add or Delete Self property right cannot be used to change the value of properties other than itself.

The Write property right includes the Add or Delete Self property.

All Properties Right versus Selected Property Right

The property rights can be assigned selectively to specific properties, or they can be applied to all the properties of an object. When a property right is assigned to all the properties of an object, it is called the All Properties right. When a property right refers to an individual or selected property, it is called Selected Property right. An example of a property right assignment is when a User object is created in a container. The User object is given the Read property right to all of its properties (All Properties). It is also given a Read/Write property right to its login script property and the Print Job Configuration Property, which enables users to modify their user login scripts and print job configurations. If you want to prevent a user from performing these activities, you must restrict these property rights.

The All Properties right is a convenient way of assigning default property rights to all properties. If some exceptions to this default are found, the Selected Property right can be used to individually set the property right of any property. The Selected Property right overrides the property right set by the All Properties right.

The Access Control List Property

Every object has an Access Control List (ACL) property, also called the Object Trustees property. This property contains a list of all trustees that have a trustee assignment to the object or its property. It does not list other objects to which this object might have rights. In order to grant a right, therefore, you must go to the object and assign a trustee.

The ACL property value can be used to specify any of the following:

◆ An object right, such as the [S B C D R] rights.

◆ A right to all properties of the object, called the "All Properties" which gives the object whatever rights are selected [S C R W A] to all properties.

◆ A right to a specific property.

Because an ACL is a property of the object that describes the trustee assignments to the object, it can include a trustee assignment to itself. This trustee assignment to the ACL property describes which of the operations defined by the property rights [S C R W A], a trustee could perform.

Consider what would happen if a trustee had a Write property right to the ACL. Such a trustee could then modify the ACL and grant and revoke privileges by changing the ACL value. To perform such modifications, the trustee would also need the Read property right and the Browse object right to the object. The trustee could grant itself Supervisor right to the object, which would give the trustee complete control over the object and its subordinates (unless blocked by an IRF or explicit assignment).

In actual practice, it is unlikely that you want to give an Admin user just the Write right to the ACL property. You probably want to give the Admin user Supervisor object right, which would provide complete control over the object and its subordinates, unless, as noted earlier, you block the Supervisor right.

Normally, you do not single out the ACL property (appears as Object Trustee property in the NetWare Administrator Tool) for giving property rights. You can, however, inadvertently grant the Write right to All Properties. This grant, in turn, grants the Write right to the ACL property, and then the problem in which a user can obtain Supervisor rights exists.

 Note Do not assign users the Write property right to the ACL property or the All Properties.

NDS Rights and the File System

A trustee who has the Write property right to the NetWare server's ACL property is granted the Supervisor file system right to the root of each of the server's volume. It is, therefore, important that you do not inadvertently give the Write right to the server's ACL property or the Write right to the server object (All Properties of the server object).

Normally, the NDS rights are independent from the file system rights. The only exception is the one mentioned previously. Actually, the exception is necessary to provide an easy way for a trustee with Supervisor rights to access files and directories in Volume objects.

A trustee who has the Write property right to the NetWare server's ACL property is granted the Supervisor file system right to the root of each of the server's volumes.

Consider the Admin user, who normally is given the Supervisor object right to the root container of the tree branch that the user is expected to manage. This user has Supervisor rights to all objects in the tree branch, unless the Supervisor right is explicitly blocked using the IRF. The Supervisor object right grants to the user the Supervisor property right to All Properties for all objects, including the server object. If the user has the Write property right to the server object, the user then inherits the Supervisor NetWare file system right to the root of all volumes for which the server is a host.

 To make a user an administrator of a tree branch, grant the user Supervisor privileges to the root of the tree branch.

The Admin user could be explicitly granted the Supervisor NetWare file system right to the root of a Volume. In general, any NDS object can be granted an explicit NetWare file system right to a file or directory in any Volume.

Figure 5.57 shows a situation in which the NDS user Admin1.CORP.ESL has been granted Supervisor, Read, and File Scan rights to the SYSTEM directory of a volume, and figure 5.58 shows that the NDS Group object Nfsgroup.CORP.ESL has been granted Read and File Scan rights.

Figure 5.57

NetWare file system right assigned to a user NDS object.

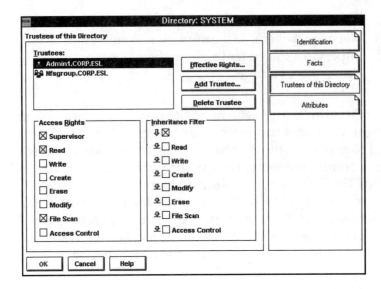

Figure 5.58

NetWare file system right assigned to a group NDS object.

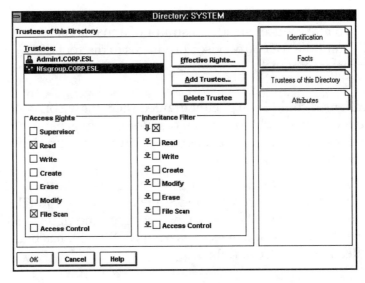

Care must be exercised when assigning a container object a right to another NDS object or a NetWare file system. A right assigned to a container object is inherited by all objects within that container, because a container acts as a logical group of NDS objects.

490

If a Supervisor NetWare file system right is granted to the [Root] object, for instance, all objects in the [Root] directory are assigned the Supervisor NetWare file system right. And because [Root] is the top-most container of an NDS tree, all objects in the NDS tree are included.

Calculating Property Effective Rights

Calculating property effective rights is similar to calculating object effective rights. The same rules of inheritance apply.

Objects property rights can be dealt with in terms of their All Property Rights or Selective Property Rights. Only All Property Rights can be inherited. Selective Property Rights cannot be inherited. Consider what happens if a Selected Property is allowed to be inherited. A selected property might have no meaning for objects farther down in the tree. Intruder detection is a property of a container object, for example, and if this property is inherited to an object, such as a User object that does not have an intruder detection property, it does not make sense. It might be convenient, however, to assign rights to information inside objects, regardless of the different types of properties NDS objects can have. This task can be done by allowing the All Properties right to be inherited.

The All Properties option and Selected Properties option have separate Inherited Rights Filters, so a right can be blocked at any level. Also, a right assigned to a Selected Property overrides the rights that can be inherited through the All Properties option.

Case Study 1—Computing Property Effective Rights

Figure 5.59 shows a directory tree for organization IBL. Drew becomes a trustee of Organization O=IBL and receives the All Properties rights of Create, Read, Add/Delete Self. The All Properties IRFs for the containers follow:

```
IRF for O=IBL          [S C R W A]
IRF for OU=CORP        [  C R W  ]
IRF for OU=MKTG        [S     W A]
```

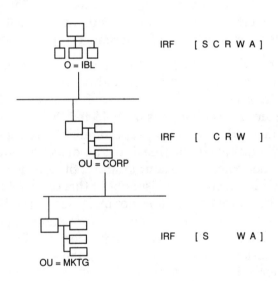

```
IRF    [ S C R W A ]

IRF    [   C R W   ]

IRF    [ S     W A ]
```

Calculate Drew's property effective rights in containers O=IBL, OU=CORP, and OU=MKTG. Assume that Drew does not inherit rights from any source other than the ones listed in the case study.

Figure 5.60 shows the completed worksheet containing the answers. The explanations for entries in the worksheet are presented next.

O = IBL		
IRF	S C R W A	
Inherited Rights	None	
Trustee Assignment	C R	A
Effective Rights	C R	A

OU = CORP		
IRF	C R W	
Inherited Rights	C R	
Trustee Assignment	None	
Effective Rights	C R	

OU = MKTG		
IRF	S W A	
Inherited Rights	No Rights	
Trustee Assignment	None	
Effective Rights	No Rights	

Figure 5.60

Property effective rights: worksheet for case study 1.

Entries for O=IBL

The IRF, according to the case study, is [S C R W A]. No rights are inherited from above, and therefore, the entry for Inherited Rights is None. An explicit trustee assignment of [C R A] has been given to the user. The explicit trustee assignment overrides any other inherited rights, so the effective rights for the user in container O=IBL are the same as the explicit trustee assignment. That is, the property effective rights of the user for O=IBL are [C R A].

Entries for OU=CORP

The IRF, according to the case study, is [C R W]. The rights inherited from above are the effective rights of the parent container masked with the IRF for this container:

```
IRF                          [    C R W      ]
Effective rights of parent   [    C R      A]
─────────────────────────────
Inherited Rights             [    C R      ]
```

The masking operation is a logical AND operation, which means that an entry needs to be in both the rights for it to be in the final result.

493

The Inherited Rights for OU=CORP are [C R]. Because no trustee assignment is made in OU=CORP, the effective rights are the same as the Inherited Rights. That is, property effective rights for OU=CORP are [C R].

Entries for OU=MKTG

The IRF, according to the case study, is [S W A]. The rights inherited from above are the effective rights of the parent container masked with the IRF for this container:

```
IRF                          [S          W A ]
Effective rights of parent   [     C R        ]
_____
Inherited Rights             [                ]
```

The Inherited Rights for OU=MKTG are [   ], or No Rights. Because no trustee assignment is made in OU=MKTG, the effective rights are the same as the Inherited Rights. That is, property effective rights for OU=MKTG are No Rights.

Case Study 2—Computing Property Effective Rights

Figure 5.61 shows a directory tree for organization IBL. James becomes a trustee of Organization O=IBL and receives the All Properties rights of Create, Read, and Write. The All Properties IRFs for the containers are shown below:

```
IRF for O=IBL        [S C R W A ]
IRF for OU=CORP      [S C R W A ]
IRF for OU=MKTG      [S   R     ]
```

Calculate James's property effective rights in containers O=IBL, OU=CORP, and OU=MKTG. Assume that James does not inherit rights from any source, other than the ones listed in the case study.

Figure 5.62 shows the completed worksheet containing the answers. The explanations for entries in the worksheet are presented next.

494

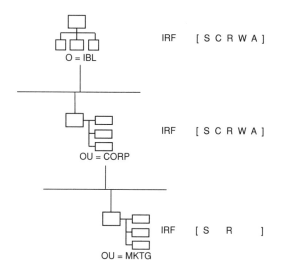

Figure 5.61

Property effective rights: NDS tree for case study 2.

O = IBL			
IRF	S C R W A		
Inherited Rights	None		
Trustee Assignment	C R W	James	
Effective Rights	C R W (A)	James	
OU = CORP			
IRF	S C R W A		
Inherited Rights	C R W (A)		
Trustee Assignment	None		
Effective Rights	C R W (A)	James	
OU = MKTG			
IRF	S R		
Inherited Rights	(C) R		
Trustee Assignment			
Effective Rights	(C) R	James	

Figure 5.62

Property effective rights: worksheet for case study 2.

Entries for O=IBL

The IRF, according to the case study, is [S C R W A]. No rights are inherited from above, and therefore, the entry for Inherited Rights is None. An explicit trustee assignment of [C R W] has been given to the user. The explicit trustee assignment overrides any other inherited rights, so the effective rights for the user in container O=IBL are the same as the explicit trustee assignment. That is, James' effective property rights for O=IBL are [C R W (A)]. The [(A)] right is implied from the Write right.

Entries for OU=CORP

The IRF, according to the case study, is [S C R W A]. The rights inherited from above are the effective rights of the parent container masked with the IRF for this container:

```
IRF                          [S   C R W  A  ]
Effective rights of parent   [    C R W (A) ]
_____

Inherited Rights             [    C R W (A) ]
```

The masking operation is a logical AND operation, which means that an entry needs to be in both the rights for it to be in the final result.

The Inherited Rights for OU=CORP are [C R W (A)]. Because no trustee assignment is made in OU=CORP, the effective rights are the same as the Inherited Rights. That is, James' effective property rights for OU=CORP are [C R W (A)].

Entries for OU=MKTG

The IRF, according to the case study, is [S R]. The rights inherited from above are the effective rights of the parent container masked with the IRF for this container:

```
IRF                          [S      R     ]
Effective rights of parent   [    C  R W (A)]
_____

Inherited Rights             [   (C) R     ]
```

The Inherited Rights for OU=MKTG are [(C) R]. The [(C)] inherited right is implied because of the presence of the Read right in the Inherited Rights. Because no trustee assignment is made in OU=MKTG, the effective rights are the same as the Inherited Rights. That is, James' effective property rights for OU=MKTG are [(C) R].

Case Study 3—Computing Property Effective Rights

Figure 5.63 shows a directory tree for organization DCS. James becomes a trustee of Organization O=DCS and receives the All

Properties rights of Create, Read, and Write. James is a member of the group ATEAM. ATEAM receives the All Properties rights Write and Add/Delete Self to OU=SALES. James also becomes a trustee of Organizational Unit OU=MKTG, and receives the All Properties of Write. The All Properties IRFs for the containers follow:

```
IRF for O=DCS         [S C R W A ]
IRF for OU=SALES      [S C R W A ]
IRF for OU=MKTG       [S   R     ]
```

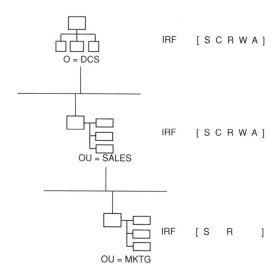

IRF   [S C R W A]

IRF   [S C R W A]

IRF   [S   R   ]

Figure 5.63

Property effective rights: NDS tree for case study 3.

Calculate James's effective property rights in containers O=DCS, OU=SALES and OU=MKTG. Assume that James does not inherit rights from any source other than the ones listed in the case study.

Figure 5.64 shows the completed worksheet containing the answers. The explanations for entries in the worksheet are presented next.

Figure 5.64

Property effective rights: worksheet for case study 3.

O = DCS			
IRF	S C R W A		
Inherited Rights	None		
Trustee Assignment	C R W	James	
Effective Rights	C R W	James	

OU = SALES			
IRF	S C R W A		
Inherited Rights	C R W (A)		
Trustee Assignment	W A	ATEAM	
Effective Rights	C R W A	James, Group ATEAM	

OU = MKTG			
IRF	S R		
Inherited Rights	(C) R	James	
Trustee Assignment	W (A)	James	
Effective Rights	W (A)	James	

Entries for O=DCS

The IRF, according to the case study, is [S C R W A]. No rights are inherited from above, and therefore, the entry for Inherited Rights is None. An explicit trustee assignment of [C R W] has been given to the user. The explicit trustee assignment overrides any other inherited rights, so the effective rights for the user in container O=DCS are the same as the explicit trustee assignment. That is, James' effective property rights for O=DCS are [C R W (A)]. The [(A)] right is implied from the Write right.

Entries for OU=SALES

The IRF, according to the case study, is [S C R W A]. The rights inherited from above are the effective rights of the parent container masked with the IRF for this container:

```
IRF                          [S  C R W  A  ]
Effective rights of parent   [   C R W (A) ]
_____

Inherited Rights             [   C R W (A) ]
```

The masking operation is a logical AND operation, which means that an entry needs to be in both the rights for it to be in the final result.

The Inherited Rights for OU=SALES are [C R W (A)]. A trustee assignment is made to Group object SALES of Write and Add/Delete Self. This would override any inherited trustee assignments for Group object ATEAM. But since no trustee assignments are inherited for Group object ATEAM, there are no rights to override. You cannot override the inherited rights of [C R W (A)], because these rights are for User object James and not Group object ATEAM.

Because James is a member of group ATEAM, his rights to OU=SALES are the sum of the inherited and effective rights.

```
Inherited Rights for user James    [  C  R  W (A) ]
Trustee Assignment for ATEAM       [        W  A  ]
_____
Effective Rights for James         [  C  R  W  A  ]
```

That is, property effective rights of User object James for OU=SALES are [C R W A]. Notice that the Add/Delete Self right is no longer an implied right [(A)], because it was explicitly assigned to group ATEAM. Also, the Write right is derived from both the Inherited Rights and trustee assignment to Group object ATEAM. If this right is removed from the trustee assignment, the Write right still exists in the effective rights because it is derived from the Inherited Rights.

Entries for OU=MKTG

The IRF, according to the case study, is [S R]. The rights inherited from above are the effective rights of the parent container masked with the IRF for this container:

```
IRF                          [S      R      ]
Effective rights of parent   [    C  R W A  ]
_____
Inherited Rights             [   (C) R      ]
```

The Inherited Rights for OU=MKTG are [(C) R]. The actual right inherited is [R], but the [(C)] inherited right is implied, because of the presence of the Read right in the Inherited Rights. Both of these rights are due to rights assigned to user James. Because an explicit trustee assignment is made in OU=MKTG to user James, the explicit trustee assignment of [W] overrides the inherited rights. That is, effective property rights for OU=MKTG are [W (A)]:

```
Inherited Rights for James     [   (C)   R            ]
Trustee Assignment for James   [                W (A) ]
_____

Effective Rights for James     [                W (A) ]
```

Guidelines for Implementing NDS Security

Novell offers the following NDS security guidelines.

1. Start with the default assignments.

   The default assignments are adequate for most users and most circumstances. The defaults are designed to give users access to information they need without giving them excessive rights.

2. Avoid assigning rights through All Properties of an object.

   All Properties rights can give users access to private information about users and other objects. In some cases, excessive rights can accrue to users, because they have rights to critical properties such as the Object Trustee (ACL) property of an object.

3. Use Selected Property rights to assign/restrict properties.

   Use Selected Property rights to assign or restrict access to individual properties. Remember that Selected Property rights override All Properties rights.

4. Be careful how you assign Write property right to the Object Trustees (ACL) property of an object.

   The Write property right to the ACL of an object enables users to add themselves as trustees to the object and give themselves Supervisor rights. Remember that if you have

All Properties Supervisor or Write property right to an object, you will automatically have Write property to the ACL of the object, unless you use the Selected property IRF for the ACL property to block the Write right.

5. Assigning Supervisor object right grants to the trustee the All Properties Supervisor property right to the object.

Because of the all inclusive privileges that are implied by Supervisor object rights, you might want to assign to the container administrator a more limited set of rights. For example, you might assign the [BCDR] object rights to the container, and selected property rights to specific properties. If you decide to use the All Properties rights, ensure that the user does not derive the Write property right to the Object Trustees (ACL) property. You can prevent inheritance of rights by using explicit trustee assignment to a property or using the selected property IRF.

6. Use caution in assigning Supervisor object right to the server object.

Assigning a trustee Supervisor object right to the server object gives to the trustee the All Properties right to the server object. The All Properties Supervisor property right to the server object gives to the user the Write property right to the ACL of the server object. The Write property right to the ACL of the server object gives to the user the Supervisor file system right to the root of all volumes attached to the server.

7. Be careful about filtering the Supervisor object right and deleting the only user who has rights to a subtree.

In decentralized administration, it is common for the container administrator to be the only user to have Supervisor object right to the container. Others are prevented from having Supervisor object right by the use of the IRF. If the only user that has Supervisor object right (the container administrator, in this case) is deleted, that particular branch of the NDS tree can no longer be managed.

501

For Profile objects and Directory Map objects, you need to assign additional NDS rights:

1. To use a Profile object, the user must have the Read property right to the Login Script property of the Profile object. If the user has the Read All Properties right to the Profile object, this implies that the user also has the Read property right to the Login Script property (unless the selected property IRF is set for the Login Script property to block the Read right).

2. To use a Directory Map object, the user must have the Read property right to the Path property of the Directory Map object. If the user has the Read All Properties right to the Directory Map object, this implies that the user also has the Read property right to the Path property (unless the selected property IRF is set for the Path property to block the Read right).

Comparing NetWare File System Security with NDS Security

Both NDS and NetWare file system security make use of the concepts of trustees, trustee rights, inheritance, and the Inherited Rights Filter. For a user to gain access to an object (NDS or file/directory), the user must be made a trustee to an object and given appropriate rights. The rights flow down the tree and can be blocked by the IRF. The actual rights a user has at any level of the tree are called effective rights.

The differences between NDS and NetWare file system security follow:

♦ NDS rights are further sub-divided into object rights and property rights.

♦ In NDS rights, the Supervisor object right and property right can be blocked by the IRF. In NetWare file system right, the Supervisor right cannot be blocked.

◆ NDS rights do not flow to a NetWare file system right, except in the following case: Any user that has the Write property right to the ACL of the server object has the Supervisor right to the root of each of the server's volume.

When a User object is created, automatic file system rights are created, except to the user's home directory, if one was specified at the time of creation. Figure 5.65 shows the rights to newly created user CN=KSS.O=IMF to the home directory USERS\KSS in volume CN=FS1_SYS.OU=SALES.O=ESL. Notice that the user has [S R W C E M F A] rights to his home directory; that is, the user has All Rights to his home directory.

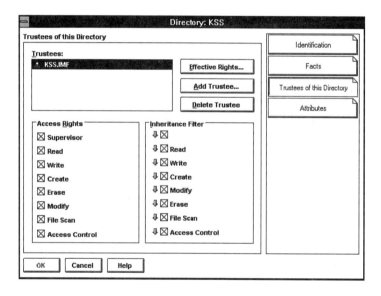

Figure 5.65

The rights of user KSS in home directory.

In NetWare 3.x, the term Inherited Rights Mask (IRM) was used to describe the mechanism to block the flow of NetWare file system rights. In NetWare 4.x, the term Inherited Rights Filter (IRF) is used for both file system rights and NDS object rights.

 Another minor distinction, though not documented in the Novell manuals, is that in NetWare 3.x the Supervisor file system rights were called Supervisory. They are now called Supervisor in NetWare 4.x.

503

As in NetWare 3.x, the file system Supervisor right granted to a directory also grants Supervisor rights to files and directories below the directory.

One major conceptual difference between the NetWare 3.x and NetWare 4.x file system is the scope of the trustee. In NetWare 3.x, the trustee could be only a user account or a group account defined in the server's bindery. In NetWare 4.x, User objects and Group objects in containers other than in the location where the volume is installed can be assigned trustees. The trustee is not limited to the User and Group objects; it can be any NDS object, such as another container object. If a container object is made a trustee of file/directory, all objects within it (including, of course, User and Group objects) inherit the trustee rights to the file or directory.

 When dealing with assigning file/directory rights, it is simpler to assign the rights using a container object, if the NDS containers and the leaf objects are properly designed to reflect usage of resources.

Any NDS object that has a Write right to the ACL property (Object Trustee property) of the NetWare server object also is granted the Supervisor right to the root of each of the volumes hosted by the NetWare server. Because a Supervisor file/directory right cannot be blocked by an IRF, this fact should be a consideration in setting up security rights.

The Write property right can be granted through the following:

1. Write right to All Properties of the NetWare server object.

2. Write right to the Selected Property ACL (Object Trustee) for the NetWare server object.

3. Supervisor right to the All Properties right or ACL property (Selected Property) for the NetWare server object.

4. Supervisor object right to the NetWare server object. This causes the object to have Supervisor right to the All Properties of the NetWare server object.

5. Security equivalence to an object that has any of the rights listed previously.

The differences between NDS and NetWare file system security are the following:

◆ NDS rights are further sub-divided into object rights and property rights.

◆ In NDS rights, the Supervisor object right and property right can be blocked by the IRF. In NetWare file system right, the Supervisor right cannot be blocked.

◆ NDS rights do not flow to a NetWare file system right, except in the following case: Any user that has the Write property right to the ACL of the server object has the Supervisor right to the root of each of the server's volume.

Directory and file attributes in NetWare 4.x are a superset of the rights for NetWare 3.x. That is, NetWare 4.x directory and file attributes include all those for NetWare 3.x, and the rights listed in table 5.6.

Table 5.6
Additional NetWare 4.x Attributes

Attribute	File/Directory	Abbreviation	Description
Migrate	File	M	Indicates that the file has migrated to near-line storage.
Don't Migrate	File/Directory	Dm	Prevents a file or the files in a directory from migrating.

505

continues

Table 5.6, Continued
Additional NetWare 4.x Attributes

Attribute	File/Directory	Abbreviation	Description
Compress	File	Co	Indicates whether a file has been compressed.
Don't Compress	File/Directory	Dc	Prevents a file or the files in a directory from being compressed.
Immediate Compress	File/Directory	Ic	Marks specified file or files in a directory for compression as soon as the OD can perform compression.
Can't Compress	File	Cc	Indicates that a file cannot be compressed because of limited space saving benefit.

The attributes Migrate (M), Compress (Co), and Can't Compress (Cc) are status attributes that indicate the status of individual files only. The other attributes, Don't Migrate (Dm), Don't Compress (Dc), and Immediate Compress (Ic), apply to both files and directories, and specify actions that are to be performed or prevented from occurring.

The attributes Migrate (M), Compress (Co), and Can't Compress (Cc) are status attributes and indicate the status of individual files only. Attributes Don't Migrate (Dm), Don't Compress (Dc), and Immediate Compress (Ic) apply to both files and directories.

The Data Migration feature is installed using INSTALL.NLM and requires a near-line-storage media that acts as a secondary to the primary hard disk storage area.

The compression feature is enabled or disabled on a volume-by-volume basis during installation. It can be further controlled by a variety of SET parameters.

The Data Migration feature is installed using INSTALL.NLM, and the compression feature is installed on a per-volume basis.

Study Guide for the Chapter

If you are preparing for the NetWare 4.x Administration CNE exams, review the chapter with the following goals:

1. Review the different types of login restrictions that can be performed in NetWare 4.x. Understand the basics of NetWare login authentication. Understand how NDS security is implemented. Use the Study Notes as a quick review.

2. Pay particular attention to the topics of NDS trustee assignments for objects and properties. Understand how inheritance and security equivalence can be used in computing effective rights. Go through the case studies and understand the reasoning behind the solutions to them. Practice assigning NDS rights using NetWare Administrator. You may be asked questions on this procedure.

3. After studying this chapter, attempt the sample test questions. If you make mistakes, review the appropriate topic.

Except for Chapter 2, "Introduction to NetWare Directory Services," on NDS fundamentals, this chapter is the most important one, because it deals with issues on NDS security, which is essential for implementing NDS effectively.

Chapter Summary

In this chapter, you learned the basics of NetWare 4.x security. NetWare security is layered. The first layer you must pass through is login authentication and login restriction. The second layer is NDS security. The last (third) layer is the NetWare file system security. You also read an explanation of how login authentication is performed.

Most of the chapter was spent in NDS security issues, because this is a new area for NetWare 3.x administrators. Several case studies were presented to help you understand how NDS security works.

Chapter Test Questions

Test questions can have a single correct answer or multiple correct answers. Where a single answer is desired, it is indicated by a ○ notation that precedes the possible answers. Some questions require you to select more than one answer; these are indicated by the □ preceding each answer. Not all the questions are multiple choice; occasionally, you might get a question that asks you to type in an answer. The answer in this case is usually a one word answer. The answer is not case sensitive. So you can type in the answer in lower- or uppercase.

Certain questions will be repeated in different ways, so that you can recognize them even when the wording is different. Taking practice quizzes will not only test your knowledge but will give you confidence when you take your exam.

For questions dealing with calculating Effective Rights, the answers should include any implied rights. For example, if the computed effective property right is [R], your answer should also include the Compare (C) right, as the Read right also includes the Compare right. Therefore the correct answer would be [C R] and not just [R]. In the case studies, the notation [(C) R] was used to indicate that the Compare right was an implied right. Unless the test question asks you to make the distinction between actual effective rights and implied rights, you should include both in your answer.

1. The _____ command logs in as a user Mona defined in the Organizational Unit ART, in the Organization RAL, given that the current context is O=ART.

   ○ A. LOGIN Mona.RAL

   ○ B. LOGIN .Mona.ART.RAL

   ○ C. LOGIN .Mona.RAL.ART

   ○ D. LOGIN Mona.ART.RAL.

2. Which of these are valid login restrictions for NetWare 4.x?

   ☐ A. Account restrictions

   ☐ B. Password authentication

   ☐ C. Station restrictions

   ☐ D. Password synchronization and time-out

   ☐ E. Time restrictions

3. Network address restrictions are properties of a _____.

   ○ A. User object

   ○ B. container object

   ○ C. Organizational Unit object

   ○ D. Organization object

   ○ E. Volume object

4. In NetWare 4.x, intruder detection _____.

   ○ A. is used to lock out a user if the user makes unauthorized access to the network

   ○ B. prevents unauthorized access by non-Admin users

   ○ C. locks a user's access to the network if an incorrect password was typed in too many times

   ○ D. prevents a server from responding to an unauthorized access request

5. In NetWare 4, authentication assures that _____.

   ○ A. the message applies to a valid user session

   ○ B. the message comes from a secure monitoring station that was used to build the initial authentication data

   ○ C. the message applies to the current session

   ○ D. the message applies to any valid user session

6. The Rename trustee assignment can be used to rename a/an _____ object.

   ☐ A. Root

   ☐ B. container

   ☐ C. leaf

   ☐ D. Organization

   ☐ E. Organizational Unit

7. The Create object right applies to _____ objects only.

   ○ A. top

   ○ B. container

   ○ C. leaf

   ○ D. Organization

   ○ E. Organizational Unit

8. Which of the following is correct for a newly created User object?

   ○ A. The [Root] object is made a trustee of the container object the user is installed in.

   ○ B. The [Root] object is made a trustee of the User object and given Rename rights.

○   C.   The [Root] object is made a trustee of the User object and given Supervisor rights.

○   D.   The [Root] object is made a trustee of the User object and given Read right to Network Address and Group Membership property.

○   E.   The [Root] object is made a trustee of the User object and given Read right to Network Address property.

9. When an NDS tree is newly created, the [Public] trustee is given _____.

○   A.   Read object rights to [Root]

○   B.   Read object rights to every container object immediately under [Root]

○   C.   Create object rights to every container object immediately under [Root]

○   D.   Browse object rights to [Root]

○   E.   Browse object rights to every container object immediately under [Root]

10. The Admin user account for a newly created NDS tree is given _____.

○   A.   Write rights to the ACL property of every server object

○   B.   Supervisor object rights to all container objects

○   C.   Supervisor object rights to all leaf objects

○   D.   Supervisor object rights to [Root]

11. Assigning rights to the [Root] container gives _____.

○   A.   container objects the right to all leaf objects in their container

○   B.   User objects that right to the entire tree

○   C.   User objects that right to the entire tree unless this right is explicitly removed using IRF

○   D.   leaf objects the right to all container objects

12. Which of the following statements about IRF is true?

   ○ A. The IRF is the same as the Inherited Rights.

   ○ B. The IRF is the same as the effective rights.

   ○ C. The default IRF for objects is all rights.

   ○ D. The IRF is set only for container objects.

13. If a user has the Write right to the Security equivalence property and Write property right to the ACL of an Admin User object _____.

   ○ A. the user can read other users' security equivalence

   ○ B. the user can modify other users' security equivalence

   ○ C. the user can become security equivalent to another user, but not the Admin user

   ○ D. the user can become security equivalent to any user including the Admin user

14. An effective right can originate from any of the following sources:

   ☐ A. Explicit trustee assignment

   ☐ B. Inherited from trustee's parent container

   ☐ C. Inherited from direct assignment to object's container

   ☐ D. Inherited from the leaf object

   ☐ E. Inherited from assignment of trustee's container to object's container

15. To compute the effective rights, which of the following can be used?

   ☐ A. Inherited Rights Mask

   ☐ B. Inherited Rights Filter

   ☐ C. Inherited Rights

   ☐ D. Explicit Trustee Assignment

   ☐ E. Public rights

16. The Selected Property right overrides the property right set by the _____.

   ○ A. object trustee rights
   ○ B. selected property rights of parent
   ○ C. All Properties right
   ○ D. Inherited Rights Filter
   ○ E. Inherited Rights

17. If a user was given a Read and Write right to the ACL property, the user _____.

   ○ A. could only assign himself the right of the parent container
   ○ B. could become an Admin user by changing the ACL
   ○ C. could become the Admin user of the container object only
   ○ D. cannot acquire Admin privileges

18. A trustee who has the Write property right to a NetWare server's ACL _____.

   ○ A. is assigned the Write privileges to the root of the volumes attached to the server
   ○ B. is assigned the Read/Write privileges to the root of the volumes attached to the server
   ○ C. is assigned the Read/File Scan/Write privileges to the root of the volumes attached to the server
   ○ D. is assigned the Supervisor privileges to the root of the volumes attached to the server

19. To make a user an administrator of a tree branch, you can minimally _____

   ○ A. grant the user Supervisor privileges to the root of the tree branch
   ○ B. grant the user Supervisor privileges to the root of the NDS tree

○ C. grant the user Write privileges to the All Properties of the root of the tree branch

○ D. grant the user Supervisor privileges to the All Properties of the root of the tree branch

20. Which of the following attributes apply to files only?

☐ A. Don't Migrate (Dm)

☐ B. Migrate (M)

☐ C. Don't Compress (Dc)

☐ D. Immediate Compress (Ic)

☐ E. Compress (Co)

☐ F. Can't Compress (Cc)

21. The NetWare 4.x compression is installed on a _____.

○ A. directory basis

○ B. file basis

○ C. volume basis

○ D. file server

22. The Don't compress (Dc) attribute _____.

○ A. indicates that the file has migrated to near-line storage

○ B. prevents a file or the files in a directory from migrating

○ C. indicates if a file has been compressed

○ D. prevents a file or the files in a directory from being compressed

○ E. specifies file or files in a directory are marked for compression as soon as the server can perform compression

○ F. indicates that a file cannot be compressed because of limited space saving benefit

23. The Can't compress (Cc) attribute _____.

○   A.   indicates that the file has migrated to near-line storage

○   B.   prevents a file or the files in a directory from migrating

○   C.   indicates if a file has been compressed

○   D.   prevents a file or the files in a directory from being compressed

○   E.   specifies file or files in a directory are marked for compression as soon as the server can perform compression

○   F.   indicates that a file cannot be compressed because of limited space saving benefit

24. The following figure shows a directory tree for organization IBL. BJoy is made a trustee of Organization O=IBL and given the rights of Supervisor, Browse, and Create. BJoy is also given a trustee assignment of Browse in OU=MKTG. The IRFs for the containers are shown as follows:

```
IRF for O=IBL          [S B C D R]
IRF for OU=CORP        [S B C    ]
IRF for OU=MKTG        [      D R]
```

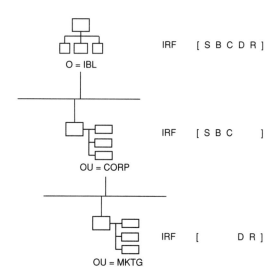

The [Public] group has been given Browse right to [Root].

What is BJoy's effective rights in container OU=MKTG? Assume that BJoy does not inherit rights from any source other than the ones listed in the case study.

- ○ A. Supervisor, Browse, Create
- ○ B. Browse
- ○ C. Browse, Create, Delete
- ○ D. Supervisor
- ○ E. Create, Delete
- ○ F. No Rights

25. The following figure shows a directory tree for organization IBL. BJoy is made a trustee of Organization O=IBL and given the All Properties rights of Supervisor, Compare, Read. The IRFs for the containers are shown as follows:

```
IRF for O=IBLS        [S C R W A]
IRF for OU=CORP       [  C R W  ]
IRF for OU=MKTG       [S     W A]
```

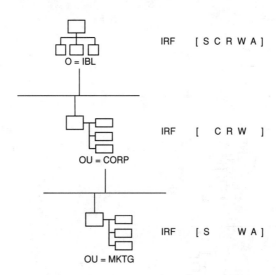

What is BJoy's effective rights in container OU=MKTG? Assume that BJoy does not inherit rights from any source other than the ones listed in the case study.

○ A. Supervisor, Compare, Write, Read

○ B. Supervisor

○ C. Supervisor, Write, Add/Delete Self

○ D. Compare, Read, Write

○ E. No Rights

26. The following figure shows a directory tree for organization IBL. BJoy is made a trustee of Organization O=IBL and given the rights of Supervisor, Read. BJoy is also given a trustee assignment of Write in OU=MKTG. The IRFs for the containers are shown as follows:

```
IRF for O=IBL        [S C R W A]
IRF for OU=CORP      [S C R    ]
IRF for OU=MKTG      [    R W A]
```

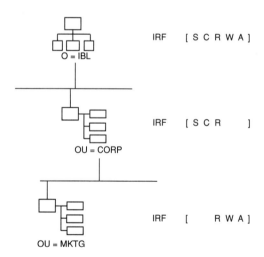

What is BJoy's effective rights in container OU=MKTG? Assume that BJoy does not inherit rights from any source other than the ones listed in the case study.

○ A. Supervisor, Compare, Write, Read, Add/Delete Self

○ B. Write, Add/Delete Self

517

    ○ C. Supervisor, Write, Add/Delete Self

    ○ D. Compare, Read, Write, Add/Delete Self

    ○ E. No Rights

27. The differences between NDS and NetWare file system security are that _____.

    ☐ A. NDS rights are further sub-divided into object rights and property rights

    ☐ B. there is no Supervisor right in NDS whereas NetWare file system has Supervisor right

    ☐ C. in NDS rights, the Supervisor object right and property right can be blocked by the IRF. In NetWare file system right the Supervisor right cannot be blocked

    ☐ D. NDS rights do not flow to a NetWare file system right, except in one important case

    ☐ E. NDS rights are the same as NetWare file system rights

28. Which of the following rights allows you to rename a leaf or container object?

    ☐ A. Supervisor

    ☐ B. Create

    ☐ C. Delete

    ☐ D. Rename

    ☐ E. Browse

29. Which one of these NDS objects cannot have Create rights?

    ○ A. Root

    ○ B. container

    ○ C. leaf

    ○ D. Organization

    ○ E. Organizational Unit

30. Which of the following statements about [Public] is true?

   A. [Public] is a special trustee that includes all users in a container object.

   B. [Public] is a special trustee that includes all users in an Organization object.

   C. [Public] is a special trustee that includes all users in an Organizational Unit object.

   D. [Public] is a special trustee that includes all users connected to the network.

31. Security equivalence is a property of the _____.

   A. leaf object

   B. container object

   C. Root object

   D. User object

   E. Group object

32. The following figure shows a directory tree for organization IBL. BJoy is made a trustee of Organization O=IBL and given the rights of Supervisor, Browse, and Create. BJoy is also given an object trustee assignment of Create and Delete in OU=MKTG. The IRFs for the containers are shown as follows:

```
IRF for O=IBL          [S B C D R]
IRF for OU=CORP         [S B C    ]
IRF for OU=MKTG         [     D R]
```

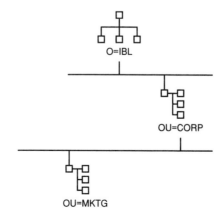

The [Public] group has been given Browse right to [Root].

What is BJoy's effective rights in container OU=MKTG? Assume that BJoy does not inherit rights from any source other than the ones listed in the case study.

○ A. Supervisor, Browse, Create

○ B. Browse

○ C. Browse, Create, Delete

○ D. Supervisor

○ E. Create, Delete

○ F. No Rights

33. The Write property right grants you _____.

○ A. the right to change any values to the property

○ B. the right to remove and change any values to the property

○ C. the right to add, remove, change any values to the property

○ D. the right to read, add, remove, change any values to the property

34. The following figure shows a directory tree for organization IBL. Amy is made a trustee of Organization O=IBL and given the rights of Supervisor, Read. Amy is also given a trustee assignment of Write in OU=MKTG. The IRFs for the containers are as follows:

```
IRF for O=IBL       [S C R W A]
IRF for OU=CORP     [S C R     ]
IRF for OU=MKTG     [    R W A]
```

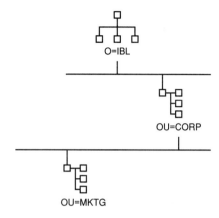

What is Amy's effective rights in container OU=MKTG? Assume that Amy does not inherit rights from any source other than the ones listed in the case study.

○ A. Supervisor, Compare, Write, Read, Add/Delete Self

○ B. Read, Write, Add/Delete Self

○ C. Supervisor, Write, Add/Delete Self

○ D. Compare, Read, Write, Add/Delete Self

○ E. No Rights

35. The following figure shows a directory tree for organization SCS. KSS is made a trustee of Organization O=SCS and given the rights of Supervisor and Create. KSS is also given a trustee assignment of Browse in OU=CORP. The IRFs for the containers are as follows:

```
IRF for O=SCS          [S B C D R]
IRF for OU=CORP        [S B C    ]
IRF for OU=MKTG        [  C D R]
```

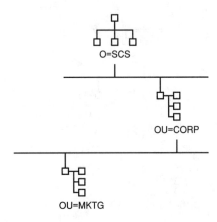

The [Public] group has been given Browse right to [Root].

What is KSS's effective rights in container OU=MKTG? Assume that KSS does not inherit rights from any source other than the ones listed in the case study.

- A. Supervisor, Browse, Create, Delete, Rename
- B. Browse
- C. Supervisor, Browse, Create
- D. Supervisor, Create
- E. Create
- F. No Rights
- G. Create, Delete, Rename

36. The figure that follows shows a directory tree for organization SCS. KSS is made a trustee of Organization O=SCS and given the rights of Supervisor. KSS is also given a trustee assignment of Delete and Rename in OU=CORP. The IRFs for the containers are as follows:

```
IRF for O=SCS          [S B C D R]
IRF for OU=CORP         [S B C    ]
IRF for OU=MKTG         [    C D  ]
```

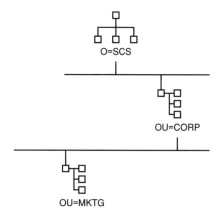

The [Public] group has been given Browse right to [Root].

What is KSS's effective rights in container OU=MKTG? Assume that KSS does not inherit rights from any source other than the ones listed in the case study.

- ○ A. Supervisor, Browse, Create, Delete, Rename
- ○ B. Browse
- ○ C. Delete
- ○ D. Supervisor, Browse, Create
- ○ E. Create, Delete
- ○ F. No Rights
- ○ G. Delete, Rename

37. The figure below shows a directory tree for organization SCS. DAVID is made a trustee of Organization O=SCS and given the rights of Create, Rename. DAVID is also given a trustee assignment of Delete in OU=MKTG. The IRFs for the containers are as follows:

```
IRF for O=SCS        [S  B C D R ]
IRF for OU=CORP      [   B C   R ]
IRF for OU=MKTG      [   B   D R ]
```

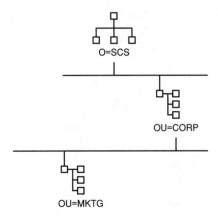

The [Public] group has been given Browse right to [Root].

What is DAVID's effective rights in container OU=MKTG? Assume that DAVID does not inherit rights from any source other than the ones listed in the case study.

- ○ A. Supervisor, Browse, Create, Delete, Rename
- ○ B. Browse, Delete
- ○ C. Delete
- ○ D. Browse, Delete, Rename
- ○ E. Browse, Create, Rename
- ○ F. No Rights
- ○ G. Browse

38. The figure below shows a directory tree for organization SCS. MARIAN is made a trustee of Organization O=SCS and given the rights of Supervisor, Create, Rename. MARIAN is also given a trustee assignment of Delete, Rename, and Create in OU=CORP and a trustee assignment of Rename in OU=MKTG. The IRFs for the containers are shown as follows:

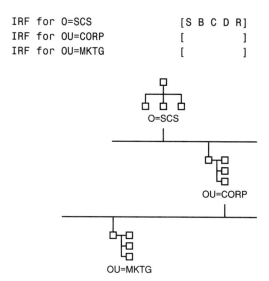

```
IRF for O=SCS          [S B C D R]
IRF for OU=CORP        [         ]
IRF for OU=MKTG        [         ]
```

O=SCS

OU=CORP

OU=MKTG

The [Public] group has been given Browse right to [Root].

What is MARIAN's effective rights in container OU=MKTG? Assume that MARIAN does not inherit rights from any source other than the ones listed in the case study.

- A. Supervisor, Browse, Create, Delete, Rename
- B. Rename
- C. Delete
- D. Supervisor, Create, Rename
- E. Delete, Create, Rename
- F. No Rights
- G. Browse

39. The following figure shows a directory tree for organization NTE. Tesla is made a trustee of Organization O=NTE and given the all property rights of Supervisor, Compare. Tesla is also given all property trustee assignment of Read and Write in OU=LAB. The IRFs for the containers follow:

```
IRF for O=NTE          [S C R W A]
IRF for OU=INVE        [S C R    ]
IRF for OU=LAB         [     R W A]
```

What is Tesla's effective rights in container OU=LAB? Assume that Tesla does not inherit rights from any source other than the ones listed in the case study.

- A. Supervisor, Compare, Write, Read, Add/Delete Self

- B. Write, Add/Delete Self

- C. Supervisor, Write, Add/Delete Self

- D. Compare, Read, Write, Add/Delete Self

- E. No Rights

40. The following figure shows a directory tree for organization NTE. Bohr is made a trustee of Organization O=NTE and given the all property rights of Read and Write. Bohr is also given all property trustee assignment of Read and Write in OU=INVE. The IRFs for the containers are as follows:

```
IRF for O=NTE          [S C R W A]
IRF for OU=INVE        [S C R    ]
IRF for OU=LAB         [     W   ]
```

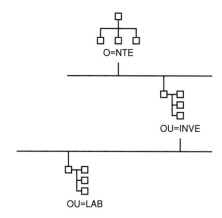

What is Bohr's effective rights in container OU=LAB? Assume that Bohr does not inherit rights from any source other than the ones listed in the case study.

- A. Supervisor, Compare, Write, Read, Add/Delete Self
- B. Write, Add/Delete Self
- C. Supervisor, Write, Add/Delete Self
- D. Compare, Read, Write, Add/Delete Self
- E. No Rights
- F. Supervisor, Compare, Read

41. The following figure shows a directory tree for organization NTE. Rutherford is made a trustee of Organization O=NTE and given the all property rights of Read. The IRFs for the containers follow:

```
IRF for O=NTE          [S        ]
IRF for OU=INVE        [S C R    ]
IRF for OU=LAB         [   R W A]
```

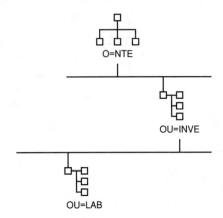

What is Rutherford's effective rights in container OU=LAB?
Assume that Rutherford does not inherit rights from any
source other than the ones listed in the case study.

- ○ A. Supervisor, Compare, Write, Read, Add/Delete
  Self
- ○ B. Write, Add/Delete Self
- ○ C. Supervisor, Write, Add/Delete Self
- ○ D. Compare, Read, Write, Add/Delete Self
- ○ E. Compare, Read
- ○ F. No Rights

42. The following figure shows a directory tree for organization
    NTE. Faraday is made a trustee of Organization O=NTE and
    given the all property rights of Supervisor. The IRFs for the
    containers are shown as follows:

```
IRF for O=NTE              [S        ]
IRF for OU=INVE            [S     A ]
IRF for OU=LAB             [         ]
```

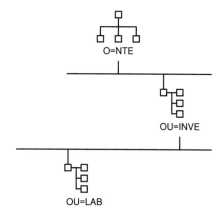

O=NTE

OU=INVE

OU=LAB

What is Faraday's effective rights in container OU=LAB? Assume that Faraday does not inherit rights from any source other than the ones listed in the case study.

- ○ A. Supervisor, Compare, Write, Read, Add/Delete Self
- ○ B. Supervisor, Add/Delete Self
- ○ C. Supervisor, Write, Add/Delete Self
- ○ D. Compare, Read, Write, Add/Delete Self
- ○ E. Supervisor
- ○ F. No Rights

43. The following figure shows a directory tree for organization NTE. Neumann is made a trustee of Organization O=NTE and given the all property rights of Supervisor. The IRFs for the containers are as follows:

```
IRF for O=NTE          [          ]
IRF for OU=INVE        [S      A ]
IRF for OU=LAB         [S        ]
```

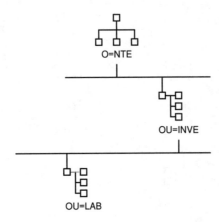

What is Neumann's effective rights in container OU=LAB?
Assume that Neumann does not inherit rights from any
source other than the ones listed in the case study.

- ○ A. Supervisor, Compare, Write, Read, Add/Delete
       Self

- ○ B. Supervisor, Add/Delete Self

- ○ C. Supervisor, Write, Add/Delete Self

- ○ D. Compare, Read, Write, Add/Delete Self

- ○ E. Supervisor

- ○ F. No Rights

44. The following figure shows a directory tree for organization
    NTE. Bose is made a trustee of Organization O=NTE and
    given the all property rights of Supervisor. Bose is also given
    the Write property to OU=LAB. The IRFs for the containers
    are as follows:

```
IRF for O=NTE          [          ]
IRF for OU=INVE        [          ]
IRF for OU=LAB         [          ]
```

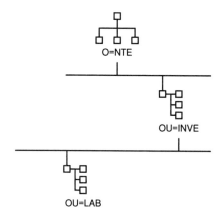

What is Bose's effective rights in container OU=LAB?
Assume that Bose does not inherit rights from any source
other than the ones listed in the case study.

- ○ A. Supervisor, Compare, Write, Read, Add/Delete
  Self
- ○ B. Write, Add/Delete Self
- ○ C. Supervisor, Write, Add/Delete Self
- ○ D. Compare, Read, Write, Add/Delete Self
- ○ E. Supervisor
- ○ F. No Rights

531

6

CHAPTER

Customizing the NetWare 4.x User Environment

Before users can use the network effectively, the network environment needs to be set up correctly. In this chapter, you'll be shown how to customize a user's network environment, a process that consists of setting up the workstation environment and login scripts, implementing user account restrictions, writing custom login scripts, and simplifying access to NetWare applications using the Novell menus.

In this chapter, you learn about the different types of login scripts used in NetWare 4.x: system, profile, user, and default. You also learn when to use each type of login script. You learn the different components of a NetWare 4.x menu system and learn to how to write a menu script file.

Defining the User Network Environment

The network environment is where the user interacts with the network. Therefore it must be set up with a great amount of planning and attention to detail. This chapter discusses the different types of start-up files for the individual DOS workstation and the network environment. Much of the attention to detail is in organizing the network start-up files, called *login scripts*.

The login script commands and script variables that make up the network start-up files will be explored, along with recommendations on how to organize the login scripts to keep them simple and understandable.

Preparing the PC as a Workstation

When DOS is used to boot a PC, the PC has no idea that it will be used as a workstation on a NetWare LAN. Most varieties of DOS do not have any inherent capability to work with a network (Novell DOS 7 does). Instead, network capability must be added to DOS, which is accomplished by running a series of TSR (terminate-and-stay-resident) programs that remain running in the background while DOS is being used on the workstation. These TSRs include the ODI drivers, Link Support Layer (LSL.COM), the VLM manager (VLM.EXE), and the driver for the network board. You need at least four files, such as LSL, NE2000, IRTODF, and VLM. Collectively, these files are called the *DOS Requester*, because they enable DOS programs to request network or local DOS services.

Even though nothing is in the CONFIG.SYS file to suggest that a PC is being used as a NetWare workstation, certain configuration commands in the CONFIG.SYS file can have an important effect on using the PC as a NetWare workstation.

How DOS Is Loaded

It's very helpful to have knowledge of what takes place behind the scenes when DOS first loads. Certain problems that can occur during the processing of network login scripts become clear when you understand the DOS load process.

When a system is first powered up, it automatically jumps to location memory 0FFFF0 hex, and begins executing the program starting at that location. This is a feature of all of the Intel 80x86 family of microprocessors—80286, 80386, 80486, and 80586 (Pentium)—and is independent of any operating system such as DOS, OS/2, or Unix that may be running on the PC. The special location 0FFFF0 hex lies in a location in the ROM of the PC, and performs a Power On Self-Test (POST) process that checks RAM integrity, the keyboard, system clock, and other devices. After a successful POST, control is transferred to the *bootstrap* program, which is part of the BIOS, as shown in figure 6.1. Most often, the process of starting a PC is called *booting*, a term derived from this bootstrap program.

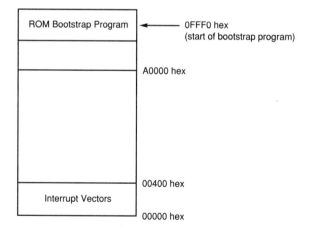

Figure 6.1

Memory map when control is transferred to bootstrap program.

The bootstrap program reads the first sector on the boot media (floppy disk in drive A or hard disk drive C), which contains the rest of the bootstrap program and information on the disk. After reading the rest of the bootstrap program in an arbitrary location in memory, the system transfers control to it (see fig. 6.2).

Figure 6.2

Memory map on
loading disk bootstrap
program.

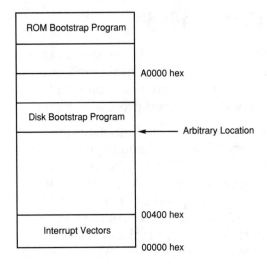

The bootstrap program then checks for the existence of a copy of
the operating system. For MS-DOS, this is done by checking for
the two files IO.SYS and MSDOS.SYS, in that order. For IBM PC-
DOS, these two files are IBMBIO.SYS and IBMDOS.SYS. If these
files are missing, you are prompted with the error message:

```
Non-System disk or disk error
Replace and strike a key when ready
```

This message appears when the NetWare workstation software is
copied onto a disk that has not been properly prepared using the
FORMAT /S or SYS commands under DOS.

If the two system files are found, they are read into memory and
control is transferred to the program in IO.SYS. In some systems
the IO.SYS loads first, and this in turn reads MSDOS.SYS in
memory. The IO.SYS file actually consists of two parts:

◆ **BIOS.**
    This contains a linked set of resident device drivers for
    standard PC devices such as CON, AUX, PRN, NUL, COM1,
    COM2, COM3, NUL, and so on. There are also some
    hardware-specific initialization programs that are run to
    initialize certain devices.

◆ **SYSINIT.**
This contains programs from Microsoft as well as the BIOS supplied by the manufacturer of the PC. SYSINIT is called by the manufacturer's BIOS initialization code. It determines the amount of contiguous RAM and then relocates itself so it can get out of the way of the DOS kernel that is loaded next.

Next, SYSINIT performs the initialization programs—in MS-DOS they carry out tasks such as:

◆ Setting up internal system tables

◆ Setting up interrupt vectors in locations 20 hex to 2F hex

◆ Calling the initialization function for each resident device driver

After the system initialization program is run, the MS-DOS copyright message is displayed. The basic MS-DOS system is loaded at this point. SYSINIT makes use of MS-DOS file services to open the CONFIG.SYS file. The details of CONFIG.SYS file processing are discussed in the next section. If it's found, the entire CONFIG.SYS file is loaded in memory and each line in the file is processed. Any device drivers loaded by DEVICE or DEVICEHIGH= commands are processed in the order in which they're found and loaded in memory. For DR DOS, a statement with a ? before it causes the system to prompt the user if that statement should be processed. With MS-DOS 6 and above, pressing the F8 key causes the system to display each line in the CONFIG.SYS file (and AUTOEXEC.BAT file) and prompt you if you want to execute this line.

After all the installable device drivers are loaded, SYSINIT closes all files it has opened and opens the console (CON), printer (PRN), and auxiliary (AUX) devices as *standard input*, *standard output*, and *standard error* devices.

Finally, SYSINIT calls the MS-DOS EXEC function to load the command-line interpreter COMMAND.COM, which is located on the boot media or specified by the SHELL= statement in CONFIG.SYS file. To save on memory, the COMMAND.COM file is actually loaded in two parts:

1. Resident part, loaded in lower memory

2. Transient part, loaded just below the 640 KB limit

The resident part, as the name implies, is always resident in RAM, whereas the transient portion of COMMAND.COM can be written over by applications that are big enough to fill the entire 640 KB. After the application exits, DOS reloads the transient portion from a copy of the COMMAND.COM indicated by the COMSPEC environment variable, whose default value is set by the COMMAND.COM path in the SHELL= statement in the CONFIG.SYS file. This last point is important to remember because it's the cause of the `Invalid COMMAND.COM_ System Halted` error message that's sometimes encountered with NetWare LANs. This issue will be discussed again later in the chapter when the setting of the login script variable COMSPEC is discussed.

To load COMMAND.COM with sufficient environment variable space, use the SHELL statement as follows:

`SHELL=COMMAND.COM /P /E:800`

The preceding statement specifies an environment variable space of 800 bytes, which should be adequate for most NetWare DOS workstations. Replace 800 with a larger value if you need additional environment variable space.

After SYSINIT performs its job, it's no longer needed and gets discarded. The final memory configuration looks similar to that shown in figure 6.3.

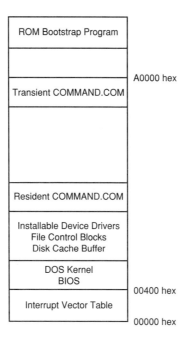

ROM Bootstrap Program
Transient COMMAND.COM
Resident COMMAND.COM
Installable Device Drivers File Control Blocks Disk Cache Buffer
DOS Kernel BIOS
Interrupt Vector Table

A0000 hex

00400 hex

00000 hex

Figure 6.3

Final DOS map showing COMMAND.COM components.

If there is an AUTOEXEC.BAT file in the root directory of the boot media, it is read into memory and processed using the command line interpreter COMMAND.COM. If the AUTOEXEC.BAT file is not found, DOS will prompt you for the date and time, which is a good reason to create an AUTOEXEC.BAT file and have at least a statement such as the PROMPT PG in the file. For a NetWare DOS workstation, there may be an additional line such as:

```
@CALL C:\NWCLIENT\STARTNET.BAT
```

in the AUTOEXEC.BAT file that calls the STARTNET.BAT file. This file loads the ODI drivers and the NetWare DOS Requester that establishes a connection with the NetWare 4.x network.

NetWare workstation configuration involves four important files (see fig. 6.4) including:

- ◆ CONFIG.SYS
- ◆ AUTOEXEC.BAT
- ◆ STARTNET.BAT
- ◆ NET.CFG

539

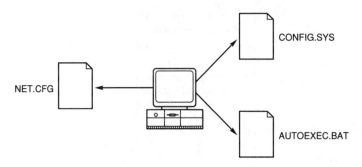

Figure 6.4
Workstation
configuration.

The processing of these files is discussed in the following sections.

The STARTNET.BAT, NET.CFG, CONFIG.SYS, and AUTOEXEC.BAT files are used to configure a NetWare DOS workstation.

DOS CONFIG.SYS Processing

A number of statements are in the CONFIG.SYS file that are important for a PC being set up as a NetWare workstation:

♦ SHELL=*pathname*/COMMAND.COM /P /E:*environmentspace*

♦ FILES=number of file handles

♦ BUFFERS=number of buffers

♦ LASTDRIVE=*last drive*

♦ DEVICEHIGH=*device path*

♦ BREAK=[ON | OFF]

The SHELL= parameter uses the /P parameter to run AUTOEXEC.BAT and make the command-line interpreter permanent. The /E parameter tells how much space DOS should reserve for the environment variables. In a NetWare environment—where many applications are being run—you might want to increase this value if you receive the message Out of environment space. A good

540

value to use is 800 bytes. Therefore, the SHELL= statement might look like the following:

```
SHELL=C:\DOS\COMMAND.COM /P /E:800
```

The C:\DOS\ specifies the *pathname* where the DOS COMMAND.COM file can be found. If you're using an earlier version of DOS (such as DOS 3.1), the environment space is measured in number of *paragraphs*, where each paragraph is 16 bytes.

The FILES= statement controls the number of files the workstation can have open locally. For example, if you want to increase the values of these parameters to 40 files, use the following statement in the CONFIG.SYS file:

```
FILES=40
```

The BUFFERS= parameter specifies the number of 512-byte blocks set aside for read and write operations. DOS reads and writes data in 512-byte sectors, and if there are a sufficient number of buffers in RAM, this can speed up file operations. In DR DOS, the HIBUFFERS= statement can be used to allocate buffers in high memory instead of conventional memory. A general rule of thumb is to have one buffer for every file you might want to open simultaneously. If you have no more than 20 files open simultaneously, set this to BUFFERS=20.

The LASTDRIVE= parameter specifies the last drive letter recognized by DOS. Its default value is E. In earlier NetWare versions where the NetWare shell was used, this value was used to determine the start of the network drives; this is the reason that the first network drive usually defaulted to the next available drive F. For the NetWare DOS Requester, you should set this value to:

```
LASTDRIVE=Z
```

The reason for this is that DOS and the NetWare DOS Requester share the same drive table (see fig. 6.5). When the older NetWare shell was used, the NetWare shell maintained a separate table for itself that was distinct from the DOS drive table.

541

Figure 6.5

Sharing of DOS drive table.

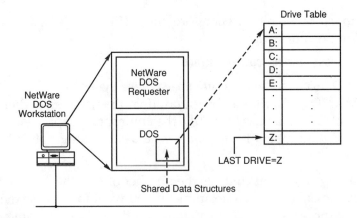

 NetWare 4.x DOS workstations should set the value of LASTDRIVE=Z in CONFIG.SYS.

Both the DEVICEHIGH= and DEVICE parameter load device drivers in memory. While the DEVICE parameter loads device drivers in conventional memory, DEVICEHIGH= loads the drivers in upper memory, leaving more space for applications to run in conventional memory. If you're interested in conserving conventional memory for applications, you should try to load as many device drivers in upper memory using DEVICEHIGH= as possible. In DR DOS, the equivalent command for loading drivers in upper memory is HIDEVICE=.

 If you're using MS DOS 6 or higher, use the memory optimizer program called MEMMAKER. MEMMAKER analyzes the current memory utilization and makes changes to the CONFIG.SYS file and AUTOEXEC.BAT file to leave more space for running applications in the *conventional memory* (memory below 640 KB).

If you use MEMMAKER, be patient; it takes quite a while to complete its analysis. You should also run MEMMAKER with the NetWare DOS Requester software loaded.

542

Setting BREAK=OFF prevents you from breaking out of programs by using Ctrl+C or Ctrl+Break keys until the program performs I/O operation on the screen or printer. Setting BREAK=OFF prevents users from breaking out of batch files.

Only the CONFIG.SYS parameters that have a more direct bearing on the network environment have been presented. For a more complete and comprehensive description of CONFIG.SYS parameters, consult your DOS manual or NRP's extensive DOS reference, *Inside MS-DOS 6.2*. In general, most other CONFIG.SYS parameters can be specified in the CONFIG.SYS file without adversely affecting the network workstation environment.

Here's an example of a CONFIG.SYS file used on one of the author's network workstations, giving you a sense of what can be placed in the CONFIG.SYS file without any problems:

```
DEVICE=C:\DOS\HIMEM.SYS
DOS=HIGH,UMB
DEVICEHIGH=C:\DOS5.0\SETVER.EXE
DEVICEHIGH=C:\DOS5.0\EMM386.EXE RAM
FILES=40
BUFFERS=20
SHELL=C:\COMMAND.COM /P /E:800
LASTDRIVE=Z
```

AUTOEXEC.BAT Processing

After the CONFIG.SYS file has been processed, DOS uses the command-line interpreter to execute the commands in the AUTOEXEC.BAT file. DOS looks for the AUTOEXEC.BAT file in the root directory of the boot media. A fundamental difference exists between CONFIG.SYS and AUTOEXEC.BAT files in terms of the kinds of statements that can be placed in these files. The statements in the CONFIG.SYS file are special statements dealing with system configuration, whereas the statements in AUTOEXEC.BAT file can be any DOS internal or external commands and any applications that you'd normally load from the DOS command line.

For setting up an automatic start-up script for logging in to a NetWare network, you can place the following commands in AUTOEXEC.BAT file:

```
@ECHO OFF
PROMPT $P$G
PATH C:\LOCAL\APPS;C:\LOCAL\BIN
CALL C:\NWCLIENT\STARTNET.BAT
```

This example has a couple of interesting points. The @ in DOS versions 3.3 and higher stops the command on that line from being displayed. The ECHO OFF stops the commands in AUTOEXEC.BAT file from being displayed as they are executed. The PATH command sets up a local path environment.

The call to STARTNET.BAT loads all drivers and the VLMs. This is discussed next.

 The call to STARTNET.BAT file is usually placed in the AUTOEXEC.BAT file.

STARTNET.BAT Processing

The AUTOEXEC.BAT file transfers control to the STARTNET.BAT file. Alternatively, the STARTNET.BAT file can be invoked from the DOS command prompt. STARTNET.BAT is the standard file that contains the commands required to start the DOS Requester.

The NET.CFG file contains configuration information for the DOS Requester. Each of the DOS Requester files can have a parameter section in NET.CFG, and you'll need to know how to customize each section to complete configuration of a DOS workstation.

Here's a sample STARTNET.BAT file:

```
@ECHO OFF
C:
CD \NWCLIENT
SET NWLANGUAGE=ENGLISH
LSL
CEODI
IPXODI
VLM
CD \
```

The above STARTNET.BAT file starts up a default DOS Requester configuration. This basic STARTNET.BAT file is produced by the NetWare DOS client INSTALL program. First, the batch file changes the directory to C:\NWCLIENT—the standard location where the files that implement the NetWare DOS Requester, ODI drivers, and VLMs are installed. The NWLANGUAGE DOS environment variable is set to the language in which NetWare menu options and Help messages should appear for the user. NetWare 4 language support includes English, Spanish, German, Italian, and French. If the NWLANGUAGE environment variable is not specified, the default language is English.

You can also specify the language environment for a user by setting the language property for the User object.

The next four commands load different components of the ODI drivers. First, the LSL.COM program is run to load the Link Support Layer. When loading, LSL.COM looks for configuration information in the Link Support section of NET.CFG.

Next, the ODI driver (also called the MLID—Multiple Link Interface Driver) is loaded. A specific ODI driver must be loaded for each brand of NIC. ODI drivers for many standard NICs are shipped with the DOS Requester files that accompany NetWare 4.x. Manufacturers also include ODI drivers on disks that accompany most NetWare-compatible NICs. In this example, the ODI driver is CEODI, which is used for Xircom's PCMCIA Credit Card Ethernet adapter driver. For a Novell NE2000 board, you replace CEODI with NE2000. When the ODI driver loads, it reads its configuration information from the Link Driver section of the NET.CFG file, which will be discussed later in this chapter.

After the ODI driver loads, the communication protocol must be loaded. The most common protocol on NetWare 4.x networks will be IPX, and in this example the IPXODI.COM is loaded. This implements the SPX/IPX protocol and the diagnostic responder. The diagnostic responder is used by some network management applications to report on network adapter statistics.

545

If the diagnostic responder isn't needed, it can be disabled using the /D switch:

```
IPXODI /D
```

Disabling the diagnostic responder can save about 3 KB of memory. SPX is used by remote console and remote printer support. NetWare core services bypass SPX and make use of IPX directly. If you're not running an application that needs SPX and you want to use less memory, you can use the following command to disable the diagnostic responder and SPX:

```
IPXODI /A
```

The /A switch results in a saving of 9 KB of memory. When the communication protocol loads, it looks for any special configuration settings for itself in the PROTCOL section of the NET.CFG file. For example, if there's more than one logical network board at the workstation, you must specify the logical board number IPX must *bind* to. This can be specified in the PROTOCOL IPX section of the NET.CFG files:

```
PROTOCOL IPX
BIND #2
```

In the preceding example, IPX is bound to board 2. The board 2 will have to be defined in the LINK DRIVER section of the NET.CFG file.

 The VLM Manager can be loaded only after the ODI interface support and the communication protocols are loaded.

NET.CFG Processing

After the communication protocol is loaded, the VLM Manager, implemented by VLM.EXE, is loaded. This loads the necessary VLMs (discussed in Chapter 1, "Introduction to NetWare 4.x") that make up the NetWare DOS Requester client software. The VLM Manager looks for its configuration information in the NetWare DOS Requester section of NET.CFG. A sample NET.CFG file is shown here:

```
Link Driver CEODI
     FRAME Ethernet_802.3
     FRAME Ethernet_802.2
     FRAME Ethernet_II
     INT  5
     PORT  380
     MEM  D0000
     IOWORDSIZE  16
Protocol IPX
     bind #2
NetWare DOS Requester
     FIRST NETWORK DRIVE = F
     NAME CONTEXT = "OU=CORP.O=SCS"
     Preferred Server=NW4KS
```

 For a NetWare 4.x workstation, one can expect to find at least the following statements in a NET.CFG file:

```
FRAME Ethernet_802.2
NetWare DOS Requester
FIRST NETWORK DRIVE
NAME CONTEXT
```

Many of the NET.CFG statements also apply to NetWare client configuration for using the older NetWare shell (NETX.COM or NETX.EXE) programs.

ETHERNET_802.2 is the standard Ethernet frame type used with NetWare 4.x. Prior to NetWare 4.x, the default frame type of ETHERNET_802.3 was used for Ethernet. This frame type did not have an explicit protocol identification field to identify whether the Ethernet frame was carrying IPX data. In a multi-protocol network environment, this made it difficult for routing devices to identify IPX packets. The ETHERNET_802.2 frame uses the LLC (Logical Link Control layer, also called the IEEE 802.2 header) header to identify the protocol data that is being carried. It uses a value of E0 (hexadecimal) in the DSAP (Destination Service Access Point) and the SSAP (Source Service Access Point) to identify that the packet data field contains an IPX packet.

Server LAN drivers written for NetWare 4.x and NetWare 3.12 use the ETHERNET_802.2 frame type by default. If all your servers use the ETHERNET_802.2 frame type, only that frame type needs to be configured on your workstations.

If a mix of older NetWare 3.11 (or earlier) networks is being used, you should also define the ETHERNET_802.3 frame so you can communicate with NetWare 3.11 servers.

If you're also using your workstation for TCP/IP client software, you should define the ETHERNET_II frame. Some TCP/IP software can work with ETHERNET_802.2 frame encapsulation, but the majority of TCP/IP software expects an ETHERNET_II frame encapsulation.

For Token Ring boards, the default frame type of TOKEN can still be used.

In the NetWare DOS Requester section, the FIRST NETWORK DRIVE is set to F:. It can be set to any other letter. A popular value is F: to maintain compatibility with the default NetWare 3.11 convention. Also, you might want to use F: if you've migrated from a NetWare 3.11 (or earlier) network to a NetWare 4.x network. Some programs and batch files might have a reference to the F: drive as a network drive. Not defining the F: drive as a network drive can cause these programs and batch files to fail.

The NAME CONTEXT defines the initial context of the workstation in the NDS tree. The context parameter must appear as a quoted string and have the complete name syntax, but should appear without a leading period. The name context value should be set to the container users can expect to have most of their resources defined.

The example of the NET.CFG shows a PREFERRED SERVER statement. This statement makes an initial attachment to the defined server. An initial attachment to a server is needed to access the LOGIN.EXE program in the SYS:LOGIN directory of a NetWare 4.x server. The LOGIN.EXE program is needed to log in to the NDS tree. When the LOGIN.EXE program runs, it prompts the user for a valid User object name and valid password.

Practical TIP If the User objects and the server the user is attached to are defined in the same context, the login name of the User object can be typed instead of typing the NDS path for the User object.

To complete the login sequence, the user must change to the network drive and run the LOGIN.EXE program:

```
F:
LOGIN
```

Because the preceding statements aren't added by default to the STARTNET.BAT by the NetWare DOS client INSTALL program, you might want to add them explicitly, as shown in figure 6.6.

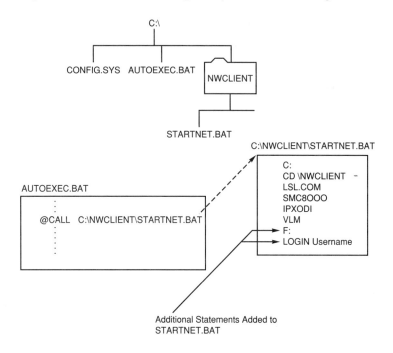

Figure 6.6

Placing LOGIN.EXE in STARTNET.BAT.

If you add the command to log in the STARTNET.BAT, you should place the call to STARTNET.BAT in the AUTOEXEC.BAT file after the PATH statement in the AUTOEXEC.BAT file. If the PATH statement is run after the STARTNET.BAT is run and the login is complete, it can wipe out your network drive mappings.

The NET.CFG file contains configuration parameters for each of the ODI layers. The following list shows which NET.CFG section contains configuration information for each of the layers:

◆ Link Support Layer (LSL.COM) parameters appear in the LINK SUPPORT section

◆ MLID (BOARDNAME.COM) parameters appear in the LINK DRIVER section

◆ Protocol (IPXODI.COM) parameters appear in the PROTOCOL section

◆ DOS Requester (VLM.EXE) parameters appear in the NetWare DOS Requester section

Login Validation and Account Restrictions

Figure 6.7 shows the login validation that takes place when a user logs in. An unusual aspect of the login name validation is that if an incorrect user name is typed, access is denied. In NetWare 3.x (and other systems), the LOGIN program waits for you to type in an incorrect password before displaying the Access denied message. In NetWare 3.x, it's not possible to guess whether you typed in the user name incorrectly or the password incorrectly.

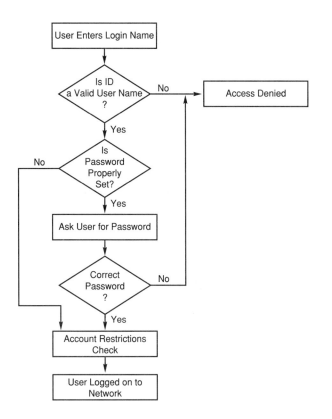

Figure 6.7

Login name and
password validation.

In NetWare 4.x, if you type in the user name incorrectly, you're
informed about it—even before you type in the complete password. This might seem to be a less secure mechanism, but it alerts
the user that the user name is incorrect early in the login process.
One reason for this could be the following: In NetWare 4.x, user
names might have to be specified using the NDS path. This is
considerably more complex than the simpler user names used
in NetWare 3.x, and many more typing mistakes can be made. By
alerting the user that the user name was typed incorrectly, the
user can take corrective action. Otherwise, it can increase
the frustration level of users and place an additional burden on
the system administrator. For sites that are concerned about security, enabling intruder detection can reduce the likelihood that
an intruder will guess a valid user ID and password combination.

After the user name and password are validated, other account restrictions may apply, including:

- Time restriction
- Station restriction
- Concurrent restriction
- Password restriction

Details of these types of restrictions were presented in Chapter 5, "NetWare Directory Services Security." These tasks can be performed using the NetWare Administrator or the NETADMIN utility.

Processing of Network Requests

When the VLM.EXE loads, it sets up the first network drive to map to the SYS:LOGIN directory of a NetWare server. The first network drive is specified in the FIRST NETWORK DRIVE statement in the NET.CFG file. Changing to this drive and invoking the LOGIN program initiates the user-authentication process. The user has to supply the correct login name and password before access to a NetWare server is granted.

After logging in, the commands typed by the user are checked by DOS to see if they're local or network commands. Network commands are sent to the network services using the DOS redirector function defined for DOS 3.1 and above. Local commands are processed by the local workstation operating system. The networking software creates the illusion that the network is an extension of the workstation operating environment. This makes it possible for single-user applications to run on the network if they're set up correctly. Figures 6.8 and 6.9 show the kind of processing that takes place at the workstation and server to keep the network transparent to DOS.

If the DOS system call is for NetWare services such as access to a file on a network drive, DOS directs this request across the network to the server. In other words, DOS plays the role of traffic policeman or a *redirector*. The request is sent as a NetWare Core Protocol (NCP) packet encapsulated in an IPX datagram and passed on to the LAN drivers for the workstation (see fig. 6.8).

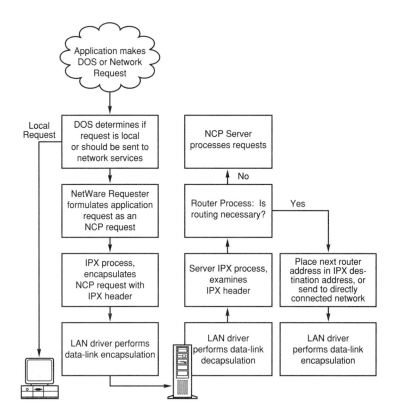

Figure 6.8

NetWare 4.x
workstation makes
system requests.

The LAN drivers encapsulate the IPX packet with data-link
headers and send this packet across the network to the server. The
server's LAN drivers strip the data-link header and pass the IPX
packet to the IPX process on the server. The IPX process passes the
IPX packet to the router process on the server. Remember: every
NetWare server is capable of acting as an IPX router. The router
process examines the destination address on the IPX packet and
checks to see whether the IPX packet is destined to a different
network than the one on which the IPX packet was received.

If the IPX packet belongs to a different network, the router process
consults its routing table to determine which router the IPX packet
should be sent to. The IPX header is then replaced by the address
of the next router. This process continues until the IPX packet gets
to its final destination.

If the router process discovers that no routing is necessary, it strips the IPX header and sends the original NCP request to the file-server process on the server.

The file server (see fig. 6.9) processes the request, and sends an NCP reply packet to the router and IPX process. The router process determines whether the packet needs to be routed. The NCP packet is encapsulated in an IPX packet and sent to the LAN drivers, which send it back to the workstation that made the request. At the workstation, the LAN drivers strip the data-link header and pass it on to the IPX software running at the workstation (IPXODI.COM). The IPX process at the workstation strips off the IPX header and sends the NCP reply packet to the NetWare Requester, which translates the original DOS request to a DOS system reply. The application that was waiting for the DOS system service then resumes—none the wiser about all the behind-the-scenes network activity it took to satisfy its request.

Figure 6.9

NetWare 4.x server replies to a workstation.

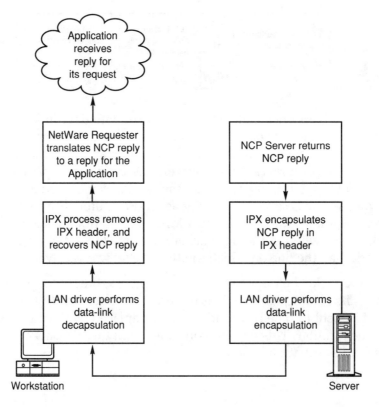

To set up the network environment, a network login script is processed when the user logs in successfully. The login script file is kept on the server and is similar in concept to the role the AUTOEXEC.BAT file plays for a single-user PC.

After the user logs in, a set of login scripts for the user can be executed. These login scripts are described in the following section.

Login Scripts

Many of the NetWare 3.x login script commands can be used with NetWare 4.x. NetWare 4.x includes a few additional login script commands, but the biggest difference is in the area of login script organization. In NetWare 3.x, there were three types of login scripts: system, user, and default login scripts. NetWare 4.x has an additional login script type called the *profile* login script. The scope of the system login script has changed also. In NetWare 3.x, the system login script applied to all user accounts defined on the file server. In NetWare 4.x, the system login script applies to user accounts for the container on which it is defined.

Login Script Types

NetWare 4.x supports four types of login scripts:

- ◆ System login scripts
- ◆ Profile login scripts
- ◆ User login scripts
- ◆ Default login scripts

The *system* login script is a property of the Organization and Organizational Unit container objects. The *profile* login script is a property of the Profile leaf object. The *user* login script is a property of the User object. The *default* login script doesn't exist as an object or a property; it's contained in the LOGIN.EXE utility used for logging in to the network. Because login scripts are properties of objects, NDS tools (such as the NETADMIN or the NetWare Administrator) can be used for creating and modifying login scripts. Each of these different login script types are discussed in the following sections.

System Login Script

The system login script is a property of the Organization and Organizational Unit container objects, and applies to all User objects defined in that container. This means that system login scripts are a convenient way of specifying the commands that should be executed for all users belonging to an organization or department (Organizational Unit) within the organization.

The NDS objects that can contain the system login script are Organization and Organizational Unit objects.

The system login script is executed for only the immediate users in that container. In figure 6.10, the system login script for organization O=SCS applies only to users Admin, KSS, and Dei that are defined in that container. They do not apply to users Lisa, Janice, or Bill in container OU=ENG.O=SCS. The container OU=ENG has its own system login script, and this applies to users Lisa, Janice, and Bill. The container OU=SALES.O=SCS, in figure 6.10, doesn't have a system login script. This means that for users Nina, John, and Dorsh, there's no system login script. If a container doesn't have a system login script, it does not inherit the system login script from a Parent container.

Inheritance of system login script from a Parent container unnecessarily complicates the network computing environment. For instance, if the system login script is removed from a Parent container, inheritance means that the user may execute the login script of the parent's Parent container. Execution of login script of a

Parent container might not make sense because the login script usually makes references to network resources that are available to users in the container. These resources might not be available to User objects several levels down on the directory information tree.

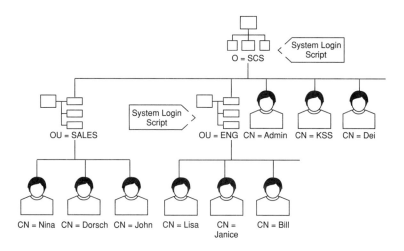

Figure 6.10

Scope of system login script.

The system login script is the first type of login script that is executed and can be used to set up the general environment for all users in that container.

To create a system login script, you must highlight the container object using NETADMIN or NetWare Administration tool, and select its Login Script property for modification.

Profile Login Script

A profile login script is a property of the Profile object. The Profile object is a leaf object whose sole purpose is to contain the profile login script (see fig. 6.11). If a group of users has common needs, that group fits a certain *profile*. In this case, a Profile object can be assigned to each of the users.

Figure 6.11

Profile login script.

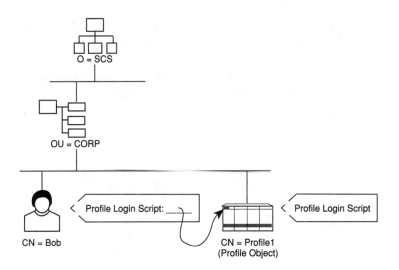

Every User object has a profile login script property (as well as a user login script property). The profile login script property for a user can contain the name of a Profile object. If the profile login property for a User object is set to a Profile object, the profile login script (property of the Profile object) is executed every time that user logs in. If the profile login property for a User object is *not* set, no profile login script is executed when that User object is logged in.

 The profile login script is set by assigning a Profile object to the User object's profile login property.

The profile login script is executed after the system login script, and only one profile login script can be assigned to a user's profile login property.

The profile login script seems to be similar to the system login script. What, then, is its purpose? The system login script applies to only User objects that are in the immediate container. There might be situations in which users belonging to different containers have a common need for setting up their user environment. The profile login script property for users can be set to the same Profile object, even if the User objects are defined in different containers. This makes it possible for users in different Parent containers to have a common login script.

Use system login scripts to meet the common needs of users in a Parent container. For most organizational structures, this should be enough. Use the Profile object only if users in different departments or organizations need to have a common login script. Using profile login scripts can complicate future maintenance if the login requirements change. You might have to change the profile login script property of every User object. Use the NLIST command to search for users who have the same Profile object value for their profile login script property.

 The profile login script is executed after the system login script, but before the user login script.

A User object can have only one profile login script.

User Login Script

Every User object has a login script property (see fig. 6.12). The value for the login script property can be a sequence of login script commands. The same type of login script commands that are used for the system and profile login script can be used for user login scripts.

 The user login script is set by entering login script commands for the User object's user login property.

The user login script is executed after the profile login script (if any).

Figure 6.12

User login script.

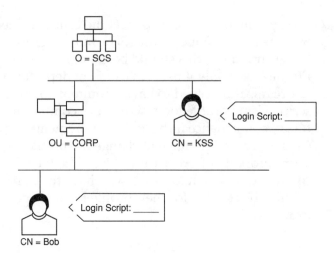

The user login script can be used to customize a user's login environment. The other login scripts (system and profile) are used to share common login script commands with other users. A user may have special needs that are not addressed by these "group" login scripts. In that case, use the user login script to further customize the user's environment.

Default Login Script

The default login script is unlike all the other login scripts in the sense that the other login scripts can be modified, but the default login script cannot. The default login script is fixed and can be considered to be "contained" in the login program, LOGIN.EXE. It's meant to provide a minimum user environment in case a user logs in and doesn't have a user login script. This is certainly true the first time the user Admin logs in to a newly installed network. A newly installed network doesn't have any system, profile, or user login script set up. The Admin user can at least perform some basic administration without having to create drive mappings.

After a user login script is created for that user, the default login script won't execute for that user. In some situations, all the login script needs of a user can be met by the system login script or the profile login script. In this case, there is no need to have a user login script. However, since the user login script has not been set, the default login script executes in addition to any system and profile login scripts. One of the default actions the default login script performs is to set up a search drive mapping to SYS:PUBLIC. If the system or profile login script already maps a search drive to SYS:PUBLIC, a second search drive mapping to SYS:PUBLIC is created unless the user login script property is set, or the NO_DEFAULT login directive exists in the system or profile login script.

The default login script is executed if the user login script is not set.

The default login script is contained in the LOGIN.EXE file.

The default login script file looks similar to the following. Comments (lines starting with REM) have been added by the author to illustrate certain points:

```
REM This sets up a greeting for the user
WRITE "Good %GREETING_TIME, %LOGIN_NAME."
REM This is similar to the DOS ECHO OFF command.
REM It stops the display of commands as they are executed.
MAP DISPLAY OFF

REM Error processing is not shown
MAP ERRORS

REM Map the first network drive (*1:) to the
REM root directory on volume SYS:
MAP *1:=SYS:

REM Map the first search drive to the SYS:PUBLIC directory
REM which contains some public system utilities that can
REM be executed by the user.
MAP S1:=SYS:PUBLIC

REM Turn on display of commands as they are processed
REM so that when the MAP command is executed, a listing
REM of the current drive mappings is displayed.
MAP DISPLAY ON
MAP
```

As you study this default login script, you'll see that the MAP command, which can be executed from the command line, can also be executed directly in the login script. Certain login script commands such as WRITE, MAP DISPLAY ON, and MAP DISPLAY OFF cannot be executed from the DOS prompt.

The commands in the login script files are interpreted by the LOGIN utility; this includes the MAP command. The MAP command is normally performed by a program named MAP.EXE, which is located in the SYS:PUBLIC directory. However, the first time you execute the MAP command in the login script you don't have a search drive mapping to the SYS:PUBLIC directory. Yet, somehow the MAP commands still work—regardless of an absence of a search path to the SYS:PUBLIC directory. The reason for this is that the MAP command is interpreted and not invoked as an external program.

The NO_DEFAULT Directive

The NO_DEFAULT directive in the system or profile login script can explicitly disable the execution of the default login script (see fig. 6.13). This is useful if you want to override the default mappings created when the user login script property is not set, but you don't want to set the user login property (because the login scripts of the system and/or profile login script are sufficient to set up the required user environment).

The NO_DEFAULT directive is used to prevent the default login script from executing and is set in the system or profile login scripts.

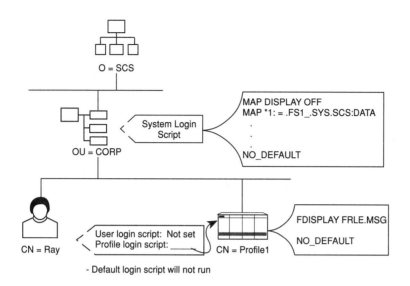

Figure 6.13
The NO_DEFAULT
login script command.

Login Script Execution Order

The order of execution for the login script types is illustrated in figure 6.14 and is also listed here. These steps are executed when the user logs in to a NetWare 4.x network:

1. If the container in which the User object resides has the system login script property set, the system login script is executed for that user.

2. If a user's profile login script property is set to a Profile object, the profile login script for that Profile object is executed for that user.

3. If a user's user login script property is set, the user login script for that User object is executed.

4. If a user's user login script property is *not* set, the default is executed *unless* the NO_DEFAULT login script command has been included in the system or profile login script.

Figure 6.14

Login script order.

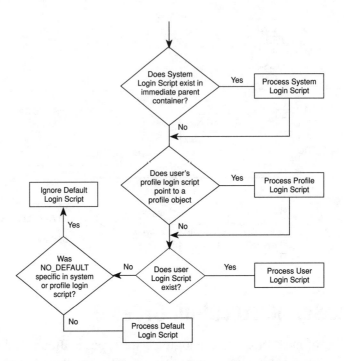

Some examples might help illustrate the above rules. Figure 6.15 shows an example of the NDS tree for organization O=TEC that has a system login script.

Figure 6.15

Example of login script execution.

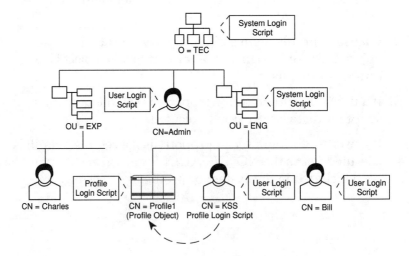

Under O=TEC there are two Organizational Unit objects. One of the Organizational Unit objects (OU=ENG) has a system login script, while the other (OU=EXP) doesn't. The users Admin, KSS, and Bill have a user login script, but user Charles does not. The user KSS also has a profile login script property set to the Profile object CN=Profile1.OU=ENG.O=TEC. The order of execution of login scripts for the different users is listed as follows:

User KSS:

User KSS's container has a system login script. Therefore, the system login script for OU=ENG is executed first. User KSS also has a profile login script. This is executed next. Finally, a check is made to see whether user KSS has a user login script. Because user KSS has a user login script, this is executed next. The order of login script executions for user KSS is:

◆ System login script for OU=ENG

◆ Profile login script for Profile object PROFILE1.ENG.TEC

◆ User login script for KSS

User Bill:

User Bill's container has a system login script. Therefore, the system login script for OU=ENG is executed first. User Bill doesn't have a profile login script. A check is made to see whether user Bill has a user login script. Because user Bill does have a user login script, this is executed next. The order of login script executions for user Bill is:

◆ System login script for OU=ENG

◆ User login script for Bill

User Admin:

User Admin's container has a system login script. Therefore, the system login script for O=TEC is executed first. User Admin does not have a profile login script. A check is made to see whether user Admin has a user login script. Because user Admin has a user login script, this is executed next. The order of login script executions for user Admin is:

- System login script for O=TEC
- User login script for Admin

User Charles:

User Charles's container OU=EXP does not have a system login script. Therefore, no system login script is executed. User Charles does not have a profile login script. A check is made to see if user Charles has a user login script. Because user Charles does not have a user login script, the default login script is executed.

The login script execution order is:

1. System login script

2. Profile login script

3. User login script or default login script if user login script property is not set

Upgrade Considerations for Login Scripts

When upgrading from an earlier NetWare version to NetWare 4.x, the first system login script encountered for a file server that's placed in a container object becomes the system login script property of that container object. Any subsequent system login scripts from file servers that are placed in the same container are ignored. It's important to upgrade the server that contains the most up-to-date version of the system login script first.

The first system login script encountered for a file server that's placed in a container object becomes the system login script property of that container object.

Even though the earlier NetWare login scripts are compatible with NetWare 4.x, you should review the upgraded login scripts to see whether you can take advantage of the new NetWare 4.x features. If the directories you want to map as network drives are on Volume objects that are in a different context than the context where the users are defined, you'll have to modify the login script MAP commands to refer to the NDS name of Volume objects.

Rights to Execute Login Script Property Value

A login script is a property of an NDS object; the system login script is a property of the Organization or Organizational Unit container; the profile login script is a property of the Profile object; and the user login script is a property of the User object. For a User object to execute the login scripts when the User object is logged in, that User object must have certain rights to that login script property.

Containers are granted the Read property right to their login script. The User object in the container must have the Browse right to the container object and the Read property right to the login script to execute the system login script. The Browse right to the container is usually granted by inheritance. For example, it's typical in most NDS trees to make [Public] a trustee of [Root] with the Browse right. Users in a container inherit the Browse right.

The User object in the container must have the Browse right to the container object and the Read property right to the login script to execute the system login script.

Containers are granted the Read property right to their login script (system login script).

Profile login scripts are assigned by setting a user's profile login script property to the name of the Profile object. The user needs to be made a trustee of the Profile object. When a user is made a trustee of the Profile object, the following rights are assigned by default to the user:

1. Browse object right to the Profile object

2. Read and Compare property rights to the All Properties of the Profile object

Because of the All Properties Read and Compare rights, the user also inherits these rights for the profile login script property.

 When a user is made a trustee of the Profile object, the user is given the Browse object right to the Profile object, and Read and Compare property rights to the All Properties of the Profile object.

Users are by default assigned Read and Write property rights to their user login script property. The Write property right lets users modify their own login scripts. In some network environments, it may not be desirable for users to modify their login scripts. In this case, the Write property right to the login script must be removed.

 By default, users are assigned Read and Write property rights to their user login script property.

NetWare Login Script Commands

As you saw in the example of the default login script earlier in this chapter, one of the most useful commands in login script processing is the MAP command.

Besides MAP, there are a number of useful commands that are discussed next. Consider the following simple login script:

```
MAP DISPLAY OFF
WRITE "Good %GREETING_TIME, %LOGIN_NAME"
MAP *1:=SYS:USERS/%LOGIN_NAME
MAP S1:=SYS:PUBLIC
```

The WRITE command displays text strings to the user's console. You might also notice in this example the use of the %GREETING_TIME and %LOGIN_NAME variables. These are called *login script identifier variables* and are discussed later. As you can probably guess, these variables represent character strings that can be used in commands such as WRITE "Good %GREETING_TIME, %LOGIN_NAME." For example, this statement may produce the following message:

```
Good Morning, KARANJIT.
```

The %GREETING_TIME evaluates to "Morning" and %LOGIN_NAME evaluates to the user's login name—in this case, KARANJIT. A word of caution, however: When used in a string, such as "Good %GREETING_TIME, %LOGIN_NAME," the script variables must be in capital letters to evaluate correctly.

In many cases, you'll be unable to accomplish a desired task using only the commands that are built into the login command processor. If you want to invoke external utilities, you must precede them with the # character. An external utility is any command that must be performed by a .COM or .EXE file. Therefore, invoking the utility NETUSER requires the following command in the login script file:

```
#NETUSER
```

Login script commands can have a maximum of 150 characters per line, and can be in upper- or lowercase. The case is not sensitive except in the case of login script variables in double quotes ("). Login script variables appearing in quotes must be preceded by % and must be in uppercase. Outside the quoted string, the login script variables can be upper- or lowercase.

Complexity of Login Script Files

One of the more powerful commands that can be used in a login script is the IF_ THEN conditional statement, which has the following general form:

```
IF <condition> THEN BEGIN
     <statements>
ELSE
     <statements>
     END
```

or

```
IF <condition> THEN <statement>
```

The IF statement in the login script file gives you the power of conditionally executing statements; that is, execute statements only if a certain condition is true. It can be used to customize a login script, but there is also a danger of making the login script too complicated, as shown in the following example of a system login script:

```
MAP DISPLAY OFF
BREAK OFF
FIRE PHASERS 3 TIMES
WRITE ""
WRITE "Good %GREETING_TIME, %LOGIN_NAME"
WRITE ""
WRITE "You have logged in to file server %FILE_SERVER"
WRITE "from station %NETWORK_ADDRESS:%P_STATION."
WRITE ""
WRITE "Your connection number is %STATION and you are"
WRITE "using shell %SHELL_TYPE on machine %SMACHINE."
WRITE "Your internal userid is %USER_ID"
WRITE ""
WRITE "Today is %DAY_OF_WEEK" %MONTH_NAME, %DAY %YEAR"
IF MEMBER OF "NONCIVILIAN" THEN
     WRITE "System time is %HOUR24:%MINUTE:%SECOND"
ELSE
     WRITE "System time is %HOUR:%MINUTE:%SECOND %AM_PM"
END

IF MONTH = "1" AND DAY = "1" THEN BEGIN

     WRITE "Happy new year %YEAR, %FULL_NAME"
END
```

```
IF SHORT_YEAR = "00" THEN WRITE "Have a nice new century!"

IF NDAY_OF_WEEK = "6" THEN
      WRITE "Have a good weekend!"

 IF NDAY_OF_WEEK > "1" AND NDAY_OF_WEEK < "7" THEN
      FDISPLAY SYS:MESSAGES/DAILY.MSG
ELSE
      DISPLAY SYS:MESSAGES/WEEKEND.MSG
END

IF MEMBER OF "ENGINEERING" THEN BEGIN
      IF DAY_OF_WEEK="TUESDAY" THEN
            WRITE "STAFF MEETING AT 3:00 PM"
      IF DAY_OF_WEEK="FRIDAY" THEN BEGIN
            WRITE "STATUS MEETING AT 3:30 PM."
            WRITE "BE THERE OR BE SQUARED!"
      END
END

MAP INS S1:=SYS:PUBLIC
MAP INS S2:=SYS:PUBLIC/%MACHINE/%OS/%OS_VERSION

IF MEMBER OF "PAYROLL" THEN BEGIN
      IF DAY_OF_WEEK="MONDAY" THEN
            WRITE "STAFF MEETING AT 1:00 PM IN CONF.RM. 303"
      IF DAY_OF_WEEK="FRIDAY" THEN
            WRITE "REVIEW MEETING AT 11:00 AM."
      END
      ATTACHB LAKSHMI/%LOGIN_NAME
      MAP L:=LAKSHMI/SYS:USERS/%LOGIN_NAME
END

COMSPEC=S2:COMMAND.COM

IF MEMBER OF "ACCOUNTING" THEN
      MAP INS S16:=SYS:APPS/AMRIT
END

IF MEMBER OF "WPUSERS" THEN
      MAP INS S16:=SYS:APPS/WP
END

IF MEMBER OF "PAYROLL" OR MEMBER OF "ACCOUNTING" THEN BEGIN
      MAP INS S16:=SYS:APPS/ADP
      MAP *2:=SYS:PAYROLL
END
```

```
IF LOGIN_NAME = "SUPERVISOR" THEN BEGIN
      MAP *1:=SYS:USERS/SUPER
      MAP *2:=SYS:SYSTEM
      MAP INS S2:=*2:
      MAP INS S3:=SYS:SYSTEM/NMUTILS
END

IF MEMBER OF "ACCOUNTING" THEN    #CAPTURE Q=ACCT_LASERQ NB TO=25

IF MEMBER OF "ENGINEERING" THEN BEGIN
      #CAPTURE Q=ENG_LASERQ NB NT TO=15
      IF ERROR_LEVEL <> "0" THEN BEGIN
            SEND "ERROR IN CAPTURE" TO TOM
            #EMAIL TOM "ERROR IN CAPTURE FOR %LOGIN_NAME"
      END
END

IF <EDITOR>="BRIEF" THEN
      MAP INS S16:=SYS:APPS/BRIEF
END

DOS SET X = "1"
ALOOP:
      SET X = [X] + "1"
      WRITE "VICTORY PARADE!"
IF <X> IS LESS THAN "7" THEN GOTO ALOOP

DRIVE *2:
DOS VERIFY ON
SET PROMPT = "$P$G"
MAP DISPLAY ON
MAP
EXIT "MENU  TOPAPPS"
```

The preceding system login script resembles a BASIC program more than a simple login script. Its only redeeming feature—besides the fact that it can work for a specific environment—is that it makes use of almost every type of script variable and login statement construct. The complexity makes the system login script difficult to maintain. When making changes for a specific group, it's easy to inadvertently make a mistake that could affect all the users on the system. The above example might seem extreme, but the author has seen more complex (worse) examples than the login script file used here.

Recommendations for Organizing Login Scripts

Over a period of time, the system login script file can become very complex (see previous section) as you try to adapt a common system login script file to a changing network environment.

You should keep the system login script file as simple as possible. The system login script should contain statements that are applicable for all users in that container. Preferably, there should be no IF ... THEN conditionals in the system login script, because these can become complex. Remember that changes you make at the system login script will be "seen" by users in that container. This also includes any mistakes that you make that will prevent users from logging in.

The system login script file can contain statements to display messages that are system-wide, as shown here:

```
REM ************************************************
REM *                                              *
REM * The system login script should  have         *
REM * simple statements of the type FDISPLAY       *
REM *                                              *
REM ************************************************

REM * Send a global display message
FDISPLAY SYS:MESSAGES/GLOBAL.MSG
```

When this system login script file is processed, it displays any global system messages that the supervisor may have kept in the message file SYS:MESSAGES/GLOBAL.MSG. Control is then transferred to the profile login script for the user—if one exists.

The profile login script can be used to group login scripts common to a group of users with similar needs (those who have a common network usage "profile" or requirement). An example of this could be users who work on a common project or have a common need for accessing directories and files. Because the users sharing a profile login script have similar needs, you should not have to use too many IF ... THEN ... ELSE statements. If you find yourself using too many IF ... THEN ... ELSE statements to implement exceptions to the rule, you probably need to make separate profile login scripts for users.

573

If a user has too many special needs and doesn't fit the profile login script, you should place the login script statements for the user in the user login script. The user login script can also be used for any special needs a user may have that cannot be accommodated easily in the system and profile login scripts.

Any of the login scripts can contain a statement of the form:

```
INCLUDE SYS:PUBLIC/SCRIPTS/COMMON.SCR
```

The INCLUDE statement means that the contents of the specified file, in this case SYS:PUBLIC/SCRIPTS/COMMON.SCR, are processed as login script commands. This is sometimes called the *subroutine* mechanism for login script processing by Novell. If all the users have a common script file, the COMMON.SCR can be used for them. The advantage of using the INCLUDE statement is that if the login script is to be changed, the COMMON.SCR file only needs to be changed once.

The individual script file can have the structure shown here:

```
MAP DISPLAY OFF
REM Greetings (optional)
WRITE "Good %GREETING_TIME, %LOGIN_NAME"

REM General logon messages
FDISPLAY SYS:USERS/MSGS/WEEKLY.TXT

REM Home Directory Mappings
MAP *1:=.CORP_SYS.CORP.SCS:USERS\%LOGIN_NAME

REM Search drive mappings
MAP INS S1:=.CORP_SYS.CORP.SCS:PUBLIC
MAP INS S2:=.CORP_SYS.CORP.SCS:PUBLIC\%MACHINE\%OS\%OS_VERSION
MAP INS S3:=.CORP_SYS.CORP.SCS:PUBLIC\BIN
MAP INS S4:=.ENG_SYS.ENG.SCS:APPS\CAD

REM Set COMSPEC environment variable
COMSPEC=S2:COMMAND.COM

REM Application directory mappings
MAP H:=.ENG_SYS.ENG.SCS:APPS\DATA

REM Any environment variable changes
SET PROMPT="$P$G"

REM Display mappings
MAP DISPLAY ON
MAP
```

The first few statements can be greeting statements. These are followed by drive mappings, including search drives. The COMSPEC variable must be set next to point to the correct copy of COMMAND.COM.

Individual messages can be printed next. Avoid using too many IF ... THEN conditionals, or else you'll have the same complexity evident in the example in the previous section. If you want to use conditionals such as IF MEMBER OF "GROUP" THEN ..., you can create a separate *group*.SCR file and specify it in the INCLUDE statement in the login script file for members of the group:

```
INCLUDE SYS:PUBLIC/SCRIPTS/group.SCR
```

Replace group with a name indicative of the group for whom special processing needs to be done. The users must have Read and File Scan rights ([R F]) in the SYS:PUBLIC/SCRIPTS directory.

The following commands can be used in login scripts:

- ◆ # (execution of external commands)
- ◆ CLS
- ◆ ATTACHB
- ◆ BREAK
- ◆ DOS BREAK
- ◆ COMSPEC
- ◆ CONTEXT
- ◆ DISPLAY
- ◆ FDISPLAY
- ◆ DOS SET or SET
- ◆ SET TIME
- ◆ DOS VERIFY
- ◆ DRIVE
- ◆ EXIT

- ◆ FIRE PHASERS
- ◆ GOTO
- ◆ IF ... THEN ... ELSE
- ◆ INCLUDE
- ◆ MACHINE
- ◆ NOSWAP and SWAP
- ◆ PAUSE
- ◆ PCCOMPATIBLE
- ◆ REMARK or REM
- ◆ SHIFT
- ◆ LASTLOGINTIME
- ◆ WRITE

These commands are discussed in the following sections.

Login Script Command:

When placed before an external command, the # character provides external program execution. The general syntax of the command is:

```
# [path]filename parameters
```

The *[path]filename* specifies the full path name of the external command. The # must be the first character in the command line. As expected, you can execute any .EXE and .COM file under DOS. To execute a DOS batch file or a DOS internal command, you must invoke the command line processor using the following command:

```
#COMMAND /C batchOrInternal
```

where *batchOrInternal* is replaced by the name of a batch file or an internal command.

For example, to clear the screen from the login script, you can use the following DOS CLS internal command:

```
#COMMAND /C CLS
```

This method was the only way to clear a screen in earlier NetWare versions. In NetWare 4.x, you can make use of the explicit login command CLS to clear the screen:

```
CLS
```

Author's Note When executing an external command, you must make sure that the proper drive mappings and search drives have been set. That's because the external command executes in the context of the NetWare environment set up at the time of execution. You must have sufficient network rights in the directory where the program is located; minimum rights should be [R F].

When the external command is executed, the login program is still resident in RAM and is not released until termination of the login script processing. Therefore, loading TSRs during login processing is not advisable; it leaves a hole (where the login program was) when login script processing terminates.

Login Script Command: ATTACHB

The ATTACHB command can be used to attach to bindery-based servers. You can attach to a maximum of *eight* file servers. This command allows the attachment to other file servers without interrupting the current execution of the login script. The general syntax of the command is:

```
ATTACHB [fileserver[/username[;password]]]
```

If the *fileserver,* *username,* and *password* are not specified, you will be prompted for the variables you have not entered.

577

Author's Note Be careful about including password information in the login script file; anyone with Read access to the login script file can read the password, and this can compromise the security of your network.

Login Script Command: BREAK

The BREAK ON command lets you terminate the execution of your login script. The general syntax of the command is:

```
BREAK [ON | OFF]
```

If BREAK is ON, the command allows you to terminate the processing of your login script using Ctrl+C or Ctrl+Break. The default value is OFF.

The BREAK command is different from the DOS BREAK command, explained next.

Login Script Command: DOS BREAK

If DOS BREAK is set to ON, it enables the Ctrl+Break checking for DOS. With the CTRL_BREAK checking enabled, whenever a program sends a request to DOS, the request can be terminated using the Ctrl+Break key. This command is equivalent to the DOS BREAK command.

Login Script Command: COMSPEC

The COMSPEC specifies the directory DOS should use to load the command line processor COMMAND.COM. The general syntax is:

```
COMSPEC=[path]COMMAND.COM
```

It's possible to use a command-line processor other than COMMAND.COM, but such implementations are rare. The COMSPEC command directly sets the COMSPEC DOS environment variable.

Earlier in this chapter, the sequence of events for when DOS loads was described. It was explained that a transient portion of COMMAND.COM is loaded in the area of memory just below 640 KB. This is shown in figure 6.16, which also shows a general memory MAP for a DOS NetWare workstation.

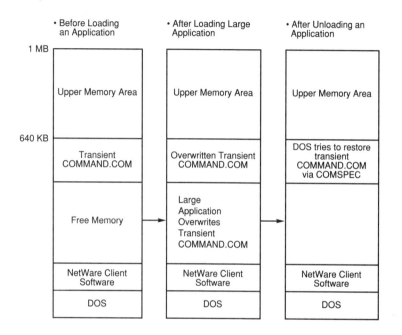

Figure 6.16

Use of COMSPEC environment variable.

When a large program loads, it can overwrite the transient portion of DOS, and when this program exits, the transient portion of COMMAND.COM needs to be restored. DOS makes use of the COMSPEC environment variable to obtain a copy of COMMAND.COM. If the COMMAND.COM in memory and the one indicated by COMSPEC are for different versions of DOS, the workstation crashes with a message, Invalid COMMAND.COM. On a network, there's a potential for users using different versions of DOS, and therefore a potential for COMSPEC pointing to an incorrect version of DOS. The COMSPEC variable should be set to the correct directory. This can be done by using the following commands:

```
MAP S2:=SYS:PUBLIC/%MACHINE/%OS/%OS_VERSION
COMSPEC=S2:COMMAND.COM
```

579

For example, the SYS:PUBLIC/%MACHINE/%OS/
%OS_VERSION evaluates to SYS:PUBLIC/IBM_PC/MSDOS/
V6.00 for MS-DOS 6.00. You can place in this directory the
MS-DOS utilities that will be used by the users on the network,
and also a copy of MS-DOS 6.0 COMMAND.COM. This allows
the sharing of DOS 6.0 utilities on the network, and also a single
place where COMMAND.COM is located.

Another technique that can be used for users who always boot
from the hard disk is to set COMSPEC as follows:

```
COMSPEC=C:\COMMAND.COM
```

This statement takes care of different versions of DOS on the
workstation's hard disk.

OS/2 users should not set their COMSPEC variable as indicated
here. In case a login script needs to be shared by OS/2 users and
users using the VDM (Virtual DOS Machine), the OS/2 users
should reset their value of the COMSPEC variable.

Login Script Command: CONTEXT

The CONTEXT statement can be used to change a user's context
from the login script. The general syntax is:

```
CONTEXT  context
```

To set your context to OU=LAB.OU=INVE.O=ETC, you can use
the login command:

```
CONTEXT OU=LAB.OU=INVE.O=ETC
```

or

```
CONTEXT LAB.INVE.ETC
```

To move one container above current context, you can use:

```
CONTEXT  .
```

To move two containers, above current context, you can use:

```
CONTEXT  ..
```

Login Script Command: DISPLAY

This command shows the contents of the specified file on the workstation screen. The exact characters are displayed including any control codes for printer and word processing formats. The general syntax is:

```
DISPLAY [pathname]file
```

where *[pathname]file* is the name of the file whose contents are displayed.

Login Script Command: FDISPLAY

This command shows the contents of the specified text file on the workstation screen. The text is formatted and filtered so that only the text itself is displayed. The general syntax is:

```
FDISPLAY [pathname]file
```

where *[pathname]file* is the name of the file whose contents are displayed.

Login Script Command: DOS SET or SET

This command can be used to set a DOS environment variable from within a login script. The general syntax is:

```
[option] [DOS] SET name = "value"
```

The *[option]* can be replaced by an optional keyword such as TEMP, TEMPORARY to signify that the variable is set only during the login script processing and does not affect the DOS environment. Replace *name* with the name of the environment variable and *value* with its actual value. The value must always be enclosed in the double quote (") characters.

Examples of the use of the SET command are:

```
SET PROMPT = "$P$G"        - for setting DOS prompt
SET FNAME =                - for removing the definition of the
                           - environment variable
SET Y = "1"
```

```
SET Y = <Y> + 1

SET UDIR = "*1:\\USERS\\%LOGIN_NAME"
```

Notice that you can refer to a DOS environment variable by using the <> brackets around it. If you want to use an environment variable in a MAP command, you must precede it with a %.

```
SET NWPATH="Z:\APPS\BIN"

MAP INS S3:=%<NWPATH>
```

If you want to use the backslash character (\) in a string value, you must specify two backslashes:

```
SET   FILENAME = "F:\\PUBLIC\\TEMP\\KSSFILE"
```

The reason for this is that the single backslash character is used to indicate special character codes as shown below:

```
\r                      carriage return
\n                      new line
\"                      embed quotation marks in string
\7                      generate a beep sound (bell)
```

Login Script Command: SET TIME [ON | OFF]

Use SET TIME ON (default) to set your workstation's time to the server you first connect to. This is the default behavior. To override this default behavior, use the SET TIME OFF. In this case, the workstation's clock will not synchronize to the server clock.

Login Script Command: DOS VERIFY ON

When set to ON, this is used to verify that the data can be written to a local drive without an error. The default is OFF and the general syntax is:

```
DOS VERIFY [ON¦OFF]
```

The NCOPY automatically does a read after write verify check and can be used to copy files to floppy disks. If you want to use the DOS COPY command, you should have:

```
DOS VERIFY ON
```

in the login script, for added reliability in making copies to floppy disks. The /V option can also be used with the DOS COPY command to produce the same effect.

Login Script Command: DRIVE

The DRIVE command can be used to specify which network drive will be the default drive. The general syntax is:

```
DRIVE [d: ¦ *n:]
```

where *d:* represents a drive letter and **n* represents a network drive number such as *1, *2, and so on. By default, the first network drive *1 is the default drive, but you can change this by specifying the new default drive in the DRIVE command.

Login Script Command: EXIT

Normally, execution terminates at the end of processing the individual user login script. The EXIT command can be used to prematurely terminate the login script processing or specify the command to be executed on termination. The general syntax is:

```
EXIT ["commandstring"]
```

where *commandstring* is replaced with the program name plus arguments of any command to be executed after login script termination. The length of *commandstring* (at the moment of writing this book) is limited to 14 characters. This is the same as the limitation in earlier NetWare versions.

Examples of the use of the EXIT command are:

```
EXIT                    - Simply terminates login processing

EXIT MENU               - Executes the MENU utility on termination

EXIT "F:USEREXEC.BAT"   - Executes USEREXEC.BAT in the default drive
                          on termination
```

Avoid using the EXIT command in all but the last line in the individual login script, because the EXIT command terminates the processing of the login script and this may not be what you want to do.

If used in the system login script file, it stops the processing of the system login script and returns control to the DOS prompt. The individual login script file will be totally bypassed.

There may be times when using the EXIT command in the individual login script file can serve as a convenient means of escaping to the DOS prompt, but for properly designed script files, this should not be necessary.

Login Script Command: FIRE PHASERS

FIRE PHASERS is a popular command that produces the sound effects of firing phasers. It doesn't work from the DOS command line. The general syntax is:

```
FIRE PHASERS n TIMES
```

where *n* is replaced by a number from one to nine.

Examples are:

```
FIRE PHASERS 4 TIMES
FIRE PHASERS %NDAY_OF_WEEK TIMES
```

Login Script Command: GOTO

The GOTO command can be used to set up a "loop" in your login script. The general syntax is:

```
GOTO label
```

The *label* can be an identifier and must be specified in the current login script. The following example should make this clear.

```
SET Y = "1"
REM The line below shows how labels can be defined
LOOP:
    REM The indentation shown below is for purposes
    REM of clarity and readability of the login script.
    REM It is not a requirement.
```

```
REM Placing <> around Y tells the login processor
REM that this is an environment variable whose value
REM needs to be evaluated.
SET Y = <Y> + "1"

REM Do whatever login script processing
REM that needs to be repeated, here.
REM Place a condition for terminating the loop, otherwise
REM you will repeat this loop indefinitely!
IF <Y> <= "45" THEN GOTO LOOP
```

Set BREAK ON in the login script before experimenting with loops, just in case you want to break out of a loop you have created unintentionally.

Login Script Command: IF ... THEN ... ELSE

This is a statement that lets you execute certain commands conditionally. The general syntax is:

```
IF conditional(s) [AND¦OR¦NOR] conditional(s) THEN
     command
ELSE
     command
END
```

If the *command* is a series of statements, you must include a BEGIN on the previous line. IF statements can be nested to a maximum of 10 nested IF statements.

The conditional(s) can be generated by using the following operators:

Equal	Not Equal
=	!=
==	<>
EQUAL	NOT EQUAL
EQUALS	DOES NOT EQUAL
	NOT EQUAL TO

Greater and Less Than Relational Operators	
>	IS GREATER THAN
<	IS LESS THAN
>=	IS GREATER THAN OR EQUAL TO
<=	IS LESS THAN OR EQUAL TO

Login Script Command: INCLUDE

The INCLUDE command indicates a level of direction for processing login scripts. It means that the content of the file specified in the INCLUDE statement is to be processed next, after which processing returns to the statement following the INCLUDE command. The general syntax is:

```
INCLUDE [pathname]filename
```

or

```
INCLUDE objectname
```

where *[pathname]filename* is the location of the file to be processed, and *objectname* is the name of the object whose login script you want to use. Container objects, Profile objects, and User objects have login scripts associated with them. For example, to execute the login script for the container OU=CORP.O=SCS, use the following:

```
INCLUDE OU=CORP.O=SCS
```

 INCLUDE commands can be nested up to any level—limited only by the memory available for processing. Don't use more than two levels of nesting or your login script will be difficult to figure out by others. You must have a minimum of [R F] rights to use the INCLUDE file.

Login Script Command: MACHINE

This can be used to set the value of the MACHINE login script variable. The MACHINE value can also be changed from the NET.CFG file. Here's the general syntax of the command:

```
MACHINE = machinename
```

where *machinename* is replaced by a name that can be up to 15 characters long. If a machine name is longer than 15 characters, it is truncated to conform to this limit. For example, to specify that a machine name is NECULTRA, use:

```
MACHINE = NECULTRA
```

Login Script Command: MAP

This has the same syntax and meaning as the NetWare MAP command found in the SYS:PUBLIC directory with a few extensions:

```
MAP DISPLAY [ON¦OFF]
MAP ERRORS [ON¦OFF]
```

The MAP DISPLAY ON shows the drive mappings when you log in. This is the default setting. To disable the MAP processing messages use MAP DISPLAY OFF.

MAP ERRORS ON displays serious error messages such as "The path to which you are mapping does not exist (not relocatable)." The default setting is ON. To disable the display of MAP errors, you can use the MAP ERRORS OFF. It's best to leave the MAP ERRORS to its default setting of ON.

When creating a login script that provides access to server volumes in other contexts, you can use the NDS name of the volume you're mapping to. For example, if you want to set a search drive to the ENGFS_SYS volume in container OU=LAB.OU=ENG.O=SCS, you can use the following:

```
MAP  INS S16: = .CN=ENGFS_SYS.OU=LAB.OU=ENG.O=SCS:PUBLIC/BIN
```

or

```
MAP INS S16: = .ENGFS_SYS.LAB.ENG.SCS:PUBLIC/BIN
```

587

Login Script Command: NO_DEFAULT

If you don't want to create a user login script and not have the default login script run, you can use the NO_DEFAULT command, which disables the execution of the default login script that would normally run if the user login script was not set.

Login Script Command: NOSWAP and SWAP

The LOGIN.EXE is normally in conventional memory when an external command is executed via the #. If there is insufficient memory available, LOGIN.EXE is swapped out to high memory, if available, or to the local hard disk. If you want to disable this swapping action, use the NOSWAP login command. In this case, if LOGIN.EXE cannot be held in conventional memory and run the external command, execution of the external command will fail.

You can revert to the default behavior by using the SWAP command.

Login Script Command: PAUSE or WAIT

This command creates a PAUSE in the execution of the login script. Its general syntax is:

PAUSE

or

WAIT

It can be used to pause the execution of the login script so that the messages do not scroll by before you have time to read them.

Login Script Command: PCCOMPATIBLE or COMPATIBLE

This is used to indicate that the workstation PC is IBM PC-compatible:

```
PCCOMPATIBLE
```

or

```
COMPATIBLE
```

If your machine is IBM PC-compatible, but you have changed the long machine or short machine name using the LONG MACHINE TYPE=, SHORT MACHINE TYPE= statements in the NET.CFG (older SHELL.CFG) file, you must use the PCCOMPATIBLE command to indicate to the shell that your machine is IBM PC-compatible. If you neglect to do this, graphical NetWare utilities such as SYSCON and FILER (that make use of the C-Worthy library routines) won't work correctly.

Login Script Command: REMARK or REM

This command is used to place comments in the login script file for enhancing the readability of the login script:

```
REM[ARK] [text]
```

or

```
* text
```

or

```
; text
```

Login Script Command: SHIFT

The LOGIN command can be used to pass variables after the LOGIN servername/username. These variables are referred to as %0, %1, %2, and so on.

Thus, in the login command:

```
LOGIN  WE_SERVE/LYDIA  PUBS  GRAPHIC
```

the following variable assignments take place:

$\qquad$ %0 =WE_SERVE

$\qquad$ %1 = LYDIA

$\qquad$ %2 = PUBS

$\qquad$ %3 = GRAPHIC

589

The %0 is always assigned to the file server being logged into, even if the file server name is not explicitly specified in the LOGIN command. The %1 is always mapped to the user's login name. The %2 and other parameters are mapped to the additional arguments on the LOGIN command line.

The SHIFT command shifts the variable assignments:

```
SHIFT [n]
```

where *n* can be a positive number for the number of variables you want to shift to the right, or a negative number for shifting to the left. If *n* is left out, the default value of 1 is assumed.

The main use of the SHIFT command is to sequence through a group of parameters specified in the command line. For instance, the following loop can be used to assign %2 to each of the parameters specified in the LOGIN command after the user name:

```
LOOP:
       IF "%2" = "VAL1" THEN Command
       IF "%2" = "VAL2" THEN Command
       IF "%2" = "VAL3" THEN Command

       SHIFT 1

IF "%2" <> "" THEN GOTO LOOP
```

This loop checks each of the parameters against a specific value, and if there's a match, performs the action specified in *Command*. The SHIFT 1 causes the %2 variable to be assigned to the next parameter, until there are no more parameters left to process; at that time, the conditional expression in the IF statement evaluates to *false*, and execution proceeds to the statement following the IF statement.

Login Script Command: LASTLOGINTIME

Used to display the last time the user logged in. Used for informational purposes.

Login Script Command: WRITE

This command is used to display a text message on the screen:

```
WRITE "text"
```

Text strings separated by a ";" are concatenated. For example, the two WRITE commands that follow will result in the same output.

```
WRITE "Good"; GREETING_TIME; ", %LOGIN_NAME"
WRITE "Good %GREETING_TIME, %LOGIN_NAME"
```

New NetWare 4.x-Specific Commands

For users already familiar with earlier versions of NetWare, the NetWare 4.x specific login script commands are summarized in table 6.1.

Table 6.1
NetWare 4.x-Specific Login Script Commands

Login Command	Description
ATTACHB	Attach to bindery-based servers. Can also attach to NetWare 4.x servers in bindery emulation mode.
CLS	Clears screen. This had to be done by the #COMMAND /C CLS in earlier NetWare versions.
CONTEXT newcontext	Can be used to change the user's context from login script.
INCLUDE NDS *objectName*	Can be used to invoke login scripts that are properties of other NDS objects. The traditional INCLUDE filename used in earlier NetWare 3.x also works in NetWare 4.x.
LASTLOGINTIME	Used to display the last time the user logged in. Used for informational purposes.
MAP CHANGE or MAP C	Change drive from ordinary network drive to search drive and vice versa.

continues

591

Table 6.1, Continued
NetWare 4.x-Specific Login Script Commands

Login Command	Description
MAP NP	No Prompt. Override existing mapping without prompting user to verify the operation.
MAP P	Map drive pointer to physical volume rather than the volume object.
NO_DEFAULT	When used in system login script or profile login script, it can disable the default login script from running.
NO_SWAP	NO_SWAP prevents LOGIN.EXE from being swapped out to high memory.
SWAP	SWAP (default) can result in LOGIN.EXE being swapped out if there is insufficient memory to run LOGIN.EXE, especially when executing # commands.
PROFILE *profobject*	Used to override the profile script assigned to a user or specified at the command line, and cause the user to execute a PROFILE script *profobject*.
SET_TIME [ON | OFF]	SET_TIME ON is used to synchronize workstation time to server that is first attached to. This is the default behavior. SET_TIME OFF disables this default behavior.

Login Script Variables

This chapter has made many references to the login variables and there are many examples of their use throughout the chapter. Table 6.2 gives a formal definition of some of these script variables. The script variables are sometimes also referred to as *login macros* because they evaluate to a specific value. When used as part of a string or a path name, the percent character must be used before the script variable name. Property values for user objects can be accessed from login scripts by using their property names. In addition, certain login script variables are defined that use compound properties (combination of more than one property). An example of this is the HOME_DIRECTORY that evaluates to a concatenation of the volume name and the path of the user's home directory.

Table 6.2
Identifier Variables

Conditional Items	Screen Display
ACCESS_SERVER	Displays TRUE if access server is functional. Displays FALSE if not functional.
ERROR_LEVEL	Displays the number of errors. If 0, no errors are found.
MEMBER OF *group*	Displays TRUE if the user is a member of a specified group. Displays FALSE if the user is not a member of a specified group.

Date	Screen Display
DAY	Displays the day from 01 to 31.
DAY_OF_WEEK	Displays the day of the week.
MONTH	Displays the month from 01 to 12.
MONTH_NAME	Displays the name of the month.
NDAY_OF_WEEK	Displays the number of the weekday.
SHORT_YEAR	Displays the year in short format, such as 94, 95, and so on.
YEAR	Displays the year in full format, such as 1994, 1995, and so on.

continues

Table 6.2, Continued
Identifier Variables

DOS Environment	Screen Display
<>	Enables you to use any DOS environment variable as a string.
NETWORK_ADDRESS	Displays the network number of the cabling system in eight hex digits.
FILE_SERVER	Displays the name of the file server.

Time	Screen Display
AM_PM	Displays the time as day or night, using a.m. or p.m.
GREETING_TIME	Displays the time of day as morning, afternoon, or evening.
HOUR	Displays the time of day in hours, from 1 to 12.
HOUR24	Displays the hour in 24-hour time, from 00 to 23.
MINUTE	Displays the minutes from 00 to 59.
SECOND	Displays the seconds from 00 to 59.

User	Screen Display
FULL_NAME	Displays the full name of the user by using SYSCON information.
LOGIN_NAME	Displays the user's login name.
USER_ID	Displays the ID number of each user.

Workstation	Screen Display
MACHINE	Displays the machine from which the shell was written, such as IBMPC.
OS	Displays the workstation's operating system, such as MS-DOS.
OS_VERSION	Displays the DOS version of the workstation.
P_STATION	Displays the station address or node address in 12 hex digits.
SMACHINE	Displays the name of the machine in short format, such as IBM.
STATION	Displays the connection number.

Novell Menus

Novell menus allow you to create a menu-driven user interface, where you have the choice of selecting the menu titles and the options in a specific menu. You can associate a number of commands with each option or specify that another submenu be invoked when an option is selected.

In NetWare 3.11 this was provided by Novell menus. The NetWare 3.11, Novell menus were adequate in simple situations, but many network administrators preferred the use of more robust third-party tools. An example of such a tool is the Saber menus. In NetWare 4.x, Novell has licensed the Saber menu technology and used it to build the Novell menus that are used with NetWare 4.x. Currently, the NetWare 4.x menus don't have the full functionality of the commercial Saber menu system package, but they're a vast improvement over the NetWare 3.x Novell menus. Starting with NetWare 3.12, the NetWare 3.x product line uses the NMENU utility. The NMENU implements the Novell menus. It is currently a batch file (NMENU.BAT) that invokes other utilities such as MENUEXE.EXE and MENUREST.EXE.

One of the improvements to the NetWare 4.x menu utility is the requirement for less memory, which allows programs that need more memory to be run from the NMENU utility.

A scripting language is used to create the source file for the NMENU utility. The source (.SRC extension) file is then compiled to produce a data file (.DAT extension). The data file is then used with an NMENU.BAT utility that interprets and executes the .DAT file. The steps to perform these operations are depicted in figure 6.17.

Figure 6.17

Novell menu compilation steps.

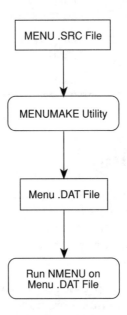

Older menu script files (.MNU extension) that were used with the scripting language of the NetWare 3.11 Novell menu utility can be converted to the NetWare 4.x menu script language by using a conversion tool called MENUCNVT.EXE. The conversion process is shown in figure 6.18.

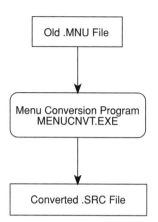

Figure 6.18
Novell menu
conversion process.

 Older menu scripts can be converted to NetWare menu scripts by using MENUCNVT.EXE.

If the older Novell menu script file is named MAIN.MNU, you can convert it by compiling and running the menu using the NetWare 4.x menu system. Perform the following steps:

MENUCNVT MAIN.MNU   (Produces a MAIN.SRC file. Examine MAIN.SRC file and edit as necessary.)

MENUMAKE MAIN.SRC   (Produces a MAIN.DAT file)

NMENU MAIN.DAT

 The MENUMAKE utility is used to compile the menu script (.SRC) file to the menu object file (.DAT).

The MENUCNVT.EXE program does not always do a complete translation. You can expect to do some manual edits to the .SRC file to make the menus behave as expected.

Menu Temporary Files

When the Novell menus are executed using the command:

```
NMENU    compiledfile
```

where *compiledfile* contains the compiled menu description, a number of temporary files are created. These default files are created in the current directory, unless special environment variables are set. To create these temporary files, the user needs the following permissions:

◆ Read (R)

◆ Write (W)

◆ Create (C)

◆ Erase (E)

◆ Modify (M)

◆ File Scan (F)

The user has these rights in the home directory and the local hard disk, so these commands can be run from the home directory or local hard disk. If the machine is turned off or stops while running the NMENU program, temporary files are left behind. Some administrators may prefer to define a common directory where these temporary files are kept, because it makes it easy for the administrator to clean up old temporary files. To set NMENU to use a specific directory for holding NMENU temporary files, you can set the S_FILEDIR environment variable. For instance, to set the NMENU to use Z:\MENUDAT as a temporary directory, you can use the following:

```
SET S_FILEDIR=Z:\MENUDAT
```

in the workstation's AUTOEXEC.BAT file. Alternatively, you can set the following:

```
SET S_FILEDIR="Z:\MENUDAT"
```

in a login script file such as the system, profile, or user login script file.

A problem with using a common directory for holding temporary files is that the temporary file names are based on the user names. As long as the user names are unique, the temporary files are unique per user, and the Novell menus will work fine. But what if a user logs in more than one time using the same user name, and uses the Novell menus? This is possible unless the concurrent connections restriction number is kept to 1. In this case, the Novell menus will try to create a separate set of temporary files with names that already exist. The resulting name collisions cause Novell menus to not work properly. The solution is to have Novell menus create temporary files based on station connection number, which is unique, per-user session. If a user logs in using the same user account, each user session will have a different connection number, and a different set of temporary files for Novell menus.

The S_FILE environment variable can be used to determine how temporary files are to be named. This can be used to change temporary files to use the station connection number using the following command in a login script:

```
SET S_FILE="%STATION"
```

To set the Novell menus to use the user's home directory for temporary files, use the following command in a login script:

```
SET S_FILEDIR="SYS:USERS/%LOGIN_NAME"
```

Example Menu Script

A sample menu script file is shown here, and figure 6.19 shows the Novell menus resulting from it:

```
menu 01,Network Utilities
        item NetAdmin
                exec NETADMIN
        item NetUser
                exec NETUSER
        item DOS Prompt
                exec DOS
        item Logout
                exec LOGOUT
```

Figure 6.19

NMENU display.

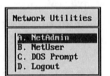

The name of the menu is called the *menu title* and is defined by the MENU command. Each of the options in the menu item are defined by the ITEM statement. The names of the programs to be executed when an option is selected is defined by the EXEC statement.

You will examine the details of the menu script in the following section.

Menu Parts

A NetWare menu can consist of four components (see fig. 6.20). The components are specified in the menu source file and are listed as follows:

1. A main menu that has a title and at least one option.

2. Commands to be executed when an option is selected.

3. Submenus that are displayed when an option is selected.

4. Prompts for user input.

The first two preceding parts are necessary. The remaining parts, such as the submenus and prompted user input, are optional.

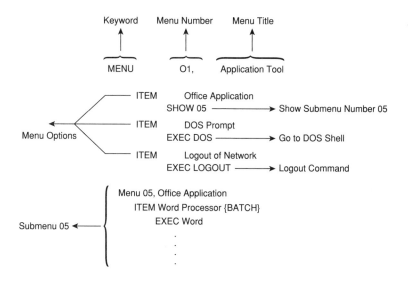

Figure 6.20
Parts of a menu.

Menu Commands

As you saw in the earlier section, the principal menu commands are MENU, ITEM, and EXEC. The MENU and ITEM commands are used for organizing the structure and appearance of the menu. The EXEC command is used for controlling the execution of commands when a particular item is selected. In general, menu commands can be divided into two categories:

◆ Organizational commands

◆ Control commands

These two categories of commands are discussed in greater detail in the following section.

 Menu commands can be divided into the categories of organizational commands and control commands.

Organizational Commands

Organizational commands are responsible for the overall organization and contents of the menu; they also determine the appearance of the menu on the screen. Currently, only two commands are defined for this category:

◆ MENU

◆ ITEM

Every menu and submenu is defined by a MENU command. The parameters for the MENU command are a menu number and the title of the menu:

```
MENU menuNumber,menuTitle
```

The *menuNumber* is unique per-menu, and it can be any number between 1 and 255. There is no special ordering relationship between the menu numbers and the menus that are displayed. The only requirement is that they be unique. There should not be any spaces between the *menuNumber*, the comma, and the *menuTitle*. The *menuTitle* is a string of characters that should not exceed 40 characters and is displayed at the top of the menu. It is used to identify the title of the menu.

 Novell menus have two organizational commands: MENU and ITEM.

If a menu is given a number of 5 and a title of "Available Options," its menu command should appear as the following:

```
MENU 5,Available Options
```

This command defines the start of the menu Available Options that's identified by the menu number 5.

The ITEM organizational command is used to define the option that is displayed for a menu. The items are listed in the order in which you want them to appear in the menu. An option consists of a text string parameter to the ITEM command. The general syntax of the ITEM command is:

```
ITEM  itemText { itemOption itemOption ... }
```

or

```
ITEM  ^tagchar itemText { itemOption itemOption ... }
```

In the first format for the ITEM command, every *itemText* is preceded by a letter that's automatically assigned by the Menu utility. The letters are from A to Z, with the first ITEM command being assigned A, the next B, and so on. These letters or *item tags* serve as a shortcut to selecting the option. Pressing the letter key corresponding to an option causes that menu item to be selected. The item tags do not determine the order in which the menu is displayed. The display order is determined by the order in which the items are listed. The *itemText* is the text string that you want displayed for the menu option. The *itemOption* is placed within { } braces, and can consist of zero or more item options that further qualify the menu option. The *itemOption* variable will be discussed in greater detail in the following section. An example of the syntax for the first format is:

```
ITEM    NetAdmin Tool { }
```

The *itemText* is "NetAdmin Tool," and there are no *itemOptions* specified. Therefore, the { } pair of braces are empty. If the braces { } are empty, they can be omitted.

```
ITEM Display Context

        EXEC CX
```

If this was the first ITEM listed under a MENU command, it would have a tag character of A; if this was the second item, its tag character would be B, and so on.

The second format for the command is similar to the first format. The difference is that *^tagchar* can precede the *itemText*. The caret (^) character followed by a single character, the *tagchar*, allows this character to override the default letter assignment for that item. For example, if you want to use digits 1 to 6 to designate the menu options, you use the following:

```
ITEM  ^1First Option { }
ITEM  ^2Second Option { }
ITEM  ^3Third Option { }
ITEM  ^4Fourth Option { }
ITEM  ^5Fifth Option { }
ITEM  ^6Sixth Option { }
```

The item options are displayed in the order in which they're listed. The menu utility makes no attempt to sort them based on any tag characters you've specified. It's possible to mix ITEM statements that have tag characters with the ITEM statements that do not have tag characters:

```
MENU 01, NLIST and NDIR Menu
ITEM  Show all objects  {PAUSE}
      EXEC NLIST * /D /S /CO "[Root]"
ITEM  LIST Help
      EXEC NLIST /? ALL
ITEM  Change Context  {PAUSE}
      EXEC CX %
ITEM  ^XEXIT
      EXEC EXIT
ITEM  ^LExit and Logout
      EXEC LOGOUT
```

ITEM Options

The *itemOptions* that are placed in the { } braces in the ITEM command further qualify how the commands associated with the ITEM are executed. The list that follows shows the ITEM command and the commands that are executed when an item is selected:

```
ITEM Menu Option Text { }
      command 1
      command 2
           :
      command N
```

The commands that are executed when the ITEM is selected are listed immediately following the ITEM. These commands are preceded by one of the following key words: EXEC, LOAD, SHOW, GETO, GETR, or GETP. These commands will be discussed in greater detail in the next section.

The commands for an ITEM follow immediately after the ITEM statement.

The commands following an ITEM statement can be EXEC, LOAD, SHOW, GETO, GETR, or GETP.

It's not necessary to indent the commands in relationship to the ITEM command. However, indenting is recommended because it makes the menu script more readable.

The *itemOption* that can be placed in { } can be any of the following:

◆ BATCH

◆ CHDIR

◆ SHOW

◆ PAUSE

The BATCH item option is used to free up additional memory when running an application. The Novell NetWare 4.x menu utility by itself takes up 32 KB of RAM. For applications that take up a large amount of memory, it is desirable to use as much RAM as possible for the application. By using the BATCH option, the commands associated with the menu are written in a temporary batch file. The menu utility is removed from memory and the batch file is run. The last command in the batch file re-invokes the menu utility. To run the NETADMIN utility using a batch file, you use the following:

```
ITEM NetAdmin Utility {BATCH}
     EXEC NETADMIN
```

 Use the BATCH option when running large programs, or when you are unable to run a program from the menu utility because of insufficient memory.

The BATCH item option is used to free up memory taken by the Novell menu utility when running an application.

The Novell NetWare 4.x menu utility takes up about 32 KB of RAM.

The CHDIR item option is used to restore the default directory to the one that existed prior to executing the command. Some programs give you the option of changing the default directory when they are run. After exiting these programs, you may be placed in a default directory that is different from the one that was in use prior to executing the program. It is often desirable to have the same default directory when programs are excepted from the menu utility.

Example:

To keep the same default directory for a progam called TELNET, throughout the execution of the menu utility, you could use the following:

```
ITEM Remote login via TELNET {CHDIR}
     EXEC TELNET
```

 The CHDIR item option is used to restore the default directory to the one that existed prior to executing the command.

The different item options can be combined. For example, to execute FILER as a batch file and to retain the same default directory, you could use the following:

```
ITEM Filer Utility {BATCH CHDIR}
     EXEC FILER
```

 To free memory taken up by the menu utility and restore the default directory to the one that existed prior to executing an application, combine the BATCH and CHDIR item options.

The order in which the item options are placed inside { } is not significant. Therefore, the preceding statements are equivalent to those listed here:

```
ITEM Filer Utility {CHDIR BATCH}
    EXEC FILER
```

 Use the CHDIR option consistently to always return to a known default directory.

The SHOW item option is used to display the name of the DOS command executed from the menu utility on the upper-left hand corner of the screen as it executes. This is particularly useful if the DOS command that is executing is passed a parameter, which is also displayed as the command executes. An example of this usage is shown as follows:

```
ITEM Directory Contents Listing {SHOW}
    EXEC DIR %
```

 The SHOW item option is used to display the name of the DOS command executed from the menu utility on the upper-left hand corner of the screen as it executes.

The PAUSE option causes the message Press any key to continue at the end of executing the command(s). This gives the user an opportunity to read the screen before proceeding to the next step. The menu utility won't proceed to the next step unless the user presses a key. An example of using the PAUSE option is shown here:

```
ITEM Search for files that have "SCS (C)opyright"  {PAUSE}
    EXEC GREP  "SCS (C)opyright"  *.*
```

Use the PAUSE option when running a utility that prints messages to the standard output or standard error stream and terminates. The standard output and standard error streams are set to the display console by default.

The PAUSE option causes the message Press any key to continue at the end of executing the command.

The PAUSE option can be combined with the SHOW option for many DOS commands that terminate after displaying their results.

Table 6.3 summarizes the different ITEM options that are discussed in this section.

Table 6.3
ITEM Options

Item Option	Description	Example
BATCH	Frees up RAM menu utility (32 KB) when a program runs.	ITEM Application {BATCH}
CHDIR	Restores default directory to that which existed prior to running the commands associated with the menu item.	ITEM Application {CHDIR}
SHOW	Shows DOS commands on upper-left corner of screen as they execute.	ITEM Application {SHOW}
PAUSE	Pauses display, and waits for user to press a key, at end of executing a command.	ITEM Application {PAUSE}

Menu Control Commands

The MENU and ITEM commands that were discussed in the previous section are used to determine the contents of a menu or submenu and the manner in which options should be displayed or run. The actual commands that are processed occur after the ITEM command. These commands are called control commands, and they are used to execute applications from within the menu utility (NMENU), load menu definitions kept in separate files, show submenus, and obtain user input. There are six control commands:

◆ EXEC

◆ LOAD

◆ SHOW

◆ GETO

◆ GETR

◆ GETP

The first three control commands (EXEC, LOAD, SHOW) deal with executing programs and loading and displaying submenus. The last three (GETO, GETR, GETP) solicit input from the user, which can then be used as parameters for commands and programs that are executed.

 The EXEC (or EXECUTE) menu command is used to run an application.

The EXEC Control Command

The EXEC (or EXECUTE) command is used to run an application. The command that is run can be an .EXE, .COM, .BAT, an internal DOS command, or any of the following:

◆ DOS

◆ EXIT

◆ LOGOUT

609

An example of using the EXEC command for a DOS internal command is shown here:

```
ITEM   ^DShow Directory listing {SHOW}
       EXEC DIR
```

An example of using the EXEC command for a NetWare .EXE program file is shown here:

```
ITEM   ^UNetwork User {BATCH}
       EXEC NETUSER
```

The EXEC DOS command runs a second copy of the command shell. For DOS, this is the COMMAND.COM command processor. When a second copy of the command shell runs, the user is presented with a command prompt and can type in any DOS or application command. The NMENU utility and the previous copy of the command shell are still loaded, so you are limited by the remaining memory available for your DOS application. An example of the use of the EXEC DOS command is shown here:

```
ITEM   Exit to DOS { }
       EXEC DOS
```

To return to the Novell menu utility, you must type the EXIT command at the command prompt. This terminates the second shell and returns you to the menu utility.

The EXEC DOS command runs a second copy of the command shell, and allows users to run DOS commands from the second command interpreter.

You should be familiar with the differences among the EXEC DOS, EXEC EXIT, and EXEC LOGOUT commands.

For secure environments, you might want to control the applications a user can run on the network. In this case, you might want to restrict the users' access to the command prompt and not use the EXEC DOS command.

To make the Novell menus secure, you should not use the EXEC DOS command in an item option.

If you want to give users the option of exiting the menu program completely and going to the DOS prompt, you can use the EXEC EXIT command. This command terminates the menu utility program, and causes the system to remove the program from memory. Control is returned to the command shell and the command prompt. If, for security reasons, you want to control a user's access to the command, you should not use the EXEC EXIT command. An example of the use of the EXEC EXIT command is shown here:

```
ITEM  Exit NMENU { }
      EXEC EXIT
```

In many environments, it's desirable to control a user's access to the command prompt; neither EXEC DOS nor EXEC EXIT are suitable for this purpose, because these give a user access to the command prompt. Yet, it's necessary for a user to terminate the use of the network and the Novell menus. To accomplish this, a special EXEC LOGOUT command has been defined. When the EXEC LOGOUT option is used, it logs the user out of the network and simultaneously terminates the Novell menu utility.

An example of the use of the EXEC LOGOUT command is shown here:

```
ITEM  Exit Novell Menus and logout { }
      EXEC LOGOUT
```

To make a menu secure, you can exit the Novell menus using the EXEC LOGOUT control command.

Table 6.4 summarizes the different EXEC commands that can be used.

Table 6.4
EXEC Command Summary

EXEC Type	Description
EXEC *command*	Replaces *command* with a DOS internal/external command, an .EXE or .COM program file, or a DOS batch file.
EXEC DOS	Starts a secondary shell and gives user access to the command prompt via the secondary shell.
EXEC EXIT	Terminates the Novell menu (NMENU) utility and returns control to the command shell and the command prompt.
EXEC LOGOUT	Terminates the Novell menu (NMENU) utility and logs user out of the network. Provides a secure option to exit the Novell menus.

The SHOW Control Command

A menu is defined using the MENU command in which you must define the menu number and the menu title. There can be many such menu commands in a single file. The first menu command in a compiled file that is passed as a parameter to the NMENU command becomes the first menu that is displayed. This is the main menu. All other menus in the file are displayed by using the SHOW command. The syntax of the SHOW command is as follows:

SHOW *menuNumber*

The *menuNumber* should be replaced with a number that represents the menu number defined in the MENU statement for the submenu that should be displayed. There can be up to 255 submenus or menu commands (menu definitions) in a single menu file.

The submenu that is displayed is *cascaded* in relationship to the previous menu. Its position on the screen is determined automatically by the Novell menu utility.

Figure 6.21 shows the SHOW commands in a menu script file. The two SHOW commands SHOW 3 and SHOW 8 refer to the indicated submenus in the script file.

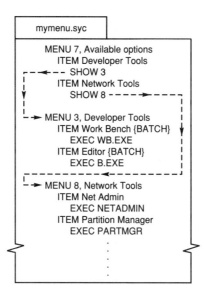

Figure 6.21

SHOW commands in a menu script file.

 The SHOW control command is used to display a menu by its menu number.

The LOAD Control Command

A menu is defined using the MENU command in which you must define the menu number and the menu title. There is a limit of up to 255 submenus or menu commands (menu definitions) in a single menu file. For large menu systems, you must place the menu definitions in separate files. You may decide to use separate files for menu systems that are not large because doing so can help you organize and manage the menu definitions. To load a menu that's in a separate file, you must use the LOAD command. The syntax of the LOAD command is:

613

LOAD *menuName*

The *menuName* should be replaced by the file name of the compiled menu file. When the LOAD command is executed, the original menu system is left running, but a second menu is added to the screen.

Figure 6.22 shows the use of the LOAD command. It shows how a large menu can be broken into smaller menus. In this figure, three menus, MENU1, MENU2, and MENU3, are shown defined in separate files MENU1.DAT, MENU2.DAT, and MENU3.DAT.

Figure 6.22

Use of menu LOAD command.

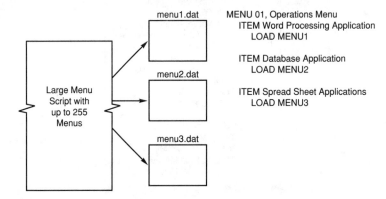

The LOAD command is used to load menus compiled in a separate file.

The GETx Commands

There are three forms of the GETx commands: GETO, GETR, and GETP. Like the other control commands, GETx commands are listed after an ITEM command and are executed when the menu item is selected. An example of some of the GETx commands is shown here:

```
ITEM    ^LDirectory Listing
        GETO  Enter directory name: {} 45,, {}
        EXEC DIR
```

The Menu GET commands obtain input from the user through the Novell menus.

The GETO Command

The GETO command is used for obtaining an optional input from the user. The O in GETO is for the word "optional." When the GETO command is executed, as shown in the previous example, a dialog box is displayed. The message in the dialog box, the width of the user input, the initial value of the user input, and so on, are passed as parameters to the GETO command.

 The GETO command is used for obtaining an optional input from the user.

With the GETO, GETR, and GETP commands, the Enter key signals that you've completed the information, and the F10 key signals that you want to continue with the menu execution.

The user has a choice of making an entry or not making an entry (optional GET). In either case, when the user presses the F10 key, execution continues. If the user makes an entry, the entered value is passed as a parameter to the command that follows. In the preceding example, the command that follows is the EXEC DIR command. In this example, if a user had made the entry F:\SYSTEM, the EXEC command that would be executed is:

```
EXEC DIR F:\SYSTEM
```

This command displays the contents of the directory F:\SYSTEM. If the user had not made any entry, but just typed in F10, the EXEC command that would be executed would be as follows:

```
EXEC DIR
```

This command displays the contents of the current directory.

The % character can be used as a placeholder for a single user input. The preceding example of the use of the GETO command can be alternatively expressed using the % placeholder.

```
ITEM   ^LDirectory Listing
       GETO  Enter directory name: {} 45,, {}
       EXEC DIR %
```

 The O in GETO stands for Optional input.

The GETR Command

The GETR command works in a manner similar to the GETO command described previously. The big difference is that the GETR command *requires* users to enter information. Just pressing F10 only (or Enter if GETR is in its own dialog box), will not cause the GETR command to continue execution. The menu display will be paused, and not continue until a valid input has been entered.

 The GETR command requires an input from the user.

An example of the use of GETR is shown here:

```
ITEM   User Command
       GETR Enter a user command: {}80,,{}
       EXEC %
```

This passes the user-typed string as a command to be executed by the EXEC command.

 The R in GETR stands for Required input.

The inputs received by the GETR and GETO commands are placed at the end of the next EXEC command line. Thus, if the next EXEC command is:

```
EXEC NNC
```

then input received by the GETR and GETO commands are placed as shown below:

```
EXEC NNC    InputViaGet
```

where InputViaGet is replaced by input received through the GETR and GETP commands.

The GETP Command

The GETP command works in a manner similar to the other GETx commands. The special feature of GETP is that it assigns a variable to the user input. This variable can then be used in other commands. An example of the use of GETP command is shown here:

```
ITEM  Network Copy {PAUSE SHOW}
      GETP Source: {} 60,, {}
      GETP Destination: {} 60,,{}
      EXEC NCOPY  %1 %2
```

The first GETP parameter assigns the user input to the variable %1, and the second GETP command assigns its user input to %2. These parameters are used in the EXEC NCOPY command as the source and destination, respectively.

The GETP command can be used to assign parameters to the user input.

Table 6.5 summarizes the different GETx commands.

Table 6.5
GETx Commands

GETx Command	Description
GETO	This is used to obtain optional user input from the user.
GETR	This is used to obtain required user input from the user.
GETP	This is used to obtain user input that is assigned to variables %1, %2, and so on.

GETx Commands—User Input Processing

While the GETR and GETO commands append the input they receive to the next EXEC command, the GETP command parses the input and breaks it down into words that are assigned to parameter variables %1, %2, %3, and so on.

Thus, if the user input is the following:

MONTHS 12 YEARS 25

the parameter variables have the following values:

%1 = MONTHS

%2 = 12

%3 = YEARS

%4 = 25

These parameter variables can be used in the next EXEC command. An example of this is shown as follows:

```
EXEC CalcInt  %3=%4  TYPE %1=%2
```

Given the previously discussed parameter values, the preceding EXEC command evaluates to:

```
EXEC CalcInt YEARS=25 TYPE MONTHS=12
```

As you can see, the GETP allows you greater control over how you can use the user typed-in values.

GETx Parameter Options

In the examples of the use of the GETx commands in the previous section, you noticed the use of the { } braces and the commas (,) as part of the syntax of the GETx command. This syntax is part of a general syntax that gives you options to control the width of the user input and the initial value that is displayed for the user. You can also modify the user input by prepending and/or appending special text string values to the user input. The syntax of these parameters is shown here:

```
GETx  promptString, {prependString}
length,prefillString,{appendString}
```

or

```
GETx  promptString, {prependString} length,prefillString,SECURE
{appendString}
```

The x in GETx is O, R, or P for the different types of GET commands. The *promptString* is the text that is displayed for the GET command, and is meant as an aid to the user to enter the appropriate value. The *prependString* placed inside the { } is a string that's attached to the beginning of the data the user enters. If there is no value that you want to prepend to the entered data, you must enter the *empty string* inside {}. An example of the use of the prepend string is shown here:

```
ITEM  ZIP code for Montana Residents
      GETR {MT }5,,{}
      EXEC RecZip %
```

In this example, the prepend string "MT" is prepended to the supplied user input. The RecZip represents a custom application that processes user-supplied data.

There's a difference between the {} braces and the { } braces. The former represents a null or empty string, and means that no value will be prepended to the user data. The latter represents a blank character that is prepended to the user data. These comments also apply to the {appendString} in the GETx command syntax.

The *length* specifies the size of the user input field. It's the number of characters the user can enter for the GET command. The *length* field is mandatory and can have a maximum value of 80 characters. The example that follows shows a maximum length field of 80 being used:

```
ITEM  Address Information
      GETR  Enter your street address {}80,,{}
      EXEC RecData %
```

The RecData in the EXEC command in the preceding example is meant as an example of a custom application (RecData) that can process the user-supplied information.

The *prefillString* is the initial value that is placed in the user's response field. It is used as the default value that the user can accept, if the user chooses not to enter a different value. The *prefillString* is optional. The *prefillString* is separated from the *length* field by a comma (,) and no spaces. If no prefill string is used, it can be omitted as shown in the following example:

```
ITEM  Get user information
      GETO Enter your company name:{}50,,{}
      EXEC RecData %
```

The next example shows a prefill string being used:

```
ITEM  Get user information
      GETO Enter your company name:{}50,IBM,{}
      EXEC RecData  %
```

In this example the "Enter your company name:" field in the dialog box for the GETO command has an initial value of IBM. The user can accept this value or override it with a different value. The user-supplied value is used as a parameter to a custom application called RecData.

The SECURE keyword is optional. If present, it must occur between the *prefillString* parameter and the *{appendString}* parameter. If the SECURE keyword exists as part of the GET command syntax, it means that the typed-in user data will not be displayed (hidden). This is useful if the user wishes to enter a password, security code, or some other confidential data. An example of the use of the SECURE keyword is shown next:

```
ITEM  Security Information
    GETR  Enter Personal Identification Number(PIN): {}4,,SE-
          CURE{}
    EXEC  ValidPIN %
```

The ValidPIN in the EXEC command is meant to signify a custom application—one that, perhaps, validates the user-supplied PIN data.

The *appendString* placed inside the {} is a string that is attached to the end (appended) of the data the user enters. If there's no value that you want to append to the entered data, you must enter the *empty string* inside {}. An example of the use of the append string is shown here:

```
ITEM  Security Information
    GETR  Enter Personal Identification Number(PIN):
          {}4,,SECURE{KXVZ}
    EXEC  ProcPIN
```

In this example, the append string "KXVZ" will be appended to the supplied user input. The ProcPIN represents a custom application that processes the user-supplied data. In this example the append string is used as a special security code that is sent in conjunction with the user-supplied data to the processing program ProcPIN.

If several GET commands are listed under an ITEM command, the GET fields are grouped in the order of occurrence with 10 GETs per dialog box. In other words, there can be a maximum of 10 GET command prompts per dialog box. If you want to override this default behavior and have a GET command appear in its own dialog box, you must use the caret (^) at the beginning of the prompt text for the GET command. The next example shows how each of the GET commands can appear in its own dialog box:

```
ITEM  Enter User Information
      GETP  ^User Name:{}50,,{}
      GETP  ^Address:{}80,,{}
      GETP  ^Password:{}30,,SECURE{}
      EXEC ProcUser %1 %2 %3
```

The ProcUser represents a custom application that processes the user-supplied input.

Another example of the use of the GET commands that prompt users for options is listed next: The user is prompted for the source and destination directories. These are used as parameters %1 and %2 in the NCOPY command:

```
ITEM  Network Copy {PAUSE SHOW}
      GETP  Source: {} 60,, {}
      GETP  Destination: {} 60,,{}
      EXEC  NCOPY  %1 %2
```

Other uses of the GET commands are shown here:

Example 1:

```
ITEM  Authenticate User
      GETR  User ID:  {} 10,guest,{}
      GETR  Password: {} 25,,SECURE{}
      EXEC  CHKUSER.EXE
```

In Example 1, the user is asked for a password. The user's response is not displayed because of the SECURE option. The user's response is used as an argument to CHKUSER.EXE.

Example 2:

```
ITEM  Directory Listing
      GETO  Directory Path: {   } 40,,{}
      EXEC  dir
```

In Example 2, the user is asked for the directory path for which a listing should be displayed. If one is not specified, the DIR command is executed without an argument—in which case, a listing for the current directory is displayed.

Example 3:

```
ITEM  Compute Mortgage {SHOW}
      GETP  Enter loan amount:   {}10,0,{}
      GETP  Interest Rate:       {}5,6.5,{}
```

```
GETP  Enter period (/m=months or+
/y=years) : {} 8, /y=30,{}
EXEC  echo  Loan amount  = %1
EXEC  echo  Interest rate  = %2
EXEC  echo  Period          = %3
EXEC  MortCalc   /l=%1  /r=%2  %3
```

In Example 3, the loan amount and interest are passed as parameters to the program MORTCALC (Mortgage Calculation). The loan amount is passed as a parameter of the form /l=*amount*. The interest rate is passed as a parameter of the form /r=*rate*. The period is displayed with a default field value of "/y=30" (30 years). The user can enter the value using the /m=*months* or /y=*years* format. This is passed as the %3 argument to the program MORTCALC.

There can be no more than 100 GET commands per ITEM command. Also, the GETO and GETR commands must be entered between the ITEM and the EXEC line that is associated with them.

The general syntax of the GETx command is shown here:

```
GETx  promptString, {prependString}
length,prefillString,[SECURE]{appendString}
```

The [ ] brackets around SECURE imply that SECURE is optional; it is not part of the syntax for GETx.

Table 6.6 summarizes the different GETx parameters that have been discussed.

Table 6.6
GETx Parameters

GETx Parameter	Description
promptString	This is the message that must be displayed to the user.
prependString	The user-entered data is prepended with the *prependString* placed in the first set of {}.
length	Maximum number of characters for the user field. Its maximum value is 80 characters.

continues

Table 6.6, Continued
GETx Parameters

GETx Parameter	Description
prefillString	The *prefillString* is used as the default response, in case the user does not enter a value.
SECURE	The user typed-in information is not displayed. It is used for secure data such as passwords and codes.
appendString	The user-entered data is appended with the *appendString* placed in the first set of {}.

 Use table 6.6 to review the GETx parameters. Also study the examples on the user of the GETx parameters in this section.

Menu Limitations

The following is a list of menu limitations:

◆ There can be up to 255 submenus or menu commands (menu definitions) in a single menu file.

◆ The maximum number of characters for the user field is 80 characters.

◆ The maximum number of characters on a line in the menu script is 80. Longer lines can continue to the next line by ending the previous line with the line continuation character.

◆ There can be no more than 100 GET commands per ITEM command.

◆ If several GET commands are listed under an ITEM command, the GET fields are grouped in the order of occurrence, with 10 GETs per dialog box.

◆ The Novell menus can have no more than one main menu, and 10 submenus (using the SHOW command), on the screen at any time. This means that the maximum level of submenu nesting cannot exceed 10.

◆ You cannot mix EXEC and SHOW submenu commands under an ITEM option. Therefore, the following is illegal:

```
ITEM Telmail option
EXEC MAP T:=FS1/SYS:INET/BIN
SHOW 06
```

Customizing Menu Colors

The menu utility COLORPAL can be used to customize color palettes for the menu utilities. The color schemes, and the default color scheme, are defined in a file called:

*shortmachine*_RUN.OVL

where *shortmachine* is replaced by the SHORT MACHINE TYPE parameter defined in the NET.CFG file. The default value of SHORT MACHINE TYPE is IBM, and therefore the default name of the color schemes file (C-Worthy overlay file) is:

IBM_RUN.OVL

If you set the SHORT_MACHINE type to a different value, such as NEC, using the following command:

SHORT MACHINE TYPE=NEC

in the NET.CFG file, you must define the overlay file NEC_RUN.OVL. This allows custom color palettes to be defined for user workstations with unusual displays that need to display a different set of color combinations from the default.

Do not change the default color combination, because it affects all workstation menu/text based utilities that use the shortmachine_RUN.OVL file. Create a special shortmachine_RUN.OVL file, with

continues

the shortmachine replaced by the value of the SHORT MACHINE TYPE parameter in the NET.CFG file. Keep this file in the SYS:PUBLIC directory on the NetWare 4.x server, where most other menu/text-based utilities are kept.

Study Guide for the Chapter

If you are preparing for the NetWare 4.x Administration CNE exams, review this chapter with the following goals:

1. Understand the different workstation files used for configuration. You should be familiar with the structure of the NET.CFG file, and special statements placed in the CONFIG.SYS and AUTOEXEC.BAT file. Use the STUDY NOTEs as a quick review.

2. Understand how login script processing works. You should be able to tell when a particular login script file (system, profile, user, default) will run for a User object in an NDS tree. You also should understand the structure of Novell menus and how to use the different EXEC command options.

3. After studying this chapter, attempt the sample test questions for this chapter. If you miss the answer to a question, review the appropriate topic until you understand the reason for the correct answer.

Chapter Summary

In this chapter, you learned about the different configuration files needed to set up the NetWare workstation configuration.

You were shown how to establish the network environment using login scripts. NetWare 4.x uses four types of login scripts: system, profile, user, and default. You learned when a particular login script type was activated. You also learned the different components of a NetWare 4.x menu system and learned to how to write a menu script file.

Chapter Test Questions

Questions are either single choice or multiple choice. Where a single answer is desired, they are indicated by a ○ that precedes the possible answers. Some questions require you to select more than one answer; these are indicated by the ☐ preceding each answer. Certain questions will be repeated in different ways, so that you can recognize them even when the wording is different. Taking practice quizzes will not only test your knowledge, but also will give you confidence when you take your exam.

1. Which of these files can be used for NetWare 4.x workstation configuration?

   ☐　A.　NET.CFG

   ☐　B.　CONFIG.SYS

   ☐　C.　CONFIG.DAT

   ☐　D.　AUTOXEC.NCF

   ☐　E.　AUTOXEC.BAT

2. The call to STARTNET.BAT file is usually placed in the _____ file.

   ○　A.　NET.CFG

   ○　B.　NETSTART.BAT

   ○　C.　START.BAT

   ○　D.　AUTOEXEC.NCF

   ○　E.　AUTOEXEC.BAT

3. Which file is normally used to load the ODI drivers in a NetWare 4.x workstation?

   ○ A. NET.CFG

   ○ B. NETSTART.BAT

   ○ C. START.BAT

   ○ D. AUTOEXEC.NCF

   ○ E. STARTNET.BAT

   ○ F. AUTOEXEC.BAT

4. The ODI drivers must be loaded _____.

   ○ A. after the VLM.EXE

   ○ B. before the LSL.COM

   ○ C. after the LSL.COM

   ○ D. after the IPXODI.COM

5. For a NetWare 4.x workstation, one can expect the following statements in a NET.CFG file:

   ☐ A. FIRST NETWORK DRIVE

   ☐ B. FRAME Ethernet_SNAP

   ☐ C. LASTDRIVE=Z

   ☐ D. VLM Requester

   ☐ E. NAME CONTEXT

6. How is the profile login script set for a user?

   ○ A. The profile login script is set by assigning a profile login script to the User object's profile login property.

   ○ B. The profile login script is set by assigning a profile login script to the user's container profile login property.

   ○ C. The profile login script is set by assigning a Profile object to the User object's profile login property.

   ○ D. The profile login script is set by assigning a Profile object to the User's container profile login property.

7. Which environment variable is set to specify languages other than English?

   ○ A. LANGUAGE

   ○ B. NWLANGUAGE

   ○ C. NWCLANGUAGE

   ○ D. NLS

   ○ E. NLSLANGUAGE

   ○ F. NLSLANG

8. A user's preference for a language can be specified by _____.

   ○ A. setting the language environment variable for the user

   ○ B. setting the language property for the user

   ○ C. loading the language driver in CONFIG.SYS

   ○ D. setting the language property in the user's container object

9. Novell menus have two organizational commands: _____ and _____.

   ☐ A. MENU

   ☐ B. EXEC

   ☐ C. GETR

   ☐ D. ITEM

   ☐ E. GETP

10. The option that can be used to free up memory taken by the Novell menu utility when running an application is _____.

   ○ A. CHDIR

   ○ B. SHOW

   ○ C. BATCH

   ○ D. PAUSE

   ○ E. MEMORY

11. Which ITEM option causes the message Press any key to continue at the end of executing the command?

    ○ A. CHDIR

    ○ B. SHOW

    ○ C. BATCH

    ○ D. PAUSE

12. To make the Novell menus secure, you should _____.

    ○ A. use the EXEC DOS command in an item option

    ○ B. not use the EXEC DOS command in an item option

    ○ C. use the EXEC SECURE command in an item option

    ○ D. use the EXEC SHELL command in an item option

13. Which menu commands obtain input from the user through the Novell menus?

    ○ A. LOAD commands

    ○ B. SHOW commands

    ○ C. PUT commands

    ○ D. GET commands

    ○ E. READ commands

    ○ F. INPUT commands

14. Which command is used for obtaining an optional input from the user?

    ○ A. GET

    ○ B. GETR

    ○ C. GETO

    ○ D. GETP

15. Which command can be used to assign parameters to the user input?

    ○ A. GET

    ○ B. GETR

    ○ C. GETO

    ○ D. GETP

16. The NDS objects that can contain the system login script are _____ and _____.

    ☐ A. Organization

    ☐ B. Organizational Unit

    ☐ C. Root

    ☐ D. User

    ☐ E. Organization Role

17. Which command is used for obtaining *required* input from the user?

    ○ A. GET

    ○ B. GETR

    ○ C. GETO

    ○ D. GETP

18. The profile login script is executed _____.

    ○ A. before the system login script but after the user login script

    ○ B. after the system login script but before the user login script

    ○ C. after the system login script but before the container's login script

    ○ D. before the system login script but after the container's login script

19. A User object can have _____ profile login script(s).

   ○ A. 1

   ○ B. 2

   ○ C. up to 8

   ○ D. any number of

20. The default login script is executed if the _____.

   ○ A. system login script is not set

   ○ B. profile login script is not set

   ○ C. system and profile login script are not set

   ○ D. user login script is not set

21. Which command is used to prevent the default login script from executing and is set in the system or profile login scripts?

   ○ A. EXIT_DEFAULT_LOGIN

   ○ B. NO_DEFAULT_LOGIN

   ○ C. SKIP_DEFAULT

   ○ D. QUIT_DEFAULT

   ○ E. ABANDON_DEFAULT

   ○ F. NO_DEFAULT

22. The User object in the container must have the _____.

   ○ A. Browse right to the container object and the Read property right to the login script in order to execute the system login script

   ○ B. Read right to the container object and the Read property right to the login script in order to execute the system login script

C. Create right to the container object and the Read and Write property rights to the login script in order to execute the system login script

D. Write right to the container object and the Read and Compare property rights to the login script in order to execute the system login script

23. Containers are granted the _____.

A. Read and Write property rights to their system login script

B. Read property right to their system login script

C. Read, Compare, and Write property rights to their system login script

D. Write property right to their system login script

24. Users are by default assigned _____.

A. Read and Write property rights to their user login script property

B. Read and Compare property rights to their user login script property

C. Read property rights to their user login script property

D. Supervisor property rights to their user login script property

25. The login script command to clear the screen is _____.

A. CLEAR

B. CLS

C. CLEAR DISPLAY

D. CLEAR SCREEN

26. The login script command to change a user's context is
    _____.

    ○ A. LCX

    ○ B. CONTEXT

    ○ C. CX

    ○ D. CHANGE CONTEXT

27. The login script command to execute other login script
    commands as if they were a subroutine is _____.

    ○ A. CALL

    ○ B. SUBROUTINE

    ○ C. INCLUDE

    ○ D. PROC

    ○ E. PROCEDURE

28. The login script command to display the last time a user
    logged in is _____.

    ○ A. LOGINDATE

    ○ B. LOGINTIME

    ○ C. LAST_LOGINDATE

    ○ D. LAST_LOGINTIME

    ○ E. LASTLOGINTIME

29. The login script command to change drive from ordinary
    network drive to search drive and vice versa is _____.

    ○ A. MAP CHANGE

    ○ B. MAP INS

    ○ C. MAP CH

    ○ D. MAP TOGGLE

30. In this figure, what is the login script execution order for user Nina, if she does not have a user login script? Assume that Nina's profile login script property is set to the Profile object CN=Profile1.O=SCS.

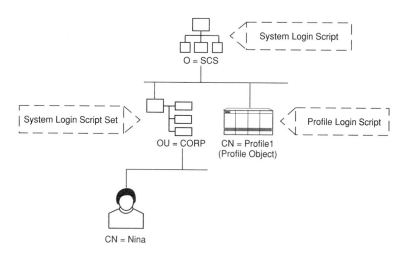

- ○ A. system login script for O=SCS, system login script for OU=CORP, user login script for CN=Nina

- ○ B. system login script for O=SCS, system login script for OU=CORP, default login script

- ○ C. system login script for O=SCS, system login script for OU=CORP, profile login script in CN=Profile1.O=SCS

- ○ D. system login script for O=CORP, profile login script in CN=Profile1.OU=SCS, default login script

31. Older menu scripts can be converted to NetWare menu scripts by using _____.

- ○ A. CNVTMENU
- ○ B. MENUCNVT
- ○ C. OLDMENU
- ○ D. OLDMENUC
- ○ E. MENUCONV

32. The utility to compile the menu script (SRC) file to the menu
    object file (DAT) is _____.

    ○ A. MAKEMENU

    ○ B. MENUMAKE

    ○ C. MENUCOMP

    ○ D. COMPMENU

    ○ E. MNUMAKE

    ○ F. MAKEMNU

7

CHAPTER

Managing NetWare Servers

Most network management functions for a NetWare 4.x server can be performed by managing its object representation in the NDS tree using tools such as NETADMIN and the NetWare Administrator. Some network management functions, however, can be done only at the server console.

This chapter discusses some of these server management functions and the programs that perform them.

Understanding NLMs

Programs that run on the server machine are written in such a manner that they can interface correctly with the NetWare operating system that runs at the server computer. These programs are different from the familiar .EXE and .COM programs used by DOS, OS/2, Windows NT, and Windows 95 workstations. Just as the .EXE and .COM programs interact with DOS, the programs that run at the server must interact with the NetWare operating system functions. These server programs are called *NetWare Loadable Modules* (NLMs).

NLMs are different from DOS .EXE and .COM program files in some significant ways, however. DOS programs run under the control of DOS, but they do not become part of DOS.

When NLMs run, they hook into the NetWare operating system, as seen in figure 7.1. Once hooked, the NLMs run as part of the operating system itself. Another way of understanding this process is to think of the NetWare operating system as producing a software NLM bus to which other NLMs can attach in the same way that adapter boards can be attached to a PC's internal bus. Figure 7.2 shows this conceptual view of the software NLM bus. The software NLM bus can support a variety of different NLMs that enhance the capability of the NetWare operating system. Some of the NLMs shown in figure 7.2 include the following:

Disk drivers (.DSK extension)

LAN drivers (.LAN extension)

Network Management NLMs (MONITOR.NLM, SERVMAN.NLM, and so on)

Communications; Additional protocol module support (TCPIP.NLM, APPLETLK.NLM, and so on)

Network Printing Support (PSERVER.NLM, NPRINTER.NLM)

Name space support NLMs (.NAM extension)

Language Support (KEYB.NLM, and so on)

Media Management

Server Monitoring

Uninterrupted Power Supply (UPS)

Application NLMs and gateways

Data Migration

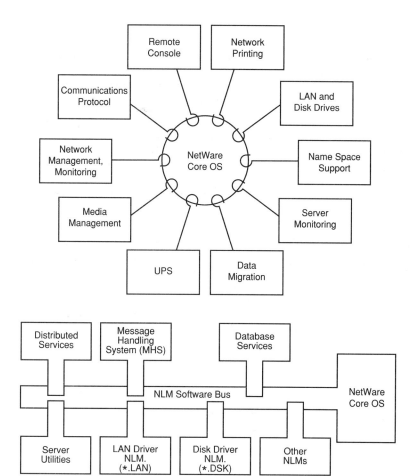

Figure 7.1

NetWare Loadable Modules and NetWare core OS.

Figure 7.2

NLM software bus.

NetWare Loadable Modules typically are stored in files that have an .NLM extension. As you can see from the preceding list, special NLMs might have a different extension that indicates the function they perform. LAN drivers have a .LAN extension, disk drivers have a .DSK extension, and name space support NLMs have a .NAM extension. Table 7.1 summarizes the different NLM extensions.

Table 7.1
Common Extensions Used for NLM Names

NLM Extension	Meaning
.DSK	Disk driver
.LAN	NIC driver
.NLM	Management utilities, server applications
.NAM	Name space modules

NLMs were introduced to enable NetWare 3.x to have a more dynamic and flexible system configuration for the NetWare operating system. NetWare 4.x uses NLMs for the same purpose. You should, however, be aware that NetWare 3.x NLMs and NetWare 4.x NLMs are not 100 percent compatible. Some of the system APIs (Application Programming Interfaces) have changed, so you should upgrade your NLM applications to those that are designed to run with NetWare 4.x.

If you are running NetWare 3 NLMs or NLMs written to NetWare 3 API standards, you will get the following message:

```
SERVER-4.10-1587:    This module is using 1 outdated
API call.  You should upgrade to a newer module when
it becomes available.
```

This is not a serious error message provided that is the only effect of running the old NLM.

NLMs also remove the need for static linking, which was used in NetWare 2.x in which object modules selected during the installation process were bound together. The static linking mechanism is called NetWare generation for NetWare 2.x.

NLMs enable software modules that run at the server to be linked at runtime, or at the time they are loaded in memory. This linking at runtime is called *dynamic linking*. Readers familiar with OS/2 or MS Windows might have heard of DLLs (Dynamic Link Libraries). The Dynamic Link Libraries in NetWare 3.x are called NetWare Loadable Modules (NLMs). NLMs are more than DLLs; they actually are processes or tasks that run under NetWare:

Dynamic Link Libraries + Processes = NLMs

NLMs can be viewed as a group of cooperating software tasks or engines.

NLMs are activated by typing the command LOAD followed by the name of the NLM:

```
LOAD NameOfNLM
```

NLMs that come with NetWare are installed on the SYS:SYSTEM directory on the server. The LOAD command, therefore, searches the SYS:SYSTEM directory for NLMs. If NLMs are installed in another location, their full path name needs to be specified or their location made known by using the SEARCH command at the console. To add SYS:MANAGE to the search path, issue this command:

```
SEARCH ADD SYS:MANAGE
```

The search path SYS:MANAGE is added at the end of the search path list. To make SYS:MANAGE the first path to be searched, use this:

```
SEARCH ADD 1 SYS:MANAGE
```

NLMs can be deactivated by unloading them via the UNLOAD command followed by the name of the NLM:

```
UNLOAD NameOfNLM
```

Practical TIP   Most NLMs come with their own internal unload procedures. It is always preferable to use the exit option within the NLM rather than a forced unload from the console.

When an NLM is loaded, it takes up a certain portion of the server RAM and competes with other processes for CPU time. The amount of memory taken by an NLM can vary depending on the task being performed and the size of its code. The actual amount of memory used can be monitored using the MONITOR.NLM. Some NLMs make system calls to allocate additional memory for the tasks they are performing. Also, this requested memory can be released during execution. The actual size of the NLM, therefore, can vary during execution. When an NLM is unloaded, all allocated resources (called resource tags) are returned to the NetWare NOS.

NLMs are written by Novell or third-party developers. Currently they are written using WATCOM's or MetaWare's 32-bit C or C++ compilers. NLMs may depend on other NLMs before they can run. The RSPX.NLM, for example, cannot be loaded until REMOTE.NLM is loaded. Also, when an NLM is loaded, it is expected that all the external interfaces it needs are already in memory. An NLM can be written to automatically load (autoload) other NLMs that it needs. If an NLM is not written to autoload its dependent NLMs, and if it cannot find the dependent NLMs already loaded in memory, an error message about unresolved external references is reported and the NLM will not load. Certain NLMs such as network card or disk drivers can accept command-line parameters or options to modify their behavior. The actual options depend on each NLM and are embedded in the program code for the NLM. In the case of disk driver and LAN adapter NLMs, if the required options are not specified, you are prompted for the parameter values. The SMC8000 NLM, for the Standard Microsystems EtherCard PLUS adapters, for example, can be loaded in the following two ways:

```
LOAD SMC8000 port=280 frame=ETHERNET_802.2
```

or

```
LOAD SMC8000
```

In the first example, all the parameters are specified on the command line in the *parameter=value* syntax.

In the second example, the parameters are not specified. On loading, SMC8000 prompts the user for these parameter values.

 Older LAN driver NLMs for Ethernet boards default to using the ETHERNET_802.3 frame type, whereas the newer LAN drivers use ETHERNET_802.2. Because NetWare 4.x uses ETHERNET_802.2 for Ethernet adapters by default, you should be aware of this difference when using older LAN drivers.

Understanding the Core Operating System

The SERVER.EXE file is the program file used to start the NetWare 4 server. It consists of two parts: the NetWare loader and program, and the core operating system called SERVER.NLM. SERVER.NLM and a number of other NLMs, such as the DS.NLM (for NetWare Directory Services), together form the core of the operating system.

The NetWare core includes the following services (see fig. 7.3):

> Authentication
>
> Directory services
>
> File services
>
> Routing
>
> Security

Both the core operating system and the NLMs use memory that is managed in a similar manner. Some of the server memory management considerations are discussed next.

Figure 7.3

NetWare core
services.

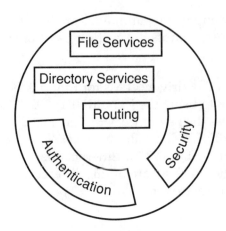

On the CNE exams, you may be asked indirect
questions in the form of "what if" scenarios. You
may be asked, for example, how you can improve
server performance under certain conditions. One
of the possible answers may be unloading un-
needed NLMs. In general, your answer depends
on understanding all of the material covered in this
section.

Examining Server Memory Considerations

Many of the commands in NetWare 4.x have been enhanced,
whereas others have remained the same from a user's interface
perspective. NetWare 4.x has a completely redesigned memory
architecture that enables it to manage memory from a global pool
rather than the separate memory pools of the NetWare 3.x architecture. Therefore, some of the problems of memory depletion
from dedicated memory pools that could occur while running
NetWare 3.x console commands and utilities have been eliminated.

NetWare 4.x uses the paged-memory architecture of the Intel processors to manage memory in units of 4 KB pages. It does not, however, implement virtual memory in the same way that general purpose operating systems such as Unix, OS/2, and Windows NT do. Virtual memory enables an operating system to swap data and programs between memory and a hard disk; this process is too slow to be of much use in a network operating system such as NetWare, which must provide rapid service to large numbers of users. All of the critical data structures and programs needed for NetWare operation reside in memory. If more memory is needed for applications to run at the server, the memory used for file caching is used up.

Using Server Commands

A new HELP command is available that enables you to learn quickly the syntax and function of a command. Figure 7.4 shows the output of typing the HELP command. To obtain more detailed help on the command LANGUAGE, you can type this command:

HELP LANGUAGE

```
ABORT REMIRROR          ADD NAME SPACE          BIND
BROADCAST               CLEAR STATION           CLS
CONFIG                  DISABLE LOGIN           DISABLE TTS
DISMOUNT                DISPLAY NETWORKS        DISPLAY SERVERS
DOWN                    ECHO OFF                ECHO ON
ENABLE LOGIN            ENABLE TTS              EXIT
FILE SERVER NAME        IPX INTERNAL NET        LANGUAGE
LIST DEVICES            LOAD                    MAGAZINE INSERTED
MAGAZINE NOT INSERTED   MAGAZINE NOT REMOVED    MAGAZINE REMOVED
MEDIA INSERTED          MEDIA NOT INSERTED      MEDIA NOT REMOVED
MEDIA REMOVED           MEMORY MAP              MEMORY
MIRROR STATUS           MODULES                 MOUNT
NAME                    OFF                     PAUSE
#                       PROTOCOL                REGISTER MEMORY
REMOVE DOS              REMIRROR PARTITION      REM
RESET ROUTER            RESTART SERVER          SCAN FOR NEW DEVICES
SEARCH                  SECURE CONSOLE          ;
SEND                    SET TIME ZONE           SET TIME
SET                     SPEED                   SPOOL
TIME                    TRACK OFF               TRACK ON
UNBIND                  UNLOAD                  VERSION
VOLUME                  HELP

Type HELP [command] to display specific command help
NW4CS:
```

Figure 7.4

The console HELP command.

645

Study Note The new console command for obtaining help on console commands is HELP.

Figure 7.5 shows help on the LANGUAGE command. Typing the LANGUAGE command displays the current language (see fig. 7.6).

Figure 7.5

The HELP LANGUAGE command.

```
NW4CS:HELP LANGUAGE
LANGUAGE                   Display current NLM language.
LANGUAGE list              Display list of available languages.
LANGUAGE name:number       Set preferred NLM language by name or number.
LANGUAGE add number name   Add a new language name and number.
LANGUAGE ren number new_name Rename the language specified by number.
 Example:  language spanish

NW4CS:
```

Figure 7.6

The LANGUAGE command.

```
NW4CS:HELP LANGUAGE
LANGUAGE                   Display current NLM language.
LANGUAGE list              Display list of available languages.
LANGUAGE name:number       Set preferred NLM language by name or number.
LANGUAGE add number name   Add a new language name and number.
LANGUAGE ren number new_name Rename the language specified by number.
 Example:  language spanish

NW4CS:LANGUAGE
  Current NLM language is (4) ENGLISH.

NW4CS:
```

Tables 7.2 through 7.5 show the NetWare 4.x commands of which you should be aware.

Table 7.2 shows the configuration commands.

Table 7.2
Configuration Commands

Commands	Description
CONFIG	Displays configuration information such as server name, IPX internal number, parameter settings for disk and LAN drivers, and binding information between protocol stacks and LAN drivers.
DISPLAY SERVERS	Displays servers and hop count information that this server knows about.

646

Commands	Description
DISPLAY NETWORKS	Displays all network numbers and their hop count/tick information that this server knows about.
MODULES	Displays a list of loaded NLMs.
NAME	Displays the server name.
TIME	Displays server date and time and whether time synchronization is active or synchronized on the network.
VOLUMES	Displays volumes currently mounted, the name spaces they support, and whether compression, suballocation, and data migration have been enabled.
UPS STATUS	Displays UPS status. Works only if the UPS NLM is loaded.
UPS TIME	Displays UPS time. Works only if the UPS NLM is loaded.

Table 7.3 shows the installation commands.

Table 7.3
Installation Commands

Commands	Description
LOAD	Used to load NLMs. During installation, disk driver and LAN card NLMs need to be loaded.
MOUNT	Once a volume is created during installation, it must be mounted before it can be accessed.
BIND	Provides an association between a transport protocol and the ODI LAN drivers.
ADD NAME SPACE	Optionally, name spaces for Macintosh, OS/2, and NFS can be added to a volume.

647

To add Windows 95 name space to a volume, add the OS/2 name space using the following server console commands:

```
LOAD OS2
ADD NAME SPACE OS2 TO VOLUME NAME
```

Table 7.4 shows the maintenance commands.

Table 7.4
Maintenance Commands

Commands	Description
CLEAR STATION	Clears a station's connection. Removes all file server resources allocated for the workstation.
DISABLE LOGIN	Disables logins. Prevents users from logging in while maintenance work is being conducted.
ENABLE LOGIN	Enables users to log in. Cancels the DISABLE command. Enables ADMIN accounts that were locked out by intruder detection.
DISMOUNT	Makes a volume unavailable for access. Can be used for volume maintenance and repairs. Other mounted volumes can still be used.
DOWN	Gracefully shuts down the server. Data in server memory is flushed to server disk. If users are logged in or are accessing files, it informs them that the server is shut down.
SECURE CONSOLE	Makes the console secure by removing DOS from the server and prevents keyboard entry into the internal debugger. Only the console operator can modify server date and time; only NLMs in the search path can be loaded.

Commands	Description
SET	View or modify current operating system parameters. The SERVMAN NLM provides an easy interface to view or modify SET parameters.
REMOVE DOS	Removes DOS from file server memory. Additionally, prevents NLMs from being loaded from DOS drives. If DOWN and EXIT commands are used, the server reboots.
UNLOAD	Unloads an NLM from server memory. Used to reinitialize and reconfigure system and application NLMs.
UNBIND	Unlinks a communication protocol from the NIC driver.

Table 7.5 shows the screen commands.

Table 7.5
Screen Commands

Commands	Description
CLS	Clears console screen.
SEND	Sends a message to a currently logged or attached user using his or her login name or connection number.
BROADCAST	Sends a message to all currently logged/attached users. Can also send messages to all currently logged/attached users. Also can send messages to a list of users or connection number.
EXIT	Returns to DOS after issuing the DOWN command.

Table 7.6 shows some of the new server console commands that have been introduced with NetWare 4.x.

Table 7.6
New Console Commands

New Console Command	Description
ABORT REMIRROR	Terminates remirroring of the specified logical partition.
REMIRROR PARTITION	Attempts to start the remirroring of the specified partition.
MIRROR STATUS	Displays a list of the mirrored logical partitions and their status.
LIST DEVICES	Displays a list of storage devices.
SCAN FOR NEW DEVICES	Registers any devices added since the server was started.
MAGAZINE	Responds to console alert messages to perform indicated actions, such as magazine insertion and removal.
MEDIA	Responds to console alert messages to perform the indicated action's insertion and removal.
RESTART SERVER	Restarts a downed server.
LANGUAGE	Enables the NLMs to use specific language files.

These commands are discussed in greater detail in the following sections.

The ABORT REMIRROR Command

The ABORT REMIRROR command stops the remirroring of the logical partition. Mirroring is the ability to have a second NetWare partition contain the same data, at all times, as a NetWare partition. It introduces redundancy at the NetWare partition level to improve its fault tolerance. The general syntax for the command is

```
ABORT REMIRROR number
```

where *number* is replaced by the logical partition for which you want to stop mirroring. Figure 7.7 shows the help that includes an example on the ABORT REMIRROR command.

```
NW4CS:HELP ABORT REMIRROR
ABORT REMIRROR partition_number
 Stops the remirroring of the specified partition.
 Example:  abort remirror 3

NW4CS:
```

Figure 7.7

Help on ABORT REMIRROR.

The ABORT REMIRROR command is the opposite of the REMIRROR PARTITION command, which is explained next.

The REMIRROR PARTITION Command

The REMIRROR PARTITION command attempts to start the remirroring of the logical partition. Its general syntax is

```
REMIRROR PARTITION number
```

where *number* is replaced by the logical partition you want to mirror. Figure 7.8 shows the help that includes an example on the REMIRROR PARTITION command.

```
NW4CS:HELP REMIRROR PARTITION
REMIRROR PARTITION partition_number
 Attempts to start the remirror of the specified partition.
 Example:  remirror partition 4

NW4CS:
```

Figure 7.8

Help on REMIRROR PARTITION.

The REMIRROR PARTITION command is the opposite of the ABORT REMIRROR command that was explained previously.

The MIRROR STATUS Command

The MIRROR STATUS command is used to display all mirrored partitions and their current status. Its syntax is

```
MIRROR STATUS
```

651

Figure 7.9 shows an example of typing the MIRROR STATUS command. Notice that because there is a lack of mirrored partitions, this fact is reported. For mirrored partitions, five possible status values exist. These status values are explained in table 7.7.

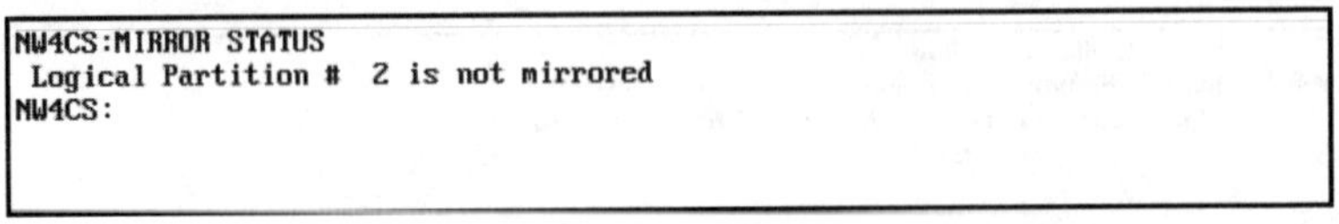

Figure 7.9

Example MIRROR
STATUS command.

```
NW4CS:MIRROR STATUS
  Logical Partition #  2 is not mirrored
NW4CS:
```

Table 7.7
Mirror Status Values

Mirror Status Value	Description
Being mirrored	This shows that the partition is in the process of being mirrored. The percentage of mirroring that has been completed is also displayed.
Fully synchronized	This indicates that the partitions are functionally identical (synchronized). This should be the normal state.
Not mirrored	This shows that the partition currently is not mirrored. This should be the status when the ABORT REMIRROR command is issued.
Orphaned state	This indicates that the partitions do not have the same data. You can use the Disk Options in the INSTALL NLM to correct this problem.
Out of synchronization	This indicates that one of the servers does not have the same data and that, therefore, they are not synchronized.

The LIST DEVICES Command

This displays a list of storage devices such as disk driver, tape driver, optical disk, or any other storage device. Its syntax is

LIST DEVICES

Figure 7.10 shows an example of typing the LIST DEVICES command. Notice that only one device is displayed. If a new device is added since the server was last started and its device driver is activated, it is often necessary to use the SCAN FOR NEW DEVICES command to register the device. The SCAN FOR NEW DEVICES command is explained in the next section.

```
NW4KS:load tapedai
Loading module TAPEDAI.DSK
  TAPE DRIVER
  Version 3.12    May 18, 1993
SERVER-4.00-30:   This module is using 3 outdated API calls
  You should upgrade to a newer module when it becomes available.
  Debug symbol information for TAPEDAI.DSK loaded
NW4KS:load tsa400
Loading module TSA400.NLM
  NetWare 4.0 Target Service Agent
  Version 4.01    June 4, 1993
  Copyright 1993 Novell, Inc.  All rights reserved.
NW4KS:load tsa_nds
Loading module TSA_NDS.NLM
  NetWare Directory Target Service Agent 4.0
  Version 4.00    February 13, 1993
  Copyright 1993 Novell, Inc.  All rights reserved.
NW4KS:list devices
 1. Device #  0 MICROP   1528-15MD1076301 DD24 (5D000000).
NW4KS:
```

Figure 7.10

Example LIST DEVICES command.

The SCAN FOR NEW DEVICES Command

The SCAN FOR NEW DEVICES command registers any new hardware and devices that have been added since the server was last started. If the server does not recognize a device as part of its boot sequence, you must issue this command after you load the driver for that device. The syntax of this command is

SCAN FOR NEW DEVICES

Typing this command does not usually produce any visible display (see fig. 7.11). You must issue the LIST DEVICES command to see any new devices that have been found by the SCAN

FOR NEW DEVICES command. Figure 7.12 shows the output of
the LIST DEVICES command after the generic SCSI tape driver
TAPEDAI.DSK has been loaded and the SCAN FOR NEW DE-
VICES command has been executed. Notice that a new device, the
HP 35470A tape drive unit, is now registered.

Figure 7.11

The SCAN FOR NEW
DEVICES command.

```
NW4KS:scan for new devices
NW4KS:
```

Figure 7.12

The LIST DEVICES
command after the
SCAN FOR NEW
DEVICES command.

```
NW4KS:scan for new devices
NW4KS:list devices
  0. Device #  1 HP - HP35470A (020000FF).
  1. Device #  0 MICROP   1528-15MD1076301 DD24 (5D000000).
NW4KS:
```

The MAGAZINE Command

A magazine holds one or more media (optical disk, tape) for
the secondary storage device used in data migration. The
MAGAZINE command is used to confirm whether magazine
requests issued by the server have been satisfied. This command
is used in conjunction with secondary storage devices used with
the data migration facility.

The MAGAZINE and the MEDIA commands
(discussed next) are reminiscent of the messages seen on the console of mainframe systems for the computer operator to mount a
new tape or disk.

The syntax of the MAGAZINE command is

MAGAZINE *request*

in which *request* is replaced by INSERTED, NOT INSERTED,
REMOVED, or NOT REMOVED.

654

Figure 7.13 shows the help message screen for the MAGAZINE INSERTED command. Notice that this command acknowledges the insertion of the specified magazine in response to the console alert message `Insert Magazine`. The MAGAZINE INSERTED command is a way of communicating to the system that the requested action has been performed. If you issue the MAGAZINE INSERTED command when no console requests have been made, no harm is done. You are told by the system that no requests are outstanding (see fig. 7.14), and your command is ignored.

```
NW4CS:HELP MAGAZINE INSERTED
MAGAZINE INSERTED
  Acknowledges the insertion of the specified media magazine in response to the
  "Insert Magazine" console alert.
  Example:  magazine inserted

NW4CS:
```

Figure 7.13

Help on MAGAZINE INSERTED command.

```
NW4CS:MAGAZINE INSERTED
There are no outstanding magazine insert requests
NW4CS:
```

Figure 7.14

The MAGAZINE INSERTED command when no requests are pending.

If you issue the MAGAZINE INSERTED command when no console request has been made, the command is ignored.

The following MAGAZINE request commands work in the same manner:

MAGAZINE NOT INSERTED

MAGAZINE REMOVED

MAGAZINE NOT REMOVED

The help messages for these commands are shown in figures 7.15, 7.16, and 7.17.

Figure 7.15

Help on MAGAZINE
NOT INSERTED
command.

```
NW4CS:HELP MAGAZINE NOT INSERTED
MAGAZINE NOT INSERTED
 Acknowledges the fact that the insertion of the specified media magazine was
 NOT performed.
 Example:  magazine not inserted

NW4CS:
```

Figure 7.16

Help on MAGAZINF
REMOVED command.

```
NW4CS:HELP MAGAZINE REMOVED
MAGAZINE REMOVED
 Acknowledges the removal of a magazine from the specified device in response
 to the "Remove Magazine" console alert.
 Example:  remove magazine

NW4CS:
```

Figure 7.17

Help on MAGAZINE
NOT REMOVED
command.

```
NW4CS:HELP MAGAZINE NOT REMOVED
MAGAZINE NOT REMOVED
 Acknowledges the fact that the removal of the magazine was NOT performed.
 Example:  magazine not removed

NW4CS:
```

The MEDIA Command

The MEDIA command is used to confirm whether media requests issued by the server have been satisfied. This command is used in conjunction with secondary storage devices that are used with the data migration facility.

The syntax of the MEDIA command is

MEDIA *request*

where *request* is replaced by INSERTED, NOT INSERTED, REMOVED, or NOT REMOVED.

Figure 7.18 shows the help message screen for the MEDIA INSERTED command. Notice that this command acknowledges the insertion of the specified media in response to the console alert message Insert Media. The MEDIA INSERTED command is a way of communicating to the system that the requested action has been performed. If you issue the MEDIA INSERTED command when no console request has been made, no harm is done. The system tells you that no requests are outstanding (see fig. 7.19), and your command is ignored.

```
NW4CS:HELP MEDIA INSERTED
MEDIA INSERTED
  Acknowledges the insertion of the specified media in response to the "Insert
  Media" console alert.
  Example:  media inserted

NW4CS:
```

Figure 7.18

Help on MEDIA INSERTED command.

```
NW4CS:MEDIA INSERTED
There are no outstanding media insert requests
NW4CS:
```

Figure 7.19

The MEDIA INSERTED command when no requests are pending.

Author's Note   If you issue the MEDIA INSERTED command when no console request has been made, the command is ignored.

The following MEDIA request commands work in the same manner:

MEDIA NOT INSERTED

MEDIA REMOVED

MEDIA NOT REMOVED

The help message screens for these commands are shown in figures 7.20, 7.21, and 7.22.

```
NW4CS:HELP MEDIA NOT INSERTED
MEDIA NOT INSERTED
  Acknowledges the fact that the insertion of the specified media was NOT
  performed.
  Example:  media not inserted

NW4CS:
```

Figure 7.20

Help on MEDIA NOT INSERTED command.

```
NW4CS:HELP MEDIA REMOVED
MEDIA REMOVED
  Acknowledges the removal of the media from the specified device in response to
  the "Remove Media" console alert.
  Example:  remove media

NW4CS:
```

Figure 7.21

Help on MEDIA REMOVED command.

657

Figure 7.22

Help on MEDIA NOT
REMOVED command.

```
NW4CS:HELP MEDIA NOT REMOVED
MEDIA NOT REMOVED
 Acknowledges the fact that the removal of the media was NOT performed.
 Example:  media not removed

NW4CS:
```

The RESTART SERVER Command

In earlier versions of NetWare, the only way to restart the server
was to issue a console command called DOWN to shut down the
server, exit to DOS, and run the SERVER.EXE program. The
RESTART SERVER command can be used to restart execution of
the server after the DOWN command has been executed but
before the EXIT command to exit to DOS.

The general syntax of this command is

```
RESTART SERVER  [optionalParameters]
```

where *optionalParameters* can be the following:

-ns   For not using the STARTUP.NCF files

-na   For not using the SYS:SYSTEM/AUTOEXEC.NCF
          file

-d   For entering into the NetWare OS low-level inter-
          nal debugger (used only by software developers)

The [ ] brackets around *optionalParameters* indicate that the parameter is optional.

Please note that you must down the server before you can run this
command.

The LANGUAGE Command

The LANGUAGE command is used to specify the language to be
used for the message files. This enables the NLMs that are written
to support internationalization to display their options and help
files in different languages. The general syntax for LANGUAGE is

```
LANGUAGE [language] [option]
```

658

The [ ] brackets around the parameters indicate that they are optional.

The *language* parameter can be the name of the language or a language identification number. The languages and assigned codes are shown in table 7.8. You should check the version of NetWare 4.x that you have for the languages available. To select the SPANISH language, for example, you can execute

LANGUAGE SPANISH

or

LANGUAGE 14

Similarly, you can use the language name or language identification number for any of the other languages listed in table 7.8, if this support has been installed at the server.

Table 7.8
Language Parameter Values for the LANGUAGE Command

Language Identification Number	Language Name
0	Canadian French
1	Chinese
2	Danish
3	Dutch
4	English
5	Finnish
6	French
7	German
8	Italian
9	Japanese
10	Korean

continues

Table 7.8, Continued
Language Parameter Values for the LANGUAGE Command

| Language
Identification Number	Language Name
11	Norwegian
12	Portuguese
13	Russian
14	Spanish
15	Swedish

Figure 7.23 shows the server console screen that has these commands issued. Figure 7.24 shows the MONITOR NLM running after the LANGUAGE command was set to use Spanish language message files. This assumes that support for the language has been installed on the server. Figure 7.24 shows that the Esc command was typed. You can see the prompt in Spanish for exiting the MONITOR NLM. Figure 7.25 shows the top level help for the MONITOR NLM.

Figure 7.23

The LANGUAGE command for Spanish.

```
NW4CS:LANGUAGE SPANISH
   Current NLM language changed to (14) SPANISH.

NW4CS:
```

Figures 7.26 through 7.33 show the MONITOR NLM and its help screen displayed in English, French, German, and Italian. You may want to compare the MONITOR screens in different languages.

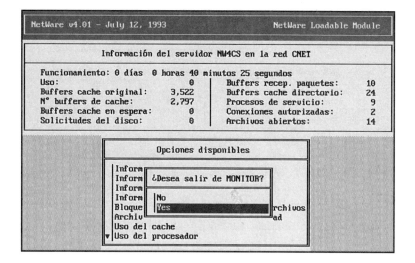

Figure 7.24

The MONITOR NLM
in Spanish.

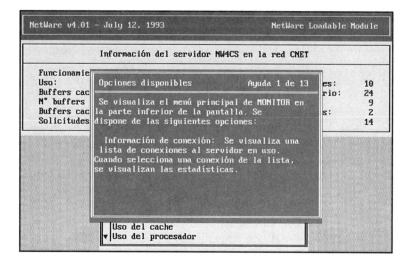

Figure 7.25

The Help screen
for MONITOR NLM
in Spanish.

Figure 7.26

The MONITOR NLM
in English.

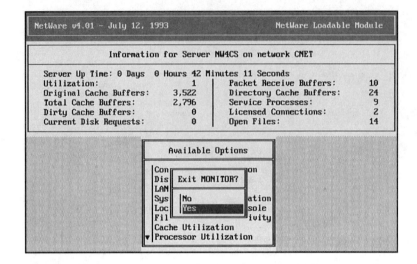

Figure 7.27

The Help screen
for MONITOR NLM
in English.

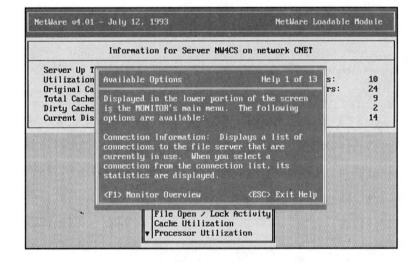

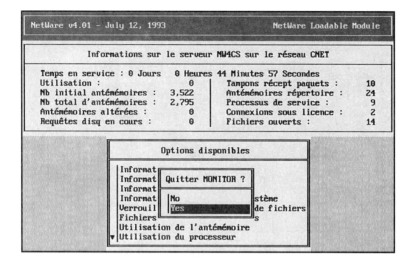

Figure 7.28

The MONITOR NLM in French.

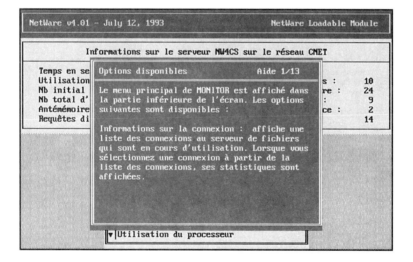

Figure 7.29

The Help screen for MONITOR NLM in French.

Figure 7.30

The MONITOR NLM in German.

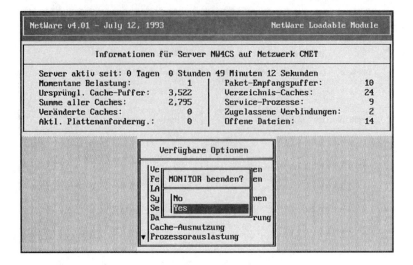

Figure 7.31

The Help screen for MONITOR NLM in German.

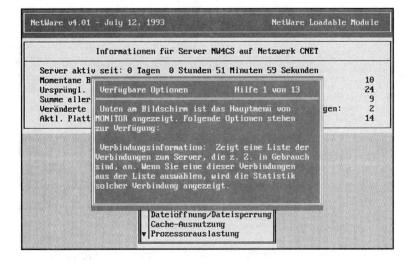

664

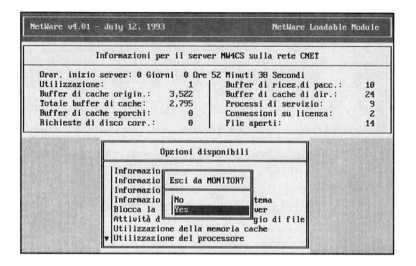

Figure 7.32

The MONITOR NLM in Italian.

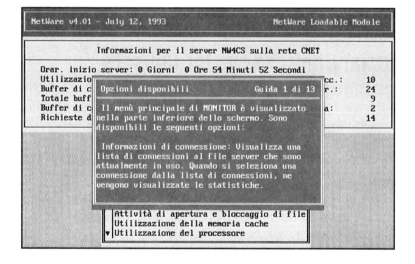

Figure 7.33

The Help screen for MONITOR NLM in Italian.

To install language support, follow these steps:

1. LOAD INSTALL (the INSTALL.NLM is a special NLM used for installing, maintaining, and upgrading a NetWare 4.x server).

2. Select "Maintenance/Selective Install."

3. Select "Other Options."

4. Select "Install an Additional Server Language from the CD-ROM" or "Install an Additional Server Language," depending on whether you have a CD-ROM or floppy distribution media.

The language message files can be installed using the INSTALL NLM.

Special Control Keys for Console Commands

The console command-line processor uses special function keys to switch between screens for different VLMs.

The Alt+Esc keys can be used to switch between screens in a cyclic manner, as shown in figure 7.34. In this figure, the display screens for three of the modules are shown. You can use Alt+Esc to go to the next console screen. If you press Alt+Esc enough times, you return to the screen where you started.

To switch between several screens quickly, you can just hold the Alt key and keep pressing the Esc key until you are at the right screen.

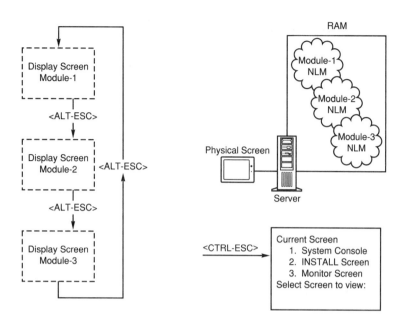

Figure 7.34

Switching between server console screens.

Pressing Ctrl+Esc displays a menu of the different screens available for viewing. These screens are numbered starting from 1. Entering a screen number causes the console display to switch to that screen.

Using System Administration NLMs

You should know about the three major categories of NLMs that follow:

- ◆ Management NLMs

- ◆ Server enhancement NLMs

- ◆ Remote management NLMs

As discussed earlier, when NLMs are executed, they are loaded and closely integrated with the NetWare 4.x operating system. NLMs are loaded with the LOAD command, entered at the server console.

Management NLMs

The management NLMs deal with those NLMs that are specifically designed for management of the server resources. These include the following NLMs:

♦ INSTALL

♦ MONITOR

♦ SERVMAN

♦ UPS

These NLMs are discussed in greater detail in the following sections.

Using INSTALL NLM

Using the INSTALL utility, you can install a new NetWare server, upgrade a NetWare 3.x server to a NetWare 4.x server, or perform a selective installation of different aspects of a server. To begin INSTALL, load it from the console with the following command:

```
LOAD INSTALL
```

The INSTALL NLM is used to install a server for the first time. You can use INSTALL to perform install and configure components of NetWare 4.x. Some of the tasks that can be performed using INSTALL include the following:

♦ Install and configure a NetWare 4.x server

♦ Install and configure other Novell and third-party products on the server

♦ Create NetWare disk partitions and mirror or unmirror them

♦ Create volumes

♦ Create and modify STARTUP.NCF and AUTOEXEC.NCF configuration files

♦ Copy SYSTEM and PUBLIC files from distribution media to the server

◆ Copy online documentation and CBT files

◆ Create upgrade and migration disks and DOS, Windows, or OS/2 client disks

◆ Install additional server languages

◆ Configure communication protocols

◆ Create registration disks

◆ Install or reinstall directory services

Using MONITOR NLM

The MONITOR NLM is the principal tool used to manage and monitor the NetWare server. It provides information about the following:

Connection information

Disk information

LAN/WAN information

System module information

Lock file server console

File open/lock activity

Cache utilization

Processor utilization

Resource utilization

Memory utilization

Scheduling information

Figure 7.35 shows the MONITOR NLM main screen. As you can see from this screen, MONITOR can be used to display information on a variety of server statistics. The MONITOR NLM is the primary tool for server management. It is complemented by the SERVMAN tool for controlling the less obvious parameter settings. Some of the new options that have been added, compared with NetWare 3.x server, are Scheduling Information and Processor Utilization. Processor Utilization was also available under the NetWare 3.x MONITOR, but it required you to start MONITOR with the P switch (LOAD MONITOR P, LOAD MONITOR /P or LOAD MONITOR -P).

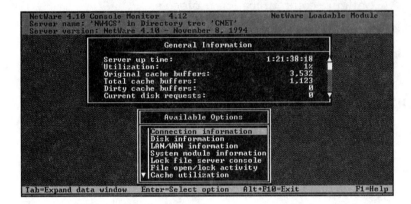

NetWare administrators can use MONITOR to keep track of resources (called *resource tags*) used by the NLMs that are running in server memory. Monitoring these resources alerts the network manager to NLMs that are using excessive resources. This precaution allows corrective action to be taken before a major problem develops.

Detailed coverage of MONITOR is beyond the scope of this chapter. It is covered in a later chapter dealing with advanced administration topics.

Using SERVMAN NLM

Many of the characteristics of a NetWare 4.x server are configured using SET parameters. These parameters can be configured using the console SET command. You will learn, however, that many SET parameters exist, and that most have long names and several possible values. They can be difficult to remember and enter correctly.

The SERVMAN tool is a new server manager NLM that provides a convenient menu interface that enables you to change and view the SET parameters, configure SPX/IPX, and view network information.

The SET commands are used to control the server performance and configuration parameters. The syntax for loading the SERVMAN NLM is

LOAD SERVMAN

Figure 7.36 shows the SERVMAN main screen. The Server Parameters option enables you to view or change the SET parameters. Changes made here are used to update the STARTUP.NCF or AUTOEXEC.NCF files. SERVMAN is also an excellent tool for obtaining quick online help concerning the meaning of each of the SET parameters. The SET parameters are organized in categories for easy reference. Figure 7.37 shows these categories when the Server Parameters option was selected from the list of Available Options. To view any of the SET parameters in a particular category, simply select that category. Figure 7.38 shows the SET TIME parameters in the Time category. As each parameter is highlighted, a brief description is displayed.

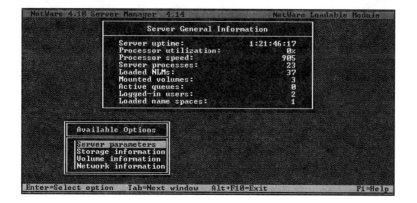

Figure 7.36

The SERVMAN main menu.

Figure 7.37

SERVMAN Server
Parameters.

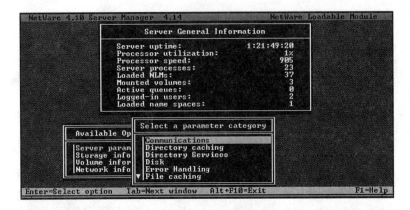

Figure 7.38

The Time category.

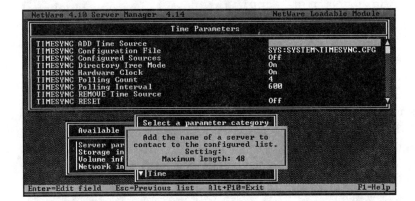

Another interesting category is the File system category. Some of
the newer parameters here deal with file compression. (File
compression was discussed in Chapter 1, "Introduction to
NetWare 4.x.") Figures 7.39 and 7.40 together show all the com-
pression-related SET parameters.

You can use these parameters to control the start time (Compression Daily Check Starting Hour) and the stop time (Compression
Daily Check Stop Hour) for the file compressor.

You can set the Minimum Compression Percentage Gain parameter to determine whether a file should be compressed. The
default value for this parameter is 2, which means that unless
there is at least a two percent reduction of the compressed file,
the system does not keep the file in the compressed state.

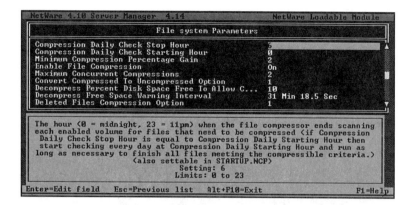

Figure 7.39

The File system category—compression parameters: Screen 1.

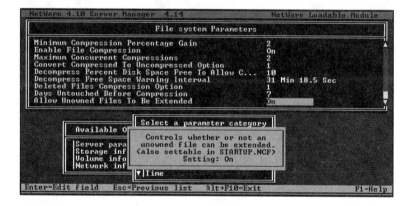

Figure 7.40

The File system category—compression parameters: Screen 2.

The Days Untouched Before Compression parameter determines how long (in days) the system waits after the file was last accessed before compressing it. The Decompress Percent Disk Space Free To Allow Commit parameter is used to determine the free disk space required before compression can begin. Its default value is 10 percent.

The Maximum Concurrent Compressions parameter can be used to limit the number of compressions going on. Compression is a low priority task and should not normally impact the server performance. You can reduce this parameter if your server performance is affected.

The SERVMAN options can be used for viewing storage information on devices, volume information, and network information. The Storage information option can be used to display information on the storage objects (see fig. 7.41). The Volume Information option can be used to display information on the mounted volumes (see fig. 7.42). Information on the highlighted volume is displayed on the top part of the screen.

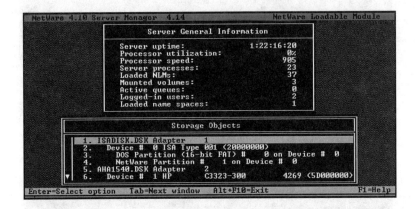

Figure 7.41

The Storage information option.

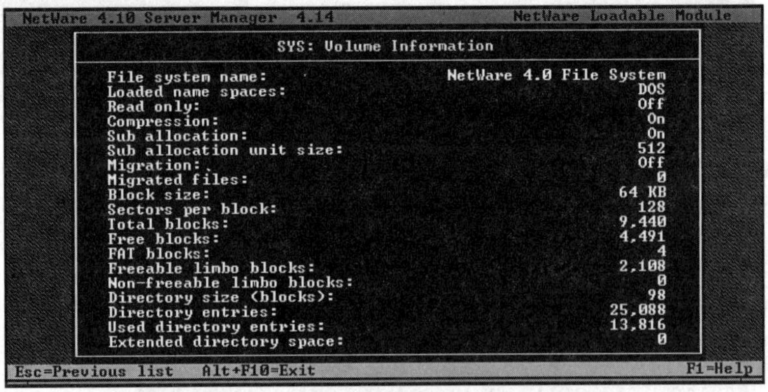

Figure 7.42

The Volume information option.

The Network information option can be used to display information on the network (see fig. 7.43). Besides monitoring the network traffic such as number of packets transmitted and received, you can use this screen for troubleshooting.

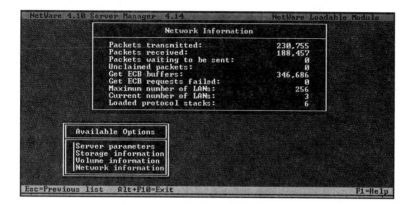

Figure 7.43

The Network information option.

A high number of Unclaimed packets indicates that an attempt is being made by network users to obtain a service that is not supported on the server. This parameter represents the number of packets for which there was no protocol stack.

If "Packets waiting to be sent" or "Get ECB requests failed" is high, that is an indication that the number of communication buffers is insufficient to handle the network traffic.

Using UPS NLM

When power is abruptly removed from a NetWare server, files on the server can be damaged, perhaps irretrievably. In all cases, it is advisable to use an Uninterruptable Power Supply (UPS) with a NetWare server. The batteries in the UPS provide a few minutes of power to the server in the event of a power failure. During those minutes, the power failure can be corrected or the server can be shut down in a controlled way so that files are not corrupted.

Because power failures can happen at any time, often when the server is unattended, it is desirable to enable the server to shut itself down in the event of a prolonged power failure that is exhausting to batteries in the UPS. The UPS NLM provides a software interface between the UPS and the NetWare server.

Most modern UPS systems have a hardware port that is connected to the server, often to a serial port, although other options also are available. The hardware driver for the UPS must be attached to the server before the UPS NLM is activated. Usually, the attachment is via one of the serial interfaces to the server. No menu screen is associated with the UPS NLM. The command to load the UPS.NLM is as follows:

LOAD UPS

You are prompted for additional parameters as the UPS NLM loads.

The power is supplied to the server via the UPS device, even under normal circumstances of no power failures. The UPS device provides a well-regulated power supply, and if the main power line fails, the UPS is able to continue supplying this power while its batteries last. If the main power supply fails, the UPS sends a signal to the server that power failure has occurred. The UPS.NLM receives the signal and is able to perform an immediate shutdown of the server or to wait a certain amount of time before initiating a shutdown. Many UPS devices are able to send a separate signal when the UPS battery is depleted, and this capability can be used to initiate server shutdown. In any case, you should refer to the UPS device documentation to learn about the details of interfacing the UPS to the server.

NetWare 4.x also provides two additional commands called UPS TIME and UPS STATUS to monitor the UPS time and status. These commands work only when the UPS NLM is loaded.

Server Enhancement NLMs

NetWare 4.x supports the following enhancements:

◆ STREAMS capability

◆ Network management (NMAGENT)

◆ Remote boot

◆ Source routing

These enhancements are implemented by special NLMs, which are called *enhancement NLMs*.

STREAMS Capability

STREAMS is a general-purpose transport protocol interface developed by AT&T that enables protocol stacks to be built dynamically. The head of the STREAMS protocol is the STREAMS interface, and the tail is usually the network card driver. On NetWare servers, the tail of the STREAMS is designed to connect with the ODI drivers loaded at the server. Between the head and the tail, any number of protocol elements can be connected as if they were part of a string or stream (see fig. 7.44). These protocol elements could be the transport and network protocols such as SPX/IPX or TCP/IP.

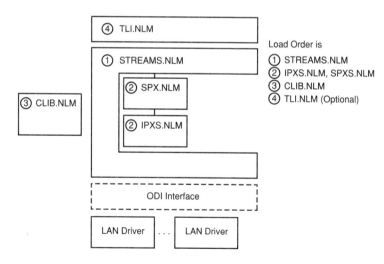

Load Order is
① STREAMS.NLM
② IPXS.NLM, SPXS.NLM
③ CLIB.NLM
④ TLI.NLM (Optional)

Figure 7.44

STREAMS enhancement.

The TLI (Transport Layer Interface), also developed by AT&T, is a higher-level interface than STREAMS. STREAMS is considered to be too low-level an interface for application programmers to use. The STREAMS interface was designed primarily to ease the process of adding additional protocols to Unix System V.

677

The NetWare TLI implementation follows the spirit of the AT&T definition but differs from it in implementation details because it works on an operating system that is unlike Unix. The STREAMS interface supports SPX/IPX and TCP/IP.

The STREAMS.NLM is required by the CLIB.NLM. If STREAMS.NLM is not loaded when CLIB.NLM loads, it is autoloaded. The SPXS.NLM and IPXS.NLM implement the SPX and IPX protocol interface to the STREAMS.NLM.

Author's Note
In addition to TLI, the BSD sockets interface can be used by application programmers. The BSD (Berkeley System Distribution) socket interface was developed as part of BSD Unix at the University of California, Berkeley. It is a very popular and simple programming interface to the TCP/IP protocols.

Network Management Agent (NMAGENT.NLM)

Network management has become increasingly important for today's more complex networks. A variety of network management tools can monitor the network for messages generated by network devices. Devices are equipped with software known as an agent, which can produce messages or even respond to queries or commands from the network management console.

NetWare 4.x provides such a network management agent. The network management agent is implemented by the NMAGENT.NLM. This NLM is autoloaded whenever a LAN driver is loaded. The NMAGENT.NLM is a network management agent that reports on network statistics collected by the LAN drivers. It can, for example, report on the number of packets transmitted or received via a particular LAN driver interface. For Ethernet networks, it can report on the number of collisions detected by the server's network adapter.

Figure 7.45 shows the NMAGENT.NLM for a LAN driver NLM. Third-party network programs can poll the NMAGENT.NLM for LAN statistics. Some of these statistics can also be viewed by the MONITOR NLM, which can poll the local network interfaces and report them.

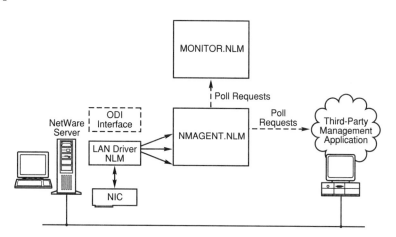

Figure 7.45

The Network management agent— NMAGENT.NLM.

Remote Boot

Remote booting for diskless workstations is implemented by the Remote Program Load NLM, called RPL.NLM. Diskless workstations do not have local disk storage devices and are used to lower the cost of workstations and to improve security. Because there is no local storage on the workstation, you cannot copy files between workstations and the network. Users are unable to install programs on the network or to copy data from the network. This eliminates a common source of computer viruses on the network.

Figure 7.46 shows that with RPL.NLM support, diskless workstations can send requests to the server to download the operating system boot image that is then used to initialize the workstation. The diskless workstation boots from the network, rather than from a local storage device.

Figure 7.46

Remote Program
Load.

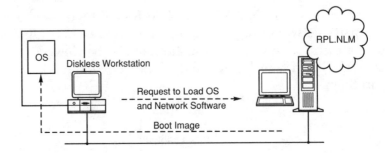

Source Routing

Source routing is used in IBM Token-Ring networks to support
data transmission in a network consisting of several interconnected Token-Ring networks (see fig. 7.47). The Token-Ring LANs
are interconnected by IBM Token-Ring bridges that follow the
source routing instructions embedded in each Token-Ring frame
to send the data to the interconnected Token-Ring LANs. The
initial route is discovered by the source station, and this is the
reason that this technique is called source routing. Once the
sending station discovers the best route to a destination, the route
path is included in every Token-Ring frame sent to that destination. The route path consists of ring number/bridge number pairs,
and the interconnected bridges simply follow the instructions in
this route path to send it to the next Token-Ring LAN. NetWare
client software is generic in nature and works with different
network topologies. To support the additional requirements of
source routing, the program's ROUTE.COM must be loaded at the
NetWare workstation. Additionally, ROUTE.NLM must be loaded
at the NetWare server.

The ROUTE.COM program must be loaded after the ODI driver is
loaded, but before loading the IPXODI.COM protocol stack. An
example of how you could modify the STARTNET.BAT in the
C:\NWCLIENT directory to support source routing in a Token-
Ring network is shown here:

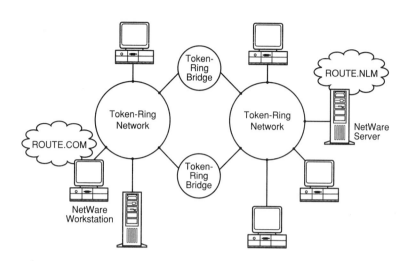

Figure 7.47

Source routing.

```
@ECHO OFF
C:
CD \NWCLIENT
SET NWLANGUAGE=ENGLISH
LSL
TOKEN.COM
ROUTE
IPXODI
VLM
CD \
```

The ROUTE.COM shown in the previous example loads with a default set of parameters. You can customize the behavior of ROUTE by using additional options. The general syntax of the ROUTE command is as follows:

```
ROUTE    U,BOARD=b,CLEAR,DEF,GBR,HOPS=hc,MBR,NODES=n,TIME=s,
➡TRA=rac,TRO=roc
```

All parameters for the ROUTE program are optional and can be entered in any order. The ROUTE command can be used to set the ROUTE parameters the first time it is loaded. If it is loaded again, it can be used to change the configuration of a previously loaded source route configuration.

The U parameter is used to unload a previously loaded ROUTE.COM from memory.

681

The BOARD=b parameter specifies the board number b assigned to the board by the ODI interface. If it is not used, the default board number 1 is assumed.

Specifying the CLEAR parameter clears all node addresses for the loaded ROUTE.COM.

The DEF parameter causes source routing to use the Send Default (Unknown) Node Addresses ALL ROUTES Broadcast. If this parameter is not entered, Single Route Broadcast is used.

The GBR parameter causes source routing to use the Send Broadcast (FFFF FFFF FFFF) Addresses ALL ROUTES Broadcast. If this parameter is not entered, Single Route Broadcast is used.

The HOPS=hc parameter specifies the number of bridge hops (hc) to configure for source routing. The default value is 7, and the maximum is 13.

The MBR parameter causes source routing to use the Send MultiCast (C000 xxxx xxxx) Addresses ALL ROUTES Broadcast. If this parameter is not entered, Single Route Broadcast is used.

The NODES=n parameter specifies the number of node addresses (n) to support. The default is 16, and the maximum is 1000. If a value less than 8 is entered, the actual value used is 8.

The TIME=s parameter specifies the number of seconds (s) to wait before declaring that a known route is timed out. The default is 10, and the maximum is 255.

The TRA=rac parameter specifies the This Ring Alternate Count (rac) for Broadcasts. The source router alternates between source-routed and nonsource-routed frames. The default is 0, and the maximum is 255.

The TRO=roc parameter specifies the This Ring Only Count (roc) for Broadcasts. The default is 0, and the maximum is 255.

For additional details of how source routing works, you can refer to *NetWare: The Professional Reference* by New Riders Publishing.

Using the Remote Console

A very useful utility for managing the server is the Remote Console utility. This utility is run at the workstation as the RCONSOLE.EXE. At the server, the NLMs REMOTE.NLM and RSPX.NLM need to be loaded. Once these NLMs are loaded, a workstation can become a server console by running the RCONSOLE.EXE program.

The order of loading the NLMs is first REMOTE.NLM and then RSPX.NLM. When REMOTE.NLM loads, you can specify a password as an argument to the LOAD REMOTE command. If you do not specify a password, the REMOTE NLM prompts you for one. The commands to run Remote Console follow.

At the server:

```
LOAD REMOTE   password
LOAD RSPX
```

At the workstation:

```
RCONSOLE     (Located in the SYS:SYSTEM directory)
```

When REMOTE is loaded, you must select if you want to use SPX or Asynchronous access, then the password used to access the server at the console can be typed on the same command line. To use a password of xyzzy, for example, you can use the following command:

```
LOAD REMOTE xyzzy
```

If a password is not specified, the REMOTE.NLM prompts you for one. If you want remote console support to be loaded whenever the server is started, you can include the commands for loading REMOTE.NLM and RSPX.NLM in the AUTOEXEC.NCF file that is kept on the server's SYS:SYSTEM directory. If a password is not specified on the command to load REMOTE.NLM, the server boot load sequence halts until you type in the password. For this reason, you may want to include the REMOTE password in the AUTOEXEC.NCF line.

Including the REMOTE password in the AUTOEXEC.NCF file introduces another problem. Anyone with access to the AUTOEXEC.NCF can see the password. If the server console is not locked, anyone can use INSTALL.NLM or EDIT.NLM to view the AUTOEXEC.NCF file. Also, anyone with access to the SYS:SYSTEM or AUTOEXEC.NCF file from a workstation can view the commands (and the password) in this file. To solve this problem, NetWare 4.x supports the E encryption option that can be used with REMOTE. Instead of specifying the actual password, you specify an encrypted key that represents the password:

```
LOAD REMOTE -E encryptedkey
```

The encrypted key is a numeric quantity that represents the password but is not the password itself. The encrypted key can be obtained after you load REMOTE.NLM. A new command called REMOTE ENCRYPT becomes available when REMOTE.NLM is loaded. You can type the following at the server:

```
REMOTE ENCRYPT
```

The command prompts you to enter a password. An encryption key will be displayed. You can use this encryption key in the LOAD REMOTE -E command in the AUTOEXEC.NCF file. If you want to use the password XYZZY, for example, you can use the following command at the console after REMOTE.NLM is loaded:

```
REMOTE ENCRYPT XYZZY
```

The encrypted key for password XYZZY is CADDA33333. You can use the following in the AUTOEXEC.NCF file:

```
LOAD REMOTE -E CADDA33333
```

Using the encrypted password preserves the integrity of the actual password used to access the server console.

The REMOTE ENCRYPT command also asks if you want to save the LOAD REMOTE command to the LDREMOTE.NCF file. If you answer Yes, it includes LDREMOTE.NCF in the AUTOEXEC.NCF file.

RSPX includes support for packet signatures. *Packet signatures* are special encryption codes used to authenticate each packet sent between workstation and server. Packet signatures make it extremely difficult to forge packets. Packet forging is a technique that is used by programs written to break the security of a network. In this technique, an illegal source duplicates the packets sent by a legal source to the server. NetWare uses packet signatures that use the MD4 (Message Digest 4) encryption algorithm to uniquely identify packets. The default for RSPX is that packet signatures are ON. RCONSOLE.EXE on earlier versions of NetWare (3.x) does not support packet signatures. If you are running a copy of RCONSOLE.EXE while logged in to a NetWare 3.x network, to connect to REMOTE.NLM running on a NetWare 4.x server you can turn packet signature off by loading RSPX with the SIGNATURES OFF parameter:

```
LOAD RSPX SIGNATURES OFF
```

Figure 7.48 shows the Remote Console components. The reason REMOTE.NLM has to be loaded before RSPX.NLM is interesting. From figure 7.48 it is clear that RSPX is lower in the functional hierarchy than REMOTE.NLM, because it implements the communication protocol stack and REMOTE.NLM implements the Remote Console Facility. For this reason, you might think that RSPX.NLM should be loaded first. When RSPX.NLM loads, it expects to logically bind to entry points in the LAN driver and the application to which it connects. The LAN drivers already are loaded when the server is activated; therefore, RSPX can bind to the LAN driver without any problem. If the REMOTE.NLM is not already loaded, RSPX.NLM is unable to logically connect to it. For this reason, REMOTE.NLM should be loaded before RSPX.NLM.

A major difference between RCONSOLE for NetWare 4.x and prior NetWare versions is that the functions of ACONSOLE, for asynchronous communications I/O, are now integrated in the NetWare 4.x RCONSOLE.

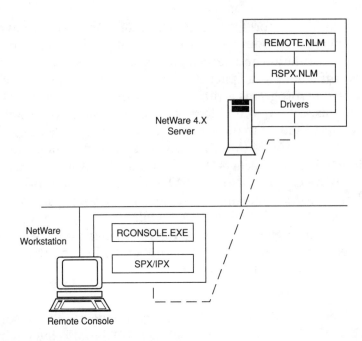

Figure 7.48

The Remote Console
components.

Figure 7.49 shows the opening screen when RCONSOLE is run at a workstation. Notice that the two options shown are Asynchronous and SPX. If the Asynchronous option is selected, you are given a list of Asynchronous Options (see fig. 7.50). The Connect To Remote Location option enables you to view a list of remote locations accessible through RCONSOLE. Before you can use this option, you must use the Configuration option to configure asynchronous operations.

Figure 7.49

The Remote Console
main screen.

Figure 7.50

Asynchronous
Options.

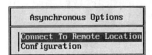

Selecting the Configuration option (see fig. 7.51) enables you to select the device and modem configuration parameters. You can select the baud rate (bits per second), the modem initialization and reset command, the modem reconnect command, the modem dial command, and the modem hang-up command.

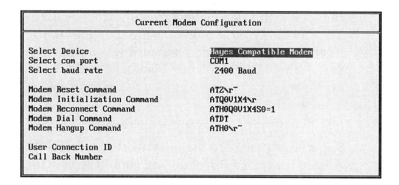

Figure 7.51

The Asynchronous Configuration option.

You can supply a user identification by which the connecting station is known to the remote server. You can also enter a call-back number. The modem type can be Hayes-compatible or a null modem. The choice of null modem cable is useful, especially when used with serial line boosters (amplifiers). You can then manage the server from fairly long distances within a local building without using the LAN. This technique is particularly useful if a problem exists with the network cabling.

When the SPX option is selected, as shown in figure 7.49, you are given a list of available servers to which to connect (see fig. 7.52). When you select a server, you are prompted for a password. After typing the password used with the REMOTE (or the first Admin password), you receive a connection to the server console (see fig. 7.53). The connection message on the screen lists the date and time the connection took place and the network number and node address of the station that was granted the connection. From figure 7.53, you can see that the network number is 000E8022 and the node address is 0000C0664E19.

Author's Note

The REMOTE and RCONSOLE utilities are bindery-based. You can use the password that was supplied with REMOTE to access the server console or the first Admin password that was assigned during NDS installation. If you change the password for the first Admin user, you cannot use this new password with RCONSOLE. You can, however, continue using the REMOTE password. If the Admin password was not specified during installation (left blank), you will not be prompted for a password when using RCONSOLE to access the server.

Specifically, this is because RCONSOLE uses the Supervisor password that is synchronised with the Admin password at install. You should be able to change the Supervisor password using SETPASS SUPERVISOR /B (provided you have a bindery context set at the server).

Figure 7.52

The RCONSOLE Available Servers list.

```
┌──────────────────────┐
│  Available Servers   │
├──────────────────────┤
│ NW4CS                │
│                      │
│                      │
│                      │
│                      │
│                      │
│                      │
│                      │
└──────────────────────┘
```

Figure 7.53

Connection granted to Remote Console.

```
10-10-93  12:43:09 pm:     RSPX-4.1-28
        Remote console connection granted for 000E8022:0000C0664E19

NW4CS:
```

In earlier NetWare versions, you could invoke the RCONSOLE menu by using the + key on the numeric pad. The control keys for NetWare 4.x RCONSOLE are different. To see the RCONSOLE menu, you must use the Alt+F1 keys. Figure 7.54 shows the RCONSOLE menu when the Alt+F1 keys are pressed.

Figure 7.54

RCONSOLE Available
Options.

The Select A Screen To View option displays a list of screens mounted on the server console. It performs the function of the Ctrl+Esc keys at the server console.

The Directory Scan option enables you to obtain a directory listing on any server volume directory or on any DOS directory on the server DOS partition. When you select this option, you are prompted for a directory name. The directory contents are displayed in a window.

The Transfer Files To Server option enables you to transfer files from a local workstation drive or a network drive (obtained by using the MAP command at the workstation) to the server volume or to the DOS partition of the server. When copying to a subdirectory on the server partition, however, you can only specify the directory name to copy to. You cannot copy file1 to the server as file2, the names must remain the same.

The End Remote Session With Server (Alt+F2) option is used to end the connection with the remote server. The Resume Remote Session With Server (Esc) option closes the RCONSOLE menu options windows and returns you to the server console screen.

The Configure Keystroke Buffering option enables you to introduce delays (milliseconds) in transmission of keystrokes, buffer keystrokes until a special key code, Alt+F8, is sent (Manual send), or enable keystroke buffering on demand by pressing Alt+F9 (On demand). This option can be used to reduce the amount of packet traffic sent over low-speed links.

The new options, when compared with NetWare 3.x, are Invoke Operating System Shell, which exits to the workstation command shell, the Workstation Address option, and Configure Keystroke Buffering. You must type **EXIT** to get back to the RCONSOLE menu. The new Workstation Address option enables you to see the workstation's node address (see fig. 7.55). In figure 7.55, the workstation address is shown in a box on the top left corner. Other shortcut keys are available. The Alt+F2 keys enable you to quit RCONSOLE. The Alt+F3 and Alt+F4 keys enable you to scroll through screen consoles (forward and backward). The Alt+F5 key enables you to view the workstation address. The RCONSOLE control keys are summarized in table 7.9.

Figure 7.55

The RCONSOLE Workstation Address option.

Table 7.9
RCONSOLE Control Keys

Control Keys	What They Do
Alt+F1	Invokes RCONSOLE menu
Alt+F2	Exits RCONSOLE
Alt+F3 and Alt+F4	Scrolls forward and backward through console screens
Alt+F5	Views workstation node (network) address

Note Remember the RCONSOLE control keys of table 7.9, because questions regarding them may appear on the test.

690

RCONSOLE.EXE normally is stored in the SYS:SYSTEM directory so that only system administrators can have access to this program. Ordinary users usually do not have access to the SYS:SYSTEM directory. If you are running RCONSOLE from a stand-alone workstation and using a modem to access the NetWare server, you must copy the following files to the stand-alone workstation from the SYS:SYSTEM directory: RCONSOLE.EXE, IBM_RUN.OVL, _RUN.OVL, IBM_AIO.OVL, and _AIO.OVL. You also must copy the following files from the SYS:SYSTEM\NLS*language* (replace *language* with ENGLISH or another supported language) directory: RCONSOLE.HEP, TEXTUTIL.MSG, TEXTUTL.HEP, and TEXTUTIL.IDX.

If you are running RCONSOLE using a modem, you need to load AIO.NLM, AIOCOMX.NLM, and RS232.NLM at the server. These NLMs must be loaded after the REMOTE.NLM is loaded. The load order for these NLMs is shown next:

1. AIO

2. AIOCOMX

3. RS232

AIO and AIOCOMX provide asynchronous I/O communications support. These NLMs implement the API support for asynchronous communications. When RS232 is loaded, it prompts you to enter the COM port number (1 for COM1, 2 for COM2) and the baud rate. Baud rates that are supported are 2400, 4800, 9600, 19200, and 38400. You can specify some of these parameters from the command line. To specify that COM1 is to be used at a data rate of 19200 bits per second, for example, you can use the following:

```
LOAD RS232 1 19200
```

Additionally, you can specify the C or N parameter to the RS232 NLM. The C parameter specifies that the callback feature is enabled. Use the N parameter to specify that a null-modem cable is being used instead of real modem devices.

When RS232 is loaded, the MODEM command becomes available. The general syntax of this command is as follows:

```
MODEM [modemstring]
```

The *modemstring* is a Hayes modem command string that is sent to the connected modem. When this command is executed, the results of executing this command are displayed on the screen. The [] around *modemstring* indicates that the modem string is optional. If the MODEM command is entered without specifying the modem string, the MODEM command prompts you for the string. The MODEM command also supports file indirection. In file indirection, the modem commands are included in an ASCII text file. This text file can be specified in place of the modem string by preceding the file's path name with an @ symbol. You can, for example, send the modem commands stored in SYS:ETC\MODCMDS\MODINIT.TXT by typing the following command:

```
MODEM  @SYS:ETC\MODCMDS\MODINIT.TXT
```

Using RCONSOLE to Install NetWare 4 System Files

You can use RCONSOLE to install NetWare 4.x system files. RCONSOLE is convenient if the CD-ROM containing the NetWare 4.x distribution is attached to the workstation and not the server machine. After loading REMOTE and RSPX at the server, you can load RCONSOLE at the workstation and connect to the server console. You can then type

```
LOAD INSTALL
```

to run the INSTALL NLM. Next, make the following selections:

1. Select the Maintenance/Selective Install option.

2. Select the Copy Files option.

3. Press F4.

4. Select the local path containing the NetWare 4.x distribution. This path should be one similar to D:\NETWARE.40*language*, where *language* should be replaced by one of the supported languages.

Using New NLMs in NetWare 4.x

Several new NLMs are supported in NetWare 4.x. These are listed in table 7.10. The sections that follow discuss their functions and capabilities.

Table 7.10
New NetWare 4.x NLMs

NLM Name	Description
DOMAIN	Creates a protected domain for running NLMs.
DSREPAIR	Enables repair of problems with the NDS database.
RTDM	Supports the Real Time Data Migration feature.
NWSNUT	NLM Utility User Interface library.
TIMESYNC	Time Synchronization NLM to ensure that server times are synchronized across the network.
DSMERGE	Used to merge roots of separate directory service trees.
CDROM	Enables a CD-ROM attached to the server to be shared.
KEYB	Enables keyboards for different languages to be used at the server console.
SERVMAN	Enables the configuration of SET, SPX/IPX, and other server parameters.
SCHDELAY	Enables priortization of server processes. You can use this to increase the scheduling delay of processes.

The DOMAIN NLM

The DOMAIN NLM uses the ring protection architecture of the Intel 80x86 processor family to create memory domains. Figure 7.56 shows the Intel ring architecture and how it is used by NetWare 4.x OS. The NetWare OS kernel runs in ring 0, the most privileged mode of the processor. Running an untested or mal-functioning NLM in this ring could crash the server.

Figure 7.56

Intel ring architecture and NetWare 4.x.

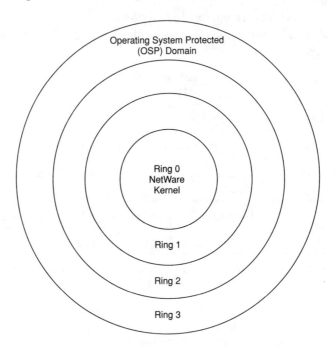

Using the ring architecture of the Intel 80386 processors, the untested NLMs can be run in an outer ring such as ring 3. NLMs in this ring obtain services from the kernel through a protected inter-ring gate call mechanism, which prevents direct access to the ring 0 memory. A small overhead is associated with the inter-gate calls, so NLMs running in a protected domain run slower than they would if they ran in ring 0 (kernel or unprotected domain). On the other hand, misbehaved NLMs running in a protected domain are prevented from altering the operating system environment.

To enable the protected OS domain capability, you must run the DOMAIN.NLM. The syntax for running the DOMAIN NLM, assuming that it is on the NLM search path, is

```
LOAD DOMAIN [/R 1 ¦ 2 ¦ 3]
```

When you run the command

```
LOAD DOMAIN
```

the protected domain is set up in the default ring of 3. You can use the /R n option to load the domain in ring number n, where n is 1, 2, or 3. Thus, to set up a protected domain using ring 2, the command is

```
LOAD DOMAIN /R 2
```

You must check your version of NetWare 4.x to see if domain support for a ring other than ring 3 is available.

The DOMAIN.NLM must be loaded before loading any other NLM, such as MONITOR or INSTALL. Once the DOMAIN loads, other domain-specific commands become available. These are described in table 7.11.

Table 7.11
Domain Commands

Domain Command	Description
DOMAIN	Displays the current domain and the modules in the current domain. Modules in other domains also are listed.
DOMAIN HELP	Displays help information on DOMAIN.
DOMAIN RING=n	Changes the OSP domain to ring n.
DOMAIN=*domain_name*	Changes current domain. *domain_name* can be OS (ring 0) or OS_PROTECTED (the ring where OSP is established). Use this command preceding any NLMs that you want to load.

When the DOMAIN NLM is loaded, you can use the command DOMAIN=OS or DOMAIN=OS_PROTECTED to change the current domain to the OS domain (ring 0) or the protected domain. NLMs loaded from the LOAD command are loaded in the current domain, so you can use this DOMAIN command to load the NLMs in the OS or OS_PROTECTED domain. The keyword OS_PROTECTED can be abbreviated to OSP. You can type DOMAIN=OSP rather than the longer DOMAIN=OS_PROTECTED command.

Figure 7.57 shows the effect of running the DOMAIN command on the top part of the screen. When the command DOMAIN is run, a list of NLMs in the domain is reported (see fig. 7.58). Figure 7.58 reports that the current domain is OS and that this is ring 0. The OS_PROTECTED domain is ring 3. All NLMs are loaded in ring 0. These include the REMOTE.NLM and the RSPX.NLM that were loaded after the LOAD DOMAIN command (see fig. 7.57).

Figure 7.57

The LOAD DOMAIN command.

```
NW4CS:LOAD DOMAIN
Loading module DOMAIN.NLM
   NetWare Domain Protection
   Version 4.01    June 14, 1993
   Copyright 1993 Novell, Inc.  All rights reserved.
   1348 RPC descriptions loaded from DOMAIN.NLM.
NW4CS:LOAD REMOTE XYZZY
Loading module REMOTE.NLM
   NetWare Remote Console
   Version 4.01    June 21, 1993
   Copyright 1993 Novell, Inc.  All rights reserved.
NW4CS:LOAD RSPX
Loading module RSPX.NLM
   NetWare Remote Console SPX Driver
   Version 4.01    June 21, 1993
   Copyright 1993 Novell, Inc.  All rights reserved.

10-10-93  2:07:06 pm:    RSPX-4.1-28
     Remote console connection granted for 000E8022:0000C0664E19

NW4CS:
```

To load the EDIT.NLM in the protected domain, you must issue the following command:

```
DOMAIN=OS_PROTECTED
```

Figure 7.59 shows the effect of executing the preceding command. Notice that the status message shows that the current domain is OS_PROTECTED. Next, you can load the EDIT NLM:

```
LOAD EDIT
```

```
NW4CS:DOMAIN
 Domain "OS" in ring 0 is the current domain.
        NetWare Remote Console SPX Driver
        NetWare Remote Console
        NetWare OS Loader
        Protected Alloc Memory
        NetWare ISA Device Driver
        NetWare Directory Services (290)
        Time Synchronization Services
        Novell Generic Media Support Module
        Novell Ethernet Topology Support Module
        SMC EtherCard PLUS Server Driver v4.16 (930503)
        NetWare Domain Protection
        NetWare Server Operating System
 Domain "OS_PROTECTED" in ring 3.
NW4CS:
```

Figure 7.58

The DOMAIN command.

```
NW4CS:DOMAIN
 Domain "OS" in ring 0 is the current domain.
        NetWare NLM Utility User Interface
        NetWare Remote Console SPX Driver
        NetWare Remote Console
        NetWare OS Loader
        Protected Alloc Memory
        NetWare ISA Device Driver
        NetWare Directory Services (290)
        Time Synchronization Services
        Novell Generic Media Support Module
        Novell Ethernet Topology Support Module
        SMC EtherCard PLUS Server Driver v4.16 (930503)
        NetWare Domain Protection
        NetWare Server Operating System
 Domain "OS_PROTECTED" in ring 3.
NW4CS:DOMAIN=OS_PROTECTED
Current Loader Domain is OS_PROTECTED
NW4CS:
```

Figure 7.59

The DOMAIN= OS_PROTECTED command.

Figure 7.60 shows that the EDIT NLM was loaded successfully. Figure 7.61 shows a list of NLMs in the different domains obtained using the DOMAIN command. Notice that the current domain (OS_PROTECTED in this case) is listed first and reports that it contains the NetWare Text Editor NLM (EDIT.NLM).

Figure 7.60

Successful load
of EDIT in
OS_PROTECTED
command.

```
NW4CS:DOMAIN
 Domain "OS" in ring 0 is the current domain.
          NetWare NLM Utility User Interface
          NetWare Remote Console SPX Driver
          NetWare Remote Console
          NetWare OS Loader
          Protected Alloc Memory
          NetWare ISA Device Driver
          NetWare Directory Services (290)
          Time Synchronization Services
          Novell Generic Media Support Module
          Novell Ethernet Topology Support Module
          SMC EtherCard PLUS Server Driver v4.16 (930503)
          NetWare Domain Protection
          NetWare Server Operating System
 Domain "OS_PROTECTED" in ring 3.
NW4CS:DOMAIN=OS_PROTECTED
Current Loader Domain is OS_PROTECTED
NW4CS:LOAD EDIT
Loading module EDIT.NLM
  NetWare Text Editor
  Version 4.00c   May 6, 1993
  Copyright 1993 Novell, Inc.  All rights reserved.
NW4CS:
```

Figure 7.61

The EDIT NLM in
OS_PROTECTED
domain.

```
NW4CS:DOMAIN=OS_PROTECTED
Current Loader Domain is OS_PROTECTED
NW4CS:LOAD EDIT
Loading module EDIT.NLM
  NetWare Text Editor
  Version 4.00c   May 6, 1993
  Copyright 1993 Novell, Inc.  All rights reserved.
NW4CS:DOMAIN
 Domain "OS_PROTECTED" in ring 3 is the current domain.
          NetWare Text Editor
 Domain "OS" in ring 0.
          NetWare NLM Utility User Interface
          NetWare Remote Console SPX Driver
          NetWare Remote Console
          NetWare OS Loader
          Protected Alloc Memory
          NetWare ISA Device Driver
          NetWare Directory Services (290)
          Time Synchronization Services
          Novell Generic Media Support Module
          Novell Ethernet Topology Support Module
          SMC EtherCard PLUS Server Driver v4.16 (930503)
          NetWare Domain Protection
          NetWare Server Operating System
NW4CS:
```

The DSREPAIR NLM

The DSREPAIR utility is used to correct problems with the
NetWare Directory Service database, such as unknown object-type
objects, or corrupted NDS objects. It also repairs NDS records,
schema, bindery object representations in the NDS, and external
references to other X.500 directories. The syntax of using
DSREPAIR is as follows:

```
LOAD DSREPAIR  [=U]  [-L logfilename]
```

The =U and -L options are optional. The =U option specifies that DSREPAIR should be run in the unattended mode without any user intervention. The -L option can be used to specify a file name *logfilename*, where errors are to be logged. The default error log file is SYS:SYSTEM\DSREPAIR.LOG.

 Note The default error log file used by DSREPAIR is SYS:SYSTEM\DSREPAIR.LOG.

Figure 7.62 shows the options when DSREPAIR is loaded. You can run the DSREPAIR.NLM in the unattended full repair mode by selecting the Unattended full repair option. This is the simplest mode for running DSREPAIR. Figure 7.63 shows the status messages being generated for the unattended full repair option. At the end of the DSREPAIR session, the repair log is displayed (see fig. 7.64). You can select the Time synchronization and Replica synchronization options to perform the indicated tasks.

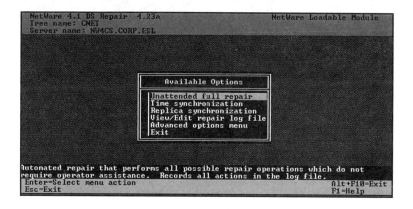

Figure 7.62

The DSREPAIR main screen.

Figure 7.63

Status messages generated when DSREPAIR is being run.

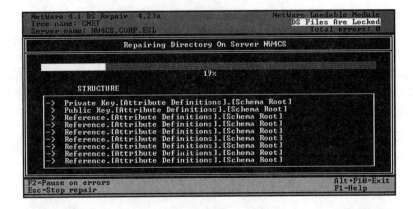

Figure 7.64

The DSREPAIR repair log.

If you select the Advanced options menu, you will see a list of advanced configuration choices (see fig 7.65). A useful option is the Create a database dump file that copies the NDS database in a compressed form in the DSREPAIR.DIB file that can be used for offline repairs (see fig. 7.66).

The RTDM NLM

The RTDM NLM is used to enable support for data migration. The syntax for loading RTDM is as follows:

```
LOAD RTDM
```

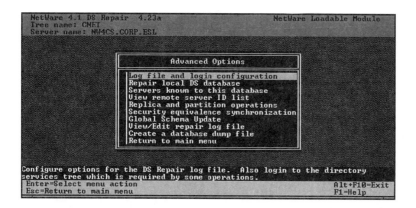

Figure 7.65

DSREPAIR Advanced Options.

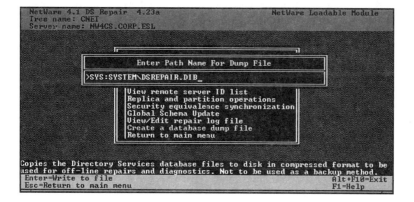

Figure 7.66

DSREPAIR—Create a database dump file option.

RTDM is the enabling module that manages the movement of data from one media type to another in a user-transparent fashion. You still need the near-line storage hardware and the drivers from the manufacturer to implement data migration.

Data migration is a feature of NetWare 4.x that permits data that has not been used in a defined period of time to be migrated to secondary storage devices.

Data migration is implemented using High Capacity Storage System (HCSS). HCSS is a storage and retrieval system that can extend the capacity of a NetWare server by integrating optical libraries into the NetWare file system. HCSS can work in conjunction with data migration so that migrated files can be moved from the faster but lower-capacity NetWare volumes to the slower but higher-capacity media that comprises the HCSS.

As far as the user is concerned, the operation of data migration and HCSS is transparent. Files that have been migrated to the HCSS are accessed with the same commands as files that reside on the NetWare volume. If a migrated file is accessed, it is automatically de-migrated.

Migration is performed on an individual file basis depending on the last time the file was accessed. This is called the least recently used criteria and the current volume usage. Least recently used criteria for files refers to files that are the least active, or that have not been accessed for the longest amount of time. If the current volume usage exceeds a capacity threshold, data migration occurs. Capacity threshold is defined as the percentage of the server's disk that is used before data migration begins.

Migration enables high capacity secondary devices to be treated as a logical extension of the server's disk storage. A volume's effective storage appears to be much larger than it really is. When data that is stored on near-line storage devices is needed, it is brought back in (de-migrated). If the data is not in use for a predefined interval of time, it is migrated back to near-line storage.

The NWSNUT NLM

The NWSNUT NLM provides the NLM Utility User Interface. It is a library NLM that exports its functions to other NLMs. It implements the server console display routines that have the look and feel of the C-Worthy libraries that are used for the workstation utilities. Management utilities like MONITOR and INSTALL make use of this library to provide a consistent, menu-driven user interface. The syntax for loading NWSNUT is as follows:

```
LOAD NWSNUT
```

NWSNUT is autoloaded by many of the modules that need its services.

For compatibility with NetWare 3.x NLMs, the NUT.NLM is provided. Normally, you do not need to worry about this NLM because it is autoloaded by the NetWare 3.x NLMs.

The TIMESYNC NLM

The TIMESYNC NLM is used to monitor the internal network time on the server and use information on time obtained from other time servers to synchronize the server time. This NLM is autoloaded whenever the NetWare server is started.

When TIMESYNC loads, it reads a file called SYS:SYSTEM\TIMESYNC.CFG that contains the time configuration parameters. These parameters can also be set by the SET commands or the SERVMAN utility. The time parameter can also be specified as an argument to TIMESYNC NLM. The general syntax for activating TIMESYNC.NLM is as follows:

```
LOAD TIMESYNC [timeParameters]
```

where *timeParameters* are the time parameters for the TIMESYNC NLM.

The DSMERGE NLM

The DSMERGE NLM is used to merge the roots of two separate NDS trees into one single tree. Remember that information between separate NDS trees (trees that have separate roots) cannot be directly shared. It may be desirable to merge the trees to share this information.

Normally, the network NDS tree should be designed beforehand so that this merger is not needed. But in the case of unforeseen events, such as corporate mergers, it may be desirable to have a single NDS tree.

You use a tool such as SBACKUP to back up the NDS database on the two trees before attempting the directory merge. The general syntax for loading DSMERGE is as follows:

```
LOAD DSMERGE
```

The preceding command should be run on the server that has the source tree that you are merging with the target tree. The objects in the source tree become part of the target tree. As a result of the DSMERGE operations, only the root objects are merged. Container objects and leaf objects maintain their identities under the newly merged root, which means that complete names of objects in the source and target trees should not change in the merged tree. You must make sure that containers at the same level in the source and target trees have unique names. If you have two containers in the separate trees that have conflicting names (same names) for a level of the tree, you cannot merge the trees. You can, however, move objects from one container into another container, delete the empty container, and then merge the trees.

In the DSMERGE utility,

◆ the objects in the source tree become part of the target tree.

◆ only the root objects are merged.

◆ container object names for the same level of the NDS tree have to be unique in the source and target trees.

The biggest conflict for unique names is at the Organization container level. Within two differently named Organization objects, it is possible to have Organizational Unit objects that have the same name. There is no conflict in this case. If the organization names in the source and target tree are different, following the suggestion of moving all objects to another container and then deleting the organization container is not a task for the faint-hearted (maybe a task for the foolhardy!). According to the NDS schema, the Rename right applies to leaf objects, not to container objects. So, Organization objects cannot be renamed, according to the current NDS definition.

Another issue concerning merging of NDS trees is that the time source for the two NDS trees must be coordinated. If an external time source is being used, both trees must have access to the external time source.

Additionally, make sure that all servers (repositories of NDS replicas) in the NDS trees are up and running before attempting DSMERGE.

When merging trees, merge the smaller tree with the larger tree for fewer problems and shorter merge times. That is, run DSMERGE on the server that has the smaller NDS database.

Also, the NDS schemas of the two trees must be the same for a merge to complete successfully.

The CDROM NLM

CD-ROM support is enabled by loading CDROM. Before doing so, you must ensure that the appropriate device drivers for your CD-ROM are running. As a precaution, you should ensure that DOS CD-ROM drivers are not loaded, because they conflict with NetWare 4.x CD-ROM drivers. For SCSI devices, you can load either ASPICD.DSK or CDNASPI.DSK. Because these drivers normally are placed in the C:\SERVER.40 directory, make sure you specify the correct path name. Alternatively, you can use the SEARCH ADD command as shown in the following:

```
SEARCH ADD C:\SERVER.40
LOAD CDNASPI
```

Figure 7.67 shows the result of loading the CDNASPI driver. The CD-ROM unit is the SONY CDU-541 and has the SCSI ID of 01. The disc drive is set to a SCSI ID of 0, and the tape drive (HP 35470A) has a SCSI ID of 1. The host bus adapter SCSI ID is 7. This ID is typical for CDs.

Figure 7.67

The LOAD CDNASPI command.

```
NW4KS:LOAD CDNASPI
Loading module CDNASPI.DSK
  Meridian Data NetWare 386 CDROM/ASPI Device Driver
  Version 2.00    June 16, 1993
  Copyright 1992 by Meridian Data, Inc. All rights reserved.
SERVER-4.00-1587:   This module is using 1 outdated API call
  You should upgrade to a newer module when it becomes available.

Meridian Data CDROM/ASPI Device Driver for NetWare 3.1x or Above, Version 2.00
Copyright 1992 by Meridian Data, Inc. All rights reserved.
Number of SCSI adapters installed: 1
Host adapter 0 is SCSI ID 7
SCSI ID: 00 is logical device 00 MICROP    1528-15MD1076301
SCSI ID: 01 is logical device 00 SONY      CD-ROM CDU-541
SCSI ID: 02 is logical device 01 HP        HP35470A
NW4KS:
```

You must next load the CDROM NLM. Figure 7.68 shows the effect of loading the CDROM driver. Notice that the CDROM NLM supports the ISO 9660 and the High Sierra format. The device is identified as device #1.

Figure 7.68

The LOAD CDROM command.

```
  Meridian Data NetWare 386 CDROM/ASPI Device Driver
  Version 2.00    June 16, 1993
  Copyright 1992 by Meridian Data, Inc. All rights reserved.
SERVER-4.00-1587:   This module is using 1 outdated API call
  You should upgrade to a newer module when it becomes available.

Meridian Data CDROM/ASPI Device Driver for NetWare 3.1x or Above, Version 2.00
Copyright 1992 by Meridian Data, Inc. All rights reserved.
Number of SCSI adapters installed: 1
Host adapter 0 is SCSI ID 7
SCSI ID: 00 is logical device 00 MICROP    1528-15MD1076301
SCSI ID: 01 is logical device 00 SONY      CD-ROM CDU-541
SCSI ID: 02 is logical device 01 HP        HP35470A
NW4KS:LOAD CDROM
Loading module CDROM.NLM
  Netware 4.xx ISO-9660 and High Sierra CD-Rom Support Module
  Version 4.02    June 28, 1993
  Copyright 1993 Novell, Inc.  All rights reserved.

10-10-93   6:37:31 pm:     SERVER-4.0-1355
    Device #  1 CDNET_DRIVE00 (A7000000) deactivated due to media dismount


For CD-ROM Support HELP enter 'cd help' on the command line.
NW4KS:
```

After the CDROM loads, a number of CD commands become available. For a list of these commands, type the following command:

`CD HELP`

Figure 7.69 shows the help screen for CD commands. Either of the CD DEVICE LIST or CD VOLUME LIST commands can be used to obtain the volume name or volume number. You need the volume name or number to mount the CD. Figures 7.70 and 7.71 show the effects of executing the CD DEVICE LIST and the CD VOLUME LIST commands.

```
CD-ROM NLM Command Line Options:
   CD DEVICE LIST
   CD VOLUME LIST
   CD MOUNT [No.] [volume name] ('/mac' or '/nfs', '/G=x' or '/R')
   CD DISMOUNT [No.] [volume name]
   CD CHANGE [No.] [volume name] ('/mac' or '/nfs', '/G=x' or '/R')
   CD DIR [No.] [volume name]
   CD GROUP ([group name] and [group num])
   CD HELP

The [volume name] can be obtained from the first 2 options.
The [No.] can be obtained from the first 2 options.
The '/mac' is used to add Macintosh Name Space Support.
The '/nfs' is used to add NFS Name Space Support.
The '/G=x' is used to set the default volume group access rights.
The 'x' is the number listed from the GROUP Command.
The [group name] is to add a group name ('del' as name will remove group name).
The [group num] is used to add a new group name to the group access list (1-9).
The '/R' is used to reuse the created data file on the 'SYS' Volume.
The '/Z' is used to remove any file with a file length of zero.

When mounting or changing a CD-ROM disc a deactivation of the selected device
will occur.   Do not be alarmed.
NW4KS:
```

Figure 7.69

The CD HELP command.

```
NW4KS:CD DEVICE LIST

r** CD ROM Device List
No. Act. Device Name                                      Volume Name    Mounted
 1   Y   Device # 1 CDNET_DRIVE00 (A7000000)              NETWARE_40       N

NW4KS:
NW4KS:
```

Figure 7.70

The CD DEVICE LIST command.

```
NW4KS:cd volume list

r** CD ROM Volume List
No. Volume Name        Mounted Device Name
 1  NETWARE_40            N    Device # 1 CDNET_DRIVE00 (A7000000)

NW4KS:
```

Figure 7.71

The CD VOLUME LIST command.

The next step is to mount the CD by using the following:

```
CD MOUNT volumename
```

or

```
CD MOUNT volumenumber
```

where *volumename* and *volumenumber* were obtained from the CD DEVICE LIST or the CD VOLUME LIST command.

Figure 7.72 shows the INSTALL screen that shows the mounted CD-ROM volume. Its default block size is 64 KB, and file compression, block suballocation, and data migration are turned to Off because they do not apply to a read-only volume. From the screen, you can see that the CD-ROM volume name is NETWARE_40. So, to map a drive H to this volume, you use the following command:

```
MAP H:=NETWARE_40:
```

Figure 7.72

The Volume Information showing the mounted CD-ROM volume.

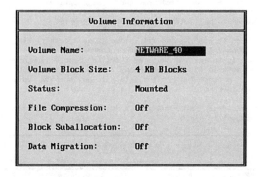

```
                  Volume Information
    Volume Name:           NETWARE_40
    Volume Block Size:     4 KB Blocks
    Status:                Mounted
    File Compression:      Off
    Block Suballocation:   Off
    Data Migration:        Off
```

When the CD-ROM is mounted, a special data file is written to the root directory on the server's SYS: volume that contains information that was used to mount the volume. You can use this file to reduce the mount time, if you need to remount the CD-ROM volume. You can use the /R switch with the CD MOUNT command to specify that the special file will be used during the re-mount process. Thus, to remount a volume, you can use the following command:

```
CD MOUNT /R
```

Because CD-ROM is a removable media, a special command called the CD CHANGE command can be used to change the CD-ROM. Typing the command

```
CD CHANGE volume
```

where *volume* is the volume name or volume number of the new disc, causes the system to prompt you to remove the current CD-ROM disc, install a new CD-ROM disc, and mount the new CD-ROM disc.

You can use any of the other CD-ROM options (such as /MAC, /NFS, /G) with the CD CHANGE option.

The /MAC option can be used with the CD MOUNT or CD CHANGE command to specify that the CD-ROM disc contains a Macintosh file system, and it should be mounted as a Macintosh file system. You can access this file system from a Macintosh workstation if you have NetWare for Macintosh running at the NetWare server.

The /NFS option can be used with the CD MOUNT or CD CHANGE command to specify that the CD-ROM disc contains a Unix file system and should be mounted as a Unix file system. You can access this file system from a Unix workstation if you have NetWare for NFS running at the NetWare server.

You can use the Group Access (/G) option with the CD MOUNT or CD CHANGE command to grant users controlled access to the CD-ROM volume. To grant controlled access, you must create an NDS group object in the same context as the server to which the CD-ROM device is attached. You can assign membership to this group. Then, you can use the CD GROUP command at the server console to assign access to this group. If you created a group object called CDUSERS, you could then give access to this group by using the following command:

```
CD GROUP CDUSERS 1
```

The preceding command registers CDUSERS as a group that can use the CD-ROM and assigns it a group number of 1. It also displays a list of currently registered groups, including the group you just registered. The group numbers can be from 0 to 9. Group 0 is by default assigned to group EVERYONE. To use group 0 with group EVERYONE, you must create a group object called EVERYONE, because this group does not exist by default in NDS. You also have the option of assigning group 0 to any other group object name.

You can use the CD DIR command to list the files in the CD-ROM. This command is particularly useful if you want to quickly determine whether the CD-ROM contains the files that you need.

To see a directory listing in the root directory for volume number 1 with name NETWARE_40, for instance, you can use the following:

```
CD DIR  1
```

or

```
CD DIR NETWARE_40
```

To dismount a volume, you can use the CD DISMOUNT command. To dismount volume number 1 with name NETWARE_40, for example, you can use the following:

```
CD DISMOUNT  1
```

or

```
CD DISMOUNT NETWARE_40
```

To see a list of groups registered with the CD-ROM, use the following command:

```
CD GROUP
```

To remove access to the CD-ROM from a specific group, use the following command:

```
CD GROUP DEL groupnumber
```

To remove the group CDUSERS that was assigned group number 1, for example, you can use the following command:

```
CD GROUP DEL 1
```

When access is granted to the CD-ROM, the users by default are given Read and File Scan ([R F]) access to the entire volume. Because the CD-ROM is a read-only volume, other NetWare file system rights such as Supervisor, Create, Write, Modify, and Access Control are not possible.

Once the CD group numbers are assigned, you can use the following:

```
CD MOUNT volume /G=groupnumber
```

To assign group 5, called READERS, access to the CD-ROM volume BOOKS, for example, you use the following:

```
LOAD CDROM
CD GROUP READERS 5
CD MOUNT BOOKS /G=5
```

If the BOOKS CD-ROM was to be mounted on volume 1, you could use the following:

```
CD MOUNT 1 /G=5
```

The KEYB NLM and International Language Support

The KEYB NLM is used to change the keyboard type for a specific language for the server console. The general syntax of the command is

```
LOAD KEYB [parameter]
```

where *parameter* is one of the following countries:

United States

United Kingdom

France

Germany

Italy

Spain

Figure 7.73 shows the effect of loading KEYB without a parameter. A brief help on the different keyboard types that are supported is presented. Figure 7.74 shows the effect of loading the keyboard of the locale France. The keyboard support for France implemented by code page 437 is loaded. This code page provides the translation to the characters used by keyboards for France. An example of the effect produced by this command on United States keyboards is that the keys Q and A are exchanged. That is, for the United States keyboard, if you press the key Q the letter A is displayed, and if you press the key A, the letter Q is displayed.

Figure 7.73

The LOAD KEYB command.

```
NW4KS:LOAD KEYB
Loading module KEYB.NLM
  NetWare National Keyboard Support
  Version 1.02    July 9, 1993
  Copyright 1993 Novell, Inc.  All rights reserved.
  Debug symbol information for KEYB.NLM loaded

Usage: Load KEYB <Keyboard Name>
Valid keyboards: United States
                 Germany
                 France
                 Italy
                 Spain

SERVER-4.00-1135:  Module initialization failed.
  Module KEYB.NLM NOT loaded
NW4KS:
```

Figure 7.74

The LOAD KEYB FRANCE command.

```
NW4KS:LOAD KEYB FRANCE
Loading module KEYB.NLM
  NetWare National Keyboard Support
  Version 1.02    July 9, 1993
  Copyright 1993 Novell, Inc.  All rights reserved.
  Debug symbol information for KEYB.NLM loaded

Keyboard support for France, code page 437 loaded

NW4KS:
```

The SCHDELAY NLM

The SCHDELAY NLM is used to prioritize server processes. Its primary purpose is to increase the scheduling delay for processes. This technique can reduce server CPU utilization if it is too high.

The general syntax for this NLM is as follows:

```
LOAD SCHDELAY [processName = number]
```

where *processName* is the name of the process and *number* is the amount of delay.

Loading SCHDELAY without any parameters shows the list of processes that are running and their current delay values (see fig. 7.75), which are 0 in this case. To increase the delay of the Media Manager process to 5, use the following command:

```
LOAD SCHDELAY MEDIA MANAGER=5
```

```
NW4KS:LOAD SCHDELAY
Loading module SCHDELAY.NLM
   NetWare 386 Scheduling Delay Control
   Version 1.02     February 1, 1993
   Copyright 1993 Novell, Inc.  All rights reserved.
   Debug symbol information for SCHDELAY.NLM loaded

   Process Name          Sch Delay
   ------------          ---------
RSPX                         0
Remote                       0
Console Command              0
TimeSyncMain                 0
Directory Service            0
Remirror                     0
Media Manager                0
Sync Clock Event             0
MakeThread                   0
NW4KS:
```

Figure 7.75

The LOAD SCHDELAY command.

Figure 7.76 shows the effect of executing the previous command. To change the delay for a particular process to 0 (no delay), use the following command:

LOAD SCHDELAY processName = 0

```
NW4KS:LOAD SCHDELAY MEDIA MANAGER=5
Loading module SCHDELAY.NLM
   NetWare 386 Scheduling Delay Control
   Version 1.02     February 1, 1993
   Copyright 1993 Novell, Inc.  All rights reserved.
   Debug symbol information for SCHDELAY.NLM loaded

   Setting "Media Manager" Scheduling Delay to 5.
NW4KS:
```

Figure 7.76

The LOAD SCHDELAY MEDIA MANAGER command.

To change the delay for all processes to 0 (no delay), use the following command:

LOAD SCHDELAY ALL PROCESSES = 0

You also can control the scheduling delay using MONITOR. Figure 7.77 shows the screen displayed when you select Scheduling Information from the Available Options in MONITOR. Notice that the scheduling delay for Media Manager is 5 from the command executed in figure 7.76. You can increase or decrease the scheduling delay by highlighting the process name and using the + or - keys.

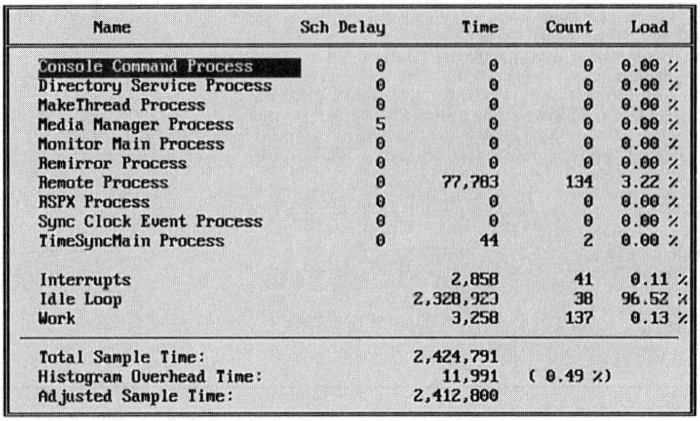

Figure 7.77

Scheduling Information in MONITOR.

Name	Sch Delay	Time	Count	Load
Console Command Process	0	0	0	0.00 %
Directory Service Process	0	0	0	0.00 %
MakeThread Process	0	0	0	0.00 %
Media Manager Process	5	0	0	0.00 %
Monitor Main Process	0	0	0	0.00 %
Remirror Process	0	0	0	0.00 %
Remote Process	0	77,783	134	3.22 %
RSPX Process	0	0	0	0.00 %
Sync Clock Event Process	0	0	0	0.00 %
TimeSyncMain Process	0	44	2	0.00 %
Interrupts		2,858	41	0.11 %
Idle Loop		2,328,923	38	96.52 %
Work		3,258	137	0.13 %
Total Sample Time:		2,424,791		
Histogram Overhead Time:		11,991	(0.49 %)	
Adjusted Sample Time:		2,412,800		

Learning Strategies for Protecting the NetWare Server

The NetWare console does not provide direct access to the NetWare file system such as commands to copy, erase, view contents, and move files. However, the EDIT.NLM can be used to view the contents of text files. In general, it is desirable to restrict access to the server machine. This goal can be accomplished by using any of the following:

◆ Controlling physical access to the server by locking up the server, or keeping the server in an area accessible to designated users only

◆ Using the SECURE CONSOLE command, which does the following:

   ◆ Removes DOS from the server

   ◆ Prevents keyboard entry into the internal debugger

   ◆ Permits only console operators to modify server date and time

   ◆ Permits only NLMs in the SYS:SYSTEM path to be loaded

◆ Selecting the Lock File Server Console option from MONITOR

714

Study Guide for the Chapter

If you are preparing for the NetWare 4.x Administration exams, review the chapter with the following goals:

1. Understand and identify all the new capabilities in NetWare 4.x. Use the Study Notes as a quick review.

2. Comprehend memory protection, NDS services, and enhanced client services. Understand how the server can be managed under different scenarios.

3. After studying this chapter, attempt the sample test questions. If you miss the answer to a question, review the appropriate topic until you understand the reason for the correct answer.

Chapter Summary

In this chapter you have learned about NLMs and their role on a NetWare 4.x server. You also learned about the different types of server console commands and the NLMs used to manage the server. You were presented with a brief overview of SERVMAN and MONITOR NLMs and how to configure Remote Console at the server.

Chapter Test Questions

Test questions are either single choice or multiple choice. Where a single answer is desired, this is indicated by a ○. Some questions require you to select more than one answer; this is indicated by the □ preceding each answer. Certain questions are repeated in different ways, so that you can recognize them even when the wording is different. Taking practice quizzes not only tests your knowledge, but it also gives you confidence when you take your exam.

1. The console command for obtaining help on NetWare 4.x console commands is _____.

   ○ A. ?

   ○ B. HELP

   ○ C. HELP CONSOLE

   ○ D. HELPCMD

2. Which server console command is used to restart a downed server?

   ○ A. MEDIA

   ○ B. MAGAZINE

   ○ C. RESTART SERVER

   ○ D. REBOOT

   ○ E. LANGUAGE

   ○ F. KEYB

3. Which server console command allows the NLMs to use language-specific message files?

   ○ A. LANGSET

   ○ B. SET LANGUAGE

   ○ C. RESTART SERVER

   ○ D. REBOOT

   ○ E. LANGUAGE

   ○ F. KEYB

4. To restart a downed server and prevent execution of the STARTUP.NCF file, the command is _____.

   ○ A. RESTART SERVER -NA

   ○ B. RESTART SERVER -N=AUTOEXEC.NCF

   ○ C. RESTART SERVER -N=STARTUP.NCF

    ○ D. RESTART SERVER -NS

    ○ E. RESTART SERVER -I

    ○ F. RESTART SERVER -D

5. The Language Message files can be installed using _____.

    ○ A. INSTALL NLM

    ○ B. MONITOR NLM

    ○ C. SERVMAN NLM

    ○ D. LANGUAGE NLM

    ○ E. ADDLANG NLM

6. Which control key invokes the RCONSOLE menu?

    ○ A. Alt+F1

    ○ B. Alt+F2

    ○ C. Alt+F3

    ○ D. Alt+F4

    ○ E. Alt+F5

7. Which control key in the RCONSOLE program displays the workstation address?

    ○ A. Alt+F1

    ○ B. Alt+F2

    ○ C. Alt+F3

    ○ D. Alt+F4

    ○ E. Alt+F5

8. Which control keys in the RCONSOLE program can be used to scroll through console screens?

    ☐ A. Alt+F1

    ☐ B. Alt+F2

☐ C. Alt+F3

☐ D. Alt+F4

☐ E. Alt+F5

9. Which NLM creates a protected domain for running NLMs?

○ A. DSREPAIR

○ B. DOMAIN

○ C. DOMPROT

○ D. OSP

10. Which NLM supports the Real Time Data Migration feature?

○ A. MEMPOOL

○ B. MIGRATE

○ C. RTDM

○ D. RTM

11. Which NLM can be used to merge roots of two NDS trees?

○ A. MERGEDS

○ B. DSMERGE

○ C. DSCOMB

○ D. DSCON

○ E. PARTMGR

12. Which NLM provides CD-ROM support?

○ A. CDROM

○ B. CD_ROM

○ C. CD-ROM

○ D. CDLIB

○ E. LIBCD

13. Which NLM can be used to view or modify SET parameters?

    ○ A. SERVMAN

    ○ B. MONITOR

    ○ C. INSTALL

    ○ D. KEYB

    ○ E. SET

14. Which of the following could be used to display SET parameters?

    ☐ A. SERVMAN

    ☐ B. MONITOR

    ☐ C. INSTALL

    ☐ D. KEYB

    ☐ E. SET

15. Which NLM needs to be loaded to enable the DOMAIN commands?

    ○ A. DOMAIN

    ○ B. RING

    ○ C. DOMLIB

    ○ D. PROTECT

16. What command is used to change the protected domain to ring 2?

    ○ A. DOMAIN=2

    ○ B. DOMAIN PROTECT=2

    ○ C. DOMAIN PROTECT RING=2

    ○ D. DOMAIN RING=2

    ○ E. DOMAIN /R 2

17. What command is used to change the current domain to the operating system domain?

    ○ A. DOMAIN OS =ON

    ○ B. DOMAIN=OS

    ○ C. DOMAIN=OS_PROTECTED

    ○ D. DOMAIN=NW

    ○ E. DOMAIN=OS_PROTECT

18. What command is used to change the current domain to the protected domain?

    ○ A. DOMAIN OS =PROTECT

    ○ B. DOMAIN=OS

    ○ C. DOMAIN=OS_PROTECTED

    ○ D. DOMAIN=NW

    ○ E. DOMAIN=OS_PROTECT

19. Which NLM allows repair of problems with the NDS database?

    ○ A. NDSREPAIR

    ○ B. VREPAIR

    ○ C. DSREPAIR

    ○ D. DIBREPAIR

20. The default error log file used by DSREPAIR is _____.

    ○ A. SYS:SYSTEM\DSLOG.TXT

    ○ B. SYS:SYSTEM\DS\DSLOG.TXT

    ○ C. SYS:SYSTEM\DS\DSREPAIR.LOG

    ○ D. SYS:SYSTEM\DSREPAIR.LOG

21. In the DSMERGE utility, _____.

   ○ A. the objects in the source tree become part of the target tree

   ○ B. the objects in the target tree become part of the source tree

   ○ C. containers in the source and target tree are merged

   ○ D. containers in the source and target tree are merged, and if there are duplicate container names the container in the target tree is renamed according to well-defined rules

22. Which option in MONITOR can be used to adjust the delay time for a task?

   ○ A. Connection Information

   ○ B. Scheduling Information

   ○ C. Lock Server Console

   ○ D. Resource Utilization

   ○ E. Delay Task

23. The NetWare console command to add additional name space is _____.

   ○ A. EXTEND SPACE

   ○ B. ADD NAME

   ○ C. EXTEND NAME SPACE

   ○ D. EXTEND NAMES

   ○ E. ADD NAME SPACE

24. Which command can be used to display configuration information on the server?

   ○ A. VOLUMES

   ○ B. SHOW CONFIG

    ○ C. CONFIG

    ○ D. LOAD CONFIG

25. Which command can be used to clear the server console screen?

    ○ A. CLEAR

    ○ B. CLS

    ○ C. CLEAR SCREEN

    ○ D. CLS SCREEN

26. What is the order of loading software for remote console support?

    ○ A. REMOTE.NLM, RSPX.NLM, REMOTE.EXE at workstation

    ○ B. RSPX.NLM, REMOTE.NLM, REMOTE.EXE at workstation

    ○ C. RS232.NLM, REMOTE.NLM, REMOTE.EXE at workstation

    ○ D. REMOTE.EXE at workstation, RS232.NLM, REMOTE.NLM

8

CHAPTER

Configuring NetWare 4.x Printing

This chapter describes the printing concepts used in NetWare 4.x and the basic components of network printing. You will learn how to create and configure Print objects. The properties of Print objects such as Print Queue, Printer, and Print Server objects are described in detail. The critical properties needed to configure these objects to provide network printing are discussed. The tools used for network print configuration are also discussed, and you are presented with a guided tour of print configuration. You are also presented with different methods used to print jobs to a network printer.

Understanding Network Printing Concepts

NetWare allows you to share printers with several users. Configuring a network printer requires that you understand how network printing works and the basic terms that are used to describe network printing.

When an application on a NetWare workstation prints, or when you use an explicit network command such as the NPRINT (Network Print) command, the data that is sent to a network printer is called a *print job*. The nature of printers is such that they can print only a single print job at a time. This is usually not a problem for single user stations that are not connected to the network and print to a local printer, because there is usually only one outstanding print job to be printed.

On a network, workstations can send print jobs to a shared network printer. Print jobs are temporarily stored in an area on a server volume called the *print queue*. The characteristics of this print queue are modeled by the NDS Print Queue object. Each print job contains information identifying the owner of the print job, the time it was submitted, the number of copies to print, and so on. The information about a print job and how it is to be printed is called the *print job configuration*.

One of the parameters in a print job configuration is the *form* parameter. A *form* is a logical description of the type of paper in the printer and is identified by a *form name* and a *form number*. If you are using 8.5 × 11 inch printer paper, you can define a form for this type of printer paper. If you use other types of printer paper, such as for invoices or checks, you can define forms for them. The form definitions are created using the PRINTDEF utility or the NetWare Administrator.

A print job will print only if the form used in the print job configuration matches the form that is currently *mounted* on the printer. The NetWare print software keeps track of the form number that is currently being used on the printer. You can use tools such as PSC or PCONSOLE to change the currently mounted form on the printer. Using forms for print job configurations and keeping track of the current form on the printer ensures that a print job will be printed only on the desired type of printer paper.

Another parameter that you can specify in a print job configuration is the *print banner*. The print banner page contains information on the user, the file or data that is being printed, and so on. The purpose of the print banner page is to identify print jobs and to separate print jobs from different users.

When you install a NetWare 4.x server, it does not have a default network print service configuration. You have to explicitly configure print services to NetWare 4.x before you can use network printing. The primary tools to add print services are as follows:

◆ NetWare Administrator Utility (NWADMIN)

◆ PCONSOLE

Other support utilities such as PRINTDEF, PRINTCON, and PSC still exist in NetWare 4.x. Because much of the scope of this book is to describe only the differences between NetWare 3.x and NetWare 4.x, these tools are not described here.

The primary tools used for network print configuration are the NetWare Administrator and PCONSOLE.

To enable printing in NetWare 4.x, you need the following:

◆ Printers

◆ Print queues

◆ Print servers

Administrators of NetWare 4.x networks will recognize that these are the same concepts that were used with NetWare 3.x. The big difference here is that these components are objects in an NDS tree. The objects model physical and logical concepts. Thus the Printer object corresponds to the printer device attached to the network (directly or via a server or workstation). In NetWare 4.x you can submit a job to the Printer object. This is done by specifying the NDS name of the Printer object when printing a job. The Printer object contains a logical association with the Print Queue and Print Server object so that the job ends up being processed by the appropriate print server and ends up in the correct network queue.

The NDS object classes needed to configure network printing are Print Queue, Printer, and Print Server.

Figure 8.1 shows the physical components of network printing, and figure 8.2 shows the logical components as part of the NDS tree. Figure 8.1 shows that print jobs submitted by the workstation are processed by the print server and stored in a queue on a storage volume, then printed to a network printer. These physical print components are represented as objects in the NDS tree in figure 8.2. The print jobs are submitted by the user objects (User A and User B) to the printer object HP_PRINTER. Printer jobs can also be submitted to the print queue object HP_QUEUE, which is the traditional way printing is done in NetWare 3.x.

If an application does not understand the network Printer objects or Print Queue objects, the CAPTURE command can be used to redirect a local printer to a Printer object or Print Queue object. The CAPTURE command for NetWare 4.x contains appropriate options to support this mode of operation.

Figure 8.1

Physical components of network printing.

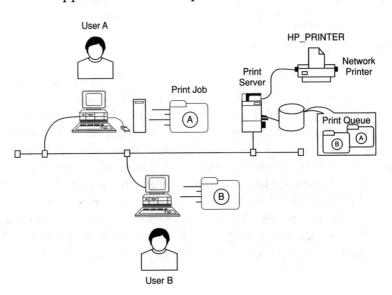

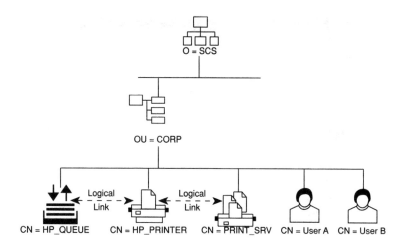

Figure 8.2

Logical (NDS) components of network printing.

Study Note

Throughout this chapter the term Print objects refers to network print-related NDS objects such as Print Queue, Printer, and Print Server objects.

Understanding the Print Queue Object

The Print Queue object is a logical representation of the physical print queue. The physical print queue is a directory on a storage volume where the print jobs are kept while they are waiting to be printed. The Print Queue object can be created using the NetWare Administrator or the PCONSOLE utility. The Print Queue object should be placed in the context in which it is most likely to be used. Figure 8.3 shows the NDS tree where the Print Queue object is placed in the O=SCS container. It is expected that users throughout the SCS organization will have access to the Print Queue object. This includes users in the departments CORP, ENG, and SALES, represented by the organizational unit containers. Figure 8.4 shows a Print Queue object in the OU=CORP.O=SCS container. The Print Queue object in this container is expected to be used by users of OU=CORP in the organization O=SCS.

Figure 8.3

The Print Queue object in an Organization container.

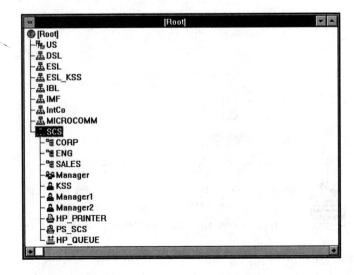

Figure 8.4

The Print Queue object in an Organizational Unit container.

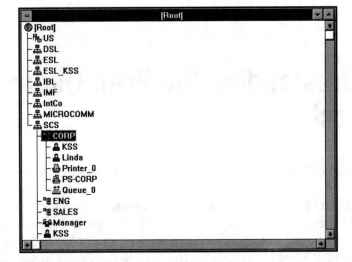

The Print Queue object is a logical representation of the physical print queue.

One of the properties of a Print Queue object is the physical location of the queue. This queue is always located on a storage volume that must be specified when the Print Queue object is created. The print queue is placed in a subdirectory of the QUEUES directory (see fig. 8.5). If the QUEUES directory does not exist at the time of creating the queue, it is automatically created.

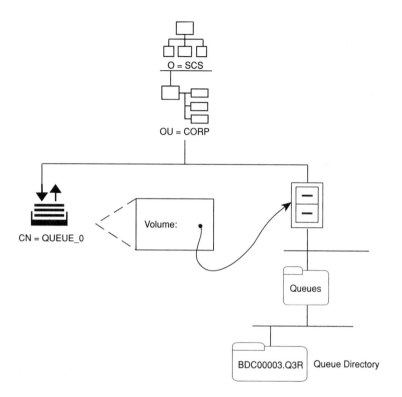

Figure 8.5

The Print Queue object and the QUEUES directory.

Study Note

The Volume property for a Print Queue object is mandatory. It describes the volume that will be used to hold print jobs waiting to be printed.

The print queue is placed as a subdirectory of the QUEUES directory.

Figure 8.6 shows the properties of the Print Queue object. Notice that the Volume property is set to CN=NW4CS_SYS.OU=CORP.O=ESL. The properties such as Other Names, Description, Location, Department, and Organization are not set when the queue is initially created via PCONSOLE. It is a good practice to set these values to a meaningful description of the Queue object.

Figure 8.6

Print Queue object
properties.

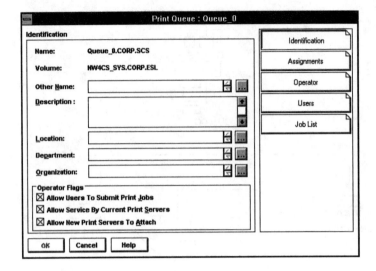

Figure 8.7 shows that the Queue_0 has the authorized print server
CN=PS-CORP.OU=CORP.O=SCS and the printer that services
this queue is CN=Printer_0.OU=CORP.O=SCS. This shows you
how the logical association to the Printer object and Print Server
object is made. The Operators property of the Print Queue object
is a list of users who can perform administrative tasks on the
queue.

Figure 8.7

Print queue
assignments.

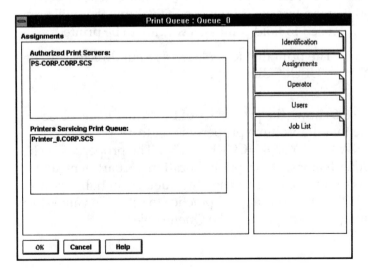

Figure 8.8 shows that the print queue operators are the creators of the print queue, CN=Admin.O=ESL, and the print server object, CN=PS-CORP.OU=CORP.O=ESL. The Users property of the queue consists of those users who can send print jobs to this queue. Figure 8.9 shows that these are the users CN=Admin.O=ESL and the container OU=CORP.O=SCS. Assigning a container to the Users property of the print queue means that all users within that container can send print jobs to the queue.

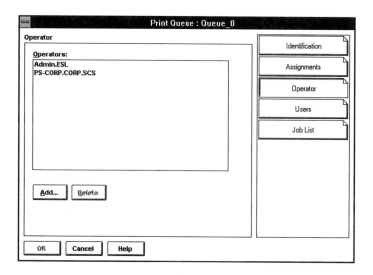

Figure 8.8

Print queue operators.

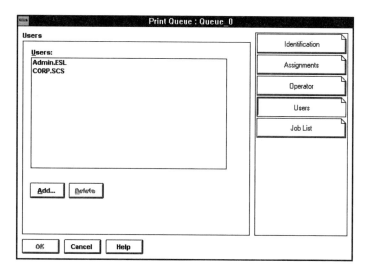

Figure 8.9

Print queue users.

Figure 8.10 shows the queue directories that were created
for the Queue objects CN=HP_QUEUE.O=SCS and
CN=Queue_0.OU=CORP.O=SCS.

Figure 8.10

Print queue
directories.

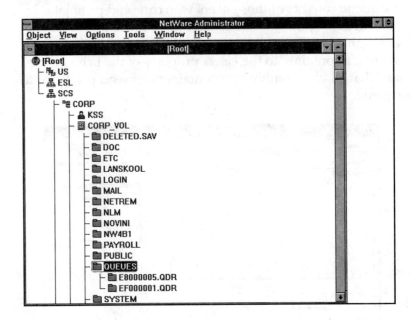

Study Note
Assigning a container object to the Users property
of the print queue means that all users within that
container can send print jobs to the queue.

From figures 8.7 through 8.10, you can tell that the Print Queue
object has the following important properties:

◆ **Volume property**

Used to describe the location of the physical print queue
directory.

◆ **Authorized Print Servers property**

List of print servers that are authorized to use the print
queue.

◆ **Printers Servicing Print Queue property**

List of printers that service the print queue.

◆ **Operators property**

List of users assigned to manage the queue.

◆ **Users property**

List of users that can print jobs to the queue.

The Job List property of the queue object can be used to view the print queue jobs (see figure 8.11). You can see that print jobs are assigned sequence numbers and a Job ID. The print job status, the name of the file being printed, and the form number used are also displayed.

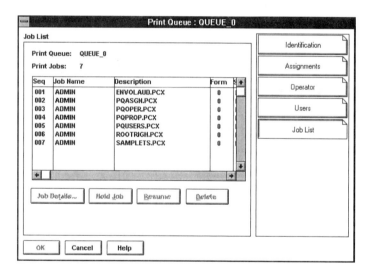

Figure 8.11

The Print Job List property.

 The Print Job List property of the Print Queue object can be used to view the print jobs in the queue.

The Printer Object

The Printer object is a logical representation of the physical printer. The physical printer can be directly connected to the network (if it has a network interface), or to a workstation or a file server. The Printer object can be created using the NetWare Administrator or the PCONSOLE utility. The Printer object should

733

be placed in the context in which it is most likely to be used. Figure 8.3 shows the NDS tree where the Printer object is placed in the O=SCS container. It is expected that users throughout the SCS organization will have access to the printer. This includes users in the departments CORP, ENG, and SALES, represented by the organization unit containers. Figure 8.4 shows a Printer object in the OU=CORP.O=SCS container. The Printer object in this container is expected to be used by users of OU=CORP in the organization O=SCS.

Figure 8.12 shows the properties of the Printer object. The Name property (Common Name) is the only property that is set on this screen. The other properties such as Other Names, Description, Location, Department, and Organization are not set when the queue is initially created. It is a good practice to set these values to a meaningful description of the Print Queue object.

Figure 8.12

Printer object properties.

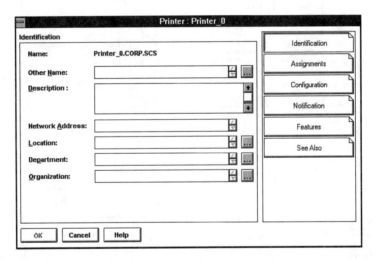

The Printer Features property, shown in figure 8.13, can be used to describe features specific to a Printer object such as the printer languages supported, amount of memory in the printer, and supported typefaces. This information can be accessed through NDS searches. For example, you could search for PostScript printers with at least 4 MB (4096 KB) of memory and the Futura font.

Figure 8.14 shows the assignments for Printer_0. The printer is assigned to the print server CN=PS-CORP.OU=CORP.O=SCS (see property Print Server), and the queue CN=Queue_0.OU=CORP.O= SCS is assigned to the Printer object (see property Print Queues). This shows you how the logical association to the Print Server object and Print Queue object is made. There can be several Print Queue objects assigned to the Printer object. One of the Print Queue objects is the Default object; if no specific Queue object is specified, the default print queue is used (see property Default Print Queue).

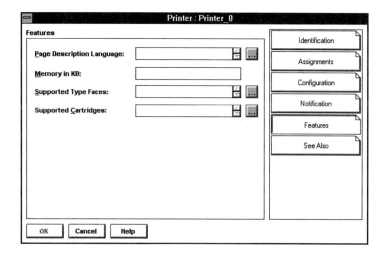

Figure 8.13
The Printer Features property.

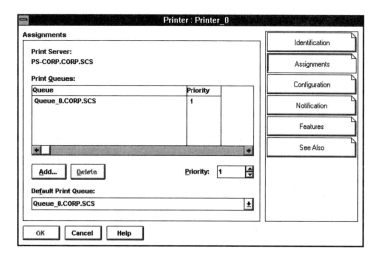

Figure 8.14
Printer assignments.

Figure 8.15 shows some of the configuration properties for the Printer object. This shows the printer type (LPT1, Parallel, Serial, AppleTalk, Unix, AIO, or XNP, for example).

Figure 8.15

Configuration properties for the Printer object.

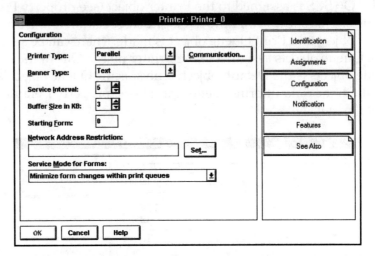

The AppleTalk printer type is used for configuring AppleTalk printers that use AppleTalk's Printer Access Protocol (PAP). If you select the AppleTalk printer type, you must also select the name by which the printer is known on the AppleTalk network (the AppleTalk *zone* name on which the printer is located). AppleTalk zones are used for logical partitioning of an AppleTalk network. A zone name value of * (asterisk) indicates any zone, and this is the default value. You can select either Hide Printer or Don't Hide Printer (the default). Hiding an AppleTalk printer prevents it from appearing on the Macintosh Chooser's list of available printers. In this case, Macintosh users cannot send print jobs to the Printer object directly; they must send the jobs to the queue associated with the printer.

The Unix printer type is used to print to a Unix printer attached to a Unix host. The Host Name field is used to enter the name of the Unix host to which the printer is connected. The NetWare server's SYS:ETC/HOSTS file should also contain an entry for the Unix host name and the Unix host's IP address. Additionally, the Unix host's /etc/hosts file should contain an entry for the NetWare server whose volume is being used to hold print queue jobs, or it should have a way of resolving the NetWare server's IP address using a name resolution protocol such as DNS (Domain Name System) or NIS (Network Information System). The Unix host's /etc/hosts.lpd file should also contain an entry for the NetWare server's host name. The Printer Name field should be set to the name of the Unix local printer. The NetWare NFS product can be used to provide printing between NetWare-based networks and Unix-based networks.

The AIO printer type is used for printers connected to an Asynchronous Communications Server using the AIO (Asynchronous Input/Output) protocol. You must follow the manufacturer's instructions for configuring this printer type.

The XNP printer type is used for configuring printers that use the Extended Network Printing protocol. You must follow the manufacturer's instructions for configuring this printer type.

The Banner Type can be Text or PostScript. The Text setting is used to print NetWare's standard print banner. If your printer uses the PostScript page description language, and you want your printer to print a PostScript banner, you can use the PostScript setting. PostScript is a special printer command language that can be used to provide graphics output. In the case of a banner page that has graphics described in a PostScript language, you should set the Banner Type to PostScript.

The Service Interval shows how often the print server checks the print queue for print jobs assigned to this printer. This can be a value from 1 second to 15 seconds. The default setting of 15 seconds works for most situations. Selecting a small value can increase the resources that the print server consumes (such as CPU utilization) when running at the server. In addition, if the print server and the volume object on which the network queue resides are not at the same server, network traffic is generated when the print server polls the queue. Decreasing the service interval will generate additional network traffic.

The Buffer Size represents how large each segment of print data sent to the printer can be. The buffer size can range from 3 KB to 255 KB and has a default value of 3 KB.

The Print Server maintains a buffer that holds the information that is sent for printing. This is different from the queue, which contains the entire print job to be printed. The print buffer holds the printing data just before it is sent for printing. If the printer seems to start and stop frequently while printing, you should increase the buffer size. Increasing the buffer size to a larger value than needed to accommodate printer data will result in an inefficient utilization of memory.

The Network Address Restrictions show the network address the printer can use. If the printer is not directly connected to the network, this is the network address of the workstation or the server the printer is connected to. The Network Address Restriction is a security feature and allows only a printer attached to a designated location to be used for printing. Without this capability, it is possible for any printer attached to the network to intercept print jobs. They can do this by running the NPRINTER program and supplying the NDS printer object name.

The restricted network address is an IPX address that consists of a network number and a node number. The network number is a four-byte (eight hexadecimal digits) number and is the cable number to which the server and the workstations are attached. This number is distinct from all other cabling segment numbers or the server's internal network numbers. The node number corresponds to the MAC (Media Access Control) address of the network boards inside a workstation or a server. The MAC address is burnt into the ROM on the network adapter for Ethernet and token ring networks but is manually set for ARCnet network adapters. You can obtain a network node's IPX address by using

```
NLIST  USER=login_name  SHOW "Network Address"
```

while logged in as user *login_name* to a workstation. Alternatively, you can use

```
NLIST USER /A  /S  /CO "[Root]"
```

to see workstation addresses of all logged in users in the NDS tree.

The Service Mode for Forms property is the policy for changing forms. It can be set to Starting Form and Service Mode for Forms. The Starting Form number is the form number that the print server assumes the printer has when the print server is started. The print server will use this form number for print jobs, and printing will occur normally until a print job calls for a different form number. The Service Mode for Forms can be set to any of the following values:

- ◆ Change Forms as Needed
- ◆ Minimize Form Changes across Print Queues
- ◆ Minimize Form Changes within Print Queues
- ◆ Service Only Currently Mounted Form

When Change Forms as Needed is selected, the print server will stop printing when a new print job requests a different form. The printing will stop unless the correct form is mounted. The print jobs will be printed according to their print queue priority, with higher priority print queues (highest queue priority is 1) being serviced before lower priority queues (lowest queue priority is 15).

When Minimize Form Changes across Print Queues is selected, the print server will print all jobs in the highest priority queue that can use the currently mounted form. Next, it will print all jobs in the next highest priority queue that can use the currently mounted form, and so on. Only when no print jobs in any of the queues can print to the currently mounted form will the print server make the request to change the currently mounted form. When this form-handling policy is selected, there is a minimum of form changes, but jobs will not be printed according to their normal queue priority. It is possible for a high priority print job to wait in the queue until a lower priority job that uses the currently mounted form is printed.

When Minimize Form Changes within Print Queues is selected, the print server will print all jobs in the highest priority queue that can use the currently mounted form. The queue priority will be honored. This means that once jobs that use the currently mounted form are printed from the highest priority queue, the print server will make a request to change the form for the remaining jobs in the high priority queue. All jobs within the queue that can use the new form type will be printed next. Only if there are no jobs in the highest priority queue will it start printing jobs in the next highest priority queue, and so on. This means that form changes within a queue are minimized.

739

When Service Only Currently Mounted Form is selected, only print jobs that can use the currently mounted form will be printed. Print jobs that need another form type are held and not printed. Moreover, the print server does not issue any requests to change the currently mounted form to print remaining print jobs. To print the remaining jobs, you have to manually check if there is a need to mount a different form type.

Figure 8.16 shows the notification form for printers. The print job owner is notified of printer status changes. The notification property contains a list of users who should be notified when there is a printer problem (such as the need to change the currently mounted form or add more paper). Some of the parameters that can be set are the number of seconds to wait to inform the users listed in the notification property about a printer problem. You can also set the number of minutes that elapse between the first notice and subsequent notices to correct the problem. You can specify that the print job owner be notified by checking the box labeled Notify Print Job Owner.

Figure 8.16

Notification properties for Printer object.

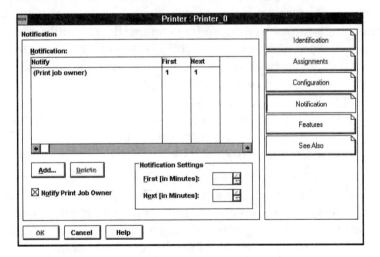

From figures 8.12 through 8.16, you can tell that the Printer object has the following important properties:

◆ **Name property**

The NDS name of the Print object. It can be used to send print jobs to the printer.

◆ **Print Server property**

Name of the print server to which the Printer is assigned.

◆ **Print Queues property**

List of print queues that are assigned to the Printer object.

◆ **Configuration property**

Used to match the physical configuration parameters of the printer specification.

◆ **Notification property**

List of users to be notified about printer problems.

Before describing the last printing object, the Print Server object, you need to understand how this object is used by the print server and the PSERVER.NLM.

The Print Server property for a Printer object is set to the print server to which the printer is assigned.

The Print Queues property for a Printer object lists the print queues that are assigned to a Printer object.

The Notification property of the Printer object lists the users to be notified about printer problems.

Understanding the Role of the Print Server and PSERVER.NLM

The Print Server object describes the print server. The Print Server object is activated by the PSERVER.NLM and can therefore run on NetWare servers only. This program takes the Print Server object name as a parameter when it is loaded:

```
LOAD PSERVER  PrintServerObjectName
```

This command can be run on any NetWare server in the NDS tree. *PrintServerObjectName* is replaced by the complete name of the Print Server object. Thus, to activate the Print Server object CN=PS-CORP.OU=CORP.O=SCS, you have to run the PSERVER NLM at one of the NetWare servers as shown:

```
LOAD PSERVER .CN=PS-CORP.OU=CORP.O=SCS
```

The PSERVER.NLM is the only type of print server program that is available from Novell. The PSERVER.EXE of NetWare 3.x is no longer supported in NetWare 4.x.

The PSERVER.NLM can support up to 256 printers. Up to 5 of the 256 printers can be attached to the server where PSERVER.NLM is run (local printers). The remaining 251 printers can be attached anywhere else on the network (remote printer). These remote printers can be on other NetWare servers, workstations, or directly attached to the network.

 The PSERVER.NLM can support 256 printers: 5 local and 251 remote printers.

Figure 8.17 shows the types of printers used with a print server, and figure 8.18 shows the operation of the PSERVER.NLM. The PSERVER.NLM monitors the queue and the printer and directs print jobs in the network print queue to the appropriate network printer.

Figure 8.17

Types of printers used with print server.

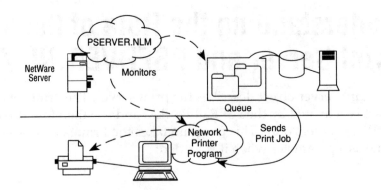

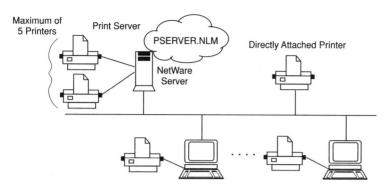

Figure 8.18
Print server operation.

With this as a background, you are now ready to understand the properties of the Print Server object.

The Print Server Object

The Print Server object is a logical representation of the print server program (PSERVER.NLM) running at a server. The Print Server object can be created using the NetWare Administrator or the PCONSOLE utility. The Printer object should be placed in the context it is most likely to be used. Figure 8.3 shows the NDS tree where the Printer object is placed in the O=SCS container. It is expected that users throughout the SCS organization will have access to this Print Server object. This includes users in the departments CORP, ENG, and SALES, represented by the organizational unit containers. Figure 8.4 shows a Print Server object in the OU=CORP.O=SCS container. The Print Server object in this container is expected to be used by users of OU=CORP in the organization O=SCS.

Figure 8.19 shows the properties of the Print Server object. Besides the Name property (Common Name), the only property that is set on this screen is the Advertising Name. Server programs in the NetWare environment, such as the PSERVER.NLM, advertise their existence using the Service Advertising Protocol (SAP).

Figure 8.19

Print Server object
properties of a
running print server.

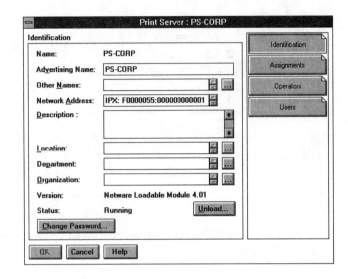

Figure 8.20 shows a packet trace captured using LAN Analyzer,
and figure 8.21 shows the packet decode of the SAP frame. Notice
that the name of the service advertised is PS-CORP, which is the
value of the property shown in figure 8.19.

Figure 8.20

Print Server SAP
protocol trace.

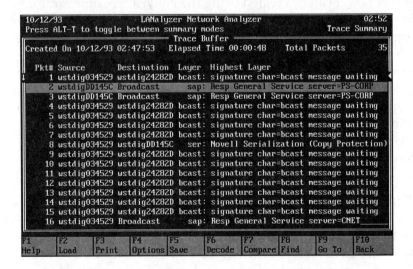

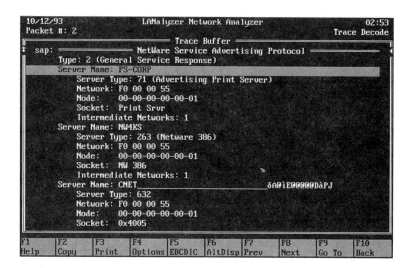

Figure 8.21

Print Server SAP packet.

Author's Note

It is interesting to note that the PS-CORP has a service type of 71 (see fig. 8.21). All SAP services are identified by their SAP type value. A well-known service such as the Print Server has a published value of 71. The NetWare 4.x server, on the other hand, has a service type of 263. This is the same type used for NetWare 3.x servers. The directory tree name CNET is advertised by server type 632. For those interested in more information on how the SAP protocol works, refer to *NetWare: The Professional Reference*, from New Riders Publishing.

Study Note

The Advertising Name property of the Print Server object is the name used by the PSERVER NLM to advertise its existence using the Service Advertising Protocol (SAP).

The other properties, such as Other Names, Description, Location, Department, and Organization, are not set when the queue is initially created. It is a good practice to set these values to a meaningful description of the Queue object. The Network Address property is set only when the print server is running. The print server in figure 8.19 is running. This is shown by the status fields and the Version property that reports the version number of the PSERVER NLM that is running. The Network Address property shows that the print server is at F0000055:000000000001. The F0000055 is the internal network number of the NetWare server on which the PSERVER is running, and 000000000001 is its node address. The internal network number is assigned to each NetWare 3.x and NetWare 4.x server to identify the NetWare services that it provides. The node address for the server on the internal network is always 1, because the internal network number uniquely identifies the NetWare services.

The Network Address property of the Print Server object is set only when the print server is running and refers to the internal network number and the NetWare server's logical node address on which the PSERVER.NLM is running.

You can unload the print server by selecting the Unload button (see fig. 8.19). The print server can also be unloaded directly from the NetWare console on which it was loaded, or through the PCONSOLE program. The print server password is used to secure access to the Print Server object and can be changed via the Change Password button.

You can unload a running print server using NetWare Administrator or PCONSOLE, or at the server where it is loaded, by typing **UNLOAD PSERVER**.

The Print Server assignments are shown in figure 8.22. The Printers property is a list of printers assigned to print servers. The figure shows that there are two printers assigned to the Print Server object PS-CORP. These printers are CN=HP_ PRINTER.O=SCS and CN=Printer_0.OU=CORP.O=SCS.

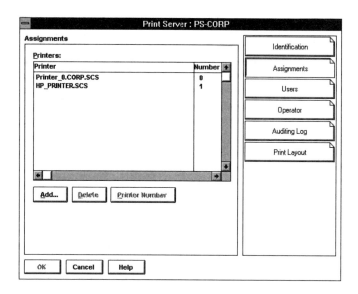

Figure 8.22

Print Server object assignments.

Figure 8.23 shows that the Operators property for PS-CORP is set to CN=Admin.O=ESL. This property describes the list of users who can perform administration tasks on the print server. In general, the Operators property of a Print Server object can include any of the following:

◆ Users

◆ Groups

◆ User Templates

◆ Organization (O) or Organizational Unit (OU) container objects

When you add a Group object, for example, to the Operator property, all members of the group become print server operators. When you add User Template to the Operator property, all users that are created using the User Template will be added as operators of the Print Server object. Adding a container such as an Organization or Organizational Unit means that all User objects in that container become print server operators.

747

Figure 8.23

Print Server
operators.

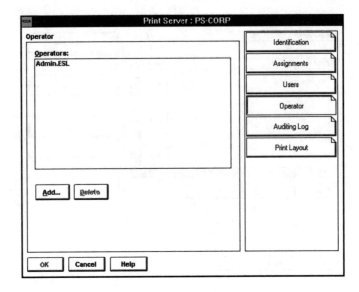

Figure 8.24 shows the Users property for PS-CORP, which is
set to OU=CORP.O=SCS. This means that all users in the
OU=CORP.O=SCS container can use the print server. You can
add containers, groups, users, and user templates to the user's
property by clicking on the Add button on the Print Server User
List dialog box.

Figure 8.24

Print Server users.

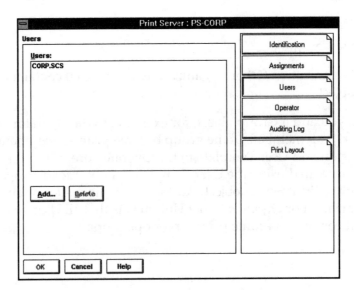

To print a job to a printer under the control of a print server, you don't need to be a print server user. You need to be a queue user for a queue assigned to the Printer object. However, making a user a print server user means that the user can, in addition to printing jobs on a printer controlled by the print server, also examine the print server's operation to see if any of its printers require attention.

To prevent unauthorized users from starting the print server (by typing the LOAD PSERVER command at a server console), you can assign a password to the print server. This can be done by selecting the Change Password button under the Identification property group of the print server.

From figures 8.19 and 8.22 through 8.24, you can tell that the Print Server object has the following important properties:

◆ **Operators property**

List of users assigned to manage the print server.

◆ **Users property**

List of users that can use the print server.

◆ **Printers property**

List of printers assigned to the print server.

◆ **Password property**

This is used to secure the print server. You need this to manage the PSERVER.NLM running at a NetWare server.

Please note that the Print Server object properties are read into the server memory when PSERVER.NLM loads. Any changes made to the Print Server object are not registered with the print server, unless you bring the print server down (unload PSERVER.NLM) and bring it up again (load PSERVER.NLM).

 The Password property of the Print Server object is used to secure the print server.

Changes made to the Print Server object properties are not registered with the print server unless you bring the print server down and up again. You can, however, create a new Print Queue object and assign it to a Printer object that has already been assigned to an active Print Server object. You can then print a job to the newly created queue, which will be printed to the printer to which the queue was assigned. This is not the same as changing a property of the Print Server object. If you were to create a new Printer object and assign it to the Printers property of an already active Print Server object, the new printer would not register with the print server unless you brought the print server down and up again.

Loading of Printer Definitions

When the PSERVER.NLM loads, it activates the Printer objects defined in the specified Print Server object's printers property list. If the printer is defined locally to the PSERVER.NLM, a program called NPRINTER.NLM is autoloaded to activate any attached local printers (see fig. 8.25). For this reason, printers attached locally to the NetWare server on which PSERVER.NLM is run are called Autoload printers. In figure 8.25 you can see that the Printer_0 was loaded successfully, but the second printer failed to load because it, too, was trying to use interrupt line 7 (which was already in use by the first printer). If the second printer was defined on a different port from LPT1, this problem would not exist.

 Printer definitions that are local to the print server are autoloaded by the NPRINTER.NLM when PSERVER.NLM is run.

```
Loading module PSERVER.NLM
   NetWare 386 Print Server
   Version 4.01    June 14, 1993
   Copyright (c) 1992-1993 Novell, Inc. All rights reserved.
      Loading module NPRINTER.NLM
   NetWare Network Printer Driver v4.01
   Version 4.01    June 30, 1993
   Copyright (c) 1992-1993 Novell, Inc. All rights reserved.
   90 program messages in ENGLISH (language #4) were loaded.
Loading module NPRINTER.NLM
   NetWare Network Printer Driver v4.01
   Version 4.01    June 30, 1993
   Copyright (c) 1992-1993 Novell, Inc. All rights reserved.
   90 program messages in ENGLISH (language #4) were loaded.

Network printer Printer_0 (number 0) loaded
and attached to print server PS-CORP.

NPRINTER-NLM-4.1-10: Interrupt number 7 or the printer port requested
by printer 1 on print server PS-CORP is not available.
(Error code 3)

Network printer not loaded.
NW4KS:
```

Figure 8.25

Load PSERVER.NLM
console messages.

Printers that are attached to other NetWare servers or workstations are called remote printers. These must have the NPRINTER program manually loaded on them. For NetWare servers, the NPRINTER program is NPRINTER.NLM; for workstations it is NPRINTER.EXE. Because the NPRINTER program has to be manually loaded for remote printers, they are referred to as Manual load printers.

Printer definitions that are remote from the print server must be manually loaded by the NPRINTER.NLM.

NPRINTER.EXE is available for both DOS and OS/2 printers.

The NPRINTER Program

The syntax for loading the NPRINTER program is as follows:

```
NPRINTER [PrintServerObjectName]    [PrinterObjectName]
```

or

```
LOAD NPRINTER PrintServerObjectName    PrinterObjectName
```

The first form is used for DOS and OS/2 workstations; the second form is used for loading the printer definition on a NetWare server. Multiple printers can be serviced at the NetWare server by running the LOAD NPRINTER command several times and specifying a different printer object each time.

The NPRINTER.EXE is used to load remote printers at a workstation.

The NPRINTER.NLM is autoloaded for local printers attached to the print server and must be manually loaded for printers attached to remote NetWare servers.

The *PrintServerObjectName* refers to the Print Server object to which the printer is assigned. Because a Print Server object can have more than one Printer object assigned to it, the second parameter, *PrinterObjectName,* further qualifies the statement by specifying the actual Printer object name. You can also load the printer definition directly by leaving out the Print Server object name. Thus, to load Printer object CN=HP_PRINTER.O=SCS at a workstation as a remote printer, you can use the following:

```
NPRINTER    .CN=HP_PRINTER.O=SCS
```

When the print server loads, it assigns printer numbers to all the Printer object definitions activated by it. Figure 8.26 shows the printer numbers assigned to the Printer objects CN=Printer_0.OU=CORP.O=SCS and CN=HP_PRINTER.O=SCS when the CN=PS-CORP.OU=CORP.O=SCS printer loads. NPRINTER supports an alternative syntax, where the printer number can be used instead of the Printer object name:

```
NPRINTER PrintServerObjectName   PrinterNumber
```

If the NPRINTER command does not work, try using a complete name for the Print Server object name.

Figure 8.26

The Printer List on the print server.

The second form of the NPRINTER syntax allows it to be compatible with the NetWare 3.x RPRINTER syntax. RPRINTER.EXE, which was used in NetWare 3.x to set up remote printing, is no longer used. Its functionality has been replaced by the NPRINTER.EXE program. You need to load NPRINTER at a workstation or server to set up a remote printer. A remote printer is a network printer that is not attached to the NetWare server where the PSERVER.NLM program runs.

An example of the second type of NPRINTER syntax is

```
NPRINTER .CN=PSERV.OU=CORP.O=ESL  1
```

where printer number is used instead of the Printer object name. Figure 8.27 shows the effect of executing this command. Notice the status message says that the HP_PRINTER (printer 1) is now installed. The NPRINTER.EXE runs as a TSR (terminate-and-stay-resident) program.

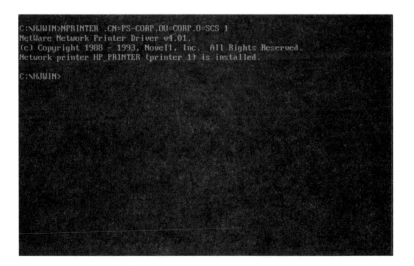

Figure 8.27

Activating a printer with the NPRINTER command.

753

If NPRINTER is used without any options, it runs as a menu utility.

To unload the NPRINTER.EXE at the workstation, use this command:

```
NPRINTER /U
```

To see the status of a printer, use this command:

```
NPRINTER /S
```

The following listing shows the output produced by running NPRINTER /S on a workstation that had NPRINTER loaded in a prior step:

```
NetWare Network Printer Driver v4.01.
 Copyright 1988 - 1993, Novell, Inc.  All Rights Reserved.

     Print server:          PS-CORP
     Printer name:          HP_PRINTER
     Printer number:     1
     Printer port:          Unknown
     Using IRQ:             None (Polled Mode)
     TSR status:            Shared Mode
     PRINTER status:  Waiting for Print Job
     Printer status:        Out of Paper
```

Figure 8.28 shows a summary of the different types of NPRINTER programs that are possible.

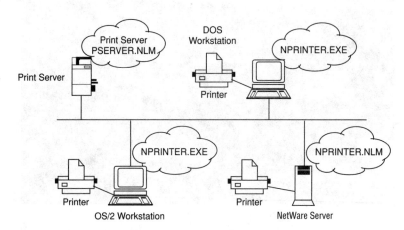

Figure 8.28

Different NPRINTER types.

If NPRINTER is used without any options, it runs as a menu utility.

Interactions Among the Print Queue, Print Server, and Printer Objects

When configuring network printing objects, certain critical properties for each of these objects need to be set up. You saw the use of some of these critical properties in the earlier discussion on Print Queue, Printer, and Print Server objects.

Figure 8.29 shows the important or critical properties for the Print Queue, Printer, and Print Server objects. The print queue is assigned to the Print Queues property of the Printer object, and the Printer object is assigned to the Printers property of the Print Server object. This assignment allows a link to be made between the different printing objects, regardless of their context. That is, the network print configuration objects (Print Queue, Printer, and Print Server) can be placed in the same context or different contexts. You should, however, try to create them in contexts where they are most likely to be used.

The diagram in figure 8.29 shows a one-to-one correspondence among the Print Queue, Printer, and Print Server objects. This is the simplest and most often-used setup. More complex many-to-one assignments can be made. Figure 8.30 shows that multiple queues can be assigned to a single Printer object, and multiple Printer objects can be assigned to a single Print Server object.

Figure 8.29

Setting of critical properties for print objects.

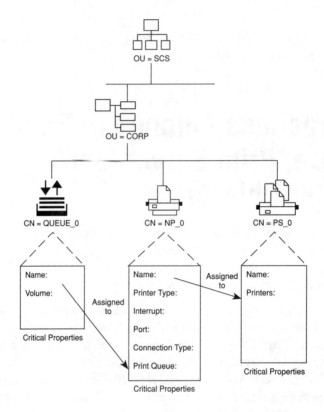

Figure 8.30

Many-to-one relationship between print objects.

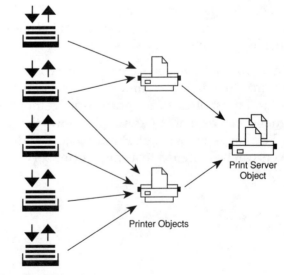

To create the print configuration objects, you should at least have the Create object right to the container where these objects will be placed. The quickest way to create these objects is to use the Quick Setup option under PCONSOLE. If you do not have the Create object right (or the Supervisor object right that implies the Create object right), this option will not be shown on the PCONSOLE menu.

To create the print configuration objects, you should have the Create object right to the container where these objects will be placed.

The quickest way to configure network printing is to use the Quick Setup option under PCONSOLE.

If you do not have the Create object right, the Quick Setup option will not be shown on the PCONSOLE menu.

By default, the creator of the print objects is made a trustee and given all object rights and property rights to that object. Figure 8.31 shows the trustee rights to object PS-CORP. The creator of the object is Admin.ESL. This user has all rights (see fig. 8.31) to Object rights (Supervisor, Browse, Delete, Rename) and the All Properties rights (Supervisor, Compare, Read, Write, Add Self).

By default, the creator of the print objects is made a trustee and given all object and property rights to that object.

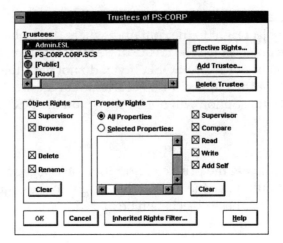

Configuring Network Print Services

As mentioned earlier, the primary tools for configuring network services are PCONSOLE and Network Administrator. But only PCONSOLE has the Quick Setup option. The other options in PCONSOLE are the same as in the PCONSOLE for NetWare 3.x, with the exception that they have been modified to work with NDS objects.

If you use the NetWare Administrator tool to create print objects, you have to make sure that their critical properties (see fig. 8.29) are defined, and also that the logical links between them are properly defined.

The NETADMIN.EXE program cannot be used to create print objects. You cannot use this tool to view or edit properties of print objects. Figure 8.32 shows that the Queue object Queue_0 cannot be edited or viewed using NETADMIN.

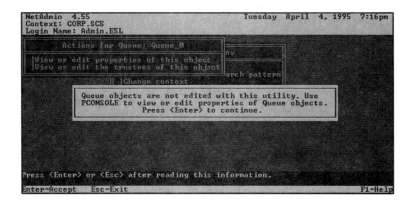

Figure 8.32

Attempt to view or
edit Queue object
from NETADMIN.

The PCONSOLE Utility

You will now be given a guided tour of setting up network printing by using the PCONSOLE utility to create Print Queue, Printer, and Print Server objects and configure them.

1. Log in as an Admin user and run PCONSOLE. You can log in as another user as long as you have Create, Delete, and Browse privileges to the container where you are creating the print objects. If you need to rename any print objects you create, you will need the Rename object right to leaf objects in the container.

   When you run PCONSOLE, you should see the screen in figure 8.33.

Figure 8.33
The PCONSOLE
main menu.

2. Select Change Context from PCONSOLE and change your context to the container where you want to place the print objects. In this guided tour the container name is OU=CORP.O=ESL_XXX. If you are practicing using PCONSOLE, you may want to create an organization with

a similar name. Substitute any characters for *XXX* so you can experiment with different organization trees. You can always delete these trees later.

You can see your context reported on the top half of the PCONSOLE screen.

3. Select Print Queues from Available Options. You should see a list of Print Queue objects defined in the OU=CORP.O=ESL_*XXX* context. The list should initially be empty (see fig. 8.34) unless you have already created Print Queue objects in this container.

Figure 8.34

Initial Print Queues.

4. Press Ins to create a Queue object. You should see a screen asking you to enter the new queue name (see fig. 8.35).

Figure 8.35

Prompt to create new queue name.

5. Enter the name of the Print Queue object as QUEUE_1. (You can choose any other name, but for the purpose of this exercise it will be referred to as QUEUE_1.) You should see a screen asking you to enter the queue's volume (see fig. 8.36). The queue has to be placed on a Volume object. It is created as a subdirectory (with the name of the Print Queue ID) under the QUEUES directory.

Print queue's volume:

Figure 8.36

Entering a queue's
volume name.

6. Enter the name of a Volume object. For the purpose of this
   exercise the volume name is referred to as CORP_VOL. You
   can use the Volume object name on your NetWare 4.x server,
   or create an Alias in your current context to the server volume, name it CORP_VOL, and use this name. If you create
   an Alias name for the Volume object, PCONSOLE replaces it
   with the name of the Aliased Volume object.

   You can also press Ins and browse through the NDS directory tree, searching for the volume on which to place the
   queue.

   After you enter the Volume name to use with the Print
   Queue object, you should see the newly created Print Queue
   object in the Print Queues list (see fig. 8.37).

Figure 8.37

A newly created
queue in the
Queue List.

7. Your next step is to create a Printer object. Return to the main
   PCONSOLE menu by pressing Esc.

8. Select the Printers option from Available Options.

   You should see a list of Printer objects defined in the
   OU=CORP.O=ESL_XXX context. The list should initially be
   empty (see fig. 8.38).

Figure 8.38

The Initial Printers list.

9. You are prompted by the New printer name box (see fig. 8.39). Enter the name of the Printer object as PRINTER_1. (You can choose any other name, but for the purpose of this exercise, it will be referred to as PRINTER_1.)

Figure 8.39

Prompt to create new printer.

You should see the newly created Printer Object in the Printers list (see fig. 8.40).

Figure 8.40

Newly created Printer object in the Printers list.

10. Select the Printer object you have created from the Printers list. You should see a screen on the printer configuration (see fig. 8.41).

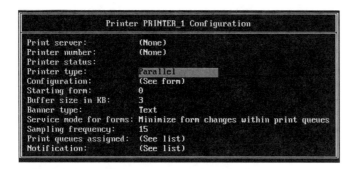

Figure 8.41

The Printer
Configuration screen.

11. Assuming that you have a parallel printer, configure the printer as follows (highlight the Configuration field and press Enter). If you have a serial printer, use one of the COMx ports.

Printer Type:	Parallel
Configuration:	
Port:	LPT1
Location:	Manual Load or Autoload
Interrupt:	7
Address restriction:	No
Print Queues Assigned:	Assign QUEUE_1 to this printer

12. After making any changes, press the F10 key to save your configuration information.

13. When you assign the Queue object that you created earlier, you select the "Print queues assigned: (list)" field from the Printer Configuration screen. You can view this list by pressing Enter. You will see a Print Queue list. Press Ins and select the name of the Queue object. You can also browse the directory tree, looking for Queue objects, by selecting the .. (parent) entry. After you make your entry, you will see a screen similar to figure 8.42.

Figure 8.42

The Print Queue Priority and Status screen.

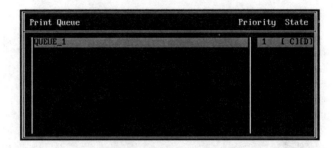

14. The Priority column displays the priority for jobs in the queue. You can select the queue name entry to change its priority from 1 (highest) to 15 (lowest).

    The State column displays codes that have the following meanings:

    A = Printer is actively servicing the queue.

    C = Printer is configured to service this queue.

    D = This is the default print queue.

15. Press Esc to return to the configuration screen.

16. In the Printer Configuration screen, you can also select the Notification field to select the users or groups that should be notified if there is a printer problem. The default Notification list contains the Print job owner value.

17. Save printer configuration changes by using the F10 key.

18. Return to the main Available Options menu.

    The last step is to create a Print Server object.

19. Select Print Servers option from Available Options.

    You should see a list of Print Server objects defined in the OU=CORP.O=ESL_*XXX* context. The list should initially be empty (see fig. 8.43).

20. Press Ins to create a Print Server object. You should see a screen asking you to enter the new print server name (see fig. 8.44).

Figure 8.43

The Printer Configuration screen.

Figure 8.44

The New print server name box.

21. Enter the name of the print server as PSRV_1 (or any other print server name). You will see a message that you should wait while the Print Server object is being created, after which you should see the newly created Printer object in the Print Servers list (see fig. 8.45).

Figure 8.45

The newly created Printer object in the Print Servers list.

22. Your next step is to configure the Print Server object. Select the Print Server object you have created from the Print Servers list. You should see a list of Print Server Information options (see fig. 8.46).

765

Figure 8.46

Print Server
Information options.

23. Select the Printers option from the Print Server Information list. You should see a list of Serviced Printers. Initially the list should be empty.

24. Press Ins. You should see a list of Printer objects that can be assigned to the print server (see fig. 8.47), or you can browse through the NDS structure to locate the desired Printer object.

Figure 8.47

Printer objects list.

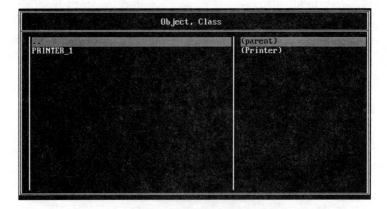

25. Select the Printer object you created earlier (PRINTER_1) and assign it to the print server. You should see a list of serviced Printer objects that are assigned to the print server (see fig. 8.48).

You can assign up to 256 Printer objects to a Print Server object. If you need to assign more than 256 printers, define another Print Server object.

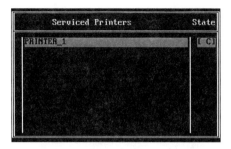

Figure 8.48

Printers assigned to print server.

26. Return to the main Available Options menu by pressing Esc a few times. You have created Print Queue, Printer, and Print Server objects and configured them properly.

The next step is to load the print server (PSERVER.NLM) on a server.

The LOAD PSERVER Command

The PSERVER command syntax is

```
LOAD PSERVER PrintServerObject
```

To load the PSERVER.NLM for the Print Server object CN=PSRV_1.OU=CORP.O=ESL_XXX that you created in the previous section, use this command:

```
LOAD PSERVER    .CN=PSRV_1.OU=CORP.O=ESL_XXX
```

When the PSERVER.NLM loads, you should see a list of Available Options for the PSERVER.NLM (see fig. 8.49). Selecting Printer Status should show the list of printers that are defined for the Print Server object (see fig. 8.49). Selecting any of the printers listed shows the printer status (see fig. 8.50). Selecting Print Server Information from Available Options shows the print server information and status (see fig. 8.51).

Figure 8.49

The PSERVER
main screen.

Figure 8.50

The PSERVER
Printer List.

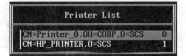

Figure 8.51

PSERVER Printer
Status.

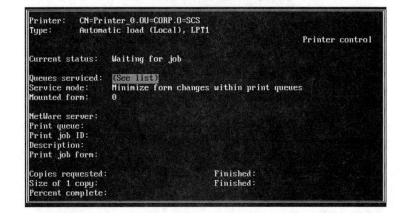

You can change the Current Status field in the Print Server Information (see fig. 8.52) from Running to Unload to unload the Print Server immediately. If you want to wait until all print jobs are finished before unloading the print server, you can set the status field to "Unload after active print jobs."

Figure 8.52

Changing printer
server status.

To activate the print server, you must run the PSERVER.NLM at a NetWare 4.x server and give it the name of the print server as a parameter.

You have a choice of loading the PSERVER.NLM on any NetWare 4.x server. To avoid the overhead of polling the print queues across the network, you should activate the print server on a NetWare 4.x server that will minimize this overhead. This can be the same server whose volume is used to hold the print queue.

Examining Print Server Status Using PCONSOLE

PCONSOLE can be used to monitor print server status, also. The steps to perform this are outlined here:

1. Start PCONSOLE and change context to where the print server is defined.

2. Select Print Servers from Available Options.

3. Select a print server to examine from the list of Print Servers.

4. Select Information and Status from the Print Server Information menu.

   You should see a screen showing print server information and status (see fig. 8.53). Comparing figure 8.53 with 8.52, you can see that they present the same type of information.

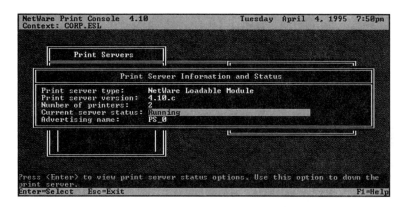

Figure 8.53

PCONSOLE Printer Server Information and Status.

Quick Setup Configuration

The Quick Setup information option in PCONSOLE can be used to create, in a single step, a Print Queue, Printer, and Print Server object that have all their critical properties defined. The Print objects are created to have the proper logical links between themselves. This means that the Print Queue object is assigned to the Printer object's Print Queues list property, and the Printer object is assigned to the Print Server object's Printers list property.

The Quick Setup option in PCONSOLE can be used to create a Print Queue, Printer, and Print Server object that have all their critical properties defined.

The Print objects that are created have default names of Q1 for the Print Queue object, P1 for the Printer object, and PS-*container* for the Print Server object. The *container* in the print server name PS-*container* is the name of the container in which the print server is defined. When you create these objects, you can change the default names to any other names (as long as they do not conflict with leaf names of other objects in the container).

Quick Setup will also make assumptions about the printer properties. For the Printer object, it defines the following property values:

```
Banner type:  Text
Printer type:  Parallel
Location:  Auto Load (Local)
Interrupt:  None (polled mode)
Port:  LPT1
```

These values can be modified during Quick Setup, but they should match your physical printer configuration.

Any of the default parameters of Quick Setup can be modified when you create Print objects by using Quick Setup.

If you want to set up a remote printer, use the Manual Load value for the Location.

You will now be presented with a guided tour of using the Quick Setup option of PCONSOLE.

1. Log in as an Admin user and run PCONSOLE.

2. If your context is not OU=CORP.O=ESL_XXX, where XXX is replaced by your group identity, select Change Context and change your context to where the Print objects will be created.

3. Select Quick Setup from Available Options.

    If your context is a container such as [Root], where Print objects cannot be created, you will not see the Quick Setup option in the Available Options menu. Change to an Organization or Organizational Unit.

    After selecting the Quick Setup option, you should see the Print Services Quick Setup screen (see fig. 8.54).

4. Change the names of these objects to whatever names you want to use.

5. Change the printer configuration to match your needs.

    The printer location to Auto Load (Local) means local printer; a value of Manual Load means remote printer.

6. Press F10 to save changes. The Printer objects will be created after a short waiting period.

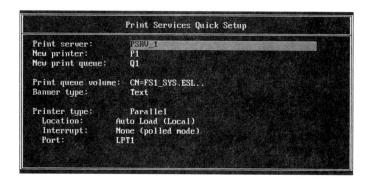

Figure 8.54

The Print Services Quick Setup screen.

Sending a Print Job

After the network printing is set up, print jobs can be submitted by using one of the following:

- NETUSER
- CAPTURE
- NPRINT
- PCONSOLE
- NWUSER

The NETUSER is a menu-driven tool that can be used to perform common network-related tasks such as network printing, messaging, drive mappings, and attaching to other servers. This is a new tool that was first introduced with NetWare 4.0.

NPRINT and CAPTURE are commands that take a number of options and can be used for sending a print job to a network printer.

The NWUSER is the Windows-based graphical User Tool. It can be used for sending print jobs and for network-related tasks such as messaging, drive mappings, and attaching to other servers.

 Network print jobs can be sent using the following:

NETUSER

CAPTURE

NPRINT

PCONSOLE

NWUSER

These printing tools will be briefly examined next. The CAPTURE, NPRINT, and PCONSOLE tools are similar to those available for NetWare 3.

Printing Using NETUSER

Figure 8.55 shows that one of the options available to NETUSER is Printing. Selecting the Printing option shows you a list of available printer ports local to your workstation. You can select any of these ports for network redirection. After selecting a port, you are given a choice of examining Print Jobs or redirecting the selected port by using Change Printers (see fig. 8.56). You cannot examine print jobs on a printer port that has not been captured (redirected to a network printer).

Figure 8.55

NETUSER options.

Figure 8.56

Available Printer Ports.

After selecting Change Printers, you are given a list of printers and queues in the current context. If no printers or queues are shown, you can use the Ins key to browse the NDS tree. Figure 8.57 shows that queue Queue_0 and printer Printer_0 NDS objects were found in the context OU=CORP.O=SCS. You can select either the Printer_0 or the Queue_0 object to direct the network print jobs. After redirecting a local printer, the Available Ports menu in NETUSER will show the queue name the port is redirected to (see fig. 8.58). You can now select the Print Jobs option to send a print job to the network queue. From this point on, the procedure for sending print jobs is similar to that for PCONSOLE: you can press Ins and browse directories for files to print.

Figure 8.57

Printers and Print Queues.

Figure 8.58

Available Printer Ports showing printer redirection.

 If you redirect your job to a Printer object, the name of the default queue for the Printer object appears in the NETUSER screen and not the name of the Printer object.

 NETUSER can be used to redirect a local printer port to a network queue or network printer and send print jobs.

Printing Using CAPTURE

The CAPTURE command is used to redirect a local printer port to a network queue or network printer. Table 8.1 shows the CAPTURE options.

Table 8.1
CAPTURE Options

Option	Description
SHow	Shows current status of local printer ports. Used as an option by itself.

Option	Description
Printer=*name*	Specifies network printer to which redirected print jobs should be sent. If *name* is a complete NDS name with embedded blanks, quotes can be used.
Local=*n*	Redirects local LPT port *n*. Please note that this option cannot be used in the NPRINT command.
Queue=*name*	Indicates queue object to which print job should be sent.
EndCap	Ends redirection to local ports.
EndCap ALL	Ends redirection of all local printer ports.
CReate=*path*	Sends print job to file *path*.
Keep	Retains print job in queue, if workstation fails.
Job=*jc*	Specifies print job configuration to use. No need to specify other options.
NoBanner	Suppresses printing of banner page.
Banner=*name*	Prints banner page. Limit is 12 characters for banner *name*. Appears in lower half of page.
NAMe=*name*	Default is name of file being printed. Indicates text in upper part of banner page. Limit is a 12-character name.
Form=*n*	Specifies form number or name that is to be used for print job.
Copies=*n*	Specifies number of copies for print job (1–255).
Tabs=*n*	Number of spaces to use for a tab character.
No Tabs	Suppresses tab expansion to space characters.
TImeout=*n*	Number of seconds to wait before closing job.

continues

Table 8.1, Continued
CAPTURE Options

Option	Description
Form Feed	Generates a form feed character at end of print job.
No Form Feed	Suppresses form feed character at end of job.
AUtoendcap	Captured data should be closed and sent to printer on exiting application.
NoAutoendcap	Captured data should *not* be closed and sent to printer on exiting application.
NOTIfy	Specifies that user receive notification of print job completion.
NoNOTIfy	Specifies that user not receive notification of print job completion.
/?	Help.
/? ALL	Displays all help screens.
Verbose	Provides detailed information on command as it is executed.

The **Printer**=*name* option can be used to specify the network Printer object name to send print jobs to.

The ENDCAP command is no longer used with NetWare 4.x. Instead CAPTURE has a new **EndCap** option to stop printer redirection. To stop the capture of local printport LPT1, you can use

```
CAPTURE EndCap
```

or

```
CAPTURE   EC
```

To stop printer redirection for all local printers, you can use the EndCap ALL option:

```
CAPTURE EndCap ALL
```

or

```
CAPTURE  EC ALL
```

Other examples that illustrate the use of the CAPTURE command are shown next.

To capture output of local printer port LPT1 and send it to the printer object NP_0 with form feed before every print job, use

```
CAPTURE  L=1  P=NP_0  FF
```

To capture output of local printer port LPT2 and send it to the printer object HP_3 with no form feed, and a user notification at the completion of a print job, use

```
CAPTURE  P=HP_3  L=2  NFF  NOTI
```

To capture output of local printer port LPT2 and send it to the Printer object .CN=PAN_NP.OU=CORP.O=ESL, with a tab setting of 8, and send printer output to the file C:\JOBS\REPT.TXT, use

```
CAPTURE  P=".CN=PAN_NP.OU=CORP.O=ESL" L=2 T=8 CR=C:\JOBS\REPT.TXT
```

To capture output of local printer port LPT3 and send it to the Printer object .CN= NP_0.OU=CORP.O=ESL, use

```
CAPTURE P=.CN=NP_0.OU=CORP.O=ESL    L=3
```

Notice that in the previous example, the quotation marks around CN=NP_0.OU=CORP.O=SCS are not required. The quotation marks are needed if any of the object names in the NDS printer path name contain blank characters.

The CAPTURE command is used to redirect a local printer port to a network queue or network printer.

The ENDCAP command of NetWare 3.x is no longer used with NetWare 4.x. Instead, CAPTURE has a new **EndCap** option to stop printer redirection.

Printing Using NPRINT

To print a job using NPRINT, use the following syntax:

```
NPRINT filename [option]
```

option can be replaced by any of the options in table 8.2.

Table 8.2
NPRINT Options

Option	Description
Server=*name*	Specifies a non-NDS server (bindery server) whose bindery contains the print queue definition.
Printer=*name*	Specifies network printer to which redirected print jobs should be sent. If *name* is a complete NDS name with embedded blanks, quotes can be used.
Local=*n*	Redirects local LPT port *n*.
Queue=*name*	Indicates Queue object to which print job should be sent.
Job=*jc*	Specifies print job configuration to use. No need to specify other options.
NoBanner	Suppresses printing of banner page.
Banner=*name*	Prints banner page. Limit is 12 characters for banner name. Appears in lower half of page.
NAMe=*name*	Default is name of file being printed. Indicates text in upper part of banner page. Limit is a 12-character name.
Form=*n*	Specifies form number or name that is to be used for print job.
Copies=*n*	Specifies number of copies for print job (1–65000).
Tabs=*n*	Number of spaces to use for a tab character, where *n* can be from 1 to 18.
No Tabs	Suppresses tab expansion to space characters.
Form Feed	Generates a form feed character at end of print job.

Option	Description
No Form Feed	Suppresses form feed character at end of job.
NOTIfy	Specifies that user receive notification of print job completion.
NoNOTIfy	Specifies that user not receive notification of print job completion.
/?	Help.
/? ALL	Displays all help screens.
Verbose	Provides detailed information on command as it is executed.

Examples that illustrate the use of the NPRINT command are shown next.

To print three copies of the file SYS:USERS\KSS\ENCFILE.C to printer object PAN_PRT, and use a banner of FYEO, use

```
NPRINT  SYS:USERS\KSS\ENCFILE.C  P=PAN_PRT C=3 B=FYEO
```

To print the file .ENG_SYS.ENG.ESL:DEVELOP\DOC\README.TXT to printer object .CN=NP_1.OU=SALES.ESL., use

```
NPRINT .ENG_SYS.ENG.ESL:DEVELOP\DOC\README.TXT
➡P=".CN=NP_1.OU=SALES.ESL"
```

To print the file MYFILE.TXT using the job configuration in the container OU=SALES.O=ESL, be notified when job is completed, suppress the banner page, and send a form feed before printing the job, use

```
NPRINT  MYFILE.TXT J="OU=SALES.O=ESL"  NOTI  FF  NB
```

Printing Using PCONSOLE

To print using PCONSOLE, select the Print Queues option from Available Options in PCONSOLE. If the print queue you want to print to is not displayed, use Change Context to change context to the container that has the Queue object.

After selecting the Queue name from the Print Queues list, you will see a menu on Print Queue Information. Select the Print Jobs option. You should see the jobs in the current queue. Press Ins, enter a directory name to print from, and press Enter. You should see a list of files in the current directory that you can select for printing (see fig. 8.59). Select the files that you want to print. You will be given a choice of Print Job Configurations to use for printing (see fig. 8.60). If no print job configurations have been defined for the current container, you can select the (Defaults) print job configuration. Figure 8.61 shows a default configuration for printing a file. You can modify any of the default values and press F10 to save your changes and send the print job to the selected queue.

Figure 8.59

Available Files for printing from PCONSOLE.

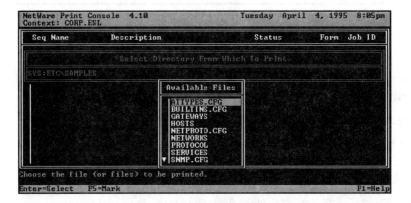

Figure 8.60

Print Job Configurations choices in PCONSOLE.

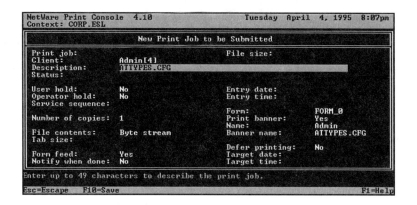

Figure 8.61

A default print job.

Network Printing Tools

Table 8.3 shows the list of network printing tools that are available for NetWare 4.x. The PCONSOLE, PSERVER, NPRINTER, and NWADMIN (Network Administrator) tools have been discussed so far. The PRINTCON and PRINTDEF tools will be discussed briefly.

Table 8.3
Network Printing Tools

Program	Extension	Executed On	Used For
PCONSOLE	EXE	Workstation	Creating and configuring print servers, print queues, and Printer objects.
PRINTCON	EXE	Workstation	Creating and configuring print job configurations.
PRINTDEF	EXE	Workstation	Defining print forms, importing/exporting print device definitions.
PSERVER	NLM	Server	Activates the Print Server object.

continues

Table 8.3, Continued
Network Printing Tools

Program	Extension	Executed On	Used For
NPRINTER	EXE	Workstation	Allows a network printer attached to a station to be shared.
NPRINTER	NLM	Server	Allows a network printer attached to a server not running PSERVER.NLM to be shared.
NWADMIN	EXE	Workstation	GUI utility to perform printer management functions.
PSC	EXE	Workstation	Command-line utility to control and see status of printers and print servers.

NetWare 4.x offers PRINTCON and PRINTDEF print job configuration. The print job configuration can be used as the Job Configuration parameter in CAPTURE and NPRINT to simplify the options by aggregating them under a print job configuration template. It is also used when submitting jobs to a queue using the Print Job option in NETUSER and PCONSOLE.

The PRINTCON Utility

Figure 8.62 shows the main menu for PRINTCON. The Edit Print Job Configuration is used to create new print job configurations. The Select Default Print Job Configuration allows you to select the print job configuration that will be used as a default. The Change Current Object allows you to change the Container object or User object for which the print job configuration will be defined.

Figure 8.62

The PRINTCON
main menu.

Print job configurations are stored as the Print Job Configuration property of an Organization, Organizational Unit, or User object. If stored in a container, all users within the container can use the print job configuration. If the print job configuration is stored as a property of a User object, only that user can make use of the print job configuration.

Print job configurations are stored as the Print Job Configuration property of an Organization, Organizational Unit, or User object.

PRINTCON can operate in the directory mode (the default) or the bindery mode. The function key F4 can be used to toggle between these two modes. This allows the NetWare 4.x PRINTCON to be used with NetWare 3.x bindery. In NetWare 3.x, print job configurations are stored in the bindery.

The following is a guided tour of using PRINTCON to set the print job configuration for a user.

1. Start PRINTCON. You should see the PRINTCON main screen as shown in figure 8.62.

2. The top part of the PRINTCON screen shows the object (user, container) for which PRINTCON can be used to set the print job configuration. The default is the User object under which you are logged.

   To change the object for which print job configuration should be created or edited, select the Change Current Object option. After you select this option, you can use Ins to browse through and select the appropriate User or Container object.

3. To edit or create a new print job configuration, select Edit Print Job Configurations from the Available Options menu.

783

You should see a list of any print job configurations for that user. Figure 8.63 shows that the user CN=Admin.O=ESL has three print job configurations available to it. The *bnc* and *onc* print job configurations have the description O=ESL next to them. This indicates that these print job configurations have been defined for the user O=ESL. The print job configuration *ujc* has been defined for the user CN=Admin.O=ESL.

The default print job configuration has an asterisk next to it.

Figure 8.63

Edit Print Job
Configurations for
PRINTCON.

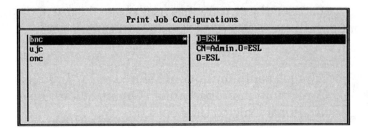

4. To create a new print job configuration, press the Ins key. You will be asked to enter the new name for the print job configuration. Enter a descriptive name and press Enter. You will see the new print job configuration name highlighted (see fig. 8.64).

Figure 8.64

New Print Job
Configuration for
PRINTCON.

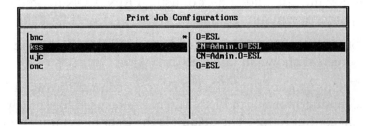

5. Press Enter at a highlighted print job configuration to see details for that print job configuration (see fig. 8.65).

The details of the print job configuration are explained following this list.

6. After you make your changes, press F10 to save the settings.

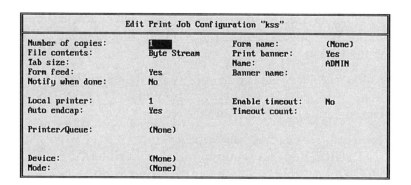

Figure 8.65

Details for Print Job Configuration using PRINTCON.

7. To make another print job configuration the default print job configuration, select Select Default Print Job Configuration from PRINTCON's Available Options. Highlight the print job configuration to become the default, and press Enter. An asterisk (*) will appear next to the default print job configuration.

The print job configuration options are as follows:

Number of copies specifies the number of print job copies that can be printed. The value can be from 1 to 65,000 and has a default value of 1.

File contents specifies whether the tab character in print jobs should be translated to spaces. Select Text if you want tabs to be translated to spaces. If you are sending graphic print jobs, select Byte Stream. The default value is Byte Stream.

> **Author's Note** If you are printing a mix of text and graphics jobs in a queue, it is best to select the Byte Stream value for File Contents. Many problems with graphics print jobs can be traced to a Text value setting for the File Contents parameter.

Tab size is set if the *File contents* is set to Text. It specifies the number of spaces that tabs in the print job are set to. The value can range from 0 to 18 and has a default value of 8.

785

Form feed is used to specify if the form feed character to eject the current page is sent at the end of a print job. The default value is Yes.

Notify when done is used to specify if a message should be sent to the print job owner's workstation when the print job is completed. The default value is No.

Local printer specifies which local printer is to be used with CAPTURE. You can set up to nine local printers using the LOCAL PRINTERS parameter in the NetWare DOS Requester section of the NET.CFG file.

Automatically End Capture can be set to Yes to have any print data that is waiting to be printed by the application sent to the print queue when the application exits, and to stop printer redirection. If a value of No is selected, you must issue a CAPTURE /EC command to process the print data and stop printer redirection. The default value is Yes.

Printer/Queue is used to select the printer or print queue where a print job is to be sent. If a printer or print queue is not specified here, you will have to specify one when using CAPTURE, PCONSOLE, NETUSER, or NPRINT. There is no default setting for this parameter.

Device is used to specify the print device to which the print job will be printed. This device is defined using PRINTDEF. When you select this parameter the print devices defined in the PRINTDEF database will be shown.

Mode is a set of printer control functions defined for the print device using PRINTDEF. Many of the newer applications use their own printer drivers to set the printer in a desired mode of operation (landscape, portrait, letter quality, and so on). Some of the older applications, or applications not properly designed for network printing, can use the Mode parameter to set the printer in an appropriate mode prior to printing.

Form name is used to select the form to be used for printing. The forms are defined in the PRINTDEF database.

Print banner specifies whether you want to have a banner page preceding each print job. The default is Yes.

Name is the username that should appear at the top of the banner page. The default is the name of the user submitting the print job or, if this is a print job configuration for a container, it is the name of the container object.

Banner name specifies the text that will appear at the bottom of the banner page. The default is the name of the file being printed.

Enable Timeout, if set to Yes, sends captured data for printing after a period defined in the *Timeout count* field. The print redirection is still in effect after the timeout period. The default is No.

Timeout count is valid only when the *Enable Timeout* parameter is set to Yes. It is the number of seconds the Requester waits before sending the captured print data. The value can be set from 1 to 1,000 seconds and has a default value of 5 seconds.

The PRINTDEF Utility

Figure 8.66 shows the main menu for PRINTDEF. The Print Devices option is used to modify printer definitions for print devices. The Print Forms option allows you to create and modify printer form definitions. The Change Current Context allows you to change the container object for which the form definition will be defined.

Figure 8.66
The PRINTDEF main menu.

Print device definitions and forms are stored in the Print Devices and Print Forms property of the container object. If stored in a container, all users and print job configurations within the container can use the print device definition.

PRINTDEF can operate in the directory mode (the default) or the Bindery mode. The function key F4 can be used to toggle between these two modes. This allows the NetWare 4.x PRINTDEF to be used with the NetWare 3.x bindery. In NetWare 3.x, print device definitions are stored in the bindery.

Print device definitions and forms are stored in the Print Devices and Print Forms property of the container object.

Use the F4 function key to toggle between directory and bindery modes for PRINTCON and PRINTDEF.

Summary of Default Assignments and Printing Capabilities

When print objects are created, many of them are automatically assigned to different printing lists. Table 8.4 summarizes the default assignments.

Table 8.4
Default Print Property List Assignments

Object	Print Server Users	Print Server Operators	Print Queue Users	Print Queue Operators	Printer Notify List
Parent container	Yes	No	Yes	No	No
Print server creator	No	Yes	Yes	Yes	No
Print job owner	No	No	No	No	Yes

In addition to default assignments, certain default capabilities are assigned; these are summarized in table 8.5.

Table 8.5
Printing Tasks for Classes of Users

Tasks	Print Server Users	Print Server Operators	Print Queue Users	Print Queue Operators	Printer Notify List	Super-visor to Container
Create and delete print queues, printers, and print servers	No	No	No	No	No	Yes
Modify print queue and print server user and opera-tor lists	No	No	No	No	No	Yes
Modify Notify lists	No	Yes	No	No	No	Yes
Modify print queue assignments	No	Yes	No	No	No	Yes
Modify printer status	No	Yes	No	No	No	No
Modify print queue operator flags	No	No	No	Yes	No	No
Use print queues	No	No	Yes	No	No	No

continues

Table 8.5, Continued
Printing Tasks for Classes of Users

Tasks	Print Server Users	Print Server Operators	Print Queue Users	Print Queue Operators	Printer Notify List	Supervisor to Container
Manipulate other print jobs in print queue	No	No	No	Yes	No	No
Manipulate own print jobs in print queue	No	No	Yes	No	No	No
Receive print error messages	Yes	No	No	No	Yes	No
Down print server	No	Yes	No	No	No	No
Monitor print server	Yes	No	No	No	No	Yes

Study Guide for the Chapter

If you are preparing for exams, review the chapter with the following goals:

1. Remember the names and understand what each printing utility covered in this chapter does. Use the Study Notes as a quick review.

2. Pay particular attention to PCONSOLE and Quick Setup.

3. After studying this chapter, attempt the sample test questions for this chapter. If you miss the answer to a question, review the appropriate topic.

Chapter Summary

This chapter described the basic printing concepts used in NetWare 4.x. The properties of Print objects such as Print Queue, Printer, and Print Server objects were covered in detail. To configure network printing, the critical properties of these objects must be set correctly. Network print configuration can be done using either PCONSOLE or the NetWare Administrator. Use of the PCONSOLE tool to configure printing using the Quick Setup and the step-by-step approach were presented in detail.

Sending print jobs on the network can be done using NETUSER, CAPTURE, NPRINT, and PCONSOLE. These methods and the options available within them were discussed.

Chapter Test Questions

Test questions can have a single correct answer or multiple correct answers. Where a single answer is desired, this is indicated by a ○ notation that precedes the possible answers. Some questions require you to select more than one answer; this is indicated by the ☐ preceding each answer.

Certain questions will be repeated in different ways so that you can recognize them even when the wording is different. Taking practice quizzes will not only test your knowledge but also will give you confidence when you take your exam.

1. The primary tools used for network print configuration are
   _____.

   ☐ A. NetWare Administrator Tool

   ☐ B. NetWare User Tool

   ☐ C. NETADMIN

   ☐ D. PRNADMIN

   ☐ E. PCONSOLE

2. The NDS objects needed to configure network printing are
_____.

☐ A. Alias objects

☐ B. Country objects

☐ C. Print Queue objects

☐ D. Print Job Configuration objects

☐ E. Printer objects

☐ F. Print Server objects

3. In NetWare 4.x a print job can be captured to a _____.

☐ A. Print Server object

☐ B. Printer object

☐ C. container object that has the Print Queue object

☐ D. Print Queue object

4. The print queue is implemented by _____.

○ A. the QUEUES directory

○ B. subdirectory of the QUEUES directory

○ C. SYS:QUEUES directory

○ D. subdirectory of the SYSTEM directory

5. Assigning a container object to the Users property of the
Print Queue object means _____.

○ A. that all users within that container are denied access to
the queue

○ B. that all users within that container and its parent container are denied access to the queue

○ C. that all users within that container can send print jobs
to the queue

○ D. that all users within that container can perform administration tasks on the queue

6. The Authorized Print Servers property for the Print Queue object is a list of _____.

   ○ A. printers and print servers that are authorized to use the print queue

   ○ B. printers that are authorized to use the print queue

   ○ C. printers that are authorized to use the print queue server

   ○ D. print servers that are authorized to use the print queue

   ○ E. printers that service the print queue

7. The Print Server property for a Printer object is set to the _____.

   ○ A. print server to which printer is assigned

   ○ B. print servers to which printer is assigned

   ○ C. print servers assigned to the Printer object

   ○ D. print server assigned to the Printer object

8. The Notification property of the Printer object _____.

   ○ A. contains the network address of the server to which console messages should be sent concerning printer problems

   ○ B. lists the vendor contact to be notified about printer problems

   ○ C. lists the Supervisor-equivalent users to be notified about printer problems

   ○ D. lists the users to be notified about printer problems

9. The PSERVER NLM used to load a Print Server object can support _____ printers.

   ○ A. 16

   ○ B. 32

   ○ C. 64

○ D. 100

○ E. 256

○ F. 512

10. The Advertising Name property of the Print Server object is the name used by the _____ to advertise its existence using the _____.

○ A. PRINTCON, NetWare Core Protocol

○ B. PSERVER, NetWare Core Protocol

○ C. PRINTCON, Service Advertising Protocol

○ D. PSERVER, Service Advertising Protocol

11. You can unload a running print server using _____.

☐ A. NetWare Administrator

☐ B. PRINTCON

☐ C. PCONSOLE

☐ D. PSERVER running on the server

☐ E. NETUSER

☐ F. NETADMIN

12. The Operators property of the Print Server object is _____.

○ A. a list of users who can use the print server

○ B. a list of users who can perform administrative tasks on the print server

○ C. a list of users with the Supervisor All Properties right to the Print Server object

○ D. Container objects whose users can perform administrative tasks on the print server

13. Changes made to the Print Server object properties of a running print server _____.

   ○ A. are not registered with the print server, unless you select the Update Configuration option from the PSERVER menu option

   ○ B. are not registered with the print server, unless you bring the print server down and up again

   ○ C. are registered with the print server immediately

   ○ D. are registered with the print server within the Poll Interval Time property value of the print server

14. Printer definitions that are local to the print server are _____.

   ○ A. autoloaded

   ○ B. manually loaded

   ○ C. autoloaded only if the Auto Load property of the Print Server object is set

   ○ D. loaded when the PSERVER.EXE loads

15. Remote printers in NetWare 4.x can be loaded using _____.

   ☐ A. PCONSOLE.EXE

   ☐ B. NPRINTER.EXE

   ☐ C. RPRINTER.EXE

   ☐ D. PSERVER.EXE

   ☐ E. NPRINTER.NLM

   ☐ F. PRINTCON.EXE

16. To create the print configuration objects, you should have a minimum of _____.

   ○ A. the Supervisor object rights to the container where these objects will be placed

   ○ B. the Create and Rename object rights to the container where these objects will be placed

    ○   C. the Create and Delete object rights to the container where these objects will be placed

    ○   D. the Create object right to the container where these objects will be placed

17. The quickest way to configure network printing is to use the _____.

    ○   A. Quick Setup option under NPRINTER

    ○   B. Fast Setup option under NPRINTER

    ○   C. Quick Setup option under PCONSOLE

    ○   D. Fast Setup option under PCONSOLE

18. To activate the print server, you must run the _____ at a NetWare 4.x server and give it the name of the _____ as a parameter.

    ○   A. NPRINTER.NLM, Print Server object

    ○   B. NPRINTER.NLM, Printer object

    ○   C. PSERVER.NLM, Print Server object

    ○   D. PSERVER.NLM, Printer object

19. The Quick Setup option in PCONSOLE can be used to _____.

    ○   A. create in a single step a Print Queue, Printer, and Print Server object, but the critical properties defined have to be defined separately

    ○   B. create in a single step a Print Queue, Printer, and Print Server object that have all their critical properties defined

    ○   C. create the Print Queue and Print Server object, but the Print Server object has to be defined separately

    ○   D. print network jobs quickly

20. Which of the following tools can be used in printing network print jobs?

☐ A. NETUSER

☐ B. CAPTURE

☐ C. PRINTCON

☐ D. PRINTDEF

21. The CAPTURE command is used to _____.

○ A. redirect a local printer port to a network printer only

○ B. redirect a local printer port to a network queue or network printer

○ C. redirect a local printer port to a network queue only

○ D. redirect a remote printer port to a network queue or network printer

22. Which command-line utility can be used to control and set status of printers and print servers?

○ A. PRINTCON

○ B. NETUSER

○ C. NPRINTER

○ D. PCONSOLE

○ E. PSC

○ F. PSERVER

23. Print job configurations can be stored as _____.

☐ A. the Print Job Configuration property of an Organization object

☐ B. the Print Job Configuration property of a Country object

☐ C. the Print Job Configuration property of a User object

☐ D. the Print Job Configuration property of an Organizational Unit object

☐ E. the Print Job Configuration property of a Print Server object

24. Print form definitions are stored in the _____.

○ A. Print Forms property of the Container object

○ B. Print Forms property of the Container or User object

○ C. Forms property of the User object

○ D. Print Forms property of the Printer object

25. Which of the following statements for NetWare 4.x printing are true?

☐ A. Printer, Print Queue, and Print Server objects can be created using NETADMIN.

☐ B. To set up a remote printer, you can use the NPRINTER.EXE program.

☐ C. Printer, Print Queue, and Print Server objects can be created using PCONSOLE.

☐ D. The password property can be set for Print Queue objects.

26. The Print Queue object can be created using _____.

☐ A. PCONSOLE

☐ B. NETADMIN

☐ C. NetWare Administrator

☐ D. FILER

27. Printer redirection can be done using _____.

☐ A. FILER

☐ B. PCONSOLE

☐ C. CAPTURE

☐ D. NPRINT

☐ E. NETUSER

9
CHAPTER

Network Fault Tolerance

This chapter discusses the system fault-tolerant capabilities of NetWare 4.x. System fault tolerance is important for preserving the integrity of data. NetWare 4.x also provides support for UPS and the native backup services. NetWare 4.x backup uses the Storage Management Services (SMS), a hardware- and software-independent method for performing backups.

This chapter also discusses the different types of backup strategies such as full backup, differential backup, and incremental backup. The principal tool for performing backups in NetWare 4.x is SBACKUP. Use of this tool is discussed at length.

Examining System Fault Tolerance

NetWare 4.x System Fault Tolerance (SFT) keeps data and software in a reliable state. This reliability is maintained dynamically while the system is up and running. NetWare 4.x provides three levels of fault tolerance:

◆ SFT Level I: Data reliability

◆ SFT Level II: Server disk and disk channel reliability

◆ SFT Level III: Server reliability

SFT Level I

System Fault Tolerance Level I provides data reliability by implementing the following:

◆ Read-after-write verification

◆ Hot fix

◆ Duplicate FAT and DETs

◆ Transaction Tracking System

SFT Level I implements *read-after-write verification* and *hot fix* (see fig. 9.1). When a block is written in any version of NetWare, it is immediately read to verify that the block that was read is the same as that which was written. This verification works by comparing the block read after it was written, giving it the name *read-after-write* verify. If the two blocks are different, the area on the disk is bad, and the block is rewritten into a special area called the *redirection area* or the *hot fix area*. About 2 percent of the disk (by default) is reserved as redirection area. The bad spot on the disk is recorded in a bad block table. The process of writing the bad block to the redirection area and marking the original bad block location in the bad block table is called *hot fix*. The bad block area of the disk never is written into until the disk is formatted and prepared again for server installation using the Surface Analysis option in INSTALL.NLM.

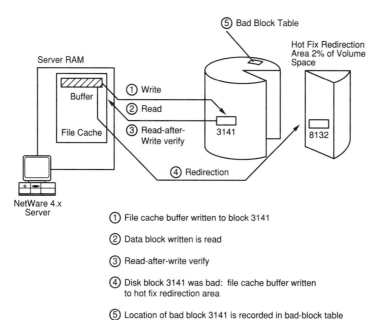

Figure 9.1

Read-after-write verify
and hot fix.

On large disks, 2 percent represents a great deal of disk space, so you might want to reduce the percentage of redirection area.

The File Allocation Table (FAT) and the Directory Entry Table (DET) are two critical data structures of the NetWare File System (see fig. 9.2). The FAT contains the location of the data blocks on the server disk, and the DET contains the directory of files in a volume. When the NetWare 4.x server is started, the FAT and DET stored on the server volume are loaded into memory: the entire FAT is cached, and needed portions of the DET also are cached. Because loss of FAT or DET can result in loss of access to data, the FAT and DET are duplicated in separate areas of the server disk. If one of the copies of FAT or DET is corrupted, it can be restored from the second copy.

Figure 9.2

Duplicate FATs and
DETs.

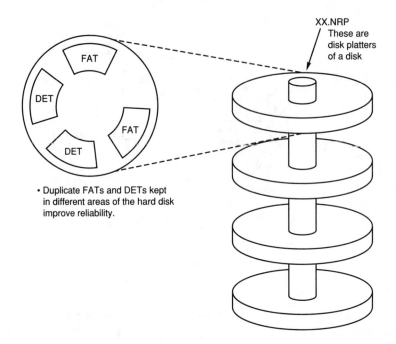

• Duplicate FATs and DETs kept
in different areas of the hard disk
improve reliability.

NetWare 4.x servers implement the Transaction Tracking System
(TTS) feature for critical data operations. TTS (see fig. 9.3) enables
you to back out incomplete file operations in the event of a crash.
You can implement TTS on a file by flagging the file with a Transaction attribute using the FLAG command. TTS uses Novell's
Btrieve database engine. Btrieve enables you to encapsulate
transactions by the Begin Transaction and End Transaction operations. If the operations defined in the transaction cannot be completed, the entire transaction can be rolled back to the Begin
Transaction point.

Figure 9.3

The Transaction
Tracking System
(TTS).

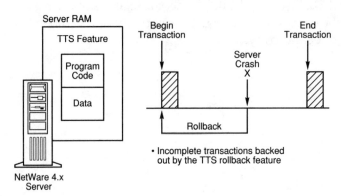

• Incomplete transactions backed
out by the TTS rollback feature

SFT Level II

SFT Level II has two options. The first option is disk mirroring. Most ISA disk controllers support two disk channels. Disks of the same size are attached to the disk controller. One of the NetWare partitions is designated as the primary partition and a NetWare partition on another disk is designated as the secondary partition (see fig. 9.4). The secondary partition acts as a mirror image of the primary. When a block is written, it is written to both partitions. When a block is read, the read command is issued to both partitions. The disk read response that is the fastest is the one used. If disks with different sizes are used for mirroring, make the mirrored partitions on the disk the same size.

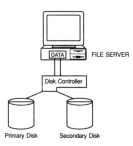

Figure 9.4

SFT Level II disk mirroring.

If the primary disk fails, control is transferred to the secondary disk. When the primary disk is repaired, the secondary disk information is transferred to the primary disk. If the disk controller fails, having a secondary disk attached to the same controller is not useful. Disk duplexing (see fig. 9.5) enables the primary and secondary disks to be attached to separate disk controllers. This feature makes the server fault tolerant toward disk controller failures. Note that SFT Level II includes the features and capabilities of SFT Level I.

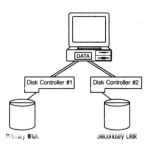

Figure 9.5

SFT Level II disk duplexing.

803

SFT Level III

SFT Level III enables a second server to act as a backup for a primary server if two servers are connected by a high-speed bus (see fig. 9.6). If the primary server fails, the secondary server takes over. SFT Level III includes SFT Level II.

Figure 9.6

SFT Level III server duplexing.

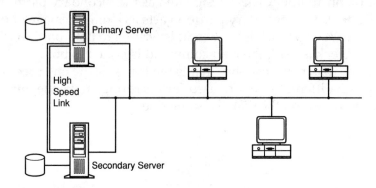

UPS Monitoring

You can use Uninterrupted Power Supply (UPS) to provide a regulated power supply and minimize the impact of power failures (see fig. 9.7). UPS guards against data loss at both the workstation and the server by keeping them up in case of power failure. The power is supplied to the server or workstations through the UPS device, even under normal circumstances with no power failures. The UPS device provides a well-regulated power supply. If the main power line fails, the UPS is capable of continuing to supply this power while its batteries last. If the main power supply fails, the UPS sends a signal to the server that power failure has occurred. The UPS.NLM, which must be loaded at the server, receives the signal and is capable of performing an immediate shutdown of the server or waiting for a certain time before initiating a shutdown. Many UPS devices are capable of sending a separate signal when the UPS battery is depleted, and this capability can be used to initiate server shutdown.

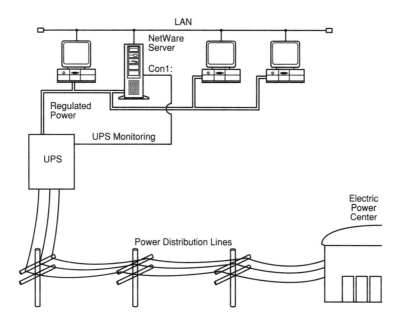

Figure 9.7
UPS monitoring.

Overview of Backup Services

In NetWare 4.x, backup services are consolidated in
SBACKUP.NLM. Because SBACKUP is an NLM, it can run only
on a NetWare server. The server on which the SBACKUP.NLM
runs should have a backup device. This server is called the *host
server*. The data source that is to be backed up and restored is
called the *target*. The target data can be file systems or databases
on network nodes such as NetWare 3.x or 4.x, or DOS or OS/2
workstations (see fig. 9.8).

NetWare 4.x backup services are consolidated in
SBACKUP.NLM.

Figure 9.8

SBACKUP host and
target machines.

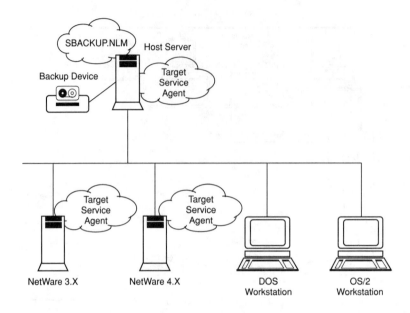

You can use many backup strategies with NetWare 4.x. These
strategies include the following:

◆ Full backup

◆ Incremental backup

◆ Differential backup

◆ Custom backup

 SBACKUP supports full backup, incremental
backup, differential backup, and custom backup.

Full Backup

In *full backup*, all data is backed up, including all diretories and
files on a volume, or all volumes on a file server. After the data is
backed up, the archive bit is cleared for all backed up files.

The archive bit indicates whether the data should be backed up. When a file is modified, the archive bit is set indicating that the file is a candidate for backup. Backup programs clear the archive bit to indicate that backup is complete.

The full backup strategy is the most comprehensive of all backup strategies because it backs up all files regardless of whether they have been modified since the last backup. Because of the large volume of data that might need to be backed up, however, full backup is the slowest of the backup strategies.

 The following points are true about full backups:

- ◆ All data, regardless of the setting of the archive bit, is backed up.

- ◆ The archive bits of all backed up files are cleared.

- ◆ Full backup is the most comprehensive of all backup strategies.

- ◆ Full backup can be the most time-consuming of all the backup strategies.

Incremental Backup

Incremental backup backs up all files modified since the last backup (full or incremental). Files that have not been modified are not backed up. To obtain a complete record of the most up-to-date versions of the files, start with the most recent full backup and add all the incremental changes recorded in each incremental backup session. Because only modified files are backed up, the incremental backup strategy tends to be very fast. If the number of files modified between incremental backup increases, the time required for an incremental backup also increases.

After performing an incremental backup, the archive bits of the backed up files are cleared.

807

The following points are true about incremental backups:

- ◆ Only modified files that have their archive bit set are backed up.

- ◆ In incremental backup, the archive bits of backed up files are cleared.

- ◆ Incremental backup usually is faster than full and differential backups.

- ◆ The incremental backup contains a sequential history of the files that have been modified.

- ◆ To restore data in incremental backup, you need the last full backup and every incremental backup after it.

Differential Backup

Differential backup backs up all files modified since the last full backup. The archive bit is not cleared at the end of the backup, as is done in the case of full and incremental backups. This means that all files backed up in the first differential backup also are backed up in the second differential backup, together with any files modified since the first differential backup. This process continues with each differential backup, and more files can be expected to be backed up with each differential backup.

To obtain a complete record of the most up-to-date versions of the files, start with the most recent full backup and add to it the files in the most recent differential backup session.

Because the differential backup contains all files modified since the last full backup, you can restore data with just two tape backup sets: the backup set for the full backup and the backup set for the last differential backup.

If the data on one of the last differential backups is corrupted, you can fall back on the next-to-the-last differential backup. On the other hand, if any data in another differential backup tape is corrupted, it does not matter as long as the data in the most recent differential backup is good.

Because all modified files are backed up, the differential backup is the same as the incremental backup for the first backup after the full backup. After that, the size of the data that needs to be backed up tends to grow with each differential backup. If all files have been modified, the differential backup session is the same as the full backup sessions. This tends not to be the case, because most network volumes contain a mix of program and data, and program files usually are not modified.

The following points are true about differential backups:

◆ The archive bits of the backed up files are not cleared.

◆ All files modified since the last full backup are backed up.

◆ You need the last full backup and the most recent differential backup to restore data in a differential backup.

◆ If any data in a differential backup tape not belonging to the last differential backup set is corrupted, the data still can be recovered from the last full backup and the most recent differential backup.

◆ If the last differential backup is bad, you can restore data only up to the next-to-the-last differential backup.

◆ The first differential backup is the same as incremental backup in terms of speed and the files that are backed up.

◆ Successive differential backups usually take longer because more files are backed up.

It is best to use either a differential backup or incremental backup strategy. Mixing these two, while theoretically possible, can lead to confusion and should therefore be avoided.

Custom Backup

Custom backups give you complete control over what files to back up or not to back up. You can include or exclude parts of the directory structure to be backed up or select different types of data items to be backed up. Custom backup options are presented in detail in a later section in this chapter.

Custom backups are useful if you want to selectively back up a few files and directories rather than wait for a scheduled backup.

Examining Storage Management Service

NetWare 4.x implements backup services using Storage Management Service (SMS). SMS enables data to be backed up and restored independent of the backup hardware and file system. The SMS supports a variety of backup hardware devices and can back up DOS, OS/2, Macintosh, and Unix file systems. The capability to back up different file systems is particularly important because NetWare-based networks support a heterogeneous workstation operating system environment. SMS provides support for the following workstations and data representation:

◆ DOS workstations

◆ OS/2 workstations

◆ Macintosh workstations (Macintosh name space)

◆ Unix workstations (NFS name space)

◆ NetWare Directory Service

◆ NetWare File Systems (2.2 to 4.x)

◆ Btrieve (SQL) databases

The primary tool that uses SMS is SBACKUP. SBACKUP runs as an NLM and relies on target service agents to communicate a data representation to it. The SBACKUP.NLM runs on the server that has the backup device. The SBACKUP.NLM is responsible for backup and restore operations. The NBACKUP function of earlier NetWare releases is now consolidated in SBACKUP.

The target service agents can run on NetWare servers and communicate with servers and workstations on the network. The target service agents have knowledge of different data representations. A target service agent called TSA410.NLM, for example, is used to back up/restore NetWare 4.x file systems, and the target service agent TSA311.NLM does the same for NetWare 3.x. Table 9.1 contains a list of TSAs installed with NetWare 4.x. These TSAs can be found in the SYS:SYSTEM directory.

Table 9.1
Target Service Agents

TSA Name	Description
TSA311.NLM	NetWare 3.11 file system TSA.
TSA312.NLM	NetWare 3.12 file system TSA.
TSA410.NLM	NetWare 4.1 file system TSA.
TSA410.NLM	NetWare 4.0, 4.01, 4.02 file system TSA
TSA220.NLM	NetWare 2.2 file system TSA.
TSADOS.NLM	TSA for backing up DOS files—runs at server.
TSASMS.COM	TSA runs at DOS workstation to be backed up/restored. Normally kept in the C:\NWCLIENT directory of the workstation.
TSANDS.NLM	NetWare 4.1 TSA for backing up NDS.
TSA_OS2.NLM	TSA for backing up OS/2 file system.

The following apply to SMS:

- ◆ The primary tool that uses SMS is SBACKUP.

- ◆ SMS enables data to be backed up and restored independent of the backup hardware and file system.

- ◆ The NBACKUP function of earlier NetWare releases now is consolidated in SBACKUP.

- ◆ SMS provides support for the following workstations and data representation:

    - ◆ DOS workstations

    - ◆ OS/2 workstations

    - ◆ Macintosh workstations (Macintosh name space)

    - ◆ Unix workstations (NFS name space)

    - ◆ NetWare Directory Service

    - ◆ NetWare File Systems (2.2 to 4.x)

    - ◆ Btrieve (SQL) databases

SMS Architecture

Besides SBACKUP.NLM and TSAs, SMS consists of a number of other support NLMs that work together to provide backup and restore operations. Figure 9.9 shows how this can be done.

SMS consists of a number of other modules, such as the Storage Management Data Requester (SMDR), that are used to pass commands between the SBACKUP and the TSAs, and device drivers that use the Storage Device Interface (SDI) to communicate between the SBACKUP program and the storage devices.

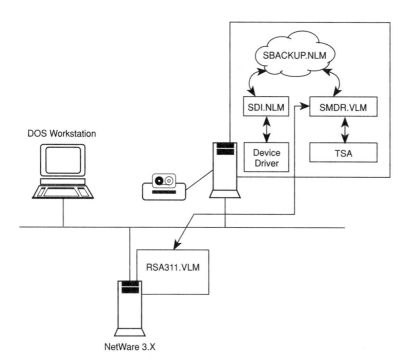

Figure 9.9

The SMS components.

 SBACKUP makes use of SDI and SMDR NLMs.

SBACKUP uses the SMDR to access the TSA. If the TSA is on the same server as the SBACKUP.NLM, the data source is on the same server. An example is using the TSA410.NLM on the host server to back up the host file system. Another example is using the TSA_NDS.NLM on the host to back up the NDS database on the host server.

 The Storage Management Data Requester (SMDR) passes commands between the SBACKUP and the TSAs.

813

The term *host* refers to the server that has the backup device. The term *target* refers to the network device (workstation or server) that has the data to be backed up or restored.

If the TSA is on a remote machine, such as a NetWare 3.x server running TSA_311.NLM, the file system on the remote machine can be backed up. It is the responsibility of the TSA to obtain the requested data and pass it on to SBACKUP through the SMDR. The TSA is the agent closest to the source data being backed up and restored. It has knowledge of the file system or data representation of the source data.

SBACKUP is capable of backing up or restoring data by communicating with the backup device through the Storage Device Interface NLM (SDI.NLM) and the backup device drivers. The Storage Device Interface detects the presence of the device and media and presents a list of devices available to the SBACKUP program. The backup operator then can select the appropriate backup device through the SBACKUP interface. The SMDR.NLM provides a high-level interface to the backup device drivers. The backup device drivers have knowledge of the backup device hardware and use commands for reading, writing, rewinding, and ejecting the storage media. The SDI.NLM, SMDR.NLM, STREAMS.NLM, CLIB.NLM, SPXS.NLM, and NWSNUT.NLM are autoloaded when SBACKUP loads.

To back up and restore workstations, a component called the Workstation Manager (WSMAN.NLM) must be loaded on the host server. WSMAN.NLM is autoloaded when TSADOS or TSA_OS2 loads. The Workstation Manager keeps an internal list of DOS TSRs (or OS/2 and Unix daemons) that have contacted it and are available for backup/restore operation.

Please note the following facts about SBACKUP-related components:

◆ SBACKUP autoloads the SDI.NLM, SMDR.NLM, STREAMS.NLM, CLIB.NLM, SPXS.NLM, and NWSNUT.NLM if they are not already loaded.

- The Storage Device Interface is used to detect the presence of the device and media and presents a list of devices available to the SBACKUP program.

- To back up and restore workstations, a component called the Workstation Manager (WSMAN.NLM) must be loaded on the host server.

- WSMAN.NLM is autoloaded when TSADOS or TSA_OS2 loads.

Using the SBACKUP Tool

The SBACKUP.NLM is loaded at the server. It is similar to the SBACKUP.NLM for NetWare 3.x servers but has been customized for the NetWare 4.x operating system.

To use SBACKUP, you first must load all the necessary drivers and TSAs for the target being backed up. NetWare 4.x ships with the tape drivers listed in table 9.2. The TAPEDAI.DSK can work with any tape device on a SCSI controller.

If the TAPEDAI.DSK driver is not installed in the SYS:SYSTEM directory on the server, you can find a copy of it in the \NW410\DISKDRV directory on the NetWare 4.x CD-ROM.

Contact the tape vendor to find out if it has specialized tape device drivers that work with NetWare 4.x SBACKUP. Specialized tape device drivers are optimized for speed and work more efficiently than

continues

generic device drivers. The list of drivers bundled with NetWare 4.x changes with time. Contact your Novell reseller or Novell at 1-800-NETWARE or 801-429-7000 for the most recent list of supported drivers.

Table 9.2
Backup Device Drivers

Device Driver	Description
TAPEDAI.DSK	A generic ASPI-compatible tape driver for SCSI controllers. It is designed to use the Advanced SCSI Programming Interface (ASPI). ASPI is a programming interface promoted by the company Adaptec. Most SCSI drive vendors have adopted it.
MNS16S.NLM and MNSDAT.DSK	Device drivers for Mountain Network Solutions, Inc. SCSI controllers and tape devices.
PS2SCSI.DSK	Work with PS/2 SCSI controllers and IBM 2.2 GB 8mm tape devices.
AHA1540.DSK, AHA1640.DSK, AHA1740.DSK, ASPITRAN.DSK	Work with devices that use the Adaptec 1540, 1640, and 1740 controllers.

To use SBACKUP, first load all the necessary drivers and TSAs for the target being backed up.

The TAPEDAI.DSK can work with any tape device on a SCSI controller.

Using SBACKUP

The following steps guide you through the basics of performing an SBACKUP.

Author's Note The actual screens presented using SBACKUP often depend on the selections you make from the SBACKUP menu for your network environment. You can select the Backup option without logging on to the Target Service first, for example. In this case, you are presented with a screen to log in to the target service first before performing the backup operation. Another example is writing labels on tapes. If you are using a new tape or completely rewriting the tape and you have not written a new label on the tape, you are given a screen to label the tape.

1. First, load the appropriate backup device drivers on the server console by typing the following command:

   ```
   LOAD TAPEDAI
   ```

   If you are using a SCSI controller, you might be able to use the generic TAPEDAI.DSK device driver.

   Figure 9.10 shows the server console screen when this device drive loads. The version number of the TAPEDAI.DSK and its date of creation are displayed. In this particular version of the TAPEDAI driver, three outdated API calls were found and a warning message was generated.

Practical TIP TAPEDAI uses the ASPI interface. ASPI does not provide sharing of tape devices between competing applications. Do not load any other device that uses ASPI when using the TAPEDAI driver.

Figure 9.10

The LOAD TAPEDAI
messages.

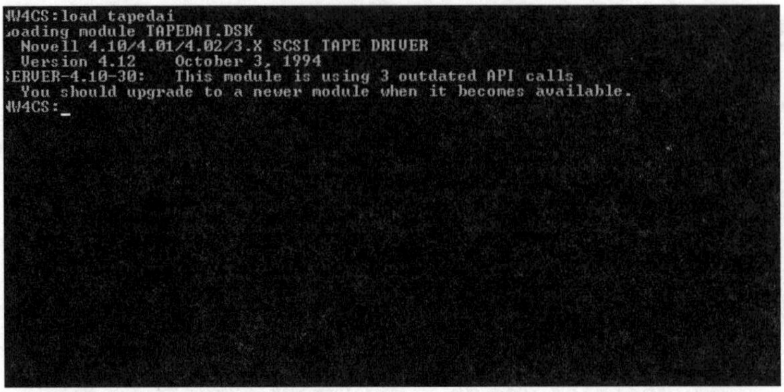

```
NW4CS:load tapedai
Loading module TAPEDAI.DSK
  Novell 4.10/4.01/4.02/3.X SCSI TAPE DRIVER
  Version 4.12    October 3, 1994
SERVER-4.10-30:   This module is using 3 outdated API calls
  You should upgrade to a newer module when it becomes available.
NW4CS:_
```

2. **Optional:** Load any other device drivers required by the manufacturer's hardware.

3. Load the TSA agents on the target. For this example, back up the NetWare 4.x file system and the NDS database. You must, therefore, load the TSA410.NLM and the TSANDS.NLM by typing the following commands:

   ```
   LOAD TSA410
   LOAD TSANDS
   ```

   Figure 9.11 shows the server console screen when the TSA for the NetWare 4.x file system loads. The version number of the TSA agent and its date of creation are displayed.

   Figure 9.12 shows the server console screen when the TSA for the NDS database loads. The version number of the TSA agent and its date of creation are displayed.

Figure 9.11

The LOAD TSA410
messages.

```
NW4CS:load tsa410
Loading module TSA410.NLM
  NetWare 4.10 Target Service Agent
  Version 4.03    October 21, 1994
  Copyright 1994 Novell, Inc.   All rights reserved.
NW4CS:
```

Figure 9.12

The LOAD TSA_NDS messages.

4. Before loading the SBACKUP.NLM, issue the command **SCAN FOR NEW DEVICES**. This command ensures that the tape device recognized by TAPEDAI is registered by NetWare 4.x.

You can use the command LIST DEVICES to see current devices. The commands below show the list of devices before and after executing the SCAN FOR NEW DEVICES command.

```
LIST DEVICES
SCAN FOR NEW DEVICES
LIST DEVICES
```

Figure 9.13 shows the output of the LIST DEVICES command. Only one device, device # 0, is listed. This is the Micropolis 1528 hard disk with 1.2 GB capacity.

```
SCAN FOR NEW DEVICES
```

```
NW4KS:load tapedai
Loading module TAPEDAI.DSK
  TAPE DRIVER
  Version 3.12    May 18, 1993
SERVER-4.00-30:   This module is using 3 outdated API calls
  You should upgrade to a newer module when it becomes available.
  Debug symbol information for TAPEDAI.DSK loaded
NW4KS:load tsa400
Loading module TSA400.NLM
  NetWare 4.0 Target Service Agent
  Version 4.01    June 4, 1993
  Copyright 1993 Novell, Inc.  All rights reserved.
NW4KS:load tsa_nds
Loading module TSA_NDS.NLM
  NetWare Directory Target Service Agent 4.0
  Version 4.00    February 13, 1993
  Copyright 1993 Novell, Inc.  All rights reserved.
NW4KS:list devices
  1. Device #  0 MICROP   1528-15MD1076301 DD24 (5D000000).
NW4KS:
```

Figure 9.13

The LIST DEVICE command before scanning for new devices.

819

Figure 9.14 shows the output of the preceding SCAN FOR NEW DEVICES command. No output is generated, but the command takes a few seconds.

Figure 9.14

Executing the SCAN FOR NEW DEVICES command.

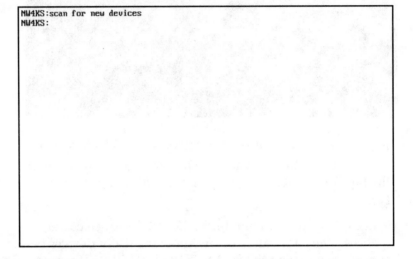

```
NW4KS:scan for new devices
NW4KS:
```

 When you execute the SCAN FOR NEW DEVICES command, the light indicators on the backup device light up when the device is accessed. If this does not happen, check for a loose cable or incorrect hardware configuration for the tape device.

Figure 9.15 shows the output of the last LIST DEVICES command after the SCAN FOR NEW DEVICES recognizes the backup device. An additional device, device # 1, is listed. This is the HP 35470A tape drive unit for DAT tapes.

5. Load the SBACKUP.NLM by entering the following commands:

```
LOAD SBACKUP
LIST DEVICES
```

820

```
NW4KS:scan for new devices
NW4KS:list devices
 8. Device #  1 HP - HP35470A (020000FF).
 1. Device #  0 MICROP   1528-15MD1076301 DD24 (5D000000).
NW4KS:
```

Figure 9.15

The LIST DEVICE command after scanning for new devices.

Practical TIP

SBACKUP has a SIZE and BUFFERS option, as shown in the following:

```
LOAD SBACKUP SIZE=sizeInKB  BUFFERS=numberOfBuffers
```

The SIZE parameter is the buffer size used by SBACKUP in KB. The value ranges from 16, 32, 64, 128, or 256 KB. The default value is 64 KB.

The BUFFERS parameter is the number of buffers reserved by SBACKUP. The value can range from 2 to 10. The default value is 4.

You can experiment with higher values to improve backup performance. If you do, take into account the additional memory required by SBACKUP. This could adversely affect server performance. Selecting a buffer size of 256 KB and 10 buffers, for example, requires an additional 2.56 MB of server RAM. Because NetWare 4.x does not use virtual memory, this is a real RAM requirement.

821

After you load SBACKUP, you can use it to perform backup and restores.

Unload SBACKUP and the support NLMs in the reverse order of their load sequence; that is, unload SBACKUP first, then the TSA NLMs, and finally the backup device drivers. An example of this unload sequence follows:

    UNLOAD SBACKUP

    UNLOAD TSANDS

    UNLOAD TSA410

    UNLOAD TAPEDAI

 Unload SBACKUP and the support NLMs in the reverse order of their load sequence; that is, unload SBACKUP first, then the TSA NLMs, and finally the backup device drivers.

Using SBACKUP to Perform a Backup

The following steps explain how to perform a backup operation. The steps assume that all the necessary drivers have already been loaded. If you have not done this, please refer to the previous section.

1. Load the SBACKUP.NLM on the host server by typing the following command:

    LOAD SBACKUP

    After SBACKUP loads, the SBACKUP main menu appears, as shown in figure 9.16.

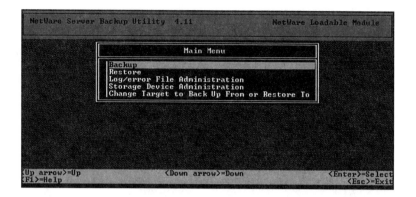

Figure 9.16

The SBACKUP Main Menu.

The Backup option enables you to specify a target to back up. It also asks you to specify the location of the session log, the device and media to use, and the type of backup to perform.

The Restore option enables you to specify the target to which you want to restore. It asks you to specify which data you want to restore and the location to which you want it restored. If a session log has been maintained, you can restore based on the session name. Alternatively, you can select the data directly from the tape. One reason for restoring directly from tape is that the session log file has been deleted or is corrupted. Restoring from a session log is convenient and quicker.

The Log/error File Administration option enables you to browse through the error log file created during a backup or restore session. This option provides a quick way to determine if any errors occurred during backup or restore operations.

The Storage Device Administration option enables you to choose the device and media to use for the backup or restore operation. This option is useful if you have more than one backup device. You also can use it to check the status of the media in the backup device.

The Change Target to Back Up From or Restore To option displays the names of the targets to which you are attached. You can select a target for performing an operation. When you do so, you are asked to specify a username/password for logging on to the target.

2. Select Storage Device Administration to see the list of backup devices (see fig. 9.17). In figure 9.17, only one backup device is shown because only one backup unit is attached to the host server. From figure 9.17, you can see that the HP 35470A device is available for use.

Figure 9.17

The list of devices.

3. Press Tab to display the status of the device, shown in figure 9.18.

   The Current operation indicates whether the device is currently reading, writing, or formatting the media. Its value is shown as None: no operation is being performed by the device. Device mode indicates whether the device is selected for reading, writing, or both. Maximum capacity indicates the storage capacity of the media in the backup device. In figure 9.18, the Maximum capacity has a value of "unknown" because the tape device driver does not report the media status.

Figure 9.18

Device status.

4. Next, label the media in the device. If the media has never been labeled, you can label it now or postpone it until later in the Backup option, when you are prompted to label the media.

   To change or add a label to the media, follow these steps:

   a. Highlight the device, press F3, and enter the media label name.

   b. To view the label for the media, highlight the backup device from the List of devices menu and press Insert.

The media for the device appears, as shown in figure 9.19.

In figure 9.19, the media has the label NETWARE_LABEL, which means that it was labeled in an earlier SBACKUP operation.

Figure 9.19

The media list.

c. Press Tab on the media listed to view the status of the media (see fig. 9.20).

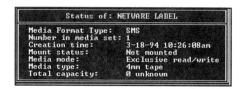

Figure 9.20

The status of the media in the backup device.

If pressing Tab doesn't work, press Esc to return to the List of devices screen and press Enter or the device you plan to use. Then try the listed steps again.

If the media was written by an SMS application (such as SBACKUP), the media owner is not displayed. If the media was written by a non-SMS application, or if it was initially "blank," the media owner is listed as "Unidentified."

Select the media you want to use by highlighting it and pressing Enter.

You are informed which media you have selected (see fig. 9.21).

825

Figure 9.21

The selected media.

In the media status box, Number in media set shows the media (tape) number within a particular media set. If the backup session takes more than one tape, the tapes are numbered consecutively in the order in which they are used. In figure 9.20, the first of these tapes is identified with the number 1.

Creation time shows the time when the media label was created and used.

Mount status indicates a value of "Mounted," "Mount Pending," "Not Mounted," or "unknown." A "Mounted" value indicates that the media is ready for reading or writing. A "Mount Pending" value indicates that the request to mount is waiting in a queue to be processed. "Not Mounted" indicates that the media is not mounted in the device.

Media mode indicates whether the media is selected for reading, writing, or reading and writing, or if the mount request is pending.

The Media type indicates the type of media in the device, such as a 4mm or 8mm tape.

Total capacity indicates the capacity of the media. If the driver does not report this value, a value of "unknown" is shown.

5. Select the Change Target to Back Up From or Restore To option from the SBACKUP Main Menu.

Figure 9.22 shows the target service choices that are running. Because the TSA410.NLM and TSA_NDS.NLM were loaded, you see that the target services are NetWare 4.0 Directory (NDS) and the NetWare 4.0 File System.

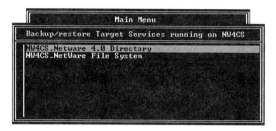

Figure 9.22

The running target services.

6. In this backup example, select the NDS database for backing up. Select the NetWare 4.0 Directory option.

   You are then prompted for the user name for the target NDSTS (NDS target service) and the password, as shown in figures 9.23 and 9.24.

Figure 9.23

The prompt for the user name of the target NDSTS.

Figure 9.24

The prompt for the password of the target NDSTS.

 If you are having a problem logging in with a user name, use the complete name. If you are logging in as user Admin in container O=ESL, for example, use the following name:

```
.CN=Admin.O=ESL
```

Some of the NLMs expect complete names with attribute type specifications.

If you are logged in correctly, a status message appears informing you that you are connected to the target service. If you do not see this message, check to see if the complete user name you typed exists and that you have entered the password correctly.

The target you are connected to always is reported on the top part of the SBACKUP screen.

7. From the SBACKUP main menu, select Backup. A box appears displaying the media and backup device to be used, as shown in figure 9.25. If you did not select the media type in step 2, a prompt appears asking you to do so.

Figure 9.25

Device media to be used for backup.

8. Another prompt appears asking you to select a location for the log and error file (see fig. 9.26). If you have been using SBACKUP for some time and already have selected this option, this screen is bypassed.

Figure 9.26

Location of log/error files.

The default location is SYS:SYSTEM/TSA/LOG. You can, however, select any other location.

828

9. Next, you are asked if you want to perform a full backup or a custom backup (see fig. 9.27). In general, the choices are Full, Differential, Incremental, and Custom. For backing up an NDS database, however, your choices are Full and Custom only. The different backup types are explained earlier in the chapter.

Figure 9.27

Type of backup.

10. For this example, select the Full backup method. The Backup Options box appears (see fig. 9.28).

Figure 9.28

Backup options.

11. Enter a description of what you want to back up.

Keep the description informative because when you select data to be restored, you are presented with a choice of the backup descriptions that you enter at this step.

12. To proceed with the backup, press F10. You are given a choice of when to start the backup (see fig. 9.29).

Figure 9.29

Proceed with backup options.

13. Select Start the Backup Later to access a form to schedule a backup at a future date and time (see fig. 9.30).

Select Start the Backup Now.

Figure 9.30

Scheduling a backup.

A status screen appears (see fig. 9.31). Press Enter to proceed to the next step.

Figure 9.31

The status screen on media label.

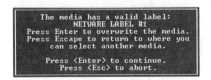

14. If the media is being completely overwritten, you are prompted for the label. Enter the name of the label for the media set.

15. As the backup proceeds, a status window on the upper right corner of the screen informs you of the status of the backup. It shows the elapsed time and the amount of data backed up, among other things. The data that is backed up appears in the upper left corner of the screen.

16. At the end of the backup, a message appears informing you that the backup is complete (see fig. 9.32).

    Press Enter to continue and exit SBACKUP.

Figure 9.32

The backup completion screen.

```
NetWare Server Backup Utility  4.11              NetWare Loadable Module
                          Target: CNET

 .CN=NW4CS_SYS.O=MI5.[Root]           Parent name: .C=IN
.O=SCS.[Root]                         Child name:
.OU=SALES.O=SCS.[Root]                Parents: 37
.OU=ENG.O=SCS.[Root]                  Children: 80
  .CN=Instructor.O=SCS.[Root]         Elapsed time: 00:00:07
.OU=CORP.O=SCS.[Root]                 Total written: 164 KB
  .CN=USER_TEMPLATE.OU=CORP.O=SCS.[Root]  Media ID: 1
.OU=CORPX.O=SCS.
  .CN=USER_TEMPL   The backup process was completed normally.
.C=US.[Root]
.C=UK.[Root]            Press <Enter> to continue.
.C=CA.[Root]

            <Escape>=Abort this backup session.
```

830

Study Note The default location of the SBACKUP error log files is SYS:SYSTEM\TSA\LOG.

Using SBACKUP to Perform a Restore

The following steps explain how to complete a restore operation. The steps assume that all necessary drivers have already been loaded.

1. Load the SBACKUP.NLM on the host server by typing the following command:

   LOAD SBACKUP

   After SBACKUP loads, the SBACKUP main menu appears. The SBACKUP options are described in the previous section, "Using SBACKUP to Perform a Backup."

2. Select Storage Device Administration to see the list of devices to which to back up.

3. Press Ins to see the media in the device (see fig. 9.33).

Figure 9.33

The media list of backup devices.

Highlight the media and press Enter to select the media to restore from (see fig. 9.34).

4. Press Tab on the media that is listed to view the status of the media.

Refer to the previous section on performing a backup using SBACKUP to see a description of the media status.

Figure 9.34

The selected media.

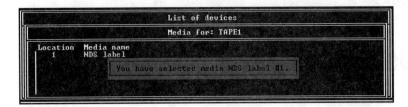

5. Select Change Target to Back Up From or Restore To from the SBACKUP main menu.

   Figure 9.35 shows the choices of target services that are running. Because the TSA410.NLM and TSA_NDS.NLM were loaded, the target services are NetWare 4.0 Directory (NDS) and the NetWare 4.0 File System.

Figure 9.35

Running restore target services.

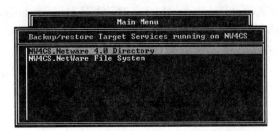

6. For this restore example, select the NDS database for restoring. If you select the NetWare 4.0 Directory option, you are prompted for the user name of the target NDSTS (NDS target service) and the password, as shown in figures 9.36 and 9.37.

Figure 9.36

Prompt for the target NDSTS user name.

Figure 9.37

Prompt for the target NDSTS password.

If you are having a problem logging in as a user name, use the complete name. If you are logging in as user Admin in container O=ESL, for example, use the following name:

.CN=Admin.O=ESL

7. If you are logged in correctly, a status message informs you that you are connected to the target service. If you do not see this message, check to see if the complete user name you typed exists, and that you have entered the password correctly.

8. From the SBACKUP main menu, select Restore. You are presented with a choice of restoring with session files or without session files (see fig. 9.38). Restoring with session files is simpler, but you might have to select restoring without session files if the log file has been deleted or corrupted.

Figure 9.38

The session restore options.

If you select Choose a Session to Restore , you are asked to select a location for the log and error files (see fig. 9.39). If you have been using SBACKUP for some time and have already selected this option, this screen is bypassed. The default location is SYS:SYSTEM/TSA/LOG. If you selected a different location at the time of backup, specify this location.

9. Figure 9.40 shows the different backup sessions that have
   been performed. The most recent session is listed first. Highlight the session you want to restore and press Enter.

If the session files are not available, use the Restore Without
Session Files option explained later in this chapter.

 Keep descriptive names of the sessions so that you
can identify them later.

10. Next, select a device and media from which to restore (see
    fig. 9.41).

Insert the media in the device, if you have not done so already.

11. Press Enter to continue. A Please wait message is displayed on-screen as the media is read. The backup device and media you are to use also are displayed (see fig. 9.42).

Figure 9.42

Media and device to be used for restoring.

12. You are presented with Restore options (see fig. 9.43). Select Restore an Entire Session.

Figure 9.43

The restore options for NDS.

13. You are asked to verify your choice (see fig. 9.44). Select Yes.

Figure 9.44

Verify the restore operation.

14. As the restore proceeds, a status window is displayed on the upper right corner of the screen, informing you of the status of the restore. You see the elapsed time and the amount of data restored, among other information. The data that is restored is shown on the upper left corner of the screen.

    At the end of the restore, a message appears informing you that the restore is complete (see fig. 9.45).

15. Press Enter. Next, exit SBACKUP.

Figure 9.45

Restore completion.

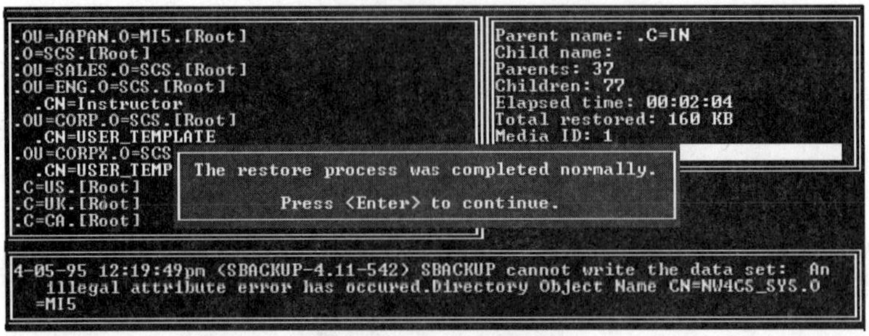

```
.OU=JAPAN.O=MIS.[Root]          Parent name:  .C=IN
.O=SCS.[Root]                   Child name:
.OU=SALES.O=SCS.[Root]          Parents: 37
.OU=ENG.O=SCS.[Root]            Children: 77
 .CN=Instructor                 Elapsed time: 00:02:04
.OU=CORP.O=SCS.[Root]           Total restored: 160 KB
 .CN=USER_TEMPLATE              Media ID: 1
.OU=CORPX.O=SCS
 .CN=USER_TEMP   The restore process was completed normally.
.C=US.[Root]
.C=UK.[Root]         Press <Enter> to continue.
.C=CA.[Root]

4-05-95 12:19:49pm <SBACKUP-4.11-542> SBACKUP cannot write the data set:  An
   illegal attribute error has occured.Directory Object Name CN=NW4CS_SYS.O
   =MIS
```

Restoring without Session Files

Occasionally, you might have a corrupted session log, or the session log might have been accidentally deleted, or the session log might not exist if you are restoring to a different server. In these cases, you must perform the restore without a session log. Perform the following steps, which complement the steps outlined in the previous section.

1. Complete steps 1 to 4 from the preceding section.

2. From the SBACKUP Main Menu, select Restore. You are given the choice of restoring with session files or without session files. Select Restore Without Session Files if the session files are corrupt or have been deleted. A message appears that indicates that you must select the device and media from which to restore.

3. Press Enter. SBACKUP identifies the media you have inserted.

4. Press Enter.

5. The restore options appear. Make the appropriate choices.

6. After selecting the restore options you want, use the F1 key if in doubt about their functions. (The meanings of these restore options are covered in the next step.)

7. Press F10. Verify that you want to continue.

8. SBACKUP reads the sessions from the media. Figure 9.46 shows the first session found.

Figure 9.46

A session description read from media and its restore options.

If this is not the session you want to restore, select No, Go on to the Next Session on the Media. When many sessions are on the media, this procedure can take a long time.

When you find the session you want to restore, select Yes, Restore This Session.

9. Proceed with the restore operations outlined in the preceding section.

Using Restore Options for Restoring a File System

The example of the restore operation was given in the context of restoring an NDS database. The restore options for restoring a file system are quite different. This section discusses the restore options peculiar to restoring a file system.

When you select the Restore a Session option from the Restore Menu for restoring a file system, you are asked to select the device/media and the name of the session from which to restore. Then the restore options shown in figure 9.47 appear.

Figure 9.47

Restore options for restoring a file system.

Select Subsets of the session to be restored from the Restore Options menu to view the data items (also called *data structure*) available for restoring (see fig. 9.48). This option classifies data items as Major TSA or Minor TSA resources. A *Major TSA* resource contains data that can be backed up as a whole when selected. Examples of Major TSAs are the file server and the volume. When you select a Major TSA resource such as a volume, all directories and files within it are considered for restore operation. A *Minor TSA* resource is contained within a directory structure of a Major TSA resource. An example of this is the directories and files within a volume.

Figure 9.48

Selecting restore subsets.

To include an entire volume for a restore operation, select Include major TSA resources. The box shown in figure 9.49 appears. Press Insert to see a list of major TSA resources available for selection (see fig. 9.50).

Figure 9.49

The Include major TSA resources box.

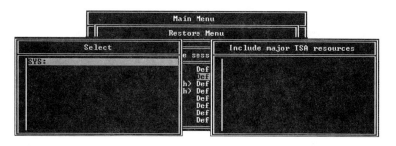

Figure 9.50

Selections for Major TSA resources.

You can use the other options for excluding or including directories or files. If you want to include a specific directory for backup, select Include directories (full path) from the Choose subsets of the session to be restored menu and press Insert to add a directory name. Figure 9.51 shows that the directory SYS:SYSTEM is selected for restore operation.

Figure 9.51

Using the Include directories option.

Select How to scan the session to be restored from the Restore Options form to view options for excluding different aspects of the file system (see fig. 9.52). This option is used for searching for the type of data contained in the data sets being restored. A *data set* is a group of data files and directories being restored.

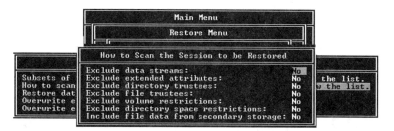

Figure 9.52

The How to Scan the Session to be Restored menu.

You can select data sets to exclude from the restore operation. If you want to restore a type of data from this list, select No; otherwise, select Yes. By default, all the Exclude options have a value of No, meaning that all aspects of the data set are to be scanned for the restore operation.

The Exclude option works in conjunction with the options Subsets of the session to be restored, and Overwrite. It narrows the types of data sets scanned for in the restore operation. You can use this to exclude or include any of the following:

◆ Extended attributes

◆ Directory trustees

◆ File trustees

◆ Volume restrictions

◆ Directory space restrictions

To restore data to a different location from where it was backed up, set the Restore data to different location field to Yes. (The default value for this field is No, which means that data is restored on top of existing data.)

While restoring files and directories, you can exclude or include any of the following:

◆ Extended attributes

◆ Directory trustees

◆ File trustees

◆ Volume restrictions

◆ Directory space restrictions

Using Custom Backup Options

The example backup operation (in the section "Using SBACKUP to Perform a Backup") was given in the context of an NDS

database. The backup options are different when the custom
Backup Method is selected for file systems.

When you select the Custom: Only Specified Data option from the
Type of Backup menu (refer to figure 9.27), the custom backup
options shown in figure 9.53 appear.

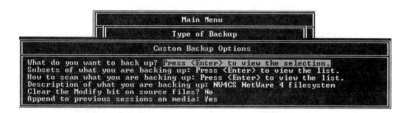

Figure 9.53

Custom backup
options for a file
system.

Select What do you want to back up? to view the Major TSA
resource that is to be backed up (see fig. 9.54). Press Ins for a
choice of other Major TSAs to back up.

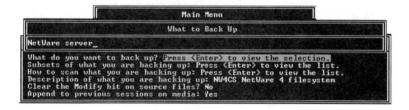

Figure 9.54

The What to Back Up
menu.

Select Subsets of what you are backing up from the What to Back
Up menu to view the data items available for backing up (see fig.
9.55). This option classifies data items as Major TSA or Minor TSA
resources.

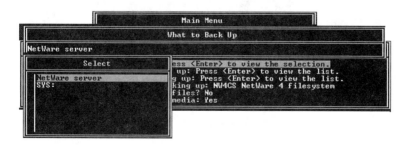

Figure 9.55

Selections for the
What do you want to
back up? option.

To include an entire volume for a restore operation, select Include major TSA resources from the Choose subsets of what you are backing up menu (see fig. 9.56). The box shown in figure 9.57 appears. Press Ins to view a list of major TSA resources available for selection (see fig. 9.58).

Figure 9.56

The Choose subsets of what you are backing up menu.

Figure 9.57

The Include major TSA resources box.

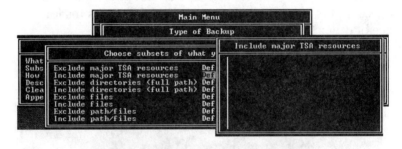

Figure 9.58

Major TSA resources available for backup.

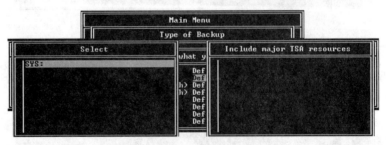

Select How to scan for what you are backing up from the What to Back Up menu to view the options for excluding different aspects of the file system (see fig. 9.59). This option shows the type of data contained in the data sets for the type of target (NetWare 4.x file system, in this case) being backed up.

Figure 9.59

The How to Scan What You Are Backing Up options.

Select the data sets you want to exclude from the backup operation. If you want to back up a type of data from this list, select No; otherwise, select Yes. By default, all the Exclude options have a value of No. This means that all aspects of the data set are scanned for the backup operation. The Exclude option works with the Choose subsets of what you are backing up option. You can exclude (Yes) or include (No) any of the following:

◆ Subdirectories

◆ Files that have not changed

◆ Hidden files and directories

◆ File and directory trustees

◆ System files and directories

◆ Directory and volume space restrictions

Using SBACKUP and Compressed Files

Using SBACKUP, you can specify whether to back up files in a compressed state. The default on NetWare 4.x volumes is that compression is enabled. This default is set at the time a volume is first created as part of the server installation.

In general, you should back up compressed files in their compressed state because the backup is faster. If you back up compressed files in the compressed state, you cannot restore them to a

NetWare server that does not support the NetWare 4.x compression.

It is not a good idea to run SBACKUP when file compression is occurring on the volume; this degrades the performance of SBACKUP. Both the default time for compressing newly created or modified files and scheduling a delayed backup is 12:00 a.m. Therefore, you should schedule SBACKUP several hours after volume compression begins.

Using SBACKUP Log and Error Files

You administer the SBACKUP session files by selecting Log/error File Administration from the SBACKUP main menu. Figure 9.60 shows the options available when this item is selected. Select View a Log File to see a list such as that shown in figure 9.61. Similarly, you can view an error file by selecting View an Error File. Select Set Location of Log and Error Files to specify the location of log and error files (see fig. 9.62).

Figure 9.60

The Log/error File Administration menu.

Figure 9.61

Selecting a log file to view.

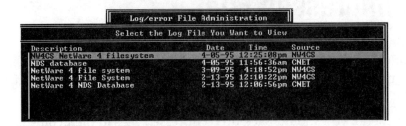

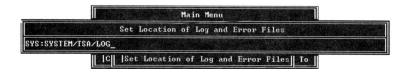

Figure 9.62

Setting the location of log and error files.

Examining SBACKUP Rights and Security Issues

Before you can use SMS, the backup operator must be able to log into NDS. To perform SBACKUP, you also need Read and File Scan rights to the file system being backed up. These rights enable the operator to read the files and scan for names of files in directories being backed up.

If you are performing an incremental or full backup, clear the archive bit at the end of the backup pass. To do this, the backup operator must have Modify rights. To back up the NDS database, you must be able to view the NDS tree structure and read the property values of the NDS object. To perform these operations, the backup operator must have Browse object trustee rights to the NDS tree, and Read property rights to All Properties. Because Browse rights are assigned to the implicit group [public], no special considerations need to be made, unless these rights are blocked by the IRF. The Read All Properties rights must be assigned to the root of the NDS subtree for which the backup operator has authority.

If the TSA at the workstation has a password set, the backup operator must have knowledge of this password.

The following guidelines apply to SBACKUP file rights:

◆ The backup operator must be able to log into NDS.

◆ The backup operator must have Read and File Scan rights to the file system being backed up.

845

◆ If you are performing an incremental or full backup, the archive bit is cleared at the end of the backup pass. To perform this, you must have Modify rights to the files being backed up.

◆ To back up the NDS database, the backup operator must have Browse object trustee rights to the NDS tree, and the Read property rights to All Properties.

Backing Up DOS Workstations

You can use SBACKUP to back up and restore DOS workstations. Specific drives and directories can be backed up at the workstation. To perform a backup/restore of the DOS workstation, follow these steps:

1. Load TSADOS.NLM at the server. This autoloads WSMAN.NLM, which is required.

2. Load TSASMS.COM at the workstation. TSASMS.COM can be found in the C:\NWCLIENT directory on the workstation.

3. Load SBACKUP and select the DOS workstation's TSA. Do this by selecting Change Target to Back Up From or Restore To from the SBACKUP main menu to see a list of the TSA agents registered with SBACKUP running on the host server.

Backing up DOS workstations is covered in more detail in the second part of this book.

Caveats when Using SBACKUP

Keep in mind these useful caveats when performing SBACKUP:

◆ SBACKUP uses temporary files (SYS:SYSTEM\TSA$TMP.*) that can be as large as 7 MB. Make sure you have enough free disk space on the server for these temporary files. The temporary files can become quite large especially if you have extended attributes or linked Unix files.

◆ Switching to the system console when running SBACKUP and manually unloading the drivers is potentially dangerous. It can crash the server.

◆ Do not mount or dismount volumes during an SBACKUP session. This could corrupt data or crash the server.

◆ When backing up a system that has global compression enabled, wait for a period of time until the compression has been completed before backing up the file system. This enables you to back up a maximum number of files in the compressed state.

◆ In general, be aware of the name space formats supported by the file system being backed up. SBACKUP shows only DOS-type file names and paths. If you are using non-DOS filenames for other types of name space support, use the DOS filename equivalents. The error and backup log files, however, show the non-DOS filename formats. SBACKUP currently supports name spaces for the following formats:

  ◆ DOS

  ◆ OS/2

  ◆ NFS

  ◆ Macintosh

  ◆ FTAM

◆ The NetWare server on which SBACKUP is run requires a minimum of 3 MB of RAM in addition to other server RAM requirements.

◆ If backing up other workstations (DOS, OS/2, and so on), you must know the workstation password, if it has been set.

◆ SBACKUP logs out when the SBACKUP session finishes. If the SBACKUP session requires more than one media (tape), it waits for one to be inserted before continuing. If no one is on hand to feed another tape drive to the backup device, SBACKUP is logged into the target, which could pose a security risk.

◆ SBACKUP does not verify the data you have backed up. That is, it does not read what it has written and compare the data. You must perform an explicit restore if you are concerned about the accuracy of SBACKUP.

 Always have an extra supply of reusable tapes on hand in case you need to back up more data than usual.

Study Guide for the Chapter

If you are preparing for passing exams, review the chapter with the following goals:

1. Understand the system fault-tolerant features of NetWare 4.x and that SMS is the principal tool used for performing SBACKUP. Use the Study Notes as a quick review.

2. Pay particular attention to the different types of backup techniques.

3. After studying this chapter, attempt the sample test questions. If you make mistakes, review the appropriate topics until you understand the reasons for the correct answers.

Chapter Summary

This chapter discusses the native backup service for NetWare 4.x. NetWare 4.x backup uses the Storage Management Services (SMS). The primary tool that uses SMS is SBACKUP.NLM.

You can use SBACKUP to support different types of backup strategies such as full backup, differential backup, and incremental backup. The advantages and disadvantages of each type of backup strategy are discussed.

The chapter explains in detail the operation of SBACKUP for backup and restoring operations.

Chapter Test Questions

Test questions can have a single correct answer or multiple correct answers. Where a single answer is desired, a ○ notation precedes the possible answers. Some questions require you to select more than one answer. These questions are indicated by the □ preceding each answer. Not all questions are multiple choice. Occasionally, a question asks you to type in an answer. The answer in this case is usually a one-word answer. The answer is not case sensitive, so you can type in the answer in lower- or uppercase.

Certain questions are repeated in different ways so you can recognize them even when the wording is different. Taking practice quizzes not only tests your knowledge, it gives you confidence when you take your exam.

1. NetWare 4.x backup services are consolidated in _____.

   ○ A. SBACKUP.NLM

   ○ B. SBACKUP.EXE

   ○ C. NBACKUP.NLM

   ○ D. NBACKUP.EXE

2. Which of the following backup methods are supported by SBACKUP?

   □ A. Full backup

   □ B. Modified backup

   □ C. Fast backup

   □ D. Incremental backup

   □ E. Differential backup

3. In full backup, _____.

   ○   A.   the archive bits of all files that are backed up are cleared

   ○   B.   only modified files that have their archive bit set are backed up

   ○   C.   the archive bits of the backed up files are not cleared

   ○   D.   the archive bits of the manually selected files are not cleared

4. In incremental backup, _____.

   ○   A.   the archive bits of all files that are backed up are cleared

   ○   B.   only modified files that have their archive bit set are backed up

   ○   C.   the archive bits of the backed up files are not cleared

   ○   D.   the archive bits of the manually selected files are not cleared

5. In differential backup, _____.

   ○   A.   the archive bits of all files that are backed up are cleared

   ○   B.   only modified files that have their archive bit set are backed up

   ○   C.   the archive bits of the backed up files are not cleared

   ○   D.   the archive bits of the manually selected files are not cleared

6. Which of the following statements about the full backup strategy is true?

   ○   A.   It takes the shortest amount of backup time.

   ○   B.   It enables files to be selectively backed up.

   ○   C.   It takes more time than incremental backup but less time than differential backup.

   ○   D.   It takes the longest amount of backup time.

7. Which of the following statements about the incremental backup strategy is true?

   ○ A. It takes the shortest amount of backup time.

   ○ B. It enables files to be selectively backed up.

   ○ C. It takes more time than differential backup but less time than full backup.

   ○ D. It takes the longest amount of backup time.

8. Which of the following backup methods contains a sequential history of the files that have been modified?

   ○ A. Full backup

   ○ B. Incremental

   ○ C. Differential

   ○ D. Custom

9. To restore data in incremental backup, you will need _____.

   ○ A. the last full backup

   ○ B. the last full backup and last incremental backup

   ○ C. the last full backup and first incremental backup

   ○ D. the last full backup and every incremental backup after it

10. If any data in a differential backup tape not belonging to the last differential backup set is corrupted, _____.

   ○ A. the data cannot be recovered

   ○ B. the data can still be recovered from the last full backup and the first differential backup

   ○ C. the data can still be recovered from the last full backup

   ○ D. the data can still be recovered from the last full backup and the most recent differential backup

11. If the last differential backup is bad, _____.

   ○ A. you can restore data only up to the next to the last differential backup

   ○ B. the data can still be recovered from the last full backup and the first differential backup

   ○ C. the data can still be recovered from the last full backup

   ○ D. the data can still be recovered from the last full backup and the most recent differential backup

12. Custom backup enables you to _____.

   ○ A. include parts of the directory structure to be backed up or select different types of data items to be backed up

   ○ B. include/exclude parts of the directory structure to be backed up or select different types of data items to be backed up

   ○ C. exclude parts of the directory structure to be backed up or select different types of data items to be backed up

   ○ D. include but not exclude parts of the directory structure to be backed up

13. Which of the following TSAs can be used for backing up a NetWare 4.x file system?

   ○ A. TSA311.NLM

   ○ B. TSA41.NLM

   ○ C. TSA410.NLM

   ○ D. TSADOS.NLM

   ○ E. TSA_DOS.NLM

   ○ F. TSANDS.NLM

   ○ G. TSA_NDS.NLM

14. Which of the following TSAs can be used for backing up an NDS database?

   ○ A. TSA311.NLM

   ○ B. TSA411.NLM

   ○ C. TSA400.NLM

   ○ D. TSADOS.NLM

   ○ E. TSA_DOS.NLM

   ○ F. TSANDS.NLM

   ○ G. TSAXNDS.NLM

15. SMS enables data to be backed up and restored _____.

   ○ A. independent of the backup hardware but dependent on the file system

   ○ B. independent of the backup hardware and file system

   ○ C. independent of the file system but dependent on the backup hardware

   ○ D. in a manner independent of the operating system

16. SBACKUP makes use of _____.

   ☐ A. SDI.NLM

   ☐ B. DIBI.NLM

   ☐ C. SMDR NLMs

   ☐ D. VLMs

   ☐ E. SQRDR.NLM

17. SBACKUP autoloads which of the following NLMs if they are not already loaded?

   ☐ A. SDI.NLM

   ☐ B. SMDR.NLM

   ☐ C. TSA410.NLM

☐ D. STREAMS.NLM

☐ E. TSA_NDS.NLM

☐ F. CLIB.NLM

☐ G. SPXS.NLM

☐ H. NWSNUT.NLM

18. Storage Management Data Requester (SMDR) is used to
_____.

○ A. pass commands between SBACKUP and the SDI NLM

○ B. pass commands between SBACKUP and the TSAs

○ C. pass commands between the SDI and the device driver

○ D. communicate with the SDR NLM

19. Which of the following NLMs are not auto-loaded by
SBACKUP?

☐ A. SDI.NLM

☐ B. SMDR.NLM

☐ C. TSA410.NLM

☐ D. STREAMS.NLM

☐ E. TSANDS.NLM

☐ F. CLIB.NLM

☐ G. SPXS.NLM

☐ H. NWSNUT.NLM

20. The Storage Device Interface is used to _____.

○ A. detect the presence of the device and media and present
a list of devices available to the SBACKUP program

○ B. communicate with the TSA

○ C. detect the presence of the correctly configured device
driver

○ D. communicate with the SMDR NLM

○ E. communicate with the SDR NLM

21. To back up and restore workstations, the _____ must be loaded on the host server.

○ A. TSA_NDS.NLM

○ B. TSA400.NLM

○ C. WSMAN.NLM

○ D. WS_MAN.NLM

22. WS_MAN.NLM is autoloaded when which of the following NLMs load?

☐ A. TSA_DOS

☐ B. TSA400

☐ C. TSA_OS2

☐ D. TSA_NDS

23. The name of the driver that can work with any tape device on a SCSI controller is _____.

○ A. TAPEDAI.DSK

○ B. TAPEDISK.NLM

○ C. TAPEASPI.DSK

○ D. TAPEASPI.NLM

24. To unload SBACKUP and the support NLMs, _____.

○ A. you must unload the TSA NLMs first, then the SBACKUP program, and finally the backup device drivers

○ B. you must unload SBACKUP first, then the backup device drivers, and finally the TSA NLMs

○ C. you must unload SBACKUP first, then the TSA NLMs, and finally the backup device drivers

○ D. you must unload device drivers first, then the TSA NLMs, and finally the SBACKUP program

855

25. The Log/error File Administration option in SBACKUP enables you to _____.

   ○ A. browse through the error log file created in the backup session only

   ○ B. browse through the error log file created during a backup or restore session

   ○ C. browse through the error log file created during a backup or restore session and edit it

   ○ D. edit the error log file created during a backup or restore session

26. The default location of the SBACKUP error log files is _____.

   ○ A. SYS:SYSTEM\TSA\LOG

   ○ B. SYS:PUBLIC\TSA\LOG

   ○ C. SYS:SYSTEM\SBACKUP\LOG

   ○ D. SYS:PUBLIC\SBACKUP\LOG

27. If you are performing an incremental or full backup you must have the _____.

   ○ A. Modify right to the files being backed up

   ○ B. Access Control right to the files being backed up

   ○ C. Supervisor right to the files being backed up

   ○ D. Delete right to the files being backed up

28. In read-after-write verification, _____.

   ○ A. data is verified by special hardware on all hard disk controllers

   ○ B. the data block written to the hard disk is read back and compared with the original

   ○ C. data blocks read are compared to previously written data

   ○ D. data is verified by error-correcting information

NetWare 4.x Messaging Services

This chapter discusses how to use NetWare 4.x networks to provide messaging services. Specifically, you learn about the NetWare MHS mail services that are bundled with NetWare 4.x.

Messaging services are used by applications such as e-mail to provide message-based communications between applications running on different nodes on a network. Message-based applications have become an important method for providing communications in an organization.

Components of Messaging Services

Messaging services transport data, called *messages*, between nodes on the network using the network's underlying communications protocol. The method of transmitting messages is called *store-and-forward*, which means that the message might be held temporarily at an intervening node on the network before its eventual delivery. The message is delivered and stored at the final destination node until the recipient is ready to read it and then either forward it, delete it, or store it. The types of messages transferred include text, binary, graphic, audio, and video information.

In a simple LAN-based messaging application (see fig. 10.1), messaging services consist of the following components:

◆ Messaging server (also called messaging engine)

◆ User mailboxes

◆ Messaging applications

Figure 10.1

Simple LAN-based
messaging services.

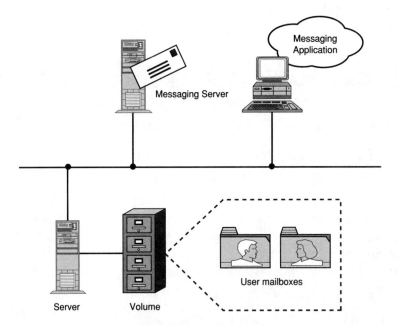

The messaging server accepts messages from an application, typically a user's e-mail client software, and delivers the message to the destination user's mailbox. In a larger network consisting of an interconnection of many different types of networks, the message might have to be routed to other messaging servers for eventual delivery.

A simple local message delivery requires the following messaging components:

- ◆ Messaging engine
- ◆ User mailboxes
- ◆ Messaging applications

User mailboxes are located on a machine local to the user. This is typically the server the user most frequently logs in to. A common method of implementing user mailboxes is to use a file system directory on the local server. You also can use methods that treat the user mailboxes as abstract mail objects.

Messaging applications include e-mail client software, groupware software such as Novell's GroupWise, calendaring software, scheduling programs, and so on.

In larger networks, other messaging service components such as mail gateways and mail routers are needed. *Mail gateways* enable the delivery of messages to a foreign e-mail system. *Mail routers* are store-and-forward computers that temporarily store messages and then forward them to their final destination or an intervening destination. In some systems, the mail router can be implemented as part of the messaging server.

NetWare 4 MHS

NetWare 4 server software comes bundled with a store-and-forward messaging engine for NetWare 4-based networks. This is implemented by the MHS.NLM installed on the server during the installation of NetWare 4 MHS.

NetWare 4 MHS also includes DOS and Windows versions of an e-mail client software called FirstMail. *FirstMail* is an NDS-aware e-mail client from Novell.

NetWare 4 Message Handling Services is implemented by the MHS.NLM that runs on the NetWare 4 server.

NetWare 4 MHS includes the FirstMail e-mail client software for DOS and Windows.

NetWare 4 MHS Installation Requirements

NetWare 4 MHS software is provided on the CD-ROM that ships with NetWare 4. The software enables you to create an unlimited number of mailboxes per NetWare server. You are, however, limited by the NetWare server license that limits the number of concurrent user sessions on the network.

The minimum hardware requirements of the NetWare server on which MHS is installed are the following:

◆ Intel 80386 processor or better

◆ 12 MB of RAM for server

◆ 65 MB of server hard disk space

◆ CD-ROM required for installation

NetWare MHS requires the following server resources:

◆ 500 KB of RAM

◆ 2.5 MB of disk space for program storage, plus additional disk space for user mailboxes. The amount of disk space for user mailboxes depends on the size and number of messages stored in them.

Novell claims that the preceding minimum requirements are not sufficient to handle more than 10 users or 100 messages per day. For networks that need to process more than 100 messages per day, the following configuration is recommended:

- Intel 80386 processor or better
- 16 MB of RAM for server plus additional RAM to maintain more than 30 percent free cache buffers
- 65 MB of server hard disk space plus an additional 5 MB per user mailbox

Installing NetWare 4 MHS

The following is a guided tour of installing NetWare 4 MHS:

1. Mount the NetWare 4 operating system CD-ROM. You can do this by using the following:

   LOAD ASPICD (For ASPI for SCSI CD-ROM)

   LOAD CDROM

   CD MOUNT *N*

   You can obtain the value of *N* by typing the following command:

   CD VOLUME LIST

   Note the volume number or name reported by the previous command.

2. Load the INSTALL.NLM at the NetWare server by typing the following command:

   LOAD INSTALL

   A screen similar to figure 10.2 appears.

Figure 10.2

The INSTALL.NLM screen.

3. Select Product options from the Installation Options menu. A screen similar to figure 10.3 appears.

Figure 10.3

Other installation options.

4. Select Choose an item or product listed above from the Other Installation Actions menu and highlight Install NetWare MHS Services in the Other Installation Items/Products menu (see fig. 10.4).

Figure 10.4

The Install NetWare MHS Services Help box.

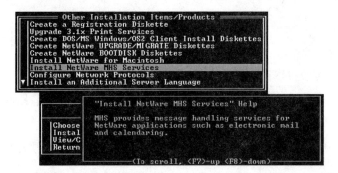

5. Press Enter. The path name from which MHS will be installed appears (see fig. 10.5).

6. Press Enter. The File Copy Status screen appears (see fig. 10.6).

7. You will see a Postmaster General Authentication screen. Supply the Admin user name and password, and press Enter.

8. If the NetWare server on which you are installing MHS has multiple volumes, select the destination volume.

9. If you are installing MHS for the first time, you will be asked whether this is the first install to the MHS tree. Answer Yes.

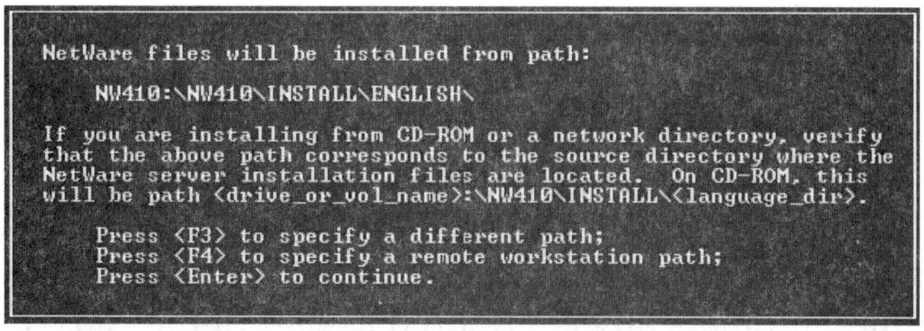

Figure 10.5

The default source
path name for
NetWare MHS
Services.

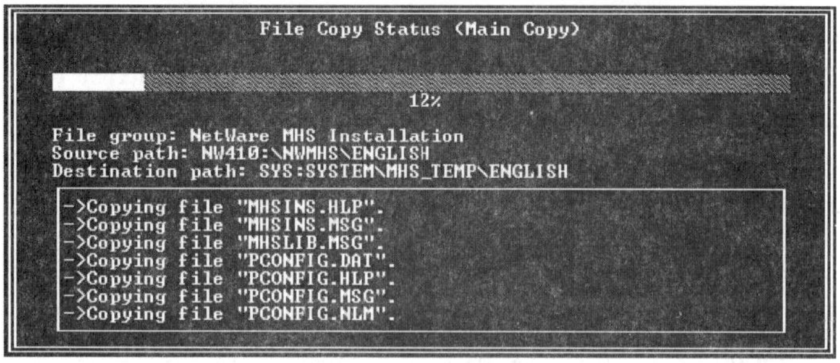

Figure 10.6

The File Copy Status
screen.

A message announcing completion of the MHS installation
appears.

10. Exit INSTALL.NLM.

11. Load the MHS NLM by typing the following command:

    LOAD MHS

    Also, place this statement in the AUTOEXEC.NCF file.

You also can install NetWare MHS during the initial NetWare 4.x
installation by completing these steps after the initial NetWare 4.x
server installation.

Post NetWare 4 MHS Installation Check

As part of the NetWare 4 MHS installation, the Messaging Server
and the Message Routing Group objects are created by default.
This section describes these objects and the changes made to the
NDS tree and the properties of these objects.

The Messaging Server object enables messaging services. This object defines the location of the message directory. This is the \MHS directory on the volume object on which MHS was installed. The Messaging Server object also identifies (via its NetWare Server property) the NetWare server on which MHS services (MHS.NLM) is running. The Messaging Server object is created and automatically configured as part of the NetWare 4 MHS service installation.

The Message Routing Group object is used to identify a cluster of messaging servers that communicate with each other for transferring messages. A default message routing group called MHS_ROUTING_GROUP is created as part of the NetWare MHS installation.

As part of the NetWare 4 MHS installation, the Messaging Server and Message Routing Group objects are created by default.

The following is a list of changes made to the NDS tree:

♦ The default Messaging Server and Message Routing Group objects are created in the context in which the NetWare 4 server is installed. Figure 10.7 shows the Messaging Server (NW4CS_MSG) and the Message Routing Group (MHS_ROUTING_GROUP) objects created in the server context OU=CORP.O=ESL.

♦ A Postmaster General (default owner) user of the Message Routing Group is assigned. This user is the Admin user specified during MHS installation. In figure 10.8, the Postmaster General is Admin.ESL.

♦ The default Messaging Server object is added to the Messaging Servers property of the Message Routing Group object (see fig. 10.9).

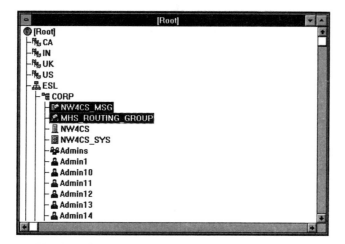

Figure 10.7

Newly created
message objects
in server context.

Figure 10.8

The Postmaster
General owner of the
Message Routing
Group object.

◆ A Postmaster for the Messaging Server object is assigned (see
fig. 10.10). This is the Admin user specified during MHS
installation.

◆ The Message Routing Groups property of the Messaging
Server object is set to the default Message Routing Group
object (see fig. 10.11).

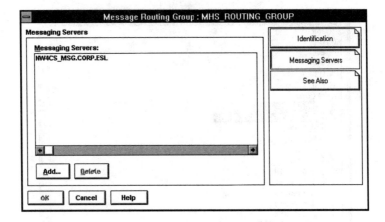

Figure 10.9

The Messaging Servers property of the Message Routing Group object.

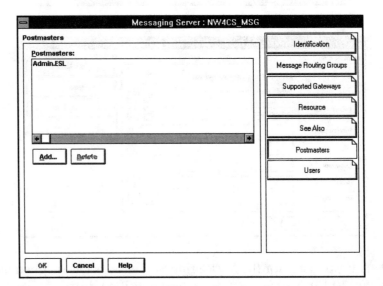

Figure 10.10

The Postmasters property of the Messaging Server object.

◆ The NetWare Server property of the Messaging Server object is set to the NetWare server on which MHS was installed. Additionally, the MHS Database Location property of the Messaging Server object is set to the volume on which MHS services was installed. Figure 10.12 shows examples of these property settings.

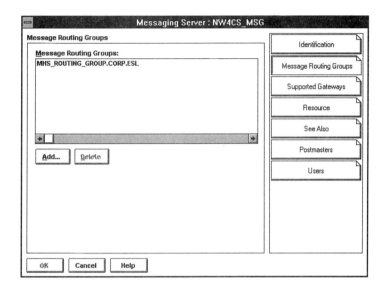

Figure 10.11

The Message Routing Groups property of the Messaging Server object.

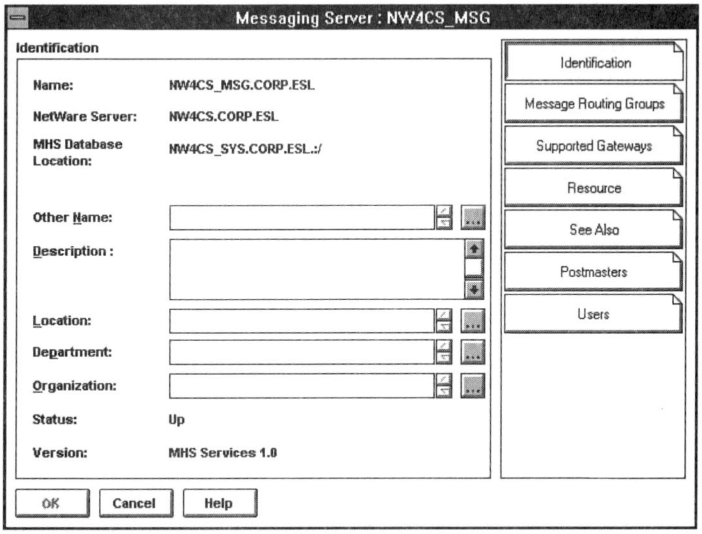

Figure 10.12

The NetWare Server and the MHS Database Location properties for a Messaging Server object.

◆ The Postmaster General (Admin) user's Mailbox Location and Mailbox ID properties are set. The Mailbox Location is set to the Messaging Server, and the Mailbox ID is set to Admin (see fig. 10.13).

Figure 10.13

The Mailbox Location and Mailbox ID properties of the Postmaster General user.

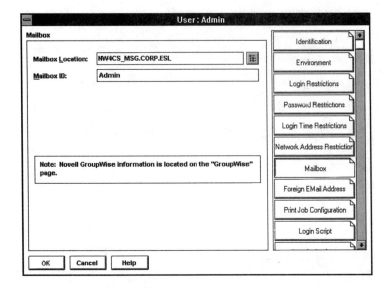

◆ The FirstMail programs for DOS (MAIL.EXE) and Windows (WMAIL.EXE) are automatically installed in the SYS:PUBLIC directory of the NetWare server on which MHS was installed.

Note that if you delete or rename the Postmaster General user (Admin user), you must make changes to the Postmaster General properties of the Messaging Server and the Message Routing Group objects. If you neglect this, messaging services will malfunction.

Assigning MHS-Related Properties to NDS Objects

The User, Group, Organizational Role, Organization, and Organizational Unit NDS objects have MHS-related properties. You can assign these properties using NWADMIN. Use the Users page button of the Messaging Server object, or select the Mailbox page button of the object whose property needs to be set.

The following steps outline how to set these properties from the Messaging Server.

1. Double-click on the Messaging Server icon from within NWADMIN.

2. Select the Users property page button. The Users property page opens (see fig. 10.14).

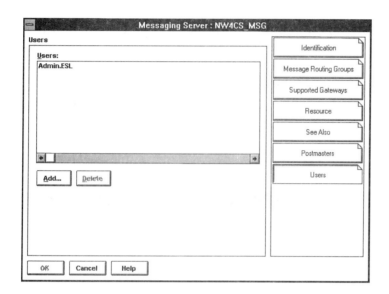

Figure 10.14

The Users property of the Messaging Server object.

3. Click on the **A**dd button. The Select Object dialog box opens (see fig. 10.15).

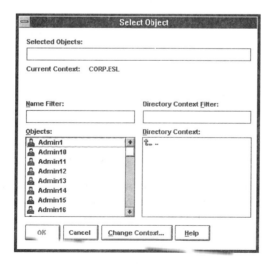

Figure 10.15

Using the Select Object dialog box to assign users to the Messaging Server object.

4. Select the objects that need to be assigned to the messaging server. Any object so selected will have its Mailbox Location property set to the Messaging Server object and its Mailbox ID property set to the object's relative distinguished name (RDN).

The following steps outline how these properties can be set from the User, Group, Organizational Role, Organization, or Organizational Unit object. In this, example, the mailbox properties are being set for the Organization O=SCS.

1. Right-click on the selected object from NWADMIN and select Details.

2. Click on the mailbox page button. The Mailbox property page opens (see fig. 10.16).

Figure 10.16

Mailbox properties of Organization O=SCS.

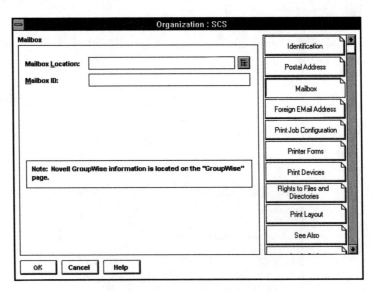

3. Select the Browse icon to the right of the Mailbox Location box. The Select Object dialog box opens (see fig. 10.17).

4. Use the Select Object dialog box to navigate the NDS tree and find the messaging server to assign to the Mailbox Location property (see fig. 10.18).

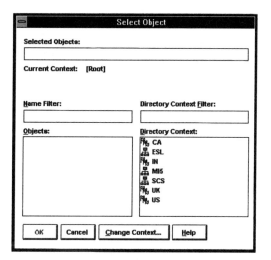

Figure 10.17

Using the Select
Object dialog box
to select the
messaging server.

Figure 10.18

A Messaging Server
object found using
the Select Object
dialog box.

5. Click on OK. The Mailbox properties set for the object appear
(see fig. 10.19).

6. Choose OK.

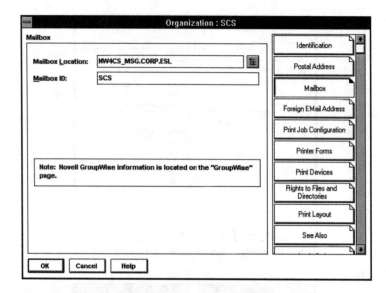

Figure 10.19

Mailbox properties set for O=SCS.

Other MHS-Related NDS Objects

Besides the Messaging Server and the Message Routing Group objects, which are created when NetWare 4 MHS is installed, two other objects deal with messaging services. These are the *External Entity* and *Distribution List* objects.

The External Entity Object

External Entity objects are nonnative NDS objects such as e-mail addresses of foreign e-mail systems. These objects are created and configured when gateway software is installed; they are not used for basic MHS services.

You can use the External Entity object as a placeholder that enables you to send messages to users who would not normally be listed in the NDS tree because they are not part of the NDS-based network.

The Distribution List Object

The Distribution List object is used for the grouping of multiple mailbox addresses. If a group of mailboxes is located on the same server, using Distribution List objects to send the same message to multiple recipients can reduce network traffic. You can send a single message to the Distribution List mailbox, for example, and then the message can be replicated for every mailbox on the distribution list.

You also can use NDS group objects to distribute mail to the members of a group. Whereas a group's membership property cannot contain other groups, the Distribution List object can contain other distribution lists. In other words, distribution lists can be *nested*. Members of a distribution list do not share login scripts or trustee assignments. The membership only serves for the convenience of sending messages to multiple recipients.

The following steps describe how to create a distribution list:

1. Right-click on the container object in which the distribution list is to be created.

2. Select Create, and select the distribution list from the list of objects. The Create Distribution List dialog box appears (see fig. 10.20).

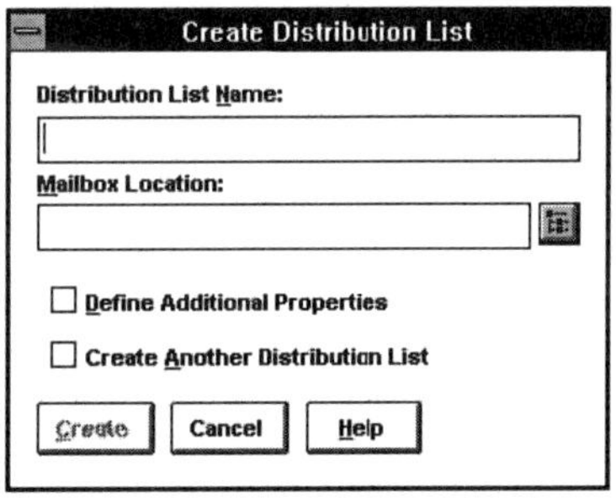

Figure 10.20

The Create Distribution List dialog box.

3. Enter the name of the distribution list.

4. Click on the Browse button to the right of the Mailbox Location field to set its value. The Select Object dialog box opens (see fig. 10.21).

5. Use the Select Object dialog box to browse the NDS tree and select the appropriate messaging server on which the distribution list is to be defined.

873

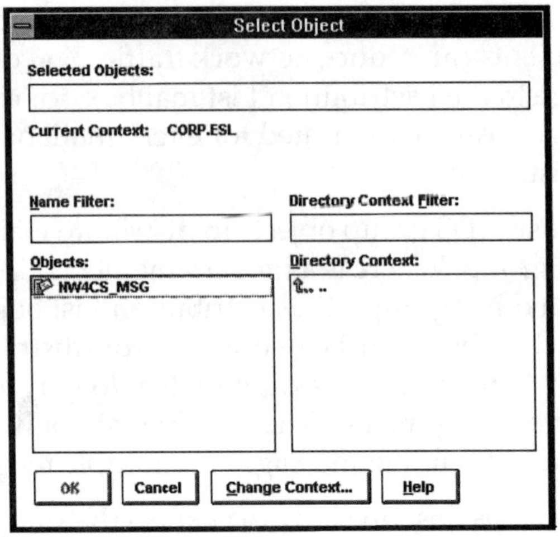

Figure 10.21

Using the Select Object dialog box to set the mailbox location.

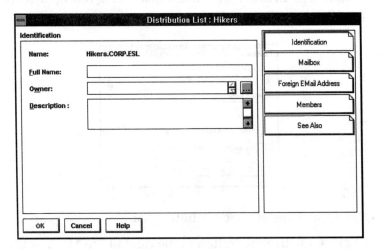

6. Check the Define Additional Properties box and select Create. The properties of the Distribution List object appear (see fig. 10.22).

Figure 10.22

Distribution List properties.

7. Select the Members page button. The Members property of the Distribution List object appears (see fig. 10.23).

874

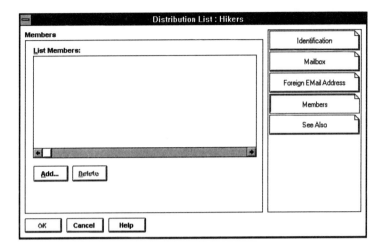

Figure 10.23

The Members
property of the
Distribution List
object.

8. Select **A**dd, and use the Select Object dialog box to assign
   members to the distribution list (see fig. 10.24).

9. Click on OK to save your changes.

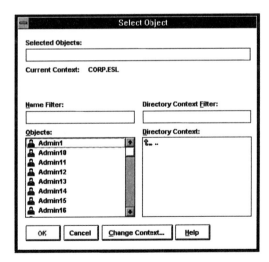

Figure 10.24

Using the Select
Object dialog box to
assign members to
the distribution list.

Using FirstMail

FirstMail is available in Windows and DOS versions. This section provides a guided tour of setting up and using FirstMail for Windows.

You must first set up a program item to use FirstMail by following these steps:

1. Select File from Program Manager.

2. Select New.

3. Select Program Item and select OK.

4. In the Program Item Properties dialog box, enter the following:

> Description: `FirstMail`

> Command Line: `Z:\PUBLIC\WMAIL.EXE`

5. Save your changes.

The following is a guided tour on using FirstMail to create, send, and receive e-mail messages. First, to create and send a message, follow these steps:

1. Double-click on the FirstMail icon. The FirstMail screen appears (see fig. 10.25).

Figure 10.25

The FirstMail screen.

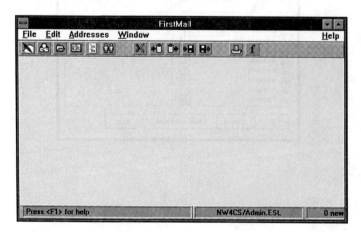

2. Select New Message from the <u>F</u>ile menu, or click on the first icon on the left of the toolbar (pen and paper).

The screen for creating messages appears (see fig. 10.26).

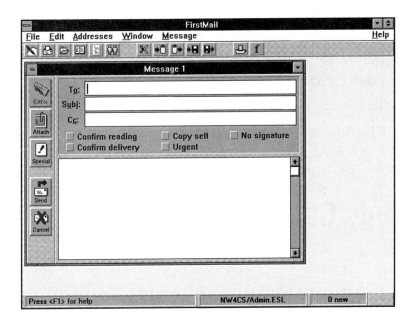

Figure 10.26

The FirstMail create message screen.

3. Enter the following information:

To: *Name of another MHS user*

S<u>u</u>bj: *Name of subject*

C<u>c</u>: *Optionally, enter another MHS user*

4. Click in the message area, and type a message.

5. Optionally, enable any of the following message options:

Confirm reading
Confirm delivery
Copy self
Urgent
No signature

6. Click on the Send button.

The recipient of the message then follows these steps to read the message:

1. Log in to the network.

2. Start FirstMail.

3. Select Read New Mail from the File menu or click on the second icon (envelope) on the toolbar.

4. Double-click on the message.

5. To save the message, highlight it.

6. Click on the Move button on the New mail folder toolbar.

7. Select the mail folder in which to save the message.

Study Guide for the Chapter

If you are preparing for exams, review the chapter with the following goals:

♦ Understand the different NDS objects for messaging services.

♦ Know about the FirstMail MHS clients for DOS and Windows. Review the properties of the MHS-related NDS objects that are created.

After studying this chapter, attempt the sample test questions. If you make mistakes, review the appropriate topics until you understand the reasons for the correct answers.

Chapter Summary

This chapter discussed how to use NetWare 4.x networks to provide messaging services. You learned about the NetWare MHS mail services bundled with NetWare 4.x, and the procedures for installing, configuring, and using these services.

Chapter Test Questions

Test questions either have a single correct answer or multiple correct answers. Where a single answer is desired, a ○ notation precedes the possible answers. Some questions require you to select more than one answer. These questions are indicated by the ☐ preceding each answer. Not all the questions are multiple choice. Occasionally, a question might ask you to type an answer. The answer in this case is usually a one-word answer. Answers are not case sensitive, so you can type the answer in lower- or uppercase.

Certain questions are repeated in different ways so you can recognize them even when the wording is different. Taking practice quizzes not only tests your knowledge, it gives you confidence when you take your exam.

1. In a simple local message delivery you can expect which of the following messaging components?

   ☐   A. Messaging engine

   ☐   B. Database engine

   ☐   C. User mailboxes

   ☐   D. Messaging applications

   ☐   E. Routing engine

2. NetWare 4 Message Handling Services is implemented by the _____ NLM that runs on the NetWare 4 server.

   ○   A. MSG.NLM

   ○   B. MESSAGE.NLM

   ○   C. MHS.NLM

   ○   D. MHS4.NLM

   ○   E. MSG_SRV.NLM

3. NetWare 4 MHS includes which of the following e-mail client software?

   ○ A. MHSX client

   ○ B. Mail First

   ○ C. FirstMail

   ○ D. cc:Mail

4. NetWare 4 MHS requires which of the following resources on the NetWare server?

   ○ A. 100 KB of RAM

   ○ B. 200 KB of RAM

   ○ C. 300 KB of RAM

   ○ D. 400 KB of RAM

   ○ E. 500 KB of RAM

5. NetWare 4 MHS takes up _____ MB for program storage:

   ○ A. 1.5

   ○ B. 2.5

   ○ C. 3.5

   ○ D. 4.5

   ○ E. 5.5

6. After the NetWare 4 MHS installation, which of the following objects are created by default?

   ☐ A. Messaging Server

   ☐ B. Distribution List

   ☐ C. Message Routing Group

   ☐ D. External Entity

7. The Messaging Server object is used to represent the _____.

   ○ A. routing server

   ○ B. messaging engine

   ○ C. user mailbox

   ○ D. e-mail client server

8. The Messaging Routing Group is a cluster of _____.

   ○ A. users that transfer messages to each other

   ○ B. messaging servers that transfer messages to each other

   ○ C. mailboxes that receive the same messages

   ○ D. NetWare 4 servers used for licensing

9. The External Entity object is used to represent an external

   _____.

   ○ A. mail server

   ○ B. mailbox

   ○ C. NetWare server

   ○ D. mail application

10. Which of the following are true for Distribution List objects?

   ☐ A. A distribution list can contain only User objects.

   ☐ B. Distribution list members do not share login scripts and trustee rights.

   ☐ C. Distribution list members share login scripts and trustee rights.

   ☐ D. Distribution lists can contain other distribution lists.

   ☐ E. Distribution lists cannot contain other distribution lists.

A

APPENDIX

NetWare 3.x and NetWare 4.x Command Comparisons

This table describes the new NetWare 4.x utilities and the NetWare 3.x utilities they replace.

Table A.1
NetWare 4.x Command/Utility Differences with NetWare 3.x

NetWare 4.0 Utility	Description
NETADMIN.EXE	Menu-driven text utility used to create NDS objects. Can also be used to assign property values and rights. Consolidates some of the features of pre-NetWare 4.0 utilities such as SYSCON, SECURITY, USERDEF, and DSPACE

continues

Table A.1, Continued
NetWare 4.x Command/Utility Differences with NetWare 3.x

NetWare 4.0 Utility	Description
NWADMIN.EXE	MS Windows and OS/2 Graphical utility to manage NDS tree and perform operations on it. This is a consolidated graphical tool for network management.
PARTMGR.EXE	Text utility for managing partitions and their replicas.
PARTMGR	Partition Manager (a menu item in the NetWare Administrator tool) is the GUI equivalent of the PARTMGR utility.
UIMPORT.EXE	Text utility for batch creation of users. Replaces the functionality of the pre-NetWare 4.0 MAKEUSER utility.
DOMAIN.NLM	Allows the creation of protected domains that allow NLMs to run in rings one, two, or three of the Intel processors. Runs as a server NLM.
MONITOR.NLM	General purpose server monitor utility for monitoring the server. Runs as a server NLM, and consolidates the functions of the pre-NetWare 4.0 MONITOR and FCONSOLE.
SERVMAN.NLM	Facilitates the easy viewing and changing of the many server SET parameters. Allows these changes to be stored in AUTOEXEC.NCF and STARTUP.NCF files. Runs as a server NLM.
RCONSOLE.EXE	RCONSOLE also performs the function REMOTE.NLM of ACONSOLE (asynchronous console). Used for remote management of server.
NWSNUT.NLM	Library interface for C-Worthy style graphical functions used by server-based graphical tools such as MONITOR and SERVMAN.

NetWare 4.0 Utility	Description
DSREPAIR.NLM	Repairs inconsistencies and problems in the NDS database. Provides the functionality of the BINDFIX and BINDREST utilities that were used to repair the bindery.
TIMESYNC.NLM	Performs time synchronization. This is set up to load via AUTOEXEC.NCF during NetWare 4.0 server installation.
CDROM.NLM	CD-ROM support for CD drives attached to the NetWare 4.0 server.
RTDM.NLM	Real Time Data Migration utility that runs at the server.
LIST DEVICES	Server console command. Lists device information.
SCAN FOR NEW DEVICES	Server console command. Scans for any new devices that have been added to the server.
MEDIA	Server console command. Used to confirm if requests to insert/remove media on the server have been performed.
MAGAZINE	Server console command. Used to confirm if requests to insert/remove magazine on the server have been performed.
MIRROR STATUS	Server console command. Used to display status of mirrored partitions.
ABORT REMIRROR	Server console command. Used to stop mirroring of partitions.
REMIRROR PARTITION	Server console command. Used to remirror partitions.
AUDITCON.EXE	Allows independent users to act as auditors. Is a superset of the pre-NetWare 4.0 ATOTAL and PAUDIT.

continues

Table A.1, Continued
NetWare 4.x Command/Utility Differences with NetWare 3.x

NetWare 4.0 Utility	Description
RIGHTS.EXE	Consolidates functions of pre-NetWare 4.0 utilities RIGHTS, GRANT, REVOKE, REMOVE, and ALLOW.
FLAG.EXE	Consolidates functions of pre-NetWare 4.0 utilities FLAG, FLAGDIR, and SMODE.
FILER	Consolidates functions of pre-NetWare 4.0 utilities FILER, SALVAGE, PURGE, DSPACE, and VOLINFO.
NPRINTER.EXE	Allows a printer attached to a workstation (DOS or OS/2) or a server to be used as a network printer.
SBACKUP.NLM	Used to perform backups across the network. Consolidates the pre-NetWare 4.0 SBACKUP and NBACKUP.
RPL.NLM	Allows remote booting for diskless workstations.
KEYB	Server console command. Allows the selection of a nationality or language for the keyboard device.
LANGUAGE	Server console command. Sets up the use of the specified language at the server.
CX.EXE	Allows users to navigate the NDS tree by changing the context. Does for NDS directory what the CD command does for file directories.
LOGIN.EXE	Used to log in or attach to a server. Uses NDS objects and consolidates pre-NetWare 4.0 utilities LOGIN and ATTACH.

NetWare 4.0 Utility	Description
NMENU.BAT	NMENU is the batch utility; MENUMAKE.EXE MENUMAKE is the menu compiler MENUCNVT.EXE utility; and MENUCNVT is the menu conversion utility. Menus are based on Saber menus.
NDIR.EXE	Consolidates the pre-NetWare 4.0 NDIR, LISTDIR, CHKDIR, and CHKVOL.
NETUSER.EXE	Replaces pre-NetWare 4.0 SESSION. Text graphical tool for performing drive mappings, printing, and network attachments.
SEND.EXE	Consolidates the pre-NetWare 4.0 SEND, CASTON, and CASTOFF.
NLIST.EXE	Consolidates the pre-NetWare 4.0 USERLIST and SLIST.
Tools Group for Windows and OS/2	Tools installed as a group in the MS Windows Program Manager and OS/2's desktop.

Strategies for Preparing for and Taking the Exams

The purpose of taking an exam is to test your knowledge of a subject area. The outcome of taking the exam, the test score, is supposed to indicate the degree to which you have mastered the subject.

Most of us who have taken exams in school or college know that while quite often the exam results indicate the degree to which you have mastered the subject, it is not always the case that the exam results reflect how much you know or don't know. There are some who really understand the subject matter extremely well, but are poor "test takers." Others who have a superficial knowledge of the subject area seem to do very well in the exams.

And there are, of course, those who know the subject area *and* do well in an exam in that subject area. The purpose of this book is to train you to fall into this third category.

How This Book Can Help You Prepare for Your Exams

As part of your preparation for taking the exams, study the information in the book so that you have a good understanding of the subject area. Sample test questions follow each chapter and are included in the on-disk test simulator that is included with this book. But no matter how well you design a test, it cannot really test all that you know or don't know.

The key to doing really well in an exam is to build your knowledge of the subject area so that you are confident about answering questions on that topic. There is no harm in over-preparing for an exam. You will not only be able to pass the exam, but as an important side effect, you will have a superior knowledge base that will help you in your career. The book and the questions are designed with this goal in mind, covering details that you will probably never be asked in an exam.

For questions that have multiple correct answers, currently the Novell tests will tell you the number of correct answers. This makes it easier to guess an answer when you are not sure. In the multiple correct answer questions in this book, no attempt has been made to give you this hint. This makes answering the questions a little harder. This has been done with the intention that it will help you increase your confidence on the subject, once you understand the reason for the right answer.

When you take your test, read the questions carefully. Many a question has been answered incorrectly, not because of a lack of knowledge, but because of *misreading* the question. You should consider the choice of answers to each question carefully. Usually one or two choices can be eliminated very easily, but you may see some choices that are quite close. In this case, you should select the answer that is most correct or applicable.

As you go through this book, it is best if you have at least one NetWare 4.x server and a workstation on a network that you can experiment with. The author realizes you may not have access to such a system at all times of the day, and even if you have access to such a system, you may not be near one when you are reading this book and preparing for your exams. To help you out, many network administration tasks are presented in a guided-tour manner with plenty of screen shots, so that you can see how a task is performed. This is the next best thing to doing hands-on network administration tasks on the network.

Author's Technique on Memorization

You need relatively little rote memorization for the NetWare 4.x exams, but if you feel that you need to memorize some facts and have a hard time remembering then, you may want to try out the following:

Before going to sleep, mentally review the facts that you want to remember (use the book to review the material in question!). On waking up, try to remember the facts and write them down. In general, writing facts that are difficult to remember on a piece of paper will help you remember them. The author has had great personal success from using this technique, especially in dealing with the hard-to-remember details of high school history before an exam! You can use the traditional cue cards, which some people find helpful.

Using the Test Questions in This Book

After going through each chapter in the book, try out the questions at the end of each chapter. Progress through the book until you are done with the last chapter. As sometimes happens, if you have not dwelt upon a particular subject, you may not remember all the details that you went over in the early chapters. If you miss a question, it may indicate that you need to review a topic in one of the chapters.

Registering for the Test

When you are ready, you can register for taking a test. The certification tests are currently given by Drake Prometrics:

> Drake Prometrics
> 8800 Queen Avenue South
> Bloomington, MN 55431
> U.S.A.

The Drake Prometrics phone number in the U.S.A. and Canada is 1-800-RED-EXAM. Table B.1 lists the phone numbers for other countries. Should you have difficulty in calling any of the numbers listed in the table, you can call Drake Training and Technologies directly at 612-921-6807 in the U.S. (the country code for North America is 1).

You can register for a test in any one of the many locations that offer Drake testing, called Drake Authorized Testing Centers (DATC). Your information is registered under an identification number. In the U.S., this is your Social Security number. If you live outside of the U.S. or you do not want to use your social security number, you can use an alternative Drake Testing identification number and can use this to track your exam status.

You can register for the test from either three hours or three days before taking the exam. The three hour option is currently available on what is called a "fast site" in North America, if an exam time slot is available. Also, you have to know the number of the test you are taking; however, because the test numbers can change, a complete list is not included in this book. You can obtain the test number and additional information on the tests by calling Novell at 1-800-233-EDUC (or 801-429-7000 for outside North America).

The fee for taking a test is $85 (U.S.) at the time of writing this book, and is payable at the time of registering for the test (by credit card). After you pay your fees, you can take the test within one year. After that period you forfeit your test fees. The test price may fluctuate, and there may be special promotional offers you will want to take advantage of. The test fee for sites outside the United States is likely to be higher; for example, it is £65 in Great

Britain at the time of writing this book. After you register, you should receive a confirmation through your postal service.

Table B.1
Drake Prometrics Phone Numbers

Country	Phone Number
U.S.A. and Canada	1-800-RED-EXAM (1-800-733-3926) 612-921-6807
Great Britain	071-437-6900
France	33147750909
Germany	4921159730
Italy	39248013554
Spain	3415774941
Belgium	3227250200
Australia	6124133077
Singapore	653228503
Taiwan	8662775383
Hong Kong	8528272223
Japan	81354811141

Taking the Test

If you have never taken a Drake test, it is advisable that you come at least 15 minutes before your exam appointment. At the time of registering at the exam site, you must be asked to present your identification. This is usually done through a photo identification such as driver's license.

The exams are computer-based; a Drake representative will act as a proctor and administer your exams. You will be given an ID to sign on to the computer. You can take a practice multiple-choice

893

test to get the feel of what it is like to take the exam. You will interact with the computer through an MS Windows-based application. You can use either the mouse or the function keys. At some sites, in the author's experience, the mouse pointing device is not particularly good. If you have this problem, be prepared to use function keys instead. You can take notes during the exams on writing paper provided by the exam site, but you cannot take the paper with you after the exam. Some sites explain these rules quite well, other sites do not.

The disk-based tests that are packaged with this book do not exactly simulate the Drake test environment, but they will give you some important experience. You will learn, for example, to identify questions that require a single answer, and questions that require several answers, by looking for the circles and squares that tag the answers. You will also learn to take tests under time pressure.

After you complete a Drake test, the results are printed for you along with the pass/fail status. Some of the results will tell you the percentage of questions answered correctly on each topic. The results are sent via modem to Drake Testing and Technology at the end of each day, and are registered with Novell within 48 hours (often sooner).

The exam proctor will give you an embossed copy of your result, which you should keep just in case there is an error in the recording of your results. Normally this should not be a problem, but the printed documentation is a fall-back in case the system fails.

If you are taking the exams as part of your certification towards CNE, ECNE, or CNA status, you should check the latest certification requirements through Novell using the 1-800-233-3382 (or 1-801-429-7000) telephone number. The fax number is 801-439-5565. You can also contact a Novell Authorized Education Center for this information. Currently you have one year to complete your CNE exam requirements, after taking the first test. The current requirement for ECNE is taking exams worth nine credits, after completing your CNE. Each exam is worth a certain number of credits. You can take the NetWare 4.x courses towards the fulfillment of CNE or ECNE exams. There are some additional rules for combining courses towards CNE/ECNE certification. Because Novell reserves the right to change these rules at any time, you should contact Novell about the latest rules.

If you are already a CNE/ECNE, Novell will mail you continuing education requirements to maintain the status of the CNE exams. For this reason, it is important to keep your address current with the CNE/ECNE/CNA administration. The mailing address for CNE/ECNE/CNA administration is:

Novell CNE/ECNE/CNA Administration
Mail Stop E-31-1
122 East 1700 South
Provo, Utah 84606
U.S.A.

Form Test Versus Adaptive Test

Novell currently favors the adaptive method of testing. However, when a test is first developed, it is offered as a form test.

A form test has a certain number of fixed questions. These are anywhere from 50 to 80 questions (or more). You can spend as long as you want on a question, but obviously not too long, because you should leave time for answering all the questions. With a form-based test, you can generally go back and review your answers. If you find a particular question difficult, you can mark it and come back to it later. You must, however, check with Drake if the form-based questions are required to be answered in strict sequence. If this is the case, you cannot spend too much time on any question, and you cannot go back to review the question.

When Novell has given an exam a number of times, it gathers the test results and generates an adaptive test based on it. It is Novell's intention that all the tests will eventually be adaptive tests. However, some of the CNE elective tests, such as the NetWare TCP/IP and NFS, are still form-based, even though they have been offered for a long time; many candidates have taken these popular tests.

In an adaptive test, each question that you are asked depends on the way you answered a previous question. The test is supposed to start out with a simple question on a particular topic. It is programmed to ask a minimum number of questions on each topic to be tested. If you answer all the questions correctly (or nearly all correct), it will ask you a minimum number of questions. This minimum number depends on the test, but is usually in a range from 10 to 15 (you can find out the minimum number from Drake Prometrics). The maximum number can be from 20 to 25. If you answer a question incorrectly, the test may ask you a similar question again. In general, if you answer a question incorrectly, you will see more than the minimum number of questions on a topic. Some test takers have assumed that if they see a similar question asked again, they must have answered the previous question incorrectly. This is not always so.

At all times, you should rely on your own certainty of the right answer. If you answer too many questions incorrectly, or answer too many incorrect questions on an important topic (such as directory services), the test will fail you. After you answer a question, you cannot go back and modify your previous answer. An adaptive test lasts about 20 to 30 minutes, though you can finish it in much less time.

The intention behind the adaptive test is to make the testing period shorter and "less painful" than the form-based test. Opinion is divided as to whether this is true. Some people prefer the shortness of the adaptive test. Others prefer the form-based test because these exams are more comprehensive.

This book prepares you to take both types of tests. You should check with Drake Technologies and Training to find out if the test is form-based or adaptive. If the test is one hour or longer, you can conclude that it is form-based. Adaptive tests are usually 30 minutes or less. You should also check to see if the questions have to be answered in the sequence they are presented, in which case you cannot go back and review the questions.

Although you can become familiar with some characteristics of the Drake test environment using the test simulator accompanying this book, the test simulator is not capable of emulating a Drake adaptive test.

C
APPENDIX

Answers to Chapter Test Questions

Chapter 1

1. C
2. B
3. C
4. B, D
5. C, D
6. B
7. A
8. C
9. B
10. A, D, E
11. A, C
12. A, B, D
13. A, C
14. B, C
15. D
16. A, C
17. C
18. B
19. D
20. C
21. C

22. A

23. D

24. B

25. B

26. C

27. A

28. B

29. D, E

30. A, C, D

31. B

32. A

33. D

34. A, C, E

Chapter 2

1. B

2. D

3. A, D

4. C, E

5. D

6. A, B, D

7. C

8. A, B

9. E

10. C

11. D

12. B

13. C

14. C

15. B

16. D

17. D

18. E

19. B

20. D

21. C

22. C

23. D

24. E

25. B

26. A

27. C

28. C

29. D

30. E

31. B, F

32. A, C

33. C

34. C

35. A

36. F

37. E

38. F

39. NWADMIN

40. NETADMIN

41. NLIST

42. Context

43. C, D, F

44. A, D, E

45. B, D

46. C, D

47. A, C

48. B, C, E

49. C

50. C

51. D

52. C

Chapter 3

1. A, C
2. C
3. A, B, D
4. A, C
5. A, C
6. D
7. B
8. SYS
9. A, E

10. B, D, F

11. D, E, F

12. B, E

13. D, E, F

14. D, F, G

15. A, C, E

16. A, C, E, F

17. B

18. E

19. A

20. C

21. C

22. C

23. A

24. B, C

25. C

26. B, D, E

27. D

28. D

29. A, C

30. D

31. D

32. A

33. D

34. C

35. D

36. C

37. D

38. C

39. B

Chapter 4

1. A

2. C

3. D

4. B

5. C

6. A

7. C

8. A

9. B

10. C

11. A

12. B

13. A

14. B

15. B

16. B

17. A

18. B

19. A

20. D

Chapter 5

1. B

2. A, C, E

3. A

4. C

5. C

6. B, C

7. B

8. D

9. D

10. D

11. C

12. C

13. D

14. A, B, D, E

15. B, C, D

16. C

17. B

18. D

19. A

20. B, E, F

21. C

22. D

23. F

24. B

25. B

26. E

27. B

28. A, C, D

29. A, D

30. C

31. D

32. D

33. E

34. C

35. B

36. E

37. C

38. B

39. B

40. D

41. B

42. E

43. F

44. A

45. B

Chapter 6

1. A, B, E

2. E

3. E

4. C

5. A, D

6. C

7. B

8. B

9. A, D

10. C

11. D

12. B

13. D

14. C

15. D

16. A, B

17. B

18. B

19. A

20. D

21. F

22. A

23. B

24. A

25. B

26. B

27. C

28. E

29. A

30. D

31. B

32. B

901

Chapter 7

1. B
2. C
3. E
4. D
5. A
6. A
7. E
8. C, D
9. B
10. C
11. B
12. A
13. A
14. A, E
15. A
16. D
17. B
18. C
19. C
20. D
21. A
22. B
23. E
24. C
25. B
26. A

Chapter 8

1. A, E
2. C, E, F
3. B, D
4. B
5. C
6. D
7. A
8. D
9. E
10. C
11. A, C, D
12. B
13. B
14. A
15. B, E
16. D
17. C
18. C
19. B
20. A, B
21. B
22. E
23. A, C, D
24. A
25. B, C

26. A, C
27. C, E

Chapter 9

1. A
2. A, D, E
3. A
4. B
5. C
6. D
7. A
8. B
9. D
10. D
11. A
12. B
13. C
14. F
15. B
16. A, C
17. A, B, D, F, G, H
18. B
19. C, E
20. A
21. D
22. A, C

23. A
24. C
25. B
26. A
27. A
28. B

Chapter 10

1. A, C, D
2. C
3. C
4. E
5. B
6. A, C
7. B
8. B
9. B
10. B, D

INDEX

Symbols

" (quotes), login script variables, 569
(number sign), login script commands, 576-577
* (asterisk), wild card, 281
. (periods)
   NDS object path names, 180, 191
   partial path names, 186
/ (slash), directory separators, 259
: (colon) delimiter, 260
<> (brackets), DOS environment variables, 582, 594
[ ] (square brackets), NDS object path names, 181
\ (backslash), directory separators, 259
{ } (braces), NDS object path names, 181
0FFFF0 hex memory location, 535

A

ABORT REMIRROR command, 650-651, 885
aborting remirroring logical partitions, 650
Abstract Syntax Notation 1 (ASN.1), 189

Access Control rights, 268, 361
ACCESS_SERVER login script variable, 593
Account Restrictions dialog box, 408
ACL (Access Control List) properties, 505-532
adaptive test, 895-896
ADD NAME SPACE command, 647
Add or Delete Self property rights, 504
addresses
   Drake Prometrics, 892
   e-mail as External Entity objects, 157
   network formats, 414
   Novell, 895
   print servers, 746
   printers, 212
   servers, 212
ADMIN user accounts, 76
Advertising Name property (Print Server objects), 745
AFP (AppleTalk Filing Protocol), 138
AFP Server objects, 138, 160
AIO (Asynchronous Input/Output) printers, 737
AIO NLM utility, 691
AIOCOMX NLM utility, 691

Alias objects, 120, 139, 160
All Properties right, 505-532
allocating disk blocks, 70-72
Alt+Esc control keys, switching
  between screens, 666
AM_PM login script variable, 594
APIs (Application Programming
  Interfaces), 25
appendString parameter (GET
  commands), 624
AppleTalk Filing Protocol (AFP), 138
AppleTalk printers, 736
AppleTalk Reference online
  manual, 54
application layer (OSI model), 25
Application Programming Interfaces,
  see APIs
applications, running, 609-612
APPS directories, 268
Archive Needed attribute (files), 379
archived files, copying, 284
ASN.1 (Abstract Syntax Notation 1), 189
assigning
  attributes
    to directories, 387, 394
    to files, 390
  container objects to Print Queue
    object Users property, 731
  drive letters to directories, 293-304
  file system rights, 344-349
  Printer objects to print servers, 766
  rights
    to directories, 388
    to files, 390
    to Group objects, 353, 358
    with container objects, 347
    with Group objects, 349
    with security equivalence, 348
  trustee rights, 391-395
  trustees
    to directories, 387
    to files, 390
  user accounts to Group objects,
    350, 357

asterisk (*), wild card, 281
Asynchronous Input/Output (AIO)
  printers, 737
ATTACHB command (login scripts),
  577-578, 591
attaching to bindery-based servers, 577
attributes
  directories
    assigning, 394
    changing with FLAG utility, 381
    security, 377-381
    setting with FILER utility, 385-388
  files, 532
    changing with FLAG utility, 381
    compression, 327-328
    data migration, 328-329
    security, 377-381
    setting with FILER utility, 388-402
  NDS object types, 136-137
  User object class, 125
  see also properties
AUDITCON utility, 79, 885
auditing networks, 77-79
auditor user accounts, 77-79
authenticating logins, 417-419
Authorized Print Servers property
  (Print Queue objects), 732
AUTOEXEC.BAT files, 539
  executing in login scripts, 576
  network connection commands, 33
  processing, 543-544
automating
  login scripts from AUTOEXEC.BAT
    files, 544
  MAP command execution at
    login, 298
Available Options menu commands
  (Edit Print Job Configurations), 783

B

backslash (\), directory separators, 259
backup devices
  drivers, 816
  labeling, 824

backups, 84-85
  DOS workstations, 846
  files, 843
  NDS trees to host servers, 813
  selecting devices, 823
  servers
    custom, 810
    differential, 808-810
    full, 806-807
    incremental, 807-808
    with SBACKUP NLM utility,
      817-831
  Storage Management Service,
    810-815
  workstations, 814
banner pages (print jobs), 775, 787
Banner Type properties (Printer
  objects), 737
base object classes, *see* parent objects
BATCH command option (ITEM
  command), 605
batch files
  executing in login scripts, 576
  network connection commands, 33
Berkeley System Distribution (BSD)
  socket interface, 678
BIND command, 647
BIND VLM utility, 45
Bindery objects, 153-154, 161
Bindery Queue objects, 154, 161
bindery services
  emulating, 154
  see also NDS
bindery-based servers, attaching to, 577
BIOS files, 536
block suballocation (hard disks), 70-72
blocking
  effective rights, 362-366
  NDS property rights, 503
booting, 535
bootstrap program, 535
braces ({ }), NDS object path names, 181
brackets (< >), DOS environment
  variables, 582, 594
BREAK command (login scripts), 578

BROADCAST command, 649
Browse object rights, 427-428
browsing NDS trees, 195-214, 420, 428
BSD (Berkeley System Distribution)
  socket interface, 678
Btrieve Installation and Reference
  Manual, 55
Buffer Size property (Printer
  objects), 737
buffers, 541
  printers, 738
  SBACKUP NLM utility, 821
Building and Auditing a Trusted
  Network Environment with
  NetWare 4 online manual, 57

C

cabling (LANs), 14-15
Can't Compress attribute (files), 380
CAPTURE command, 726, 774-777
capturing printer port output, 777
Carrier Sense Multiple Access with
  Collision Detect (CSMA/CD), 14
case sensitivity (NDS objects), 126
CCITT (Consultative Committee for
  International Telephone and
  Telegraphy), 111
CD commands, 706
  CHANGE, 708
  DIR, 709
  DISMOUNT, 710
CD-ROM drives
  listing file contents, 709
  mapping to, 708
  mounting, 707, 861
  NetWare 4.x support, 705-711
  user access, removing, 710
CDROM NLM utility, 705-711, 885
CHANGE command option (MAP
  command), 302-303
Change Forms as Needed property
  (Printer objects), 739
CHDIR command option (ITEM
  command), 606

classes (NDS objects), 117-125
CLEAR STATION command, 648
Client for DOS and MS Windows
  Technical Reference online
  manual, 55
Client for DOS and MS Windows User
  Guide online manual, 55
Client for OS/2 User Guide online
  manual, 56
client software
    loading at DOS workstations, 33
    NetWare 4.x improvements, 82-84
    see also workstations
CLS command, 591, 649
CN objects, *see* leaf objects
colon (:) delimiter, 260
color (menus), customizing, 625-626
COLORPAL utility, 625-626
command options
    CAPTURE command, 774-776
    CX command-line utility, 204-205
    defining, 604-608
    EXEC command, 612
    FILER utility, 382
    MAP command
        CHANGE, 302-303
        INS S16, 299
        NEXT, 300
        NP, 301-302
        ROOT, 300-301
    NDIR command, 280
    NLIST VOLUME command, 273
    NPRINT command, 778-779
    SEND command, 66
    VLMs, 41
command-line utilities, 65-67
    see also commands; utilities
COMMAND.COM files, loading,
  537, 578
commands
    ABORT REMIRROR, 650-651, 885
    ADD NAME SPACE, 647
    Available Options menu, 783
    BIND, 647
    BROADCAST, 649

CAPTURE, 726, 774-777
CD, 706
    CHANGE, 708
    DIR, 709
    DISMOUNT, 710
CLEAR STATION, 648
CLS, 649
CONFIG, 646
console (servers), 650-667
defining, 602-608
directory-related, 282-291, 606
DISABLE LOGIN, 648
DISMOUNT, 648
DISPLAY NETWORKS, 647
DISPLAY SERVERS, 646
domain-related, 695
DOWN, 648
ENABLE LOGIN, 648
EXEC, 609-612
EXIT, 610, 649
FILER, 886
FLAG, 381
GETO, 615-624
GETP, 617-624
GETR, 616-624
HELP, 646
IPXODI, 36
ITEM, 602-608
KEYB, 886
LANGUAGE, 646, 650, 658-666, 886
LIST DEVICES, 650, 653, 819, 885
LOAD, 613-614, 647
LOAD PSERVER, 767-769
login scripts, 568-569, 575-592
    ATTACHB, 577-578, 591
    BREAK, 578
    CLS, 591
    COMPATIBLE, 588-589
    COMSPEC, 578-580
    CONTEXT, 580, 591
    DISPLAY, 581
    DOS BREAK, 578
    DOS SET, 581-582
    DOS VERIFY OFF, 582-583
    DOS VERIFY ON, 582-583

DRIVE, *583*
EXIT, *583-584*
FDISPLAY, *581*
FIRE PHASERS, *584*
GOTO, *584-585*
INCLUDE, *586*
INCLUDE NDS, *591*
LASTLOGINTIME, *590-591*
MACHINE, *587*
MAP, *587, 591*
NO_DEFAULT, *588, 592*
NO_SWAP, *592*
NOSWAP, *588*
PAUSE, *588*
PCCOMPATIBLE, *588-589*
PROFILE, *592*
REMARK, *589*
SET, *581-582*
SET TIME OFF, *582, 592*
SET TIME ON, *582, 592*
SHIFT, *589-590*
SWAP, *588, 592*
WAIT, *588*
WRITE, *569, 591*
LSL ?, 37
MAGAZINE, 650, 654-655, 885
MAP, 293-304, 568
    NDS syntax, 309-311
    optimizing with directory map
        objects, 141
MEDIA, 650, 656-657, 885
MENU, 602
menus
    control, 609-624
    organizational, 602-608
MIRROR STATUS, 650-652, 885
MODULES, 647
MOUNT, 647
NAME, 647
names, displaying, 607
NCOPY, 282-285
NDIR, 273-281
NLIST VOLUME, 272-273
NPRINT, 724, 778-779
Other Installation Actions menu, 862

pausing, 607
REMIRROR PARTITION,
    650-651, 885
REMOVE DOS, 649
RENDIR, 282
RESTART SERVER, 650, 658
Restore menu, 837
RIGHTS, 367-377
SCAN FOR NEW DEVICES, 650,
    653-654, 819, 885
screen (servers), 649-667
SEARCH, 641
SEARCH ADD, 705
SECURE CONSOLE, 648
SEND, 65, 649
servers, 645-667
    configuration, 646-647
    installation, 647
    maintenance, 648-649
SET, 649
SHOW, 612-613
TIME, 647
Type of Backup menu, 841
UNBIND, 649
UNLOAD, 649
UPS STATUS, 647
UPS TIME, 647
VLMs, 40-41
VOLUMES, 647
comments (login script files), 589
communication protocols, 23
    loading, 545
    stacks, 32
Compare property rights, 503
COMPATIBLE command (login
  scripts), 588-589
Compress attribute (files), 380
compressed files, copying, 284
compressing files, 73, 327-328
Computer objects, 141, 160
    see also workstations
computing
    effective rights, 363-366
    NDS property rights, 508-532
COMSPEC command (login scripts),
  578-580

COMSPEC variables (login scripts), 575

Concepts online glossary, 55

conditional statements (login scripts)
 IF...THEN...ELSE, 573, 585-586
 IF_THEN, 570

CONFIG command, 646

CONFIG directories, 269

CONFIG.SYS files
 contents, 537
 processing, 540-543

configuration commands (servers), 646-647

Configuration property (Printer objects), 741

configurations
 MLID, 28
 network printing services, 757-767
 ODI layers, 550
 print jobs, 724, 775, 780
  creating, 784
  defaults, 785
  displaying details, 784
  editing, 783
  forms, 739
  options, 785-787
  with PRINTCON utility, 782-787
  with PRINTDEF utility, 787-788
 Print Queue objects, 760
 Print Server objects, 764
 print services, 725
 Printer objects, 736, 761
 server commands, 646-647
 VLM Manager, 546-547

confirming
 drive mappings, 304
 magazine requests (servers), 654-655
 media requests (servers), 656-657

CONN VLM utility, 45

connections
 user account-to-network, 22-30
 workstation-to-network, 30-34

console commands (servers), 650-667

Consultative Committee for International Telephone and Telegraphy (CCITT), 111

container objects, 115-118, 125, 347
 assigning
  rights with, 347
  to Print Queue object Users property, 731
 typeless names, 192
 viewing, 197

Containment Class rules (NDS objects), 119

context
 NDS objects, 176-179
  changing with CX utility, 195-205
  promoting, 191
  workstation settings, 193-194
 user accounts, 580
 workstations, 548

CONTEXT command (login scripts), 580, 591

control commands (menus), 609-624

control keys
 Alt+Esc, switching between screens, 666
 console commands (servers), 666-667
 Ctrl+Esc, displaying screen menus, 667
 DOS text-based utilities, 61
 Remote Console utility, 690

conventional memory, loading DOS Requester in, 41

converting
 search drives to network drives, 302
 tabs in print jobs to spaces, 785

Copy Inhibit attribute (files), 379

copying
 archived files, 284
 compressed files, 284
 directories from servers, 282-285
 files
  from servers, 282-285
  in sparse format, 284, 385

core operating system, 643-644

corruption
 Unknown object indications, 158-161
 NDS, repairing, 698

Country container objects, 116, 119, 133

Create Distribution List dialog box, 873
Create object rights, 428-429
Create rights, 360
CSMA/CD (Carrier Sense Multiple Access with Collision Detect), 14
Ctrl+Esc control keys, displaying screen menus, 667
current directories, setting, 383
custom backups
    file systems, 840-843
    servers, 810
customizing
    color for menus, 625-626
    user login environments, 560
CX utility, 194-205, 886

D

data link layer (OSI model), 24
data migration
    attributes, 328-329
    files, 74-75
    NetWare 4.x, 700-702
    verifying copies to local drives, 582
databases, *see* NDs
dates (international formats), 86
DAY login script variable, 593
DAY_OF_WEEK login script variable, 593
defaults
    file settings, 288
    login scripts, 560-562, 588
    NDS object rights, 435-439
    network drives, 583
    print job configurations, 785
defining
    command options, 604-608
    commands, 602-608
    menus, 602
    printers, 750-751
Delete Inhibit attribute (directories/ files), 378-379
Delete object rights, 429-430

deleted files
    purging, 288, 320
    salvaging, 320, 384
deleted Volume objects, recovering, 429
deleting
    directory trustees, 394
    drive mappings, 306
    NDS objects, 429-430
        with NETADMIN utility, 176
        with NWADMIN utility, 172
    network drive mappings, 52
    search drive mappings, 307
    user accounts from Group objects, 352
DETs (Directory Entry Tables), 801
device drivers
    backups, 816
    loading to memory, 542
    MLID, 27-28
        configurations, 28
        loading, 32, 545
    network drivers, 25
    ODI drivers, 545
    loading to memory, 542
diagnostic responders, disabling, 546
diagnostics (VLMs), displaying, 41
dialog boxes
    Account Restrictions, 408
    Create Distribution List, 873
    NetWare Settings, 53
    Organization container object, 170
    Organizational Unit container object, 171
    Password Restrictions, 410
    Select Object, 139, 351, 869
    Time Restrictions, 413
DIB (Directory Information Base), *see* NDS tree
differential backups (servers), 808-810
directories, 125
    APPS directories, 268
    attributes
        assigning, 394
        changing with FLAG utility, 381
        setting with FILER utility, 385-388

changing for commands, 606
commands, 282-291
CONFIG directories, 269
contents
  displaying, 273-281, 382
  listing, 286-287
copying from servers, 282-285
current directories, setting, 383
custom backups, 840-843
default structure, 262-265
drive letters, 252, 293-304
drive mappings, 291-329
effective rights, 363
files, 274-281, 388-402
finding, 274-281, 288
home directories (user accounts), 268
LOGIN directories, 264
MAIL directories, 265
management utilities, 319
multiple-volume structure, 270-271
naming, 257
ownership, changing, 326-327
paths, selecting, 288
PUBLIC directories, 265
referencing, 141
renaming, 282
restoring, 837-840
rights, 359-362
  assigning to Group objects, 353, 358
  displaying, 370
  editing, 358
  granting, 371-375
  revoking, 371-375
  setting with FILER utility, 385-388
search patterns, 382
searching, 295
selecting, 287
separators, 259
Shared data directories, 269
single-volume structures, 269
structure, 266-271
SYSTEM directories, 263-265
trustees
  assigning, 387
  listing, 370-371, 386
  removing, 376, 387, 394

rights, 360
  setting with FILER utility, 385-388
volumes, 257-261
Directory Entry Tables (DETs), 801
Directory Information Base (DIB), *see*
  NDS tree
Directory Map objects, 160, 311-317
  creating, 317-322
  NDS rights, 526
DISABLE LOGIN command, 648
disk subsystems (servers), 252-257
diskless workstations, remote
  booting, 679
disks
  block suballocation, 70-72
  duplexing, 253, 803
  mirroring, 253, 803
  subsystems, 252-257
DISMOUNT command, 648
DISPLAY command (login scripts), 581
DISPLAY NETWORKS command, 647
DISPLAY SERVERS command, 646
displaying
  command names, 607
  CONFIG.SYS file contents, 537
  directories
    attributes, 387
    contents, 273-281, 382
    trustees, 386
  drive mappings, 303
  effective rights, 366, 393
  files
    contents, 273-281, 581
    data migration statistics, 329
    deleted files, 288
    trustees, 389
  inheritance for user rights, 375-376
  menus, 612
  NetWare 4.x settings, 53
  print jobs
    priority, 764
    queue status, 733
  print server status, 769
  printers
    port status, 774
    status, 754, 767

properties for NDS objects, 103
search drive mappings, 303
user login times, 590
user rights to directories, 370
values for NDS objects, 212
VLM diagnostics, 41
volumes
  space information, 322-323
  statistics, 273-281, 288, 383
**distinguished names (NDS objects),
180-182**
**Distribution List objects, 154-155, 161,
872-881**
distribution lists (messages), 872-875
DOMAIN NLM utility, 694-697, 884
domains
  commands, 695
  protected domains, creating for
    NLMs, 694-697
**Don't Compress attribute (directories/
files), 380**
**Don't Migrate attribute (directories/
files), 380**
DOS
  AUTOEXEC.BAT files, 539, 543-544
  bootstrap program, 535
  COMMAND.COM files, loading, 537
  commands
    BREAK, 578
    executing in login scripts, 577
    SET, 581-582
    VERIFY OFF, 582-583
    VERIFY ON, 582-583
  CONFIG.SYS files, processing,
    540-543
  directory structures, 267
  environment variables, setting from
    login scripts, 581
  IO.SYS files, 536
  loading, 535-540
  login script variables, 267, 594
  search paths (network drives), 306
  STARTNET.BAT files, 539, 544-546
  text-based utilities, 60-65

workstations
  backups, 846
  connecting to networks, 31-32
DOS Requester, 34-38, 534
  components, 38-39
  drive assignments, 548
  loading, 41
  starting, 544
DOWN command, 648
Drake Prometrics
  address, 892
  phone number, 892-893
DRIVE command (login scripts), 583
drive letters, 291
  assigning to directories, 293-304
  DOS recognition, 541
  DOS Requester assignments, 548
  search drives, 297
drive mappings, 291-329
  confirming, 304
  creating, 50
  deleting, 52, 305
drivers
  backup device drivers, 816
  loading to memory, 542
  MLID, 27-28
    configurations, 28
    loading, 32, 545
  network drivers, 25
  ODI drivers, 545
drives
  DOS search paths, 306
  mapping
    displaying, 303
    with Directory Map objects, 311-317
  networks
    defaults, 583
    mappings, 304-309
  rooting to network directories, 300
  search drives
    converting to network drives, 302
    drive letters, 297
    mapping, 295-299

DSMERGE NLM utility, 114, 703-705
DSREPAIR NLM utility, 698-700, 885
duplexing disks, 253, 803
dynamic building (protocol stacks), 677
dynamic linking (NLMs), 641
DynaText utility, 54-60

E

e-mail
  addresses as External Entity
    objects, 157
  FirstMail client program, 859, 868,
    876-878
Edit Print Job Configurations command (Available Options menu), 783
editing
  print job configurations, 783
  rights, 358
effective object classes, 124-130
effective rights, 445-451
  blocking, 362-366
  computing, 363-366, 451-484
  displaying, 366
  for trustees, 393
emulating bindery services, 154
ENABLE LOGIN command, 648
ENDCAP command, see CAPTURE
  command
environment variables (DOS), setting
  from login scripts, 581
Erase rights, 360
ERROR_LEVEL login script
  variable, 593
errors (printers), user notification, 764
Ethernet
  ETHERNET_802.2 frame types, 547
  ETHERNET_II frame types, 548
  network address format, 414
exam
  adaptive test, 895-896
  answers to chapter samples, 897-904
  cost, 892
  form test, 895-896
  registering for, 892
  strategies, 889-896
EXEC control command, 609-612
Execute Only attribute (files), 379
EXIT command, 583-584, 610, 649
expanded memory, loading DOS
  Requester in, 41
explicit trustee rights, 365
extended memory, loading DOS
  Requester in, 41
eXtended Network Printing (XNP)
  protocol, 737
External Entity objects, 156-158,
  161, 872

F

F1 function key, Help, 67
F4 function key
  toggling between PRINTCON utility
    modes, 783
  toggling between PRINTDEF utility
    modes, 788
F6 function key, NetWare Hotkey, 53
F10 function key, saving printer object
  configurations, 763
FAT (File Allocation Table) file
  systems, 801
fault tolerances, 799-804
  see also SFT
FDISPLAY command (login
  scripts), 581
File Allocation Tables, see FAT file
  systems
file cache memory, 80-82
file extensions (NLMs), 640
file management utilities, 320
File Scan rights, 361
File Server objects, 20, 162
file servers, 20
  see also servers
file systems, 249-252
  custom backups, 840-843
  DETs, 801
  directories, 125, 271

FAT, 801
management, 75-77
NetWare 4.x improvements, 70-75
relationship to NDS property
  rights, 507
restoring, 837-840
security, 75-77, 343-359, 527-532
**FILE_SERVER login script
variable, 594**
FILER utility, 286-289, 382-395, 886
files
archived, copying, 284
attributes
  changing with FLAG utility, 381
  setting with FILER utility, 388-402
backups, 843
compressed, copying, 284
compressing, 72-73, 327-328
contents, displaying, 273-281,
  286, 581
copying
  from servers, 282-285
  in sparse format, 284, 385
custom backups, 840-843
data migration, 74-75, 328-329
default settings, 288
deleted
  displaying, 288
  purging, 288, 320
  recovering/salvaging, 288, 320, 384
finding, 274-281
  by access date, 324
  by ownership, 324
  by size, 324
  with FILER utility, 288
information, listing, 287
listing, 287
login scripts, 570-572
naming, 259-261
near-line storage, 75
Novell menus, 598-599
off-line storage, 75
ownership, changing, 326-327
rights, 359-362
  assigning, 344-349
  assigning to Group objects, 353, 358

  editing, 358
  granting, 371-375
  listing, 287
  revoking, 371-375
  setting with FILER utility, 388-402
search patterns, 382
sparse files, 288, 385
Storage Management Service,
  810-815
storing in sparse format, 288
trustee rights, 361
trustees, removing, 376
TTS (Transaction Tracking
  System), 802
volumes, 257-261
finding
directories, 274-281, 288
files, 274-281
  by access date, 324
  by ownership, 324
  by size, 324
  with FILER utility, 288
IPX addresses for network nodes, 738
NDS objects
  by property values, 213
  with NLIST utility, 205-214
  with NWADMIN utility, 216-218
network addresses
  for printers, 212
  for servers, 212
NLM paths, 641
Print Queue objects, 763
property values for NDS objects, 211
Volume objects, 289
FIO VLM utility, 45
**FIRE PHASERS command (login
  scripts), 584**
**FirstMail e-mail client program, 859,
  868, 876-878**
FLAG utility, 381, 886
foreign languages
installing support for, 666
keyboard support, 711
NetWare 4.x support, 86-87
parameters, 659-660
user environments, 545

form test, 895-896
formats (network addresses), 414
forms (print jobs), 786-788
   changing, 724
   configurations, 739
   feeds, 786
   parameters, 724
frame types
   ETHERNET_802.2, 547
   ETHERNET_II, 548
   TOKEN, 548
full backups (servers), 806-807
FULL_NAME login script variable, 594
function keys
   F1, Help, 67
   F4
      *toggling between PRINTCON utility
      modes, 783*
      *toggling between PRINTDEF utility
      modes, 788*
   F6, NetWare Hotkey, 53
   F10, saving printer object configurations, 763

G

GENERAL VLM utility, 45
GETO command, 615-616, 618-624
GETP command, 617-624
GETR command, 616-624
global network management, 68
GOTO command (login scripts),
  584-585
granting rights, 371-375
GREETING_TIME login script
  variable, 594
Group objects, 142-144, 160-161, 347
   creating
      with NETADMIN utility, 355-359
      with NWADMIN utility, 349-354
   properties, 350, 357
   rights
      assigning, 353, 358
      displaying, 354
   user accounts, assigning, 350, 357

group user accounts, 346
   explicit versus implicit, 432
   referencing, 142

H

hard disks
   block suballocation, 70-72
   duplexing, 253
   mirroring, 253
   subsystems, 252-257
hardware
   backup devices
      drivers, 816
      labeling, 824
   CD-ROM drives
      enabling for NetWare 4.x, 705-711
      listing file contents, 709
      mapping to, 708
      mounting, 707, 861
      NetWare 4.x support, 705-711
      user access, removing, 710
   listing, 653
   MHS requirements, 860-861
   storage devices, listing, 653
HCSS (High Capacity Storage
  System), 74
heirarchy (NDS objects), 109, 113-125
Help
   CD commands, 706
   command-line utilities, 67
   CX command-line utility, 203
   NLIST utility, 214
HELP command, 646
Hidden attribute (directories/files),
  378-379
High Capacity Storage System
  (HCSS), 74
Higher Privileges attribute (User object
  class), 125
home directories (user accounts), 268
host servers, 814
hot fixes, implementing, 800
HOUR login script variable, 594
HOUR24 login script variable, 594

I

identifying print jobs, 724
IF…THEN…ELSE statements (login scripts), 573, 585-586
IF_ THEN conditional statement (login scripts), 570
Immediate Compress attribute (directories/files), 380
implicit group accounts, 432
importing objects into NDS, 156
INCLUDE command (login scripts), 586
INCLUDE NDSobjectName command (login scripts), 591
INCLUDE statements (login scripts), 574
increasing buffer size for printers, 738
incremental backups (servers), 807-808
Indexed attribute (files), 379
inheritance
    NDS objects, 120
    rights, 422, 375-376
        NDS object rights, 439-441
        trustee rights, 347
    system login scripts, 556
Inherited Rights Filter, 362-366, 376-377, 422, 442-443
INS S16 command option (MAP command), 299
INSTALL NLM utility, 668-669, 861
installation
    FirstMail e-mail client program, 868
    language support, 666
    MHS, 861-878
    NetWare 4.x
        from CD-ROM s, 87
        system files, 692
    servers, 647, 668-669
Installation online manual, 55
Installing and using NetSync online manual, 56
instantiated object classes (NDS), 118
interfaces
    BSD socket interface, 678
    NLM Utility User interface, 702

SDI, 812
STREAMS, 677
TLI, 677
international languages
    installing support for, 666
    keyboard support, 711
    NetWare 4.x support, 86-87
    parameters, 659-660
    user environments, 545
International Organization of Standards (ISO), 121
internationalization, 87
Internet Packet Exchange protocol, *see* IPX protocol
Introduction to NDS online manual, 56
intruder limits (logins), 416-417
IO.SYS files (DOS), 536
IPX (Internet Packet Exchange) protocol, 23, 36
    addresses, finding, 738
    Router Reference online manual, 55
IPX/SPX network address format, 414
IPXNCP VLM utility, 45
IPXODI commands, 36
IRF (Inherited Rights Filter), 362-366, 376-377, 422, 442-443
ISO (International Organization of Standards), 121
ISODE (ISO Development Environment), 190
ITEM command, 602-608

J–K–L

Job List property (Print Queue objects), 733
jukeboxes, 75

KEYB command, 886
KEYB NLM utility, 711
keyboard (language support), 711

labeling backup devices, 824
LANGUAGE command, 646, 650, 658-666, 886

languages
   installing support for, 666
   keyboard support, 711
   NetWare 4.x support, 86-87
   parameters, 659-660
   user environments, 545
LANs (local area networks), 13-15
Large Internet Packet (LIP) protocol, 83
LASTLOGINTIME command (login
   scripts), 590-591
layers
   ODI, configurations, 550
   OSI model, 24
leaf objects, 116-117, 137-161
   see also objects
length parameter (GET commands), 623
letter codes (RIGHTS utility), 374
Link Support Layer (LSL), 27, 31
LIP (Large Internet Packet) protocol, 83
LIST DEVICES command, 650, 653,
   819, 885
listing
   CD-ROM file contents, 709
   directories
      contents, 286-287
      trustees, 370-371, 386
   drive mappings, 303
   files, 287, 324
      attributes, 390
      contents, 286
      information, 287
      rights, 287
      trustees, 389
   hardware, 653
   print queue availability, 773
   printer availability, 773
   properties for User objects, 208-209
   storage devices, 653
   TSAs, 842
   volume contents, 290-291
   Volume object information, 272, 290
LOAD command, 613-614, 647
LOAD PSERVER command, 767-769

loading
   client software at DOS work-
      stations, 33
   COMMAND.COM files, 537, 578
   communication protocol stacks at
      workstations, 32
   communication protocols, 545
   device drivers to memory, 542
   DOS, 535-540
   DOS Requester, 41
   LSL (Link Support Layer), 31
   menus, 613-614
   MHS NLM utility, 863
   MLID drivers, 32, 545
   NLMs, 641
   ODI drivers, 545
   printer definitions, 752
   protocol modules at workstations, 29
   PSERVER NLM utility, 767-769
   remote printers at workstations, 752
   SBACKUP NLM utility, 820, 831
   TSAs, 818
   VLMs, 546
      at workstations, 32
      from other directories, 40
local area networks (LANs), 13-15
log files (backup sessions),
   viewing, 823
logical partitions
   mirrored status, 651
   remirroring, 650-651
LOGIN directories, 264
login scripts, 141, 298, 534, 555
   automating from AUTOEXEC.BAT
      files, 544
   commands, 568-569, 575-592
      ATTACHB, 577-578, 591
      BREAK, 578
      CLS, 591
      COMPATIBLE, 588-589
      COMSPEC, 578-580
      CONTEXT, 580, 591
      DISPLAY, 581
      DOS BREAK, 578

DOS SET, 581-582
DOS VERIFY OFF, 582-583
DOS VERIFY ON, 582-583
DRIVE, 583
EXIT, 583-584
FDISPLAY, 581
FIRE PHASERS, 584
GOTO, 584-585
INCLUDE, 586
INCLUDE NDS, 591
LASTLOGINTIME, 590, 591
MACHINE, 587
MAP, 587, 591
NO_DEFAULT, 588, 592
NO_SWAP, 588, 592
PAUSE, 588
PCCOMPATIBLE, 588-589
PROFILE, 592
REMARK, 589
SET, 581-582
SET TIME OFF, 582, 592
SET TIME ON, 582, 592
SHIFT, 589-590
SWAP, 588, 592
WAIT, 588
WRITE, 569, 591
comments, 589
default login scripts, 560-562, 588
DOS variables, 267
execution order, 563-566
files, 570-572
IF...THEN...ELSE statements (login scripts), 573, 585-586
IF_ THEN conditional statement, 570
INCLUDE statements, 574
loops, 584-585
NO_DEFAULT directive, 562
organizing, 573-592
pausing, 588
processing, 586
profile login scripts, 557-559
Profile objects, 150
rights, 567-568
swapping in memory, 588
system login scripts, 556-557

terminating, 578, 583-584
upgrading to NetWare 4.x, 566-567
user login scripts, 559-560
variables, 569, 592-595
    COMSPEC, 575
    shifting, 589-590
writing text messages to screen, 591
LOGIN.EXE utility, 886
LOGIN_NAME login script variable, 594
logins, 21-22, 42-44
    account restrictions, 407-408
    authentication, 417-419
    displaying last user logins, 590
    intruder limits, 416-417
    restrictions, 550-552
    security, 404-417
    time restrictions, 411-413
    validation, 550-552
    with NWUSER utility, 52
    workstation restrictions, 413-415
logouts, 52
loops (login scripts), 584-585
LSL (Link Support Layer), 27, 31
LSL ? command, 37
LSL.COM program, 545

M

MACHINE command (login scripts), 587
MACHINE login script variable, 595
machine names (workstations), 587
Macintosh File and Print Services online manual, 55
MAGAZINE command, 650, 654-655, 885
magazine requests (servers), confirming, 654-655
MAIL directories, 265
mail gateways, 859
mail routers, 859
Mailbox Location property (NDS objects), 870
Mailbox property page, 870

mailboxes
NDS objects, 154-155
user accounts, 859
**MAIN.MNU files, upgrading to
NetWare 4.x, 597**
Management NLMs, 668-676
manual load printers, *see* **remote
printers**
manuals (online), 54-57
MAP commands, 293-304, 568
login scripts, 587, 591
NDS syntax, 309-311
optimizing with directory map
objects, 141
mapping
drives, 291-329
displaying, 303
to root directories, 300
with Directory Map objects, 311-317
network drives, 304-309
search drives, 295-299, 301
to CD-ROM drives, 708
Master Index online manual, 54
MEDIA command, 650, 656-657, 885
**media requests (servers), confirming,
656-657**
MEMBER OF login script variable, 593
MEMMAKER program, 542
memory
0FFFF0 hex, 535
conventional, loading DOS Requester in, 41
domains, creating for NLMs, 694-697
expanded, loading DOS Requester
in, 41
extended, loading DOS Requester
in, 41
management, 79-82
NLM requirements, 642
optimizing
*by disabling diagnostic
responder, 546*
by disabling SPX, 546
with MEMMAKER program, 542

servers, management, 644-645
virtual memory, 645
VLMs, 41
MENU command, 602
MENUMAKE.EXE utility, 887
menus
color, customizing, 625-626
commands
control, 609-624
organizational, 602-608
components, 600
defining, 602
displaying, 612
limitations, 624-625
loading, 613-614
Novell menus, 595-598
executing, 598
temporary files, 598-599
script files, 596, 599-600
merging NDS trees, 114, 703-705
Message Handling System, *see* **MHS**
**Message Routing Group objects,
155-156, 864**
Message Routing objects, 161
**Message Server attribute (User object
class), 125**
Message Transfer Agents (MTAs), 158
messages, 857
distribution lists, 872-875
mail gateways, 859
Postmasters, 156
receiving from external e-mail
addresses, 876-878
routing, 155-156, 158
sending
*to external e-mail addresses, 872,
876-878*
with NETUSER utility, 61-65
with NWUSER utility, 49
Messaging Server objects, 158, 161, 864
messaging servers, 858
**Messaging Servers property (Message
Routing Group object), 864**
messaging services, 857-859

MHS (Message Handling System), 156, 860-878
   installation, 861-863
   installation requirements, 860-878
   online manual, 56
   server requirements, 860
   verifying installation, 863-868
MHS NLM utility, 859, 863
Migrate file attribute (directories/ files), 380
migrating file data, 74-75
Minimize Form Changes across Print Queues property (Printer objects), 739
Minimize Form Changes within Print Queues property (Printer objects), 739
MINUTE login script variable, 594
MIRROR STATUS command, 650-652, 885
mirrored partitions, 651
mirroring disks, 253, 803
MLIDs (Multiple Link Interface Drivers), 26-28, 32, 545
modemstring (Hayes command string), 692
modules (protocols), loading at workstations, 29
MODULES command, 647
MONITOR NLM utility, 669-670, 884
monitoring resources, 670
MONTH login script variable, 593
MONTH_NAME login script variable, 593
MOUNT command, 647
mounting CD-ROM drives, 707, 861
MTAs (Message Transfer Agents), 158
Multiple Link Interface Driver (MLID), 26-28, 32, 545

N

NAME command, 647
Name property (Printer objects), 734, 740

naming
   directories, 257
   files, 259-261
   NDS objects, 126-129
   temporary files for Novell menus, 599
   volumes, 254-257
NCOPY command, 282-285
NCP (NetWare Core Protocol), 25
NDAY_OF_WEEK login script variable, 593
NDIR command, 273-281, 887
NDS (Network Directory Services), 18-20, 100-101
   corruption, 158-161
   DIB (Directory Information Base), 112
   object rights, 423-431
      Browse, 427-428
      Create, 428-429
      defaults, 435-439
      Delete, 429-430
      inheritance, 439-441
      Rename, 430-431
      Supervisor, 427
   objects, 20, 101-105
      accessing, 419
      ACL properties, 505-532
      AFP Server, 138, 159
      Alias, 120, 139, 160
      attribute types, 136-137
      Bindery, 153-154, 161
      Bindery Queue, 154, 161
      case sensitivity, 126
      classes, 117-125
      complete path names, 180-182
      Computer, 141, 160
      container, 115-118, 125, 347
      Containment Class rules, 119
      context, 176-179, 195-205
      Country container, 116, 133
      creating, 123, 428
      creating with NETADMIN utility, 172-176

creating with NWADMIN utility, 168-172

deleting, 429-430

deleting with NETADMIN utility, 176

deleting with NWADMIN utility, 172

Directory Map, 141, 160, 311-322

Distribution List, 154-155, 161, 872-881

effective classes, 124-130

effective rights, 445-484

External Entity, 156-158, 161, 872

File Server, 20, 162

finding with NLIST utility, 205-214

finding with NWADMIN utility, 216-218

Group, 142-144, 160-161, 347-359

heirarchy, 109, 113-125

inheritance, 120

IRFs, 442-443

leaf, 116-117, 137-161

mailboxes, 154-155

Message Routing, 161

Message Routing Group, 155-156, 864

Messaging Server, 158, 161, 864

MHS property assignments, 868-871

naming, 126-129

NetWare Server, 144-145, 161

noneffective classes, 123

Organization container, 116, 134

Organizational Person class, 121

Organizational Role, 146-147, 160

Organizational Unit container, 110, 116, 134-136, 347

organizing in container objects, 115

parent, 120

partial path names, 183-191

path names, 191

Person class, 121

print configuration, 757

Print Queue, 148, 160, 727-733, 755-757, 760, 770-771, 788

Print Server, 147, 160, 741-750, 755-757, 764, 770-771, 788

Printer, 148-149, 160, 733-741, 755-757, 761, 770-771, 788

Profile, 150, 160

properties, 162-167

property rights, 502

property values, 162

QUIPU naming scemes, 190

referencing, 139

renaming, 430

Residential Person class, 122

rights, 77

[Root], 114, 130-132

schema, 117-125

searching by property values, 213

security equivalence, 444-445

trustees, 505-532

typeless names, 192-193

Unknown, 158-161

User, 121, 151-152, 161

values, displaying, 212

Volume, 152-153, 161, 219, 256, 272, 289-290

partitions, 100

property rights, 423-425, 484-491

computing, 508-532

file system considerations, 507

to login scripts, 567

repairing, 698-700

security, 403-404, 420-422

guidelines, 519-532

versus file system security, 527-532

storage, 109

trees, 112-114

backups to host servers, 813

browsing, 195-214, 420, 428

case study, 163-166

depth limits, 125

merging, 114, 703-705

object context, 176-179

viewing, 169

versus bindery services, 105-108

near-line storage (files), 75
nesting mail distribution lists, 155, 873
NETADMIN utility, 172-176, 605, 883
NetSync utility, 56
NETUSER utility, 61, 772-774, 887
NetWare 3.x
    accessing NetWare 4.x servers, 154
    bindery services
        emulating, 154
        versus NDS, 105-108
    print queues in NDS trees, 154
    RPRINTER.EXE utility, 753
    utilities versus NetWare 4.x, 883
NetWare 4.x
    CD-ROM drive support, 705-711
    CD-ROM installation, 87
    data migration, 700-702
    network logins, 42-44
    NLMs, 693-713
    servers, synchronizing, 703
    settings, displaying, 53
    system files, installing with
        RCONSOLE utility, 692
    utilities versus NetWare 3.x, 883
NetWare Core Protocol (NCP), 25
NetWare Graphical User Interface
    utilities, 46-60
NetWare Loadable Modules, *see* NLMs
NetWare Server objects, 144-145, 161
NetWare Server property (Messaging
    Server object), 866
NetWare Settings dialog box, 53
network adapters (protocol stack
    support), 26
Network Address property (Print
    Server objects), 745
Network Address Restrictions property
    (Printer objects), 738
Network Administrator Tool, *see*
    NWADMIN utility
Network Directory Services, *see* NDS
network drivers, 25
network drive mappings, 304-309
Network Interface Cards, *see* NICs
network layer (OSI model), 25

Network Management Agent
    (NMAGENT) NLM utility, 678-679
NETWORK_ADDRESS login script
    variable, 594
networks
    address formats, 414
    auditing, 77-79
    backups, 84-85
    components, 11-13
    connections (user accounts), 22-30
    drives
        defaults, 583
        mapping, 50-52, 291-329
    global management, 68
    logical organization, 19-20
    logins, 21-23, 42-44
    NDS tree case study, 163-166
    nodes (IPX addresses), finding, 738
    printing services, 723-727
        configurations, 757-767
        NetWare 4.x improvements, 85-86
    printing utilities, 781-790
    requests, processing, 552-555
    resources
        server locations, 68
        user access, 15-17
        see also *objects (NDS)*
    user environments (setup), 534-555
    workstation connections, 30-34
NETX VLM utility, 46
New Features online manual, 56
NEXT command option (MAP
    command), 300
NICs (Network Interface Cards), 23
NLIST utility, 205-214, 887
NLIST VOLUME command, 272-273
NLMs (NetWare Loadable Modules),
    637-643
    AIO, 691
    AIOCOMX, 691
    CDROM, 705-711, 885
    DOMAIN, 694-697, 884
    DSMERGE, 703-705
    DSREPAIR, 698-700, 885
    dynamic linking, 641

file extensions, 640
INSTALL, 668-669, 861
KEYB, 711
loading, 81, 641
Management, 668-676
memory requirements, 642
MHS, 859, 863
MONITOR, 669-670, 884
NetWare version compatibility, 640
NMAGENT (Network Management
Agent), 678-679
NPRINTER, 750, 782
NWSNUT, 702-703, 884
parameters, 642
paths, searching, 641
protected domains, creating, 694-697
PSERVER, 742-743, 767-769, 781
REMOTE, 683-692
ROUTE (Source routing), 680-682
RPL (Remote Program Load),
679, 886
RSPX, 683-692
RTDM, 700-702, 885
SBACKUP, 84, 805, 811, 815-822, 886
    backups, performing, 822
    buffers, 821
    caveats, 846-848
    error files, 844
    file backups in compressed format,
        843-844
    loading, 820, 831
    log files, 844
    restores, performing, 831-835
    restores, performing without session
        log files, 836-837
    security, 845-846
    unloading, 822
SCHDELAY, 712-713
SDI, 814
server enhancement, 676-693
SERVMAN, 670-675, 884
SMDR, 814
STREAMS, 677-678
TIMESYNC, 703, 885
TSA_NDS, 813, 818

TSA410, 811, 818
unloading, 641
UPS, 675-676, 804
Utility User interface, 702
versus VLMs, 38
WSMAN, 814
NMAGENT (Network Management
Agent) NLM utility, 678-679
NMENU utility, 595, 887
NO_DEFAULT command (login
scripts), 562, 588, 592
NO_SWAP command (login
scripts), 592
node addresses
node IPX addresses
    finding, 738
    print servers, 746
non-native NDS objects, 156
noneffective object classes, 123
NOSWAP command (login scripts), 588
Notification property (Printer
objects), 741
notification property (printer
forms), 740
Novell
    address, 895
    menus, 595-598
        color, customizing, 625-626
        executing, 598
        limitations, 624-625
        temporary files, 598-599
    phone numbers, 892
NP option (MAP command), 301-302
NPRINT command, 724, 778-779
NPRINTER NLM utility, 750-755,
782, 886
number sign (#), login script commands, 576-577
numbers (international formats), 86
NWADMIN (Network Administrator)
utility, 167-172, 216-218, 285-286,
391-395, 782, 884
NWP VLM utility, 46
NWSNUT NLM utility, 702-703, 884
NWUSER (NetWare User) utility, 47-53

O

Object Property rights, 77
object rights (NDS), 423-431
Browse, 427-428
Create, 428-429
defaults, 435-439
Delete, 429-430
inheritance, 439-441
Rename, 430-431
Supervisor, 427
Object Trustee property, *see* **ACL property**
objects (NDS), 20, 101-105
accessing, 419
ACL properties, 505-532
AFP Server, 138, 160
Alias, 120, 139, 160
attribute types, 136-137
Bindery, 153-154, 161
Bindery Queue, 154, 161
case sensitivity, 126
classes, 117-125
complete path names, 180-182
Computer, 141, 160
container, 115-118, 125, 347
    assigning rights with, 347
    viewing, 197
Containment Class rules, 119
context, 176-179
    changing with CX utility, 195-205
    promoting, 191
Country, 116, 133
creating, 123, 428
    with NETADMIN utility, 172-176
    with NWADMIN utility, 168-172
deleting, 429-430
    with NETADMIN utility, 176
    with NWADMIN utility, 172
Directory Map, 141, 160, 311-317
    creating, 317-322
    NDS rights, 526
Distribution List, 154-155, 161, 872-881
effective classes, 124-130

effective rights, 445-484
External Entity, 156-158, 161, 872
File Server, 20, 162
finding
    with NLIST utility, 205-214
    with NWADMIN utility, 216-218
Group, 142-144, 160-161, 347
    assigning rights, 353, 358
    assigning user accounts to, 350, 357
    creating with NETADMIN utility, 355-359
    creating with NWADMIN utility, 349-354
    displaying rights, 354
    properties, 350, 357
heirarchy, 109, 113-125
importing into NDS, 156
inheritance, 120
IRFs, 442-443
leaf, 116-117, 137-161
mailboxes, 154-155
Message Routing, 161
Message Routing Group, 155-156, 864
Messaging Server, 158, 161, 864
MHS property assignments, 868-871
naming, 126-129
NetWare Server, 144-145, 161
noneffective classes, 123
Organization container, 116, 134
    creating with NETADMIN utility, 174
    creating with NWADMIN utility, 170
    system login scripts, 556-557
Organizational Person class, 121
Organizational Role, 146-147, 160-161
Organizational Unit container, 110, 116, 134-136, 347
    creating with NETADMIN utility, 175
    creating with NWADMIN utility, 171
    system login scripts, 556-557
organizing in container objects, 115

parent, 120
partial path names, 183-191
path names, 191
Person class, 121
print configuration, 757
Print Queue, 148, 160, 727-733, 755
    configurations, 760
    creating, 760
    finding, 763
    print list assignments, 788
    Quick Setup configurations, 770-771
    user tasks, 789-790
Print Server, 147, 160, 741-750, 755
    configurations, 764
    creating, 764
    print list assignments, 788
    Quick Setup configurations, 770-771
    user tasks, 789-790
Printer, 148-149, 160, 733-741, 755
    assigning to print servers, 766
    configurations, 761
    creating, 761
    print list assignments, 788
    Quick Setup configurations, 770-771
    user tasks, 789-790
Profile, 150, 160
    login scripts, 557-559
    NDS rights, 526
properties, 162-167
property values, 162, 211
QUIPU naming scemes, 190
referencing, 139
renaming, 430
Residential Person class, 122
rights, 77
[Root] container, 114, 130-132
schema, 117-125
searching by property values, 213
security equivalence, 444-445
trustees (ACL), 505-532
typeless names, 192-193
Unknown, 158-161
User, 121, 151-152, 161
    login scripts, 559-560
    profile login script property, 558
    properties, listing, 208-209

values, 212
Volume, 152-153, 161, 219, 256
    finding, 289
    listing information, 272, 290
    User Space Limits property, 324
ODI (Open Datalink Interface), 83
drivers, loading, 545
layer configurations, 550
offline storage (files), 75
online manuals, 54-57
Only Specified Data command (Type of Backup menu), 841
operating systems, 12, 643-644
Operators property
Print Queue objects, 730, 733
Print Server objects, 747, 749
optical disks (jukeboxes), 75
optimizing
MAP commands with directory map objects, 141
memory
    by disabling diagnostic responder, 546
    by disabling SPX, 546
    with MEMMAKER program, 542
options (commands)
CAPTURE command, 774-776
CX command-line utility, 204-205
defining, 604-608
EXEC command, 612
FILER utility, 382
MAP command
    CHANGE, 302-303
    INS S16, 299
    NEXT, 300
    NP, 301-302
    ROOT, 300-301
NDIR command, 280
NLIST VOLUME command, 273
NPRINT command, 778-779
SEND command, 66
VLMs, 41
Organization container object dialog box, 170

Organization container objects,
116, 134
   Containment Class rules, 119
   creating
      with NETADMIN utility, 174
      with NWADMIN utility, 170
   system login scripts, 556-557
organizational commands (menus),
602-608
Organizational Person object class, 121
Organizational Role objects, 146-147,
160-161
Organizational Unit container object
dialog box, 171
Organizational Unit container objects,
110, 116, 134-136, 347
   Containment Class rules, 119
   creating
      with NETADMIN utility, 175
      with NWADMIN utility, 171
   system login scripts, 556-557
OS login script variable, 595
OS_VERSION login script
variable, 595
OSI (Open Standard Interface)
model, 24
   application layer, 25
   data link layer, 24
   network layer, 25
   physical layer, 24
   session layer, 25
   transport layer, 25
Other Installation Actions menu
commands, 862
output (printer ports), capturing, 777
overriding search drive mappings, 301
ownership
   directories, 326-327
   files, 326-327

P

P_STATION login script variable, 595
packet burst protocol, 83

packets
   routing, 553-555
   transmission, 83
PAP (Printer Access Protocol), 736
parameters
   GET commands, 619-624
   languages, 659-660
   NLMs, 642
   SET parameters (servers), 670-675
parent objects, 120
partial path names (NDS objects),
183-186
partitions
   mirrored status, 651
   NDS, 100
   remirroring, 650-651
PARTMGR.EXE utility, 884
Password property (Print Server
objects), 749
Password Restrictions dialog box, 410
passwords
   print servers, 746, 749
   Remote Console utility, 684
path names (NDS objects), 180-191
paths
   directories, 288
   NLMs, searching, 641
PAUSE command (login scripts), 588
PAUSE command option (ITEM
command), 607
pausing
   commands, 607
   login scripts, 588
PCCOMPATIBLE command (login
scripts), 588-589
PCONSOLE utility, 759-771, 779-781
periods (.), NDS object path names,
180, 191
Person object class, 121
phone numbers
   Drake Prometrics, 892-893
   Novell, 892
physical layer (OSI model), 24
PNW VLM utility, 46

ports (printers)
   capturing output, 777
   redirecting, 773-777
   status, 774
POST (Power On Self-Test)
   process, 535
Postmaster General users, 864
Postmaster users, 156, 865
PostScript banners (Printer
   objects), 737
Power On Self-Test (POST)
   process, 535
prefillString parameter (GET com-
   mands), 624
prependString parameter (GET
   commands), 623
print banner parameters (print
   jobs), 724
Print Configuration objects, 757
print jobs, 724
   banner pages, 787
     printing, 775
     suppressing, 775
   configurations, 724, 775, 780
     creating, 784
     defaults, 785
     displaying details, 784
     editing, 783
     options, 785-787
     with PRINTCON utility, 782-787
     with PRINTDEF utility, 787-788
   displaying queue status, 733
   forms, 786-788
     configurations, 739
     feeds, 786
     parameters, 724
   identifying, 724
   print banner parameters, 724
   print queue specifications, 786
   printer specifications, 786
   priority
     displaying, 764
     setting, 739
   retaining in print queues, 775

sending, 725
   from print servers, 749
   to file paths, 775
   to Printer objects, 149
   with CAPTURE command, 774-777
   with NETUSER utility, 773-774
   with NPRINT command, 778-779
   with PCONSOLE utility, 779
tabs, converting to spaces, 785
user notification upon completion,
   776, 786
usernames, 787
Print Queue objects, 148, 160, 727-733
   Authorized Print Servers
     property, 732
   configurations, 760
   creating, 727, 760
   finding, 763
   interaction with other printing
     objects, 755
   Job List property, 733
   Operators property, 730, 733
   print list assignments, 788
   Printers Servicing Print Queue
     property, 732
   properties, 755
   Quick Setup configurations, 770-771
   storage location, 728
   user access, 727
   user tasks, 789-790
   Users property, 731, 733
   Volume property, 729
print queues, 724
   checking for print jobs (time
     intervals), 737
   listing availability, 773
   NetWare 3.x in NDS trees, 154
Print Queues property (Printer
   objects), 741
Print Server objects, 147, 160, 743-750
   activating, 741-743
   Advertising Name property, 745
   configurations, 764
   creating, 743, 764
   interaction with other printing
     objects, 755

Network Address property, 745
Operators property, 747-749
Password property, 749
print list assignments, 788
Printers property, 746, 749
properties, 743, 755
Quick Setup configurations, 770-771
user tasks, 789-790
Users property, 748-749
**Print Server property (Printer objects),
738, 741**
print servers
activating, 768
node addresses, 746
passwords, 746, 749
printer assignments, 746, 766
running status, 746
status displays, 769
unloading, 746, 768
user access, 747
print service configurations, 725
Print Services online manual, 56
PRINT VLM utility, 46
PRINTCON utility, 781-787
PRINTDEF utility, 724, 781, 787-788
Printer Access Protocol (PAP), 736
**Printer Features property (Printer
objects), 734**
Printer objects, 148-149, 160, 733-741
assigning to print servers, 766
Banner Type properties, 737
Buffer Size property, 737
Change Forms as Needed
property, 739
Configuration property, 741
configurations, 736, 761
creating, 733, 761
interaction with other printing
objects, 755
Minimize Form Changes across Print
Queues property, 739
Minimize Form Changes within Print
Queues property, 739
Name property, 734, 740
Network Address Restrictions
property, 738

Notification property, 741
PostScript banners, 737
print list assignments, 788
print queue assignments, 735
Print Queues property, 741
Print Server property, 738, 741
Printer Features property, 734
properties, 755
Quick Setup configurations, 770-771
server assignments, 735
Service Interval property, 737
Service Mode for Forms
property, 738
Service Only Currently Mounted
Form property, 740
types, 736
user tasks, 789-790
printers
AIO (Asynchronous Input/
Output), 737
AppleTalk, 736
buffers, 738
defining, 750-751
definitions, 752
errors (user notification), 764
forms
changing, 724
notification property, 740
listing availability, 773
network addresses
finding, 212
restrictions, 738
ports
capturing output, 777
redirecting, 773-777
status, 774
print server assignments, 752
queue assignments, 763
redirecting to NDS Printer/Queue
objects, 726
remote printers, 751-752
status displays, 754, 767
Unix, 736
XNP, 737

Printers property (Print Server objects), 746, 749

Printers Servicing Print Queue property (Print Queue objects), 732

printing
  banner pages for print jobs, 775
  network printing services, 723-727, 757-767
  with CAPTURE command, 774-777
  with NETUSER utility, 773-774
  with NPRINT command, 778-779
  with PCONSOLE utility, 779
  see also print jobs

printing services (NetWare 4.x improvements), 85-86

prioritizing server processes, 712-713

priority (print jobs)
  displaying, 764
  setting, 739

processes (servers), prioritizing, 712-713

processing
  AUTOEXEC.BAT files, 543-544
  CONFIG.SYS files, 540-543
  login scripts, 586
  network requests, 552-555
  STARTNET.BAT files, 544-546

profile login scripts, 557-559

Profile objects, 150, 160
  login scripts, 557-559
  NDS rights, 526

PROFILE profobject command (login scripts), 592

profiles (user accounts), 150

programs, breaking out of, 543

promoting context in NDS objects, 191, 197

promptString parameter (GET commands), 623

properties
  Distribution List objects, 874
  Group objects, 350, 357
  mail distribution lists, 155
  Message Routing Group objects, 864
  Messaging Server objects, 866

NDS objects, 101, 162-167
  ACL, 505-532
  MHS assignments, 868-871
  Print Queue objects, 729, 755
  Print Server objects, 743, 755
  Printer objects, 734, 755
  User objects, 151
    listing, 208-209
    login scripts, 559
    profile login scripts, 558

property rights (NDS), 423-425, 502
  computing, 508-532
  file system considerations, 507
  to login scripts, 567

property values (NDS objects), 103, 105, 162, 211

protected domains (NLMs), 694-697

protocols
  AFP, 138
  AIO, 737
  communication protocols, 23, 545
  IPX, 23, 36
  LIP, 83
  modules, loading at workstations, 29
  NCP, 25
  packet burst, 83
  PAP, 736
  SAP, 743
  SMTP, 157
  SPX, 36
  stacks
    dynamic building, 677
    LSL support, 29
    network adapter support, 26
  X.500
    NDS compliance, 111
    NDS object property specifications, 104
  XNP, 737

PSC utility, 782

PSERVER NLM utility, 742-743 767-769, 781

[Public] trustees, 347, 431-435

PUBLIC directories, 265

Purge attribute (directories/files), 378-379

purging deleted files, 288, 320

Q–R

queues, *see* print queues; Print Queue objects

Quick Setup configurations (printing objects), 770-771

QUIPU (NDS object naming), 190

quotes ("), login script variables, 569

RCONSOLE.EXE (Remote Console) utility, 683-692, 884

RDNs (Relative Distinguished Names)
NDS objects, 183, 187-191
see also partial path names

Read only attribute (files), 379

Read property rights, 504

Read rights, 360

Read Write attribute (files), 379

read-after-write verification, 800

receiving messages from external e-mail addresses, 876-878

recovering
deleted files, 288, 320, 384
deleted Volume objects, 429

REDIR VLM utility, 46

redirecting
printer ports, 773-777
printers to NDS Printer/Print Queue objects, 726

referencing
directories, 141
group user accounts, 142
NDS objects, 139
servers, 145

registering for test, 892

Relative Distinguished Names (RDNs)
NDS objects, 183, 187-191
see also partial path names

REMARK command (login scripts), 589

REMIRROR PARTITION command, 650-651, 885

remirroring logical partitions, 650-651

remote booting (diskless workstations), 679

Remote Console (RCONSOLE.EXE) utility, 683-692

REMOTE NLM utility, 683-692

remote printers, 751-752

Remote Program Load (RPL) NLM utility, 679

REMOVE DOS command, 649

removing
directories
attributes, 387
rights, 388
trustees, 376, 387, 394
files
rights, 390
trustees, 390
user access to CD-ROM drives, 710

Rename Inhibit attribute (directories/ files), 378-379

Rename object rights, 430-431

renaming
directories, 282
NDS objects, 430

RENDIR command, 282

repairing NDS, 698-700

requests (networks), processing, 552-555

Residential Person object class, 122

resolving partial path names for NDS objects, 183-186

resources (networks)
accessing, 419
monitoring, 670
server locations, 68
user access, 15-17
see also objects

RESTART SERVER command, 650, 658

restarting servers, 658

Restore a Session command (Restore menu), 837

Restore menu commands, 837

restoring
directories, 837-840
file systems, 837-840
servers
with SBACKUP NLM utility, 831-835
without session log files, 836-837

volumes, 838, 842
workstations, 814
restricting
logins, 550-552
volume space for users, 324-326
revoking rights, 371-375
rights
Access Control rights (user
accounts), 268
assigning
with container objects, 347
with Group objects, 349
with security equivalence, 348
directories, 359-362
displaying, 370
setting with FILER utility, 385-388
editing, 358
effective rights, 445-451
blocking, 362
computing, 363-366, 451-484
displaying, 366
for trustees, 393
files, 359-362
assigning, 344-349
listing, 287
setting with FILER utility, 388-402
granting, 371-375
Group objects
assigning, 353, 358
displaying, 354
inheritance, 375-376, 422
Inherited Rights Filter, 362-366, 376,
422-443
login scripts, 567-568
NDS, 423-425
[Public], 347, 431-435
revoking, 371-375
SBACKUP NLM utility, 845-846
security equivalence, 444-445
Supervisor, 268, 366
trustee rights, 75, 425-426
assigning with NWADMIN utility,
391-395
directories, 360
explicit, 365

files, 361
inheritance, 347
print objects, 757
user accounts, 347
RIGHTS utility, 362, 367-377, 886
[Root] container objects, 114, 119,
130-132
ROOT option (MAP command),
300-301
rooting drives to network
directories, 300
ROUTE (source routing) NLM utility,
680-682
routers, 553, 859
routing
messages, 155-158
packets, 553-555
RPL (Remote Program Load) NLM
utility, 679, 886
RPRINTER.EXE utility, 753
RSA VLM utility, 46
RSPX NLM utility, 683-692
RTDM NLM utility, 700-702, 885
running
applications, 609-612
NETADMIN utility from batch
files, 605

S

salvaging deleted files, 320, 384
SAP (Service Advertising Protocol), 743
saving printer object configura-
tions, 763
SBACKUP NLM utility, 84, 805, 811,
815-822, 886
backups, performing, 822
buffers, 821
caveats, 846-848
error files, 844
file backups in compressed format,
843-844
loading, 820, 831
log files, 844

restores
    performing, 831-835
    performing without session log files,
        836-837
    security, 845-846
    unloading, 822
SCAN FOR NEW DEVICES command,
    650, 653-654, 819, 885
SCHDELAY NLM utility, 712-713
schema (NDS objects), 117-125
screen commands (servers), 649-667
script files (menus), 596, 599-600
SDI (Storage Device Interface), 812
SDI NLM utility, 814
SEARCH ADD command, 705
SEARCH command, 641
search drives
    converting to network drives, 302
    drive letters, 297
    mappings, 295-299
        deleting, 307
        displaying, 303
        overriding, 301
searching
    directories, 288, 295
    files, 274-281, 288
    NDS objects
        by property values, 213
        with NLIST utility, 205-214
        with NWADMIN utility, 216-218
    NLM paths, 641
    property values for NDS objects, 211
    Volume objects, 289
SECOND login script variable, 594
SECURE CONSOLE command, 648
SECURE parameter (GET com-
    mands), 624
security
    directories, 377-381
    file systems, 75-77, 343-359, 527-532
    files with attributes, 377-381
    logins, 404-417
    NDS, 403-404, 420-422
        guidelines, 522-532
        versus file system security, 527-532
    SBACKUP NLM utility, 845-846

security equivalence, 444-445
Select Object dialog box, 139, 351, 869
Selected Property right, 505-532
SEND command, 65, 649, 887
sending
    messages
        to external e-mail addresses, 872,
            876-878
        with NETUSER utility, 61-65
        with NWUSER utility, 49
    print jobs, 725
        from print servers, 749
        to file paths, 775
        to Printer objects, 149
        with CAPTURE command, 774-777
        with NETUSER utility, 773-774
        with NPRINT command, 778-779
        with PCONSOLE utility, 779
separators (directories), 259
Sequenced Packet eXchange (SPX)
    protocol, 36
servers, 12
    AFP, 138
    backups, 805-810
        custom, 810
        differential, 808-810
        full, 806-807
        incremental, 807-808
        with SBACKUP NLM utility,
            817-831
    bindery-based, 577
    commands, 645-667
    console commands, 650-667
    disk subsystems, 252-257
        duplexing, 803
        mirroring, 803
    enhancement NLMs, 676-693
    fault tolerance, 799-804
    host servers, 814
    installation, 668-669
    installation commands, 647
    magazine requests, confirming,
        654-655
    maintenance commands, 648-649
    management from remote worksta-
        tions, 683-692

media requests, confirming, 656-657
memory management, 644-645
messaging servers, 858
MHS requirements, 860
network addresses, finding, 212
processes, prioritizing, 712-713
protecting, 714
referencing, 145
restarting, 658
restoring
    with SBACKUP NLM utility, 831-835
    without session log files, 836-837
screen commands, 649-667
SET parameters, 670-675
synchronizing, 703
TSAs, 811
    listing, 842
    loading, 818
    selecting, 823
uninterruptable power supply, 675-676
upgrading, 668-669
volumes, 152-153, 252-257
    contents, listing, 290-291
    details, 253
    directories, 257-261, 291-293
    disk spanning, 253
    displaying statistics, 273-281, 383
    files, 257-261
    object names, 256-257
    physical names, 254-255
    restoring, 838, 842
    restricting space for users, 324-326
    space information displays, 322-323
    space management, 322
    statistic displays, 273-281, 288, 383
Service Advertising Protocol (SAP), 743
Service Interval property (Printer objects), 737
Service Mode for Forms property (Printer objects), 738
Service Only Currently Mounted Form property (Printer objects), 740
SERVMAN NLM utility, 670-675, 884
session layer (OSI model), 25

SET command, 581-582, 649
SET parameters (servers), 670-675
SET TIME OFF command (login scripts), 582, 592
SET TIME ON command (login scripts), 582, 592
setup
    user network environments, 534-555
    workstations, 534
SFT (System Fault Tolerance), 799-800
    Level I, 800-802
    Level II, 803
    Level III, 804
Sharable attribute (files), 379
Shared data directories, 269
SHIFT command (login scripts), 589-590
shifting login script variables, 589-590
SHORT_YEAR login script variable, 593
SHOW control command, 607, 612-613
Simple Mail Transfer Protocol (SMTP), 157
slash (/), directory separators, 259
SMACHINE login script variable, 595
SMDR (Storage Management Data Requester) NLM utility, 812-814
SMS (Storage Management Service), 84-85, 810-815
SMTP (Simple Mail Transfer Protocol), 157
software, *see* client software
sound effects (firing phasers), 584
source routing NLM utility, 680-682
sparse files, 284, 288, 385
SPX (Sequenced Packet eXchange) protocol, 36
square brackets [ ], NDS object path names, 181
stacks (protocols)
    dynamic building, 677
    LSL support, 29
    network adapter support, 26
starting
    DOS Requester, 544
    DynaText utility, 57-60

STARTNET.BAT files, 33, 539, 544-546
STATION login script variable, 595
storage
 HCSS, 74
 NDS, 109
Storage Device Interface (SDI), 812
storage devices, listing, 653
Storage Management Data Requester (SMDR), 812
Storage Management Service (SMS), 84-85, 810-815
store-and-forward messaging, 857
storing files in sparse format, 288
STREAMS interface, 677
STREAMS NLM utility, 677-678
suballocating disk blocks, 70-72
Supervising the Network online manual, 56
Supervisor rights, 366
 object rights, 427
 property rights, 503
 user accounts, 268
suppressing banner page printing, 775
SWAP command (login scripts), 588, 592
swapping login scripts in memory, 588
synchronizing
 NetWare 4.x servers, 703
 workstation time with servers, 582
SYS: directories, 263-265
SYS: volumes, 254
SYSINIT program, 537
System attribute (directories/files), 378-379
System Fault Tolerance, see SFT
system login scripts, 556-557
System Messages online manual, 57

T

tabs (print jobs), converting to spaces, 785
tape backups, 75

target service agents (TSAs), 811
 accessing, 813
 listing, 842
 loading, 818
 selecting, 823
TCP/IP (Transmission Control Protocol/Internet Protocol), 414
TCP/IP Reference online manual, 57
telephone numbers
 Drake Prometrics, 892-893
 Novell, 892
terminate-and-stay-resident programs, see TSRs
terminating login scripts, 578, 583-584
test
 adaptive test, 895-896
 answers to chapter samples, 897-904
 cost, 892
 form test, 895-896
 registering for, 892
 strategies, 889-896
testing drive mappings, 304-309
text-based utilities (DOS), 60-65
time (international formats), 86
TIME command, 647
time restrictions (logins), 411-413
Time Restrictions dialog box, 413
TIMESYNC NLM utility, 703, 885
TLI (Transport Layer Interface), 677
TOKEN frame types, 548
Tokenring network address format, 414
trailing periods (.), partial path names, 186
TRAN VLM utility, 46
Transaction Tracking System (TTS), 802
Transactional attribute (files), 379
transmitting packets, 83
transport layer (OSI model), 25
Transport Layer Interface (TLI), 677
trees (NDS), 112-114
 backups to host servers, 813
 browsing, 195-214, 420, 428
 case studies, 163-166

depth limits, 125
merging, 114, 703-705
object context, 176-179
viewing, 169
trustee rights, 75, 425-426
assigning with NWADMIN utility, 391-395
directories, 360
explicit, 365
files, 361
inheritance, 347
print objects, 757
trustees (user accounts), 424-426
Access Control Lists, 505-532
directories
assigning, 387
listing, 370-371, 386
removing, 376, 387, 394
setting with FILER utility, 385-388
files, 388-402
[Public] trustees, 431-435
TSA_NDS NLM utility, 813, 818
TSA410 NLM utility, 811, 818
TSAs (target service agents), 811
accessing, 813
listing, 842
loading, 818
selecting, 823
TSRs (terminate-and-stay-resident) programs, 534, 753
TTS (Transaction Tracking System), 802
Type of Backup menu commands, 841
typeless names (NDS objects), 192-193

U

UIMPORT.EXE utility, 884
UNBIND command, 649
Uninterrupted Power Supplies (UPS), 675-676, 804
Unix printers, 736
Unknown objects, 158-161
UNLOAD command, 649

unloading
NLMs, 641
NPRINTER utility, 754
print servers, 746, 768
SBACKUP NLM utility, 822
VLMs, 41
Upgrade and Migration online manual, 57
upgrading
login scripts to NetWare 4.x, 566-567
MAIN.MNU files to NetWare 4.x, 597
servers, 668-669
UPS (Uninterruptable Power Supplies), 675-676, 804
UPS NLM utility, 675-676, 804
UPS STATUS command, 647
UPS TIME command, 647
user accounts
Access Control rights, 268
ADMIN user accounts, 76
assigning to Group objects, 350, 357
auditors, 77-79
context, changing, 580
deleting from Group objects, 352
effective rights, 445-451
blocking, 362-366
computing, 451-484
groups, 346
home directories, 268
language environments, 545
login scripts, 298, 559-560
logins, 21-22
authentication, 417-419
customizing environment, 560
displaying last logins, 590
intruder limits, 416-417
restrictions, 407-408, 550-552
security, 404-417
time restrictions, 411-413
validation, 550-552
workstation restrictions, 413-415
mailboxes, 859
NDS object right defaults, 438-439
network connections, 22-30

network environments, 534-555
Postmaster Generals, 864
Postmasters, 156, 865
print server access, 747
printer error notification, 764
profiles, 150
resource access, 15-17
rights
    granting, 371-375
    inheritance, 375-376
    [Public], 347
    revoking, 371-375
security equivalence, 444-445
Supervisor rights, 268
trustee rights, 75
trustees, 424-426
    assigning, 387
    displaying assignments, 386
    effective rights, 393
    listing, 370-371, 389
    removing, 376, 387, 394
User objects, 121, 151-152, 161
  Higher Privileges attribute, 125
  login scripts, 559-560
  Message Server attribute, 125
  profile login script property, 558
  properties, listing, 208-209
User Space Limits property (Volume objects), 324
USER_ID login script variable, 594
usernames (print jobs), 787
Users property
  Print Queue objects, 731, 733
  Print Server objects, 748-749
Users property page, 869
using MacNDS client for NetWare 4 online manual, 55
utilities
  AUDITCON, 79, 885
  COLORPAL, 625-626
  command line utilities, 65-67
  CX, 194-205, 886
  directory management, 319
  DSMERGE, 114
  DynaText, 54-60
  file management, 320
  FILER, 286-289, 382-395

FLAG, 381, 886
LOGIN.EXE, 886
MENUMAKE.EXE, 887
NDIR.EXE, 887
NETADMIN, 172-176, 605, 883
NetSync, 56
NETUSER, 61, 772-774, 887
NetWare 4.x versus NetWare 3.x, 883
NetWare Graphical User Interface, 46-60
network printing utilities, 781-790
NLIST, 205-214, 887
NLMs
  AIO, 691
  AIOCOMX, 691
  CDROM, 705-711, 885
  DOMAIN, 694-697, 884
  DSMERGE, 703-705
  DSREPAIR, 698-700, 885
  INSTALL, 668-669, 861
  KEYB, 711
  loading in memory, 81
  MHS, 859, 863
  MONITOR, 669-670, 884
  NMAGENT, 678-679
  NPRINTER, 750, 782
  NWSNUT, 702-703, 884
  PSERVER, 742-743, 767-769, 781
  REMOTE, 683-692
  ROUTE (Source routing), 680-682
  RPL, 679, 886
  RSPX, 683-692
  RTDM, 700-702, 885
  SBACKUP, 84, 805, 811, 815-822, 831-835, 843-848, 886
  SCHDELAY, 712-713
  SDI, 814
  SERVMAN, 670-675, 884
  SMDR, 814
  STREAMS, 677-678
  TIMESYNC, 703, 885
  TSA_NDS, 813, 818
  TSA410, 811, 818
  UPS, 675-676, 804
  WSMAN, 814

NMENU, 595, 887
NPRINTER, 751-755, 782, 886
NWADMIN, 167-172, 216-218,
   285-286, 391-395, 782, 884
NWUSER (NetWare User), 47-53
PARTMGR.EXE, 884
PCONSOLE, 759-771, 779-780, 781
PRINTCON, 781-787
PRINTDEF, 724, 781, 787-788
PSC, 782
RCONSOLE.EXE, 683-692, 884
RIGHTS, 362, 367-377, 886
RPRINTER.EXE, 753
SEND.EXE, 887
text-based (DOS), 60-65
UIMPORT.EXE, 884
VLMs, 32, 36-39, 83
   BIND, 45
   CONN, 45
   displaying diagnostics, 41
   FIO, 45
   GENERAL, 45
   IPXNCP, 45
   loading, 546
   loading from other directories, 40
   memory types, selecting, 41
   NETX, 46
   NWP, 46
   PNW, 46
   PRINT, 46
   REDIR, 46
   RSA, 46
   TRAN, 46
   unloading, 41
Utilities Reference online manual, 57

V

validating logins, 550-552
values (NDS objects), 212
variables
   DOS login scripts, 267
   login scripts, 569, 592-595
      COMSPEC, 575
      shifting, 589-590
verifying
   data migration to local drives, 582
   MHS installation, 863-868
viewing
   container objects, 197
   NDS trees, 169
Virtual Loadable Modules, *see* **VLMs**
virtual memory, 645
VLM /? command, 40
VLM Manager, 39-40, 546-547
VLMs (Virtual Loadable Modules), 32,
   36-39, 83
   BIND, 45
   CONN, 45
   diagnostic displays, 41
   FIO, 45
   GENERAL, 45
   IPXNCP, 45
   loading, 40, 546
   memory types, selecting, 41
   NETX, 46
   NWP, 46
   PNW, 46
   PRINT, 46
   REDIR, 46
   RSA, 46
   TRAN, 46
   unloading, 41
   versus NLMs, 38

Volume objects, 152-153, 161, 219, 256
finding, 289
listing information, 272, 290
recovering, 429
User Space Limits property, 324
Volume property (Print Queue objects), 729
volumes (servers), 152-153, 252-257
contents, listing, 290-291
details, 253
directories, 257-261
assigning drive letters to, 293
drive mappings, 291
disk spanning, 253
files, 257-261
object names, 256-257
physical names, 254-255
restoring, 838, 842
restricting space for users, 324-326
space information displays, 322-323
space management, 322
statistic displays, 273-281, 288, 383
VOLUMES command, 647

W

WAIT command (login scripts), 588
WANs (wide area networks), 13-15
warning messages online manual, 57
Workstation Manager, 814
workstations, 12
backups, 814
buffers, 541
client software, 82-84
CONFIG.SYS files, 540-543
context, 548
context settings, 193-194

diskless, remote booting, 679
DOS
backups, 846
connecting to networks, 31-32
IBM compatibility, 588
loading
communication protocol stacks, 32
DOS, 535-540
LSL, 31
MLID drivers, 32
protocol modules, 29
remote printers, 752
VLMs, 32
login restrictions, 413-415
machine names, 587
network connections, 30-34
restoring, 814
setup, 534
SMS support, 810
synchronizing time with servers, 582
see also Computer objects
WRITE command, 569, 591
Write property rights, 504, 531
Write rights, 360
WSMAN NLM utility, 814

X–Y–Z

X.500 protocol
NDS compliance, 111
NDS object property specifications, 104
XNP (eXtended Network Printing) protocol, 737

YEAR login script variable, 593

zones (AppleTalk), 736

PLUG YOURSELF INTO...

THE MACMILLAN INFORMATION SUPERLIBRARY™

Free information and vast computer resources from the world's leading computer book publisher—online!

FIND THE BOOKS THAT ARE RIGHT FOR YOU!

A complete online catalog, plus sample chapters and tables of contents give you an in-depth look at *all* of our books, including hard-to-find titles. It's the best way to find the books you need!

- STAY INFORMED with the latest computer industry news through our online newsletter, press releases, and customized Information SuperLibrary Reports.

- GET FAST ANSWERS to your questions about MCP books and software.

- VISIT our online bookstore for the latest information and editions!

- COMMUNICATE with our expert authors through e-mail and conferences.

- DOWNLOAD SOFTWARE from the immense MCP library:
  - Source code and files from MCP books
  - The best shareware, freeware, and demos

- DISCOVER HOT SPOTS on other parts of the Internet.

- WIN BOOKS in ongoing contests and giveaways!

TO PLUG INTO MCP: →

WORLD WIDE WEB: http://www.mcp.com

GOPHER: gopher.mcp.com

FTP: ftp.mcp.com

WANT MORE INFORMATION?

CHECK OUT THESE RELATED TOPICS OR SEE YOUR LOCAL BOOKSTORE

CAD

As the number one CAD publisher in the world, and as a Registered Publisher of Autodesk, New Riders Publishing provides unequaled content on this complex topic under the flagship *Inside AutoCAD*. Other titles include *AutoCAD for Beginners* and *New Riders' Reference Guide to AutoCAD Release 13*.

Networking

As the leading Novell NetWare publisher, New Riders Publishing delivers cutting-edge products for network professionals. We publish books for all levels of users, from those wanting to gain NetWare Certification, to those administering or installing a network. Leading books in this category include *Inside NetWare 3.12*, *Inside TCP/IP Second Edition*, *NetWare: The Professional Reference*, and *Managing the NetWare 3.x Server*.

Graphics and 3D Studio

New Riders provides readers with the most comprehensive product tutorials and references available for the graphics market. Best-sellers include *Inside Photoshop 3*, *3D Studio IPAS Plug In Reference*, *KPT's Filters and Effects*, and *Inside 3D Studio*.

Internet and Communications

As one of the fastest growing publishers in the communications market, New Riders provides unparalleled information and detail on this ever-changing topic area. We publish international best-sellers such as *New Riders' Official Internet Yellow Pages, 2nd Edition*, a directory of over 10,000 listings of Internet sites and resources from around the world, as well as *VRML: Browsing and Building Cyberspace, Actually Useful Internet Security Techniques, Internet Firewalls and Network Security*, and *New Riders' Official World Wide Web Yellow Pages*.

Operating Systems

Expanding off our expertise in technical markets, and driven by the needs of the computing and business professional, New Riders offers comprehensive references for experienced and advanced users of today's most popular operating systems, including *Inside Windows 95, Inside Unix, Inside OS/2 Warp Version 3*, and *Building a Unix Internet Server*.

Orders/Customer Service **1-800-653-6156**   Source Code **NRP95**

New Riders Publishing   201 West 103rd Street ◆ Indianapolis, Indiana 46290 USA

REGISTRATION CARD

CNE Training Guide: NetWare 4.1 Administration, Second Edition

Name _____ Title _____

Company _____ Type of business _____

Address _____

City/State/ZIP _____

Have you used these types of books before? ☐ yes   ☐ no

If yes, which ones? _____

_____

How many computer books do you purchase each year? ☐ 1–5   ☐ 6 or more

How did you learn about this book? _____

Where did you purchase this book? _____

Which applications do you currently use? _____

_____

Which computer magazines do you subscribe to? _____

_____

What trade shows do you attend? _____

_____

Comments: _____

_____

_____

Would you like to be placed on our preferred mailing list? ☐ yes   ☐ no

☐ **I would like to see my name in print!** You may use my name and quote me in future New Riders products and promotions. My daytime phone number is: _____

New Riders Publishing   201 West 103rd Street ◆ Indianapolis, Indiana 46290 USA

Fax to **317-581-4670**   Orders/Customer Service **1-800-653-6156**   Source Code **NRP95**

Fold Here

BUSINESS REPLY MAIL
FIRST-CLASS MAIL PERMIT NO. 9918 INDIANAPOLIS IN
POSTAGE WILL BE PAID BY THE ADDRESSEE

NEW RIDERS PUBLISHING
201 W 103RD ST
INDIANAPOLIS IN 46290-9058